asian cooking

asian cooking

The complete encyclopedia of aromatic Asian food

Contributing Editor: Linda Doeser

This edition published in 2001 by Hermes House

Hermes House is an imprint of
Anness Publishing Limited
Hermes House
88–89 Blackfriars Road
London SE1 8HA

This edition published in the USA by Hermes House
Anness Publishing Inc., 27 West 20th Street
New York, NY 10011

A CIP catalogue record for this book is available from the British Library

Publisher: Joanna Lorenz
Project Editor: Linda Doeser
Copy Editor: Harriette Lanzer
Designer: Ian Sandom
Photography: Karl Adamson, Edward Allwright, David Armstrong, Steve Baxter, James Duncan, Michelle Garrett, Amanda Heywood, Patrick McLeavey, Michael Michaels and Thomas Odulate
Styling: Madeleine Brehaut, Michelle Garrett, Maria Kelly, Blake Minton and Kirsty Rawlings
Food for Photography: Carla Capalbo, Kit Chan, Elizabeth Wolf-Cohen, Joanne Craig, Nicola Fowler, Carole Handslip, Jane Hartshorn, Shehzad Husain, Wendy Lee, Lucy McKelvie, Annie Nichols, Jane Stevenson and Steven Wheeler
Illustrations: Madeleine David

Printed and bound in China

1 3 5 7 9 10 8 6 4 2

For all recipes, quantities are given in both metric and imperial measures and, where appropriate, in standard cups and spoons. Follow one set, but not a mixture because they are not interchangeable.

CONTENTS

Introduction *6*

Soups *15*

Starters and Snacks *49*

Fish and Seafood *101*

Meat *175*

Poultry *235*

Vegetables *291*

Salads *347*

Noodles *383*

Rice *435*

Desserts *467*

Sauces, Sambals and Accompaniments *495*

Index *506*

INTRODUCTION

Chinese and Asian cooking have become increasingly popular in the West with the proliferation of Chinese, Thai, Indonesian, Japanese and Balti restaurants. This superb collection of recipes now provides the opportunity for Western cooks to recreate the unique flavours and textures of the East in their own kitchens.

The cuisines of each country that have inspired these mouth-watering recipes have their own distinctive and special qualities: from the subtle spiciness of Thai cooking to the harmonious mixing of colour, texture and flavour in Chinese stir-fries, from the fiery heat of Indonesian dishes to the almost painterly elegance of Japanese presentation. Yet they have many things in common, too – a careful blending of herbs and spices, a thoughtful combining of complementary ingredients and, of course, the widespread use of the wok. This multi-purpose pan, closely related to the karahi or Balti pan, is ideal for poaching, steaming and deep-frying, as well as stir-frying. Western cooks have been quick to recognize the ease and speed of wok cookery and so recipes that marry the best of East and West are also featured.

The book includes a basic introduction to looking after and using a wok and a guide to other useful kitchen equipment. This is followed by notes on some of the more exotic ingredients, as well as standard Chinese and Asian sauces, spices and herbs. All the recipes are beautifully illustrated in colour with easy-to-follow, step-by-step instructions. Hints and tips throughout the book advise on variations, best buys and ways of preparing some of the more unfamiliar ingredients.

Whether your tastes tend towards a full Chinese banquet, a satisfying curry for a midweek family supper, a quick and easy lunchtime treat or simply a different dessert, you will find just what you are looking for among the hundreds of recipes here.

INGREDIENTS

Bamboo shoots Mild-flavoured, tender shoots of the young bamboo, widely available fresh, or sliced or halved in cans.

Basil Several different types of basil are used in Asian cooking. Thai cooks use two varieties, holy and sweet basil, but ordinary basil works well.

Bean curd See under Tofu.

Beansprouts Shoots of the mung bean, usually available from supermarkets. They add a crisp texture to stir-fries.

Black bean sauce Made of salted black beans crushed and mixed with flour and spices (such as ginger, garlic or chilli) to form a thickish paste. It is sold in jars or cans and, once opened, should be kept in the refrigerator.

Cardamom pods Available both as small green pods and larger black pods containing seeds, they have a strong aromatic quality.

Cashew nuts Whole cashew nuts feature prominently in Chinese stir-fries, especially those with chicken.

Cassia bark A form of cinnamon, but with a more robust flavour.

Chilli bean sauce Made from fermented bean paste mixed with hot chilli and other seasonings. Sold in jars, some chilli bean sauces are quite mild, but some are very hot. You will have to try out the various brands yourself to see which one is to your taste.

Chilli oil Made from dried red chillies, garlic, onions, salt and vegetable oil, this is used more as a dip than as a cooking ingredient.

Chilli sauce A very hot sauce made from chillies, vinegar, sugar and salt. Usually sold in bottles, it should be used sparingly in cooking or as a dip. Tabasco sauce can be a substitute.

Chillies There is a wide range of fresh and dried chillies from which to choose. Generally the larger the chilli, the milder the flavour, but there are some exceptions, and the only way to gauge potency is by taste. Remove the seeds for a milder flavour. Whether using dried or fresh chillies, take care when preparing them as their seeds and flesh can "burn": wash your hands immediately afterwards or, better still, wear rubber gloves – and never rub your eyes.

Chinese cabbage Also known as Chinese leaves, two sorts are widely available. The most commonly seen variety has a pale green colour and tightly wrapped elongated head, and about two-thirds of the cabbage is stem which has a crunchy texture. The other type has a shorter and fatter head with curlier, pale yellow or green leaves, and white stems.

Chinese chives Better known as garlic chives, these are sometimes sold with their flowers.

Chinese five-spice powder This flavouring contains star anise, pepper, fennel, cloves and cinnamon.

Chinese pancakes Thin flour and water pancakes with no added seasonings or spices. They are available fresh or frozen.

Chinese rice wine Made from glutinous rice, this is also known as yellow wine – *huang jin* or *chiew* – because of its colour. The best variety is called Shao Hsing or Shaoxing and comes from the south-east of China. Dry sherry may be used as a substitute.

Coconut milk and cream Coconut milk should not be confused with the "milk" or juice found inside a fresh coconut (though the latter makes a refreshing drink). The coconut milk used for cooking is produced from the white flesh of the nut. If left to stand, the thick part of the milk will rise to the surface like cream.

To make your own, break open a fresh coconut and remove the brown inner skin from the flesh. Grate sufficient flesh to measure 400ml/14 fl oz/1⅔ cups. Place the grated flesh, together with 300ml/½ pint/1¼ cups water, in a blender or food processor fitted with a metal blade and process for 1 minute. Strain the mixture through a sieve lined with muslin into a bowl. Gather up the corners of the muslin and squeeze out the liquid. The coconut milk is then ready to use, but you should stir it before use.

Coconut milk is also available in cans, as a soluble powder and as creamed coconut which is sold in block form. Powder and creamed coconut make a poor milk, but are useful for sauces and dressings.

Coriander Fresh coriander has a strong, pungent smell that combines well with other rich flavours. The white coriander root is used when the green colouring is not required. The seeds are also used, whole and ground.

Cornflour paste To make cornflour paste, mix 4 parts cornflour with about 5 parts cold water until smooth.

Cumin Available as whole seeds and as a powder, cumin has a strong, slightly bitter flavour and is used mainly in Indian recipes, and also in many Asian dishes.

Curry paste Curry paste is traditionally made by pounding fresh herbs and spices in a mortar with a pestle. The two types of Thai curry paste, red and green, are made with red and green chillies respectively. Other ingredients vary with individual cooks, but red curry paste typically contains ginger, shallots, garlic, coriander and cumin seeds and lime juice, as well as chillies. Herbs and flavourings in green curry paste usually include spring onions, fresh coriander, kaffir lime leaves, ginger, garlic and lemon grass. Making curry paste is time-consuming, but it tastes excellent and keeps well. Ready-made pastes, available in packets and tubs, are satisfactory substitutes.

Top shelf, left to right: *garlic, ginger, lemon grass, dried shrimps, Thai fish sauce, Szechuan peppercorns, sweet chilli sauce, ground coriander, galangal, Chinese five-spice powder, fresh green chillies*
Middle shelf: *dried red chillies, peanuts (skins on), cardamom pods, cashew nuts (in jar), peanuts (skins off), kaffir lime leaves, tamarind, hoisin sauce, salted black beans, chilli oil*
Bottom shelf, back row: *sake, rice vinegar, Chinese rice wine*
Bottom shelf, middle row: *sesame oil, mirin, peanut oil, fresh coriander, cumin seeds*
Bottom shelf, front row: *basil, dried shrimp paste, red and green chillies, flaked coconut and creamed coconut, light soy sauce, oyster sauce, pieces of coconut, whole coconut*

Dashi Light Japanese stock, available in powder form. The flavour derives from kelp seaweed. Diluted vegetable stock made from a cube may be substituted.

Dried shrimps and shrimp paste Dried shrimps are tiny shrimps that are salted and dried. They are used as a seasoning for stir-fried dishes. Soak them first in warm water until soft, then either process them in a blender or food processor or pound them in a mortar with a pestle. Shrimp paste, also known as *terasi*, is a dark, odorous paste made from fermented shrimps. Use sparingly.

Fish sauce The most commonly used flavouring in Thai food. Fish sauce (*nam pla*) is used in Thai cooking in the same way as soy sauce is used in Chinese dishes. It is made from salted anchovies and has a strong, salty flavour.

Galangal Fresh galangal, also known as *lengkuas*, tastes and looks a little like ginger with a pinkish tinge to its skin. Prepare it in the same way. It is also available dried and ground.

Garlic Garlic, together with ginger, is an indispensable ingredient in Chinese and Asian cooking.

Ginger Fresh ginger root has a sharp, distinctive flavour. Choose firm, plump pieces of fresh root with unwrinkled, shiny skins.

Gram flour Made from ground chick-peas, this flour has a unique flavour and is worth seeking out in Indian food stores.

Hoisin sauce A thick, dark brownish-red sauce which is sweet and spicy.

Kaffir lime leaves These are used rather like bay leaves, but to give an aromatic lime flavour to dishes. The fresh leaves are available from oriental food stores and can be frozen for future use.

Lemon grass Also known as citronella, lemon grass has a long, pale green stalk and a bulbous end similar to that of a spring onion. Only the bottom 13cm/5in are used. It has a woody texture and an aromatic, lemony scent. Unless finely chopped, it is always removed before serving because it is so fibrous.

Lengkuas See under Galangal.

Mirin A mild, sweet, Japanese rice wine used in cooking.

Miso A fermented bean paste that adds richness and flavour to Japanese soups.

Mooli A member of the radish family with a fresh, slightly peppery taste and white skin and flesh. Unlike other radishes, it is good when cooked, but should be salted and allowed to drain first, as it has a high water content. It is widely used in Chinese cooking and may be carved into an elaborate garnish.

Mushrooms Chinese shiitake mushrooms are used both fresh and dried to add texture and flavour to a dish. Wood ears are used in their dried form. All dried mushrooms need to be soaked in warm water for 20–30 minutes before use. Dried mushrooms are expensive, but a small quantity goes a long way.

Noodles: Cellophane noodles, also known as bean thread, transparent or glass noodles, are made from ground mung beans. Dried noodles must be soaked in hot water before cooking.

Egg noodles are made from wheat flour, egg and water. The dough is flattened and then shredded or extruded through a pasta machine to the required shape and thickness.

Rice noodles are made from ground rice and water. They range in thickness from very thin to wide ribbons and sheets. Dried ribbon rice noodles are usually sold tied together in bundles. Fresh rice noodles are also available. Rinse rice noodles in warm water and drain before use.

Rice vermicelli are thin, brittle noodles that look like white hair and are sold in large bundles. They cook almost instantly in hot liquid, provided the noodles are first soaked in warm water. They can also be deep-fried.

Somen noodles are delicate, thin, white Japanese noodles made from wheat flour in dried form, usually tied in bundles held together with a paper band.

Udon noodles, also Japanese, are made of wheat flour and water. They are usually round, but can also be flat and are available fresh, precooked or dried.

Nori Paper-thin sheets of Japanese seaweed.

Oyster sauce Made from oyster extract, this is used in many Asian fish dishes, soups and sauces.

Pak choi Also known as bok choi, this is a leaf vegetable with long, smooth, milky white stems and dark green foliage.

Palm sugar Strongly flavoured, hard brown sugar made from the sap of the coconut palm tree. It is available in oriental stores. If you have trouble finding it, use soft dark brown sugar instead.

Peanut oil This oil can be heated to a high temperature, making it perfect for stir-frying and deep-frying.

Peanuts Used in wok cookery to add flavour and a crunchy texture. The thin red skins must be removed before cooking, by immersing the peanuts in boiling water for a few minutes and then rubbing off the skins.

Red bean paste A reddish-brown paste made from puréed red beans and crystallized sugar. It is sold in cans.

Rice Long-grain rice is generally used for savoury dishes. There are many high-quality varieties, coming from a range of countries. Basmati, which means fragrant in Hindi, is generally acknowledged as the king of rices. Thai jasmine rice is also fragrant and slightly sticky.

Rice vinegar There are two basic types of rice vinegar: red vinegar is made from fermented rice and has a distinctive dark colour and depth of flavour; white vinegar is stronger in flavour as it is distilled from rice. If rice vinegar is unavailable, cider vinegar may be substituted.

Sake A strong, powerful, fortified rice wine from Japan.

Dried noodles
1 ribbon noodles, 2 somen noodles, 3 udon noodles, 4 soba noodles, 5 egg ribbon noodles, 6 medium egg noodles, 7 cellophane noodles, 8 rice sheets, 9 rice vermicelli, 10 egg noodles, 11 rice ribbon noodles

Sesame oil This is used more for flavouring than for cooking. It is very intensely flavoured, so only a little is required.

Soy sauce A major seasoning ingredient in Asian cooking, this is made from fermented soy beans combined with yeast, salt and sugar. Chinese soy sauce falls into two main categories: light and dark. Light soy sauce has more flavour than the sweeter dark soy sauce, which gives food a rich, reddish colour.

Spring roll wrappers Paper-thin wrappers made from wheat or rice flour and water. Wheat wrappers are usually sold frozen and should be thawed and separated before use. Rice flour wrappers are dry and must be soaked before use.

Sweet potato The sweet richness of this red tuber marries well with the hot-and-sour flavours of South-east Asia. In Japan the sweet potato is used to make delicious candies and sweetmeats.

Szechuan peppercorns Also known as farchiew, these aromatic, red peppercorns are best used roasted and ground. They are not so hot as either white or black peppercorns, but do add a unique taste.

Tamarind The brown, sticky pulp of the bean-like seed pod of the tamarind tree. It is used in Thai and Indonesian cooking to add tartness to recipes, rather as western cooks use vinegar or lemon juice. It is usually sold dried or pulped. The pulp is diluted with water and strained before use. Soak 25g/1oz tamarind pulp in 150ml/¼ pint/⅔ cup warm water for about 10 minutes. Squeeze out as much tamarind juice as possible by pressing all the liquid through a sieve.

Terasi See under Dried Shrimps and Shrimp Paste.

Tofu This custard-like preparation of puréed and pressed soya beans, also known as bean curd, is high in protein. Plain tofu is bland in flavour but readily absorbs the flavours of the food with which it is cooked. Tofu is also available smoked and marinated. Firm blocks of tofu are best suited to stir-frying.

Turmeric A member of the ginger family, turmeric is a rich, golden-coloured root. If you are using the fresh root, wear rubber gloves when peeling it to avoid staining your skin. Turmeric is also available in powder form.

Wasabi This is an edible root, which is used in Japanese cooking to make a condiment with a sharp, pungent and fiery flavour. It is very similar to horseradish and is available fresh, and in powder and paste form.

Water chestnuts Walnut-sized bulbs from an Asian water plant that look like sweet chestnuts. They are sold fresh by some oriental food stores, but are more readily available canned.

Wonton wrappers Small, paper-thin squares of wheat-flour and egg dough.

Top shelf, left to right: *fresh egg noodles, wonton wrappers, water chestnuts, cellophane noodles, gram flour, spring roll wrappers*
Middle shelf: *dried Chinese mushrooms, pak choi, tofu, dried egg noodles, Chinese pancakes*
Bottom shelf, at back: *rice; (in basket) mangetouts, baby sweetcorn, shallots, shiitake mushrooms; Chinese cabbage, rice vermicelli*
Bottom shelf, at front: *bamboo shoots, beansprouts, wood ears (mushrooms), spring onions, yard-long beans*

Yard-long beans Long, thin beans similar to French beans but three or four times longer. Cut into smaller lengths and use just like ordinary green beans.

Yellow bean sauce A thick paste made from salted, fermented yellow soya beans, crushed with flour and sugar.

EQUIPMENT

You don't need specialist equipment to produce a Chinese or Asian meal – you can even use a heavy-based frying pan instead of a wok in many instances. However, the items listed below will make your oriental dishes easier and more pleasant to prepare.

Wok There are many different varieties of wok available. All are bowl-shaped with gently sloping sides that allow the heat to spread rapidly and evenly over the surface. One that is about 35cm/14in in diameter is a useful size for most families, allowing adequate room for deep-frying, steaming and braising, as well as stir-frying.

Originally always made from cast iron, woks are now manufactured in a number of different metals. Cast iron remains very popular as it is an excellent conductor of heat and develops a patina over a period of time that makes it virtually non-stick. Carbon steel is also a good choice, but stainless steel tends to scorch. Non-stick woks are available but are not really very efficient because they cannot withstand the high heat required for wok cooking. They are also expensive.

Woks may have an ear-shaped handle or two made from metal or wood, a single long handle or both. Wooden handles are safer.

Seasoning the wok New woks, apart from those with a non-stick lining, must be seasoned. Many need to be scrubbed first with a cream cleanser to remove the manufacturer's protective coating of oil. Once the oil has been removed, place the wok over a low heat and add about 30ml/2 tbsp vegetable oil. Rub the oil over the entire inside surface of the wok with a pad of kitchen paper. Heat the wok slowly for 10–15 minutes, then wipe off the oil with more kitchen paper. The paper will become black. Repeat this process of coating, heating and wiping several times until the paper is clean. Once the wok has been seasoned, it should not be scrubbed again. After use, just wash it in hot water without using any detergent, then wipe it completely dry before storage.

Wok accessories There is a range of accessories available to go with woks, but they are by no means essential.

Lid This is a useful addition, particularly if you want to use the wok for steaming and braising, as well as frying. Usually made of aluminium, it is a close-fitting, dome-shaped cover. Some woks are sold already supplied with matching lids. However, any snug-fitting, dome-shaped saucepan lid is an adequate substitute.

Stand This provides a secure base for the wok when it is used for steaming, braising or deep-frying and is a particularly useful accessory. Stands are always made of metal but vary in form, usually either a simple open-sided frame or a solid metal ring with holes punched around the sides.

Trivet This is essential for steaming to support the plate above the water level. Trivets are made of wood or metal.

Scoop This is a long, often wooden-handled, metal spatula with a wooden end used to toss ingredients during stir-frying. Any good, long-handled spoon can be used instead, although it does not have quite the same action.

Bamboo steamer This fits inside the wok where it should rest safely perched on the sloping sides. Bamboo steamers range in size from small for dumplings and dim sum to those large enough to hold a whole fish.

Bamboo strainer This wide, flat, metal strainer with a long bamboo handle makes lifting foods from steam or hot oil easier. A slotted metal spoon can also be used.

Other equipment Most equipment required for cooking the recipes in this book will be found in any kitchen. However, specialist tools are generally simple and inexpensive, especially if you seek out authentic implements from oriental stores.

A selection of cooking utensils, clockwise from top: bamboo steamer, pestle and mortar, chopping board with cleaver, chef's knife and small paring knife, wok with lid and draining wire, wok scoop

Cleaver No Chinese cook would be without one. This is an all-purpose cutting tool, available in various weights and sizes. It is easy to use and serves many purposes from chopping up bones to precision cutting, such as deveining prawns. It is a superb instrument for slicing vegetables thinly. It must be kept very sharp.

Pestle and mortar Usually made of earthenware or stone, this is extremely useful for grinding small amounts of spices and for pounding ingredients together to make pastes.

Food processor This is a quick and easy alternative to the pestle and mortar for grinding spices and making pastes. It can also be used for chopping and slicing vegetables.

COOKING TECHNIQUES

STIR-FRYING

This quick technique retains the fresh flavour, colour and texture of ingredients, and its success depends upon having all that you require ready prepared before starting to cook.

1 Heat an empty wok over a high heat. This prevents food sticking and will ensure an even heat. Add the oil and swirl it around so that it coats the base and half-way up the sides of the wok. It is important that the oil is hot when the food is added, so that it will start to cook immediately.

2 Add the ingredients in the order specified in the recipe. Aromatics (garlic, ginger, spring onions) are usually added first: do not wait for the oil to get so hot that it is almost smoking or they will burn and become bitter. Toss them in the oil for a few seconds. Next add the main ingredients that require longer cooking, such as dense vegetables or meat. Follow with the faster-cooking items. Toss the ingredients from the centre of the wok to the sides using a wok scoop, long-handled spoon or wooden spatula.

DEEP-FRYING

A wok is ideal for deep-frying as it uses far less oil than a deep-fat fryer. Make sure that it is fully secure on its stand before adding the oil and never leave the wok unattended.

1 Put the wok on a stand and half-fill with oil. Heat until the required temperature registers on a thermometer. Alternatively, test it by dropping in a small piece of food: if bubbles form all over the surface of the food, the oil is ready.

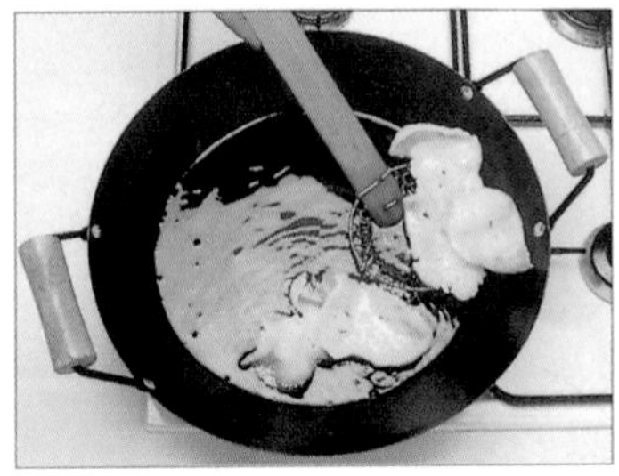

2 Carefully add the food to the oil, using long wooden chopsticks or tongs, and move it around to prevent it sticking. Use a bamboo strainer or slotted spoon to remove the food. Drain on kitchen paper before serving.

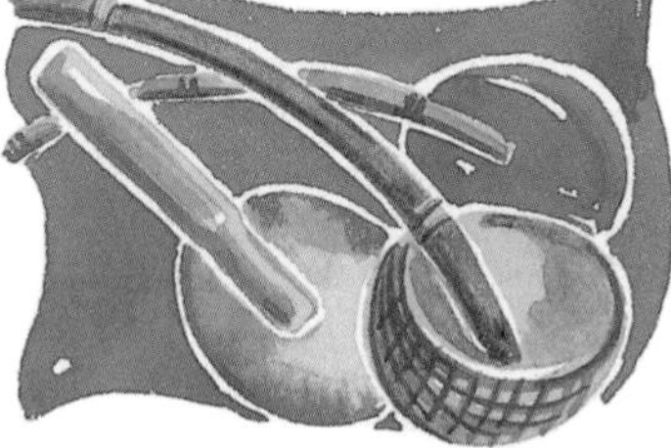

STEAMING

Steamed foods are cooked by a gentle moist heat, which must circulate freely in order for the food to cook. Steaming is increasingly popular with health-conscious cooks as it preserves flavour and nutrients. It is perfect for vegetables, meat, poultry and especially fish. The easiest way to steam food in a wok is using a bamboo steamer.

USING A BAMBOO STEAMER

1 Put the wok on a stand. Pour in sufficient boiling water to come about 5cm/2in up the sides and bring back to simmering point. Carefully put the bamboo steamer into the wok so that it rests securely against the sloping sides without touching the surface of the water.

2 Cover the steamer with its matching lid and cook for the time recommended in the recipe. Check the water level from time to time and top up with boiling water if necessary.

USING A WOK AS A STEAMER

Put a trivet in the wok, then place the wok securely on its stand. Pour in sufficient boiling water to come just below the trivet. Carefully place a plate containing the food to be steamed on the trivet. Cover the wok with its lid, bring the water back to the boil, then lower the heat so that it is simmering gently. Steam for the time recommended in the recipe. Check the water level from time to time and top up with boiling water if necessary.

SOUPS

The delicious soups in this chapter can be served as a first course, a light lunch or as part of a selection of main course dishes, as they usually do in China. Some familiar favourites include Corn and Crab Meat Soup, Hot and Sour Soup, Three Delicacy Soup and Chicken Wonton Soup with Prawns. For a change, why not try Pork and Pickled Mustard Greens Soup, Balinese Vegetable Soup or Hanoi Beef and Noodle Soup? There is even an unusual and satisfying Japanese breakfast soup, which will set up the whole family for the day ahead!

Basic Stock

This stock is used not only as the basis for soup making, but also for general cooking whenever liquid is required instead of plain water.

Ingredients

Makes 2.25 litres/4 pints/10½ cups

675g/1½lb chicken pieces, skinned
675g/1½lb pork spareribs
3.25 litres/6 pints/15 cups cold water
3–4 pieces fresh ginger root, unpeeled and crushed
3–4 spring onions, each tied into a knot
45–60ml/3–4 tbsp Chinese rice wine or dry sherry

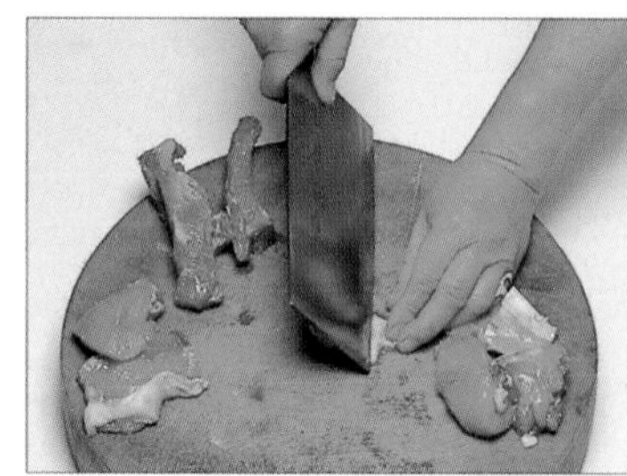

1 Trim off any excess fat from the chicken and spareribs and chop them into large pieces.

2 Place the chicken, spareribs and water in a large saucepan. Add the ginger and spring onion knots.

3 Bring to the boil and, using a sieve, skim off the froth. Reduce the heat and simmer, uncovered, for 2–3 hours.

4 Strain the stock, discarding the chicken, pork, ginger and spring onions, and return it to the pan. Add the rice wine or dry sherry and bring to the boil. Simmer for 2–3 minutes. Refrigerate the stock when cool. It will keep for up to 4–5 days. Alternatively, it can be frozen in small containers and defrosted when required.

Chicken Wonton Soup with Prawns

This soup is a more luxurious version of the familiar, basic Wonton Soup and is almost a meal in itself.

INGREDIENTS

Serves 4
275g/10oz boneless chicken breast, skinned
200g/7oz prawn tails, raw or cooked
5ml/1 tsp finely chopped fresh root ginger
2 spring onions, finely chopped
1 egg
10ml/2 tsp oyster sauce (optional)
1 packet wonton wrappers
15ml/1 tbsp cornflour paste
900ml/1½ pints/3¾ cups chicken stock
¼ cucumber, peeled and diced
salt and ground black pepper
1 spring onion, roughly shredded, 4 sprigs fresh coriander and 1 tomato, skinned, seeded and diced, to garnish

1 Place the chicken breast, 150g/5oz of the prawn tails, the ginger and spring onions in a food processor and process for 2–3 minutes. Add the egg, oyster sauce and seasoning and process briefly. Set aside.

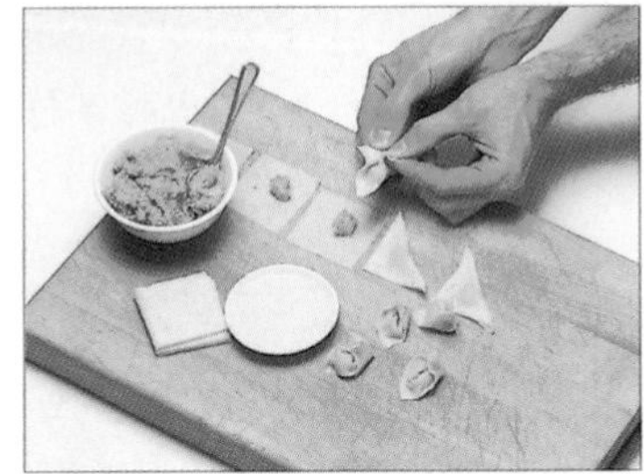

2 Place 8 wonton wrappers at a time on a surface, moisten the edges with cornflour paste and place 2.5ml/½ tsp of the chicken and prawn mixture in the centre of each. Fold them in half and pinch to seal. Simmer in salted water for 4 minutes.

3 Bring the chicken stock to the boil, add the remaining prawn tails and the cucumber and simmer for 3–4 minutes. Add the filled wontons and simmer for 3–4 minutes to warm through. Garnish with the spring onion, coriander and diced tomato and serve hot

Thai Chicken Soup

The subtle combination of herbs, spices and creamed coconut makes this satisfying soup a special treat.

Ingredients

Serves 4

15ml/1 tbsp vegetable oil
1 garlic clove, finely chopped
2 x 6oz boneless chicken breasts, skinned and chopped
2.5ml/½ tsp ground turmeric
1.5ml/¼ tsp hot chilli powder
75g/3oz creamed coconut
900ml/1½ pints/3¾ cups hot chicken stock
30ml/2 tbsp lemon or lime juice
30ml/2 tbsp crunchy peanut butter
350g/12oz thread egg noodles, broken into small pieces
15ml/1 tbsp finely chopped spring onion
15ml/1 tbsp chopped fresh coriander
salt and ground black pepper
30ml/2 tbsp desiccated coconut and ½ fresh red chilli, seeded and finely chopped, to garnish

1 Heat the oil in a large pan and fry the garlic for 1 minute until lightly golden. Add the chicken, turmeric and chilli powder and stir-fry for a further 3–4 minutes.

2 Crumble the creamed coconut into the hot chicken stock and stir until dissolved. Pour on to the chicken and add the lemon or lime juice, peanut butter and egg noodles.

3 Cover and simmer for about 15 minutes. Add the spring onion and coriander, then season well and cook for a further 5 minutes.

4 Meanwhile, place the desiccated coconut and chopped chilli in a small frying pan and heat for 2–3 minutes, stirring frequently, until the coconut is lightly browned.

5 Serve the soup in bowls sprinkled with the fried coconut and chilli.

Chinese Tofu and Lettuce Soup

This light, clear soup is brimful of nourishing, tasty vegetables.

INGREDIENTS

Serves 4

30ml/2 tbsp groundnut or sunflower oil
200g/7oz smoked or marinated tofu, cubed
3 spring onions, sliced diagonally
2 garlic cloves, cut in thin strips
1 carrot, thinly sliced in rounds
1 litre/1¾ pints/4 cups vegetable stock
30ml/2 tbsp soy sauce
15ml/1 tbsp dry sherry or vermouth
5ml/1 tsp sugar
115g/4oz Cos lettuce, shredded
salt and ground black pepper

1 Heat the oil in a preheated wok, then stir-fry the tofu cubes until browned. Drain and set aside on kitchen paper.

2 Add the onions, garlic and carrot to the wok and stir-fry for 2 minutes. Pour in the stock, soy sauce, dry sherry or vermouth, sugar and lettuce. Heat through gently for 1 minute, season to taste and serve hot.

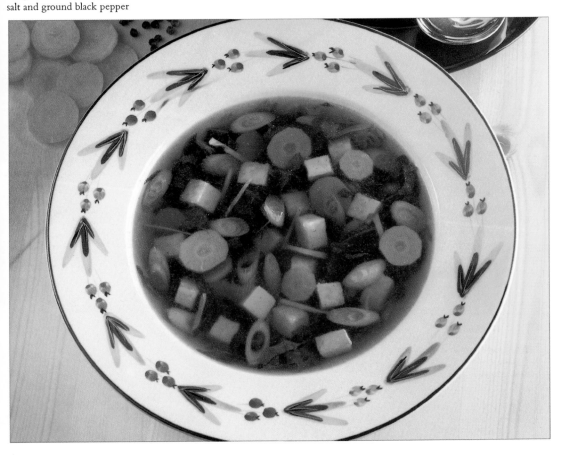

Crab and Egg Noodle Broth

This delicious broth is the ideal solution when you are hungry, time is short and you need a fast, nutritious and filling meal.

Ingredients

Serves 4

75g/3oz thin egg noodles
25g/1oz/2 tbsp unsalted butter
1 small bunch spring onions, chopped
1 celery stick, sliced
1 medium carrot, cut into batons
1.2 litres/2 pints/5 cups chicken stock
60ml/4 tbsp dry sherry
115g/4oz white crab meat, fresh or frozen
pinch of celery salt
pinch of cayenne pepper
10ml/2 tsp lemon juice
1 small bunch coriander or flat-leaf parsley, roughly chopped, to garnish

1 Bring a large saucepan of salted water to the boil. Toss in the egg noodles and cook according to the instructions on the packet. Cool under cold running water and leave immersed in water until required.

Cook's Tip

Fresh and frozen crab meat have a better flavour than canned crab, which tends to taste rather bland.

2 Heat the butter in another large pan, add the spring onions, celery and carrot, cover and cook the vegetables over a gentle heat for 3-4 minutes until soft.

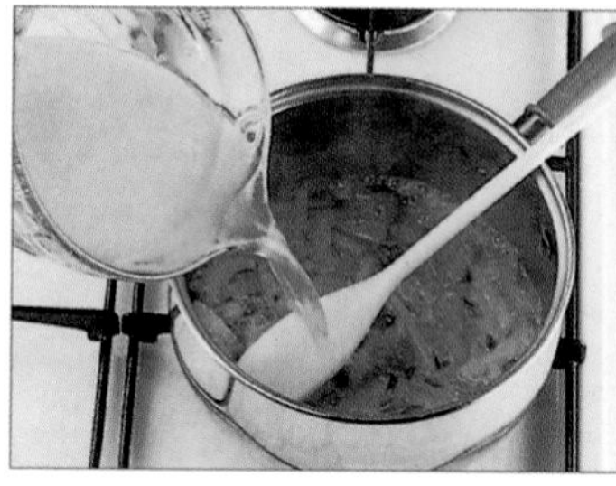

3 Add the chicken stock and dry sherry, bring to the boil and simmer for a further 5 minutes.

4 Flake the crab meat between your fingers on to a plate and remove any stray pieces of shell.

5 Drain the noodles and add to the broth together with the crab meat. Season to taste with celery salt and cayenne pepper and stir in the lemon juice. Return to a simmer.

6 Ladle the broth into shallow soup plates, scatter with roughly chopped coriander or parsley and serve immediately.

Cheat's Shark's Fin Soup

Shark's fin soup is a renowned delicacy. In this poor man's vegetarian version cellophane noodles, cut into short lengths, mimic shark's fin needles.

Ingredients

Serves 4–6
4 dried Chinese mushrooms
25ml/1½ tbsp dried wood ears
115g/4oz cellophane noodles
30ml/2 tbsp vegetable oil
2 carrots, cut into fine strips
115g/4oz canned bamboo shoots, rinsed, drained and cut into fine strips
1 litre/1¾ pints/4 cups vegetable stock
15ml/1 tbsp soy sauce
15ml/1 tbsp arrowroot or potato flour
30ml/2 tbsp water
1 egg white, beaten (optional)
5ml/1 tsp sesame oil
salt and freshly ground black pepper
2 spring onions, finely chopped, to garnish
Chinese red vinegar, to serve (optional)

1 Soak the mushrooms and wood ears separately in warm water for 20 minutes. Drain well. Remove and discard the stems from the mushrooms and slice the caps thinly. Cut the wood ears into fine strips, discarding any hard bits. Soak the noodles in hot water until soft. Drain and cut into short lengths. Leave until required.

2 Heat the oil in a large saucepan. Add the mushrooms and stir-fry for 2 minutes. Add the wood ears, stir-fry for 2 minutes, then stir in the carrots, bamboo shoots and noodles.

3 Add the stock to the pan. Bring to the boil, reduce the heat and simmer gently for 15–20 minutes. Season with salt, pepper and soy sauce.

4 Blend the arrowroot or potato flour with a little water. Pour into the soup, stirring all the time to prevent lumps from forming as the soup continues to simmer.

5 Remove the pan from the heat. Stir in the egg white if using, so that it sets to form small threads in the hot soup. Stir in the sesame oil, then pour the soup into individual bowls. Sprinkle each portion with chopped spring onions and offer the Chinese red vinegar separately, if using.

Miso Breakfast Soup

Miso is a fermented bean paste that adds richness and flavour to many of Japan's favourite soups. It is available in health food stores. This unusual soup provides a nourishing start to the day.

Ingredients

Serves 4

3 shiitake mushrooms, fresh or dried
1.2 litres/2 pints/5 cups vegetable stock
60ml/4 tbsp miso paste
115g/4oz tofu, cut into large dice
1 spring onion, green part only, sliced, to garnish

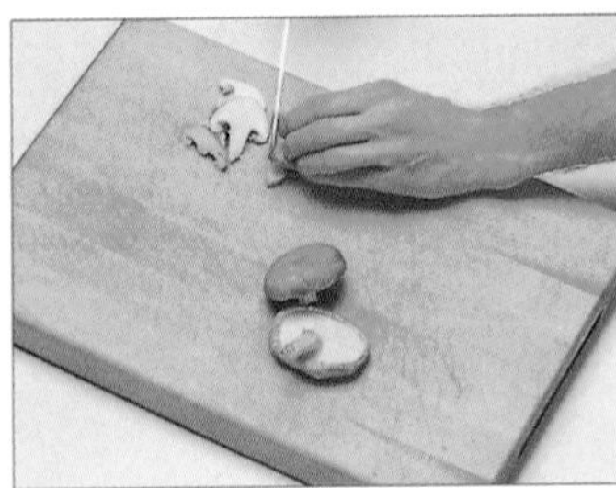

1 If using dried mushrooms, soak them in hot water for 3–4 minutes, then drain. Slice the mushrooms thinly and set aside.

2 Bring the stock to the boil in a large saucepan. Stir in the miso paste and mushrooms, lower the heat and simmer for 5 minutes.

3 Ladle the broth into 4 soup bowls and divide the tofu between them. Sprinkle over the spring onion and serve immediately.

Noodle Soup with Pork and Szechuan Pickle

Ingredients

Serves 4

1 litre/1¾ pints/4 cups chicken stock
350g/12oz egg noodles
15ml/1 tbsp dried shrimps, soaked in water
30ml/2 tbsp vegetable oil
225g/8oz lean pork, finely shredded
15ml/1 tbsp yellow bean paste
15ml/1 tbsp soy sauce
115g/4oz Szechuan hot pickle, rinsed, drained and shredded
pinch of sugar
salt and freshly ground black pepper
2 spring onions, finely sliced, to garnish

1 Bring the stock to the boil in a large saucepan. Add the noodles and cook until almost tender. Drain the dried shrimps, rinse them under cold water, drain again and add to the stock. Lower the heat and simmer for a further 2 minutes. Keep hot. Heat the oil in a frying pan or wok. Add the pork and stir-fry over a high heat for about 3 minutes.

2 Add the bean paste and soy sauce to the pork; stir-fry for 1 minute more. Add the hot pickle with a pinch of sugar. Stir-fry for 1 minute more.

3 Divide the noodles and soup among individual serving bowls. Spoon the pork mixture on top, then sprinkle with the spring onions and serve at once.

Snapper, Tomato and Tamarind Noodle Soup

Tamarind gives this light, fragrant noodle soup a slightly sour taste.

Ingredients

Serves 4

2 litres/3½ pints/8 cups water
1kg/2¼lb red snapper (or other red fish such as mullet)
1 onion, sliced
50g/2oz tamarind pods
15ml/1 tbsp fish sauce
15ml/1 tbsp sugar
30ml/2 tbsp vegetable oil
2 garlic cloves, finely chopped
2 lemon grass stalks, very finely chopped
4 ripe tomatoes, roughly chopped
30ml/2 tbsp yellow bean paste
225g/8oz rice vermicelli, soaked in warm water until soft
115g/4oz beansprouts
8–10 basil or mint sprigs
25g/1oz roasted peanuts, ground
salt and freshly ground black pepper

1 Bring the water to the boil in a saucepan. Lower the heat and add the fish and onion, with 2.5ml/½ tsp salt. Simmer gently until the fish is cooked through.

2 Remove the fish from the stock; set aside. Add the tamarind, fish sauce and sugar to the stock. Cook for 5 minutes, then strain the stock into a large jug or bowl. Carefully remove all of the bones from the fish, keeping the flesh in big pieces.

3 Heat the oil in a large frying pan. Add the garlic and lemon grass and fry for a few seconds. Stir in the tomatoes and bean paste. Cook gently for 5–7 minutes, until the tomatoes are soft. Add the stock, bring back to a simmer and adjust the seasoning.

4 Drain the vermicelli. Plunge it into a saucepan of boiling water for a few minutes, drain and divide among individual serving bowls. Add the beansprouts, fish and basil or mint, and sprinkle the ground peanuts on top. Top up each bowl with the hot soup.

Beef Noodle Soup

A steaming bowl, packed with delicious flavours and a taste of the Orient, will be welcome on cold winter days.

Ingredients

Serves 4

10g/¼oz dried porcini mushrooms
150 ml/¼ pint/⅔ cup boiling water
6 spring onions
115g/4oz carrots
350g/12oz rump steak
about 30 ml/2 tbsp sunflower oil
1 garlic clove, crushed
2.5 cm/1in piece fresh root ginger, peeled and finely chopped
1.2 litres/2 pints /5 cups beef stock
45 ml/3 tbsp light soy sauce
60 ml/4 tbsp Chinese rice wine or dry sherry
75g/3oz thin egg noodles
75g/3oz spinach, shredded
salt and ground black pepper

1 Break the mushrooms into small pieces, place in a bowl and pour over the boiling water. Set aside to soak for 15 minutes.

2 Shred the spring onions and carrots into 5cm/2in-long fine strips. Trim any fat off the rump steak and slice into thin strips.

3 Heat the oil in a large saucepan and cook the beef in batches until browned, adding a little more oil if necessary. Remove the beef with a slotted spoon and set aside to drain on kitchen paper.

4 Add the garlic, ginger, spring onions and carrots to the pan and stir-fry for 3 minutes.

5 Add the beef stock, the mushrooms and their soaking liquid, the soy sauce, rice wine or dry sherry and plenty of seasoning. Bring to the boil and simmer, covered, for 10 minutes.

6 Break up the noodles slightly and add to the pan, with the spinach. Simmer gently for 5 minutes, or until the beef is tender. Adjust the seasoning before serving.

Pork and Noodle Broth with Prawns

This delicately flavoured Vietnamese soup is very quick and easy to make, but tastes really special.

INGREDIENTS

Serves 4–6

350g/12oz pork chops or fillet
225g/8oz raw prawn tails or cooked prawns
150g/5oz thin egg noodles
15ml/1 tbsp vegetable oil
10ml/2 tsp sesame oil
4 shallots or 1 medium onion, sliced
15ml/1 tbsp finely sliced fresh root ginger
1 garlic clove, crushed
5ml/1 tsp sugar
1.5 litres/2½ pints/6¼ cups chicken stock
2 kaffir lime leaves
45ml/3 tbsp fish sauce
juice of ½ lime
4 sprigs fresh coriander and 2 spring onions, green parts only, chopped, to garnish

1 If you are using pork chops, trim away any fat and the bones. Place the meat in the freezer for 30 minutes to firm, but not freeze, it. Slice the pork thinly and set aside. Peel and devein the prawns, if using raw prawn tails.

2 Bring a large saucepan of salted water to the boil and simmer the noodles according to the instructions on the packet. Drain and refresh under cold running water. Set aside.

3 Heat the vegetable and sesame oils in a preheated wok, add the shallots or onion and stir-fry for 3–4 minutes, until evenly browned. Remove from the wok and set aside.

4 Add the ginger, garlic, sugar and chicken stock to the wok and bring to a simmer. Add the lime leaves, fish sauce and lime juice. Add the pork, then simmer for 15 minutes. Add the prawns and noodles and simmer for 3–4 minutes to heat through. Serve in shallow bowls, garnished with coriander sprigs, the green parts of the spring onion and the browned shallots or onion.

Hanoi Beef and Noodle Soup

Millions of North Vietnamese eat this fragrant soup for breakfast.

Ingredients

Serves 4–6

1 onion
1.5kg/3–3½lb beef shank with bones
2.5cm/1in fresh root ginger
1 star anise
1 bay leaf
2 whole cloves
2.5ml/½ tsp fennel seeds
1 piece of cassia bark or cinnamon stick
3 litres/5 pints/12½ cups water
fish sauce, to taste
juice of 1 lime
150g/5oz fillet steak
450g/1lb fresh flat rice noodles
salt and freshly ground black pepper

For the accompaniments

1 small red onion, sliced into rings
115g/4oz beansprouts
2 red chillies, seeded and sliced
2 spring onions, finely sliced
handful of coriander leaves
lime wedges

1 Cut the onion in half. Grill under a high heat, cut side up, until the exposed sides are caramelized, and deep brown. Set aside.

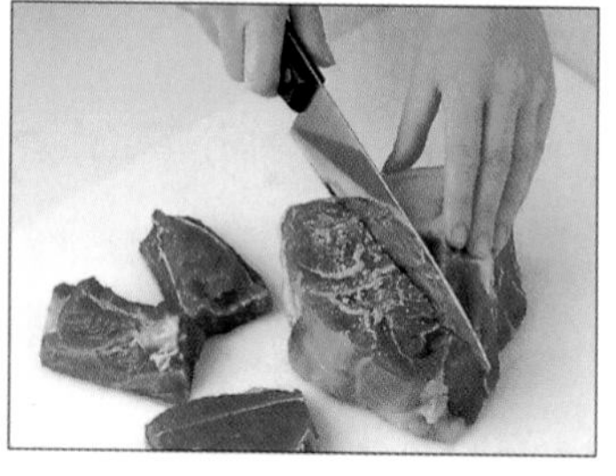

2 Cut the meat into large chunks and then place with the bones in a large saucepan or stock pot. Add the caramelized onion with the ginger, star anise, bay leaf, cloves, fennel seeds and cassia bark or cinnamon stick.

3 Add the water, bring to the boil, reduce the heat and simmer gently for 2–3 hours, skimming off the fat and scum from time to time.

4 Using a slotted spoon, remove the meat from the stock; when cool enough to handle, cut into small pieces, discarding the bones. Strain the stock and return to the pan or stock pot together with the meat. Bring back to the boil and season with the fish sauce and lime juice.

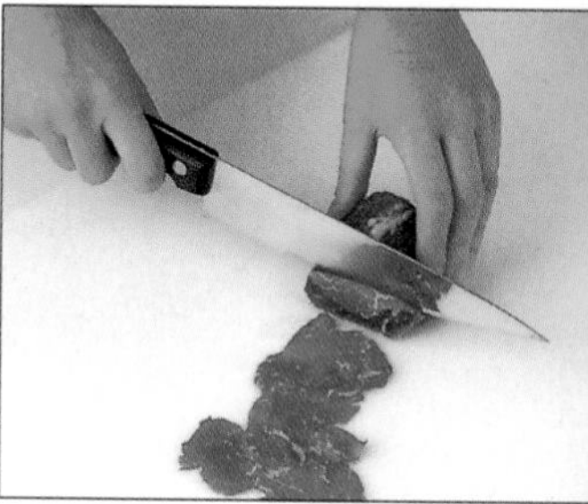

5 Slice the fillet steak very thinly and then chill until required. Place the accompaniments in separate bowls.

6 Cook the noodles in a large saucepan of boiling water until just tender. Drain and divide among individual serving bowls. Arrange the thinly sliced steak over the noodles, pour the hot stock on top and serve, offering the accompaniments separately so that each person may garnish their soup as they like.

Tamarind Soup with Peanuts and Vegetables

Sayur Asam is a colourful and refreshing soup from Jakarta with more than a hint of sharpness.

INGREDIENTS

Serves 4 or 8 as part of a buffet

For the spice paste

- 5 shallots or 1 medium red onion, sliced
- 3 garlic cloves, crushed
- 2.5cm/1in *lengkuas*, peeled and sliced
- 1–2 fresh red chillies, seeded and sliced
- 25g/1oz raw peanuts
- 1cm/½in cube *terasi*, prepared
- 1.2 litres/2 pints/5 cups well-flavoured stock
- 50–75g/2–3oz salted peanuts, lightly crushed
- 15–30ml/1–2 tbsp dark brown sugar
- 5ml/1 tsp tamarind pulp, soaked in 75ml/5 tbsp warm water for 15 minutes
- salt

For the vegetables

- 1 chayote, thinly peeled, seeds removed, flesh finely sliced
- 115g/4oz French beans, trimmed and finely sliced
- 50g/2oz sweetcorn kernels (optional)
- handful green leaves, such as watercress, rocket or Chinese leaves, finely shredded
- 1 fresh green chilli, sliced, to garnish

1 Prepare the spice paste by grinding the shallots or onion, garlic, *lengkuas*, chillies, raw peanuts and *terasi* to a paste in a food processor or with a pestle and mortar.

2 Pour in some of the stock to moisten and then pour this mixture into a pan or wok, adding the rest of the stock. Cook for 15 minutes with the lightly crushed peanuts and sugar.

3 Strain the tamarind, discarding the seeds, and reserve the juice.

4 About 5 minutes before serving, add the chayote slices, beans and sweetcorn, if using, to the soup and cook fairly rapidly. At the last minute, add the green leaves and salt to taste.

5 Add the tamarind juice and taste for seasoning. Serve, garnished with slices of green chilli.

Sweetcorn and Chicken Soup

This popular classic Chinese soup is delicious and extremely easy to make in a wok.

INGREDIENTS

Serves 4–6

1 chicken breast fillet, about 115g/4oz, skinned and cubed
10ml/2 tsp light soy sauce
15ml/1 tbsp Chinese rice wine or dry sherry
5ml/1 tsp cornflour
60ml/4 tbsp cold water
5ml/ 1 tsp sesame oil
30ml/2 tbsp groundnut oil
5ml/1 tsp grated fresh root ginger
1 litre/1¾ pints/4 cups chicken stock
425g/15oz can creamed sweetcorn
225g/8oz can sweetcorn kernels
2 eggs, beaten
salt and ground black pepper
2–3 spring onions, green parts only, cut into tiny rounds, to garnish

1 Mince the chicken in a food processor or blender, taking care not to over-process. Transfer the chicken to a bowl and stir in the soy sauce, rice wine or sherry, cornflour, water, sesame oil and seasoning. Cover and leave for about 15 minutes to absorb the flavours.

2 Heat a wok over a medium heat. Add the groundnut oil and swirl it around. Add the ginger and stir-fry for a few seconds. Add the stock, creamed sweetcorn and sweetcorn kernels. Bring to just below boiling point.

3 Spoon about 90ml/6 tbsp of the hot liquid into the chicken mixture and stir until it forms a smooth paste. Add to the wok. Slowly bring to the boil, stirring constantly, then simmer for 2–3 minutes until cooked.

4 Pour the beaten eggs into the soup in a slow, steady stream, using a fork or chopsticks to stir the top of the soup in a figure-of-eight pattern. The egg should set in lacy threads. Serve immediately with the spring onions sprinkled over.

Chicken and Asparagus Soup

This is a very delicate and delicious soup, with chicken and asparagus simply and quickly prepared in a wok.

INGREDIENTS

Serves 4
150g/5oz chicken breast fillet
5ml/1 tsp egg white
5ml/1 tsp cornflour paste
115g/4oz fresh or canned asparagus
750ml/1¼ pints/3 cups stock
salt and ground black pepper
fresh coriander leaves, to garnish

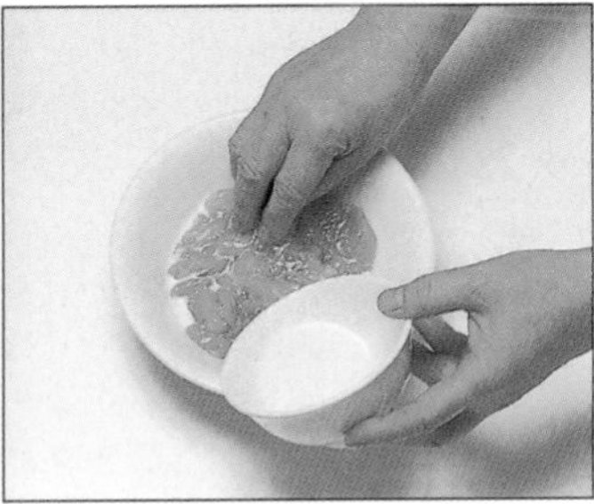

1 Cut the chicken meat into thin slices, each about the size of a postage stamp. Mix with a pinch of salt, then add the egg white and finally the cornflour paste.

2 Discard the tough stems of the asparagus, and cut the tender spears diagonally into short lengths.

3 Bring the stock to a rolling boil in a wok. Add the asparagus, bring back to the boil and cook for 2 minutes. (This is not necessary if you are using canned asparagus.)

4 Add the chicken, stir to separate and bring back to the boil once more. Adjust the seasoning to taste. Serve hot, garnished with fresh coriander leaves.

Corn and Crab Meat Soup

Surprisingly, this soup originated in the United States, but it has since been introduced into mainstream Chinese cookery. It is important that you make sure you use creamed sweetcorn in the recipe to achieve exactly the right consistency.

Ingredients

Serves 4

115g/4oz crab meat or chicken breast fillet
2.5ml/½ tsp finely chopped root ginger
2 egg whites
30ml/2 tbsp milk
15ml/1 tbsp cornflour paste
600ml/1 pint/2½ cups stock
225g/8oz can creamed sweetcorn
salt and ground black pepper
finely chopped spring onions, to garnish

1 Flake the crab meat roughly with chopsticks or chop the chicken breast. Mix the crab meat or chicken with the chopped root ginger.

2 Beat the egg whites until frothy, add the milk and cornflour paste and beat again until smooth. Blend with the crab meat or chicken breast.

3 Bring the stock to the boil in a wok. Add the creamed sweetcorn and bring back to the boil once more.

4 Stir in the crab meat or chicken breast and egg-white mixture, adjust the seasoning and simmer gently until cooked. Serve garnished with finely chopped spring onions.

Hot-and-sour Soup

This must surely be the best-known and all-time favourite soup in Chinese restaurants and take-aways throughout the world. It is fairly simple to make once you have got all the necessary ingredients together.

INGREDIENTS

Serves 4

4–6 dried Chinese mushrooms, soaked in warm water
115g/4oz pork or chicken
1 packet tofu
50g/2oz sliced bamboo shoots, drained
600ml/1pint/2½ cups stock
15ml/1 tbsp Chinese rice wine or dry sherry
15ml/1 tbsp light soy sauce
15ml/1 tbsp rice vinegar
salt and ground white pepper
15ml/1 tbsp cornflour paste

1 Squeeze the soaked mushrooms dry, then discard the hard stalks. Thinly shred the mushrooms, meat, tofu and bamboo shoots.

2 Bring the stock to a rolling boil in a wok and add the shredded ingredients. Bring back to the boil and simmer for about 1 minute.

3 Add the wine or sherry, soy sauce and vinegar and season. Bring back to the boil, then add the cornflour paste, stir until thickened and serve.

Spinach and Tofu Soup

If fresh young spinach leaves are not available, watercress or lettuce can be used instead. Sorrel leaves may also be used as a substitute, but they have a stronger and slightly more bitter flavour than spinach.

Ingredients

Serves 4
1 packet tofu
115g/4oz spinach leaves
750ml/1¼ pints/3 cups stock
15ml/1 tbsp light soy sauce
salt and ground black pepper

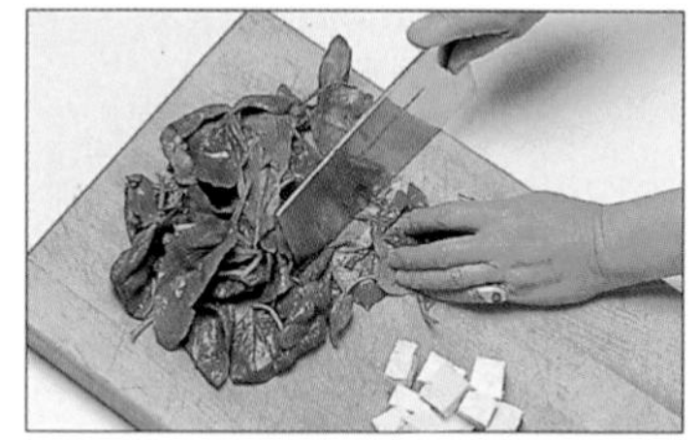

1 Cut the tofu into 12 small pieces, each about 5mm/¼in thick. Wash the spinach leaves and cut them into small pieces.

2 Bring the stock to a rolling boil in a wok. Add the tofu and soy sauce, bring back to the boil and simmer for about 2 minutes.

3 Add the spinach and simmer for a further minute. Skim the surface to make it clear, then adjust the seasoning and serve immediately.

Cook's Tip

Fresh tofu is sold in cakes about 7.5cm/3in square in Chinese food stores. Do not confuse it with fermented tofu, which is much stronger-tasting, quite salty and usually used as a condiment.

Sliced Fish and Coriander Soup

It is not necessary to remove the skin from the fish, as it helps to keep the flesh together when poached in the wok.

Ingredients

Serves 4
225g/8oz white fish fillets, such as lemon sole or plaice
15ml/1 tbsp egg white
10ml/2 tsp cornflour paste
750ml/1¼ pints/3 cups stock
15ml/1 tbsp light soy sauce
about 50g/2oz fresh coriander leaves, chopped
salt and ground black pepper

1 Cut the fish into slices, each about the size of a matchbox. Mix with the egg white and cornflour paste.

2 Bring the stock to a rolling boil in a wok and poach the fish slices for about 1 minute.

3 Add the soy sauce and coriander leaves, adjust the seasoning and serve immediately.

Three Delicacy Soup

This delicious soup combines the three ingredients of chicken, ham and prawns.

Ingredients

Serves 4
115g/4oz chicken breast fillet
115g/4oz honey-roast ham
115g/4oz peeled prawns
750ml/1¼ pints/3 cups stock
salt

> **Cook's Tip**
>
> Fresh, uncooked prawns impart the best flavour. If these are not available, you can use ready-cooked prawns. They must be added at the last stage to prevent over-cooking.

1 Thinly slice the chicken and ham into small pieces. Devein the prawns and, if they are large, cut each in half lengthways.

2 Bring the stock to a rolling boil in a wok. Add the chicken, ham and prawns. Bring back to the boil, add the salt and simmer for 1 minute. Serve the soup hot.

Lamb and Cucumber Soup

This is a variation on hot and sour soup, but it is even simpler to prepare.

Ingredients

Serves 4
225g/8oz lamb steak
15ml/1 tbsp light soy sauce
15ml/1 tbsp Chinese rice wine or dry sherry
2.5ml/½ tsp sesame oil
7.5cm/3in piece cucumber
750ml/1¼ pints/3 cups stock
15ml/1 tbsp rice vinegar
salt and ground white pepper

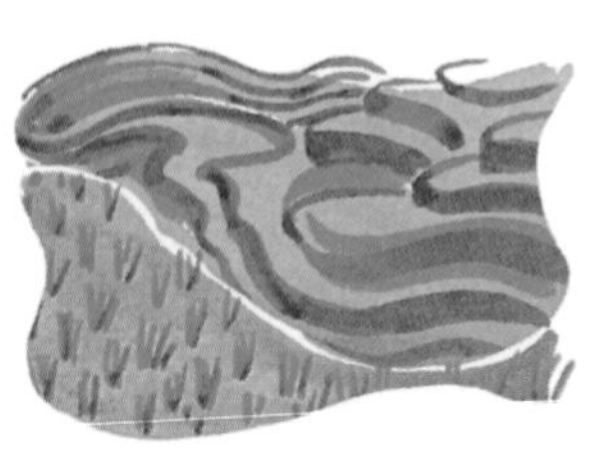

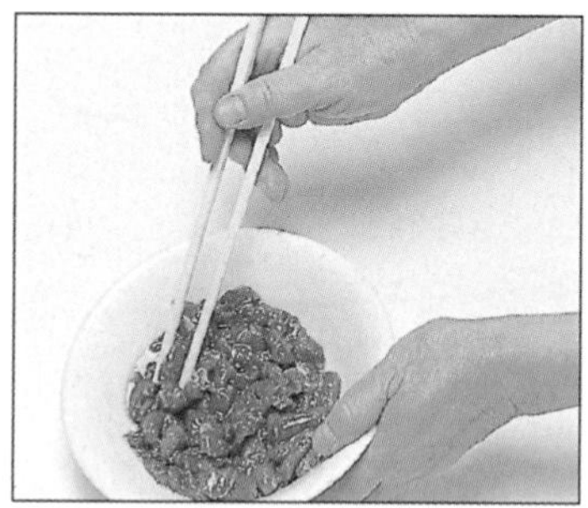

1 Trim off any excess fat from the lamb and discard. Thinly slice the lamb into small pieces. Put it into a shallow dish and add the soy sauce, rice wine or sherry and sesame oil. Set aside to marinate for 25–30 minutes. Discard the marinade.

2 Halve the cucumber piece lengthways (do not peel), then cut it into thin slices diagonally.

3 Bring the stock to a rolling boil in a wok. Add the lamb and stir to separate. Return to the boil, then add the cucumber slices, vinegar and seasoning. Bring to the boil once more, and serve at once.

Wonton Soup

In China, wonton soup is served as a snack or dim sum rather than as a soup course during a large meal.

Ingredients

Serves 4

175g/6oz pork, not too lean, roughly chopped
50g/2oz peeled prawns, finely minced
5ml/1tsp light brown sugar
15ml/1 tbsp Chinese rice wine or dry sherry
15ml/1 tbsp light soy sauce
5ml/1 tsp finely chopped spring onions
5ml/1 tsp finely chopped root ginger
24 ready-made wonton skins
about 750ml/1¼ pints/3 cups stock
15ml/1 tbsp light soy sauce
finely chopped spring onions, to garnish

1 In a bowl, mix the chopped pork and minced prawns with the sugar, rice wine or sherry, soy sauce, spring onions and chopped ginger root. Blend well and set aside for 25–30 minutes for the flavours to blend.

2 Place about 5ml/1 tsp of the filling at the centre of each wonton skin.

3 Wet the edges of each wonton with a little water and press them together with your fingers to seal, then fold each wonton over.

4 To cook, bring the stock to a rolling boil in a wok, add the wontons and cook for 4–5 minutes. Transfer to individual soup bowls, season with the soy sauce and garnish with the spring onions. Serve.

Seafood Laksa

For a special occasion serve creamy rice noodles in a spicy coconut-flavoured soup, topped with seafood. There is a fair amount of work involved in the preparation but you can make the soup base ahead.

Ingredients

Serves 4

4 red chillies, seeded and roughly chopped
1 onion, roughly chopped
1 piece *blacan*, the size of a stock cube
1 lemon grass stalk, chopped
1 small piece fresh root ginger, roughly chopped
6 macadamia nuts or almonds
60ml/4 tbsp vegetable oil
5ml/1 tsp paprika
5ml/1 tsp ground turmeric
475ml/16fl oz/2 cups stock or water
600ml/1 pint/2½ cups coconut milk
fish sauce (see method)
12 king prawns, peeled and deveined
8 scallops
225g/8oz prepared squid, cut into rings
350g/12oz rice vermicelli or rice noodles, soaked in warm water until soft
salt and freshly ground black pepper
lime halves, to serve

For the garnish

¼ cucumber, cut into matchsticks
2 red chillies, seeded and finely sliced
30ml/2 tbsp mint leaves
30ml/2 tbsp fried shallots or onions

1 In a blender or food processor, process the chillies, onion, *blacan*, lemon grass, ginger and nuts until smooth in texture.

Cook's Tip

Blacan is dried shrimp or prawn paste. It is sold in small blocks and you will find it in oriental supermarkets.

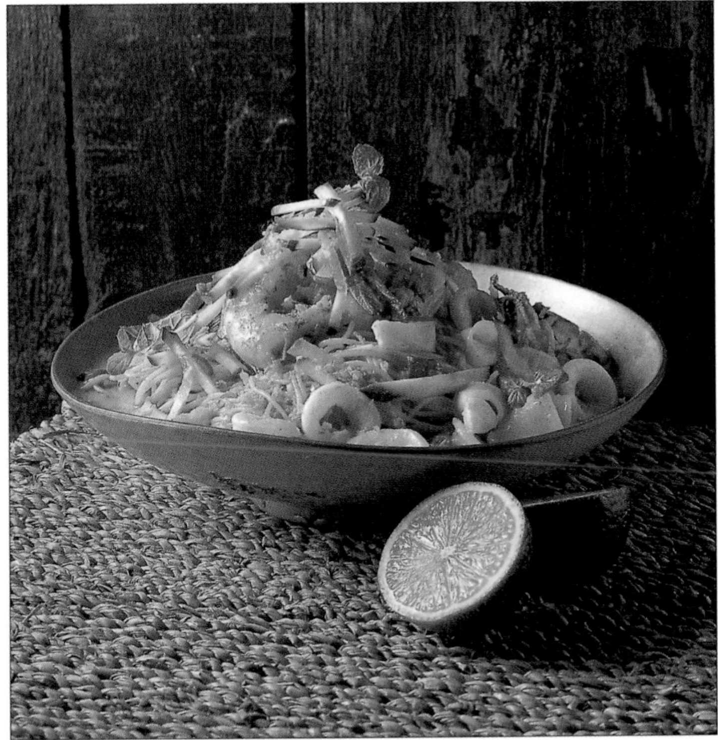

2 Heat 45ml/3 tbsp of the oil in a large saucepan. Add the chilli paste and fry for 6 minutes. Stir in the paprika and turmeric and fry for about 2 minutes more.

3 Add the stock or water and the coconut milk to the pan. Bring to the boil, reduce the heat and simmer gently for 15–20 minutes. Season to taste with fish sauce.

4 Season the seafood with salt and pepper. Heat the remaining oil in a frying pan, add the seafood and fry quickly for 2–3 minutes until cooked.

5 Add the noodles to the soup and heat through. Divide among individual serving bowls. Place the fried seafood on top, then garnish with the cucumber, chillies, mint and fried shallots or onions. Serve with the limes.

Chicken and Buckwheat Noodle Soup

Buckwheat or soba noodles are widely enjoyed in Japan. The simplest way of serving them is in hot seasoned broth. Almost any topping can be added and the variations are endless.

Ingredients

Serves 4

225g/8oz skinless, boneless chicken breasts
120ml/4fl oz/½ cup soy sauce
15ml/1 tbsp saké
1 litre/1¾ pints/4 cups chicken stock
2 pieces young leek, cut into 2.5cm/1in pieces
175g/6oz spinach leaves
300g/11oz buckwheat or soba noodles
sesame seeds, toasted, to garnish

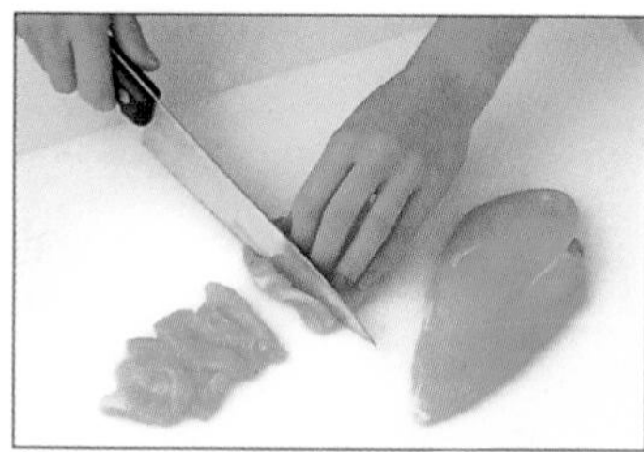

1 Slice the chicken diagonally into bite-size pieces. Combine the soy sauce and sake in a saucepan. Bring to a simmer. Add the chicken and cook gently for about 3 minutes until it is tender. Keep hot.

2 Bring the stock to the boil in a saucepan. Add the leek and simmer for 3 minutes, then add the spinach. Remove from the heat but keep warm.

3 Cook the noodles in a large saucepan of boiling water until just tender, following the manufacturer's directions on the packet.

4 Drain the noodles and divide among individual serving bowls. Ladle the hot soup into the bowls, then add a portion of chicken to each. Serve at once, sprinkled with sesame seeds.

Cook's Tip

Home-made chicken stock makes the world of difference to noodle soup. Make a big batch of stock, use as much as you need and freeze the rest until required. Put about 1.5kg/3–3½lb meaty chicken bones into a large saucepan, add 3 litres/5 pints/12½ cups water and slowly bring to the boil, skimming off any foam that rises to the top. Add 2 slices fresh root ginger, 2 garlic cloves, 2 celery sticks, 4 spring onions, a handful of coriander stalks and about 10 peppercorns, crushed, then reduce the heat and simmer the stock for 2–2½ hours. Remove from the heat and leave to cool, uncovered and undisturbed. Strain the stock into a clean bowl, leaving the last dregs behind as they tend to cloud the soup. Use as required, removing any fat that congeals on top.

Pork and Pickled Mustard Greens Soup

INGREDIENTS

Serves 4–6

225g/8oz pickled mustard leaves, soaked
50g/2oz cellophane noodles, soaked
15ml/1 tbsp vegetable oil
4 garlic cloves, finely sliced
1 litre/1¾ pints/4 cups chicken stock
450g/1lb pork ribs, cut into large chunks
30ml/2 tbsp fish sauce
pinch of sugar
freshly ground black pepper
2 red chillies, seeded and finely sliced, to garnish

1 Cut the pickled mustard leaves into bite-size pieces. Taste to check the seasoning. If they are too salty, then soak them for a little bit longer.

2 Drain the cellophane noodles and cut them into short lengths.

3 Heat the oil in a small frying pan, add the garlic and stir-fry until golden. Transfer the mixture to a bowl and set aside.

4 Put the stock in a saucepan, bring to the boil, then add the pork and simmer gently for 10–15 minutes.

5 Add the pickled mustard leaves and cellophane noodles. Bring back to the boil. Season to taste with fish sauce, sugar and freshly ground black pepper. Serve hot, topped with the fried garlic and red chillies.

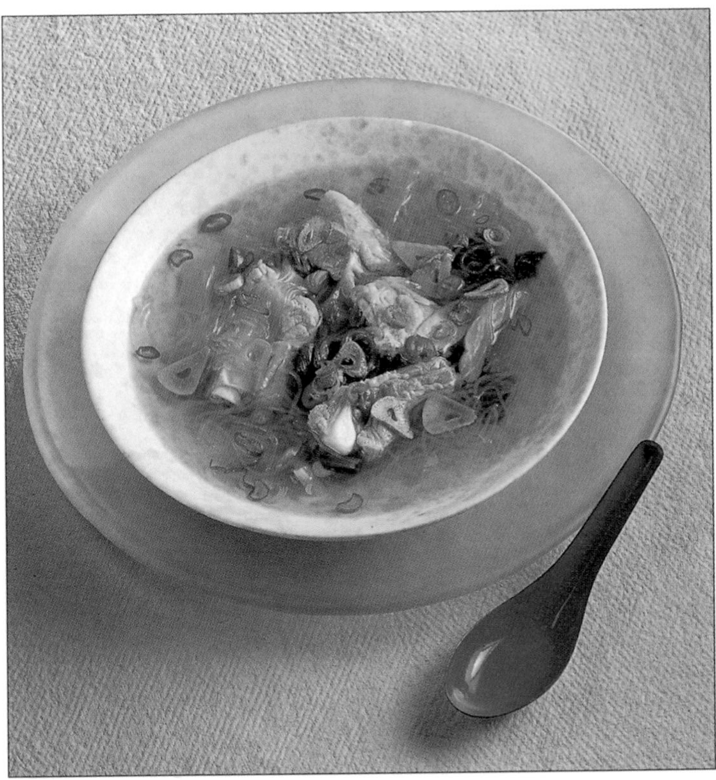

Clear Soup with Meatballs

Ingredients

Serves 8

For the meatballs

175g/6oz very finely minced beef
1 small onion, very finely chopped
1–2 garlic cloves, crushed
15ml/1 tbsp cornflour
a little egg white, lightly beaten
salt and freshly ground black pepper

For the soup

4–6 Chinese mushrooms, soaked in warm water for 30 minutes
30ml/2 tbsp groundnut oil
1 large onion, finely chopped
2 garlic cloves, finely crushed
1cm/½ in fresh root ginger, bruised
2 litres/3½ pints/8 cups beef or chicken stock, including soaking liquid from the mushrooms
30ml/2 tbsp soy sauce
115g/4oz curly kale, spinach or Chinese leaves, shredded

1 First prepare the meatballs. Mix the beef with the onion, garlic, cornflour and seasoning in a food processor and then bind with sufficient egg white to make a firm mixture. With wetted hands, roll into tiny, bite-size balls and set aside.

2 Drain the mushrooms and reserve the soaking liquid to add to the stock. Trim off and discard the stalks. Slice the caps finely and set aside.

3 Heat a wok or large saucepan and add the oil. Fry the onion, garlic and ginger to bring out the flavour, but do not allow to brown.

4 When the onion is soft, pour in the stock. Bring to the boil, then stir in the soy sauce and mushroom slices and simmer for 10 minutes. Add the meatballs and cook for 10 minutes.

5 Just before serving, remove the ginger. Stir in the shredded curly kale, spinach or Chinese leaves. Heat through for 1 minute only: no longer or the leaves will be overcooked. Serve the soup immediately.

Balinese Vegetable Soup

Any seasonal vegetables can be used in *Sayur Oelih*.

INGREDIENTS

Serves 8

225g/8oz green beans
1.2 litres/2 pints/5 cups boiling water
400ml/14fl oz/1⅔ cups coconut milk
1 garlic clove
2 macadamia nuts or 4 almonds
1cm/½ in cube *terasi*
10–15ml/2–3 tsp coriander seeds, dry-fried and ground
oil for frying
1 onion, finely sliced
2 *duan salam* or bay leaves
225g/8oz beansprouts
30ml/2 tbsp lemon juice
salt

1 Top and tail the green beans and cut into small pieces. Cook the beans in the salted, boiling water for 3–4 minutes. Drain the beans and reserve the cooking water.

2 Spoon off 45–60ml/3–4 tbsp of the cream from the top of the coconut milk and reserve it.

3 Grind the garlic, nuts, *terasi*, and ground coriander together to a paste in a food processor or with a pestle and mortar.

4 Heat the oil in a wok or saucepan, and fry the onion until transparent. Remove and reserve. Fry the paste for 2 minutes without browning. Pour in the reserved vegetable water and coconut milk. Bring to the boil and add the *duan salam* or bay leaves. Cook, uncovered, for 15–20 minutes.

5 Just before serving, add the beans, fried onion, beansprouts, reserved coconut cream and lemon juice. Taste for seasoning and adjust it, if necessary. Serve at once.

Cook's Tip

Even in the East, cooks use canned coconut milk. Any leftovers can be chilled for 3–4 days or frozen immediately, then thawed before use.

Pumpkin and Coconut Soup

Ingredients

Serves 4–6

2 garlic cloves, crushed
4 shallots, finely chopped
2.5ml/½ tsp shrimp paste
15ml/1 tbsp dried shrimps soaked for 10 minutes and drained
1 stalk lemon grass, chopped
2 green chillies, seeded
salt, to taste
600ml/1 pint/2½ cups chicken stock
450g/1lb pumpkin, cut into 2cm/¾in thick chunks
600ml/1 pint/2½ cups coconut cream
30ml/2 tbsp fish sauce
5ml/1 tsp granulated sugar
115g/4oz small cooked shelled prawns
freshly ground black pepper
2 red chillies, seeded and finely sliced, to garnish
10–12 basil leaves, to garnish

1 Grind the garlic, shallots, shrimp paste, dried shrimps, lemon grass, green chillies and salt into a paste.

2 In a large saucepan, bring the chicken stock to the boil, add the ground paste and stir to dissolve.

3 Add the pumpkin and simmer for about 10–15 minutes or until the pumpkin is tender.

4 Stir in the coconut cream, then bring back to a simmer. Add the fish sauce, sugar and ground black pepper to taste.

5 Add the prawns and cook until they are heated through. Serve garnished with the sliced red chillies and basil leaves.

Cook's Tip

Shrimp paste, which is made from ground shrimps fermented in brine, is used to give food a savoury flavour.

Chiang Mai Noodle Soup

A signature dish of the city of Chiang Mai, this delicious noodle soup has Burmese origins and is the Thai equivalent of the Malaysian 'Laksa'.

INGREDIENTS

Serves 4–6

600ml/1 pint/2½ cups coconut milk
30ml/2 tbsp red curry paste
5ml/1 tsp ground turmeric
450g/1lb chicken thighs, boned and cut into bite-size chunks
600ml/1 pint/2½ cups chicken stock
60ml/4 tbsp fish sauce
15ml/1 tbsp dark soy sauce
salt and freshly ground black pepper
juice of ½–1 lime
450g/1lb fresh egg noodles, blanched briefly in boiling water

For the garnish

3 spring onions, chopped
4 red chillies, chopped
4 shallots, chopped
60ml/4 tbsp sliced pickled mustard leaves, rinsed
30ml/2 tbsp fried sliced garlic
coriander leaves
4 fried noodle nests (optional)

1 In a large saucepan, add about one third of the coconut milk and bring to the boil, stirring often with a wooden spoon until it separates.

2 Add the curry paste and ground turmeric, stir to mix completely and cook until fragrant.

3 Add the chicken and stir-fry for about 2 minutes, ensuring that all the chunks are coated with the paste.

4 Add the remaining coconut milk, chicken stock, fish sauce and soy sauce. Season with salt and freshly ground black pepper to taste. Simmer gently for 7–10 minutes. Remove from the heat and stir in the lime juice.

5 Reheat the noodles in boiling water, drain and divide between individual bowls. Divide the chicken between the bowls and ladle in the hot soup. Top each serving with a few of each of the garnishes.

Ginger, Chicken and Coconut Soup

This aromatic soup is rich with coconut milk and intensely flavoured with galangal, lemon grass and kaffir lime leaves.

Ingredients

Serves 4–6

750ml/1¼ pints/3 cups coconut milk
475ml/16fl oz/2 cups chicken stock
4 stalks lemon grass, bruised and chopped
2.5cm/1in piece galangal, thinly sliced
10 black peppercorns, crushed
10 kaffir lime leaves, torn
300g/11oz boneless chicken, cut into thin strips
115g/4oz button mushrooms
50g/2oz baby sweetcorn
60ml/4 tbsp lime juice
45ml/3 tbsp fish sauce
2 red chillies, chopped, to garnish
chopped spring onions, to garnish
coriander leaves, to garnish

1 Bring the coconut milk and chicken stock to the boil. Add the lemon grass, galangal, peppercorns and half the kaffir lime leaves, reduce the heat and simmer gently for 10 minutes.

2 Strain the stock into a clean pan. Return to the heat, then add the chicken, button mushrooms and baby sweetcorn. Cook for about 5–7 minutes or until the chicken is cooked.

3 Stir in the lime juice, fish sauce to taste and the rest of the lime leaves. Serve hot, garnished with red chillies, spring onions and coriander.

Hot And Sour Prawn Soup with Lemon Grass

This is a classic Thai seafood soup – *Tom Yam Goong* – and is probably the most popular and well known soup from Thailand.

Ingredients

Serves 4–6

450g/1lb king prawns
1 litre/1¾ pints/4 cups chicken stock or water
3 stalks lemon grass
10 kaffir lime leaves, torn in half
225g/8oz can straw mushrooms, drained
45ml/3 tbsp fish sauce
50ml/2fl oz/¼ cup lime juice
30ml/2 tbsp chopped spring onion
15ml/1 tbsp coriander leaves
4 red chillies, seeded and chopped
2 spring onions, finely chopped

1 Shell and devein the prawns and set aside. Rinse the prawn shells and place in a large saucepan with the stock or water and bring to the boil.

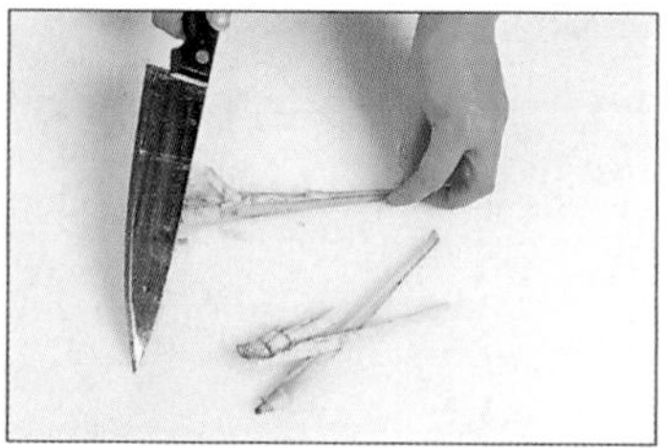

2 Bruise the lemon grass stalks with the blunt edge of a chopping knife and add them to the stock together with half of the lime leaves. Simmer gently for 5–6 minutes, until the stalks change colour and the stock is fragrant.

3 Strain the stock and return to the saucepan and reheat. Add the mushrooms and prawns, then cook until the prawns turn pink.

4 Stir in the fish sauce, lime juice, spring onions, coriander, red chillies and the rest of the lime leaves. Taste and adjust the seasoning. It should be sour, salty, spicy and hot.

Starters and Snacks

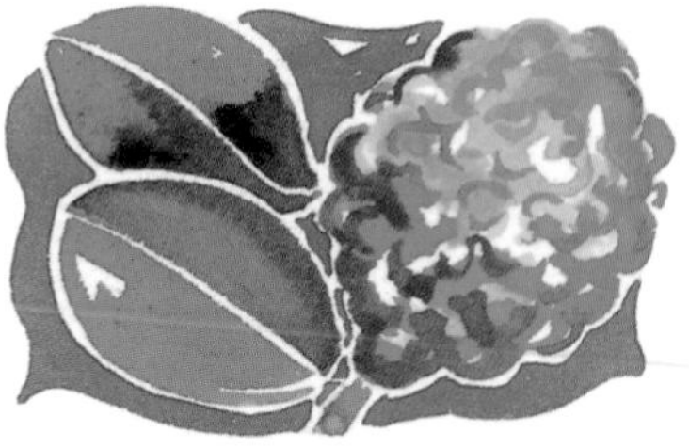

Recipes in this chapter range from robust, spicy and filling snacks to delicately flavoured, melt-in-the-mouth morsels to tempt the taste buds. Many of the mouthwatering starters – a variety of spring rolls with spicy dipping sauces, dim sum, wontons and tempura – need no introduction, as they are long-established favourites in the West. Others are lesser known but just as tasty. Try Lacy Duck Egg Nets from Thailand, Spiced Honey Chicken Wings from China or Spicy Meat Patties with Coconut from Indonesia, for example.

Prawn Crackers

These are a popular addition to many Chinese and other Far Eastern dishes and are often served before guests come to the table. Freshly cooked prawn crackers are more delicious than the ready-to-eat variety.

INGREDIENTS

Serves 4–6

300ml/½ pint/1¼ cups vegetable oil
50g/2oz uncooked prawn crackers
fine table salt, to serve

1 Line a tray with kitchen paper. Heat the oil in a large wok until it begins to smoke. Reduce the heat to maintain a steady temperature. Drop 3 or 4 prawn crackers into the oil.

2 After they swell up, remove them from the oil almost immediately before they start to colour. Transfer to the paper-lined tray to drain. Serve sprinkled with salt.

Hot Chilli Prawns

These can be prepared up to 8 hours in advance and are delicious either grilled or barbecued.

INGREDIENTS

Serves 4–6

1 garlic clove, crushed
1cm/½in piece fresh root ginger, finely chopped
1 small fresh red chilli, seeded and chopped
10ml/2 tsp sugar
15ml/1 tbsp light soy sauce
15ml/1 tbsp vegetable oil
5ml/1 tsp sesame oil
juice of 1 lime
675g/1½lb raw prawns
175g/6oz cherry tomatoes
½ cucumber, cut into chunks
salt
1 small bunch coriander, roughly chopped, to garnish
lettuce leaves, to serve

1 Pound the garlic, ginger, chilli and sugar to a paste in a mortar with a pestle. Add the soy sauce, vegetable and sesame oils, lime juice and salt to taste. Place the prawns in a shallow dish and pour over the marinade. Set aside to marinate for up to 8 hours. Soak some bamboo skewers.

2 Thread the prawns, tomatoes and cucumber chunks on to bamboo skewers. Cook under a preheated grill or on a barbecue for 3–4 minutes. Transfer to a serving dish, scatter over the coriander and serve on a bed of lettuce.

Spring Rolls with Sweet Chilli Dipping Sauce

Miniature spring rolls make a delicious starter or unusual finger-food for serving at a party.

INGREDIENTS

Makes 20–24
25g/1oz rice vermicelli noodles
groundnut oil, for deep-frying
5ml/1 tsp grated fresh root ginger
2 spring onions, finely shredded
50g/2oz carrot, finely shredded
50g/2oz mangetouts, shredded
25g/1oz young spinach leaves
50g/2oz fresh beansprouts
15ml/1 tbsp chopped fresh mint
15ml/1 tbsp chopped fresh coriander
30ml/2 tbsp fish sauce
20–24 spring roll wrappers, each 13cm/5in square
1 egg white, lightly beaten

For the dipping sauce
50g/2oz caster sugar
50ml/2fl oz rice vinegar
30ml/2 tbsp water
2 fresh red chillies, seeded and finely chopped

1 First make the dipping sauce. Place the sugar, vinegar and water in a small pan. Heat gently, stirring until the sugar dissolves, then boil rapidly until it forms a light syrup. Stir in the chillies and leave to cool.

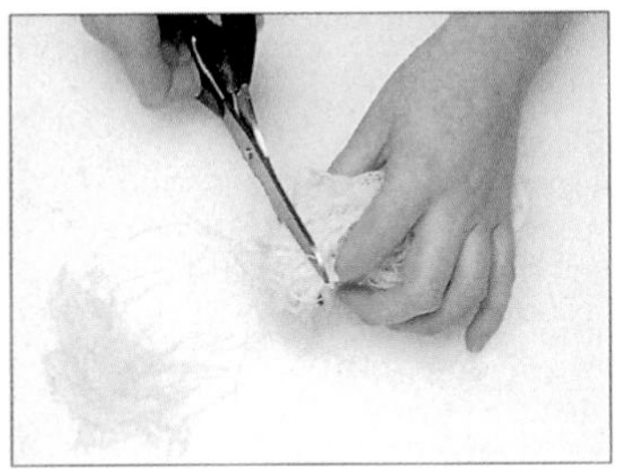

2 Soak the noodles according to the packet instructions, then rinse and drain well. Using scissors, snip the noodles into short lengths.

3 Heat 15ml/1 tbsp of the oil in a preheated wok and swirl it around. Add the ginger and spring onions and stir-fry for 15 seconds. Add the carrot and mangetouts and stir-fry for 2–3 minutes. Add the spinach, beansprouts, mint, coriander, fish sauce and noodles and stir-fry for a further minute. Set aside to cool.

4 Soften the spring roll wrappers, following the directions on the packet. Take one spring roll wrapper and arrange it so that it faces you in a diamond shape. Place a spoonful of filling just below the centre, then fold up the bottom point over the filling.

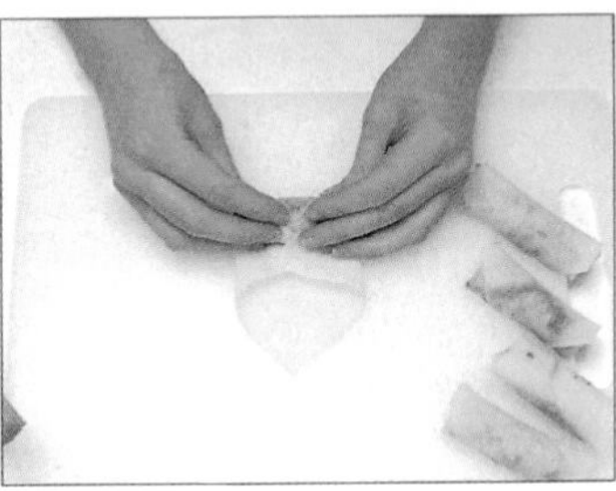

5 Fold in each side, then roll up tightly. Brush the end with beaten egg white to seal. Repeat until all the filling has been used up.

6 Half-fill a wok with oil and heat to 180°C/350°F. Deep-fry the spring rolls in batches for 3–4 minutes until golden and crisp. Drain on kitchen paper. Serve hot with the sweet chilli dipping sauce.

COOK'S TIP

You can cook the spring rolls 2–3 hours in advance, then reheat them on a foil-lined baking sheet at 200°C/400°F/Gas 6 for about 10 minutes.

Crab Spring Rolls and Dipping Sauce

Chilli and grated ginger add a hint of heat to these sensational treats. Serve them as a starter or with other Chinese dishes as part of a main course.

Ingredients

Serves 4–6

15ml/1 tbsp groundnut oil
5ml/1 tsp sesame oil
1 garlic clove, crushed
1 fresh red chilli, seeded and finely sliced
450g/1lb fresh stir-fry vegetables, such as beansprouts and shredded carrots, peppers and mangetouts
30ml/2 tbsp chopped coriander
2.5cm/1in piece of fresh root ginger, grated
15ml/1 tbsp Chinese rice wine or dry sherry
15ml/1 tbsp soy sauce
350g/12oz fresh dressed crab meat (brown and white meat)
12 spring roll wrappers
1 small egg, beaten
oil, for deep-frying
salt and ground black pepper
lime wedges and fresh coriander, to garnish

For the dipping sauce

1 onion, thinly sliced
oil, for deep-frying
1 fresh red chilli, seeded and finely chopped
2 garlic cloves, crushed
60ml/4 tbsp dark soy sauce
20ml/4 tsp lemon juice or 15–25ml/1–1½ tbsp prepared tamarind juice
30ml/2 tbsp hot water

1 First make the sauce. Spread the onion out on kitchen paper and leave to dry for 30 minutes. Then half-fill a wok with oil and heat to 190°C/375°F. Fry the onion in batches until crisp and golden, turning all the time. Drain on kitchen paper.

2 Mix together the chilli, garlic, soy sauce, lemon or tamarind juice and hot water in a bowl.

3 Stir in the onion and leave to stand for 30 minutes.

4 Heat the groundnut and sesame oils in a clean, preheated wok. When hot, stir-fry the crushed garlic and chilli for 1 minute. Add the vegetables, coriander and ginger and stir-fry for 1 minute more. Drizzle over the rice wine or dry sherry and soy sauce. Allow the mixture to bubble up for 1 minute.

5 Using a slotted spoon, transfer the vegetables to a bowl. Set aside until cool, then stir in the crab meat and season with salt and pepper.

6 Soften the spring roll wrappers, following the directions on the packet. Place some of the filling on a wrapper, fold over the front edge and the sides and roll up neatly, sealing the edges with a little beaten egg. Repeat with the remaining wrappers and filling.

7 Heat the oil for deep-frying in the wok and fry the spring rolls in batches, turning several times, until brown and crisp. Remove with a slotted spoon, drain on kitchen paper and keep hot while frying the remainder. Serve at once, garnished with lime wedges and coriander, with the dipping sauce.

Mini Spring Rolls

Eat these irresistibly light and crisp parcels with your fingers. If you like slightly spicier food, sprinkle them with a little cayenne pepper before serving.

Ingredients

Makes 20

1 green chilli
120ml/4fl oz/½ cup vegetable oil
1 small onion, finely chopped
1 garlic clove, crushed
75g/3oz cooked boneless chicken breast, skinned
1 small carrot, cut into fine matchsticks
1 spring onion, finely sliced
1 small red pepper, seeded and cut into fine matchsticks
25g/1oz beansprouts
5ml/1 tsp sesame oil
4 large sheets filo pastry
1 small egg white, lightly beaten
long chives, to garnish (optional)
45ml/3 tbsp light soy sauce, to serve

1 Carefully remove the seeds from the chilli and chop finely, wearing rubber gloves to protect your hands, if necessary.

2 Heat 30ml/2 tbsp of the vegetable oil in a preheated wok. Add the onion, garlic and chilli and stir-fry for 1 minute.

3 Slice the chicken breast very thinly, then add to the wok and fry over a high heat, stirring constantly, until browned.

4 Add the carrot, spring onion and red pepper and stir-fry for 2 minutes. Add the beansprouts, stir in the sesame oil and leave to cool.

5 Cut each sheet of filo pastry into 5 short strips. Place a small amount of filling at one end of each strip, then fold in the long sides and roll up the pastry. Seal and glaze the parcels with the egg white, then chill, uncovered, for 15 minutes before frying.

6 Wipe the wok with kitchen paper, reheat it and add the remaining vegetable oil. When the oil is hot, fry the rolls in batches until crisp and golden brown. Drain on kitchen paper and serve dipped in light soy sauce.

Cook's Tip

Be careful to avoid touching your face or eyes when seeding and chopping chillies because they are very potent and may cause burning and irritation to the skin. Try preparing chillies under running water.

Thai Spring Rolls

These crunchy spring rolls are as popular in Thai cuisine as they are in the Chinese. Thais fill their version with a garlic, pork and noodle filling.

INGREDIENTS

Makes about 24

4–6 dried Chinese mushrooms, soaked
50g/2oz bean thread noodles, soaked
30ml/2 tbsp vegetable oil
2 garlic cloves, chopped
2 red chillies, seeded and chopped
225g/8oz minced pork
50g/2oz chopped cooked prawns
30ml/2 tbsp fish sauce
5ml/1 tsp granulated sugar
1 carrot, finely shredded
50g/2oz bamboo shoots, chopped
50g/2oz beansprouts
2 spring onions, chopped
15ml/1 tbsp chopped coriander
30ml/2 tbsp flour
24 x 15cm/6in square spring roll wrappers
freshly ground black pepper
oil for frying

1 Drain and chop the mushrooms. Drain the noodles and cut into short lengths, about 5cm/2in.

2 Heat the oil in a wok or frying pan, add the garlic and chillies and fry for 30 seconds. Add the pork, stirring until the meat is browned.

3 Add the noodles, mushrooms and prawns. Season with fish sauce, sugar and pepper. Tip into a bowl.

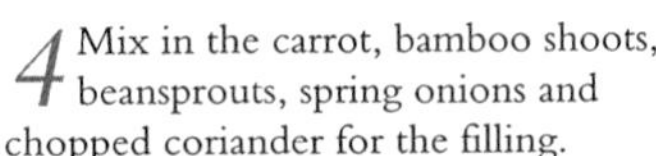

4 Mix in the carrot, bamboo shoots, beansprouts, spring onions and chopped coriander for the filling.

5 Put the flour in a small bowl and mix with a little water to make a paste. Place a spoonful of filling in the centre of a spring roll wrapper.

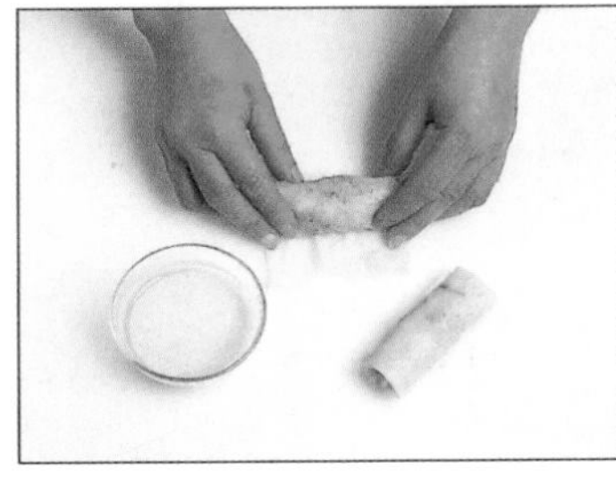

6 Turn the bottom edge over to cover the filling, then fold in the left and right sides. Roll the wrapper up almost to the top edge. Brush the top edge with flour paste and seal. Repeat with the rest of the wrappers.

7 Heat the oil in a wok or deep-fat fryer. Slide in the spring rolls a few at a time and fry until crisp and golden brown. Remove with a slotted spoon and drain on kitchen paper. Serve hot with Thai sweet chilli sauce to dip them into, if liked.

Chinese Crispy Spring Rolls

These small and dainty vegetarian stir-fried rolls are ideal served as starters or cocktail snacks. For a non-vegetarian, just replace the mushrooms with chicken or pork, and substitute prawns for the carrots.

INGREDIENTS

Makes 40 rolls

225g/8oz fresh bean sprouts
115g/4oz tender leeks or spring onions
115g/4oz carrots
115g/4oz bamboo shoots, sliced
115g/4oz white mushrooms
45–60ml/3–4 tbsp vegetable oil
5ml/1 tsp salt
5ml/1 tsp light brown sugar
15ml/1 tbsp light soy sauce
15ml/1 tbsp Chinese rice wine or dry sherry
20 frozen spring roll skins, thawed
15ml/1 tbsp cornflour paste
flour, for dusting
oil, for deep frying
soy sauce, to serve (optional)

1 Cut all the vegetables into thin shreds, roughly the same size and shape as the bean sprouts.

COOK'S TIP

To make cornflour paste, mix 4 parts dry cornflour with about 5 parts cold water until smooth.

2 Heat the oil in a wok and stir-fry the vegetables for about 1 minute. Add the salt, sugar, soy sauce and rice wine or sherry and continue stirring for 1½–2 minutes. Remove and drain the excess liquid, then leave to cool.

3 To make the spring rolls, cut each spring roll skin in half diagonally, then place about 15ml/1 tbsp of the vegetable mixture one third of the way down on the skin, with the triangle pointing away from you.

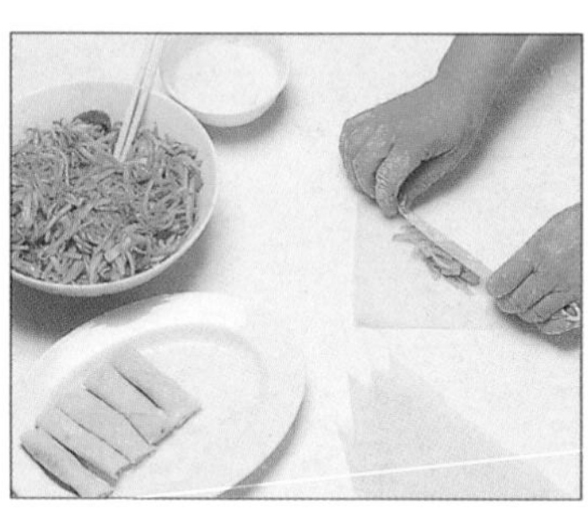

4 Lift the lower flap over the filling and roll it up once.

5 Fold in both ends and roll once more, then brush the upper edge with a little cornflour paste, and roll into a neat pack. Lightly dust a tray with flour and place the spring rolls on the tray with the flap side down.

6 To cook, heat the oil in a wok until hot, then reduce the heat to low. Deep fry the spring rolls in batches (about 8–10 at a time) for 2–3 minutes or until golden and crisp, then remove and drain. Serve the spring rolls hot with soy sauce, if liked.

Vietnamese Spring Rolls with Nuoc Cham Sauce

Ingredients

Makes 25

6 dried Chinese mushrooms, soaked in hot water for 30 minutes
225g/8oz lean ground pork
115g/4oz uncooked prawns, peeled, deveined and chopped
115g/4oz white crabmeat, picked over
1 carrot, shredded
50g/2oz cellophane noodles, soaked in water, drained and cut into short lengths
4 spring onions, finely sliced
2 garlic cloves, finely chopped
30ml/2 tbsp fish sauce
juice of 1 lime
freshly ground black pepper
25 x 10cm/4in Vietnamese rice sheets
oil for deep frying
lettuce leaves, cucumber slices and coriander leaves, to garnish

For the nuoc cham sauce

2 garlic cloves, finely chopped
30ml/2 tbsp white wine vinegar
juice of 1 lime
30ml/2 tbsp sugar
120ml/4fl oz/½ cup fish sauce
120ml/4fl oz/½ cup water
2 red chillies, seeded and chopped

1 Drain the mushrooms, squeezing out the excess moisture. Remove the stems and thinly slice the caps into a bowl. Add the pork, prawns, crabmeat, carrot, cellophane noodles, spring onions and garlic.

2 Season with the fish sauce, lime juice and pepper. Set the mixture aside for about 30 minutes to allow the flavours to blend.

3 Meanwhile make the nuoc cham sauce. Mix together the garlic, vinegar, lime juice, sugar, fish sauce, water and chillies in a serving bowl, then cover and set aside.

4 Assemble the spring rolls. Place a rice sheet on a flat surface and brush with warm water until it is pliable. Place about 10ml/2 tsp of the filling near the edge of the rice sheet. Fold the sides over the filling, fold in the two ends, then roll up, sealing the ends of the roll with a little water. Make more rolls in the same way until all the filling is used up.

5 Heat the oil for deep frying to 180°C/350°F or until a cube of dry bread added to the oil browns in 30–45 seconds. Add the rolls, a few at a time, and fry until golden brown and crisp. Drain on kitchen paper. Serve the spring rolls hot, garnished with the lettuce, cucumber and coriander. Offer the nuoc cham sauce separately.

Crab and Tofu Dumplings

These little crab and ginger-flavoured dumplings are usually served as a delicious side dish as part of a Japanese meal.

INGREDIENTS

Serves 4–6

115g/4oz frozen white crab meat, thawed
115g/4oz tofu
1 egg yolk
30ml/2 tbsp rice flour or wheat flour
30ml/2 tbsp finely chopped spring onion, green part only
2cm/¾in fresh root ginger, grated
10ml/2 tsp light soy sauce
salt
vegetable oil, for deep-frying
50g/2oz mooli, very finely grated, to serve

For the dipping sauce
120ml/4fl oz vegetable stock
15ml/1 tbsp sugar
45ml/3 tbsp dark soy sauce

1 Squeeze as much moisture out of the crab meat as you can. Press the tofu through a fine strainer with the back of a tablespoon. Combine the tofu and crab meat in a bowl.

2 Add the egg yolk, rice or wheat flour, spring onion, ginger and soy sauce and season to taste with salt. Mix thoroughly to form a light paste.

3 To make the dipping sauce, combine the stock, sugar and soy sauce in a serving bowl.

4 Line a tray with kitchen paper. Heat the vegetable oil in a wok or frying pan to 190°C/375°F. Meanwhile, shape the crab and tofu mixture into thumb-sized pieces. Fry in batches of three at a time for 1–2 minutes. Drain on the kitchen paper and serve with the sauce and mooli.

Dim Sum

Popular as a snack in China, these tiny dumplings are fast becoming fashionable in many fast-food, as well as specialist, restaurants in the West.

INGREDIENTS

Serves 4

For the dough

150g/5oz/1¼ cups plain flour
50ml/2fl oz/¼ cup boiling water
25ml/1½ tbsp cold water
7.5ml/½ tbsp vegetable oil

For the filling

75g/3oz minced pork
45ml/3 tbsp canned chopped bamboo shoots
7.5ml/½ tbsp light soy sauce
5ml/1 tsp dry sherry
5ml/1 tsp demerara sugar
2.5ml/½ tsp sesame oil
5ml/1 tsp cornflour
lettuce leaves such as iceberg, frisée or Webbs, soy sauce, spring onion curls, sliced fresh red chilli and prawn crackers, to serve

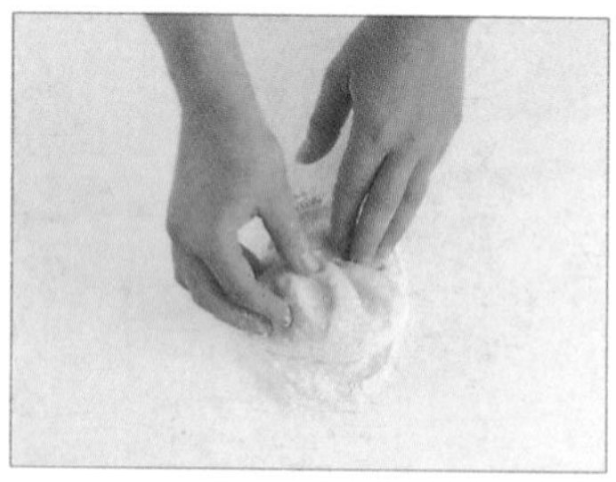

1 To make the dough, sift the flour into a bowl. Stir in the boiling water, then the cold water together with the oil. Mix to form a dough and knead until smooth.

2 Divide the mixture into 16 equal pieces and shape into circles.

3 For the filling, mix together the pork, bamboo shoots, soy sauce, dry sherry, sugar and oil.

4 Add the cornflour and stir well until thoroughly combined.

5 Place a little of the filling in the centre of each dim sum circle. Pinch the edges of the dough together to form little "purses".

6 Line a steamer with a damp tea towel. Place the dim sum in the steamer and steam for 5–10 minutes. Arrange the lettuce leaves on four individual serving plates, top with the dim sum and serve with soy sauce, spring onion curls, sliced red chilli and prawn crackers.

VARIATION

You can replace the pork with cooked, peeled prawns. Sprinkle 15ml/1 tbsp sesame seeds on to the dim sum before cooking, if wished.

Pork Dumplings

These dumplings, when shallow fried, make a good starter to a multi-course meal. They can also be steamed and served as a snack or poached in large quantities for a complete meal.

INGREDIENTS

Makes about 80–90
450g/1lb plain flour
about 475ml/16fl oz/2 cups water
flour, for dusting
salt

For the filling
450g/1lb Chinese leaves or white cabbage
450g/1lb minced pork
15ml/1 tbsp finely chopped spring onions
5ml/1 tsp finely chopped fresh root ginger
10ml/2 tsp salt
5ml/1 tsp light brown sugar
30ml/2 tbsp light soy sauce
15ml/1 tbsp Chinese rice wine or dry sherry
10ml/2 tsp sesame oil

For the dipping sauce
30ml/2 tbsp red chilli oil
15ml/1 tbsp light soy sauce
15ml/1 tbsp finely chopped garlic
15ml/1 tbsp finely chopped spring onions

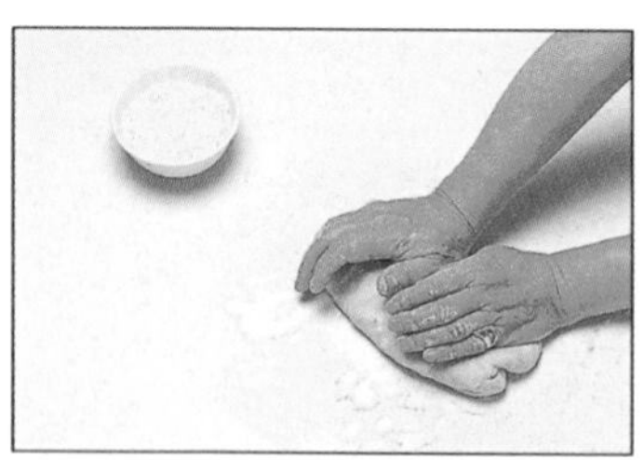

1 Sift the flour into a bowl, then pour in the water and mix to a firm dough. Knead until smooth on a lightly floured surface, then cover with a damp cloth and set aside for 25–30 minutes.

2 For the filling, blanch the Chinese leaves or cabbage until soft. Drain and chop finely. Mix the cabbage with the pork, spring onions, ginger, salt, sugar, soy sauce, wine and sesame oil.

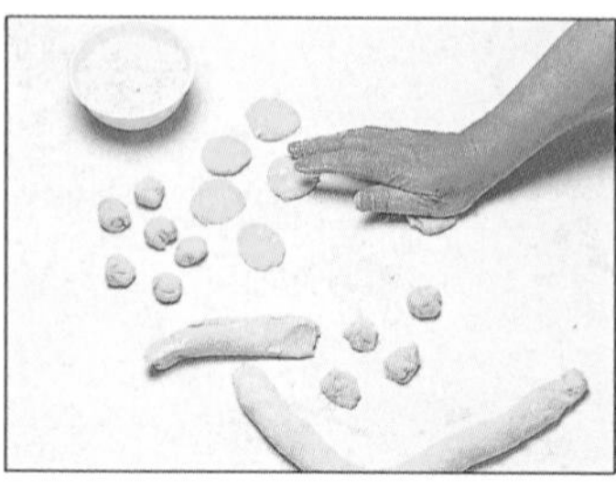

3 Lightly dust a work surface with the flour. Knead and roll the dough into a long sausage about 2.5cm/1in in diameter. Cut the sausage in about 80–90 small pieces and flatten each piece with the palm of your hand.

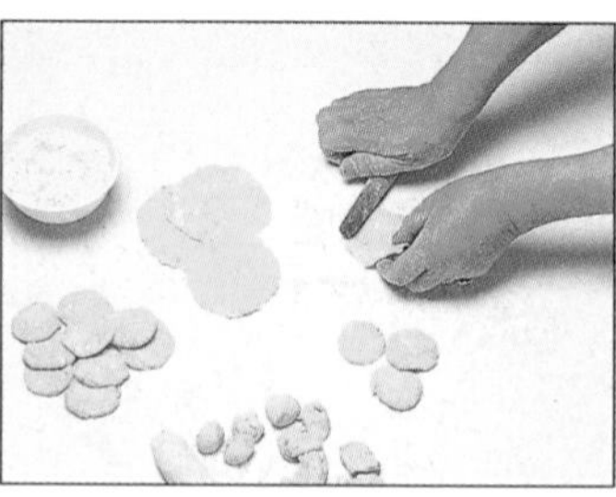

4 Using a rolling pin, roll out each piece into a thin pancake about 6cm/2½in in diameter.

5 Place about 25ml/1½ tbsp of the filling in the centre of each pancake and fold into a half-moon pouch.

6 Pinch the edges firmly so that the dumpling is tightly sealed.

7 Bring 150ml/¼ pint/⅔ cup salted water to the boil in a wok. Add the dumplings and poach for 2 minutes. Remove the wok from the heat and leave the dumplings in the water for a further 15 minutes.

8 Make the dipping sauce by combining all the sauce ingredients in a bowl and mixing well. Serve in a small bowl with the dumplings.

Seafood Wontons with Coriander Dressing

These tasty wontons resemble tortellini. Water chestnuts add a light crunch to the filling.

INGREDIENTS

Serves 4

225g/8oz raw prawns, peeled and deveined
115g/4oz white crabmeat, picked over
4 canned water chestnuts, finely diced
1 spring onion, finely chopped
1 small green chilli, seeded and finely chopped
2.5ml/½ tsp grated fresh root ginger
1 egg, separated
20–24 wonton wrappers
salt and ground black pepper
coriander leaves, to garnish

For the coriander dressing

30ml/2 tbsp rice vinegar
15ml/1 tbsp chopped pickled ginger
90ml/6 tbsp olive oil
15ml/1 tbsp soy sauce
45ml/3 tbsp chopped coriander
30ml/2 tbsp finely diced red pepper

1 Finely dice the prawns and place them in a bowl. Add the crabmeat, water chestnuts, spring onion, chilli, ginger and egg white. Season with salt and pepper and stir well.

2 Place a wonton wrapper on a board. Put about 5ml/1 tsp of the filling just above the centre of the wrapper. With a pastry brush, moisten the edges of the wrapper with a little of the egg yolk. Bring the bottom of the wrapper up over the filling. Press gently to expel any air, then seal the wrapper neatly in a triangle.

3 For a more elaborate shape, bring the two side points up over the filling, overlap the points and pinch the ends firmly together. Space the filled wontons on a large baking sheet lined with greaseproof paper, so that they do not stick together.

4 Half fill a large saucepan with water. Bring to simmering point. Add the filled wontons, a few at a time and simmer for 2–3 minutes. The wontons will float to the surface. When ready the wrappers will be translucent and the filling should be cooked. Remove the wontons with a large slotted spoon, drain them briefly, then spread them on trays. Keep warm while cooking the remaining wontons.

5 Make the coriander dressing by whisking all the ingredients together in a bowl. Divide the wontons among serving dishes, drizzle with the dressing and serve garnished with a handful of coriander leaves.

Steamed Pork and Water Chestnut Wontons

Ginger and Chinese five-spice powder flavour this version of steamed dumplings – a favourite snack in many teahouses.

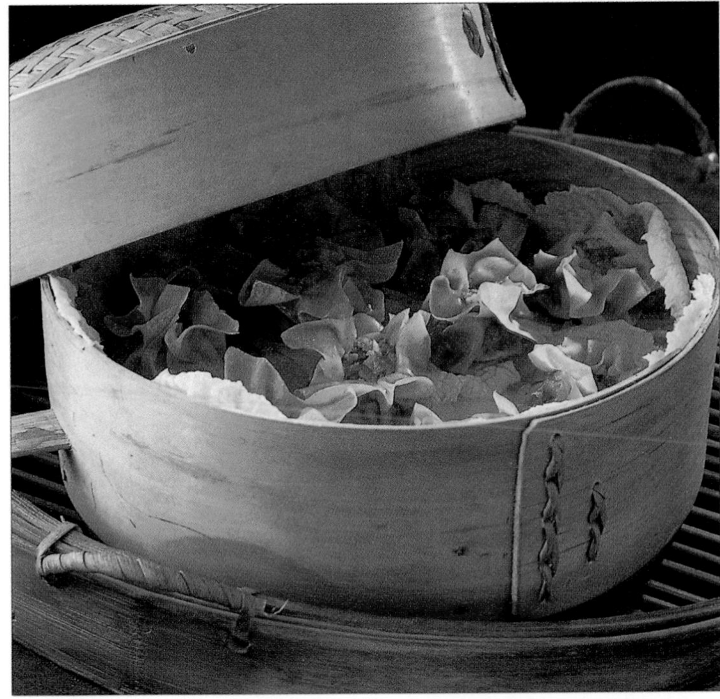

INGREDIENTS

Makes about 36

- 2 large Chinese cabbage leaves, plus extra for lining the steamer
- 2 spring onions, finely chopped
- 1cm/½in fresh root ginger, chopped
- 50g/2oz canned water chestnuts, rinsed and finely chopped
- 225g/8oz minced pork
- 2.5ml/½ tsp Chinese five-spice powder
- 15ml/1 tbsp cornflour
- 15ml/1 tbsp light soy sauce
- 15ml/1 tbsp Chinese rice wine or dry sherry
- 10ml/2 tsp sesame oil
- generous pinch of caster sugar
- about 36 wonton wrappers, each 7.5cm/3in square
- light soy sauce and hot chilli oil, for dipping

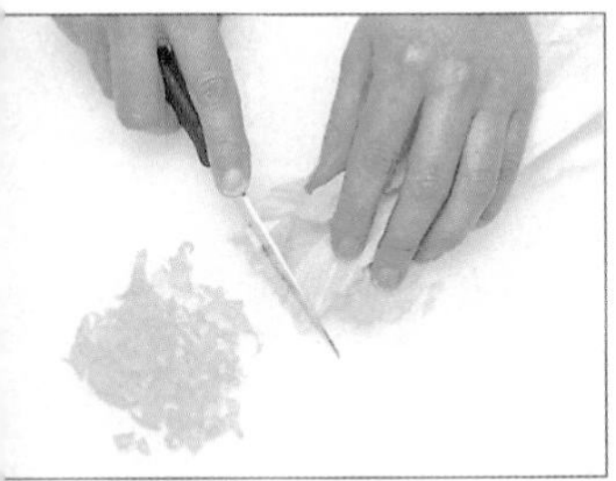

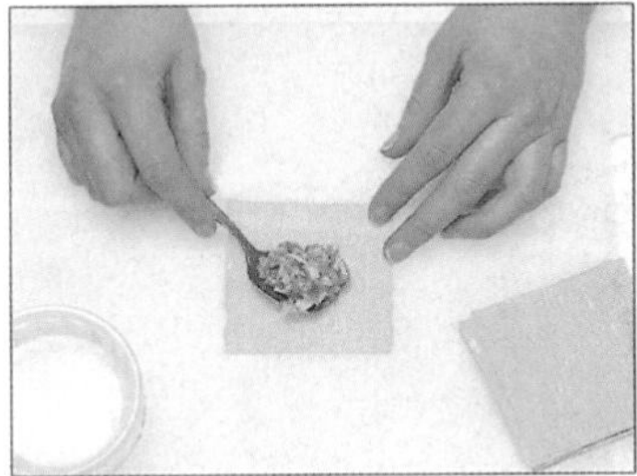

1 Place the Chinese cabbage leaves on top of one another. Cut them lengthways into quarters and then across into thin shreds.

2 Place the shredded Chinese cabbage leaves in a bowl. Add the spring onions, ginger, water chestnuts, pork, five-spice powder, cornflour, soy sauce, rice wine or dry sherry, sesame oil and sugar and mix well.

3 Place a heaped teaspoon of the filling in the centre of the wrapper. Lightly dampen the edges with water.

4 Lift the wrapper up around the filling, gathering it to form a "purse". Squeeze the wrapper firmly around the middle, then tap the bottom to make a flat base. The top should be open. Place the wonton on a tray and cover with a damp tea towel. Repeat.

5 Line a steamer with cabbage leaves and steam the dumplings for 12–15 minutes, until tender. Remove each batch from the steamer as soon as they are cooked, cover with foil and keep warm. Serve hot with soy sauce and chilli oil for dipping.

Seared Scallops with Wonton Crisps

Quick seared scallops with crisp vegetables in a lightly spiced sauce make a delightful starter.

INGREDIENTS

Serves 4
16 medium scallops, halved
oil for deep frying
8 wonton wrappers
45ml/3 tbsp olive oil
1 large carrot, cut into long thin strips
1 large leek, cut into long thin strips
juice of 1 lemon
juice of ½ orange
2 spring onions, finely sliced
30ml/2 tbsp coriander leaves
salt and freshly ground black pepper

For the marinade
5ml/1 tsp Thai red curry paste
5ml/1 tsp grated fresh root ginger
1 garlic clove, finely chopped
15ml/1 tbsp soy sauce
15ml/1 tbsp olive oil

1 Make the marinade by mixing all the ingredients in a bowl. Add the scallops, toss to coat and leave to marinate for about 30 minutes.

2 Heat the oil in a large heavy-based saucepan or deep fryer and deep fry the wonton wrappers in small batches until crisp and golden.

3 When the wrappers are ready, drain them on kitchen paper and set aside until required.

4 Heat half the olive oil in a large frying pan. Add the scallops, with the marinade, and sear over a high heat for about 1 minute or until golden, taking care not to overcook (they should feel firm to the touch but not rubbery). Using a slotted spoon, transfer the scallops to a plate.

5 Add the remaining olive oil to the pan. When hot, add the carrot and leek strips. Toss and turn the vegetables until they start to wilt and soften, but remain crisp. Season to taste with salt and pepper, stir in the lemon and orange juices, and add a little more soy sauce if needed.

6 Return the scallops to the pan, mix lightly with the vegetables and heat for just long enough to warm through. Transfer to a bowl and add the spring onions and coriander. To serve, sandwich a quarter of the mixture between two wonton crisps. Make three more "sandwiches" in the same way and serve at once.

Wonton Flowers with Sweet-and-sour Sauce

These melt-in-the-mouth, crisp dumplings make a delicious first course or snack – and take hardly any time at all to prepare.

INGREDIENTS

Serves 4–6
16–20 wonton wrappers
vegetable oil, for deep-frying

For the sauce
15ml/1 tbsp vegetable oil
30ml/2 tbsp light brown sugar
45ml/3 tbsp rice vinegar
15ml/1 tbsp light soy sauce
15ml/1 tbsp tomato ketchup
45–60ml/3–4 tbsp stock or water
15ml/1 tbsp cornflour paste

1 Pinch the centre of each wonton wrapper and twist it around to form a floral shape.

2 Heat the oil in a wok and deep-fry the floral wontons for 1–2 minutes, until crisp. Remove and drain on kitchen paper.

3 To make the sauce, heat the oil in a wok or frying pan and add the sugar, vinegar, soy sauce, tomato ketchup and stock or water.

4 Stir in the cornflour paste to thicken the sauce. Continue stirring until smooth. Pour a little sauce over the wontons and serve immediately with the remaining sauce.

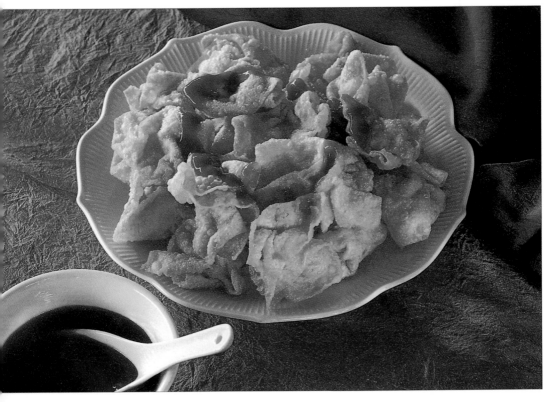

Butterfly Prawns

For best results, use uncooked giant or king prawns in their shells for this deep fried dish. Sold headless, they are about 8–10cm/3–4in long, and you should get 18–20 prawns per 450g/1lb.

INGREDIENTS

Serves 6–8

450g/1lb uncooked prawns in their shells, headless
5ml/1 tsp ground Szechuan peppercorns
15ml/1 tbsp light soy sauce
15ml/1 tbsp Chinese rice wine or dry sherry
10ml/2 tsp cornflour
2 eggs, lightly beaten
60–75ml/4–5 tbsp breadcrumbs
vegetable oil, for deep frying
2–3 spring onions, to garnish
lettuce leaves or crispy "seaweed", to serve

1 Peel the prawns but leave the tails on. Split the prawns in half from the underbelly, about three-quarters of the way through, leaving the tails still firmly attached.

2 Put the prawns in a bowl with the pepper, soy sauce, rice wine or sherry and cornflour and set aside to marinate for 10–15 minutes.

3 Pick up one prawn at a time by the tail, and dip it in the beaten egg.

4 Roll the egg-covered prawns in breadcrumbs.

5 Heat the oil in a wok until medium-hot. Gently lower the prawns into the oil.

6 Deep fry the prawns in batches until golden brown. Remove and drain. Garnish with spring onions, which are either raw or have been soaked for about 30 seconds in hot oil. To serve, arrange the prawns neatly on a bed of lettuce leaves or crispy "seaweed".

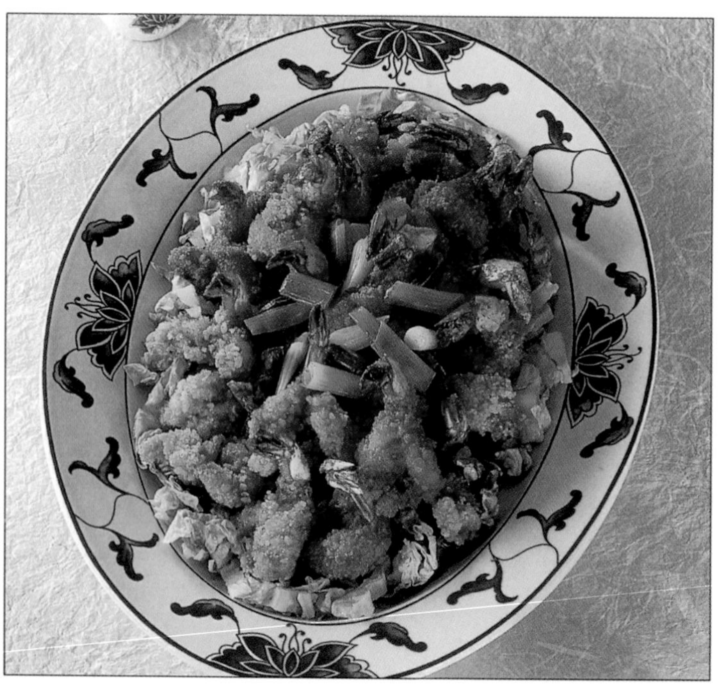

Deep-fried Squid with Spicy Salt and Pepper

This recipe is one of the specialities of the Cantonese school of cuisine. Southern China is famous for its seafood, often flavoured with ginger.

INGREDIENTS

Serves 4

450g/1lb squid
5ml/1 tsp ginger juice, see Cook's Tip
15ml/1 tbsp Chinese rice wine or dry sherry
about 575ml/1 pint/2½ cups boiling water
vegetable oil, for deep frying
spicy salt and pepper
fresh coriander leaves, to garnish

1 Clean the squid by discarding the head and the transparent backbone as well as the ink bag; peel off and discard the thin skin, then wash the squid and dry well on kitchen paper. Open up the squid and, using a sharp knife, score the inside of the flesh in a criss-cross pattern.

2 Cut the squid into pieces, each about the size of a postage stamp. Marinate in a bowl with the ginger juice and rice wine or sherry for 25–30 minutes.

3 Blanch the squid in boiling water for a few seconds – each piece will curl up and the criss-cross pattern will open out to resemble ears of corn. Remove and drain. Dry well.

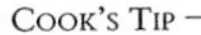

COOK'S TIP

To make ginger juice, mix finely chopped or grated fresh root ginger with an equal quantity of cold water and place in a piece of damp muslin. Twist tightly to extract the juice. Alternatively, crush the ginger in a garlic press.

4 Heat sufficient oil for deep frying in a wok. Deep fry the squid for 15–20 seconds only, remove quickly and drain. Sprinkle with the spicy salt and pepper and serve garnished with fresh coriander leaves.

Quick-fried Prawns with Hot Spices

These spicy prawns are stir-fried in moments to make a wonderful starter. Don't forget that you will need to provide your guests with finger bowls.

INGREDIENTS

Serves 4

450g/1lb large raw prawns
2.5cm/1in fresh root ginger, grated
2 garlic cloves, crushed
5ml/1 tsp hot chilli powder
5ml/1 tsp ground turmeric
10ml/2 tsp black mustard seeds
seeds from 4 green cardamom pods, crushed
50g/2oz/4 tbsp ghee or butter
120ml/4fl oz/½ cup coconut milk
salt and ground black pepper
30–45ml/2–3 tbsp chopped fresh coriander, to garnish
naan bread, to serve

1 Peel the prawns carefully, leaving the tails attached.

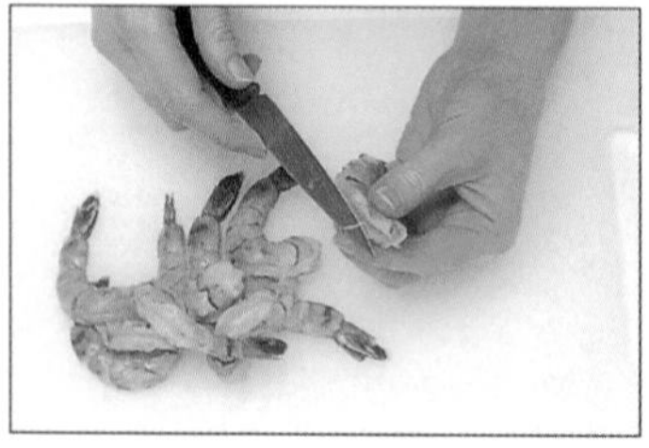

2 Using a small sharp knife, make a slit along the back of each prawn and remove the dark vein. Rinse under cold running water, drain and pat dry.

3 Put the ginger, garlic, chilli powder, turmeric, mustard seeds and cardamom seeds in a bowl. Add the prawns and toss to coat completely with spice mixture.

4 Heat a wok until hot. Add the ghee or butter and swirl it around until foaming.

5 Add the marinated prawns and stir fry for 1–1½ minutes until they are just turning pink.

6 Stir in the coconut milk and simmer for 3–4 minutes until the prawns are just cooked through. Season to taste with salt and pepper. Sprinkle over the coriander and serve at once with naan bread.

Crab, Pork and Mushroom Spring Rolls

If you cannot obtain minced pork, use the meat from the equivalent weight of best-quality pork sausages. Filled spring rolls can be made in advance and kept in the refrigerator until they are ready for frying.

INGREDIENTS

Serves 4–6

25g/1oz rice noodles
50g/2oz shiitake mushrooms, fresh or dried
vegetable oil, for deep-frying
4 spring onions, chopped
1 small carrot, grated
175g/6oz minced pork
115g/4oz white crab meat
5ml/1 tsp fish sauce (optional)
12 frozen spring roll wrappers, defrosted
30ml/2 tbsp cornflour paste
salt and ground black pepper
1 iceberg or bib lettuce, separated into leaves
1 bunch fresh mint or basil, coarsely chopped
1 bunch fresh coriander leaves, coarsely chopped
½ cucumber, sliced

1 Bring a large saucepan of salted water to the boil, add the noodles and simmer for 8 minutes. Cut the noodles into finger-length pieces. If the mushrooms are dried, soak them in boiling water for 10 minutes, then drain. Slice the mushrooms thinly.

2 To make the filling, heat 15ml/1 tbsp of the oil in a wok or frying pan, add the spring onions, carrot and pork and cook for 8–10 minutes. Remove from the heat, then add the crab meat, fish sauce, if using, and seasoning. Add the noodles and mushrooms and set aside.

3 To fill the rolls, brush one spring roll wrapper at a time with the cornflour paste, then place 5ml/1 tsp of the filling on to the skin. Fold the edges towards the middle and roll evenly to make a neat cigar shape. The paste will help seal the wrapper.

4 Heat the oil for deep-frying in a wok or deep-fryer until hot. Fry the spring rolls two at a time for 6–8 minutes. Make sure the oil is not too hot or the filling will not heat through properly. Arrange the salad leaves, mint or basil, coriander and cucumber on a serving platter and top with the spring rolls.

Hot Spicy Crab Claws

Crab claws are used to delicious effect in this quick stir-fried starter based on an Indonesian dish called *kepiting pedas*.

Ingredients

Serves 4

12 fresh or frozen and thawed cooked crab claws
4 shallots, roughly chopped
2–4 fresh red chillies, seeded and roughly chopped
3 garlic cloves, roughly chopped
5ml/1 tsp grated fresh root ginger
2.5ml/½ tsp ground coriander
45ml/3 tbsp groundnut oil
60ml/4 tbsp water
10ml/2 tsp sweet soy sauce (*kecap manis*)
10–15ml/2–3 tsp lime juice
salt
fresh coriander leaves, to garnish

1 Crack the crab claws with the back of a heavy knife to make eating them easier and set aside. In a mortar, pound the chopped shallots with the pestle until pulpy. Add the chillies, garlic, ginger and ground coriander and pound until the mixture forms a fairly coarse paste.

2 Heat the wok over a medium heat. Add the oil and swirl it around. When it is hot, stir in the chilli paste. Stir-fry for about 30 seconds. Increase the heat to high. Add the crab claws and stir-fry for another 3–4 minutes.

3 Stir in the water, sweet soy sauce, lime juice and salt to taste. Continue to stir-fry for 1–2 minutes. Serve at once, garnished with fresh coriander. The crab claws are eaten with the fingers, so it is helpful to provide finger bowls.

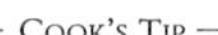

Cook's Tip

If whole crab claws are unavailable, look out for frozen ready-prepared crab claws. These are shelled with just the tip of the claw attached to the whole meat. Stir-fry for about 2 minutes until hot through.

Steamed Seafood Packets

Very neat and delicate, these steamed packets make an excellent starter or a light lunch.

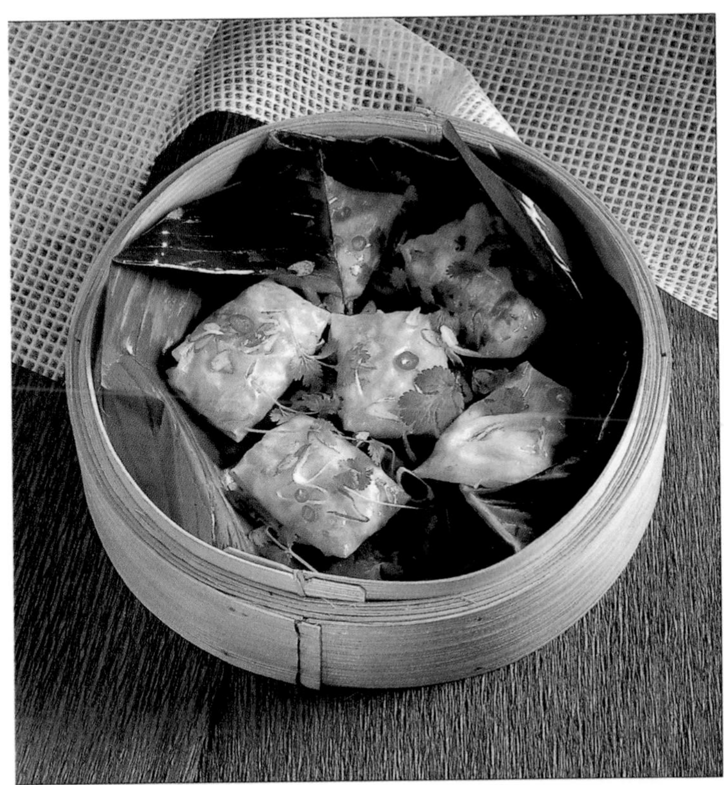

Ingredients

Serves 4

225g/8oz crab meat
50g/2oz shelled prawns, chopped
6 water chestnuts, chopped
30ml/2 tbsp chopped bamboo shoots
15ml/1 tbsp chopped spring onion
5ml/1 tsp chopped root ginger
15ml/1 tbsp soy sauce
15ml/1 tbsp fish sauce
12 rice sheets
banana leaves
oil for brushing
15ml/1 tbsp soy sauce
2 spring onions, shredded, to garnish
2 red chillies, seeded and sliced, to garnish
coriander leaves, to garnish

1 Combine the crab meat, chopped prawns, chestnuts, bamboo shoots, spring onion and ginger in a bowl. Mix well, then add the soy sauce and fish sauce. Stir until blended.

2 Take a rice sheet and dip it in warm water. Place it on a flat surface and leave for a few seconds to soften.

3 Place a spoonful of the filling in the centre of the sheet and fold into a square packet. Repeat with the rest of the rice sheets and seafood mixture.

4 Use banana leaves to line a steamer, then brush them with oil. Place the packets, seam-side down, on the leaves and steam over a high heat for 6–8 minutes or until the filling is cooked. Transfer to a plate and garnish with the remaining ingredients.

Cook's Tip

The seafood packets will spread out when steamed so be sure to space them well apart to prevent them sticking together.

Crisp-fried Crab Claws

Ingredients

Serves 4

50g/2oz rice flour
15ml/1 tbsp cornflour
2.5ml/½ tsp granulated sugar
1 egg
60ml/4 tbsp cold water
1 stalk lemon grass, finely chopped
2 garlic cloves, finely chopped
15ml/1 tbsp chopped coriander
1–2 red chillies, seeded and chopped
5ml/1 tsp fish sauce
oil for frying
12 half-shelled crab claws
freshly ground black pepper

Chilli vinegar dip
45ml/3 tbsp sugar
120ml/4fl oz/½ cup water
120ml/4fl oz/½ cup red wine vinegar
15ml/1 tbsp fish sauce
2–4 red chillies, seeded and chopped

1 To make the chilli dip, put the sugar and water in a saucepan and bring to the boil, stirring until the sugar dissolves. Lower the heat and simmer for 5–7 minutes. Stir in the rest of the ingredients and set aside.

2 Combine the rice flour, cornflour and sugar in a large bowl. Beat the egg with the cold water, then stir the liquid into the flour mixture and mix well until it forms a light batter.

3 Add the lemon grass, garlic, coriander, red chillies, fish sauce and freshly ground black pepper.

4 Heat the oil in a wok or deep fat fryer. Pat dry the crab claws and dip one at a time in the batter. Gently drop the battered claws in the hot oil, a few at a time. Fry until golden brown. Drain on kitchen paper. Serve hot with the chilli vinegar dip.

Golden Pouches

These crisp pouches are delicious served as an appetizer or to accompany drinks at a party.

Ingredients

Makes about 20

115g/4oz minced pork
115g/4oz crab meat
2–3 wood ears, soaked and chopped
15ml/1 tbsp chopped coriander
5ml/1 tsp chopped garlic
30ml/2 tbsp chopped spring onion
1 egg
15ml/1 tbsp fish sauce
5ml/1 tsp soy sauce
pinch of granulated sugar
freshly ground black pepper
20 wonton wrappers
20 chives, blanched (optional)
oil for deep frying
plum or sweet chilli sauce, to serve

1 In a mixing bowl, combine the pork, crab meat, wood ears, coriander, garlic, spring onions and egg. Mix well and season with fish sauce, soy sauce, sugar and freshly ground black pepper.

2 Take a wonton wrapper and place it on a flat surface. Put a heaped teaspoonful of filling in the centre of the wrapper, then pull up the edges of the pastry around the filling.

3 Pinch together to seal. If you like, you can go a step further and tie it with a long chive. Repeat with the remaining pork mixture.

4 Heat the oil in a wok or deep fat fryer. Fry the wontons in batches until they are crisp and golden brown. Drain on kitchen paper and serve immediately with either a plum or sweet chilli sauce.

Rice Cakes with Spicy Dipping Sauce

Rice cakes are a classic Thai appetizer. They are easy to make and can be kept in an airtight box almost indefinitely.

Ingredients

Serves 4–6
175g/6oz/1 cup jasmine rice
350ml/12fl oz/1½ cups water
oil for frying and greasing

For the spicy dipping sauce
6–8 dried chillies
2.5ml/½ tsp salt
2 shallots, chopped
2 garlic cloves, chopped
4 coriander roots
10 white peppercorns
250ml/8fl oz/1 cup coconut milk
5ml/1 tsp shrimp paste
115g/4oz minced pork
115g/4oz cherry tomatoes, chopped
15ml/1 tbsp fish sauce
15ml/1 tbsp palm sugar
30ml/2 tbsp tamarind juice
30 ml/2 tbsp coarsely chopped roasted peanuts
2 spring onions, finely chopped

1 Stem the chillies and remove most of the seeds. Soak the chillies in warm water for 20 minutes. Drain and transfer to a mortar.

2 Add the salt and grind with a pestle until the chillies are crushed. Add the shallots, garlic, coriander roots and peppercorns. Pound together until you have a coarse paste.

3 Pour the coconut milk into a saucepan and boil until it begins to separate. Add the pounded chilli paste. Cook for 2–3 minutes until it is fragrant. Stir in the shrimp paste. Cook for another minute.

4 Add the pork, stirring to break up any lumps. Cook for about 5–10 minutes. Add the tomatoes, fish sauce, palm sugar and tamarind juice. Simmer until the sauce thickens.

5 Stir in the chopped peanuts and spring onions. Remove from the heat and leave to cool.

6 Wash the rice in several changes of water. Put in a saucepan, add the water and cover with a tight-fitting lid. Bring to the boil, reduce the heat and simmer gently for about 15 minutes.

7 Remove the lid and fluff up the rice. Turn out on to a lightly greased tray and press down with the back of a large spoon. Leave to dry out overnight in a very low oven until it is completely dry and firm.

8 Remove the rice from the tray and break into bite-size pieces. Heat the oil in a wok or deep-fat fryer.

9 Deep fry the rice cakes in batches for about 1 minute, until they puff up, taking care not to brown them too much. Remove and drain. Serve accompanied with the dipping sauce.

Fish Cakes with Cucumber Relish

'hese wonderful small fish cakes re a very familiar and popular ppetizer. They are usually ccompanied with Thai beer.

NGREDIENTS

lakes about 12

00g/11oz white fish fillet, such as cod, cut into chunks
0ml/2 tbsp red curry paste
egg
0ml/2 tbsp fish sauce
ml/1 tsp granulated sugar
0ml/2 tbsp cornflour
kaffir lime leaves, shredded
5ml/1 tbsp chopped coriander
0g/2oz green beans, finely sliced
il for frying
'hinese mustard cress, to garnish

'or the cucumber relish

0ml/4 tbsp Thai coconut or rice vinegar
0ml/4 tbsp water
0g/2oz sugar
head pickled garlic
cucumber, quartered and sliced
shallots, finely sliced
5ml/1 tbsp finely chopped root ginger

1 To make the cucumber relish, bring the vinegar, water and sugar to the oil. Stir until the sugar dissolves, then emove from the heat and cool.

2 Combine the rest of the relish ingredients together in a bowl and our over the vinegar mixture.

3 Combine the fish, curry paste and egg in a food processor and process well. Transfer the mixture to a bowl, add the rest of the ingredients, except for the oil and garnish, and mix well.

4 Mould and shape the mixture into cakes about 5cm/2in in diameter and 5mm/¼in thick.

5 Heat the oil in a wok or deep-fat fryer. Fry the fish cakes, a few at a time, for about 4–5 minutes or until golden brown. Remove and drain on kitchen paper. Garnish with Chinese mustard cress and serve with the cucumber relish.

Vegetable Tempura

These deep-fried fritters are based on *kaki-age*, a Japanese dish that often incorporates fish and prawns as well as vegetables.

INGREDIENTS

Serves 4
2 medium courgettes
½ medium aubergine
1 large carrot
½ small Spanish onion
1 egg
120ml/4fl oz/½ cup iced water
115g/4oz/1 cup plain flour
salt and ground black pepper
vegetable oil, for deep-frying
sea salt flakes, lemon slices and Japanese soy sauce (*shoyu*), to serve

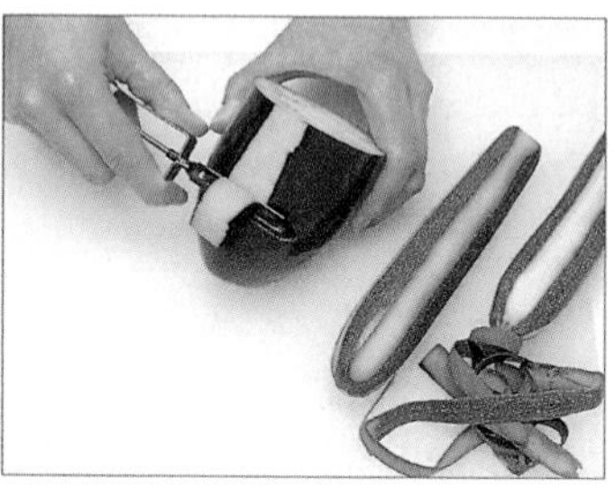

1 Using a potato peeler, pare strips of peel from the courgettes and aubergine to give a striped effect.

2 Cut the courgettes, aubergine and carrot into strips about 7.5–10cm/3–4in long and 3mm/⅛in wide.

3 Put the courgettes, aubergine and carrot into a colander and sprinkle liberally with salt. Leave for about 30 minutes, then rinse thoroughly under cold running water. Drain well.

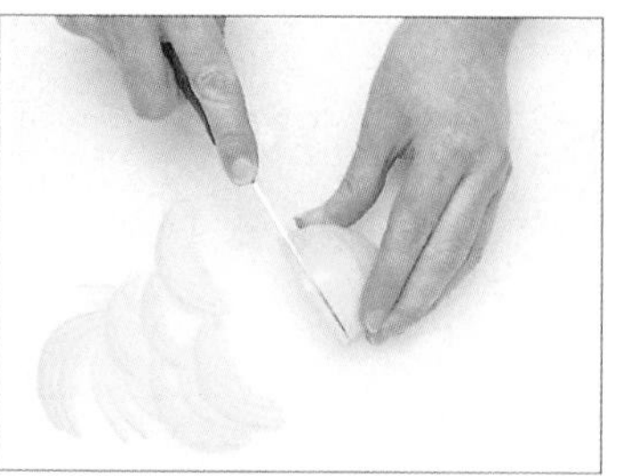

4 Thinly slice the onion from top to base, discarding the plump pieces in the middle. Separate the layers so that there are lots of fine, long strips. Mix all the vegetables together and season with salt and pepper.

5 Make the batter immediately before frying. Mix the egg and ice water in a bowl, then sift in the flour. Mix briefly with a fork or chopsticks. Do not overmix; the batter should remain lumpy. Add the vegetables to the batter and mix to combine.

6 Half-fill a wok with oil and heat to 180°C/350°F. Scoop up one heaped tablespoon of the mixture at a time and carefully lower it into the oil. Deep-fry in batches for about 3 minutes, until golden brown and crisp. Drain on kitchen paper. Serve each portion with salt, slices of lemon and a tiny bowl of Japanese soy sauce for dipping.

Spicy Spareribs

Fragrant with spices, this authentic Chinese dish makes a great – if slightly messy – starter to an informal meal.

Ingredients

Serves 4

675–900g/1½–2lb meaty pork spareribs
5ml/1 tsp Szechuan peppercorns
30ml/2 tbsp coarse sea salt
2.5ml/½ tsp Chinese five-spice powder
25ml/1½ tbsp cornflour
groundnut oil, for deep-frying
coriander sprigs, to garnish

For the marinade

30ml/2 tbsp light soy sauce
5ml/1 tsp caster sugar
15ml/1 tbsp Chinese rice wine or dry sherry
ground black pepper

1 Using a sharp, heavy cleaver, chop the spareribs into pieces about 5cm/2in long, or ask your butcher to do this for you. Place them in a shallow dish and set aside.

2 Heat a wok to medium heat. Add the Szechuan peppercorns and salt and dry-fry for about 3 minutes, stirring constantly, until the mixture colours slightly. Remove from the heat and stir in the five-spice powder. Set aside to cool.

3 Grind the cooled spice mixture in a mortar with a pestle to a fine powder.

4 Sprinkle 5ml/1 tsp of the spice powder over the spareribs and rub in well with your hands. Add all the marinade ingredients and toss the ribs to coat thoroughly. Cover and leave in the refrigerator to marinate for about 2 hours, turning occasionally.

5 Pour off any excess marinade from the spareribs. Sprinkle the ribs with the cornflour and mix to coat evenly.

6 Half-fill a wok with oil and heat to 180°C/350°F. Deep-fry the spareribs in batches for 3 minutes until golden. Remove and set aside. When all the batches have been cooked, reheat the oil to 180°C/350°F and deep-fry the ribs for a second time for 1–2 minutes, until crisp and thoroughly cooked. Drain on kitchen paper. Transfer the ribs to a warm serving platter and sprinkle over 5–7.5ml/1–1½ tsp of the remaining spice powder. Garnish with coriander sprigs and serve immediately.

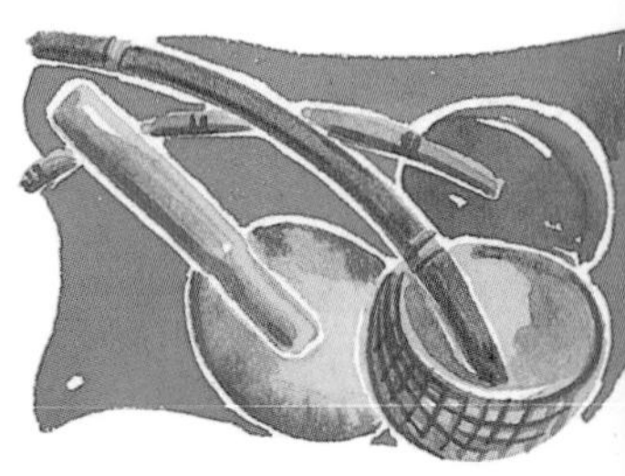

Cook's Tip

Any leftover spice powder can be kept in a screw-top jar for several months. Use to rub on the flesh of duck, chicken or pork before cooking.

Deep-fried Ribs with Spicy Salt and Pepper

INGREDIENTS

Serves 4–6

10–12 finger ribs, about 675g/1½lb, with excess fat and gristle trimmed
about 30–45ml/2–3 tbsp flour
vegetable oil, for deep frying

For the marinade

1 clove garlic, crushed and finely chopped
15ml/1 tbsp light brown sugar
15ml/1 tbsp light soy sauce
15ml/1 tbsp dark soy sauce
30ml/2 tbsp Chinese rice wine or dry sherry
2.5ml/½ tsp chilli sauce
few drops sesame oil

For the spicy salt and pepper

15ml/1 tbsp salt
10ml/2 tsp ground Szechuan peppercorns
5ml/1 tsp five-spice powder

1 Chop each rib into three or four pieces, then mix with all the marinade ingredients and marinate for at least 2–3 hours.

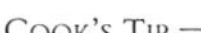

COOK'S TIP

Ideally, each sparerib should be chopped into three or four bite-sized pieces before or after deep frying in a wok. If this is not possible, then serve the ribs whole.

2 Coat the ribs with flour and deep fry in medium-hot oil for 4–5 minutes, stirring to separate. Remove from the oil and drain.

3 Heat the oil to high and deep fry the ribs once more for about 1 minute, or until the colour is an even dark brown. Remove and drain.

4 To make the spicy salt and pepper heat all the ingredients in a preheated dry wok for about 2 minut over a low heat, stirring constantly. Serve with the ribs.

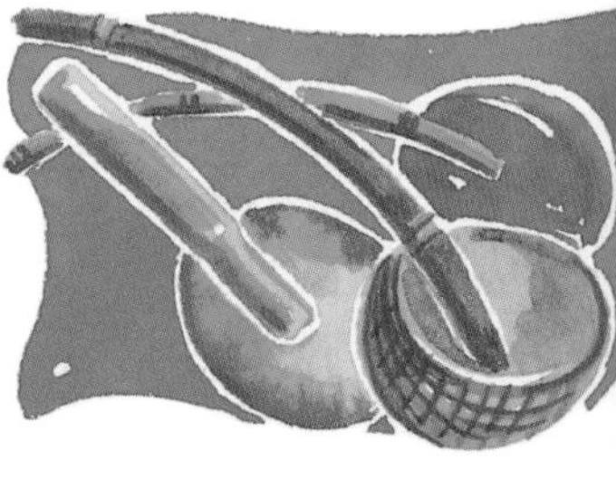

Lacy Duck Egg Nets

These parcels are very attractive. Thais have a special dispenser for naking the nets. It is cone-shaped vith holes at the bottom, to allow he egg mixture to dribble out in hreads. You can use a small-hole unnel, a piping bag with a small nozzle or a squeezy bottle.

NGREDIENTS

Aakes about 12–15

For the filling

4 coriander roots
2 garlic cloves
10 white peppercorns
pinch of salt
45ml/3 tbsp oil
1 small onion, finely chopped
115g/4oz lean minced pork
75g/3oz shelled prawns, chopped
50g/2oz roasted peanuts, ground
5ml/1 tsp palm sugar
fish sauce, to taste

For the egg nets

6 duck eggs
oriander leaves, to serve, plus extra to garnish
pring onion tassels, to garnish
liced red chillies, to garnish

1 Using a pestle and mortar, grind the coriander roots, garlic, white peppercorns and salt into a paste.

2 Heat 30ml/2 tbsp of the oil, add the paste and fry until fragrant. Add the onion and cook until softened. Add the pork and prawns and continue to stir-fry until the meat is cooked.

3 Add the peanuts, palm sugar, salt and fish sauce, to taste. Stir the mixture and continue to cook until it becomes a little sticky. Remove from the heat. Transfer the mixture into a bowl and set aside.

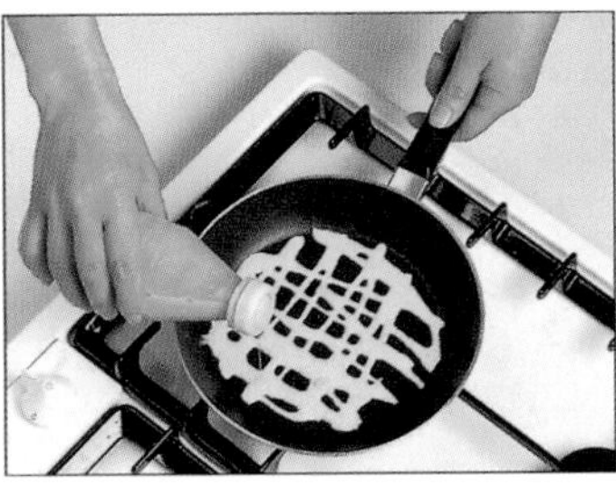

4 Beat the duck eggs in a bowl. Grease a non-stick frying pan with the remaining oil and heat. Using a special dispenser or one of the alternatives, trail the eggs across the pan to make a net pattern, about 13cm/5in in diameter.

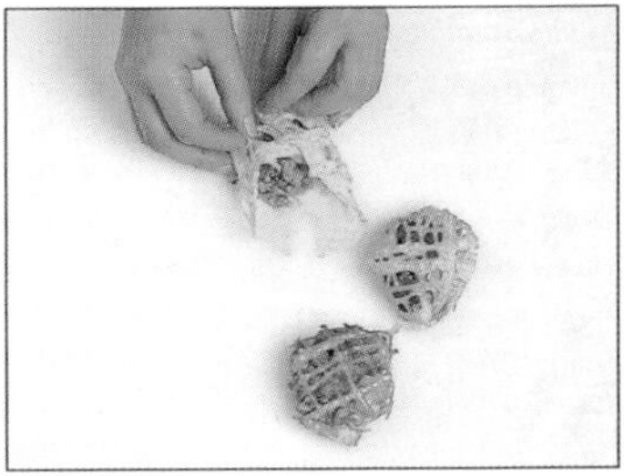

5 When the net is set, carefully remove it from the pan, and repeat until all the eggs have been used up.

6 To assemble, lay a net on a board, lay a few coriander leaves on it and top with a spoonful of the filling. Turn in the edges to make a neat square shape. Repeat with the rest of the nets. Arrange on a serving dish, garnish with spring onion tassels, coriander leaves and chillies.

Son-in-law Eggs

This fascinating name comes from a story about a prospective bridegroom who wanted to impress his future mother-in-law and devised a recipe from the only other dish he knew how to make – boiled eggs. The hard-boiled eggs are deep fried and then drenched with a sweet piquant tamarind sauce.

Ingredients

Serves 4–6

75g/3oz palm sugar
75ml/5 tbsp fish sauce
90ml/6 tbsp tamarind juice
oil for frying
6 shallots, finely sliced
6 garlic cloves, finely sliced
6 red chillies, sliced
6 hard-boiled eggs, shelled
lettuce, to serve
sprigs of coriander, to garnish

1 Combine the palm sugar, fish sauce and tamarind juice in a small saucepan. Bring to the boil, stirring until the sugar dissolves, then simmer for about 5 minutes.

2 Taste and add more palm sugar, fish sauce or taramind juice, if necessary. It should be sweet, salty and slightly sour. Transfer the sauce to a bowl and set aside.

3 Heat the oil in a wok or deep-fat fryer. Meanwhile, heat a couple of spoonfuls of the oil in a frying pan and fry the shallots, garlic and chillies until golden brown. Transfer the mixture to a bowl and set aside.

4 Deep-fry the eggs in the hot oil for 3–5 minutes until golden brown. Remove and drain on kitchen paper. Cut the eggs in quarters and arrange on a bed of lettuce. Drizzle with the sauce and scatter over the shallots. Garnish with sprigs of coriander.

Fried Clams with Chilli and Yellow Bean Sauce

Seafood is abundant in Thailand, especially at all of the beach holiday resorts. This delicous dish, which is simple to prepare, is one of the favourites.

Ingredients

Serves 4–6

1kg/2¼lb fresh clams
30ml/2 tbsp vegetable oil
4 garlic cloves, finely chopped
15ml/1 tbsp grated root ginger
4 shallots, finely chopped
30ml/2 tbsp yellow bean sauce
6 red chillies, seeded and chopped
15ml/1 tbsp fish sauce
pinch of granulated sugar
handful of basil leaves, plus extra to garnish

1 Wash and scrub the clams. Heat the oil in a wok or large frying pan. Add the garlic and ginger and fry for 30 seconds, add the shallots and fry for a further minute.

2 Add the clams. Using a fish slice or spatula, turn them a few times to coat with the oil. Add the yellow bean sauce and half the red chillies.

3 Continue to cook, stirring often, until all the clams open, about 5–7 minutes. You may need to add a splash of water. Adjust the seasoning with fish sauce and a little sugar.

4 Finally add the basil and transfer to individual bowls or a platter. Garnish with the remaining red chillies and basil leaves.

Pickled Sweet-and-sour Cucumber

The "pickling" can be done in minutes rather than days – but the more time you have, the better the result.

INGREDIENTS

Serves 6–8

1 slender cucumber, about 30cm/12in long
5ml/1 tsp salt
10ml/2 tsp caster sugar
5ml/1 tsp rice vinegar
2.5ml/½ tsp red chilli oil (optional)
few drops of sesame oil

1 Halve the unpeeled cucumber lengthways. Scrape out the seeds and cut the cucumber into thick chunks.

2 In a bowl, sprinkle the cucumber chunks with the salt and mix well. Leave for at least 20–30 minutes – longer if possible – then pour the juice away.

3 Mix the cucumber with the sugar, vinegar and chilli oil. Sprinkle with the sesame oil just before serving.

Hot-and-sour Cabbage

This popular dish from Szechuan in western China can be served hot or cold.

INGREDIENTS

Serves 6–8

450g/1lb pale green or white cabbage
45–60ml/3–4 tbsp vegetable oil
10–12 red Szechuan peppercorns
few whole dried red chillies
5ml/1 tsp salt
15ml/1 tbsp light brown sugar
15ml/1 tbsp light soy sauce
30ml/2 tbsp rice vinegar
few drops of sesame oil

1 Cut the cabbage leaves into small pieces each roughly 2.5 x 1cm/ 1 x ½in.

2 Heat the oil in a preheated wok until smoking, then add the peppercorns and chillies.

3 Add the cabbage to the wok and stir-fry for about 1–2 minutes. Add the salt and sugar, continue stirring for 1 minute more, then add the soy sauce, vinegar and sesame oil. Blend well and serve immediately.

Crispy "Seaweed"

Surprisingly, the very popular and rather exotic-sounding "seaweed" served in Chinese restaurants is, in fact, just ordinary spring greens.

INGREDIENTS

Serves 4
450g/1lb spring greens
vegetable oil, for deep frying
2.5ml/½ tsp salt
5ml/1 tsp caster sugar
15ml/1 tbsp ground fried fish, to garnish (optional)

1 Cut off the hard stalks in the centre of each spring green leaf. Pile the leaves on top of each other, and roll into a tight sausage shape. Thinly cut the leaves into fine shreds. Spread them out to dry.

2 Heat the oil in a wok until hot. Deep fry the shredded greens in batches, stirring to separate them.

3 Remove the greens with a slotted spoon as soon as they are crispy, but before they turn brown. Drain. Sprinkle the salt and sugar evenly all over the "seaweed", mix well, garnish with ground fish, if liked, and serve.

Sesame Seed Prawn Toasts

Use uncooked prawns for this dish, as ready-cooked ones will tend to separate from the bread during cooking.

INGREDIENTS

Serves 4
225g/8oz uncooked prawns, peeled
25g/1oz lard
1 egg white, lightly beaten
5ml/1 tsp finely chopped spring onions
2.5ml/½ tsp finely chopped root ginger
15ml/1 tbsp Chinese rice wine or dry sherry
15ml/1 tbsp cornflour paste
115–150g/4–5oz/white sesame seeds
6 large slices white bread
vegetable oil, for deep frying
salt and ground black pepper

1 Chop together the prawns with the lard to form a smooth paste. In a bowl, mix with all the other ingredients except the sesame seeds and bread.

2 Spread the sesame seeds evenly on a large plate or tray; spread the prawn paste thickly on one side of each slice of bread, then press, spread side down, on to the seeds.

3 Heat the oil in a wok until medium-hot; fry 2–3 slices of the sesame bread at a time, spread side down, for 2–3 minutes. Remove and drain. Cut each slice into six or eight fingers (without crusts).

Sweet Potato and Pumpkin Prawn Cakes

Serve these fried cakes warm with a fish sauce.

Ingredients

Serves 4–6
200g/7oz strong white bread flour
2.5ml/½ tsp salt
2.5ml/½ tsp dried yeast
175ml/6fl oz/¾ cup hand-hot water
1 egg, beaten
200g/7oz fresh prawn tails, peeled and roughly chopped
150g/5oz sweet potato, peeled and grated
225g/8oz pumpkin, peeled, seeded and grated
2 spring onions, chopped
50g/2oz water chestnuts, sliced and chopped
2.5ml/½ tsp chilli sauce
1 clove garlic, crushed
juice of ½ lime
30–45ml/2–3 tbsp vegetable oil
spring onions, to garnish

1 Sift the flour and salt into a mixing bowl and make a well in the centre. Dissolve the yeast in the water, then pour into the well. Pour in the egg and leave for a few minutes until bubbles appear. Mix to a batter.

2 Place the peeled prawns in a saucepan and cover with water. Bring to the boil and simmer for 10–1 minutes. Drain, refresh in cold water and drain again. Roughly chop and se the prawns aside.

3 Add the sweet potato and pumpk to the batter, then add the spring onions, water chestnuts, chilli sauce, garlic, lime juice and prawns. Heat a little oil in a wok or frying pan. Spoo in the batter in small heaps and fry un golden. Drain and serve, garnished with spring onions.

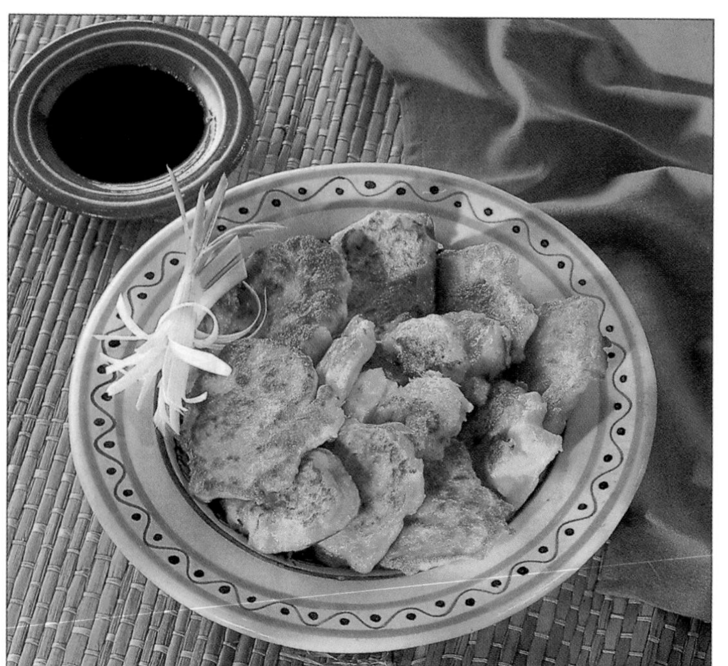

Spicy Meat-filled Parcels

In Indonesia the finest gossamer dough is made for *Martabak*. You can achieve equally good results using ready-made filo pastry or spring roll wrappers.

INGREDIENTS

Makes 16

450g/1lb lean minced beef
2 small onions, finely chopped
2 small leeks, very finely chopped
2 garlic cloves, crushed
10ml/2 tsp coriander seeds, dry-fried and ground
5ml/1 tsp cumin seeds, dry-fried and ground
5–10ml/1–2 tsp mild curry powder
2 eggs, beaten
400g/14oz packet filo pastry
45–60ml/3–4 tbsp sunflower oil
salt and freshly ground black pepper
light soy sauce, to serve

1 To make the filling, mix the meat with the onions, leeks, garlic, coriander, cumin, curry powder and seasoning. Turn into a heated wok, without oil, and stir all the time, until the meat has changed colour and looks cooked, about 5 minutes.

2 Allow to cool and then mix in enough beaten egg to bind to a soft consistency. Any leftover egg can be used to seal the edges of the dough; otherwise, use milk.

3 Brush a sheet of filo with oil and lay another sheet on top. Cut the sheets in half. Place a large spoonful of the filling on each double piece of filo. Fold the sides to the middle so that the edges just overlap. Brush these edges with either beaten egg or milk and fold the other two sides to the middle in the same way, so that you now have a square parcel shape. Make sure that the parcel is as flat as possible, to speed cooking. Repeat with the remaining fifteen parcels and place on a floured tray in the fridge.

4 Heat the remaining oil in a shallow pan and cook several parcels at a time, depending on the size of the pan. Cook for 3 minutes on the first side and then turn them over and cook for a further 2 minutes, or until heated through. Cook the remaining parcels in the same way and serve hot, sprinkled with light soy sauce.

5 If preferred, these spicy parcels can be cooked in a hot oven at 200°C/400°F/Gas 6 for 20 minutes. Glaze with more beaten egg before baking for a rich, golden colour.

Spicy Meat Patties with Coconut

Spicy meat patties, known as *Rempah*, with a hint of coconut, often feature as one of the delicious accompaniments in an Indonesian-style buffet.

Ingredients

Makes 22

115g/4oz freshly grated coconut, or desiccated coconut, soaked in 60–90ml/4–6 tbsp boiling water
350g/12oz finely minced beef
2.5ml/½ tsp each coriander and cumin seeds, dry-fried
1 garlic clove, crushed
a little beaten egg
15–30ml/1–2 tbsp plain flour
groundnut oil for frying
salt
thin lemon or lime wedges, to serve

1 Mix the moistened coconut with the minced beef.

2 Grind the dry-fried coriander and cumin seeds with a pestle and mortar. Add the ground spices to the meat and coconut mixture together with the garlic, salt to taste, and sufficient beaten egg to bind.

3 Divide the meat into evenly sized portions, the size of a walnut, and form into patty shapes.

4 Dust with flour. Heat the oil and then fry the patties for 4–5 minute until both sides are golden brown and cooked through. Serve with lemon or lime wedges, to squeeze over.

Sweetcorn Fritters

There is no doubt that freshly cooked sweetcorn is best for this recipe, called *Perkedel Jagung*. Do not add salt to the water, because this toughens the outer husk.

Ingredients

Makes 20

2 fresh corn on the cob, or 350g/12oz can sweetcorn kernels
2 macadamia nuts or 4 almonds
1 garlic clove
1 onion, quartered
1cm/½in fresh *lengkuas*, peeled and sliced
5ml/1 tsp ground coriander
30–45ml/2–3 tbsp oil
3 eggs, beaten
30ml/2 tbsp desiccated coconut
2 spring onions, finely shredded
a few celery leaves, finely shredded (optional)
salt

1 Cook the corn on the cob in boiling water for 7–8 minutes. Drain, cool slightly and, using a sharp knife, strip the kernels from the cob. If using canned sweetcorn, drain well.

2 Grind the nuts, garlic, onion, *lengkuas* and coriander to a fine paste in a food processor or pestle and mortar. Heat a little oil and fry the paste until it gives off a spicy aroma.

3 Add the fried spices to the beaten eggs with the coconut, spring onions and celery leaves, if using. Add salt to taste with the corn kernels.

4 Heat the remaining oil in a shallow frying pan. Drop large spoonfuls of batter into the pan and cook for 2–3 minutes until golden. Flip the fritters over with a fish slice and cook until golden brown and crispy. Only cook three or four fritters at a time.

Spiced Honey Chicken Wings

Be prepared to get very sticky when you eat these stir-fried wings, as the best way to enjoy them is by eating them with your fingers. Provide individual finger bowls for your guests.

INGREDIENTS

Serves 4
1 red chilli, finely chopped
5ml/1 tsp chilli powder
5ml/1 tsp ground ginger
rind of 1 lime, finely grated
12 chicken wings
60ml/4 tbsp sunflower oil
15ml/1 tbsp fresh coriander, chopped
30ml/2 tbsp soy sauce
50ml/3½ tbsp clear honey
lime rind and fresh coriander sprigs, to garnish

1 Mix the fresh chilli, chilli powder, ground ginger and lime rind together. Rub the mixture into the chicken skins and leave for at least 2 hours to allow the flavours to penetrate.

2 Heat a wok and add half the oil. When the oil is hot, add half the wings and stir-fry for 10 minutes, turning regularly until crisp and golden. Drain on kitchen paper. Repeat with the remaining oil and chicken wings.

3 Add the coriander to the hot wok and stir-fry for 30 seconds, then return the wings to the wok and stir-fry for 1 minute.

4 Stir in the soy sauce and honey, and stir-fry for 1 minute. Serve the chicken wings hot with the sauce drizzled over them and garnished with lime rind and coriander sprigs.

Pork Satay

)riginating in Indonesia, satay re skewers of meat marinated vith spices and grilled quickly ver charcoal. It's street food at ts best, prepared by vendors vith portable grills who set up talls at every street corner and narket place. You can make atay with chicken, beef or lamb.

NGREDIENTS

Makes about 20
150g/1lb lean pork
ml/1 tsp grated root ginger
stalk lemon grass, finely chopped
garlic cloves, finely chopped
15ml/1 tbsp medium curry paste
ml/1 tsp ground cumin
ml/1 tsp ground turmeric
0ml/4 tbsp coconut cream
0ml/2 tbsp fish sauce
ml/1 tsp granulated sugar
20 wooden satay skewers
il for cooking

For the satay sauce
250 ml/8fl oz/1 cup coconut milk
0ml/2 tbsp red curry paste
75g/3oz crunchy peanut butter
.20ml/4fl oz/½ cup chicken stock
5ml/3 tbsp brown sugar
0ml/2 tbsp tamarind juice
5ml/1 tbsp fish sauce
.5ml/½ tsp salt

1 Cut the pork thinly into 5cm/2in strips. Mix together the ginger, lemon grass, garlic, medium curry paste, cumin, turmeric, coconut cream, fish sauce and sugar.

2 Pour over the pork and leave to marinate for about 2 hours.

3 Meanwhile, make the sauce. Heat the coconut milk over a medium heat, then add the red curry paste, peanut butter, chicken stock and sugar.

4 Cook and stir until smooth, about 5–6 minutes. Add the tamarind juice, fish sauce and salt to taste.

5 Thread the meat on to skewers. Brush with oil and grill over charcoal or under a preheated grill for 3–4 minutes on each side, turning occasionally, until cooked and golden brown. Serve with the satay sauce.

Bon-bon Chicken with Sesame Sauce

The chicken meat is tenderized by being beaten with a stick (called a *bon* in Chinese), hence the name for this very popular Szechuan dish.

Ingredients

Serves 6–8

1 chicken, about 1kg/2¼lb
1.2 litre/2 pints/5 cups water
15ml/1 tbsp sesame oil
shredded cucumber, to garnish

For the sauce

30ml/2 tbsp light soy sauce
5ml/1 tsp sugar
15ml/1 tbsp finely chopped spring onions
5ml/1 tsp red chilli oil
2.5ml/½ tsp ground Szechuan peppercorns
5ml/1 tsp white sesame seeds
30ml/2 tbsp sesame paste or 30ml/2 tbsp peanut butter creamed with a little sesame oil

1 Clean the chicken well. Bring the water to a rolling boil in a wok, add the chicken. Reduce the heat, cover and cook for 40–45 minutes. Remove the chicken and immerse in cold water to cool.

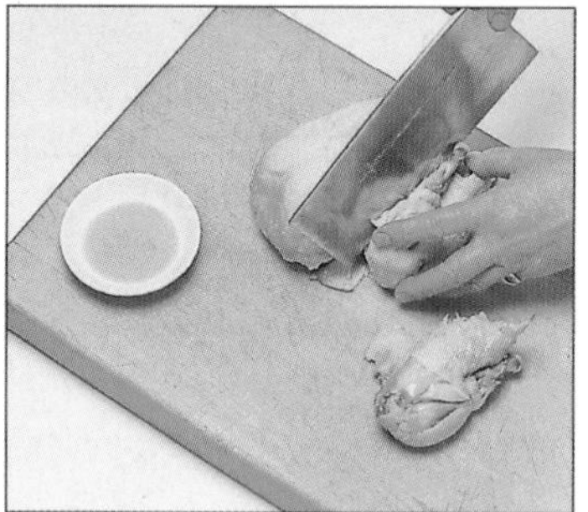

2 After at least 1 hour, remove the chicken and drain; dry well with kitchen paper and brush on a coating of sesame oil. Carve the meat off the legs, wings and breast and pull the meat off the rest of the bones.

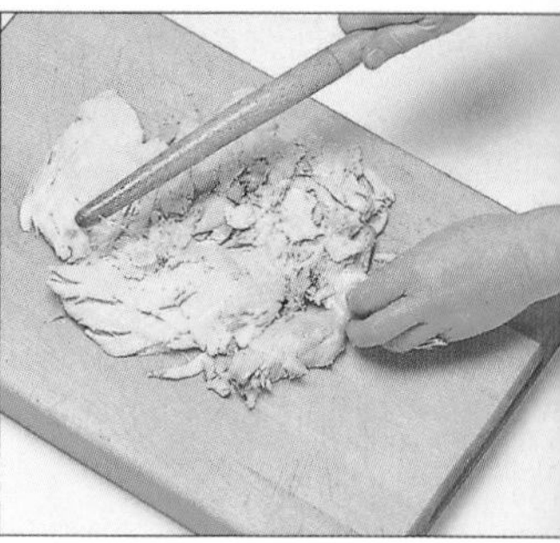

3 On a flat surface, pound the meat with a rolling pin, then tear the meat into shreds with your fingers.

4 Place the meat in a dish with the shredded cucumber around the edge. In a bowl, mix together all the sauce ingredients, keeping a few spring onions to garnish. Pour the sauce over the chicken and serve.

Barbecue-glazed Chicken Skewers

Known as *yakitori*, this mouth-watering appetizer is often served with pre-dinner drinks in Japan.

NGREDIENTS

Makes 12 skewers and 8 wing pieces
chicken thighs, skinned
spring onions, blanched and cut into short lengths
chicken wings
5ml/1 tbsp grated mooli, to serve (optional)

For the sauce
Oml/4 tbsp sake
5ml/5 tbsp dark soy sauce
Oml/2 tbsp tamari sauce
5ml/3 tbsp sweet sherry
Oml/4 tbsp sugar

1 Bone the chicken thighs and cut the meat into large dice. Thread the pring onions and chicken on to 12 amboo skewers.

2 To prepare the chicken wings, remove the tip at the first joint. Chop through the second joint, revealing the two narrow bones. Take hold of the bones with a clean cloth and pull, turning the meat around the bones inside out. Remove the smaller bone and set the meat aside.

3 Put all the sauce ingredients into a stainless steel or enamel saucepan and simmer until reduced by two-thirds. Set aside to cool.

4 Cook the skewers of chicken and the wings under a preheated grill without brushing on any oil. When juices begin to emerge from the chicken, baste liberally with the sauce. Cook the chicken on the skewers for a further 3 minutes and cook the wings for a further 5 minutes. Serve with grated mooli, if liked.

Lamb Satés

Ingredients

Makes 25–30 skewers
1kg/2¼lb leg of lamb, boned
3 garlic cloves, crushed
3–4 fresh chillies, seeded and ground, or 5–10ml/1–2 tsp chilli powder
60–90ml/4–6 tbsp dark soy sauce
juice of 1 lemon
salt and freshly ground black pepper
oil for brushing

For the sauce
6 garlic cloves, crushed
2–3 fresh chillies, seeded and ground
90ml/6 tbsp dark soy sauce
25ml/1½ tbsp lemon juice
30ml/2 tbsp boiling water

To serve
small onion pieces
cucumber wedges

1 Cut the lamb into thick slices and then into neat 1cm/½in cubes. Remove any pieces of gristle but do not trim off any of the fat because this keeps the *satés* moist during cooking and enhances the flavour.

Variation

Lamb neck fillet is now widely available in supermarkets and can be used instead of boned leg. Brush the lamb fillet with oil before grilling.

2 Blend the garlic, ground fresh chillies or chilli powder, soy sauce, lemon juice and seasoning to a paste in a food processor or with a pestle and mortar. Pour over the lamb. Cover and leave in a cool place for at least an hour. Soak wooden or bamboo skewers in water so that they won't burn during cooking.

3 Prepare the sauce. Put the garlic cloves into a bowl. Add the chillies, soy sauce, lemon juice and boiling water. Stir well.

4 Thread the meat on to the skewers. Brush with oil and cook under the grill, turning often. Brush each *saté* with a little of the sauce and serve hot, with small pieces of onion and cucumber. Serve with the remaining sauce.

Chicken and Sticky Rice Balls

'hese balls can either be steamed r deep fried. The fried versions re crunchy and are excellent for erving at drinks parties.

NGREDIENTS

Iakes about 30

50g/1lb minced chicken
egg
5ml/1 tsp tapioca flour
spring onions, finely chopped
0ml/2 tbsp chopped coriander
0ml/2 tbsp fish sauce
inch of granulated sugar
eshly ground black pepper
25g/8oz cooked sticky rice
anana leaves
il for brushing
small carrot, shredded, to garnish
red pepper, cut into strips, to garnish
nipped chives, to garnish
weet chilli sauce, to serve

1 In a mixing bowl, combine the minced chicken, egg, tapioca flour, pring onions and coriander. Mix well nd season with fish sauce, sugar and eshly ground black pepper.

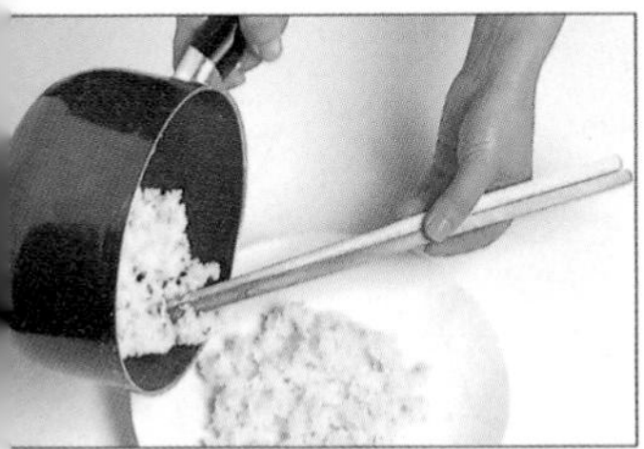

2 Spread the cooked sticky rice on a plate or flat tray.

3 Place a teaspoonful of the chicken mixture on the bed of rice. With damp hands, roll and shape the mixture in the rice to make a ball about the size of a walnut. Repeat with the rest of the chicken mixture.

Cook's Tip

Sticky rice, also known as glutinous rice, has a very high gluten content. It is so called because the grains stick together when it is cooked. It can be eaten both as a savoury and as a sweet dish.

4 Line a bamboo steamer with banana leaves and lightly brush them with oil. Place the chicken balls on the leaves, spacing well apart to prevent them sticking together. Steam over a high heat for about 10 minutes or until cooked.

5 Remove and arrange on serving plates. Garnish with shredded carrots, red pepper and chives. Serve with sweet chilli sauce to dip in.

Fish and Seafood

The many islands in the Pacific and the long coastline of mainland China ensure an abundance of wonderful fish and seafood recipes in the cuisines of Asia. Whole fish and fillets are combined with fragrant herbs and marinades and then steamed, baked or fried quickly. The different ways of preparing prawns, mussels, scallops, squid and other seafood are almost endless, from the subtly aromatic Pan-steamed Mussels with Thai Herbs to the robust and spicy Prawns with Chayote in Turmeric Sauce. All are highly nutritious and utterly delicious.

Steamed Fish with Ginger and Spring Onions

Firm and delicate fish steaks, such as salmon or turbot, can be cooked by this same method.

Ingredients

Serves 4–6

1 sea bass, trout or grey mullet, weighing about 675g/1½lb, gutted
2.5ml/½ tsp salt
15ml/1 tbsp sesame oil
2–3 spring onions, cut in half lengthways
30ml/2 tbsp light soy-sauce
30ml/2 tbsp Chinese rice wine or dry sherry
15ml/1 tbsp finely shredded fresh ginger
30ml/2 tbsp vegetable oil
finely shredded spring onions, to garnish

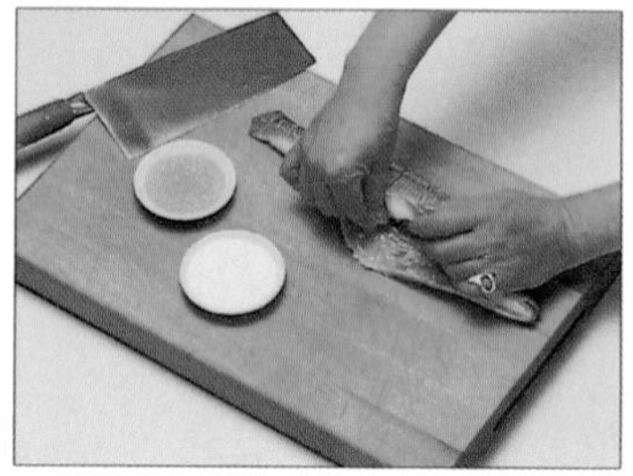

1 Using a sharp knife, score both sides of the fish as far down as the bone with diagonal cuts about 2.5cm/1in apart. Rub the fish all over, inside and out, with salt and sesame oil.

2 Sprinkle the spring onions over a heatproof platter and place the fish on top. Blend together the soy sauce and rice wine or dry sherry with the ginger shreds and pour evenly all over the fish.

3 Place the platter in a very hot steamer (or inside a wok on a rack) and steam vigorously, under cover, for 12–15 minutes.

4 Heat the vegetable oil until hot. Remove the platter from the steamer, place the shredded spring onions on top of the fish, then pour the hot oil along the whole length of the fish. Serve immediately.

Chinese-spiced Fish Fillets

Ingredients

Serves 4

65g/2½oz/generous ½ cup plain flour
5ml/1 tsp Chinese five-spice powder
8 skinless fillets of fish, such as plaice or lemon sole, about 800g/1¾lb in total
1 egg, lightly beaten
40–50g/1½–2oz/scant 1 cup fine fresh breadcrumbs
groundnut oil, for frying
25g/1oz/2 tbsp butter
4 spring onions, cut diagonally into thin slices
350g/12oz tomatoes, seeded and diced
30ml/2 tbsp soy sauce
salt and ground black pepper
red pepper strips and chives, to garnish

1 Sift the flour together with the Chinese five-spice powder and salt and pepper to taste on to a plate. Dip the fish fillets first in the seasoned flour, then in the beaten egg and finally in breadcrumbs.

2 Pour oil into a large frying pan to a depth of 1cm/½ in. Heat until it is very hot and starting to sizzle. Add the coated fillets, a few at a time, and fry for 2–3 minutes on each side, depending on their thickness, until just cooked and golden brown. Do not crowd the pan, or the temperature of the oil will drop and the fish will absorb too much of it.

3 Drain the fillets on kitchen paper, then transfer to serving plates and keep warm. Pour off all the oil from the frying pan and wipe it out with kitchen paper.

4 Cook the spring onions and tomatoes in the butter for 1 minute, then add the soy sauce.

5 Spoon the tomato mixture over the fish, garnish with red pepper strips and chives and serve.

Whole Fish with Sweet-and-sour Sauce

Ingredients

Serves 4

1 whole fish, such as red snapper or carp, about 1kg/2¼lb
30–45ml/2–3 tbsp cornflour
oil for frying
salt and freshly ground black pepper
boiled rice, to serve

For the spice paste

2 garlic cloves
2 lemon grass stems
2.5cm/1in fresh *lengkuas*
2.5cm/1in fresh root ginger
2cm/¾in fresh turmeric or 2.5ml/½ tsp ground turmeric
5 macadamia nuts or 10 almonds

For the sauce

15ml/1 tbsp brown sugar
45ml/3 tbsp cider vinegar
about 350ml/12fl oz/1½ cups water
2 lime leaves, torn
4 shallots, quartered
3 tomatoes, skinned and cut in wedges
3 spring onions, finely shredded
1 fresh red chilli, seeded and shredded

1 Ask the fishmonger to gut and scale the fish, leaving on the head and tail, or you may do this yourself. Wash and dry the fish thoroughly and then sprinkle it inside and out with salt. Set aside for 15 minutes, while preparing the other ingredients.

2 Peel and crush the garlic cloves. Use only the lower white part of the lemon grass stems and slice thinly. Peel and slice the fresh *lengkuas*, the fresh root ginger and fresh turmeric, if using. Grind the nuts, garlic, lemon grass, *lengkuas*, ginger and turmeric to a fine paste in a food processor or with a pestle and mortar.

3 Scrape the paste into a bowl. Stir in the brown sugar, cider vinegar, seasoning to taste and the water. Add the lime leaves.

4 Dust the fish with the cornflour and fry on both sides in hot oil for about 8–9 minutes or until almost cooked through. Drain the fish on kitchen paper and transfer to a serving dish. Keep warm.

5 Pour off most of the oil and then pour in the spicy liquid and allow to come to the boil. Reduce the heat and cook for 3–4 minutes. Add the shallots and tomatoes, followed a minute later by the spring onions and chilli. Taste and adjust the seasoning.

6 Pour the sauce over the fish. Serve at once, with plenty of rice.

Sesame Baked Fish with a Hot Ginger Marinade

lthough tropical varieties of ish are found increasingly requently in supermarkets, riental food stores usually have wider selection suitable for this Malaysian dish.

NGREDIENTS

erves 4–6

red snapper, parrot fish or monkfish tails, each weighing about 350g/12oz
0ml/2 tbsp vegetable oil, plus extra for greasing
0ml/2 tsp sesame oil
0ml/2 tbsp sesame seeds
.5cm/1in fresh root ginger, thinly sliced
garlic cloves, crushed
small fresh red chillies, seeded and finely chopped
shallots or 1 medium onion, halved and sliced
0ml/2 tbsp water
cm/½in square shrimp paste or 15ml/1 tbsp fish sauce
0ml/2 tsp sugar
.5ml/½ tsp cracked black pepper
uice of 2 limes
–4 banana leaves (optional)

1 Clean and dry the fish well. Slash both sides of the fish deeply with sharp knife. If using parrot fish, rub with fine salt and leave to stand for 5 minutes to remove the rather chalky oral flavour.

2 To make the marinade, heat the vegetable and sesame oils in a preheated wok. Add the sesame seeds and fry until golden. Add the ginger, garlic, chillies and shallots or onion and stir-fry 1–2 minutes, until softened. Add the water, shrimp paste or fish sauce, sugar, pepper and lime juice and simmer for 2–3 minutes. Remove from the heat and allow to cool.

COOK'S TIP

Banana leaves are available from Indian and South-east Asian food stores.

3 If using banana leaves, remove and discard the central stems. Soften the leaves by dipping them in boiling water. To keep them supple, rub the surfaces with vegetable oil. Spread the sesame seed marinade over the fish, then wrap them separately in the banana leaves, secured with a skewer, or enclose them in foil. Set aside in a cool place to allow the flavours to mingle, for up to 3 hours.

4 Place the fish parcels on a baking sheet and cook in a preheated oven at 180°C/350°F/Gas 4 or on a glowing barbecue for 35–40 minutes. Serve hot.

Sea Bass with Chinese Chives

Chinese chives are widely available in oriental supermarkets but if you are unable to buy them, use half a large Spanish onion, finely sliced, instead.

Ingredients

Serves 4

2 sea bass, about 450g/1lb in total
15ml/1 tbsp cornflour
45ml/3 tbsp vegetable oil
175g/6oz Chinese chives
15ml/1 tbsp Chinese rice wine or dry sherry
5ml/1 tsp caster sugar
salt and ground black pepper
Chinese chives with flowerheads, to garnish

1 Remove the scales from the bass by scraping them with the back of a knife, working from the tail end towards the head end. Fillet the fish.

2 Cut the fillets into large chunks and dust them lightly with cornflour, salt and pepper.

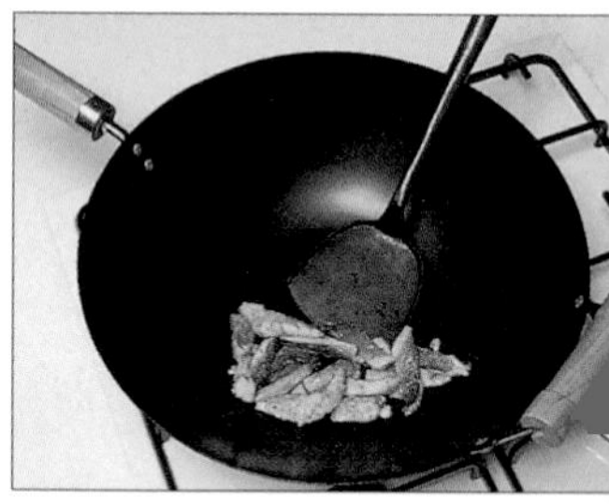

3 Heat 30ml/2 tbsp of the oil in a preheated wok. When the oil is hot, toss the chunks of fish in the wok briefly to seal, then set aside. Wipe out the wok with kitchen paper.

4 Cut the Chinese chives into 5cm/2in lengths and discard the flower Reheat the wok and add the remainin oil, then stir-fry the Chinese chives fo 30 seconds. Add the fish and rice wine or dry sherry, then bring to the boil and stir in the sugar. Serve hot, garnished with some flowering Chinese chives.

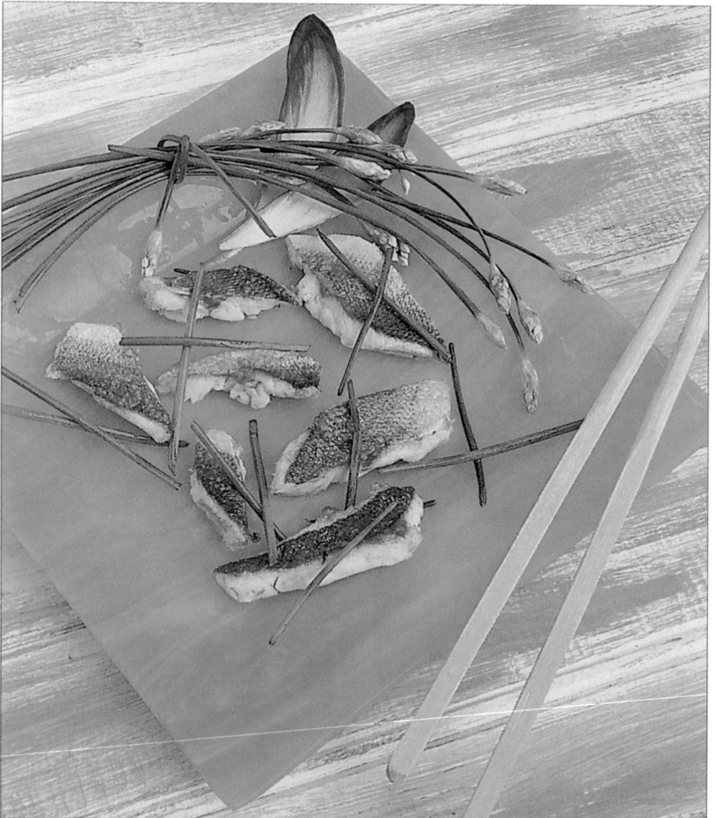

Sizzling Chinese Steamed Fish

Steamed whole fish is very popular in China, and the wok is used as a steamer. In this recipe the fish is flavoured with garlic, ginger and spring onions cooked in sizzling hot oil.

INGREDIENTS

Serves 4

4 rainbow trout, about 250g/9oz each
1.5ml/¼ tsp salt
2.5ml/½ tsp sugar
2 garlic cloves, finely chopped
15ml/1 tbsp finely diced fresh root ginger
5 spring onions, cut into 5cm/2in lengths and finely shredded
60ml/4 tbsp groundnut oil
5ml/1 tsp sesame oil
45ml/3 tbsp light soy sauce
thread egg noodles and stir-fried vegetables, to serve

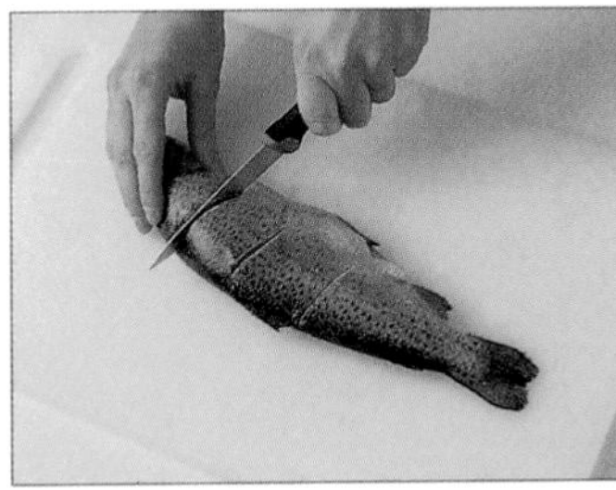

1 Make three diagonal slits on both sides of each fish and lay them on a heatproof plate. Place a small rack or trivet in a wok half-filled with water, cover and heat until just simmering.

2 Sprinkle the fish with the salt, sugar, garlic and ginger. Place the plate securely on the rack or trivet and cover. Steam gently for about 10–12 minutes, or until the flesh has turned pale pink and feels quite firm.

3 Turn off the heat, remove the lid and scatter the spring onions over he fish. Replace the lid.

4 Heat the groundnut and sesame oils in a small pan over a high heat until just smoking, then quickly pour a quarter over the spring onions on each of the fish – the shredded onions will sizzle and cook in the hot oil. Sprinkle the soy sauce over the top. Serve the fish and juices immediately with boiled noodles and stir-fried vegetables.

Salmon Teriyaki

Marinating the salmon makes it so wonderfully tender, it just melts in the mouth, and the crunchy condiment provides an excellent foil.

Ingredients

Serves 4

675g/1½lb salmon fillet
30ml/2 tbsp sunflower oil
watercress, to garnish

For the teriyaki sauce

5ml/1 tsp caster sugar
5ml/1 tsp dry white wine
5ml/1 tsp sake, rice wine or dry sherry
30ml/2 tbsp dark soy sauce

For the condiment

5cm/2in fresh root ginger, grated
pink food colouring (optional)
50g/2oz mooli, grated

1 For the teriyaki sauce, mix together the sugar, white wine, sake or rice wine or dry sherry and soy sauce, stirring until the sugar dissolves.

2 Remove the skin from the salmon using a very sharp filleting knife.

3 Cut the fillet into strips, then place in a non-metallic dish. Pour over the teriyaki sauce and set aside to marinate for 10–15 minutes.

4 To make the condiment, place the ginger in a bowl and add a little pink food colouring if you wish. Stir in the mooli.

5 Lift the salmon from the teriyaki sauce and drain.

6 Heat the oil in a preheated wok. Add the salmon in batches and stir fry for 3–4 minutes, until it is cooked. Transfer to serving plates, garnish with the watercress and serve with the mooli and ginger condiment.

Salt-grilled Mackerel

ı Japan salt is applied to oily fish ɛfore cooking to draw out the ɪvours. Mackerel, snapper and ɪrfish are the most popular ıoices for this treatment, known *Shio-yaki* in Japanese. All of ɪem develop a unique flavour ıd texture when treated with lt. The salt is washed away ɛfore cooking.

ɴGREDIENTS

rves 2

small or 1 large mackerel, snapper or garfish, gutted and cleaned, with head on
)ml/2 tbsp fine table salt
medium carrot, shredded, to serve

ɔr the soy ginger dip

)ml/4 tbsp dark soy sauce
)ml/2 tbsp sugar
5cm/1in piece fresh root ginger

or the Japanese horseradish

5ml/3 tbsp *wasabi* powder
)ml/2 tsp water

1 To make the soy ginger dip, put the soy sauce, sugar and ginger in a ainless steel saucepan. Bring to the ɔil, lower the heat and simmer for 2–3 ɪinutes. Strain and set aside to cool. To ɪake the Japanese horseradish, put the *ɪsabi* powder into a small bowl and ir in the water to make a stiff paste. hape the mixture into a neat ball and t aside.

2 Rinse the fish under cold, running water and pat thoroughly dry with kitchen paper. Slash the fish several times on both sides, cutting down as far as the bone. Sprinkle the salt inside the fish and rub it well into the skin. Set aside on a plate for 40 minutes.

3 Wash the fish in plenty of cold water to remove all traces of salt. Shape the fish into a gentle curve and secure in position with two bamboo skewers inserted along the length of the body, one above and one below the eye.

4 Cook the fish under a preheated grill or on a barbecue for 10–12 minutes, turning once. The skin can be basted with a little of the soy ginger dip part way through cooking, if liked. Transfer the fish to a serving plate and arrange carrot, Japanese horseradish and soy ginger dip decoratively around it.

COOK'S TIP

Wasabi is the ground root of an oriental type of horseradish. It is very sharp and aromatic and often served with raw fish and shellfish. In the West, it is usually available only as a powder, which has to be mixed with water to make a paste.

Fried Monkfish Coated with Rice Noodles

These marinated medallions of fish are coated in rice vermicelli and deep fried – they taste as good as they look.

Ingredients

Serves 4
450g/1lb monkfish
5ml/1 tsp grated fresh root ginger
1 garlic clove, finely chopped
30ml/2 tbsp soy sauce
175g/6oz rice vermicelli
50g/2oz cornflour
2 eggs, beaten
salt and freshly ground black pepper
oil for deep frying
banana leaves, to serve (optional)

For the dipping sauce
30ml/2 tbsp soy sauce
30ml/2 tbsp rice vinegar
15ml/1 tbsp sugar
2 red chillies, thinly sliced
1 spring onion, thinly sliced

1 Trim the monkfish and cut into 2.5cm/1in thick medallions. Place in a dish and add the ginger, garlic and soy sauce. Mix lightly and leave to marinate for 10 minutes.

2 Meanwhile, make the dipping sauce. Combine the soy sauce, vinegar and sugar in a small saucepan. Bring to the boil. Add salt and pepper to taste. Remove from the heat, add the chillies and spring onion and set aside until required.

3 Using kitchen scissors, cut the noodles into 4cm/1½in lengths. Spread them out in a shallow bowl.

4 Coat the fish medallions in cornflour, dip in beaten egg and cover with noodles, pressing them on to the fish so that they stick.

5 Deep fry the coated fish in hot oil, 2–3 pieces at a time, until the noodle coating is fluffy, crisp and light golden brown. Drain and serve hot on banana leaves, if you like, accompanied by the dipping sauce.

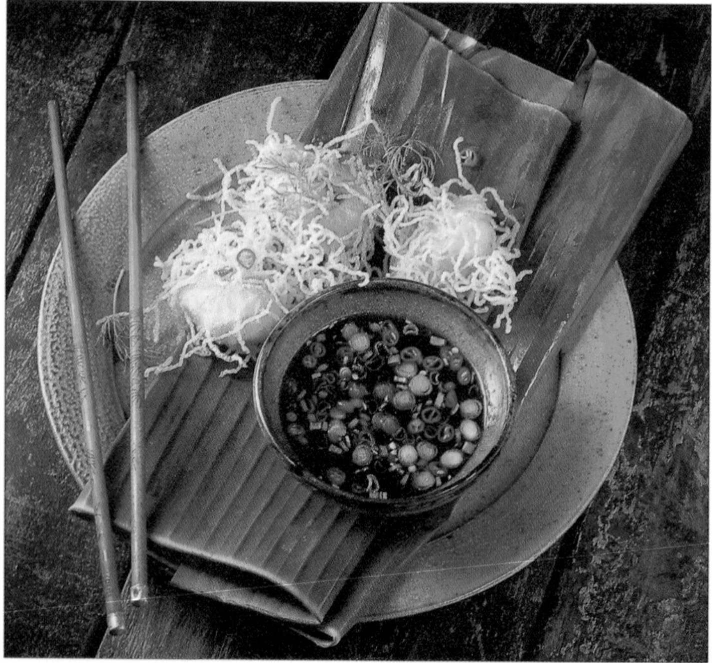

Fish with a Cashew Ginger Marinade

› capture the sweet, spicy ıvour of this Indonesian vourite, marinated fish are rapped in parcels before baking. 'hen they are unwrapped at the ble, their delicious aroma will ake your mouth water.

IGREDIENTS

rves 4

1kg/2½lb sea bass or pomfret, scaled and cleaned
0g/5oz/1¼ cups raw cashew nuts
shallots or 1 small onion, finely chopped
m/½in fresh root ginger, finely chopped
garlic clove, crushed
small fresh red chilli, seeded and finely chopped
ml/2 tbsp vegetable oil
ml/1 tbsp shrimp paste
ml/2 tsp sugar
ml/2 tbsp tamarind sauce
ml/2 tbsp tomato ketchup
ice of 2 limes
t

1 Slash the fish 3–4 times on each side with a sharp knife. Set aside.

2 Grind the cashew nuts, shallots or onion, ginger, garlic and chilli to a ıe paste in a mortar with a pestle or a food processor. Add the vegetable l, shrimp paste and sugar and season taste with salt. Blend, then add the marind sauce, tomato ketchup and ne juice and blend again.

3 Cover both sides of the fish with the paste and set aside in the refrigerator for up to 8 hours to allow the flavours to mingle.

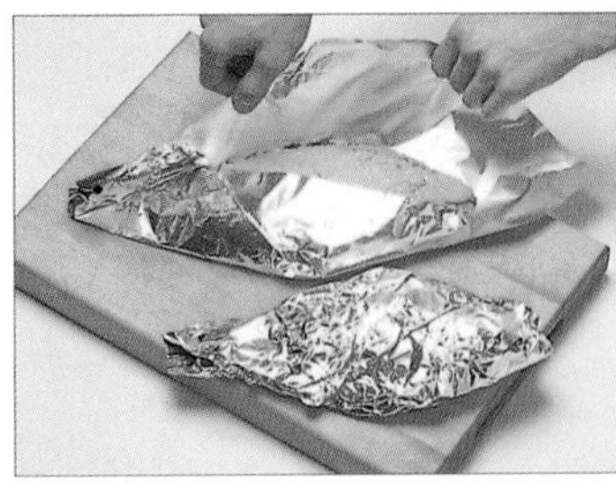

4 Wrap the fish in foil, securing the parcels carefully. Bake in a preheated oven at 180°C/350°F/Gas 4 for 30–35 minutes.

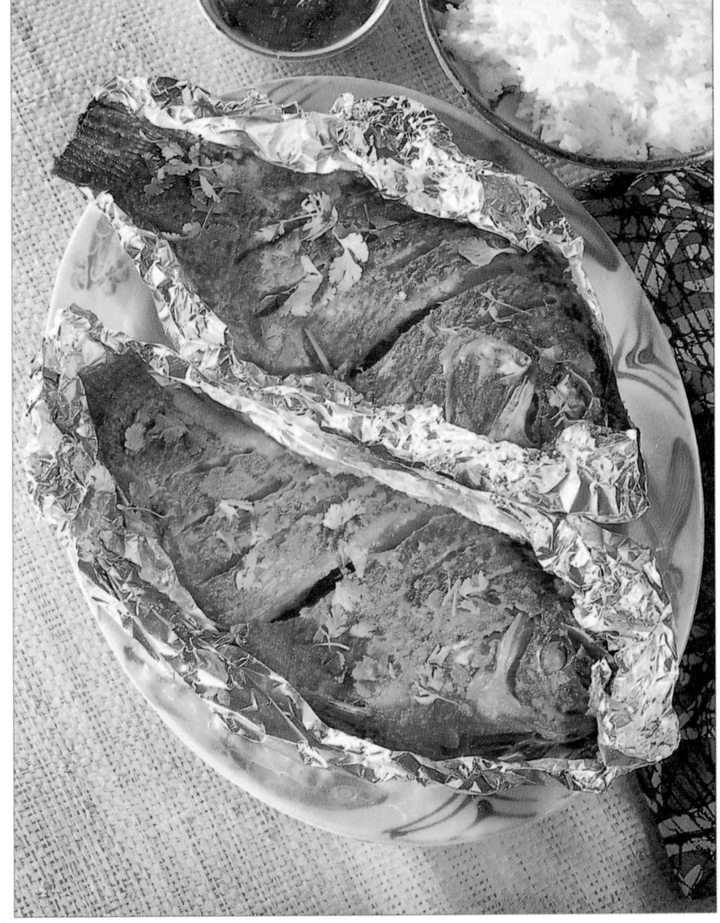

Fish Balls with Chinese Greens

These tasty fish balls are steamed over a wok with a selection of green vegetables – pak choi is available from oriental stores.

Ingredients

Serves 4

For the fish balls

450g/1lb white fish fillets, skinned, boned and cubed
3 spring onions, chopped
1 back bacon rasher, rinded and chopped
15ml/1 tbsp Chinese rice wine
30ml/2 tbsp light soy sauce
1 egg white

For the vegetables

1 small head pak choi
5ml/1 tsp cornflour
15ml/1 tbsp light soy sauce
150ml/¼ pint/⅔ cup cup fish stock
30ml/2 tbsp groundnut oil
2 garlic cloves, sliced
2.5cm/1in fresh root ginger, cut into thin shreds
75g/3oz green beans
175g/6oz mangetouts
3 spring onions, sliced diagonally into 5–7.5cm/2–3in lengths
salt and ground black pepper

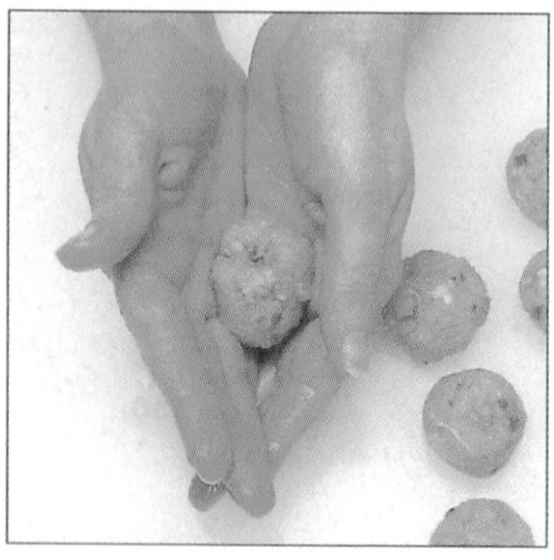

1 Put the fish, spring onions, bacon, rice wine, soy sauce and egg white in a food processor and process until smooth. With wetted hands, form the mixture into about 24 small balls.

2 Steam the fish balls in batches in a lightly greased bamboo steamer in a wok for 5–10 minutes until cooked through and firm. Remove from the steamer and keep warm.

3 Meanwhile trim the pak choi, removing any discoloured leaves or damaged stems, then tear into manageable pieces.

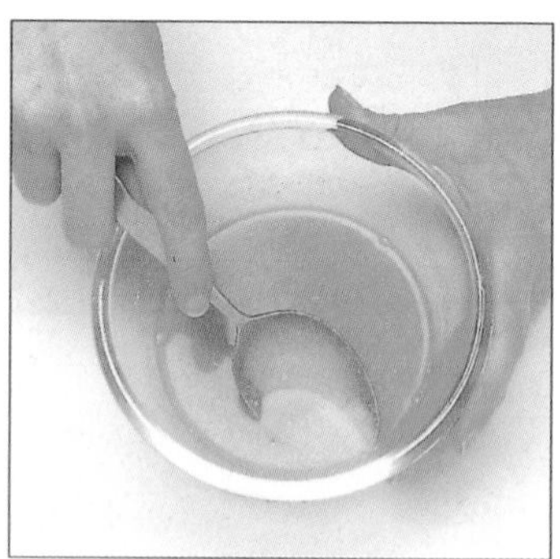

4 Blend together the cornflour, soy sauce and stock in a small bowl and set aside.

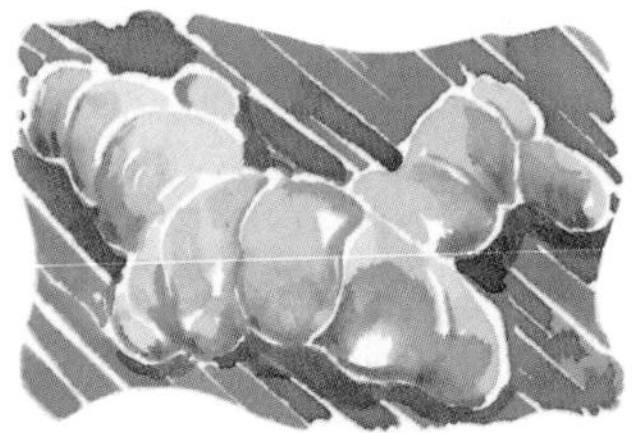

5 Heat a wok until hot, add the oil and swirl it around. Add the garlic and ginger and stir-fry for 2–3 minutes. Add the beans and stir-fry for 2–3 minutes, then add the mangetouts, spring onions and pak choi. Stir-fry for 2–3 minutes.

6 Add the sauce to the wok and cook, stirring, until it has thickened and the vegetables are tender but crisp. Taste and adjust the seasoning, if necessary. Serve with the fish balls.

Cook's Tip

You can replace the mangetouts and green beans with broccoli florets. Blanch them before stir-frying.

Balti Fried Fish

Both freshwater and sea fish are widely eaten in Pakistan. The coastal city of Karachi is particularly famous for its delicious seafood.

Ingredients

Serves 4–6

675g/1½lb white cod fillet
1 onion, sliced
15ml/1 tbsp lemon juice
5ml/1 tsp salt
5ml/1 tsp garlic pulp
5ml/1 tsp crushed dried red chillies
7.5ml/1½ tsp garam masala
30ml/2 tbsp chopped fresh coriander
2 tomatoes
30ml/2 tbsp cornflour
150ml/¼ pint/⅔ cup corn oil
apricot chutney and paratha (optional), to serve

1 Skin the fish and cut it into small cubes. Place in a bowl and chill in the refrigerator.

2 In a bowl mix together the onion, lemon juice, salt, garlic pulp, crushed red chillies, garam masala and chopped coriander. Set aside.

3 Place the tomatoes in boiling water for a few seconds. Remove with a slotted spoon and peel off the skins. Roughly chop the tomatoes and add to the onion mixture.

4 Transfer the onion mixture to a food processor or blender and process for about 30 seconds.

5 Remove the fish from the refrigerator and add the onion mixture from the food processor or blender. Mix thoroughly.

6 Add the cornflour and mix thoroughly again until the fish pieces are well coated.

7 Heat the oil in a preheated wok or frying pan. Lower the heat slightly and add the fish pieces, a few at a time. Cook, turning them gently with a slotted spoon, for about 5 minutes or until lightly browned.

8 Remove the fish with a slotted spoon and drain on kitchen paper. Keep warm while you cook the remaining fish pieces in the same way. Serve immediately with apricot chutney and paratha, if liked.

Thai Fish Stir-fry

This is a substantial dish, best served with crusty bread, for mopping up all the spicy juices.

Ingredients

Serves 4

675g/1½lb mixed seafood, such as red snapper and cod, filleted and skinned, and raw prawn tails
300ml/½ pint/1¼ cups coconut milk
15ml/1 tbsp vegetable oil
salt and ground black pepper
crusty bread, to serve

For the sauce

2 large red fresh chillies
1 onion, roughly chopped
5cm/2in fresh root ginger, peeled and sliced
5cm/2in lemon grass stalk, outer leaf discarded, roughly sliced
5cm/2in piece galangal peeled and sliced
6 blanched almonds, chopped
2.5ml/½ tsp turmeric
2.5ml/½ tsp salt

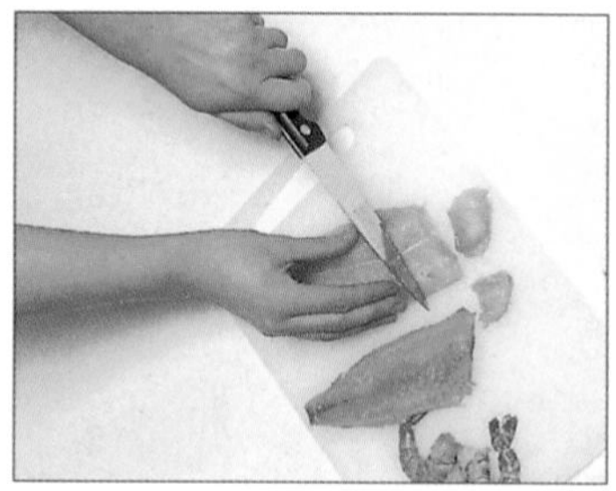

1 Cut the filleted fish into large chunks. Peel the prawns, keeping their tails intact.

Cook's Tip

Galangal, also spelt galingale, is a rhizome from the same family as ginger, with a similar but milder flavour. It is peeled and sliced, chopped or grated in the same way as root ginger. It is an important spice in South-east Asian cooking, particularly in Indonesia, Malaysia and Thailand.

2 To make the sauce, carefully remove the seeds from the chillies and chop the flesh roughly. Put the chillies and the other sauce ingredients in a food processor or blender with 45ml/3 tbsp of the coconut milk. Process until smooth.

3 Heat a wok, then add the oil. When the oil is hot, stir-fry the seafood for 2–3 minutes, then remove.

4 Add the sauce and the remaining coconut milk to the wok, then return the seafood. Bring to the boil, season well and serve with crusty bread

Boemboe Bali of Fish

'he island of Bali has wonderful
sh, surrounded as it is by
parkling blue sea. This simple
sh "curry" is packed with many
f the characteristic flavours
ssociated with Indonesia.

NGREDIENTS

erves 4–6

75g/1½lb cod or haddock fillet
cm/½in cube *terasi*
red or white onions
.5cm/1in fresh root ginger, peeled and sliced
cm/½in fresh *lengkuas*, peeled and sliced, or 5ml/1 tsp *lengkuas* powder
garlic cloves
–2 fresh red chillies, seeded, or 5–10ml/1–2 tsp chilli powder
0ml/6 tbsp sunflower oil
5ml/1 tbsp dark soy sauce
ml/1 tsp tamarind pulp, soaked in 30ml/2 tbsp warm water
50ml/8fl oz/1 cup water
elery leaves or chopped fresh chilli, to garnish
oiled rice, to serve

1 Skin the fish, remove any bones and then cut the flesh into bite-size ieces. Pat dry with kitchen paper and t aside.

2 Grind the *terasi*, onions, ginger, *lengkuas*, garlic and fresh chillies, if sing, to a paste in a food processor or vith a pestle and mortar. Stir in the hilli powder and *lengkuas* powder, f using.

3 Heat 30ml/2 tbsp of the oil and fry the spice mixture, stirring, until it gives off a rich aroma. Add the soy sauce. Strain the tamarind and add the juice and water. Cook for 2–3 minutes.

Variation

Substitute 450g/1lb cooked tiger prawns. Add them 3 minutes before the end.

4 In a separate pan, fry the fish in the remaining oil for 2–3 minutes. Turn once only so that the pieces stay whole. Lift out with a draining spoon and put into the sauce.

5 Cook the fish in the sauce for a further 3 minutes and serve with boiled rice. Garnish the dish with feathery celery leaves or a little chopped fresh chilli, if liked.

Balti Fish Fillets in Spicy Coconut Sauce

Use fresh fish fillets to make this dish if you can, as they have much more flavour than frozen ones. However, if you are using frozen fillets, ensure that they are completely thawed before using.

Ingredients

Serves 4

30ml/2 tbsp corn oil
5ml/1 tsp onion seeds
4 dried red chillies
3 garlic cloves, sliced
1 onion, sliced
2 tomatoes, sliced
30ml/2 tbsp desiccated coconut
5ml/1 tsp salt
5ml/1 tsp ground coriander
4 flatfish fillets, such as plaice, sole or flounder, each about 75g/3oz
150ml/¼ pint/⅔ cup water
15ml/ 1 tbsp lime juice
15ml/1 tbsp chopped fresh coriander
boiled rice, to serve (optional)

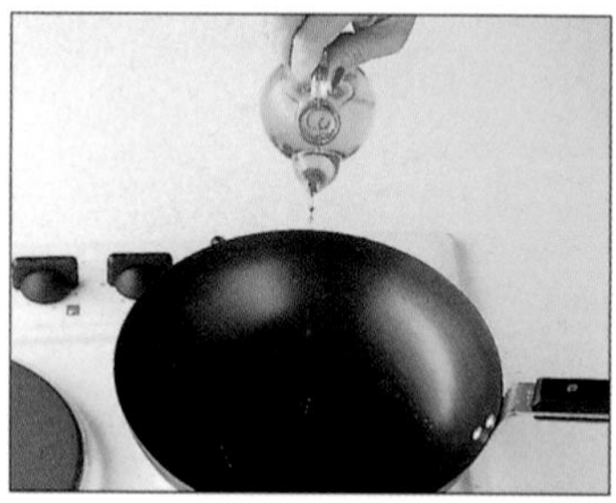

1 Heat the oil in a wok. Lower the heat slightly and add the onion seeds, dried red chillies, garlic slices and onion. Cook for 3–4 minutes, stirring once or twice.

2 Add the tomatoes, coconut, salt and coriander and stir thoroughly.

3 Cut each fish fillet into three pieces. Drop the fish pieces into the mixture and turn them over gently until they are well coated.

4 Cook for 5–7 minutes, lowering the heat if necessary. Add the water, lime juice and fresh coriander and cook for a further 3–5 minutes until the water has mostly evaporated. Serve immediately with rice, if liked.

Cook's Tip

The Balti equivalent of the Chinese wok is the karahi, also known as a Balti pan. They are usually round-bottomed with two carrying handles. Like the wok, the karahi is traditionally made of cast iron in order to withstand the high temperatures and hot oil used in cooking. They are now made in a variety of different metals and are available in a range of sizes, including small ones for individual servings.

Braised Whole Fish in Chilli and Garlic Sauce

This is a classic Szechuan recipe. When it is served in a restaurant, the fish's head and tail are usually discarded before cooking, and used in other dishes. A whole fish may be used, however, and always looks impressive, especially for special occasions and formal dinner parties.

Ingredients

Serves 4–6

1 carp, bream, sea bass, trout, grouper or grey mullet, weighing about 675g/1½lb, gutted
15ml/1 tbsp light soy sauce
15ml/1 tbsp Chinese rice wine or dry sherry
vegetable oil, for deep frying

For the sauce

2 cloves garlic, finely chopped
2–3 spring onions, finely chopped with the white and green parts separated
5ml/1 tsp finely chopped fresh root ginger
30ml/2 tbsp chilli bean sauce
15ml/1 tbsp tomato purée
10ml/2 tsp light brown sugar
15ml/1 tbsp rice vinegar
120ml/4fl oz/½ cup chicken stock
15ml/1 tbsp cornflour paste
few drops of sesame oil

1 Rinse and dry the fish well. Using a sharp knife, score both sides of the fish down to the bone with diagonal cuts about 2.5cm/1in apart. Rub both sides of the fish with the soy sauce and rice wine or sherry. Set aside for 10–15 minutes to marinate.

2 Heat sufficient oil for deep frying in a wok. When it is hot, add the fish and fry for 3–4 minutes on both sides, until golden brown.

3 To make the sauce pour away all but about 15ml/1 tbsp of the oil. Push the fish to one side of the wok and add the garlic, the white part of the spring onions, the ginger, chilli bean sauce, tomato purée, sugar, vinegar and stock. Bring to the boil and braise the fish in the sauce for 4–5 minutes, turning it over once. Add the green of the spring onions. Stir in the cornflour paste to thicken the sauce. Sprinkle over a little sesame oil and serve.

Seafood Balti with Vegetables

The spicy seafood is cooked separately and combined with vegetables at the last minute.

INGREDIENTS

Serves 4

For the seafood

225g/8oz cod, or any other firm, white fish
225g/8 oz peeled, cooked prawns
6 crab sticks, halved lengthways
15ml/1 tbsp lemon juice
5ml/1 tsp ground coriander
5ml/1 tsp chilli powder
5ml/1 tsp salt
5ml/1 tsp ground cumin
60ml/4 tbsp cornflour
150ml/¼ pint/⅔ cup corn oil

For the vegetables

150ml/¼ pint/⅔ cup corn oil
2 onions, chopped
5ml/1 tsp onion seeds
½ cauliflower, cut into florets
115g/4oz French beans, cut into 2.5cm/1in lengths
175g/6oz sweetcorn
5ml/1 tsp shredded fresh root ginger
5ml/1 tsp chilli powder
5ml/1 tsp salt
4 fresh green chillies, sliced
30ml/2 tbsp chopped fresh coriander
lime slices, to garnish (optional)

1 Skin the fish and cut into small cubes. Put it into a mixing bowl with the prawns and crab sticks.

COOK'S TIP

Raita makes a delicious accompaniment to this seafood dish. Whisk 300ml/½ pint/1¼ cups natural yogurt, then whisk in 120ml/4 fl oz/½ cup water. Stir in 5ml/1 tsp salt, 30ml/2 tbsp chopped fresh coriander and 1 finely chopped green chilli. Garnish with slices of cucumber and one or two sprigs of mint.

2 In a separate bowl, mix together the lemon juice, ground coriander, chilli powder, salt and ground cumin. Pour this over the seafood and mix together thoroughly using your hands.

3 Sprinkle on the cornflour and mix again until the seafood is well coated. Set aside in the refrigerator for about 1 hour to allow the flavours to develop fully.

4 To make the vegetable mixture, heat the oil in a preheated wok. Add the onions and the onion seeds and stir-fry until lightly browned.

5 Add the cauliflower, French beans, sweetcorn, ginger, chilli powder, salt, green chillies and fresh coriander. Stir-fry for about 7–10 minutes over a medium heat, making sure that the cauliflower florets retain their shape.

6 Spoon the fried vegetables around the edge of a shallow dish, leaving space in the middle for the seafood, an keep warm.

7 Wash and dry the pan, then heat the oil to fry the seafood pieces. Fry the seafood pieces in two or three batches, until they turn a golden brown. Remove with a slotted spoon and drain on kitchen paper.

8 Arrange each batch of seafood in the middle of the dish of vegetable and keep warm while you fry the remaining batches. Garnish with lime slices and serve immediately.

Braised Fish Fillet with Mushrooms

This is the Chinese stir-fried version of the French *filets de sole bonne femme* (sole cooked with mushrooms and wine sauce).

Ingredients

Serves 4

450g/1lb lemon sole or plaice fillets
5ml/1 tsp salt
½ egg white
30ml/2 tbsp cornflour paste
about 600ml/1 pint/2½ cups vegetable oil
15ml/1 tbsp finely chopped spring onions
2.5ml/½ tsp finely chopped fresh root ginger
115g/4oz white mushrooms, thinly sliced
5ml/1 tsp light brown sugar
15ml/1 tbsp light soy sauce
30ml/2 tbsp Chinese rice wine or dry sherry
15ml/1 tbsp brandy
about 120ml/4fl oz/⅔ cup stock
few drops sesame oil

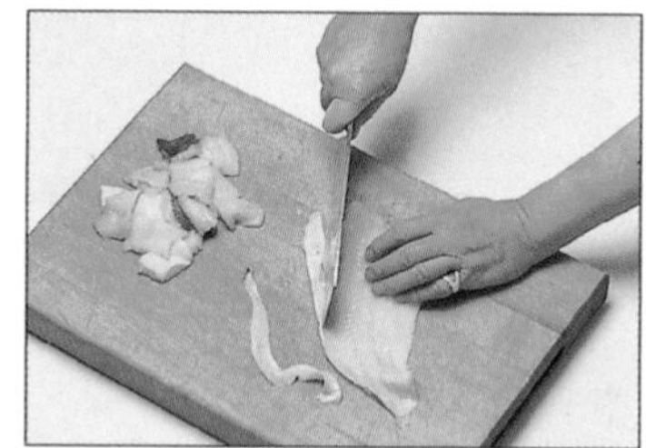

1 Trim off the soft bones along the edge of the fish, but leave the skin on. Cut each fillet into bite-sized pieces. Mix the fish with a little salt, the egg white and about half of the cornflour paste.

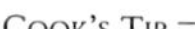

Cook's Tip

You could substitute straw mushrooms, so called because they are grown on beds of rice straw. They have a subtle flavour and a slightly slippery texture.

2 Heat the oil in a preheated wok until medium-hot, add the fish, slice by slice, and stir gently so the pieces do not stick. Remove after about 1 minute and drain. Pour off the excess oil, leaving about 30ml/2 tbsp in the wok.

3 Stir-fry the spring onions, ginger and mushrooms for 1 minute. Add the sugar, soy sauce, rice wine or sherry, brandy and stock. Bring to the boil. Return the fish to the wok and braise for 1 minute. Stir in the remaining cornflour paste to thicken the sauce and sprinkle with sesame oil.

Prawn Fu-yung

This is a very colourful dish that is simple to make in a wok. Most of the preparation can be done well in advance.

Ingredients

Serves 4

3 eggs, beaten, reserving 5ml/1 tsp egg white
15ml/1 tbsp finely chopped spring onions
45–60ml/3–4 tbsp vegetable oil
225g/8oz uncooked prawns, peeled
10ml/2 tsp cornflour paste
175g/6oz green peas
15ml/1 tbsp Chinese rice wine or dry sherry
salt

1 Beat the eggs with a pinch of the salt and a few pieces of the spring onions. Heat a little oil in a preheated wok over a moderate heat. Add the egg mixture and stir to scramble. Remove the scrambled eggs and reserve.

2 Mix the prawns with a little salt, 5ml/1 tsp egg white and the cornflour paste. Stir-fry the peas in hot oil for 30 seconds Add the prawns.

3 Add the spring onions. Stir-fry for 1 minute, then stir the mixture into the scrambled egg with a little salt and the wine or sherry and serve.

Thai Fish Cakes

Bursting with flavours of chillies, lime and lemon grass, these little fish cakes make a wonderful starter or light lunch dish.

INGREDIENTS

Serves 4

450g/1lb cod or haddock fillets
3 spring onions, sliced
1 lemon grass stalk, finely chopped
30ml/2 tbsp chopped fresh coriander
30ml/2 tbsp Thai red curry paste
1 fresh green chilli, seeded and chopped
10ml/2 tsp grated lime rind
15ml/1 tbsp lime juice
30ml/2 tbsp groundnut oil
salt
crisp lettuce leaves, shredded spring onions, fresh red chilli slices, coriander sprigs and lime wedges, to serve

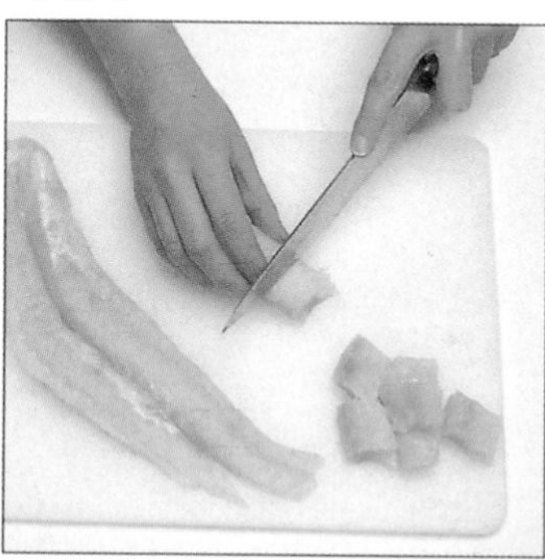

1 Cut the fish into chunks, then place them in a blender or food processor.

2 Add the spring onions, lemon grass, coriander, curry paste, chilli, lime rind and juice to the fish. Season with salt. Process until finely minced.

3 Using lightly floured hands, divide the mixture into 16 pieces and shape each one into a small cake about 4cm/1½in across. Place the fish cakes on a plate, cover with clear film and chill for about 2 hours until firm.

4 Heat a wok over a high heat until hot. Add the oil and swirl it around. Fry the fish cakes, a few at a time, for 6–8 minutes, turning them over carefully until evenly browned. Drain each batch on kitchen paper and keep hot while you are cooking the remainder. Serve on a bed of crisp lettuce leaves with shredded spring onions, red chilli slices, fresh coriander sprigs and lime wedges.

Sweet-and-sour Fish

Vhen fish is cooked in this way he skin becomes crispy on the utside, while the flesh remains noist and juicy inside. The sweet nd sour sauce, with its colourful herry tomatoes, complements he fish beautifully.

NGREDIENTS

erves 4–6

- large or 2 medium-size fish such as snapper or mullet, heads removed
- 0ml/4 tsp cornflour
- 20ml/4fl oz/½ cup vegetable oil
- 5ml/1 tbsp chopped garlic
- 5ml/1 tbsp chopped root ginger
- 0ml/2 tbsp chopped shallots
- 25g/8oz cherry tomatoes
- 0ml/2 tbsp red wine vinegar
- 0ml/2 tbsp granulated sugar
- 0ml/2 tbsp tomato ketchup
- 5ml/1 tbsp fish sauce
- 5ml/3 tbsp water
- lt and freshly ground black pepper
- oriander leaves, to garnish
- hredded spring onions, to garnish

1 Thoroughly rinse and clean the fish. Score the skin diagonally on oth sides of the fish.

2 Coat the fish lightly on both sides with 15ml/1 tbsp cornflour. Shake ff any excess.

3 Heat the oil in a wok or large frying pan and slide the fish into the wok. Reduce the heat to medium and fry the fish until crisp and brown, about 6–7 minutes on both sides.

4 Remove the fish with a fish slice and place on a large platter.

5 Pour off all but 30ml/2 tbsp of the oil and add the garlic, ginger and shallots. Fry until golden.

6 Add the cherry tomatoes and cook until they burst open. Stir in the vinegar, sugar, tomato ketchup and fish sauce. Simmer gently for 1–2 minutes and adjust the seasoning.

7 Blend the remaining 5ml/1 tsp cornflour with the water. Stir into the sauce and heat until it thickens. Pour the sauce over the fish and garnish with coriander leaves and shredded spring onions.

Spiced Salmon Stir-fry

Marinating the salmon allows all the flavours to develop, and the lime juice tenderizes the fish beautifully, so it needs very little stir-frying – be careful not to overcook it.

INGREDIENTS

Serves 4
4 salmon steaks, about 225g/8oz each
4 whole star anise
1 dried chilli
2 lemon grass stalks, sliced
juice and finely grated rind of 3 limes
30ml/2 tbsp clear honey
30ml/2 tbsp grapeseed oil
salt and ground black pepper
lime wedges, to garnish

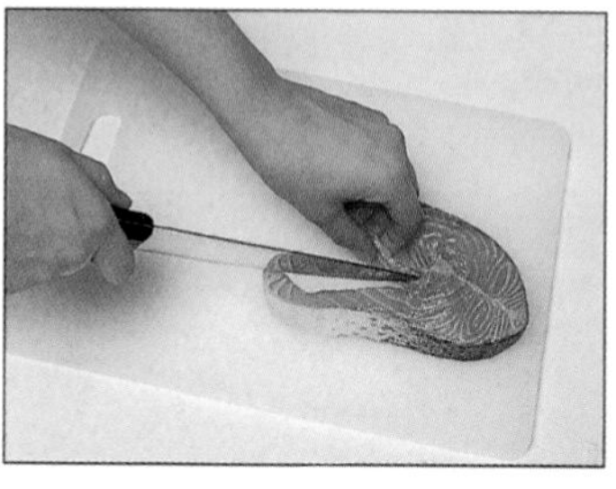

1 Remove the middle bone from each steak, using a very sharp filleting knife, to make two strips from each steak.

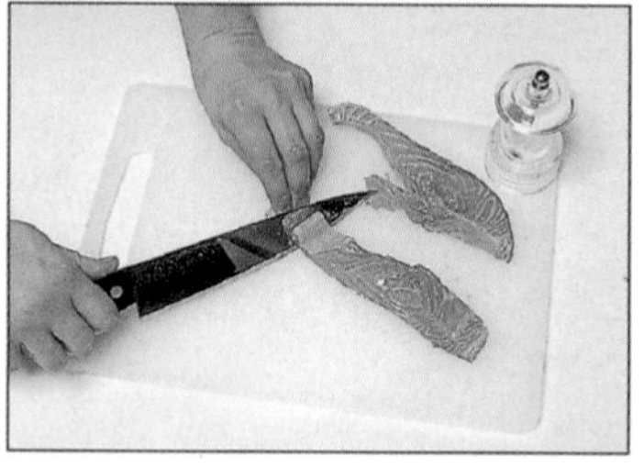

2 Remove the skin by inserting the knife at the thin end of each piece of salmon. Sprinkle 5ml/1 tsp salt on the cutting board to prevent the fish slipping while removing the skin. Slice into pieces, cutting diagonally.

3 Roughly crush the star anise and chilli in a mortar with a pestle. Place the salmon in a non-metallic dish and add the star anise, lemon grass, lime juice and rind and honey. Season well with salt and pepper. Turn the salmon strips to coat. Cover and leave in the refrigerator overnight.

4 Carefully drain the salmon from the marinade, pat dry on kitchen paper and reserve the marinade.

5 Heat a wok, then add the oil. When the oil is hot, add the salmon and stir-fry, stirring constantly until cooked. Increase the heat, pour over the marinade and bring to the boil. Garnish with lime wedges and serve.

COOK'S TIP

Star anise contains the same oil as the more familiar Mediterranean spice, anise or aniseed, but looks completely different. Its star-shaped pods are particularly attractive, so it is often used whole in Chinese cooking for its decorative effect. It is also becoming increasingly popular with western cooks for the same reason. It is an essential ingredient in many classic Chinese recipes and is one of the spices that constitute five-spice powder. The flavour of star anise is very strong and liquorice-tasting with rather deeper undertones than its European counterpart.

Malaysian Fish Curry

Fish gently cooked in a wok of coconut milk makes a mouth-watering curry for any occasion.

INGREDIENTS

Serves 4–6

675g/$1\frac{1}{2}$lb monkfish, hokey or red snapper fillet
salt, to taste
45ml/3 tbsp grated or desiccated coconut
30ml/2 tbsp vegetable oil
2.5cm/1in galangal or fresh root ginger, peeled and thinly sliced
2 small red chillies, seeded and finely chopped
2 cloves garlic, crushed
5cm/2in lemon grass stalk, shredded
1 piece shrimp paste, 1cm/$\frac{1}{2}$in square or 15ml/1 tbsp fish sauce
400g/14oz canned coconut milk
600ml/1 pint/$2\frac{1}{2}$ cups chicken stock
2.5ml/$\frac{1}{2}$ tsp turmeric
15ml/1 tbsp sugar
juice of 1 lime, or $\frac{1}{2}$ lemon
boiled rice, to serve (optional)

1 Cut the fish into large chunks, season with salt and set aside.

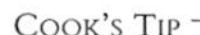

COOK'S TIP

Sambal, a fiery hot relish, is traditionally served with this curry. Mix together 2 skinned and chopped tomatoes, 1 finely chopped onion, 1 finely chopped green chilli and 30ml/2 tbsp lime juice. Season to taste with salt and pepper and sprinkle over 30ml/2 tbsp grated or desiccated coconut.

2 Dry fry the coconut in a large wok until evenly brown. Add the vegetable oil, galangal or ginger, chillies, garlic and lemon grass and fry briefly. Stir in the shrimp paste or fish sauce. Strain the coconut milk through a sieve, then add to the wok.

3 Add the chicken stock, turmeric, sugar, a little salt and the lime or lemon juice. Simmer for 10 minutes. Add the fish and simmer for 6–8 minutes. Stir in the thick part of the coconut milk and simmer to thicken. Garnish with coriander and lime slices and serve with rice, if liked.

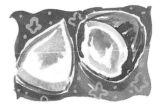

Vinegar Fish

ish cooked in a spicy mixture hat includes chillies, ginger and inegar is an Indonesian peciality. It is a method that ends itself particularly well to trong-flavoured, oily fish, such s the mackerel used here.

NGREDIENTS

erves 2–3

–3 mackerel, filleted
-3 red chillies, seeded
macadamia nuts or 8 almonds
red onion, quartered
garlic cloves, crushed
cm/½in piece root ginger, peeled and sliced
ml/1 tsp ground turmeric
5ml/3 tbsp coconut or vegetable oil
5ml/3 tbsp wine vinegar
50ml/¼ pint/⅔ cup water
alt
eep-fried onions and finely chopped chilli, to garnish
oiled or coconut rice, to serve (optional)

1 Rinse the mackerel fillets in cold water and dry well on kitchen aper. Set aside.

2 Put the chillies, macadamia nuts or almonds, onion, garlic, ginger, turmeric and 15ml/1 tbsp of the oil in a food processor and process to form a paste. Alternatively, pound them together in a mortar with a pestle to form a paste. Heat the remaining oil in a wok. When it is hot, add the paste and cook for 1–2 minutes without browning. Stir in the vinegar and water and season with salt to taste. Bring to the boil, then lower the heat.

3 Add the mackerel fillets to the sauce and simmer for 6–8 minutes or until the fish is tender and cooked.

4 Transfer the fish to a warm serving dish. Bring the sauce to a boil and cook for 1 minute or until it has reduced slightly. Pour the sauce over the fish, garnish with the deep-fried onions and chopped chilli and serve with rice, if liked.

Cook's Tip

To make coconut rice, put 400g/14oz washed long grain rice in a heavy saucepan with 2.5ml/½ tsp salt, a 5cm/2in piece of lemon grass and 25g/1oz creamed coconut. Add 750ml/1¼ pints/3 cups boiling water and stir once to prevent the grains sticking together. Simmer over a medium heat for 10–12 minutes. Remove the pan from the heat, cover and set aside for 5 minutes. Fluff the rice with a fork or chopsticks before serving.

Fragrant Swordfish with Ginger and Lemon Grass

Swordfish is a firm-textured, meaty fish which cooks well in a wok if it has been marinated as steaks rather than cut in strips. It is sometimes a little dry, but this is counteracted by the marinade. If you cannot get swordfish, use any variety of fresh tuna.

Ingredients

Serves 4

1 kaffir lime leaf
45ml/3 tbsp rock salt
75ml/5 tbsp brown sugar
4 swordfish steaks, about 225g/8oz each
1 lemon grass stalk, sliced
2.5cm/1in fresh root ginger, cut into matchsticks
1 lime
15ml/1 tbsp grapeseed oil
1 large ripe avocado, peeled and stoned
salt and ground black pepper

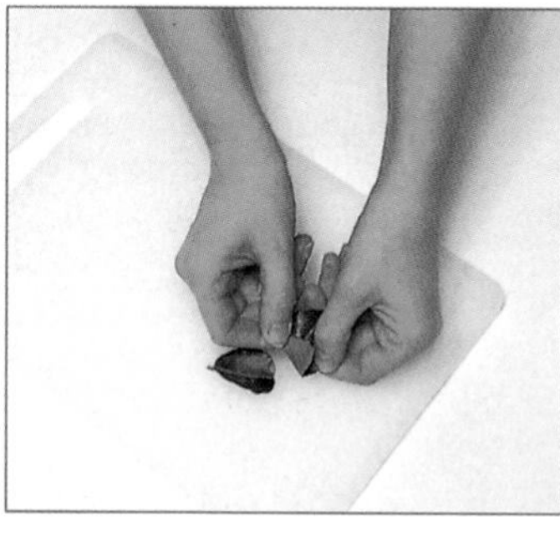

1 Bruise the lime leaf by crushing slightly, to release the flavour.

Cook's Tip

Kaffir lime leaves are intensely aromatic with a distinctive figure-of-eight shape. They are used extensively in Indonesian and Thai cooking, and Thai cuisine also makes use of the fruit rind of the lime from this particular type of tree.

2 To make the marinade, process the rock salt, brown sugar and lime leaf together in a food processor or blender until thoroughly blended.

3 Place the swordfish steaks in a bowl. Sprinkle the marinade over them and add the lemon grass and root ginger matchsticks. Leave for 3–4 hours to marinate.

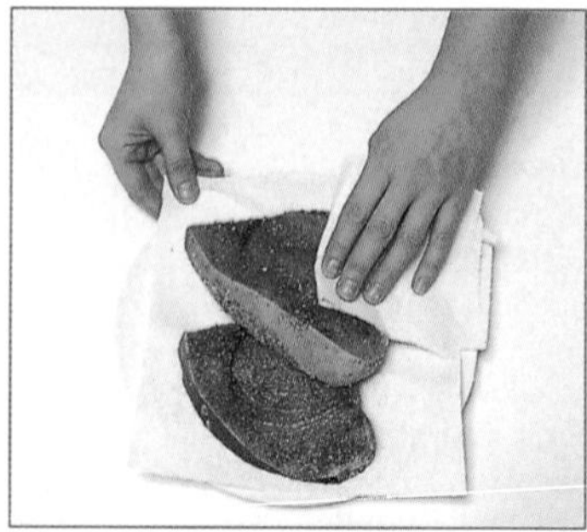

4 Rinse off the marinade and pat the fish dry with kitchen paper.

5 Peel the lime. Remove any excess pith from the peel. Cut the peel into very thin strips. Squeeze the juice from the fruit.

6 Heat a wok, then add the oil. When the oil is hot, add the lime rind and then the swordfish steaks. Stir-fry for 3–4 minutes. Add the lime juice. Remove the wok from the heat, slice the avocado and add to the fish. Season to taste and serve.

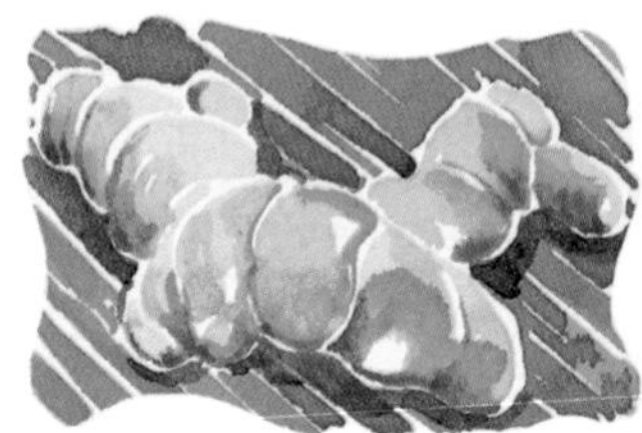

Balti Prawns in Hot Sauce

This sizzling prawn dish is cooked in a fiery hot and spicy sauce. Not only does the sauce contain chilli powder, it is further enhanced by the addition of ground green chillies and other spices.

Ingredients

Serves 4

2 onions, roughly chopped
30ml/2 tbsp tomato purée
5ml/1 tsp ground coriander
1.5ml/¼ tsp turmeric
5ml/1 tsp chilli powder
3 fresh green chillies
45ml/3 tbsp chopped fresh coriander
30ml/2 tbsp lemon juice
5ml/1 tsp salt
45ml/3 tbsp corn oil
16 peeled cooked king prawns

1 Put the onions, tomato purée, ground coriander, turmeric, chilli powder, 2 of the green chillies, 30ml/2 tbsp of the chopped coriander, the lemon juice and salt into a food processor. Process for about 1 minute. If the mixture seems too thick, add a little water to loosen it. Chop the remaining chilli and reserve for garnishing the dish.

2 Heat the oil in a preheated wok or frying pan. Lower the heat, add the spice mixture and fry for 3–5 minutes or until the sauce has thickened slightly.

3 Add the prawns and stir-fry over a medium heat until they are heated through, but not overcooked.

4 Transfer to a serving dish and garnish with the remaining chilli and chopped fresh coriander. Serve immediately.

Battered Fish, Prawns and Vegetables

his is a recipe for tempura, one ˙the few dishes that was ought to Japan from the West. he idea came from Spanish and ortuguese missionaries who ttled in southern Japan in the te sixteenth century.

IGREDIENTS

rves 4–6
sheet nori
large raw prawn tails
'5g/6oz whiting or monkfish fillet, cut into fingers
small aubergine
spring onions, trimmed
fresh shiitake mushrooms
getable oil, for deep-frying
our, for dusting
ne salt
ml/5 tbsp soy or tamari sauce, to serve

or the batter
egg yolks
)0ml/ ½ pint/1¼ cups iced water
25g/8oz/2 cups flour
5ml/½ tsp salt

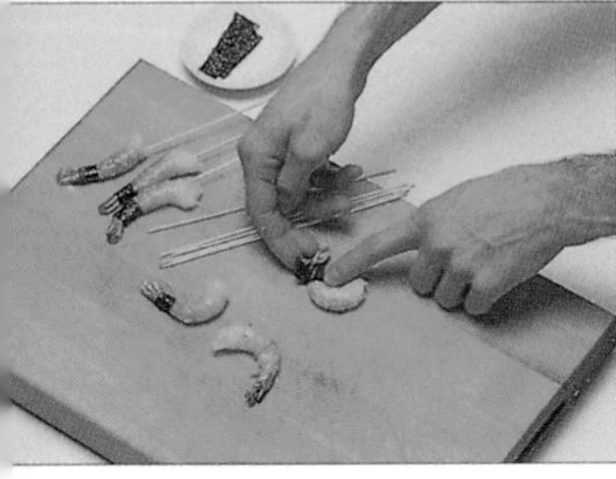

1 Cut the nori into strips 1cm/½in wide and 5cm/2in long. Moisten ne end of each strip with water and rap it round the tail end of each rawn. Skewer the prawns along their ngth to straighten them. Skewer the ngers of white fish and set aside.

2 Slice the aubergine into neat sections, sprinkle with salt and arrange in layers on a plate. Press lightly with your hand to expel the bitter juices, then leave for 20–30 minutes. Rinse thoroughly under cold water, dry well and place on bamboo skewers. Skewer the spring onions and shiitake mushrooms.

3 Make the batter just before using. Beat together the egg yolks and half the iced water. Sift in the flour and salt and stir lightly with chopsticks without mixing to a dry paste. Add the remaining water and stir to make a smooth batter. Avoid over-mixing.

4 Heat the oil to 180°C/350°F in a wok fitted with a wire draining rack. Dust the vegetables and fish in flour, not more than three at a time. Dip them into the batter to coat, then fry for 1–2 minutes, until crisp and golden. Drain well, sprinkle with salt and drain on kitchen paper. Serve with soy or tamari sauce for dipping.

Green Curry of Prawns

A popular fragrant creamy curry that also takes very little time to prepare. It can also be made with thin strips of chicken meat.

Ingredients

Serves 4–6

30ml/2 tbsp vegetable oil
30ml/2 tbsp green curry paste
450g/1lb king prawns, shelled and deveined
4 kaffir lime leaves, torn
1 stalk lemon grass, bruised and chopped
250ml/8fl oz/1 cup coconut milk
30ml/2 tbsp fish sauce
½ cucumber, seeded and cut into thin batons
10–15 basil leaves
4 green chillies, sliced, to garnish

1 Heat the oil in a frying pan. Add the green curry paste and fry until bubbling and fragrant.

2 Add the prawns, kaffir lime leaves and lemon grass. Fry for 1–2 minutes, until the prawns are pink.

3 Stir in the coconut milk and bring to a gentle boil. Simmer, stirring occasionally, for about 5 minutes or until the prawns are tender.

4 Stir in the fish sauce, cucumber, and basil, then top with the green chillies and serve.

Prawn Satés

For *Saté Udang*, king prawns look spectacular and taste wonderful. The spicy coconut marinade marries beautifully with the prawns and is also excellent when used with firm cubes of monkfish or halibut and cooked in the same way.

INGREDIENTS

Makes 4 skewers

12 uncooked king prawns

For the marinade

5mm/¼in cube *terasi*
1 garlic clove, crushed
1 lemon grass stem, lower 6cm/2½in sliced, top reserved
3–4 macadamia nuts or 6–8 almonds
2.5ml/½ tsp chilli powder
salt
oil for frying
120ml/4fl oz/½ cup coconut milk
2.5ml/½ tsp tamarind pulp, soaked in 30ml/2 tbsp water, then strained and juice reserved

To serve

cucumber cubes (optional)
lemon wedges

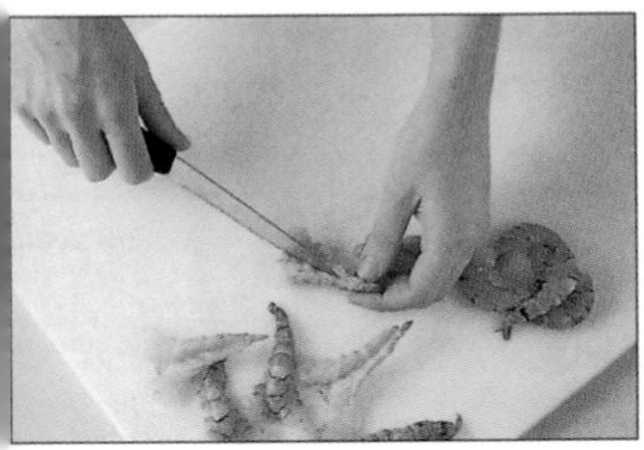

1 Remove the heads from the prawns. Peel the prawns and remove the spinal cord, if liked. Using a small sharp knife, make an incision along the underbody of each prawn, without cutting it completely in half and open it up like a book. Thread 3 of the prawns on to each skewer.

2 Make the marinade. Grind the *terasi*, garlic, lemon grass slices, nuts, chilli powder and a little salt to a paste in a food processor or with a pestle and mortar.

3 Fry the paste in oil, for 1 minute. Add the coconut milk and tamarind juice. Simmer for 1 minute. Cool. Pour over the prawns and leave for 1 hour.

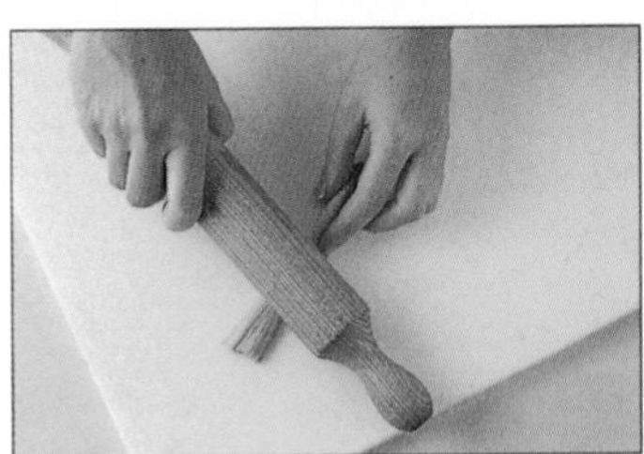

4 Cook the prawns under a hot grill or on the barbecue for 3 minutes or until cooked through. Beat the top part of the lemon grass with the end of a rolling pin, to make it into a brush. Use this to brush the prawns with the marinade during cooking.

5 Serve on a platter, with the rice shapes and cucumber cubes, if using, and lemon wedges.

Prawns with Chayote in Turmeric Sauce

This delicious, attractively coloured dish is called *Gule Udang Dengan Labu Kuning*.

Ingredients

Serves 4

1–2 chayotes or 2–3 courgettes
2 fresh red chillies, seeded
1 onion, quartered
5mm/¼in fresh *lengkuas*, peeled
1 lemon grass stem, lower 5cm/2in sliced, top bruised
2.5cm/1in fresh turmeric, peeled
200ml/7fl oz/scant 1 cup water
lemon juice
400ml/14fl oz can coconut milk
450g/1lb cooked, peeled prawns
salt
red chilli shreds, to garnish (optional)
boiled rice, to serve

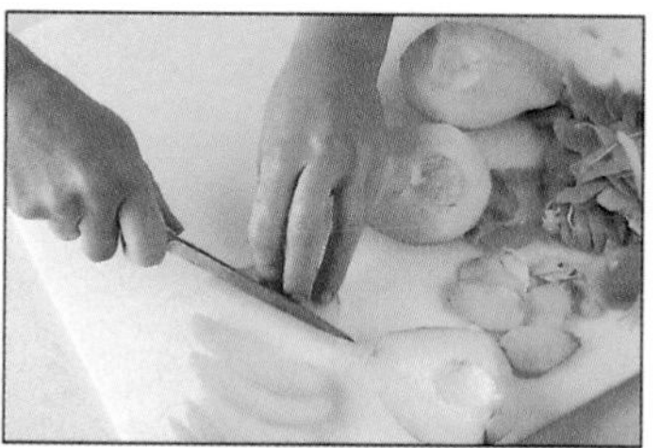

1 Peel the chayotes, remove the seeds and cut into strips. If using courgettes, cut into 5cm/2in strips.

2 Grind the fresh red chillies, onion, sliced *lengkuas*, sliced lemon grass and the fresh turmeric to a paste in a food processor or with a pestle and mortar. Add the water to the paste mixture, with a squeeze of lemon juice and salt to taste.

3 Pour into a pan. Add the top of the lemon grass stem. Bring to the boil and cook for 1–2 minutes. Add the chayote or courgette pieces and cook for 2 minutes. Stir in the coconut milk. Taste and adjust the seasoning.

4 Stir in the prawns and cook gently for 2–3 minutes. Remove the lemon grass stem. Garnish with shreds of chilli, if using, and serve with rice.

Doedoeh of Fish

Haddock or cod fillet may be substituted in this recipe.

Ingredients

Serves 6–8

1kg/2¼lb fresh mackerel fillets, skinned
30ml/2 tbsp tamarind pulp, soaked in 200ml/7fl oz/scant 1 cup water
1 onion
1cm/½in fresh *lengkuas*
2 garlic cloves
1–2 fresh red chillies, seeded, or 5ml/1 tsp chilli powder
5ml/1 tsp ground coriander
5ml/1 tsp ground turmeric
2.5ml/½ tsp ground fennel seeds
15ml/1 tbsp dark brown sugar
90–105ml/6–7 tbsp oil
200ml/7fl oz/scant 1 cup coconut cream
salt and freshly ground black pepper
fresh chilli shreds, to garnish

1 Rinse the fish fillets in cold water and dry them well on kitchen paper. Put into a shallow dish and sprinkle with a little salt. Strain the tamarind and pour the juice over the fish fillets. Leave for 30 minutes.

2 Quarter the onion, peel and slice the *lengkuas* and peel the garlic. Grind the onion, *lengkuas*, garlic and chillies or chilli powder to a paste in a food processor or with a pestle and mortar. Add the ground coriander, turmeric, fennel seeds and sugar.

3 Heat half of the oil in a frying pan. Drain the fish fillets and fry for 5 minutes, or until cooked. Set aside.

4 Wipe out the pan and heat the remaining oil. Fry the spice paste, stirring all the time, until it gives off a spicy aroma. Do not let it brown. Add the coconut cream and simmer gently for a few minutes. Add the fish fillets and gently heat through.

5 Taste for seasoning and serve scattered with shredded chilli.

Red and White Prawns with Green Vegetables

The Chinese name for this dish is *Yuan Yang* prawns. Pairs of mandarin ducks are also known as *yuan yang*, or love birds, because they are always seen together. They symbolize affection and happiness.

Ingredients

Serves 4–6

450g/1lb raw prawns
½ egg white
15ml/1 tbsp cornflour paste
175g/6oz mangetouts
about 600ml/1 pint/2½ cups vegetable oil
5ml/1 tsp light brown sugar
15ml/1 tbsp finely chopped spring onion
5ml/1 tsp finely chopped fresh root ginger
15ml/1 tbsp light soy sauce
15ml/1 tbsp Chinese rice wine or dry sherry
5ml/1 tsp chilli bean sauce
15ml/1 tbsp tomato purée
salt

1 Peel and devein the prawns and mix with the egg white, cornflour paste and a pinch of salt. Top and tail the mangetouts.

2 Heat 30–45ml/2–3 tbsp of the oil in a preheated wok and stir-fry the mangetouts for about 1 minute. Add the sugar and a little salt and continue stirring for 1 more minute. Remove and place in the centre of a warmed serving platter.

3 Add the remaining oil to the wok and cook the prawns for 1 minute. Remove and drain.

4 Pour off all but about 15ml/1 tbsp of the oil. Add the spring onion and ginger to the wok.

5 Return the prawns to the wok and stir-fry for 1 minute, then add the soy sauce and rice wine or dry sherry. Blend the mixture thoroughly. Transfer half the prawns to one end of the serving platter.

6 Add the chilli bean sauce and tomato purée to the remaining prawns in the wok, blend well and place the "red" prawns at the other end of the platter. Serve.

Cook's Tip

All raw prawns have an intestinal tract that runs just beneath the outside curve of the tail. The tract is not poisonous, but it can taste unpleasant. It is, therefore, best to remove it – devein. To do this, peel the prawns, leaving the tail intact. Score each prawn lightly along its length to expose the tract. Remove the tract with a small knife or Chinese cleaver.

Karahi Prawns and Fenugreek

The black-eyed beans, prawns and paneer in this mean that it is rich in protein. The combination of both ground and fresh fenugreek makes this a very fragrant and delicious dish.

Ingredients

Serves 4–6

60ml/4 tbsp corn oil
2 onions, sliced
2 medium tomatoes, sliced
7.5ml/1½ tsp garlic pulp
5ml/1 tsp chilli powder
5ml/1 tsp ginger pulp
5ml/1 tsp ground cumin
5ml/1 tsp ground coriander
5ml/1 tsp salt
150g/5oz paneer, cubed
5ml/1 tsp ground fenugreek
1 bunch fresh fenugreek leaves
115g/4oz cooked prawns
2 fresh red chillies, sliced
30ml/2 tbsp chopped fresh coriander
50g/2oz canned black-eyed beans, drained
15ml/1 tbsp lemon juice

1 Heat the oil in a preheated wok. Lower the heat slightly and add the onions and tomatoes. Fry, stirring occasionally, for about 3 minutes.

2 Add the garlic, chilli powder, ginger, ground cumin, ground coriander, salt, paneer and the ground and fresh fenugreek. Lower the heat and stir-fry for about 2 minutes.

3 Add the prawns, red chillies, fresh coriander and the black-eyed beans and mix well. Cook for a further 3–5 minutes, stirring occasionally, or until the prawns are heated through.

4 Finally sprinkle over the lemon juice and serve.

Spiced Prawns with Coconut

his spicy dish is based on the aditional Indonesian dish *sambal reng udang*. Sambals are ıngent, very hot dishes popular ıroughout south India and ɔuth-east Asia.

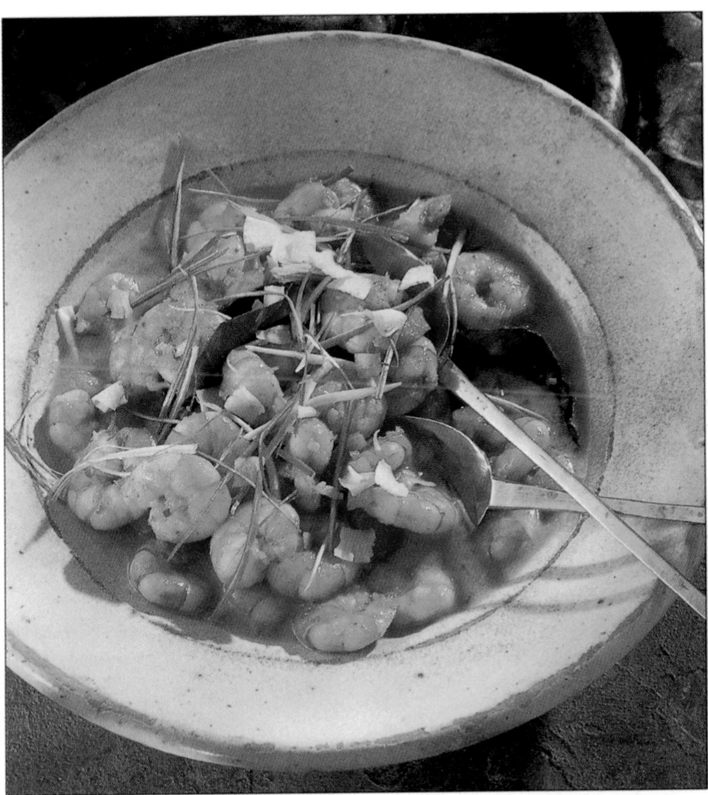

IGREDIENTS

rves 3–4

-3 red chillies, seeded and chopped
shallots, chopped
lemon grass stalk, chopped
garlic cloves, chopped
ıin sliver of dried shrimp paste
5ml/½ tsp ground galangal
nl/1 tsp ground turmeric
nl/1 tsp ground coriander
5ml/1 tbsp groundnut oil
50ml/8fl oz/1 cup water
fresh kaffir lime leaves
nl/1 tsp light brown soft sugar
tomatoes, skinned, seeded and chopped
50ml/8fl oz/1 cup coconut milk
75g/1½lb large raw prawns, peeled and deveined
ueeze of lemon juice
lt
ıredded spring onions and flaked coconut, to garnish

1 In a mortar, pound together the chillies, shallots, lemon grass, garlic, hrimp paste, galangal, turmeric and oriander with a pestle until the nixture forms a paste.

2 Heat a wok, add the oil and swirl it around. Add the spice paste and stir-fry for 2 minutes. Pour in the water and add the kaffir lime leaves, sugar and tomatoes. Simmer for 8–10 minutes until most of the liquid has evaporated.

Cook's Tip

Dried shrimp paste, widely used in South-east Asian cooking, is available from oriental food stores. Ground galangal, which is similar to ground ginger and comes from the same family, is also available from oriental food stores.

3 Add the coconut milk and prawns and cook gently, stirring, for 4 minutes until the prawns are pink. Season with lemon juice and salt to taste. Transfer the mixture to a warmed serving dish, garnish with the spring onions and flaked coconut and serve.

Paneer Balti with Prawns

Although paneer is not widely eaten in Pakistan, it makes an excellent substitute for red meat. Here it is combined with king prawns to make a memorable stir-fry dish.

INGREDIENTS

Serves 4

12 cooked king prawns
175g/6oz paneer
30ml/2 tbsp tomato purée
60ml/4 tbsp Greek-style yogurt
7.5ml/1½ tsp garam masala
5ml/1 tsp chilli powder
5ml/1 tsp garlic pulp
5ml/1 tsp salt
10ml/2 tsp mango powder
5ml/1 tsp ground coriander
115g/4oz butter
15ml/1 tbsp corn oil
3 fresh green chillies, chopped
45ml/3 tbsp chopped fresh coriander
150ml/¼ pint/⅔ cup single cream

1 Peel the king prawns and cube the paneer.

2 Blend together the tomato purée, yogurt, garam masala, chilli powder, garlic, salt, mango powder and ground coriander in a mixing bowl and set aside.

3 Melt the butter with the oil in a wok. Lower the heat slightly and stir-fry the paneer and prawns for about 2 minutes. Remove with a slotted spoon and drain on kitchen paper. Set aside.

4 Pour the spice mixture into the butter and oil left in the pan and stir-fry for about 1 minute.

5 Add the paneer and prawns, and cook for 7–10 minutes, stirring occasionally, until the prawns are heated through.

6 Add the fresh chillies and most of the coriander, and pour in the cream. Heat through for about 2 minutes, garnish with the remaining fresh coriander and serve.

COOK'S TIP

To make paneer at home, bring 1 litre/1¾ pints/4 cups milk to the boil over a low heat. Add 30ml/2 tbsp lemon juice, stirring continuously and gently until the milk thickens and begins to curdle. Strain the curdled milk through a sieve lined with muslin. Set aside under a heavy weight for about 1½–2 hours to press to a flat shape about 1cm/½in thick.

Make the paneer a day before you plan to use it in a recipe; it will then be firmer and easier to handle. Cut and use as required; it will keep for about one week in the refrigerator.

Stir-fried Prawns with Broccoli

This is a very colourful dish, highly nutritious and at the same time extremely delicious; furthermore, it is not time-consuming or difficult to prepare.

Ingredients

Serves 4

175–225g/6–8oz prawns, shelled and deveined
5ml/1 tsp salt
15ml/1 tbsp Chinese rice wine or dry sherry
½ egg white
15ml/1 tbsp cornflour paste
225g/8oz broccoli
about 300ml/½ pint/1¼ cups vegetable oil
1 spring onion, cut into short sections
5ml/1 tsp light brown sugar
about 30ml/2 tbsp stock or water
5ml/1 tsp light soy sauce
few drops sesame oil

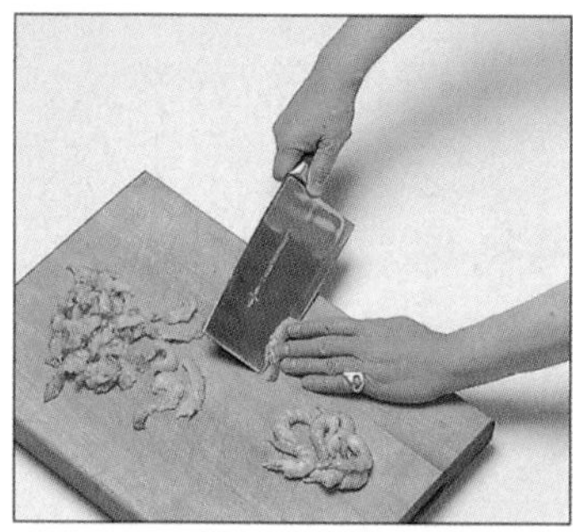

1 Cut each prawn in half lengthways. Mix with a pinch of salt and about 5ml/1 tsp of the rice wine, egg white and cornflour paste.

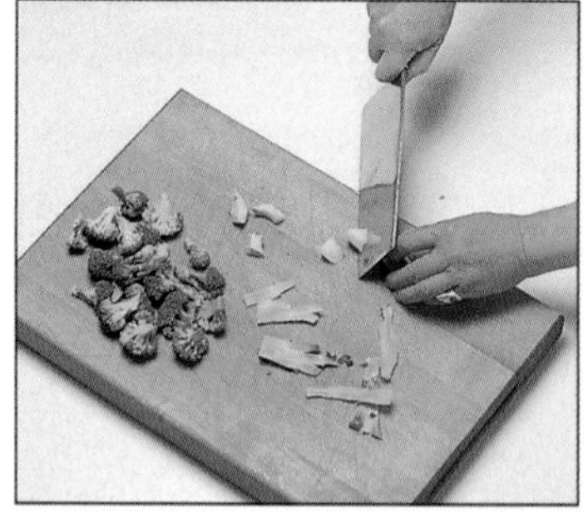

2 Cut the broccoli heads into florets; remove the rough skin from the stalks, then slice the florets diagonally into diamond-shaped chunks.

3 Heat the oil in a preheated wok and stir-fry the prawns for about 30 seconds. Remove with a slotted spoon and drain thoroughly.

4 Pour off the excess oil, leaving 30ml/2 tbsp in the wok. Add the broccoli and spring onion, stir-fry for about 2 minutes, then add the remaining salt and the sugar, followed by the prawns and stock or water. Add the soy sauce and remaining rice wine or sherry. Blend well, then finally add the sesame oil and serve.

Stir-fried Prawns with Tamarind

'he sour, tangy flavour that is haracteristic of many Thai ishes comes from tamarind. resh tamarind pods from the ımarind tree can sometimes be ought, but preparing them for ooking is a laborious process. 'he Thais, however, usually refer to use compressed blocks f tamarind paste, which is mply soaked in warm water and ıen strained.

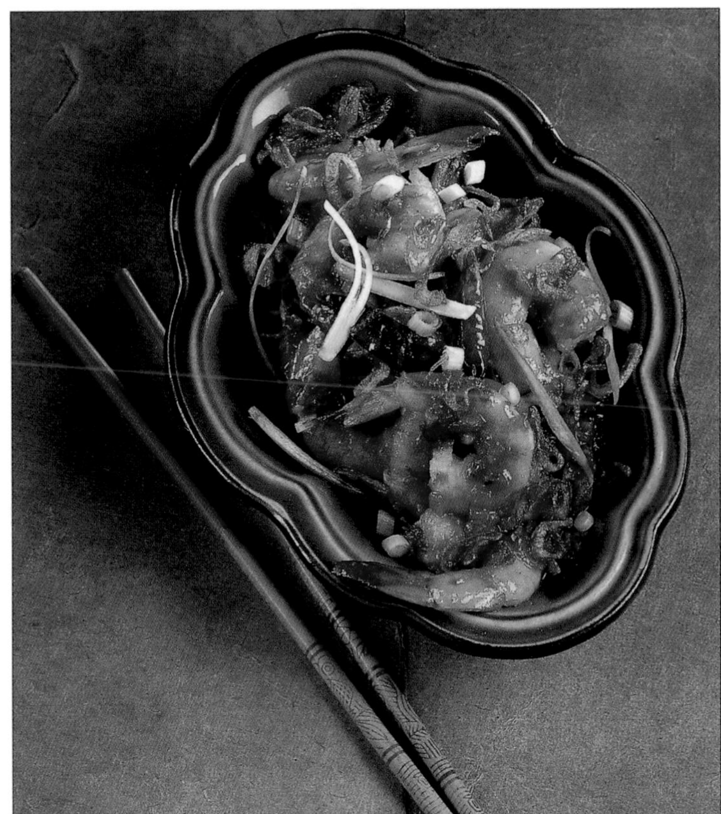

NGREDIENTS

erves 4–6

0g/2oz tamarind paste
50ml/¼ pint/⅔ cup boiling water
0ml/2 tbsp vegetable oil
0ml/2 tbsp chopped onion
0ml/2 tbsp palm sugar
0ml/2 tbsp chicken stock or water
5ml/1 tbsp fish sauce
dried red chillies, fried
50g/1lb uncooked shelled prawns
5ml/1 tbsp fried chopped garlic
0ml/2 tbsp fried sliced shallots
spring onions, chopped, to garnish

1 Put the tamarind paste in a small bowl, pour over the boiling water ıd stir well to break up any lumps. eave for 30 minutes. Strain, pushing much of the juice through as ossible. Measure 90ml/6 tbsp of the ıice, the amount needed, and store the mainder in the fridge. Heat the oil in wok. Add the chopped onion and fry ntil golden brown.

2 Add the sugar, stock, fish sauce, dried chillies and the tamarind juice, stirring well until the sugar dissolves. Bring to the boil.

3 Add the prawns, garlic and shallots. Stir-fry until the prawns are cooked, about 3–4 minutes. Garnish with the spring onions.

Satay Prawns

An enticing and tasty dish. Serve with greens and jasmine rice.

Ingredients

Serves 4–6
450g/1lb king prawns, shelled, tail ends left intact and deveined
½ bunch coriander leaves, to garnish
4 red chillies, finely sliced, to garnish
spring onions, cut diagonally, to garnish

For the peanut sauce
45ml/3 tbsp vegetable oil
15ml/1 tbsp chopped garlic
1 small onion, chopped
3–4 red chillies, crushed and chopped
3 kaffir lime leaves, torn
1 stalk lemon grass, bruised and chopped
5ml/1 tsp medium curry paste
250ml/8fl oz/1 cup coconut milk
1.5cm/½in cinnamon stick
75g/3oz crunchy peanut butter
45ml/3 tbsp tamarind juice
30ml/2 tbsp fish sauce
30ml/2 tbsp palm sugar
juice of ½ lemon

1 To make the sauce, heat half the oil in a wok or large frying pan and add the garlic and onion. Cook until it softens, about 3–4 minutes.

2 Add the chillies, kaffir lime leaves, lemon grass and curry paste. Cook for a further 2–3 minutes.

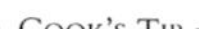

Cook's Tip

Curry paste has a far superior, authentic flavour to powdered varieties. Once opened, they should be kept in the fridge and used within 2 months.

3 Stir in the coconut milk, cinnam stick, peanut butter, tamarind jui fish sauce, palm sugar and lemon juic

4 Reduce the heat and simmer gently for 15–20 minutes until th sauce thickens, stirring occasionally tc ensure the sauce doesn't stick to the bottom of the wok or frying pan.

5 Heat the rest of the oil in a wok large frying pan. Add the prawns and stir-fry for about 3–4 minutes or until the prawns turn pink and are slightly firm to the touch.

6 Mix the prawns with the sauce. Serve garnished with coriander leaves, red chillies and spring onions.

Prawn Curry with Quail's Eggs

This luscious Indonesian recipe is haracterized by the mix of lavours – galangal, chillies, urmeric and coconut milk.

NGREDIENTS

erves 4

2 quail's eggs
0ml/2 tbsp vegetable oil
shallots or 1 medium onion, finely chopped
.5cm/1in fresh galangal or root ginger, chopped
garlic cloves, crushed
cm/2in lemon grass, finely shredded
–2 small, fresh red chillies, seeded and finely chopped
.5ml/½ tsp ground turmeric
cm/½in square shrimp paste or 15ml/1 tbsp fish sauce
00g/2lb raw prawn tails, peeled and deveined
00ml/14fl oz/1⅔ cup coconut milk
00ml/½ pint/1¼ cups chicken stock
15g/4oz Chinese leaves, roughly shredded
0ml/2 tsp sugar
alt
spring onions, green part only, shredded, and 30ml/2 tbsp shredded fresh coconut, to garnish

1 Put the quail's eggs in a saucepan, cover with water and boil for minutes. Refresh in cold water, peel y dipping in cold water to release the hells and set aside.

2 Heat the oil in a preheated wok. Add the shallots or onion, galangal or ginger and garlic and stir-fry for 1 minute, until soft but not coloured. Add the lemon grass, chillies, turmeric and shrimp paste or fish sauce and stir-fry for 1 minute.

3 Add the prawns to the wok and stir-fry for 1 minute. Strain the coconut milk and add the thin liquid to the wok, together with the chicken stock. Add the Chinese leaves and sugar and season to taste with salt. Bring to the boil, reduce the heat and simmer for 6–8 minutes.

4 Turn the curry out on to a serving dish. Halve the quail's eggs and toss them in the sauce. Scatter over the spring onions and shredded coconut and serve immediately.

COOK'S TIP

Quail's eggs are available from speciality grocers and delicatessens. If you cannot find them, use hens' eggs – one hen's egg is the equivalent of four quail's eggs.

Balti Prawns and Vegetables in Thick Sauce

Tender prawns, crunchy vegetables and a thick curry sauce combine to produce a dish rich in flavour and texture.

INGREDIENTS

Serves 4

45ml/3 tbsp corn oil
5ml/1 tsp mixed fenugreek, mustard and onion seeds
2 curry leaves
½ medium cauliflower, cut into florets
8 baby carrots, halved lengthways
6 new potatoes, thickly sliced
50g/2oz frozen peas
2 medium onions, sliced
30ml/2 tbsp tomato purée
7.5ml/1½ tsp chilli powder
5ml/1 tsp ground coriander
5ml/1 tsp ginger pulp
5ml/1 tsp garlic pulp
5ml/1 tsp salt
30ml/2 tbsp lemon juice
450g/1lb peeled cooked prawns
30ml/2 tbsp chopped fresh coriander
1 fresh red chilli, seeded and sliced
120ml/4fl oz/½ cup single cream

1 Heat the oil in a preheated wok or frying pan. Lower the heat slightly and add the fenugreek, mustard and onion seeds and the curry leaves.

2 Add the cauliflower, carrots, potatoes and peas, increase the heat and stir-fry until the vegetables are cooked. Remove from the wok or frying pan with a slotted spoon and drain on kitchen paper.

3 Add the onions to the oil left in the wok or frying pan and fry over a medium heat until golden brown.

4 Meanwhile, mix together the tomato purée, chilli powder, ground coriander, ginger pulp, garlic pulp, salt and lemon juice. When the onions are cooked, pour the spice paste over them.

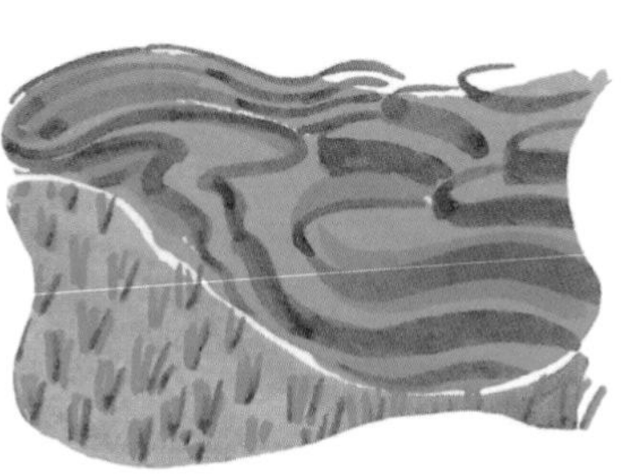

5 Lower the heat, add the prawns to the wok or frying pan and stir-fry for about 5 minutes or until heated through.

6 Return the fried vegetables to the wok or frying pan and mix together thoroughly.

7 Add the chopped fresh coriander and red chilli to the wok or frying pan and pour over the cream. Bring to the boil and serve immediately.

COOK'S TIP

Monkfish is an excellent alternative to the prawns used in this recipe, as it is a firm-flesh fish that will not break up when fried. Cut the monkfish into chunks, add to the onion and spice mixture at Step 5 and stir-fry over a low heat for 5–7 minutes or until cooked through.

Lemon Grass Prawns on Crisp Noodle Cake

INGREDIENTS

Serves 4

300g/11oz thin egg noodles
60ml/4 tbsp vegetable oil
500g/1¼lb medium raw king prawns, peeled and deveined
2.5ml/½ tsp ground coriander
15ml/1 tbsp ground turmeric
2 garlic cloves, finely chopped
2 slices fresh root ginger, finely chopped
2 lemon grass stalks, finely chopped
2 shallots, finely chopped
15ml/1 tbsp tomato purée
250ml/8fl oz/1 cup coconut cream
4–6 kaffir lime leaves (optional)
15–30ml/1–2 tbsp fresh lime juice
15–30ml/1–2 tbsp fish sauce
1 cucumber, peeled, seeded and cut into 5cm/2in batons
1 tomato, seeded and cut into strips
2 red chillies, seeded and finely sliced
salt and freshly ground black pepper
2 spring onions, finely sliced, and a few coriander sprigs, to garnish

1 Cook the egg noodles in a saucepan of boiling water until just tender. Drain, rinse under cold running water and drain well.

2 Heat 15ml/1 tbsp of the oil in a large frying pan. Add the noodles, distributing them evenly, and fry for 4–5 minutes until crisp and golden. Turn the noodle cake over and fry the other side. Alternatively, make four individual cakes. Keep hot.

3 In a bowl, toss the prawns with the ground coriander, turmeric, garlic, ginger and lemon grass. Add salt and pepper to taste.

4 Heat the remaining oil in a large frying pan. Add the shallots, fry fo 1 minute, then add the prawns and fry for 2 minutes more. Using a slotted spoon remove the prawns.

5 Stir the tomato purée and coconut cream into the mixture remaining in the pan. Stir in lime juice to taste and season with the fish sauce. Bring the sauce to a simmer, return the prawns to the sauce, then add the kaffi lime leaves, if using, and the cucumbe Simmer gently until the prawns are cooked and the sauce is reduced to a nice coating consistency.

6 Add the tomato, stir until just warmed through, then add the chillies. Serve on top of the crisp noodle cake(s), garnished with sliced spring onions and coriander sprigs.

Gingered Seafood Stir-fry

This cornucopia of scallops, rawns and squid in an aromatic auce makes a refreshing summer upper, served with plenty of rusty bread to mop up the juices - together with a glass of chilled dry white wine. It would also nake a great dinner-party starter or four people.

NGREDIENTS

erves 2

5ml/1 tbsp sunflower oil
ml/1 tsp sesame oil
.5cm/1in fresh root ginger, finely chopped
bunch spring onions, sliced
red pepper, seeded and finely chopped
15g/4 oz small queen scallops
large raw prawns, peeled
15g/4oz squid rings
5ml/1 tbsp lime juice
5ml/1 tbsp light soy sauce
0ml/4 tbsp coconut milk
alt and ground black pepper
nixed salad leaves and lime slices, to serve

1 Heat the sunflower and sesame oils in a preheated wok or large frying an and cook the ginger and spring nions for 2–3 minutes, or until olden. Stir in the red pepper and cook or a further 3 minutes.

2 Add the scallops, prawns and squid rings and cook over a medium heat for about 3 minutes, until the seafood is just cooked.

3 Stir in the lime juice, soy sauce and coconut milk. Simmer, uncovered, for 2 minutes, until the juices begin to thicken slightly.

4 Season well. Arrange the salad leaves on 2 serving plates and spoon over the seafood mixture with the juices. Serve with lime slices for squeezing over the seafood.

Chilli Prawns

This delightful, spicy combination makes a lovely, light main course for a casual supper. Serve with rice, noodles or even freshly cooked pasta and a leafy green salad.

INGREDIENTS

Serves 3–4

45ml/3 tbsp olive oil
2 shallots, chopped
2 garlic cloves, chopped
1 fresh red chilli, chopped
450g/1lb ripe tomatoes, skinned, seeded and chopped
15ml/1 tbsp tomato purée
1 bay leaf
1 thyme sprig
90ml/6 tbsp dry white wine
450g/1lb cooked large prawns, peeled
salt and ground black pepper
roughly torn basil leaves, to garnish

1 Heat the oil in a pan, then add the shallots, garlic and chilli and fry until the garlic starts to brown.

2 Add the tomatoes, tomato purée, bay leaf, thyme, wine and seasoning. Bring to the boil, then reduce the heat and cook gently for about 10 minutes, stirring occasionally, until the sauce has thickened. Discard the herbs.

3 Stir the prawns into the sauce and heat through for a few minutes. Taste and adjust the seasoning. Scatter over the basil leaves and serve at once.

COOK'S TIP

For a milder flavour, remove all the seeds from the chilli.

Scallops with Ginger

Scallops are at their best in the winter, but are available frozen throughout the year. Rich and creamy, this dish is very simple to make and utterly scrumptious.

INGREDIENTS

Serves 4

8–12 scallops, shelled
40g/1½oz/3 tbsp butter
2.5cm/1in fresh root ginger, finely chopped
1 bunch spring onions, sliced diagonally
60ml/4 tbsp white vermouth
250ml/8fl oz/1 cup crème fraîche
salt and ground black pepper
chopped fresh parsley, to garnish

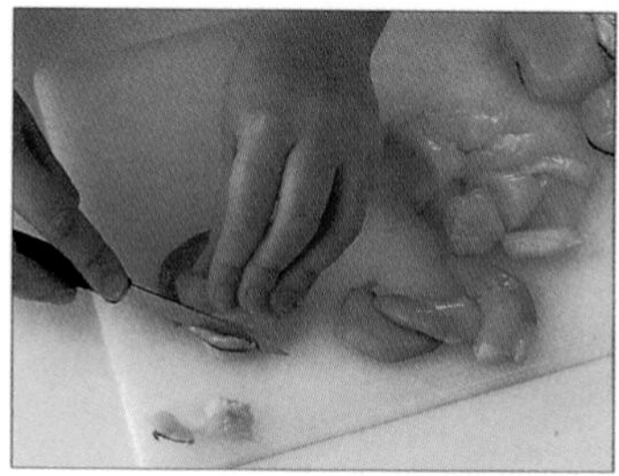

1 Remove the tough muscle opposite the coral on each scallop. Separate the coral and cut the white part of the scallop in half horizontally.

2 Melt the butter in a frying pan. Add the scallops, including the corals, and sauté for about 2 minutes until lightly browned. Take care not to overcook the scallops as this will make them tough.

3 Lift out the scallops with a slotted spoon and transfer to a warmed serving dish. Keep warm.

4 Add the ginger and spring onions to the pan and stir-fry for 2 minutes. Pour in the vermouth and allow to bubble until it has almost evaporated. Stir in the crème fraîche and cook for a few minutes until the sauce has thickened. Taste and adjust the seasoning.

5 Pour the sauce over the scallops, sprinkle with parsley and serve immediately.

Oriental Scallops with Ginger Relish

Buy scallops in their shells to be absolutely sure of their freshness; your fishmonger will open them for you if you find this difficult. Remember to ask for the shells, which make excellent and attractive serving dishes. Queen scallops are particularly prized for their delicate-tasting coral or roe.

Ingredients

Serves 4

8 king or queen scallops
4 whole star anise
25g/1oz unsalted butter
salt and ground white pepper
fresh chervil sprigs and whole star anise, to garnish

For the relish

½ cucumber, peeled
salt, for sprinkling
5cm/2in fresh root ginger, peeled
10ml/2 tsp caster sugar
45ml/3 tbsp rice wine vinegar
10ml/2 tsp ginger juice, strained from a jar of stem ginger
sesame seeds, to garnish

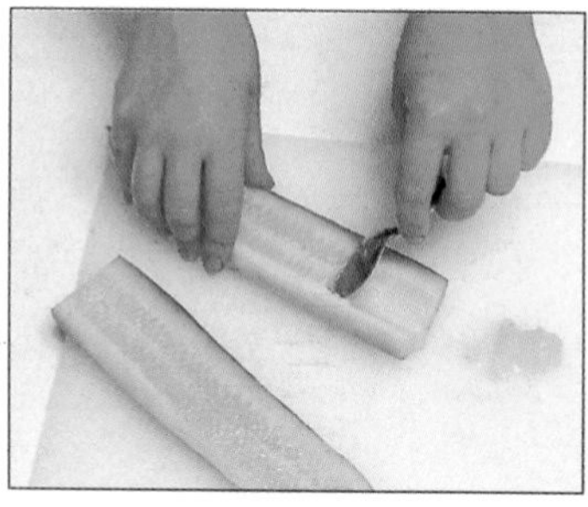

1 To make the relish, halve the cucumber lengthways and scoop out the seeds with a teaspoon and discard.

2 Cut the cucumber into 2.5cm/1in pieces, place in a colander and sprinkle liberally with salt. Set aside for 30 minutes.

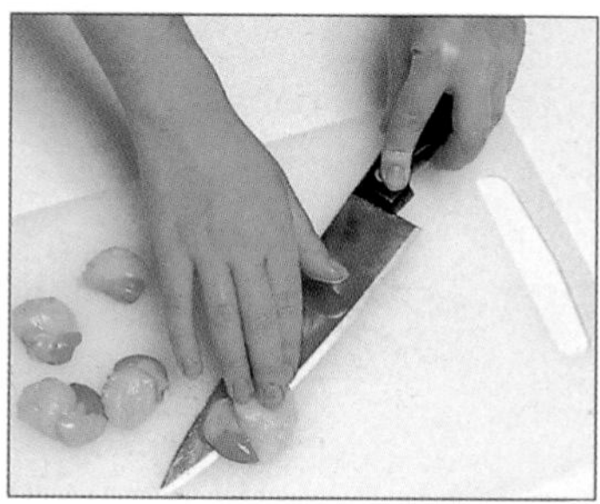

3 Open the scallop shells, detach the scallops and remove the edible parts. Cut each scallop into two or three slices and reserve the corals. Coarsely grind the star anise in a mortar with a pestle.

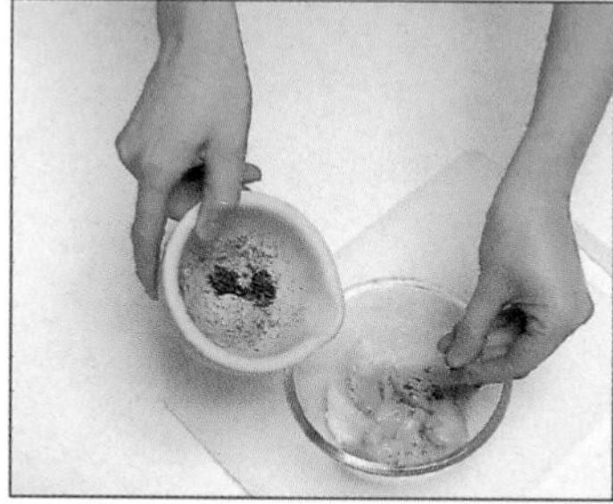

4 Place the scallop slices and corals in a bowl, sprinkle over the star anise and season with salt and pepper. Set aside to marinate for about 1 hour.

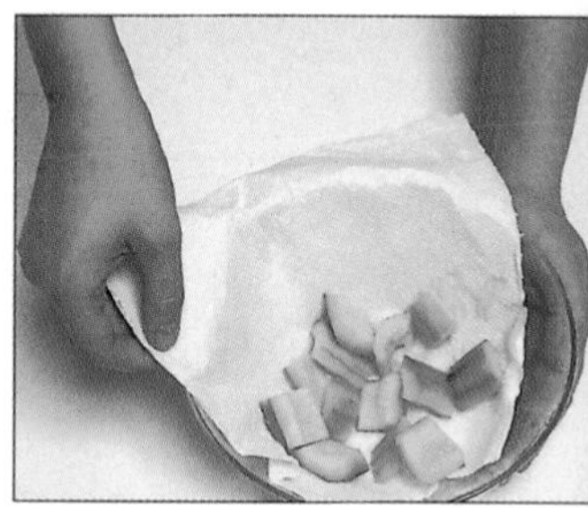

5 Rinse the cucumber under cold water, drain well and pat dry on kitchen paper. Cut the ginger into thin julienne strips and mix with the cucumber, sugar, vinegar and ginger juice. Cover and chill until needed.

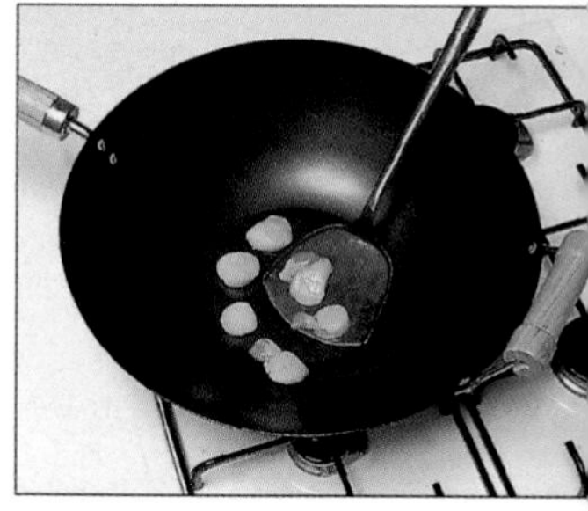

6 Heat a wok and add the butter. When the butter is hot, add the scallop slices and corals and stir-fry for 2–3 minutes. Garnish with sprigs of chervil and whole star anise, and serve with the cucumber relish, sprinkled with sesame seeds.

Cook's Tip

To prepare scallops, hold the shell, flat side up, and insert a strong knife between the shells to cut through the muscle. Separate the two shells. Slide the knife blade underneath the scallop in the bottom shell to cut the second muscle. Remove the scallop and separate the edible parts – the white muscle and orange coral or roe. The skirt can be used for making fish stock, but the other parts should be discarded.

Baked Fish in Banana Leaves

Fish that is prepared in this way is particularly succulent and flavourful. Fillets are used here rather than whole fish – easier for those who don't like to mess about with bones. It is a great dish for outdoor barbecues.

INGREDIENTS

Serves 4

250ml/8fl oz/1 cup coconut milk
30ml/2 tbsp red curry paste
45ml/3 tbsp fish sauce
30ml/2 tbsp caster sugar
5 kaffir lime leaves, torn
4 x 175g/6oz fish fillets, such as snapper
175g/6oz mixed vegetables, such as carrots or leeks, finely shredded
4 banana leaves
30ml/2 tbsp shredded spring onions, to garnish
2 red chillies, finely sliced, to garnish

1 Combine the coconut milk, curry paste, fish sauce, sugar and kaffir lime leaves in a shallow dish.

2 Marinate the fish in this mixture for about 15–30 minutes. Preheat the oven to 200°C/400°F/Gas 6.

3 Mix the vegetables together and lay a portion on top of a banana leaf. Place a piece of fish on top with a little of its marinade.

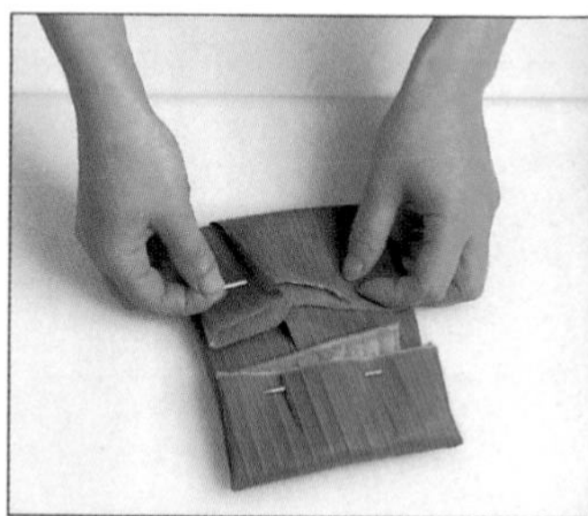

4 Wrap the fish up by turning in th sides and ends of the leaf and secure with cocktail sticks. Repeat wi the rest of the leaves and fish.

5 Bake in the hot oven for 20–25 minutes or until the fish is cooke Alternatively, cook under the grill or on the barbeque. Just before serving, garnish the fish with a sprinkling of spring onions and sliced red chillies.

Stir-fried Scallops with Asparagus

Asparagus is extremely popular among the Chinese Thai. The combination of garlic and black pepper gives this dish its spiciness. You can substitute the scallops with prawns or other firm fish.

INGREDIENTS

Serves 4–6

60ml/4 tbsp vegetable oil
1 bunch asparagus, cut into 5cm/2in lengths
4 garlic cloves, finely chopped
2 shallots, finely chopped
450g/1lb scallops, cleaned
30ml/2 tbsp fish sauce
2.5ml/½ tsp coarsely ground black pepper
120ml/4fl oz/½ cup coconut milk
coriander leaves, to garnish

1 Heat half the oil in a wok or large frying pan. Add the asparagus and stir-fry for about 2 minutes. Transfer the asparagus to a plate and set aside.

2 Add the rest of the oil, garlic and shallots to the same wok and fry until fragrant. Add the scallops and cook for another 1–2 minutes.

3 Return the asparagus to the wok. Add the fish sauce, black pepper and coconut milk.

4 Stir and cook for another 3–4 minutes or until the scallops and asparagus are cooked. Garnish with th coriander leaves.

Spiced Scallops in their Shells

Scallops are excellent steamed. When served with this spicy sauce, they make a delicious, yet simple, starter for four people or a light lunch for two. Each person spoons sauce on to the scallops before eating them.

Ingredients

Serves 2

8 scallops, shelled (ask the fishmonger to reserve the cupped side of 4 shells)
2 slices fresh root ginger, shredded
½ garlic clove, shredded
2 spring onions, green parts only, shredded
salt and ground black pepper

For the sauce

1 garlic clove, crushed
15ml/1 tbsp grated fresh root ginger
2 spring onions, white parts only, chopped
1–2 fresh green chillies, seeded and finely chopped
15ml/1 tbsp light soy sauce
15ml/1 tbsp dark soy sauce
10ml/2 tsp sesame oil

1 Remove the dark beard-like fringe and tough muscle from the scallops.

2 Place 2 scallops in each shell. Season lightly with salt and pepper, then scatter the ginger, garlic and spring onions on top. Place the shells in a bamboo steamer in a wok and steam for about 6 minutes, until the scallops look opaque (you may have to do this in batches).

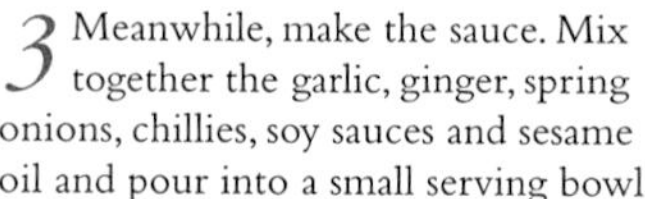

3 Meanwhile, make the sauce. Mix together the garlic, ginger, spring onions, chillies, soy sauces and sesame oil and pour into a small serving bowl.

4 Carefully remove each shell from the steamer, taking care not to spill the juices, and arrange them on a serving plate with the sauce bowl in the centre. Serve at once.

Lemon-grass-and-basil-scented Mussels

The classic Thai flavourings of emon grass and basil are used in his fragrant dish.

NGREDIENTS

erves 4
.75kg/4–4½lb fresh mussels in their shells
: lemon grass stalks
–6 fresh basil sprigs
cm/2in fresh root ginger
: shallots, finely chopped
50ml/¼ pint/⅔ cup fish stock

1 Scrub the mussels under cold running water, scraping off any arnacles with a small, sharp knife. Pull or cut off the hairy "beards". Discard ny mussels with damaged shells and ny that remain open when they are harply tapped.

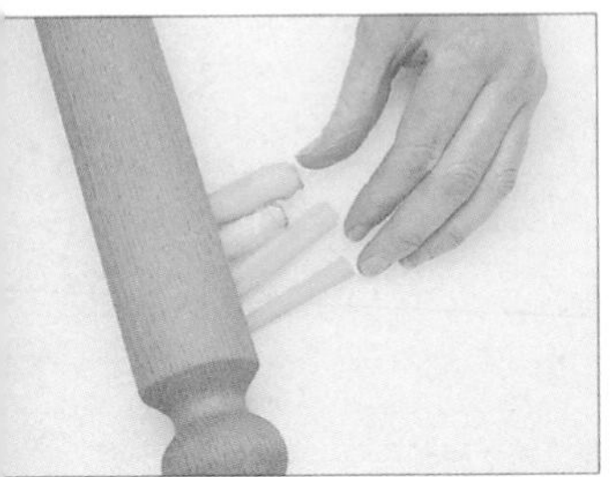

2 Cut each lemon grass stalk in half and bruise with a rolling pin.

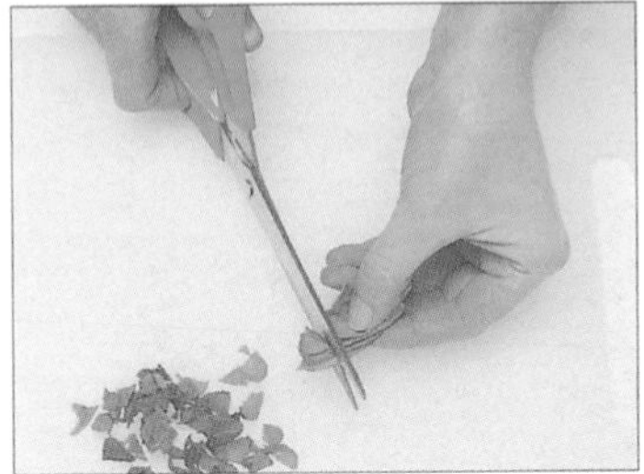

3 Pull the basil leaves off the stems and roughly chop half of them. Reserve the remainder.

4 Put the mussels, lemon grass, chopped basil, ginger, shallots and stock in a wok. Bring to the boil, cover and simmer for 5 minutes. Discard the lemon grass and any mussels that remain closed, scatter over the reserved basil leaves and serve immediately.

Pineapple Curry with Prawns and Mussels

The delicate sweet and sour flavour of this curry comes from the pineapple and although it seems an odd combination, it is rather delicious. Use the freshest shellfish that you can find.

INGREDIENTS

Serves 4–6

600ml/1 pint/2½ cups coconut milk
30ml/2 tbsp red curry paste
30ml/2 tbsp fish sauce
15ml/1 tbsp granulated sugar
225g/8oz king prawns, shelled and deveined
450g/1lb mussels, cleaned and beards removed
175g/6oz fresh pineapple, finely crushed or chopped
5 kaffir lime leaves, torn
2 red chillies, chopped, to garnish
coriander leaves, to garnish

1 In a large saucepan, bring half the coconut milk to the boil and heat, stirring, until it separates.

2 Add the red curry paste and cook until fragrant. Add the fish sauce and sugar and continue to cook for a few moments.

3 Stir in the rest of the coconut milk and bring back to the boil. Add the king prawns, mussels, pineapple and kaffir lime leaves.

4 Reheat until boiling and then simmer for 3–5 minutes, until the prawns are cooked and the mussels have opened. Remove any mussels th have not opened and discard. Serve garnished with chopped red chillies ar coriander leaves.

Curried Prawns in Coconut Milk

A curry-like dish where the prawns are cooked in a spicy coconut gravy.

INGREDIENTS

Serves 4–6

600ml/1 pint/2½ cups coconut milk
30ml/2 tbsp yellow curry paste (see Cook's Tip)
15ml/1 tbsp fish sauce
2.5ml/½ tsp salt
5ml/1 tsp granulated sugar
450g/1lb king prawns, shelled, tails left intact and deveined
225g/8oz cherry tomatoes
juice of ½ lime, to serve
2 red chillies, cut into strips, to garnish
coriander leaves, to garnish

1 Put half the coconut milk into a pan or wok and bring to the boil.

2 Add the yellow curry paste to the coconut milk, stir until it disperses, then simmer for about 10 minutes.

3 Add the fish sauce, salt, sugar and remaining coconut milk. Simmer for another 5 minutes.

4 Add the prawns and cherry tomatoes. Simmer very gently for about 5 minutes until the prawns are pink and tender.

5 Serve sprinkled with lime juice an garnish with chillies and coriande

COOK'S TIP

To make yellow curry paste, process together 6–8 yellow chillies, 1 chopped lemon grass stalk, 4 peeled shallots, 4 garlic cloves, 15ml/1 tbsp peeled chopped fresh root ginger, 5ml/1 tsp coriander seeds, 5ml/1 tsp mustard powder, 5ml/1 tsp salt, 2.5ml/½ tsp ground cinnamon, 15ml/1 tbsp light brown sugar and 30ml/2 tbsp oil in a blender or food procesor. When a paste has formed, transfer to a glass jar and keep in the fridge.

Baked Crab with Spring Onions and Ginger

This recipe is far less complicated than it looks and will delight the eyes as much as the taste buds.

Ingredients

Serves 4

1 large or 2 medium crabs, about 675g/1½lb in total
30ml/2 tbsp Chinese rice wine or dry sherry
1 egg, lightly beaten
15ml/1 tbsp cornflour
45–60/3–4 tbsp vegetable oil
15ml/1 tbsp finely chopped fresh root ginger
3–4 spring onions, cut into short lengths
30ml/2 tbsp soy sauce
5ml/1 tsp light brown sugar
about 75ml/5 tbsp Basic Stock
few drops of sesame oil

1 Cut the crab in half from the underbelly. Break off the claws and crack them with the back of a cleaver. Discard the legs and crack the shell, breaking it into several pieces. Discard the feathery gills and the sac. Put the pieces of crab in a bowl.

2 Mix together the rice wine or dry sherry, egg and cornflour and pour over the crab. Leave to marinate for 10–15 minutes.

3 Heat the oil in a preheated wok Add the crab pieces, ginger and spring onions and stir-fry for about 2–3 minutes.

4 Add the soy sauce, sugar and stock and blend well. Bring to the boil, reduce the heat, cover and braise for 3–4 minutes. Transfer the crab to a serving dish, sprinkle with the sesame oil and serve.

Cook's Tip

For the very best flavour, buy a live crab and cook it yourself. However, if you prefer to buy a cooked crab, look for one that feels heavy for its size. This is an indication that it has fully grown into its shell and that there will be plenty of meat. Male crabs have larger claws, so will yield a greater proportion of white meat. However, females – identifiable by a broader, less-pointed tail flap – may contain coral, which many people regard as a delicacy.

Pan-steamed Mussels with Thai Herbs

nother simple dish to prepare. 'he lemon grass adds a refreshing ing to the mussels.

NGREDIENTS

erves 4–6
kg/2¼lb mussels, cleaned and beards removed
stalks lemon grass, finely chopped
shallots, chopped
kaffir lime leaves, roughly torn
red chillies, sliced
5ml/1 tbsp fish sauce
0ml/2 tbsp lime juice
spring onions, chopped, to garnish
oriander leaves, to garnish

1 Place all the ingredients, except for the spring onions and coriander, in large saucepan and stir thoroughly.

2 Cover and steam for 5–7 minutes, shaking the saucepan occasionally, ntil the mussels open. Discard any nussels that do not open.

3 Transfer the cooked mussels to a serving dish.

4 Garnish the mussels with chopped spring onions and coriander leaves. Serve immediately.

Chilli Crabs

It is possible to find variations on *Kepitang Pedas* all over Asia. It will be memorable whether you eat in simple surroundings or in a sophisticated restaurant.

Ingredients

Serves 4

2 cooked crabs, about 675g/1½lb
1cm/½in cube *terasi*
2 garlic cloves
2 fresh red chillies, seeded, or 5ml/ 1 tsp chopped chilli from a jar
1cm/½in fresh root ginger, peeled and sliced
60ml/4 tbsp sunflower oil
300ml/½ pint/1¼ cups tomato ketchup
15ml/1 tbsp dark brown sugar
150ml/¼ pint/⅔ cup warm water
4 spring onions, chopped, to garnish
cucumber chunks and hot toast, to serve (optional)

1 Remove the large claws of one crab and turn on to its back, with the head facing away from you. Use your thumbs to push the body up from the main shell. Discard the stomach sac and "dead men's fingers", i.e. lungs and any green matter. Leave the creamy brown meat in the shell and cut the shell in half, with a cleaver or strong knife. Cut the body section in half and crack the claws with a sharp blow from a hammer or cleaver. Avoid splintering the claws. Repeat with the other crab.

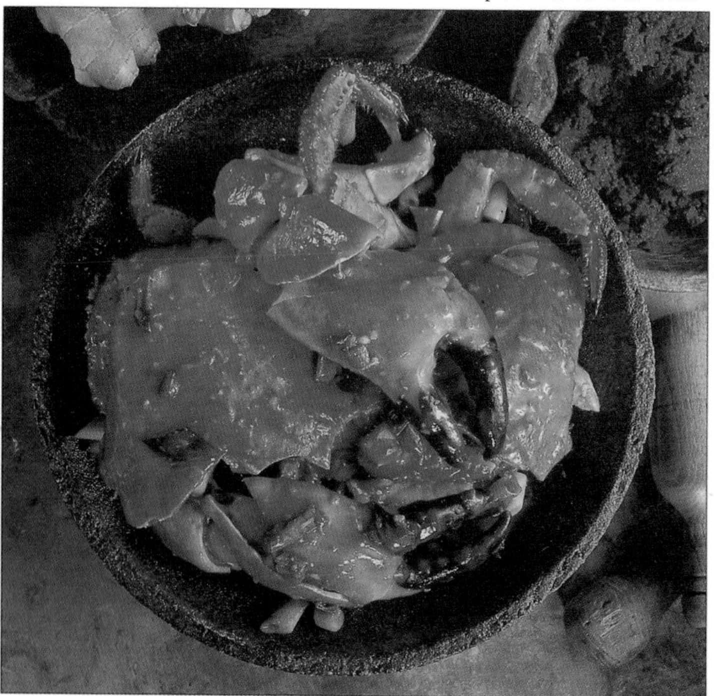

2 Grind the *terasi*, garlic, chillies and ginger to a paste in a food processor or with a pestle and mortar.

3 Heat a wok and add the oil. Fry the spice paste, stirring it all the time, without browning.

4 Stir in the tomato ketchup, sugar and water and mix the sauce well When just boiling, add all the crab pieces and toss in the sauce until well-coated and hot. Serve in a large bowl, sprinkled with the spring onions. Place in the centre of the table for everyone to help themselves. Accompany this finger-licking dish with cool cucumber chunks and hot toast for mopping up the sauce, if you like.

Baked Lobster with Black Beans

he term "baked", as used on ost Chinese restaurant menus, not strictly correct – pot-roasted" or "pan-baked" is ore accurate.

NGREDIENTS

rves 4–6

large or 2 medium lobsters, about 800g/1¾lb in total
getable oil, for deep-frying
garlic clove, finely chopped
nl/1 tsp finely chopped fresh root ginger
-3 spring onions, chopped
)ml/2 tbsp black bean sauce
)ml/2 tbsp Chinese rice wine or dry sherry
20ml/4fl oz/½ cup Basic Stock
esh coriander leaves, to garnish

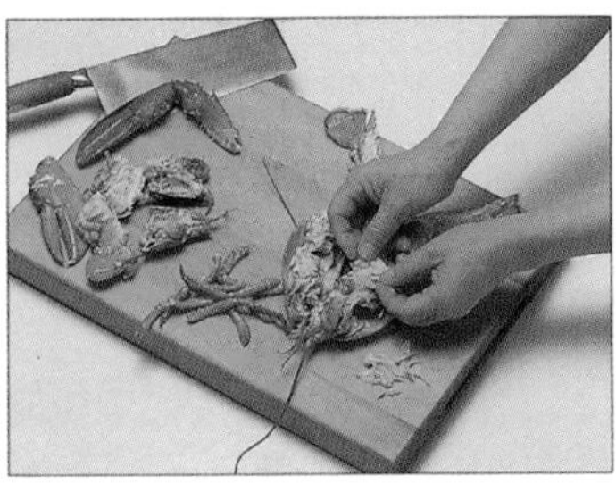

1 Starting from the head, cut the lobster in half lengthways. Discard the legs, remove the claws and crack them with the back of a cleaver. Discard the feathery lungs and intestine. Cut each half into 4–5 pieces.

2 Heat the oil in a preheated wok and deep-fry the lobster pieces for about 2 minutes, or until the shells turn bright orange. Remove the pieces from the wok and drain on kitchen paper.

3 Pour off the excess oil, leaving about 15ml/1 tbsp in the wok. Add the garlic, ginger, spring onions and black bean sauce and stir-fry for 1 minute.

4 Add the lobster pieces to the sauce and blend well. Add the rice wine or dry sherry and stock, bring to the boil, cover and cook for 2–3 minutes. Serve garnished with coriander leaves.

Cook's Tip

Ideally, buy live lobsters and cook them yourself. Ready-cooked ones have usually been boiled for far too long and have lost much of their delicate flavour and texture.

Ragout of Shellfish with Sweet-scented Basil

Green curry paste, so called because it is made with green chillies, is an essential part of Thai cuisine. It can be used to accompany many other dishes and will keep for up to three weeks in the refrigerator. Ready-made curry pastes are available, but they are not as full of flavour as the home-made variety.

Ingredients

Serves 4–6

450g/1lb mussels in their shells
60ml/4 tbsp water
225g/8oz medium cuttle fish or squid
400ml/14fl oz/1⅔ cups coconut milk
300ml/½ pint/1¼ cups chicken or vegetable stock
375g/12oz monkfish, hoki or red snapper, skinned
150g/5oz raw or cooked prawn tails, peeled and deveined
4 scallops, shelled and sliced
75g/3oz French beans, trimmed and cooked
50g/2oz canned bamboo shoots, drained
1 tomato, skinned, seeded and roughly chopped
4 sprigs large-leaf basil, torn, to garnish
boiled rice, to serve

For the green curry paste

10ml/2 tsp coriander seeds
2.5ml/½ tsp caraway or cumin seeds
3–4 medium fresh green chillies, finely chopped
20ml/4 tsp sugar
10ml/2 tsp salt
7.5cm/3in lemon grass
2cm/¾in fresh galangal or ginger root, peeled and finely chopped
3 garlic cloves, crushed
4 shallots or 1 medium onion, finely chopped
2cm/¾in square shrimp paste
50g/2oz fresh coriander leaves, finely chopped
45ml/3 tbsp finely chopped fresh basil
2.5ml/½ tsp grated nutmeg
30ml/2 tbsp vegetable oil

1 Scrub the mussels in cold running water and pull off the "beards". Discard any that do not shut when sharply tapped. Put them in a saucepan with the water, cover and cook for 6–8 minutes. Discard any mussels that remain closed and remove three-quarters of the mussels from their shells. Set aside. Strain the cooking liquid and set aside.

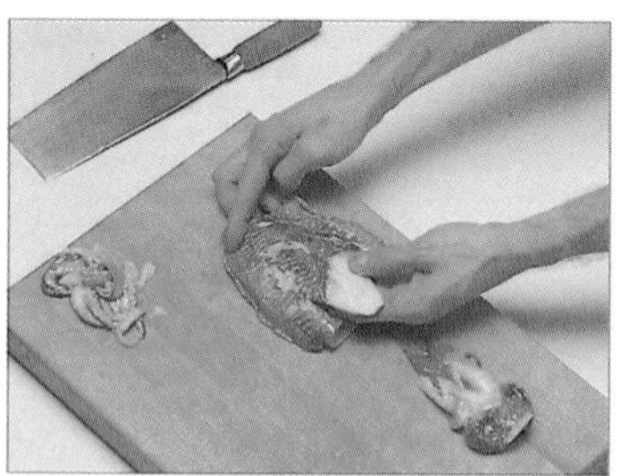

2 To prepare the cuttle fish or squid, trim off the tentacles and discard the gut. Remove the cuttle shell from inside the body and rub off the skin. Cut the body open and score in a criss-cross pattern with a sharp knife. Cut into strips and set aside.

3 To make the green curry paste, dry-fry the coriander and caraway or cumin seeds in a wok. Grind the chillies with the sugar and salt in a pestle with a mortar or in a food processor. Add the coriander and caraway or cumin seeds, lemon grass, galangal or ginger, garlic and shallots or onion and grind. Add the shrimp paste, fresh coriander, chopped basil, nutmeg and oil and combine thoroughly.

4 Strain the coconut milk and pour the thin liquid into a wok with the chicken or vegetable stock and reserve cooking liquid from the mussels. Reserve the thick part of the coconut milk. Add 60–75ml/4–5 tbsp of the green curry paste to the wok and bring the mixture to the boil. Boil rapidly for a few minutes, until the liquid has reduced completely.

5 Add the thick part of the coconut milk, then add the cuttle fish or squid and monkfish, hoki or red snapper. Simmer for 15–20 minutes. Then add the prawns, scallops, mussels, beans, bamboo shoots and tomato. Simmer for 2–3 minutes until heated through. Transfer to a warmed serving dish, garnish with torn basil leaves and serve immediately with boiled rice.

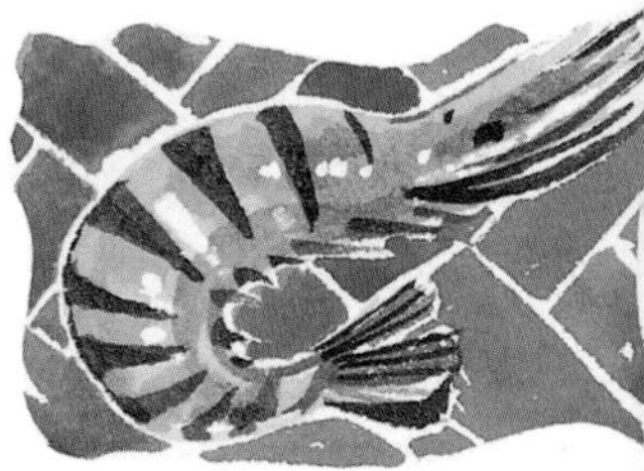

Vietnamese Stuffed Squid

The smaller the squid, the sweeter the dish will taste. Be very careful not to overcook the flesh, as it becomes tough extremely quickly.

Ingredients

Serves 4

8 small squid
50g/2oz cellophane noodles
30ml/2 tbsp groundnut oil
2 spring onions, finely chopped
8 shiitake mushrooms, halved if large
250g/9oz minced pork
1 garlic clove, chopped
30ml/2 tbsp fish sauce
5ml/1 tsp caster sugar
15ml/1 tbsp finely chopped fresh coriander
5ml/1 tsp lemon juice
salt and ground black pepper

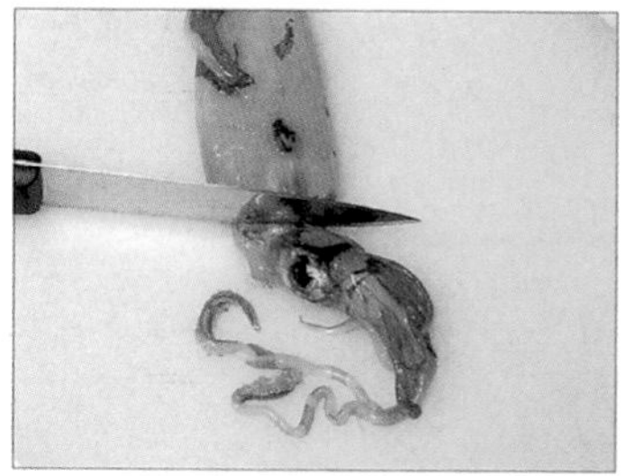

1 Cut off the tentacles of the squid just below the eye. Remove the transparent "quill" from inside the body and rub off the skin on the outside. Wash thoroughly in cold water and set aside.

2 Bring a saucepan of water to the boil and add the noodles. Remove from the heat and set aside to soak for 20 minutes.

3 Heat 15ml/1 tbsp of the oil in a preheated wok and stir-fry the spring onions, shiitake mushrooms, pork and garlic for 4 minutes until the meat is golden.

4 Drain the noodles and add to the wok, with the fish sauce, sugar, coriander, lemon juice and salt and pepper to taste.

5 Stuff the squid with the mixture and secure with cocktail or satay sticks. Arrange the squid in an ovenproof dish, drizzle over the remaining oil and prick each squid twice. Bake in a preheated oven at 200°C/400°F/Gas 6 for 10 minutes. Serve hot.

Stir-fried Five-spice Squid

Squid is perfect for stir-frying as it should be cooked quickly. The spicy sauce makes the ideal accompaniment.

INGREDIENTS

Serves 6

450g/1lb small squid, cleaned
45ml/3 tbsp oil
2.5cm/1 in fresh root ginger, grated
1 garlic clove, crushed
8 spring onions, cut diagonally into 2.5cm/1in lengths
1 red pepper, seeded and cut into strips
1 fresh green chilli, seeded and thinly sliced
6 mushrooms, sliced
5ml/1 tsp Chinese five-spice powder
30ml/2 tbsp black bean sauce
30ml/2 tbsp soy sauce
5ml/1 tsp sugar
15ml/1 tbsp Chinese rice wine or dry sherry

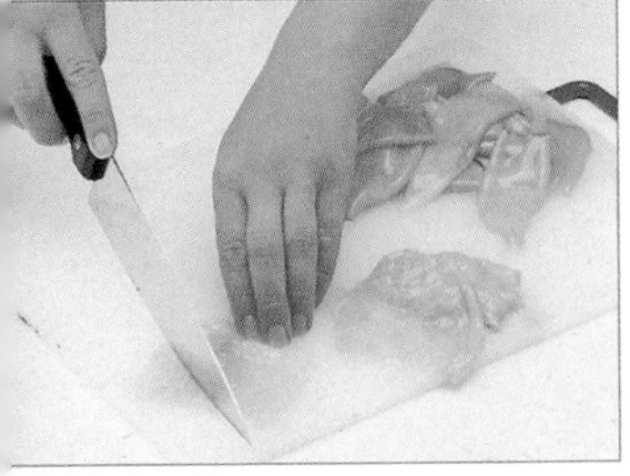

1 Rinse the squid and pull away the outer skin. Dry on kitchen paper. Slit the squid open and score the inside into diamonds with a sharp knife. Cut the squid into strips.

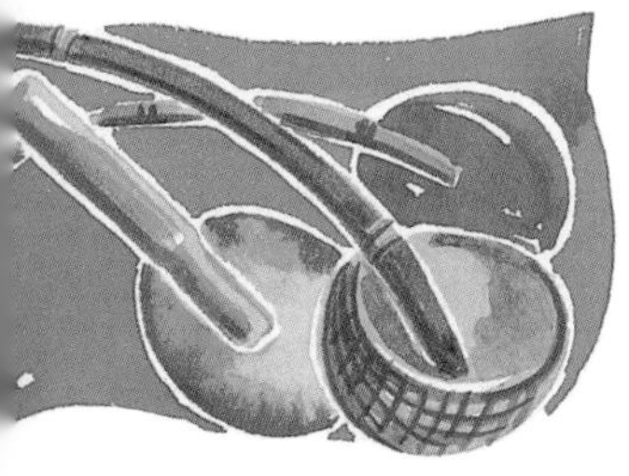

2 Heat the oil in a preheated wok. Stir-fry the squid quickly. Remove the squid strips from the wok with a slotted spoon and set aside. Add the ginger, garlic, spring onions, red pepper, chilli and mushrooms to the oil remaining in the wok and stir-fry for 2 minutes.

3 Return the squid to the wok and stir in the five-spice powder. Stir in the black bean sauce, soy sauce, sugar and rice wine or dry sherry. Bring to the boil and cook, stirring, for 1 minute. Serve immediately.

Clay Pot of Chilli Squid and Noodles

Ingredients

Serves 4
675g/1½lb fresh squid
30ml/2 tbsp vegetable oil
3 slices fresh root ginger, finely shredded
2 garlic cloves, finely chopped
1 red onion, finely sliced
1 carrot, finely sliced
1 celery stick, diagonally sliced
50g/2oz sugar snap peas, topped and tailed
5ml/1 tsp sugar
15ml/1 tbsp chilli bean paste
2.5ml/½ tsp chilli powder
75g/3oz cellophane noodles, soaked in hot water until soft
120ml/4fl oz/½ cup chicken stock or water
15ml/1 tbsp soy sauce
15ml/1 tbsp oyster sauce
5ml/1 tsp sesame oil
pinch of salt
coriander leaves, to garnish

1 Prepare the squid. Holding the body in one hand, gently pull away the head and tentacles. Discard the head; trim and reserve the tentacles. Remove the transparent "quill" from inside the body of the squid. Peel off the brown skin on the outside of the body. Rub a little salt into the squid and wash thoroughly under cold running water. Cut the body of the squid into rings or split it open lengthways, score criss-cross patterns on the inside of the body and cut it into 5 x 4cm/2 x 1½in pieces.

2 Heat the oil in a large clay pot or flameproof casserole. Add the ginger, garlic and onion, and fry for 1–2 minutes. Add the squid, carrot, celery and sugar snap peas. Fry until the squid curls up. Season with salt and sugar, and stir in the chilli bean paste and powder. Transfer the mixture to a bowl and set aside until required.

3 Drain the soaked noodles and add them to the clay pot or casserole. Stir in the stock or water, soy sauce and oyster sauce. Cover and cook over a medium heat for about 10 minutes or until the noodles are tender.

4 Return the squid and vegetables to the pot. Cover and cook for about 5–6 minutes more, until all the flavours are combined. Season to taste.

5 Just before serving, drizzle with the sesame oil and sprinkle with the coriander leaves.

Cook's Tip

These noodles have a smooth, light texture that readily absorbs the other flavours in the dish. To vary the flavour, the vegetables can be altered according to what is available.

Squid with Green Pepper and Black Bean Sauce

This dish is a product of the Cantonese school and makes an attractive meal that is just as delicious as it looks.

INGREDIENTS

Serves 4

375–400g/12–14oz squid
1 medium green pepper, cored and seeded
45–60ml/3–4 tbsp vegetable oil
1 garlic clove, finely chopped
2.5ml/½ tsp finely chopped fresh root ginger
15ml/1 tbsp finely chopped spring onion
5ml/1 tsp salt
15ml/1 tbsp black bean sauce
15ml/1 tbsp Chinese rice wine or dry sherry
few drops of sesame oil

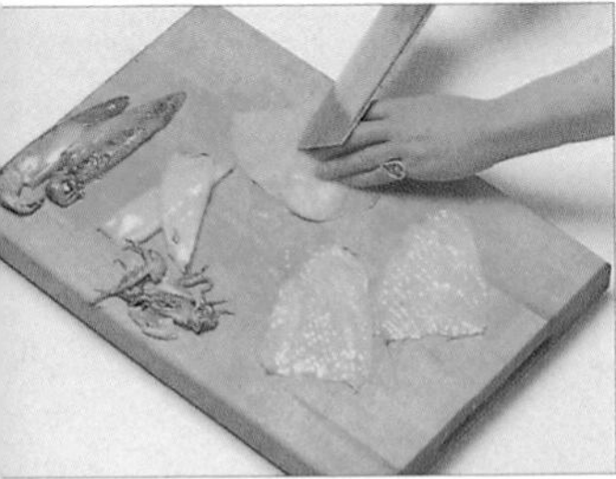

1 To clean the squid, cut off the tentacles just below the eye. Remove the "quill" from inside the body. Peel off and discard the skin, then wash the squid and dry well. Cut open the squid and score the inside of the flesh in a criss-cross pattern.

2 Cut the squid into pieces each about the size of an oblong postage stamp. Blanch the squid in a pan of boiling water for a few seconds. Remove and drain. Dry well.

3 Cut the green pepper into small triangular pieces. Heat the oil in a preheated wok and stir-fry the green pepper for about 1 minute.

4 Add the garlic, ginger, spring onion, salt and squid, then stir for 1 minute. Add the black bean sauce, rice wine or dry sherry and sesame oil and serve.

Spicy Fish

If you make *Ikan Kecap* a day ahead, put it straight on to a serving dish after cooking and then pour over the sauce, cover and chill until required.

INGREDIENTS

Serves 3–4

450g/1lb fish fillets, such as mackerel, cod or haddock
30ml/2 tbsp plain flour
groundnut oil for frying
1 onion, roughly chopped
1 small garlic clove, crushed
4cm/1½in fresh root ginger, peeled and grated
1–2 fresh red chillies, seeded and sliced
1cm/½in cube *terasi,* prepared
60ml/4 tbsp water
juice of ½ lemon
15ml/1 tbsp brown sugar
30ml/2 tbsp dark soy sauce
salt
roughly torn lettuce leaves, to serve

1 Rinse the fish fillets under cold water and dry well on absorbent kitchen paper. Cut into serving portions and remove any bones.

2 Season the flour with salt and use it to dust the fish. Heat the oil in a frying pan and fry the fish on both sides for 3–4 minutes, or until cooked. Lift on to a plate and set aside.

3 Rinse out and dry the pan. Heat a little more oil and fry the onion, garlic, ginger and chillies just to bring out the flavour. Do not brown.

4 Blend the *terasi* with a little water, to make a paste. Add it to the onion mixture, with a little extra wate if necessary. Cook for 2 minutes and then stir in the lemon juice, brown sugar and soy sauce.

5 Pour over the fish and serve, hot or cold, with roughly torn lettuce

COOK'S TIP

For a buffet dish cut the fish into bite-size pieces or serving portions.

Squid from Madura

This squid dish, *Cumi Cumi Madura*, is popular in Indonesia. It is quite usual to be invited into the restaurant kitchen and given a warm welcome.

INGREDIENTS

Serves 2–3

450g/1lb cleaned and drained squid, body cut in strips, tentacles left whole
3 garlic cloves
1.5ml/¼ tsp ground nutmeg
1 bunch of spring onions
60ml/4 tbsp sunflower oil
250ml/8fl oz/1 cup water
15ml/1 tbsp dark soy sauce
salt and freshly ground black pepper
1 lime, cut in wedges (optional)
boiled rice, to serve

1 Squeeze out the little central "bone" from each tentacle. Heat a wok, toss in all the squid and stir-fry for 1 minute. Remove the squid.

2 Crush the garlic with the nutmeg and some salt and pepper. Trim the roots from the spring onions, cut the white part into small pieces, slice the green part and then set aside.

3 Heat the wok, add the oil and fry the white part of the spring onions Stir in the garlic paste and the squid.

4 Rinse out the garlic paste container with the water and soy sauce and add to the pan. Half-cover and simmer for 4–5 minutes. Add the spring onion tops, toss lightly and serve at once, with lime, if using, and rice.

Meat

Satisfying beef curries, quick and easy stir-fried steak, fragrant lamb dishes and, of course, sweet and sour pork – the range of Chinese and Asian meat recipes is immense, offering something special for all tastes and budgets. The recipes in this chapter include inexpensive and easy-to-prepare weekday family meals, such as Balti Lamb Tikka and Pork and Vegetable Stir-fry, as well as impressive and unusual dinner party dishes, such as Beef and Vegetables in Table-top Broth and Braised Birthday Noodles with Hoisin Lamb.

Lemon Grass Pork

Chillies and lemon grass flavour this simple stir-fry, while peanuts add crunch.

INGREDIENTS

Serves 4
675g/1½lb boneless loin of pork
2 lemon grass stalks, finely chopped
4 spring onions, thinly sliced
5ml/1 tsp salt
12 black peppercorns, coarsely crushed
30ml/2 tbsp groundnut oil
2 garlic cloves, chopped
2 fresh red chillies, seeded and chopped
5ml/1 tsp light brown soft sugar
30ml/2 tbsp Thai fish sauce (*nam pla*), or to taste
25g/1oz roasted unsalted peanuts, chopped
salt and ground black pepper
coriander leaves, to garnish
rice noodles, to serve

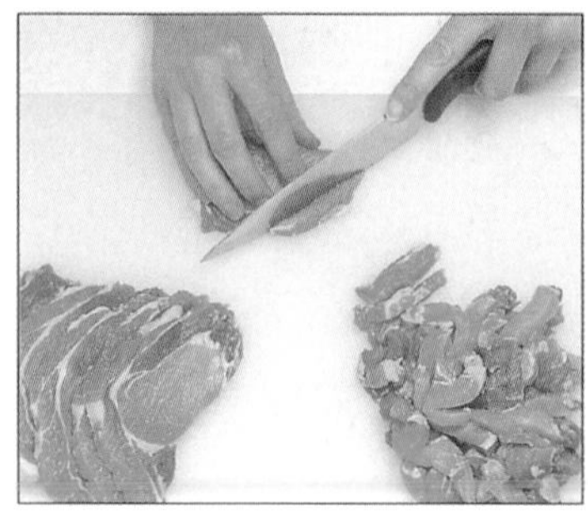

1 Trim any excess fat from the pork. Cut the meat across into 5mm/¼in thick slices, then cut each slice into 5mm/¼in strips. Put the pork into a bowl with the lemon grass, spring onions, salt and crushed peppercorns. Mix well, then cover and leave to marinate for 30 minutes.

2 Heat a wok until hot, add the oil and swirl it around. Add the pork mixture and stir-fry for 3 minutes.

3 Add the garlic and chillies and stir fry for a further 5–8 minutes over medium heat until the pork no longer looks pink.

4 Add the sugar, fish sauce and chopped peanuts and toss to mix. Taste and adjust the seasoning, if necessary. Serve at once, garnished wi roughly torn coriander leaves on a be of rice noodles.

Stir-fried Pork with Lychees

ispy pieces of pork with fleshy
chees make an unusual stir-fry
at is ideal for a dinner party.

GREDIENTS

ves 4
0g/1lb fatty pork, such as belly pork
ml/2 tbsp hoi-sin sauce
pring onions, sliced
5g/6oz lychees, peeled, stoned and
cut into slivers
and ground black pepper
sh lychees and fresh parsley sprigs, to
garnish

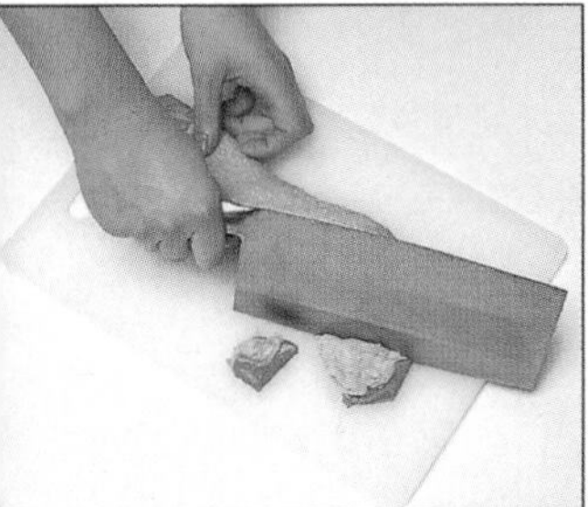

Cut the pork into bite-sized pieces.

Pour the hoi-sin sauce over the
pork and marinate for 30 minutes.

3 Heat the wok, then add the pork and stir-fry for 5 minutes until crisp and golden. Add the spring onions and stir-fry for a further 2 minutes.

4 Scatter the lychee slivers over the pork, and season well with salt and pepper. Garnish with fresh lychees and parsley, and serve.

Cook's Tip

f you cannot buy fresh lychees, this dish
can be made with drained canned lychees.

Savoury Pork Ribs with Snake Beans

This is a rich and pungent dish. If snake beans are hard to find, you can substitute fine green or runner beans.

INGREDIENTS

Serves 4–6

675g/1½lb pork spare ribs or belly of pork
30ml/2 tbsp vegetable oil
120ml/4fl oz/½ cup water
15ml/1 tbsp palm sugar
15ml/1 tbsp fish sauce
150g/5oz snake beans, cut into 5cm/2in lengths
2 kaffir lime leaves, finely sliced
2 red chillies, finely sliced, to garnish

For the chilli paste

3 dried red chillies, seeded and soaked
4 shallots, chopped
4 garlic cloves, chopped
5ml/1 tsp chopped galangal
1 stalk lemon grass, chopped
6 black peppercorns
5ml/1 tsp shrimp paste
30ml/2 tbsp dried shrimp, rinsed

1 Put all the ingredients for the chilli paste in a mortar and grind together with a pestle until it forms a thick paste.

2 Slice and chop the spare ribs (or belly pork) into 4cm/1½in lengths.

3 Heat the oil in a wok or frying pan. Add the pork and fry for about 5 minutes, until lightly browned.

4 Stir in the chilli paste and continue to cook for another 5 minutes, stirring constantly to stop the paste from sticking to the pan.

5 Add the water, cover and simme for 7–10 minutes or until the spa ribs are tender. Season with palm sug and fish sauce.

6 Mix in the snake beans and kaffi lime leaves and fry until the bean are cooked. Serve garnished with slic red chillies.

Thai Sweet-and-sour Pork

Sweet and sour is traditionally a Chinese creation but the Thais do it very well. This version has an altogether fresher and cleaner flavour and it makes a good one-dish meal when served over rice.

INGREDIENTS

Serves 4

350g/12oz lean pork
30ml/2 tbsp vegetable oil
4 garlic cloves, finely sliced
1 small red onion, sliced
30ml/2 tbsp fish sauce
15ml/1 tbsp granulated sugar
1 red pepper, seeded and diced
½ cucumber, seeded and sliced
2 plum tomatoes, cut into wedges
115g/4oz pineapple, cut into small chunks
freshly ground black pepper
2 spring onions, cut into short lengths
coriander leaves, to garnish
spring onions, shredded, to garnish

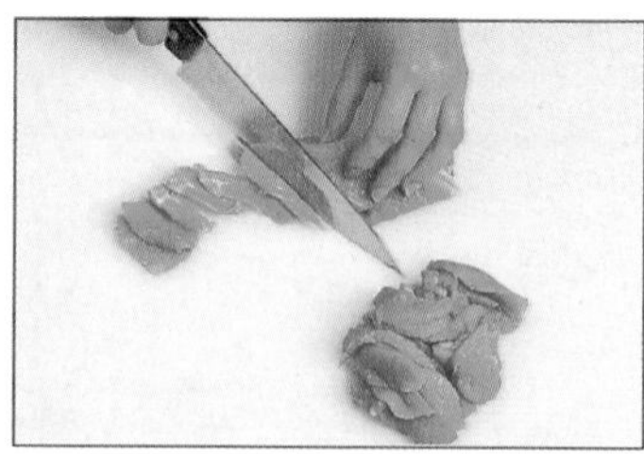

1 Slice the pork into thin strips. Heat the oil in a wok or large frying pan.

2 Add the garlic and fry until golden, then add the pork and stir-fry for about 4–5 minutes. Add the onion.

3 Season with fish sauce, sugar and freshly ground black pepper. Stir and cook for 3–4 minutes, or until the pork is cooked.

4 Add the rest of the vegetables, the pineapple and spring onions. You may need to add a few tablespoons of water. Continue to stir-fry for another 3–4 minutes. Serve hot garnished with coriander leaves and spring onion.

Pork Chow Mein

. perfect, speedy meal, this
ımily favourite is flavoured with
:same oil for an authentic
riental taste.

NGREDIENTS

erves 4
75g/6oz medium egg noodles
50g/12oz pork fillet
)ml/2 tbsp sunflower oil
5ml/1 tbsp sesame oil
garlic cloves, crushed
spring onions, sliced
red pepper, seeded and roughly chopped
green pepper, seeded and roughly chopped
)ml/2 tbsp dark soy sauce
5ml/3 tbsp Chinese rice wine or dry sherry
75g/6oz beansprouts
5ml/3 tbsp chopped fresh flat-leaf parsley
5ml/1 tbsp toasted sesame seeds

1 Soak the noodles according to the packet instructions. Drain well.

2 Thinly slice the pork fillet. Heat the sunflower oil in a preheated wok or large frying pan and cook the pork over a high heat until golden brown and cooked through.

3 Add the sesame oil to the wok or frying pan, with the garlic, spring onions and peppers. Cook over a high heat for 3–4 minutes, or until the vegetables are beginning to soften.

4 Reduce the heat slightly and stir in the noodles, with the soy sauce and rice wine or dry sherry. Stir-fry for 2 minutes. Add the beansprouts and cook for a further 1–2 minutes. If the noodles begin to stick, add a splash of water. Stir in the parsley and serve sprinkled with the sesame seeds.

Pork with Eggs and Mushrooms

Traditionally, this stir-fried dish is served as a filling wrapped in thin pancakes, but it can also be served on its own with plain rice.

INGREDIENTS

Serves 4
15g/½ oz dried Chinese mushrooms
175–225g/6–8oz pork fillet
225g/8oz Chinese leaves
115g/4oz bamboo shoots, drained
2 spring onions
3 eggs
5ml/1 tsp salt
60ml/4 tbsp vegetable oil
15ml/1 tbsp light soy sauce
15ml/1 tbsp Chinese rice wine or dry sherry
few drops sesame oil

1 Rinse the mushrooms thoroughly in cold water and then soak in warm water for 25–30 minutes. Rinse thoroughly again and discard the hard stalks, if any. Dry the mushrooms and thinly shred.

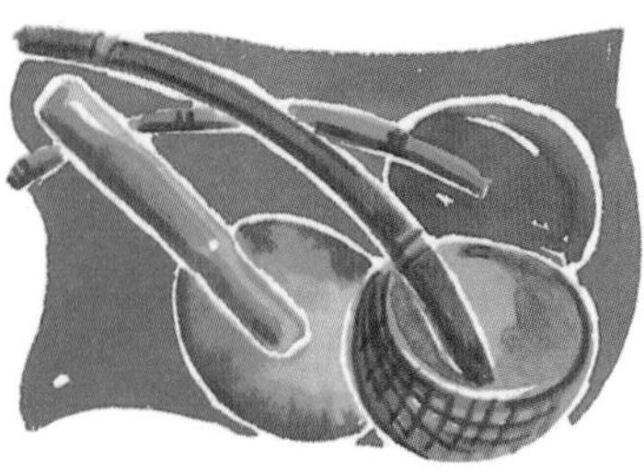

2 Cut the pork fillet into matchstick-size shreds. Thinly shred the Chinese leaves, bamboo shoots and spring onions.

3 Beat the eggs with a pinch of salt. Heat a little oil in a wok, add the eggs and lightly scramble, but do not make too dry. Remove from the wok.

4 Heat the remaining oil in the wok and stir-fry the pork for about 1 minute, or until the colour changes.

5 Add the vegetables to the wok and stir-fry for 1 minute. Add the remaining salt, the soy sauce and rice wine or sherry. Stir for 1 further minute before adding the scrambled eggs. Break up the scrambled eggs and blend well. Sprinkle with sesame oil and serve.

COOK'S TIP

Chinese fungi grow on trees and are valued more for their unusual texture than their flavour – often they have very little flavour at all. Wood ears are the most frequently used in authentic Chinese cookery, especially in stir-fries with meat or fish. They are available dried from oriental food stores and should be well rinsed, then soaked in warm water for 20 minutes and rinsed again before use. Other types of dried mushrooms and fungi are also available from oriental stores.

Hot-and-sour Pork

This tasty dish is cooked in the oven and uses less oil than a stir-fry. Trim all visible fat from the pork before cooking, for a healthy, low-fat recipe.

INGREDIENTS

Serves 4
350g/12oz pork fillet
5ml/1 tsp sunflower oil
2.5cm/1in fresh root ginger, grated
1 fresh red chilli, seeded and finely chopped
5ml/1 tsp Chinese five-spice powder
15ml/1 tbsp sherry vinegar
15ml/1 tbsp soy sauce
225g/8oz can pineapple chunks in natural juice
175ml/6fl oz/¾ cup chicken stock
20ml/4 tsp cornflour
15ml/1 tbsp water
1 small green pepper, seeded and sliced
115g/4oz baby sweetcorn, halved
salt and ground black pepper
sprig of flat-leaf parsley, to garnish
boiled rice, to serve

1 Trim away any visible fat from the pork and cut into 1cm/½in-thick slices using a sharp knife.

2 Brush the sunflower oil over the base of a flameproof casserole. Heat over a medium heat, then fry the pork for about 2 minutes on each side or until lightly browned.

3 Blend together the ginger, chilli, Chinese five-spice powder, sherry vinegar and soy sauce.

4 Drain the pineapple chunks, reserving the juice. Make the stock up to 300ml/½ pint/1¼ cups with the reserved juice, mix together with the spices and pour over the pork.

5 Slowly bring the stock to the boi Blend the cornflour with the wat and gradually stir into the pork. Add the green pepper and baby sweetcorn and season to taste.

6 Cover and cook in a preheated oven at 160°C/325°F/Gas 3 for 3 minutes or until the pork is tender. Sti in the pineapple and cook for a furthe 5 minutes. Garnish with flat-leaf parsle and serve with boiled rice.

COOK'S TIP

Chinese five-spice powder is available from oriental food stores and some large supermarkets. However, if you cannot find it, you can use ground mixed spice instead, although the flavour will be slightly different.

Chinese Sweet-and-sour Pork

Sweet-and-sour pork must be one of the most popular dishes served in Chinese restaurants and take-aways in the Western world. Unfortunately, it is often spoiled by cooks who use too much tomato ketchup in the sauce. Here is a classic recipe from Canton, the city of its origin.

INGREDIENTS

Serves 4

350g/12oz lean pork
1.5ml/¼ tsp salt
2.5ml/½ tsp ground Szechuan peppercorns
15ml/1 tbsp Chinese rice wine or dry sherry
115g/4oz bamboo shoots
30ml/2 tbsp plain flour
1 egg, lightly beaten
vegetable oil, for deep-frying

For the sauce

15ml/1 tbsp vegetable oil
1 garlic clove, finely chopped
1 spring onion, cut into short sections
1 small green pepper, seeded and diced
1 fresh red chilli, seeded and thinly shredded
15ml/1 tbsp light soy sauce
30ml/2 tbsp light brown sugar
30–45ml/2–3 tbsp rice vinegar
15ml/1 tbsp tomato purée
about 120ml/4fl oz/½ cup Basic Stock or water

1 Cut the pork into small bite-sized cubes and place in a shallow dish. Add the salt, peppercorns and rice wine or dry sherry and set aside to marinate for 15–20 minutes.

2 Drain the bamboo shoots, if canned, and cut them into small cubes the same size as the pork.

3 Dust the pork with flour, dip in the beaten egg and coat with more flour. Heat the oil in a preheated wok and deep-fry the pork in moderately hot oil for 3–4 minutes, stirring to separate the pieces. Remove and drain.

4 Reheat the oil until hot, return the pork to the wok and add the bamboo shoots. Fry for about 1 minute, or until the pork is golden. Remove and drain well.

5 To make the sauce, heat the oil ir clean wok or frying pan and add the garlic, spring onion, green pepper and red chilli. Stir-fry for 30–40 seconds, then add the soy sauce, sugar rice vinegar, tomato purée and stock water. Bring to the boil, then add the pork and bamboo shoots. Heat throu and stir to mix, then serve.

Pork and Vegetable Stir-fry

A quick and easy stir-fry of pork and a mixture of vegetables, this makes an excellent family lunch or supper dish.

INGREDIENTS

Serves 4

225g/8oz can pineapple chunks
15ml/1 tbsp cornflour
30ml/2 tbsp light soy sauce
15ml/1 tbsp Chinese rice wine or dry sherry
15ml/1 tbsp soft brown sugar
15ml/1 tbsp white wine vinegar
5ml/1 tsp Chinese five-spice powder
10ml/2 tsp olive oil
1 red onion, sliced
1 garlic clove, crushed
1 fresh red chilli, seeded and chopped
2.5cm/1in fresh root ginger
350g/12oz lean pork tenderloin, cut into thin strips
175g/6oz carrots
1 red pepper, seeded and sliced
175g/6oz mangetouts, halved
115g/4oz beansprouts
200g/7oz can sweetcorn kernels
30ml/2 tbsp chopped fresh coriander
salt
15ml/1 tbsp toasted sesame seeds, to garnish

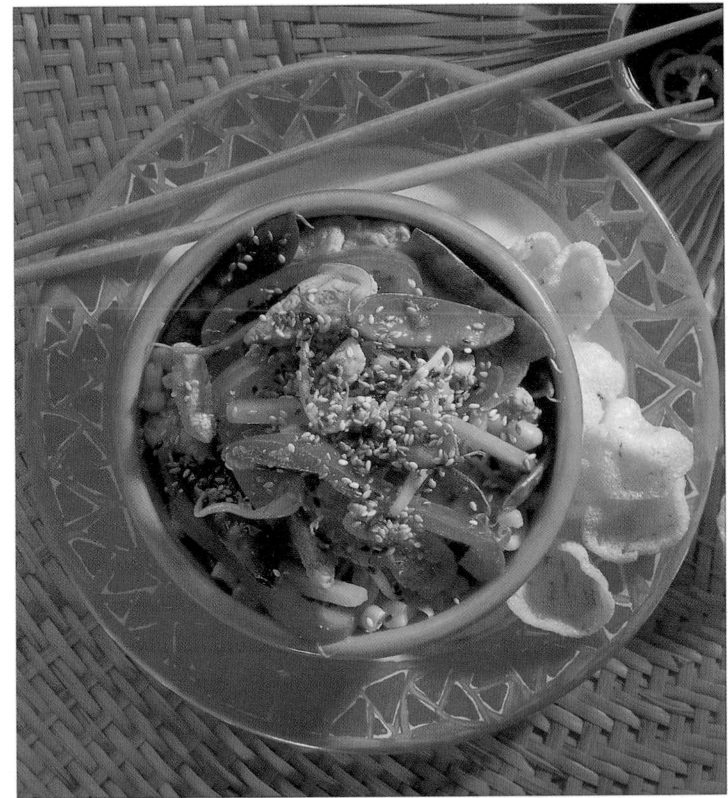

1 Drain the pineapple, reserving the juice. In a small bowl, blend the cornflour with the reserved pineapple juice. Add the soy sauce, rice wine or dry sherry, sugar, vinegar and five-spice powder, stir to mix and set aside.

2 Heat the oil in a preheated wok or large, non-stick frying pan. Add the onion, garlic, chilli and ginger and stir-fry for 30 seconds. Add the pork and stir-fry for 2–3 minutes.

3 Cut the carrots into matchstick strips. Add to the wok with the red pepper and stir-fry for 2–3 minutes. Add the mangetouts, beansprouts and sweetcorn and stir-fry for 1–2 minutes.

4 Pour in the sauce mixture and the reserved pineapple and stir-fry until the sauce thickens. Reduce the heat and stir-fry for a further 1–2 minutes. Stir in the coriander and season to taste. Sprinkle with sesame seeds and serve immediately.

Sweet-and-sour Pork and Prawn Soup

This main-course soup has a sour, rich flavour.

Ingredients

Serves 4–6

225g/8oz raw or cooked prawns, peeled
30ml/2 tbsp tamarind sauce
juice of 2 limes
350g/12oz lean pork, diced
1 small green guava, peeled, halved and seeded
1 small under-ripe mango, peeled, stoned and chopped
1.5 litres/2½ pints/6¼ cups chicken stock
15ml/1 tbsp fish sauce or soy sauce
275g/10oz sweet potato, peeled and cut into even-sized pieces
225g/8oz unripe tomatoes, quartered
115g/4oz green beans, halved
1 star fruit, thickly sliced
75g/3oz green cabbage shredded
salt and ground black pepper
lime wedges, to garnish

1 Devein the prawns and set aside. Put the tamarind sauce and lime juice into a saucepan.

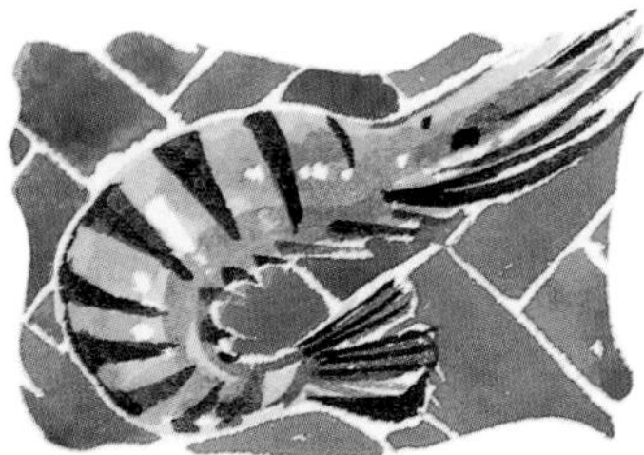

2 Add the pork, guava and mango t the pan and pour in the stock. Ad the fish sauce or soy sauce, bring to th boil, reduce the heat and simmer for 30 minutes.

3 Add the remaining fruit and vegetables and the prawns and simmer for a further 10–15 minutes. Season to taste. Transfer to a serving dish and garnish with lime wedges.

Savoury Pork Pies

This recipe from the Philippines is a legacy of sixteenth-century Spanish colonialism, with a unique Eastern touch.

Ingredients

Serves 6

15ml/1 tbsp vegetable oil
1 medium onion, chopped
1 garlic clove, crushed
5ml/1 tsp chopped fresh thyme
115g/4oz minced pork
5ml/1 tsp paprika
1 hard-boiled egg, chopped
1 medium gherkin, chopped
30ml/2 tbsp chopped fresh parsley
350g/12oz frozen pastry, thawed
salt and ground black pepper
vegetable oil, for deep-frying

1 To make the filling, heat the oil in a saucepan, add the onions, garlic and thyme and fry for 3–4 minutes. Add the pork and paprika and stir-fry until the meat is evenly browned. Season and turn the mixture into a bowl. Set aside to cool. Add the hard-boiled egg, gherkin and parsley.

2 Lightly knead the pastry on a floured surface, then roll out to a 37.5cm/15in square. Cut out 12 circles, 12.5cm/5in in diameter. Place 15ml/ 1 tbsp of the filling on each circle, moisten the edges with a little water, fold over into a half-moon shape and press the edges together to seal.

3 Heat the vegetable oil in a deep-fryer to 196°C/385°F. Deep-fry th pies, three at a time, for 1–2 minutes, until golden brown. Drain on kitchen paper and keep warm while you fry th remaining pies. Serve warm.

Lion's Head Casserole

The name of this dish – *shi zi tou* in Chinese – derives from the rather strange idea that the meatballs look like a lion's head and the Chinese leaves resemble its mane.

INGREDIENTS

Serves 4–6

450g/1lb minced pork
10ml/2 tsp finely chopped spring onion
5ml/1 tsp finely chopped fresh root ginger
50g/2oz mushrooms, chopped
50g/2oz cooked prawns, peeled, or crab meat, finely chopped
15ml/1 tbsp light soy sauce
5ml/1 tsp light brown sugar
15ml/1 tbsp Chinese rice wine or dry sherry
15ml/1 tbsp cornflour
675g/1½lb Chinese leaves
45–60ml/3–4 tbsp vegetable oil
5ml/1 tsp salt
300ml/½ pint/1¼ cups Basic Stock or water

1 Mix together the pork, spring onion, ginger, mushrooms, prawns or crab meat, soy sauce, brown sugar, rice wine or dry sherry and cornflour. Shape the mixture into 4–6 meatballs.

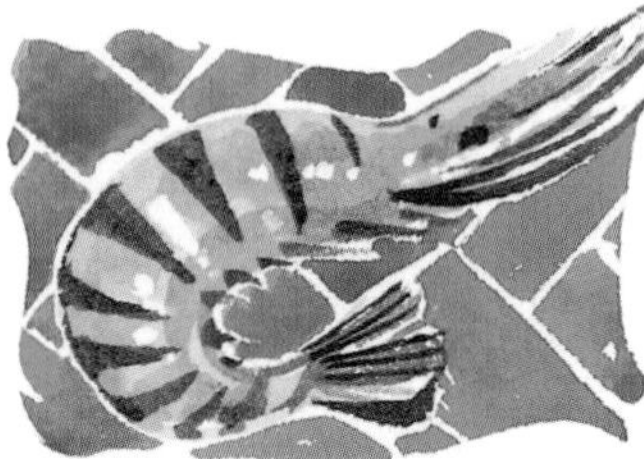

2 Cut the Chinese leaves into large pieces, all about the same size.

3 Heat the oil in a preheated wok or large frying pan. Add the Chinese leaves and salt and stir-fry for 2–3 minutes. Add the meatballs and the stock, bring to the boil, cover and simmer gently for 30–45 minutes. Serve immediately.

Stir-fried Pork with Tomatoes and Courgettes

This dish is a perfect example of the Chinese way of balancing and harmonizing colours, flavours and textures.

INGREDIENTS

Serves 4

225g/8oz pork fillet, thinly sliced
15ml/1 tbsp light soy sauce
5ml/1 tsp light brown sugar
5ml/1 tsp Chinese rice wine or dry sherry
10ml/2 tsp cornflour paste
115g/4oz firm tomatoes, skinned
175g/6oz courgettes
1 spring onion
60ml/4 tbsp vegetable oil
5ml/1 tsp salt (optional)
Basic Stock or water, if necessary

1 Put the pork in a bowl with 5ml/1 tsp of the soy sauce, the sugar, rice wine or dry sherry and cornflour paste. Set aside to marinate. Cut the tomatoes and courgettes into wedges. Slice the spring onion.

2 Heat the oil in a preheated wok and stir-fry the pork for 1 minute, or until it colours. Remove with a slotted spoon, set aside and keep warm.

3 Add the vegetables to the wok and stir-fry for 2 minutes. Add the salt, if using, the pork and a little stock or water, if necessary, and stir-fry for 1 minute. Add the remaining soy sauce, mix well and serve.

Stuffed Green Peppers

Stuffed peppers are given a different treatment here where they are deep fried in a wok and served with a tangy sauce.

INGREDIENTS

Serves 4

225–275g/8–10oz minced pork
4–6 water chestnuts, finely chopped
2 spring onions, finely chopped
2.5ml/½ tsp finely chopped fresh root ginger
15ml/1 tbsp light soy sauce
15ml/1 tbsp Chinese rice wine or dry sherry
3–4 green peppers, cored and seeded
15ml/1 tbsp cornflour
vegetable oil, for deep frying

For the sauce

10ml/2 tsp light soy sauce
5ml/1 tsp light brown sugar
1–2 fresh hot chillies, finely chopped (optional)
about 75ml/5 tbsp stock or water

1 Mix together the minced pork, water chestnuts, spring onions, ginger, soy sauce and rice wine or sherry in a bowl.

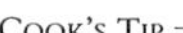

COOK'S TIP

You could substitute minced beef or lamb for the minced pork used in this recipe.

2 Cut the green peppers into halves or quarters. Stuff the sections wit the pork mixture and sprinkle with a little cornflour.

3 Heat the oil in a preheated wok and deep fry the stuffed peppers, with the meat side down, for 2–3 minutes, then remove and drain.

4 Pour off the excess oil, then retur the stuffed green peppers to the wok with the meat side up. Add the sauce ingredients, shaking the wok gently to make sure they do not stick to the bottom, and braise for 2–3 minutes. Carefully lift the stuffed peppers on to a serving dish, meat sid up, and pour the sauce over them.

Stir-fried Pork with Vegetables

'his is a basic recipe for stir-ying any meat with any egetables, according to seasonal ailability and preference.

NGREDIENTS

rves 4
25g/8oz pork fillet
5ml/1 tbsp light soy sauce
nl/1 tsp light brown sugar
nl/1 tsp Chinese rice wine or
dry sherry
)ml/2 tsp cornflour paste
15g/4oz mangetouts
15g/4oz white mushrooms
carrot
spring onion
)ml/4 tbsp vegetable oil
nl/1 tsp salt
ock (optional)
w drops sesame oil

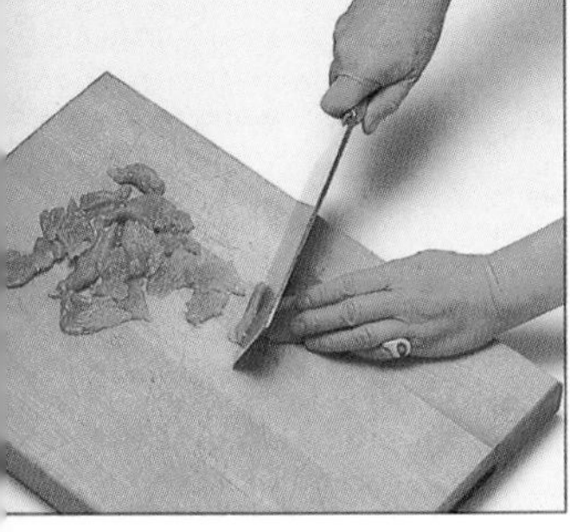

1 Cut the pork into thin slices, each about the size of a postage stamp. larinate with about 5ml/1 tsp of the y sauce, sugar, rice wine or sherry d cornflour paste.

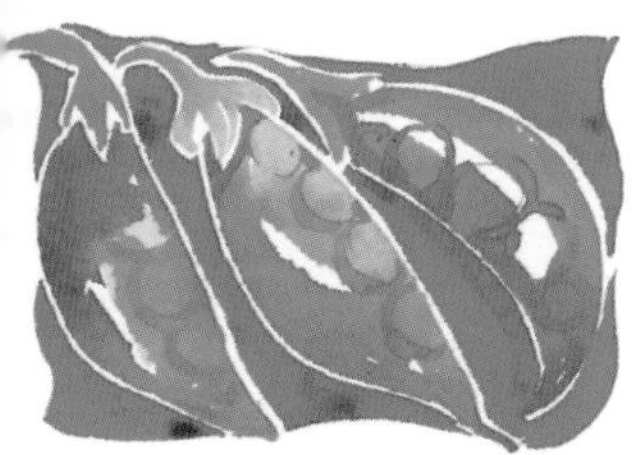

2 Top and tail the mangetouts. Thinly slice the mushrooms. Cut the carrot into pieces roughly the same size as the pork and cut the spring onion into short sections.

3 Heat the oil in a preheated wok and stir-fry the pork for about 1 minute or until its colour changes. Remove with a slotted spoon and keep warm while you cook the vegetables.

4 Add the vegetables to the wok and stir-fry for about 2 minutes. Add the salt and the partly cooked pork, and a little stock or water if necessary. Continue cooking and stirring for about 1 minute, then add the remaining soy sauce and blend well. Sprinkle with the sesame oil and serve.

Fragrant Thai Meatballs

INGREDIENTS
Serves 4–6
450g/1lb lean minced pork or beef
15ml/1 tbsp chopped garlic
1 stalk lemon grass, finely chopped
4 spring onions, finely chopped
15ml/1 tbsp chopped fresh coriander
30ml/2 tbsp red curry paste
15ml/1 tbsp lemon juice
15ml/1 tbsp fish sauce
1 egg
salt and freshly ground black pepper
rice flour for dusting
oil for frying
sprigs of coriander, to garnish

For the peanut sauce
15ml/1 tbsp vegetable oil
15ml/1 tbsp red curry paste
30ml/2 tbsp crunchy peanut butter
15ml/1 tbsp palm sugar
15ml/1 tbsp lemon juice
250ml/8fl oz/1 cup coconut milk

1 Make the peanut sauce. Heat the oil in a small saucepan, add the curry paste and fry for 1 minute.

2 Stir in the rest of the ingredients and bring to the boil. Lower the heat and simmer for 5 minutes, until the sauce thickens.

3 Make the meatballs. Combine all the ingredients except for the rice flour, oil and coriander, and add some seasoning. Mix and blend everything together well.

4 Roll and shape the meat into sm balls about the size of a walnut. Dust the meatballs with rice flour.

5 Heat the oil in a wok until hot a deep fry the meatballs in batches until nicely browned and cooked through. Drain on kitchen paper. Se garnished with sprigs of coriander an accompanied with the peanut sauce.

Stuffed Thai Omelette

INGREDIENTS
Serves 4
30ml/2 tbsp vegetable oil
2 garlic cloves, finely chopped
1 small onion, finely chopped
225g/8oz minced pork
30ml/2 tbsp fish sauce
5ml/1 tsp granulated sugar
freshly ground black pepper
2 tomatoes, peeled and chopped
15ml/1 tbsp chopped fresh coriander

For the omelette
5–6 eggs
15ml/1 tbsp fish sauce
30ml/2 tbsp vegetable oil
sprigs of coriander, to garnish
red chillies, sliced, to garnish

1 First heat the oil in a wok or frying pan. Add the garlic and onion and fry for 3–4 minutes until softened. Stir in the pork and fry for about 7–10 minutes, until lightly browned.

2 Add the fish sauce, sugar, freshly ground pepper and tomatoes. Stir to combine and simmer until the sauce thickens slightly. Mix in the chopped fresh coriander.

3 To make the omelettes, whisk together the eggs and fish sauce.

4 Heat 15ml/1 tbsp of the oil in an omelette pan or wok. Add half the beaten egg and tilt the pan to spread the egg into a thin even sheet.

5 When set, spoon half the filling over the centre of the omelette. Fold in opposite sides; first the top an bottom, then the right and left sides t make a neat square parcel.

6 Slide out on to a warm serving dish, folded-side down. Repeat with the rest of the oil, eggs and fillin Serve garnished with sprigs of coriander and red chillies.

Spicy Meat Fritters

Ingredients

Makes 30

450g/1lb potatoes, boiled and drained
450g/1lb lean minced beef
1 onion, quartered
1 bunch spring onions, chopped
3 garlic cloves, crushed
5ml/1 tsp ground nutmeg
15ml/1 tbsp coriander seeds, dry-fried and ground
10ml/2 tsp cumin seeds, dry-fried and ground
4 eggs, beaten
oil for shallow-frying
salt and freshly ground black pepper

1 While the potatoes are still warm, mash them in the pan until they are well broken up. Add to the minced beef and mix well together.

2 Finely chop the onion, spring onions and garlic. Add to the meat with the ground nutmeg, coriander and cumin. Stir in enough beaten egg to give a soft consistency which can be formed into fritters. Season to taste.

3 Heat the oil in a large frying par Using a dessertspoon, scoop out 6–8 oval-shaped fritters and drop th into the hot oil. Allow to set, so that they keep their shape (this will take about 3 minutes) and then turn over and cook for a further minute.

4 Drain well on kitchen paper and keep warm while cooking the remaining fritters.

Barbecued Pork Spareribs

Ingredients

Serves 4

1kg/2¼lb pork spareribs
1 onion
2 garlic cloves
2.5cm/1in fresh root ginger
75ml/3fl oz/⅓ cup dark soy sauce
1–2 fresh red chillies, seeded and chopped
5ml/1 tsp tamarind pulp, soaked in 75ml/3fl oz/⅓ cup water
15–30ml/1–2 tbsp dark brown sugar
30ml/2 tbsp groundnut oil
salt and freshly ground black pepper

1 Wipe the pork ribs and place them in a wok, wide frying pan or large flameproof casserole.

2 Finely chop the onion, crush the garlic and peel and slice the ginger. Blend the soy sauce, onion, garlic, ginger and chopped chillies together to a paste in a food processor or with a pestle and mortar. Strain the tamarind and reserve the juice. Add the tamarind juice, brown sugar, oil and seasoning to taste to the onion mixture and mix well together.

3 Pour the sauce over the ribs and toss well to coat. Bring to the bo and then simmer, uncovered and stirring frequently, for 30 minutes. A extra water if necessary.

4 Put the ribs on a rack in a roastir tin, place under a preheated grill, on a barbecue or in the oven at 200°C/400°F/Gas 6 and continue cooking until the ribs are tender, abo 20 minutes, depending on the thickn of the ribs. Baste the ribs with the sau and turn them over from time to tim

Peking Beef and Pepper Stir-fry

This quick and easy stir-fry is perfect for today's busy cook and tastes superb.

INGREDIENTS

Serves 4

350g/12oz rump or sirloin steak, sliced into strips
30ml/2 tbsp soy sauce
30ml/2 tbsp medium sherry
15ml/1 tbsp cornflour
5ml/1 tsp brown sugar
15ml/1 tbsp sunflower oil
15ml/1 tbsp sesame oil
1 garlic clove, finely chopped
15ml/1 tbsp grated fresh root ginger
1 red pepper, seeded and sliced
1 yellow pepper, seeded and sliced
115g/4oz sugar snap peas
4 spring onions, cut into 5cm/2in lengths
30ml/2 tbsp oyster sauce
60ml/4 tbsp water
cooked noodles, to serve

1 In a bowl, mix together the steak strips, soy sauce, sherry, cornflour and brown sugar. Cover and leave to marinate for 30 minutes.

2 Heat the sunflower and sesame o in a preheated wok or large fryin pan. Add the garlic and ginger and st fry for about 30 seconds. Add the peppers, sugar snap peas and spring onions and stir-fry for 3 minutes.

3 Add the beef, together with the marinade juices, to the wok or frying pan and stir-fry for a further 3–4 minutes. Pour in the oyster sauce and water and stir until the sauce has thickened slightly. Serve immediately with cooked noodles.

Stir-fried Beef and Broccoli

[T]his spicy beef may be served [w]ith noodles or on a bed of [b]oiled rice for a speedy and low-[c]alorie Chinese meal.

[I]NGREDIENTS

[S]erves 4

- [3]50g/12oz rump steak
- [1]5ml/1 tbsp cornflour
- [5]ml/1 tsp sesame oil
- [3]50g/12oz broccoli, cut into small florets
- [4] spring onions, sliced diagonally
- [1] carrot, cut into matchstick strips
- [1] garlic clove, crushed
- [2].5cm/1in fresh root ginger, cut into very fine strips
- [1]20ml/4fl oz/½ cup beef stock
- [3]0ml/2 tbsp soy sauce
- [3]0ml/2 tbsp dry sherry
- [1]0ml/2 tsp soft light brown sugar
- [s]pring onion tassels, to garnish (optional)
- [n]oodles or rice, to serve

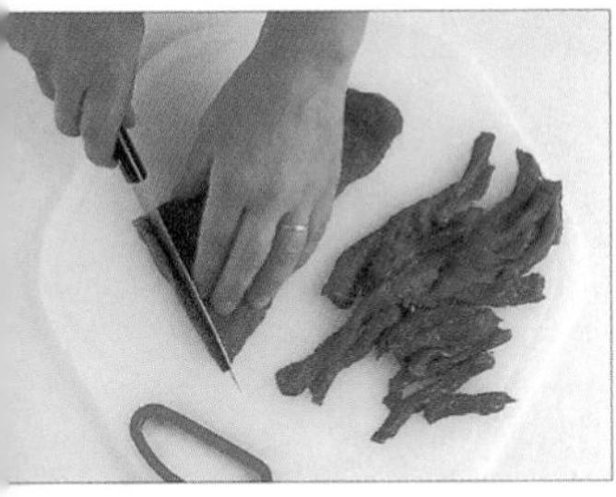

1 Trim the beef and cut into thin slices across the grain. Cut each [sl]ice into thin strips. Toss in the [c]ornflour to coat thoroughly.

2 Heat the sesame oil in a preheated wok or large non-stick frying pan. Add the beef strips and stir-fry over a brisk heat for 3 minutes. Remove and set aside.

3 Add the broccoli, spring onions, carrot, garlic, ginger and stock to the wok or frying pan. Cover and simmer for 3 minutes. Uncover and cook, stirring, until all the stock has reduced entirely.

4 Mix the soy sauce, dry sherry and brown sugar together and add to the wok or frying pan with the beef. Cook for 2–3 minutes, stirring continuously. Spoon into a warmed serving dish and garnish with spring onion tassels, if liked. Serve on a bed of noodles or rice.

COOK'S TIP

To make spring onion tassels, trim the bulb base, then cut the green shoot so that the onion is 7.5cm/3in long. Shred to within 2.5cm/1in of the base and put into iced water for 1 hour.

Beef Stir-fry with Crisp Parsnips

Wonderful crisp shreds of parsnip add extra crunchiness to this unusual stir-fry – a great supper dish to share with friends.

INGREDIENTS

Serves 4
350g/12oz parsnips
450g/1lb rump steak
450g/1lb trimmed leeks
2 red peppers, seeded
350g/12oz courgettes
90ml/6 tbsp vegetable oil
2 garlic cloves, crushed
45ml/3 tbsp hoisin sauce
salt and ground black pepper

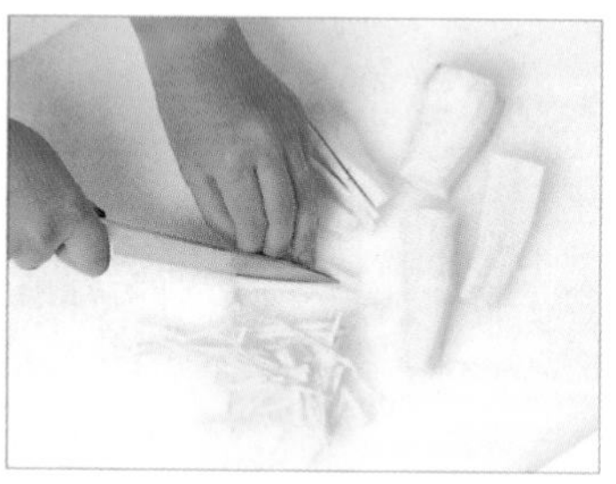

1 Peel the parsnips and cut in half lengthways. Place the flat surface on a chopping board and cut them into thin strips. Finely shred each piece. Rinse in cold water and drain thoroughly. Dry the parsnips on kitchen paper, if necessary.

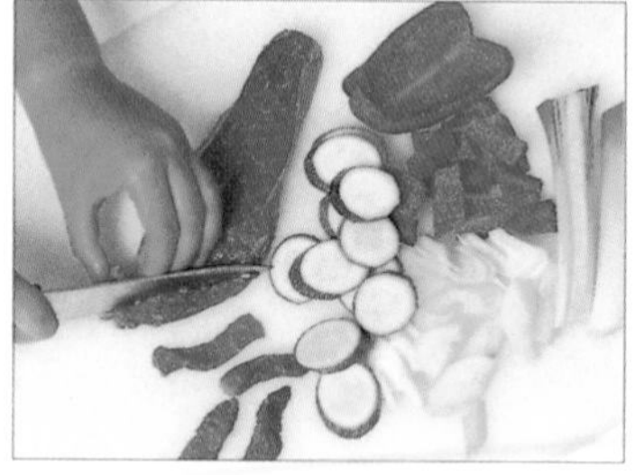

2 Cut the steak into thin strips. Split the leeks in half lengthways and thickly slice at an angle. Roughly chop the peppers and thinly slice the courgettes.

3 Heat the oil in a preheated wok or large frying pan. Fry the parsnips until crisp and golden. You may need to do this in batches, adding a little more oil if necessary. Remove with a slotted spoon and drain on kitchen paper.

4 Stir-fry the steak in the wok or frying pan until golden and cooked through. You may need to do this in batches, adding more oil if necessary. Remove and drain on kitchen paper.

5 Stir-fry the garlic, leeks, peppers and courgettes for about 10 minutes, or until golden brown and beginning to soften but still retaining little bite. Season the mixture well.

6 Return the meat to the pan with the hoisin sauce. Stir-fry for 2–3 minutes, or until piping hot. Adjust th seasoning and serve with the crisp parsnips piled on top.

Beef with Cantonese Oyster Sauce

This is a classic Cantonese recipe in which any combination of vegetables can be used. Broccoli may be used instead of mangetouts, bamboo shoots instead of baby corn cobs, and white or black mushrooms instead of straw mushrooms, for example.

INGREDIENTS

Serves 4

275–350g/10–12oz rump steak
5ml/1 tsp light brown sugar
15ml/1 tbsp light soy sauce
10ml/2 tsp Chinese rice wine or dry sherry
10ml/2 tsp cornflour paste
115g/4oz mangetouts
115g/4oz baby corn cobs
115g/4oz straw mushrooms
1 spring onion
300ml/½ pint/1¼ cups vegetable oil
few small pieces of fresh root ginger
2.5ml/½ tsp salt
30ml/2 tbsp oyster sauce

1 Cut the beef into thin strips. Place in a bowl and add the sugar, soy sauce, rice wine or dry sherry and cornflour paste. Mix well and set aside to marinate for 25–30 minutes.

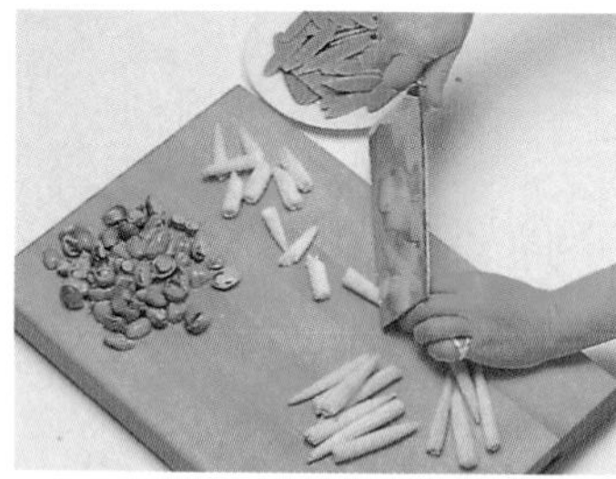

2 Top and tail the mangetouts and cut the baby corn cobs in half. If using canned straw mushrooms, drain them. If the straw mushrooms are large, cut them in half, but leave whole if they are small. Cut the spring onion into short sections.

3 Heat the oil in a preheated wok and stir-fry the beef until the colour changes. Remove with a perforated spoon and drain.

4 Pour off the excess oil, leaving about 30ml/2 tbsp in the wok, then add the spring onion, ginger and the vegetables. Stir-fry for about 2 minutes with the salt, then add the beef and the oyster sauce. Blend well and serve.

Beef Strips with Orange and Ginger

tir-frying is one of the best ways o cook with the minimum of t. This recipe is ideal for people ying to lose weight, those equiring a low-fat and low-holesterol diet or, in fact, anyone ho wants to eat healthily.

NGREDIENTS

erves 4

50g/1lb lean rump, fillet or sirloin steak, cut into thin strips
nely grated rind and juice of 1 orange
5ml/1 tbsp light soy sauce
ml/1 tsp cornflour
.5cm/1in fresh root ginger, finely chopped
0ml/2 tsp sesame oil
large carrot, cut into matchstick strips
spring onions, thinly sliced
ice noodles or boiled rice, to serve

1 Place the steak strips in a bowl and sprinkle over the orange rind and uice. Set aside to marinate for about 0 minutes.

2 Drain the liquid from the steak and reserve. Mix together the steak, soy auce, cornflour and ginger.

3 Heat the oil in a preheated wok or large frying pan, then add the steak and stir-fry for 1 minute, until lightly coloured. Add the carrot and stir-fry for a further 2–3 minutes.

4 Stir in the spring onions and reserved marinade liquid. Cook, stirring constantly, until boiling and thickened. Serve hot with rice noodles or plain boiled rice.

Thick Beef Curry in Sweet Peanut Sauce

This curry is deliciously rich and thicker than most other Thai curries. Serve with boiled jasmine rice and salted duck's eggs, if liked.

INGREDIENTS

Serves 4–6

600ml/1 pint/2½ cups coconut milk
45ml/3 tbsp red curry paste
45ml/3 tbsp fish sauce
30ml/2 tbsp palm sugar
2 stalks lemon grass, bruised
450g/1lb rump steak, cut into thin strips
75g/3oz roasted ground peanuts
2 red chillies, sliced
5 kaffir lime leaves, torn
salt and freshly ground black pepper
2 salted eggs, to serve
10–15 Thai basil leaves, to garnish

1 Put half the coconut milk into a heavy-bottomed saucepan and heat, stirring, until it boils and separates.

2 Add the red curry paste and cook until fragrant. Add the fish sauce, palm sugar and lemon grass.

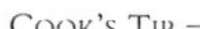

COOK'S TIP

If you don't have the time to make your own red curry paste, you can buy a ready-made Thai curry paste. There is a wide range available in most supermarkets.

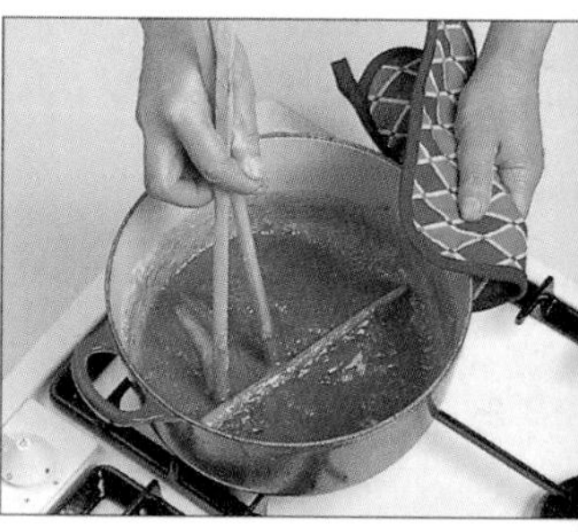

3 Continue to cook until the colou deepens. Add the rest of the coconut milk. Bring back to the boil.

4 Add the beef and ground peanuts Stir and cook for 8–10 minutes o until most of the liquid has evaporate

5 Add the chillies and kaffir lime leaves. Adjust the seasoning to taste. Serve with salted eggs and garni with Thai basil leaves.

Sizzling Steak

his Malaysian method of sizzling chly marinated meat on a cast on grill can be applied with qual success to sliced chicken pork.

GREDIENTS

rves 4–6
garlic clove, crushed
5cm/1in fresh root ginger, finely chopped
ml/2 tsp black peppercorns
ml/1 tbsp sugar
ml/2 tbsp tamarind sauce
ml/3 tbsp dark soy sauce
ml/1 tbsp oyster sauce
slices rump steak, each about 200g/7oz
getable oil, for brushing

or the dipping sauce
ml/5 tbsp beef stock
ml/2 tbsp tomato ketchup
nl/1 tsp chilli sauce
ice of 1 lime

1 Pound together the garlic, ginger, peppercorns, sugar and tamarind uce in a mortar with a pestle. Mix in e soy sauce and oyster sauce, then oon over the steaks. Set aside in the frigerator to marinate for up to hours.

2 Heat a cast iron grilling plate over high heat until very hot. Scrape the marinade from the meat and reserve. Brush the meat with oil and grill for 2 minutes on each side for rare and 3–4 minutes on each side for medium, depending on thickness.

3 Meanwhile, make the sauce. Pour the marinade into a saucepan and add the stock, tomato ketchup, chilli sauce and lime juice. Set over a low heat and simmer to heat through. Serve the steak and hand the dipping sauce separately.

Sesame Steak

Toasted sesame seeds bring their distinctive smoky aroma to this scrumptious oriental marinade.

INGREDIENTS

Serves 4

450g/1lb rump steak
30ml/2 tbsp sesame seeds
15ml/1 tbsp sesame oil
30ml/2 tbsp vegetable oil
115g/4oz small mushrooms, quartered
1 large green pepper, seeded and cut into strips
4 spring onions, chopped diagonally
boiled rice, to serve

For the marinade

10ml/2 tsp cornflour
30ml/2 tbsp Chinese rice wine or dry sherry
15ml/1 tbsp lemon juice
15ml/1 tbsp soy sauce
few drops of Tabasco sauce
2.5cm/1in fresh root ginger, grated
1 garlic clove, crushed

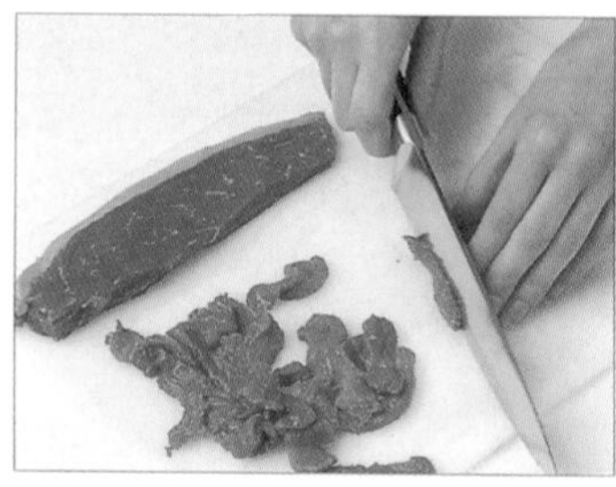

1 Trim the steak and cut into thin strips about 1 x 5cm/½ x 2in.

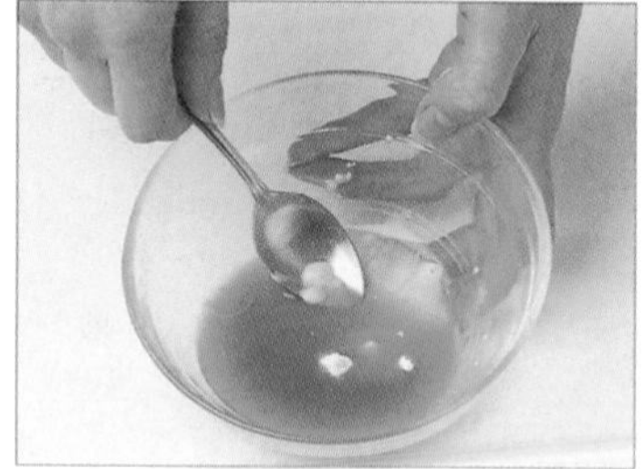

2 Make the marinade. In a bowl, blend the cornflour with the rice wine or dry sherry, then stir in the lemon juice, soy sauce, Tabasco sauce, ginger and garlic. Stir in the steak strips, cover and leave in a cool place for 3–4 hours.

3 Place the sesame seeds in a wok or large frying pan and dry-fry over a moderate heat, shaking the pan, until the seeds are golden. Set aside.

4 Heat the sesame and vegetable oils in the wok or frying pan. Drain the steak, reserving the marinade, and stir-fry a few pieces at a time until browned. Remove with a slotted spoon.

5 Add the mushrooms and green pepper and stir-fry for 2–3 minutes. Add the spring onions and cook for 1 minute more.

6 Return the steak to the wok or frying pan, together with the reserved marinade, and stir over a moderate heat for a further 2 minutes until the ingredients are evenly coated with glaze. Sprinkle over the sesame seeds and serve immediately with boiled rice.

COOK'S TIP

This marinade would also be good with pork or chicken.

Stir-fried Beef with Mangetouts

The crisp texture and fresh taste of mangetouts perfectly complement the melt-in-the-mouth tenderness of the steak, all served in a richly aromatic sauce.

INGREDIENTS

Serves 4

450g/1lb rump steak
45ml/3 tbsp soy sauce
30ml/2 tbsp Chinese rice wine or dry sherry
15ml/1 tbsp soft brown sugar
2.5ml/½ tsp cornflour
15ml/1 tbsp vegetable oil
15ml/1 tbsp finely chopped fresh root ginger
15ml/1 tbsp finely chopped garlic
225g/8oz mangetouts

1 Cut the steak into even-sized, very thin strips.

2 Combine the soy sauce, rice wine or dry sherry, brown sugar and cornflour. Mix well and set aside.

3 Heat the oil in a preheated wok. Add the ginger and garlic and stir-fry for 30 seconds. Add the steak and stir-fry for 2 minutes, or until evenly browned.

4 Add the mangetouts and stir-fry fc a further 3 minutes.

5 Stir the soy sauce mixture until smooth, then add to the wok. Bring to the boil, stirring constantly, lower the heat and simmer until the sauce is thick and smooth. Serve immediately.

Braised Beef in a Rich Peanut Sauce

ike many dishes brought to the hilippines by the Spanish, this ow-cooking stew, renamed *kari ari*, retains much of its original harm, while at the same time it as acquired a uniquely oriental avour. Rice and peanuts are sed to thicken the juices, elding a rich, glossy sauce.

IGREDIENTS

rves 4–6

)0g/2lb braising steak
)ml/2 tbsp vegetable oil
iml/1 tbsp annatto seeds
medium onions, chopped
garlic cloves, crushed
'5g/10oz celeriac or swede, roughly chopped
'5ml/16fl oz/2 cups beef stock
'5g/12oz new potatoes, peeled and cut into large dice
iml/1 tbsp fish or anchovy sauce
ml/2 tbsp tamarind sauce
)ml/2 tsp sugar
bay leaf
fresh thyme sprig
iml/3 tbsp long-grain rice
)g/2oz/½ cup peanuts or 30ml/2 tbsp peanut butter
iml/1 tbsp white wine vinegar
lt and ground black pepper

1 Cut the beef into 2.5cm/1in cubes and set aside. Heat the oil in a ımeproof casserole, add the annatto eds and stir until the oil is dark red in lour. Remove the seeds with a otted spoon and discard.

2 Add the onions, garlic and celeriac or swede to the casserole and fry r 3–5 minutes, until softened but not loured. Add the beef and fry until ghtly and evenly browned. Add the ock, potatoes, fish or anchovy sauce, marind sauce, sugar, bay leaf and yme. Bring to a simmer, cover and ok for 2 hours.

3 Meanwhile, place the rice in a bowl, cover with cold water and set aside for 30 minutes. Roast the peanuts, if using, under a preheated grill for 2 minutes. Remove and rub off the skins with a clean tea towel. Drain the rice and grind with the peanuts or peanut butter in a mortar with a pestle or in a food processor.

4 When the beef is tender, add 60ml/4 tbsp of the cooking liquid to the rice and nut mixture. Blend until smooth, then stir into the casserole. Simmer gently, uncovered, for 15–20 minutes, until thickened. Stir in the wine vinegar and season to taste.

COOK'S TIP

Annatto seeds have little flavour, although they are edible. They are used to colour oil or lard to a rich reddish-orange shade. If you cannot find them, substitute 5ml/1 tsp paprika and a pinch of turmeric, adding these to the casserole with the beef.

Beef and Vegetables in a Table-top Broth

In Japanese, this dish is called *Shabu Shabu*, which refers to the swishing sound made as wafer-thin slices of beef, tofu and vegetables cook in a special broth. This is a delicious and easy all-in-one main course for a dinner party.

INGREDIENTS

Serves 4–6
450g/1lb sirloin steak, trimmed
1.75 litres/3 pints/7½ cups water
½ sachet instant *dashi* powder or ½ vegetable stock cube
150g/5oz carrots
6 spring onions, sliced
150g/5oz Chinese leaves, roughly chopped
225g/8oz mooli, shredded
115g/4oz canned bamboo shoots, drained and sliced
175g/6oz tofu, cut into large dice
10 shiitake mushrooms, fresh or dried
salt
275g/10oz udon noodles, cooked, to serve

For the sesame dipping sauce
50g/2oz sesame seeds or 30ml/2 tbsp tahini paste
120ml/4fl oz/½ cup instant *dashi* stock or vegetable stock
60ml/4 tbsp dark soy sauce
10ml/2 tsp sugar
30ml/2 tbsp sake (optional)
10ml/2 tsp *wasabi* powder (optional)

For the ponzu dipping sauce
45ml/3 tbsp lemon juice
15ml/1 tbsp rice vinegar or white wine vinegar
45ml/3 tbsp dark soy sauce
15ml/1 tbsp tamari sauce
15ml/1 tbsp mirin or 5ml/1 tsp sugar
1.5ml/¼ tsp instant *dashi* powder or ¼ vegetable stock cube

1 Place the beef in the freezer for 30 minutes, or until firm but not frozen. Slice it very thinly using a cleaver or large, sharp knife. Arrange it decoratively on a serving plate, cover and set aside. Bring the water to the boil in a Japanese *donabe*, a fondue pot or any other covered flameproof casserole with an unglazed outside. Stir in the *dashi* powder or stock cube, cover and simmer for 8–10 minutes. Transfer the container to a heat source (its own stand or a hot plate) at the dining table.

2 Meanwhile, prepare the vegetables and bring a saucepan of lightly salted water to the boil. With a canelle knife, cut a series of grooves along the length of the carrots, then slice thinly. Blanch the carrots, spring onions, Chinese leaves and mooli, separately, for 2–3 minutes each and drain thoroughly. Arrange the vegetables decoratively on serving dishes, together with the bamboo shoots and tofu. If using dried mushrooms, put them in a bowl, cover with hot water and leave to soak for 3–4 minutes, then drain. Slice the shiitake mushrooms.

3 To make the sesame dipping sauce, dry-fry the sesame seeds, if using, in a heavy frying pan over medium heat. Grind them in a mortar with a pestle or in a food processor.

4 Mix together the ground sesame seeds or tahini paste, stock, soy sauce, sugar, sake and *wasabi* powder, if using. Combine thoroughly and pour into a shallow dish.

5 To make the ponzu dipping sauce put all the ingredients in a screw-top jar and shake vigorously. Pour into a shallow dish.

6 To serve, arrange the plates of vegetables and dishes of sauce around the broth and provide your guests with chopsticks and individual bowls so that they can help themselves to what they want, cook it in the broth and then serve themselves. Towards the end of the meal, each guest can take a portion of noodles and ladle a little stock over them before eating.

COOK'S TIP

Tahini paste is a purée of toasted sesame seeds that is used mainly in Greek, Turkish and some Middle Eastern cooking. It makes a quick alternative to using sesame seeds in this recipe and is readily available from large supermarkets and delicatessens.

Sukiyaki Beef

This Japanese dish, with its mixture of meat, vegetables, noodles and tofu, is a meal in itself. If you want to do it properly, eat the meal with chopsticks and then use a spoon to collect the stock juices.

INGREDIENTS

Serves 4

450g/1lb thick rump steak
200g/7oz Japanese rice noodles
15ml/1 tbsp shredded suet
200g/7oz firm tofu, cut into cubes
8 shiitake mushrooms, hard stems trimmed
2 medium leeks, sliced into 2.5cm/1in lengths
90g/3½oz baby spinach, to serve

For the stock

15ml/1 tbsp caster sugar
90ml/6 tbsp sake, Chinese rice wine or dry sherry
45ml/3 tbsp dark soy sauce
120ml/4fl oz/½ cup water

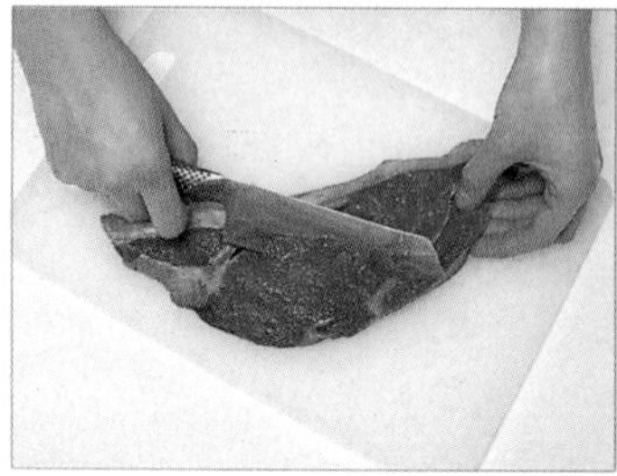

1 Cut the steak into thin slices using a cleaver or sharp knife.

2 Blanch the noodles in boiling water for 2 minutes. Drain thoroughly and set aside.

3 Make the stock: mix together the sugar, sake, rice wine or dry sherry, soy sauce and water.

4 Melt the suet in a preheated wok. Add the steak and stir-fry for 2–3 minutes, or until cooked through but still pink.

5 Pour the stock over the beef.

6 Add the tofu, mushrooms and leek and cook for 4 minutes, or until th leeks are tender. Serve a selection of th different ingredients, together with a few baby spinach leaves, to each persor

Beef Saté with Hot Mango Dip

romatic beef is served with a picy fruit sauce. Just add a green alad and plain boiled rice for the erfect balance of flavours and extures.

NGREDIENTS

erves 4
50g/1lb sirloin steak
5ml/1 tbsp coriander seeds
ml/1 tsp cumin seeds
0g/2oz/½ cup raw cashew nuts
5ml/1 tbsp vegetable oil
shallots or 1 small onion, finely chopped
cm/½in fresh root ginger, finely chopped
garlic clove, crushed
0ml/2 tbsp tamarind sauce
0ml/2 tbsp dark soy sauce
0ml/2 tsp sugar
ml/1 tsp rice vinegar or white wine vinegar
alad leaves, to serve

or the hot mango dip
ripe mango
–2 small fresh red chillies, seeded and finely chopped
5ml/1 tbsp fish sauce
uice of 1 lime
0ml/2 tsp sugar
0ml/2 tbsp chopped fresh coriander
alt

1 Slice the beef into long, narrow strips and thread, zig-zag style, on o 12 bamboo skewers. Put them on a lat plate and set aside.

2 Dry-fry coriander seeds, cumin seeds and cashew nuts in a preheated wok until evenly brown. Transfer to a mortar and crush with a pestle or crush finely in a food processor. Mix together the crushed spices and nuts, vegetable oil, shallots or onion, ginger, garlic, tamarind sauce, soy sauce, sugar and vinegar. Spoon this mixture over the beef and set aside to marinate for up to 8 hours.

3 Cook the steak skewers under a preheated grill for 6–8 minutes, turning occasionally to ensure an even colour.

4 Meanwhile, make the mango dip. Peel the mango and cut the flesh from the stone. Place in a food processor with the chillies, fish sauce, lime juice and sugar and process until smooth. Stir in the coriander and season with salt to taste. Serve the skewers on a bed of salad leaves, with the sauce separately.

Green Beef Curry with Thai Aubergine

INGREDIENTS

Serves 4–6
15ml/1 tbsp vegetable oil
45ml/3 tbsp green curry paste
600ml/1 pint/2½ cups coconut milk
450g/1lb beef sirloin
4 kaffir lime leaves, torn
15–30ml/1–2 tbsp fish sauce
5ml/1 tsp palm sugar
150g/5oz small Thai aubergines, halved
a small handful of Thai basil
2 green chillies, to garnish

For the green curry paste
15 hot green chillies
2 stalks lemon grass, chopped
3 shallots, sliced
2 garlic cloves
15ml/1 tbsp chopped galangal
4 kaffir lime leaves, chopped
2.5ml/½ tsp grated kaffir lime rind
5ml/1 tsp chopped coriander root
6 black peppercorns
5ml/1 tsp coriander seeds, roasted
5ml/1 tsp cumin seeds, roasted
15ml/1 tbsp sugar
5ml/1 tsp salt
5ml/1 tsp shrimp paste (optional)
30ml/2 tbsp vegetable oil

1 Make the green curry paste. Combine all the ingredients, except for the oil. Pound in a pestle and mortar or process in a food processor until smooth. Add the oil a little at a time and blend well between each addition. Keep in a glass jar in the fridge until required.

2 Heat the oil in a large saucepan or wok. Add 45ml/3 tbsp curry paste and fry until fragrant.

3 Stir in half the coconut milk, a little at a time. Cook for about 5–6 minutes, until an oily sheen appears.

4 Cut the beef into long thin slices and add to the saucepan with the kaffir lime leaves, fish sauce, sugar and aubergines. Cook for 2–3 minutes, th stir in the remaining coconut milk.

5 Bring back to a simmer and cook until the meat and aubergines are tender. Stir in the Thai basil just befor serving. Finely shred the green chillies and use to garnish the curry.

Oriental Beef

his sumptuous stir-fried beef elts in the mouth, and is erfectly complemented by the elicious crunchy relish.

GREDIENTS

rves 4
50g/1lb rump steak
5ml/1 tbsp sunflower oil
whole radishes, to garnish

or the marinade
cloves garlic, crushed
0ml/4 tbsp dark soy sauce
0ml/2 tbsp dry sherry
0ml/2 tsp soft dark brown sugar

or the relish
radishes
0cm/4in piece cucumber
piece stem ginger

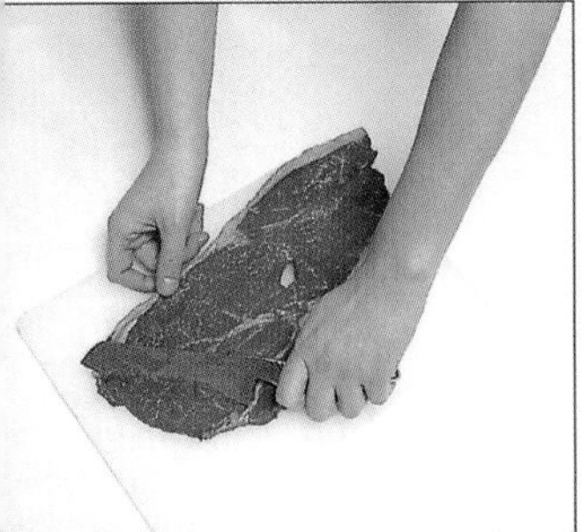

1 Cut the beef into thin strips. Place in a bowl.

2 To make the marinade, mix together the garlic, soy sauce, erry and sugar in a bowl. Pour it over e beef and leave to marinate ernight.

COOK'S TIP

Dark soy sauce has a stronger, more robust flavour than light soy sauce. It is particularly useful for imparting a rich, dark colour to meat dishes.

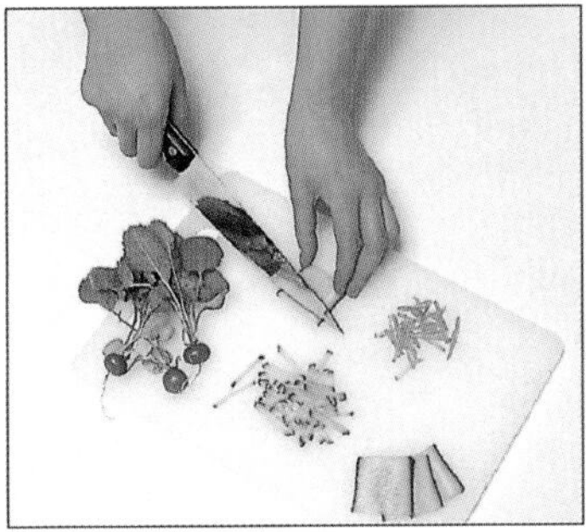

3 To make the relish, chop the radishes and cucumber into short matchsticks, then cut the ginger into small matchsticks. Mix thoroughly together in a bowl.

4 Heat a wok, then add the oil. When the oil is hot, add the meat and the marinade and stir-fry for 3–4 minutes. Serve with the relish, and garnish with a whole radish on each plate.

Chilli Beef with Basil

This is a dish for chilli lovers! It is very easy to prepare – all you need is a wok.

INGREDIENTS

Serves 2

about 90ml/6 tbsp groundnut oil
16–20 large fresh basil leaves
275g/10oz rump steak
30ml/2 tbsp Thai fish sauce (*nam pla*)
5ml/1 tsp dark brown soft sugar
1–2 fresh red chillies, sliced into rings
3 garlic cloves, chopped
5ml/1 tsp chopped fresh root ginger
1 shallot, thinly sliced
30ml/2 tbsp finely chopped fresh basil leaves, plus extra to garnish
squeeze of lemon juice
salt and ground black pepper
Thai jasmine rice, to serve

1 Heat the oil in a wok and, when hot, add the whole basil leaves and fry for about 1 minute until crisp and golden. Drain on kitchen paper. Remove the wok from the heat and pour off all but 30ml/2 tbsp of the oil.

COOK'S TIP

Although not so familiar to western cooks, Thai fish sauce is as widely used in Thai cooking as soy sauce is in Chinese cuisine. In fact, they are not dissimilar in appearance and taste. Called *nam pla*, Thai fish sauce is available at oriental food stores, but if you cannot get it, soy sauce is an adequate substitute.

2 Cut the steak across the grain into thin strips. Mix together the fish sauce and sugar in a bowl. Add the beef, mix well, then leave to marinate for about 30 minutes.

3 Reheat the oil until hot, add the chilli, garlic, ginger and shallot and stir-fry for 30 seconds. Add the beef and chopped basil, then stir-fry for about 3 minutes. Flavour with lemon juice and salt and pepper to taste.

4 Transfer to a warmed serving plate, scatter over the basil leaves to garnish and serve immediately with Thai jasmine rice.

Spicy Meatballs

erve *Pergedel Djawa* with either *sambal* or spicy sauce.

GREDIENTS

akes 24

large onion, roughly chopped
-2 fresh red chillies, seeded and chopped
garlic cloves, crushed
cm/½in cube *terasi*, prepared
5ml/1 tbsp coriander seeds
nl/1 tsp cumin seeds
50g/1lb lean minced beef
0ml/2 tsp dark soy sauce
nl/1 tsp dark brown sugar
ice of ½ lemon
little beaten egg
l for shallow-frying
lt and freshly ground black pepper
esh coriander sprigs, to garnish

1 Put the onion, chillies, garlic and *terasi* in a food processor. Process but do not over-chop or the onion will become too wet and spoil the consistency of the meatballs. Dry-fry the coriander and cumin seeds in a preheated pan for about 1 minute, to release the aroma. Do not brown. Grind with a pestle and mortar.

2 Put the meat in a large bowl. Stir in the onion mixture. Add the ground coriander and cumin, soy sauce, seasoning, sugar and lemon juice. Bind with a little beaten egg and shape into small, even-size balls.

3 Chill the meatballs briefly to firm up, if necessary. Fry in shallow oil, turning often, until cooked through and browned. This will take 4–5 minutes, depending on their size.

4 Remove from the pan, drain well on kitchen paper and serve, garnished with coriander sprigs.

Sizzling Beef with Celeriac Straw

The crisp celeriac matchsticks look like fine pieces of straw when stir-fried, and they have a mild celery-like flavour that is quite delicious.

INGREDIENTS

Serves 4
450g/1lb celeriac
150ml/¼ pint/⅔ cup vegetable oil
1 red pepper
6 spring onions
450g/1lb rump steak
60ml/4 tbsp beef stock
30ml/2 tbsp sherry vinegar
10ml/2 tsp Worcestershire sauce
10ml/2 tsp tomato purée
salt and ground black pepper

1 Peel the celeriac and then cut into fine matchsticks, using a cleaver.

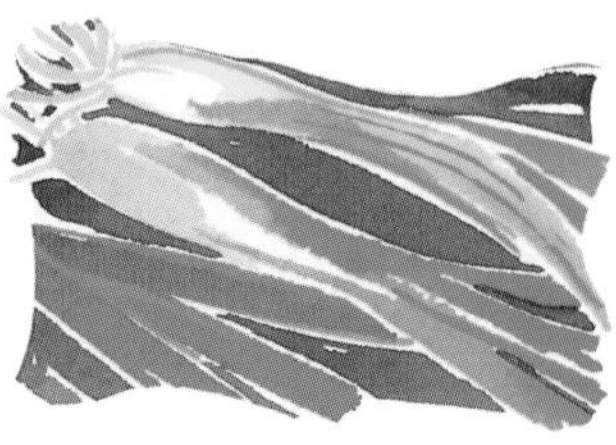

2 Heat a wok, then add two-thirds of the oil. When the oil is hot, fry the celeriac matchsticks in batches until golden brown and crispy. Drain well on kitchen paper.

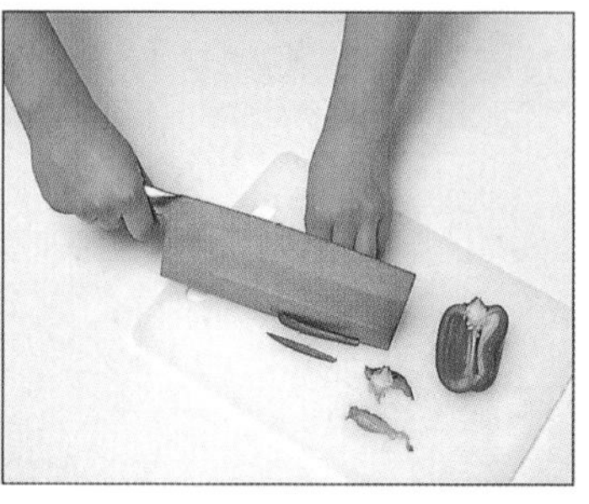

3 Halve, core and seed the red pepper, then slice diagonally into 2.5cm/1in lengths. Slice the spring onions diagonally into 2.5cm/1in lengths.

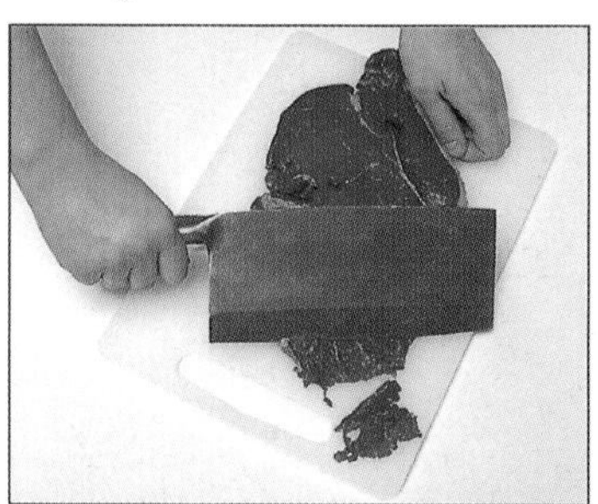

4 Chop the beef into thin strips, across the grain of meat.

5 Heat the wok again and add the remaining oil. When the oil is hot stir-fry the chopped red pepper and spring onion for 2–3 minutes.

6 Add the beef strips and stir-fry for further 3–4 minutes until browned. Add the stock, vinegar, Worcestershire sauce and tomato purée. Season to taste and serve with the celeriac straw.

COOK'S TIP

Avoid buying very large celeriac roots, as they tend to be woody or otherwise unpleasant in texture. As it is rather an unwieldy and knobbly vegetable, celeriac is easier to peel properly if you cut it into more or less even-sized slices first. Then peel each slice individually using a very sharp knife. They need to be peeled quite thickly to obtain a neat edge. You can then easily cut the slices into thin strips.

Stir-fried Beef in Oyster Sauce

Another simple but delicious recipe. In Thailand fresh straw mushrooms are readily available, but oyster mushrooms make a good substitute. To make the dish even more interesting, use several types of mushroom.

Ingredients

Serves 4–6

450g/1lb rump steak
30ml/2 tbsp soy sauce
15ml/1 tbsp cornflour
45ml/3 tbsp vegetable oil
15ml/1 tbsp chopped garlic
15ml/1 tbsp chopped root ginger
225g/8oz mixed mushrooms such as shiitake, oyster and straw
30ml/2 tbsp oyster sauce
5ml/1 tsp granulated sugar
4 spring onions, cut into short lengths
freshly ground black pepper
2 red chillies, cut into strips, to garnish

1 Slice the beef, on the diagonal, into long thin strips. Mix together the soy sauce and cornflour in a large bowl, stir in the beef and leave to marinate for 1–2 hours.

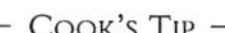

Cook's Tip

Made from extracts of oysters, oyster sauce is velvety smooth and has a savoury sweet and meaty taste. There are several types available; buy the best you can afford.

2 Heat half the oil in a wok or fryi pan. Add the garlic and ginger ar fry until fragrant. Stir in the beef. Stir to separate the strips, let them colour and cook for 1–2 minutes. Remove from the pan and set aside.

3 Heat the remaining oil in the wo Add the shiitake, oyster and straw mushrooms. Cook until tender.

4 Return the beef to the wok with the mushrooms. Add the oyster sauce, sugar and freshly ground black pepper to taste. Mix well.

5 Add the spring onions. Mix together. Serve garnished with strips of red chilli.

Dry Fried Shredded Beef

'y frying is a unique Szechuan
oking method, in which the
ıin ingredient is firstly stir-fried
wly over a low heat until dry,
en finished off quickly with a
xture of other ingredients over
ıigh heat.

GREDIENTS

ves 4

)–400g/12–14oz beef steak
ırge or 2 small carrots
3 sticks celery
ml/2 tbsp sesame oil
ml/1 tbsp Chinese rice wine or
lry sherry
ml/1 tbsp chilli bean sauce
nl/1 tbsp light soy sauce
love garlic, finely chopped
ıl/1 tsp light brown sugar
3 spring onions, finely chopped
ml/½ tsp finely chopped fresh
oot ginger
ound Szechuan pepper

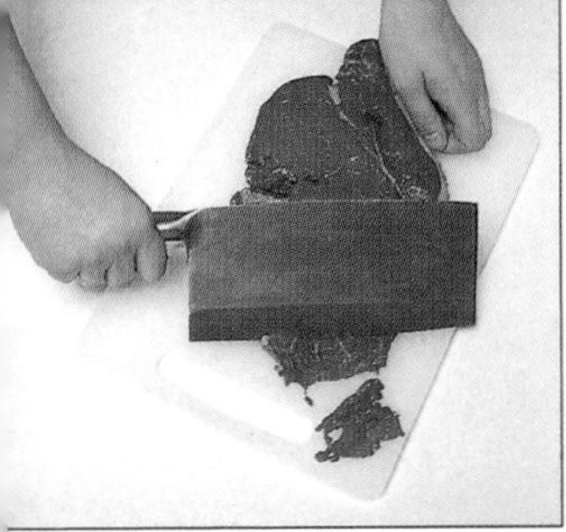

1 Cut the beef into matchstick-sized strips. Thinly shred the carrots and lery sticks.

2 Heat the sesame oil in a preheated wok (it will smoke very quickly). educe the heat and stir-fry the beef reds with the rice wine or sherry til the colour changes.

3 Pour off the excess liquid and reserve. Continue stirring until the meat is absolutely dry.

4 Add the chilli bean sauce, soy sauce, garlic and sugar. Blend well, then add the carrot and celery shreds. Increase the heat to high and add the spring onions, ginger and the reserved liquid. Continue stirring, and when all the juice has evaporated, season with Szechuan pepper and serve.

Beef and Aubergine Curry

Ingredients

Serves 6

120ml/4fl oz/½ cup sunflower oil
2 onions, thinly sliced
2.5cm/1in fresh root ginger, sliced and cut in matchsticks
1 garlic clove, crushed
2 fresh red chillies, seeded and very finely sliced
2.5cm/1in fresh turmeric, peeled and crushed, or 5ml/1 tsp ground turmeric
1 lemon grass stem, lower part sliced finely, top bruised
675g/1½ lb braising steak, cut in even-size strips
400ml/14fl oz can coconut milk
300ml/½ pint/1¼ cups water
1 aubergine, sliced and patted dry
5ml/1 tsp tamarind pulp, soaked in 60ml/4 tbsp warm water
salt and freshly ground black pepper
finely sliced chilli, (optional) and Deep-fried Onions, to garnish
boiled rice, to serve

1 Heat half the oil and fry the onions, ginger and garlic until they give off a rich aroma. Add the chillies, turmeric and the lower part of the lemon grass. Push to one side and then turn up the heat and add the steak, stirring until the meat changes colour.

Cook's Tip

If you want to make this curry, *Gulai Terung Dengan Daging*, ahead, prepare to the end of step 2 and finish later.

2 Add the coconut milk, water, lemon grass top and seasoning to taste. Cover and simmer gently for 1½ hours, or until the meat is tender.

3 Towards the end of the cooking time heat the remaining oil in a frying pan. Fry the aubergine slices until brown on both sides.

4 Add the browned aubergine slices to the beef curry and cook for a further 15 minutes. Stir gently from time to time. Strain the tamarind and stir the juice into the curry. Taste and adjust the seasoning. Put into a warm serving dish. Garnish with the sliced chilli, if using, and Deep-fried Onions and serve with boiled rice.

Braised Birthday Noodles with Hoisin Lamb

China, the egg symbolizes ntinuity and fertility so it is ·quently included in birthday hes. The noodles traditionally ·ved at birthday celebrations · left long: it is considered bad ·k to cut them since this might orten one's life.

GREDIENTS

ves 4
0g/12oz thick egg noodles
g/2¼lb lean neck fillets of lamb
ml/2 tbsp vegetable oil
5g/4oz fine green beans, topped and ailed, and blanched
: and freshly ground black pepper
ıard-boiled eggs, halved, and
2 spring onions, finely chopped, o garnish

r the marinade
garlic cloves, crushed
ml/2 tsp grated fresh root ginger
ml/2 tbsp soy sauce
ml/2 tbsp rice wine
2 dried red chillies
ml/2 tbsp vegetable oil

r the sauce
ml/1 tbsp cornflour
ml/2 tbsp soy sauce
ml/2 tbsp rice wine
ıted rind and juice of ½ orange
ml/1 tbsp hoisin sauce
ml/1 tbsp wine vinegar
ıl/1 tsp soft light brown sugar

1 Bring a large saucepan of water to the boil. Add the noodles and cook · 2 minutes only. Drain, rinse under ·ld water and drain again. Set aside.

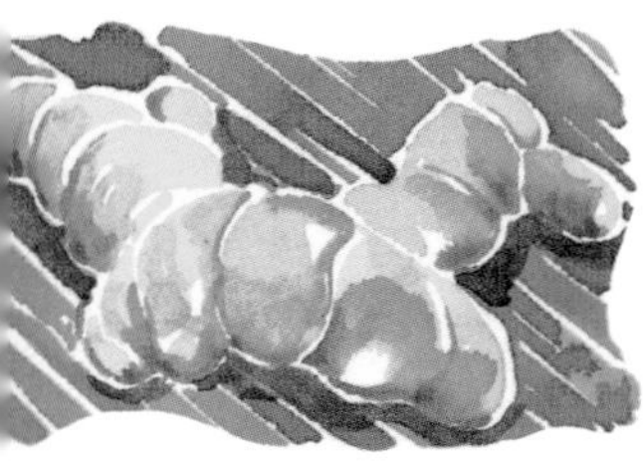

2 Cut the lamb into 5cm/2in thick medallions. Mix the ingredients for the marinade in a large shallow dish. Add the lamb and leave to marinate for at least 4 hours or overnight.

3 Heat the oil in a heavy-based saucepan or flameproof casserole. Fry the lamb for 5 minutes until browned. Add just enough water to cover the meat. Bring to the boil, skim, then reduce the heat and simmer for 40 minutes or until the meat is tender, adding more water as necessary.

4 Make the sauce. Blend the cornflour with the remaining ingredients in a bowl. Stir into the lamb and mix well without breaking up the meat.

5 Add the noodles to the lamb with the beans. Simmer gently until both the noodles and the beans are cooked. Add salt and pepper to taste. Divide the noodles, lamb and beans among four large bowls, garnish each portion with half a hard-boiled egg, sprinkle with spring onions and serve.

Spiced Lamb with Spinach

INGREDIENTS

Serves 3–4

45ml/3 tbsp vegetable oil
500g/1¼lb lean boneless lamb, cut into 2.5cm/1in cubes
1 onion, chopped
3 garlic cloves, finely chopped
1cm/½in fresh root ginger, finely chopped
6 black peppercorns
4 whole cloves
1 bay leaf
3 green cardamom pods, crushed
5ml/1 tsp ground cumin
5ml/1 tsp ground coriander
generous pinch of cayenne pepper
150ml/¼ pint/⅔ cup water
2 tomatoes, peeled, seeded and chopped
5ml/1 tsp salt
400g/14oz fresh spinach, trimmed, washed and finely chopped
5ml/1 tsp garam masala
crisp-fried onions and fresh coriander sprigs, to garnish
naan bread or spiced basmati rice, to serve

1 Heat a wok until hot. Add 30ml/2 tbsp of the oil and swirl it around. When hot, stir-fry the lamb in batches until evenly browned. Remove the lamb and set aside. Add the remaining oil, onion, garlic and ginger and stir-fry for 2–3 minutes.

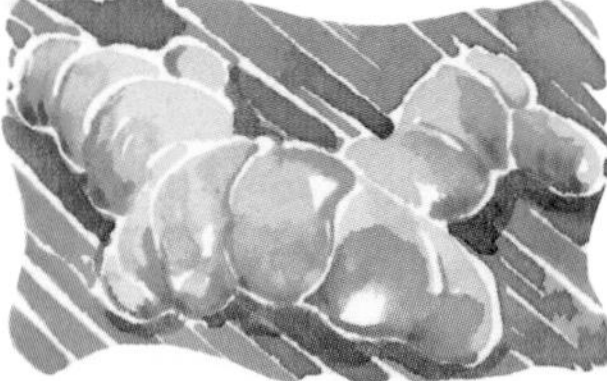

2 Add the peppercorns, cloves, bay leaf, cardamom pods, cumin, ground coriander and cayenne pepper. Stir-fry for 30–45 seconds. Return the lamb and add the water, tomatoes and salt and bring to the boil. Simmer, covered over a very low heat for about 1 hour, stirring occasionally until the meat is cooked and tender.

3 Increase the heat, then gradually add the spinach to the lamb, stirring to mix. Keep stirring and cooking until the spinach wilts completely and most, but not all, of the liquid has evaporated and you are left with a thick green sauce. Stir in the garam masala. Garnish with crisp-fried onions and coriander sprigs. Serve with naan bread or spiced basmati rice.

Glazed Lamb

emon and honey make a assical stir-fry combination in veet dishes, and this lamb recipe iows how well they work gether in savoury dishes, too. erve with a fresh mixed salad to omplete this delicious dish.

IGREDIENTS

rves 4
i0g/1lb boneless lean lamb
ml/1 tbsp grapeseed oil
'5g/6oz mangetouts, topped and tailed
spring onions, sliced
)ml/2 tbsp clear honey
ice of ½ lemon
)ml/2 tbsp chopped fresh coriander
ml/1 tbsp sesame seeds
.t and ground black pepper

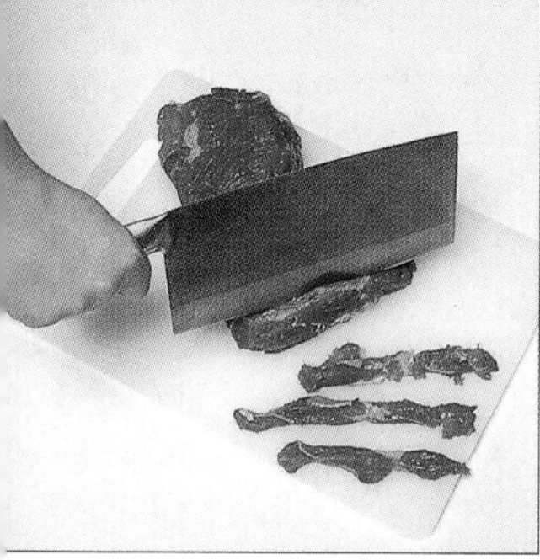

1 Using a cleaver, cut the lamb into thin strips.

COOK'S TIP

This recipe would work just as well made with pork or chicken instead of lamb. You could substitute chopped fresh basil for the coriander if using chicken.

2 Heat the wok, then add the oil. When the oil is hot, stir-fry the lamb until browned all over. Remove from the wok and keep warm.

3 Add the mangetouts and spring onions to the hot wok and stir-fry for 30 seconds.

4 Return the lamb to the wok and add the honey, lemon juice, chopped coriander and sesame seeds and season well. Stir thoroughly to mix. Bring to the boil, then allow to bubble vigorously for 1 minute until the lamb is completely coated in the honey mixture. Serve immediately.

Balti Lamb Tikka

One of the best ways of tenderizing meat is to marinate it in papaya, which must be unripe or it will lend too much sweetness to what should be a savoury dish. Papaya, also known as pawpaw, is readily available from most large supermarkets.

INGREDIENTS

Serves 4

675g/1½lb lean lamb, cubed
1 unripe papaya
45ml/3 tbsp natural yogurt
5ml/1 tsp ginger pulp
5ml/1 tsp chilli powder
5ml/1 tsp garlic pulp
1.5ml/¼ tsp ground turmeric
10ml/2 tsp ground coriander
5ml/1 tsp ground cumin
30ml/2 tbsp lemon juice
15ml/1 tbsp chopped fresh coriander, plus extra for garnishing
1.5ml/¼ tsp red food colouring
300ml/½ pint/1¼ cups corn oil
salt
lemon wedges and onion rings, to garnish
raita and naan, to serve

1 Place the cubed lamb in a large mixing bowl. Peel the papaya, cut in half and scoop out the seeds. Cut the flesh into cubes, place in a food processor or blender and blend until it is pulped, adding about 15ml/1 tbsp water if necessary.

COOK'S TIP

A good-quality meat tenderizer, available from supermarkets, can be used in place of the papaya. However, the meat will need a longer marinating time and should ideally be left to tenderize overnight.

2 Pour about 30ml/2 tbsp of the papaya pulp over the lamb cubes and rub it in well with your fingers. Set aside to marinate for at least 3 hours.

3 Meanwhile, mix together the yogurt, ginger, chilli powder, garlic, turmeric, ground coriander, cumin, lemon juice, fresh coriander, red food colouring and 30ml/2 tbsp of the oil. Season with salt and set aside.

4 Spoon the yogurt mixture over th lamb and mix together well.

5 Heat the remaining oil in a wok. When it is hot, lower the heat slightly and add the lamb cubes, a few at a time. Deep fry the batches of lam for 5–7 minutes or until the lamb is cooked and tender. Transfer each batc to a warmed serving dish and keep warm while you cook the next batch.

6 When all the batches of lamb hav been cooked, garnish with the lemon wedges, onion rings and fresh coriander. Serve with raita and naan.

Paper-thin Lamb with Spring Onions

Spring onions lend a delicious flavour to the lamb in this simple supper dish.

Ingredients

Serves 3–4

450g/1lb lamb neck fillet
30ml/2 tbsp Chinese rice wine or dry sherry
10ml/2 tsp light soy sauce
2.5ml/½ tsp roasted and ground Szechuan peppercorns
2.5ml/½ tsp salt
2.5ml/½ tsp dark brown soft sugar
20ml/4 tsp dark soy sauce
15ml/1 tbsp sesame oil
30ml/2 tbsp groundnut oil
2 garlic cloves, thinly sliced
2 bunches spring onions, cut into 7.5cm/3 in lengths, then shredded
30ml/2 tbsp chopped fresh coriander

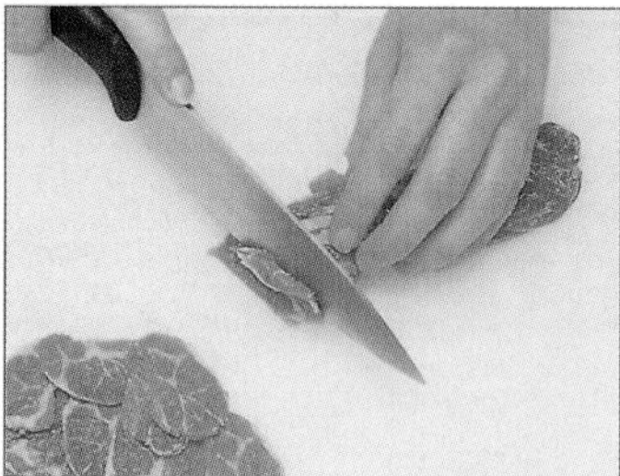

1 Wrap the lamb and place in the freezer for about 1 hour until just frozen. Cut the meat across the grain into paper-thin slices. Put the lamb slices in a bowl, add 10ml/2 tsp of the rice wine or sherry, the soy sauce and ground Szechuan peppercorns. Mix well and set aside to marinate for 15–30 minutes.

2 Make the sauce: in a bowl mix together the remaining rice wine or sherry, the salt, brown sugar, soy sauce and 10ml/2 tsp of the sesame oil. Set aside.

3 Heat the groundnut oil in a preheated wok. Add the garlic and let it sizzle for a few seconds, then add the lamb. Stir-fry for about 1 minute, until the lamb is no longer pink. Pour in the sauce and stir briefly to mix.

4 Add the spring onions and coriander and stir-fry for 15–20 seconds, until the spring onions just wilt. The finished dish should be slightly dry in appearance. Serve at once, sprinkled with the remaining sesame oil.

Cook's Tip

Some large supermarkets sell very thinly sliced lean lamb ready for stir-frying, which makes this dish even quicker to prepare.

Minted Lamb Stir-fry

amb and mint have a long-
stablished partnership that
orks particularly well in this
ill-flavoured stir-fry. Serve with
lenty of crusty bread.

NGREDIENTS

rves 2
75g/10oz lamb neck fillet
)ml/2 tbsp sunflower oil
)ml/2 tsp sesame oil
onion, roughly chopped
garlic cloves, crushed
fresh red chilli, seeded and
finely chopped
5g/3oz fine green beans, halved
25g/8oz fresh spinach
)ml/2 tbsp oyster sauce
)ml/2 tbsp fish sauce
5ml/1 tbsp lemon juice
nl/1 tsp caster sugar
5ml/3 tbsp chopped fresh mint
lt and ground black pepper
esh mint sprigs, to garnish
usty bread, to serve

1 Trim the lamb of any excess fat and cut into thin slices. Heat the nflower and sesame oils in a eheated wok or large frying pan and ir-fry the lamb over a high heat until owned. Remove with a slotted spoon id drain on kitchen paper.

2 Add the onion, garlic and chilli to the wok and cook for 2–3 minutes. Add the beans to the wok and stir-fry for 3 minutes.

3 Stir in the spinach with the browned lamb, oyster sauce, fish sauce, lemon juice and sugar. Stir-fry for a further 3–4 minutes, or until the lamb is cooked through.

4 Sprinkle over the mint, adjust the seasoning and garnish with mint sprigs. Serve piping hot, with plenty of crusty bread to mop up all the juices.

Stir-fried Lamb with Spring Onions

This is a classic Beijing "meat and veg" recipe, in which the lamb can be replaced with either beef or pork, and the spring onions by other strongly flavoured vegetables, such as leeks or onions.

INGREDIENTS

Serves 4

350–400g/12–14oz leg of lamb fillet
5ml/1 tsp light brown sugar
15ml/1 tbsp light soy sauce
15ml/1 tbsp Chinese rice wine or dry sherry
10ml/2 tsp cornflour paste
15g/½oz dried wood ears
300ml/½ pint/1¼ cups vegetable oil
6–8 spring onions
few small pieces of fresh root ginger
30ml/2 tbsp yellow bean sauce
few drops of sesame oil

1 Slice the lamb thinly and place in a shallow dish. Mix together the sugar, soy sauce, rice wine or dry sherry and cornflour paste, pour over the lamb and set aside to marinate for 30–45 minutes. Soak the wood ears in water for 25–30 minutes, then drain and cut into small pieces. Finely chop the spring onions.

2 Heat the oil in a preheated wok and stir-fry the lamb for about 1 minute, or until the colour changes. Remove with a slotted spoon, drain and set aside.

3 Pour off all but about 15ml/1 tbsp oil from the wok, then add the spring onions, ginger, wood ears and yellow bean sauce. Blend well, then add the meat and stir for about 1 minute. Sprinkle with the sesame oil and serve.

Five-spice Lamb

:his aromatic and mouth-vatering lamb dish is perfect for n informal supper party.

NGREDIENTS

erves 4

0ml/2 tbsp oil
.5kg/3–3½lb leg of lamb, boned and cubed
onion, chopped
0ml/2 tsp grated fresh root ginger
garlic clove, crushed
ml/1 tsp Chinese five-spice powder
0ml/2 tbsp hoisin sauce
5ml/1 tbsp light soy sauce
00ml/½ pint/1¼ cups passata
50ml/8fl oz/1 cup lamb stock
red pepper, seeded and diced
yellow pepper, seeded and diced
0ml/2 tbsp chopped fresh coriander
5ml/1 tbsp sesame seeds, toasted
ılt and ground black pepper
oiled rice, to serve

1 Heat 30ml/2 tbsp of the oil in a flameproof casserole and brown the amb in batches over a high heat. Remove and set aside.

2 Add the onion, ginger and garlic to the casserole with a little more oil, f necessary, and cook for about 5 ninutes, until softened.

3 Return the lamb to the casserole. Stir in the five-spice powder, hoisin and soy sauces, passata, stock and seasoning. Bring to the boil, cover and cook in a preheated oven at 160°C/325°F/Gas 3 for 1¼ hours.

4 Remove the casserole from the oven, stir in the peppers, then cover and return to the oven for a further 15 minutes, or until the lamb is cooked and very tender.

5 Sprinkle with the coriander and sesame seeds. Serve hot with rice.

Balti Minced Lamb Koftas with Vegetables

These koftas look most attractive served on their bed of mixed fresh vegetables, especially if you make them quite small.

Ingredients

Serves 4
450g/1lb lean minced lamb
5ml/1 tsp garam masala
5ml/1 tsp ground cumin
5ml/1 tsp ground coriander
5ml/1 tsp garlic pulp
5ml/1 tsp chilli powder
5ml/1 tsp salt
15ml/1 tbsp chopped fresh coriander
1 small onion, finely diced
150ml/¼ pint/⅔ cup corn oil

For the vegetables
45ml/3 tbsp corn oil
1 bunch spring onions, roughly chopped
½ large red pepper, seeded and chopped
½ large green pepper, seeded and chopped
175g/6 oz sweetcorn
225g/8 oz canned butter beans, drained
½ small cauliflower, cut into florets
4 fresh green chillies, chopped

For the garnish
5ml/1 tsp chopped fresh mint
fresh coriander sprigs
15ml/1 tbsp shredded fresh root ginger
½ lime, thinly sliced
15ml/1 tbsp lemon juice

1 Put the minced lamb into a food processor or blender and process for about 1 minute.

2 Transfer the lamb to a bowl and add the garam masala, ground cumin, ground coriander, garlic pulp, chilli powder, salt, fresh coriander and onion. Mix thoroughly using your fingers. Cover the bowl and set aside in the refrigerator.

3 Heat the oil for the vegetables in a preheated wok or frying pan. Add the spring onions and stir-fry for about 2 minutes.

4 Add the red and green peppers, sweetcorn, butter beans, cauliflower and green chillies and stir-fry over a high heat for about 2 minutes. Set the wok or frying pan aside.

5 Remove the kofta mixture from the refrigerator. Using your hands, roll small pieces of the mixture into portions about the size of golf balls. The mixture will make 12–16 koftas.

6 Heat the oil for the koftas in a frying pan. Lower the heat and add the koftas, a few at a time. Shallow fry each batch, turning the koftas, until they are evenly browned. Remove from the oil with a slotted spoon and drain on kitchen paper.

7 Return the wok or frying pan with the vegetables to a medium heat and add the cooked koftas. Stir the mixture gently for about 5 minutes, or until heated through.

8 Transfer to a serving dish and garnish with the mint, coriander, shredded ginger and lime slices. Just before serving, sprinkle over the lemon juice.

Poultry

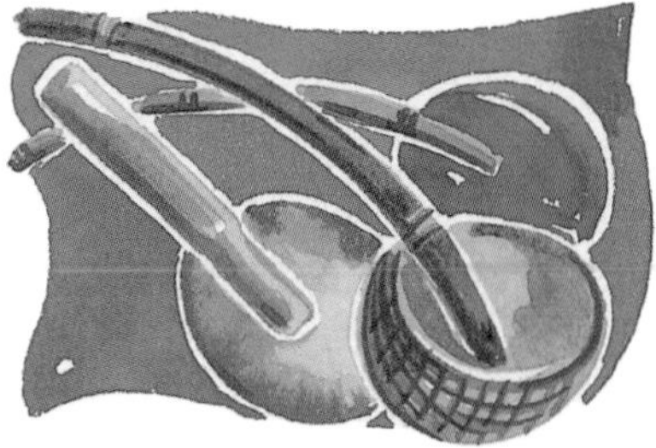

The versatility of chicken has never been so apparent – stir-fried with ginger, baked with spices, braised in coconut milk and even barbecued Thai-style – and, of course, this chapter also includes mouth-watering recipes for other types of poultry. Some dishes are familiar favourites, such as Indonesian-style Satay Chicken and Peking Duck, while others offer new and exciting combinations of ingredients. Try Chilli Duck with Crab and Cashew Sauce, Sweet-sour Duck with Mango, Khara Masala or Balti Baby Chicken in Tamarind Sauce.

Chicken Curry with Rice Vermicelli

Lemon grass gives this South East Asian curry a wonderful lemony flavour and fragrance.

INGREDIENTS

Serves 4

1 chicken, about 1.5kg/3–3½lb
225g/8oz sweet potatoes
60ml/4 tbsp vegetable oil
1 onion, finely sliced
3 garlic cloves, crushed
30–45ml/2–3 tbsp Thai curry powder
5ml/1 tsp sugar
10ml/2 tsp fish sauce
600ml/1 pint/2½ cups coconut milk
1 lemon grass stalk, cut in half
350g/12oz rice vermicelli, soaked in hot water until soft
1 lemon, cut into wedges, to serve

For the garnish
115g/4oz beansprouts
2 spring onions, finely sliced diagonally
2 red chillies, seeded and finely sliced
8–10 mint leaves

1 Skin the chicken. Cut the flesh into small pieces and set aside. Peel the sweet potatoes and cut them into large chunks, about the size of the chicken pieces.

2 Heat half the oil in a large heavy saucepan. Add the onion and garlic and fry until the onion softens.

3 Add the chicken pieces and stir-fry until they change colour. Stir in the curry powder. Season with salt and sugar and mix thoroughly, then stir in the fish sauce.

4 Pour in the coconut milk and ad the lemon grass. Cook over a low heat for 15 minutes.

5 Meanwhile, heat the remaining oi in a large frying pan. Fry the swee potatoes until lightly golden. Using a slotted spoon, add them to the chicke Cook for 10–15 minutes more, or until both the chicken and sweet potatoes are tender.

6 Drain the rice vermicelli and cook it in a saucepan of boiling water f 3–5 minutes. Drain well. Place in shallow bowls, with the chicken curry Garnish with beansprouts, spring onions, chillies and mint leaves and serve with lemon wedges.

Gingered Chicken Noodles

blend of ginger, spices and
conut milk flavours this
elicious supper dish, which is
iade in minutes. For a real
riental touch, add a little fish
uce to taste, just before serving.

IGREDIENTS

rves 4
50g/12oz boneless chicken breasts, skinned
25g/8oz courgettes
75g/10oz aubergine
)ml/2 tbsp vegetable oil
m/2in fresh root ginger, finely chopped
spring onions, sliced
ml/2 tsp Thai green curry paste
)0ml/14fl oz/1⅔ cups coconut milk
75ml/16fl oz/2 cups chicken stock
15g/4oz medium egg noodles
5ml/3 tbsp chopped fresh coriander
5ml/1 tbsp lemon juice
lt and ground black pepper
opped fresh coriander, to garnish

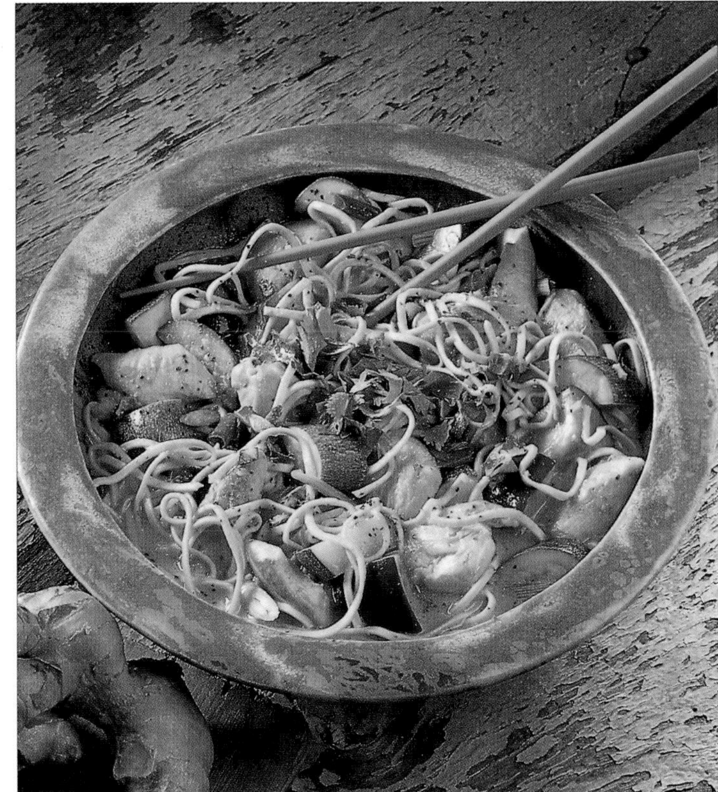

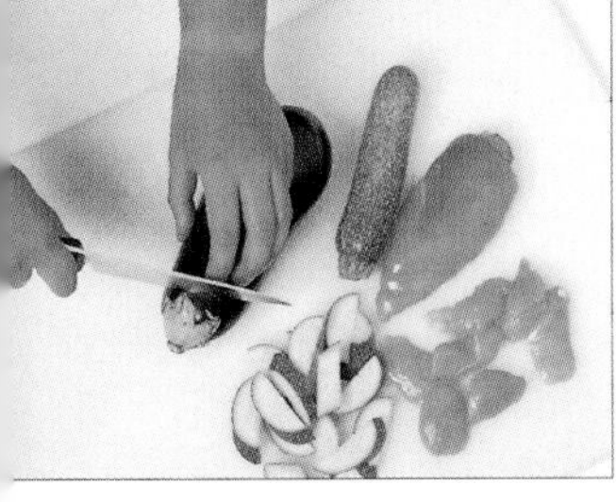

1 Cut the chicken into bite-sized pieces. Halve the courgettes ngthways and roughly chop them. oughly chop the aubergine.

2 Heat the oil in a large saucepan and cook the chicken until golden. emove with a slotted spoon and drain n kitchen paper.

3 Add a little more oil, if necessary, and cook the ginger and spring onions for 3 minutes. Add the courgettes and cook for 2–3 minutes, or until beginning to turn golden. Stir in the Thai curry paste and cook for 1 minute.

4 Add the coconut milk, stock, aubergine and chicken and simmer for 10 minutes. Add the noodles and cook for a further 5 minutes, or until the chicken is cooked and the noodles are tender. Stir in the coriander and lemon juice and adjust the seasoning. Serve immediately garnished with chopped fresh coriander.

Spicy Chicken Stir-fry

The chicken is marinated in an aromatic blend of spices and stir-fried with crisp vegetables. If you find it too spicy, serve with a spoonful of soured cream or yogurt. It's delicious hot or cold.

INGREDIENTS

Serves 4

2.5ml/½ tsp ground turmeric
2.5ml/½ tsp ground ginger
5ml/1 tsp salt
5ml/1 tsp ground black pepper
10ml/2 tsp ground cumin
15ml/1 tbsp ground coriander
15ml/1 tbsp caster sugar
450g/1lb boneless chicken breasts, skinned
1 bunch spring onions
4 celery sticks
2 red peppers, seeded
1 yellow pepper, seeded
175g/6oz courgettes
175g/6oz mangetouts or sugar snap peas
sunflower oil, for frying
15ml/1 tbsp lime juice
15ml/1 tbsp clear honey

1 Mix together the turmeric, ginger, salt, pepper, cumin, coriander and sugar in a bowl until well combined.

2 Cut the chicken into bite-sized strips. Add to the spice mixture and stir to coat the chicken pieces thoroughly. Set aside.

3 Prepare the vegetables. Cut the spring onions, celery and peppers into 5cm/2in-long, thin strips. Cut the courgettes at a slight angle into thin rounds and top and tail the mangetouts or sugar snap peas.

4 Heat 30ml/2 tbsp of oil in a preheated wok or large frying pan. Stir-fry the chicken in batches until cooked through and golden brown, adding a little more oil if necessary. Remove from the pan and keep warm.

5 Add a little more oil to the pan and cook the spring onions, celery, peppers and courgettes over a medium heat for about 8–10 minutes, until beginning to soften and turn golden. Add the mangetouts or sugar snap peas and cook for a further 2 minutes.

6 Return the chicken to the pan, with the lime juice and honey. Cook for 2 minutes. Serve immediately.

Spicy Clay-pot Chicken

Clay-pot cooking stems from the practice of burying a glazed pot in the embers of an open fire. The gentle heat surrounds the base and keeps the liquid inside at a slow simmer, similar to the modern-day casserole.

INGREDIENTS

Serves 4–6

1.5kg/3–3½lb chicken
45ml/3 tbsp freshly grated coconut
30ml/2 tbsp vegetable oil
2 shallots or 1 small onion, finely chopped
2 garlic cloves, crushed
5cm/2in lemon grass
2.5cm/1in galangal or fresh root ginger, thinly sliced
2 small fresh green chillies, seeded and finely chopped
1cm/½ in square shrimp paste or 15ml/1 tbsp fish sauce
400ml/14fl oz/1⅔ cups canned coconut milk
300ml/½ pint/1¼ cups chicken stock
2 kaffir lime leaves (optional)
15ml/1 tbsp sugar
15ml/1 tbsp rice vinegar or white wine vinegar
2 ripe tomatoes, to garnish and 30ml/2 tbsp chopped coriander leaves, to garnish

1 To joint the chicken, remove the legs and wings with a chopping knife. Skin the pieces and divide the drumsticks from the thighs and, using a pair of kitchen scissors, remove the lower part of the chicken, leaving the breast piece. Remove as many of the bones as you can, to make the dish easier to eat. Cut the breast piece into four and set aside.

2 Dry-fry the coconut in a large wok until evenly brown. Add the vegetable oil, shallots or onion, garlic, lemon grass, galangal or ginger, chillies and shrimp paste or fish sauce. Fry briefly to release the flavours. Add the chicken pieces to the wok and brown evenly with the spices for 2–3 minutes.

3 Strain the coconut milk and reserve the thick part. Add the thi part to the wok, together with the chicken stock, lime leaves, if using, sugar and vinegar. Transfer to a glazed clay pot, cover and bake in a preheatec oven at 180°C/350°F/Gas 4 for 50–5 minutes or until the chicken is tender. Stir in the thick part of the coconut milk and return to the oven for 5–10 minutes to simmer and thicken.

4 Place the tomatoes in a bowl and cover with boiling water to loosen and remove the skins. Halve the tomatoes, discard the seeds and cut int large dice. Add the tomatoes to the finished dish, scatter with the chopped coriander and serve.

Green Curry Coconut Chicken

he recipe given here for green ırry paste takes time to make roperly. Pork, prawns and fish n all be used instead of ıicken, but cooking times must adjusted accordingly.

IGREDIENTS

rves 4–6

1kg/2½lb chicken
0ml/1 pint/2½ cups canned coconut milk
0ml/¾ pint/1¾ cups chicken stock
kaffir lime leaves
0g/12oz sweet potatoes, roughly chopped
0g/12oz winter squash, seeded and roughly chopped
5g/4oz French beans, halved
small bunch fresh coriander, shredded, to garnish

or the green curry paste

ml/2 tsp coriander seeds
5ml/½ tsp caraway or cumin seeds
-4 medium fresh green chillies, finely chopped
ml/4 tsp sugar
ml/2 tsp salt
5cm/3in lemon grass
m/¾in galangal or fresh root ginger, finely chopped
garlic cloves, crushed
shallots or 1 medium onion, finely chopped
m/¾in square shrimp paste
ml/3 tbsp finely chopped fresh coriander
ml/3 tbsp finely chopped fresh mint
5ml/½ tsp ground nutmeg
ml/2 tbsp vegetable oil

1 To prepare the chicken, remove the legs, then separate the thighs from e drumsticks. Separate the lower part the chicken carcass by cutting ough the rib section with kitchen ssors. Divide the breast part in half wn the middle, then chop each half two. Remove the skin from all the eces and discard.

2 Strain the coconut milk into a bowl, reserving the thick part. Place the chicken in a stainless steel or enamel saucepan, pour in the thin part of the coconut milk and the stock. Add the lime leaves and simmer, uncovered, for 40 minutes. Remove the chicken from the saucepan and allow to cool. Reserve the cooking liquid. Remove the cooled meat from the bone and set aside.

3 To make the curry paste, dry-fry the coriander seeds and caraway or cumin seeds. Grind the chillies with the sugar and salt in a mortar with a pestle to make a smooth paste. Combine the seeds from the wok with the chilli paste, the lemon grass, galangal or ginger, garlic and shallots or onion, then grind smoothly. Add the shrimp paste, coriander leaves, mint, nutmeg and vegetable oil.

4 Place 250ml/8fl oz/1 cup of the reserved cooking liquid in a large wok. Add 60–75ml/4–5 tbsp of the curry paste to the liquid, according to taste. Boil rapidly until the liquid has reduced completely. Add the chicken stock, chicken meat, sweet potatoes, squash and beans. Simmer for 10–15 minutes until the potatoes are cooked. Stir in the thick part of the coconut milk and simmer gently to thicken. Serve garnished with coriander.

Chicken Cooked in Coconut Milk

Traditionally, the chicken pieces would be part-cooked by frying, but I think that roasting in the oven is a better option. *Ayam Opor* is an unusual recipe in that the sauce is white as it does not contain chillies or turmeric, unlike many other Indonesian dishes. The dish is served with crisp Deep-fried Onions.

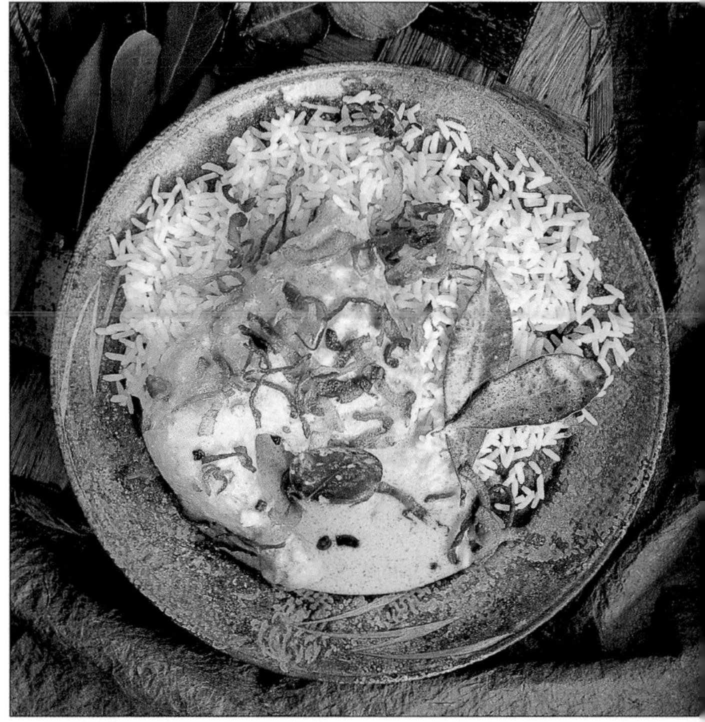

Ingredients

Serves 4

1.5kg/3–3½ lb chicken or 4 chicken quarters
4 garlic cloves
1 onion, sliced
4 macadamia nuts or 8 almonds
15ml/1 tbsp coriander seeds, dry-fried, or 5ml/1 tsp ground coriander
45ml/3 tbsp oil
2.5cm/1in fresh *lengkuas*, peeled and bruised
2 lemon grass stems, fleshy part bruised
3 lime leaves
2 bay leaves
5ml/1 tsp sugar
600ml/1 pint/2½ cups coconut milk
salt
boiled rice and deep-fried onions, to serve

1 Preheat the oven to 190°C/375°F/Gas 5. Cut the chicken into four or eight pieces. Season with salt. Put in an oiled roasting tin and cook in the oven for 25–30 minutes. Meanwhile prepare the sauce.

2 Grind the garlic, onion, nuts and coriander to a fine paste in a food processor or with a pestle and mortar. Heat the oil and fry the paste to bring out the flavour. Do not allow it to brown.

3 Add the part-cooked chicken pieces to a wok together with the *lengkuas*, lemon grass, lime and bay leaves, sugar, coconut milk and salt to taste. Mix well to coat in the sauce.

4 Bring to the boil and then reduce the heat and simmer gently for 30–40 minutes, uncovered, until the chicken is tender and the coconut sauce is reduced and thickened. Stir t mixture occasionally during cooking.

5 Just before serving remove the bruised *lengkuas* and lemon grass. Serve with boiled rice sprinkled with crisp deep-fried onions.

Chicken Teriyaki

simple bowl of boiled rice is
e ideal accompaniment to this
btle Japanese chicken dish.

GREDIENTS

ves 4
0g/1lb boneless chicken breasts,
kinned
ange segments and mustard and cress,
o garnish

r the marinade
ıl/1 tsp sugar
ml/1 tbsp sake
ml/1 tbsp dry sherry
ml/2 tbsp dark soy sauce
ıted rind of 1 orange

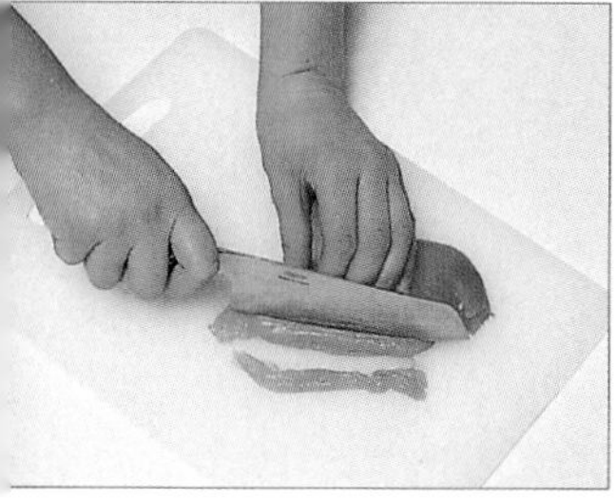

Slice the chicken into long, thin strips using a cleaver or sharp knife.

Mix together the sugar, sake, dry sherry, soy sauce and grated orange d in a bowl.

3 Place the chicken in a separate bowl, pour over the marinade and set aside to marinate for 15 minutes.

4 Add the chicken and the marinade to a preheated wok and stir-fry for 4–5 minutes. Serve garnished with orange segments and mustard and cress.

Shredded Chicken with Celery

The tender chicken breast contrasts with the crunchy texture of the celery, and the red chillies add colour and flavour.

INGREDIENTS

Serves 4

275g/10oz boneless chicken breast, skinned
5ml/1 tsp salt
½ egg white, lightly beaten
10ml/2 tsp cornflour paste
475ml/16fl oz/2 cups vegetable oil
1 celery heart, thinly shredded
1–2 fresh red chillies, seeded and thinly shredded
1 spring onion, thinly shredded
few strips of fresh root ginger, thinly shredded
5ml/1 tsp light brown sugar
15ml/1 tbsp Chinese rice wine or dry sherry
few drops of sesame oil

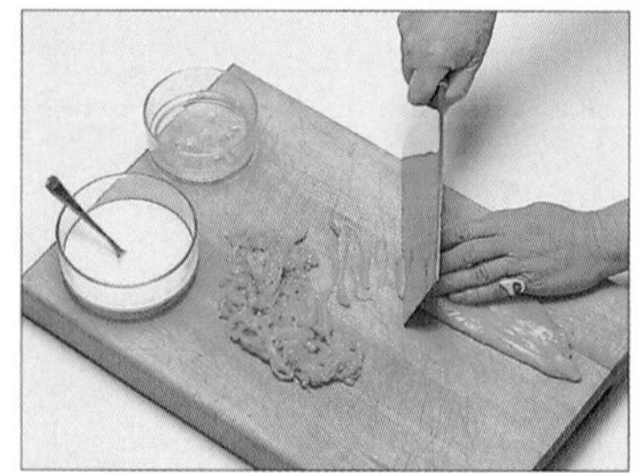

1 Using a sharp knife, thinly shred the chicken. In a bowl, mix together a pinch of the salt, the egg white and cornflour paste. Stir in the chicken.

2 Heat the oil in a preheated wok, add the chicken and stir to separate the shreds. When the chicken turns white, remove with a strainer and drain. Keep warm.

3 Pour off all but 30ml/2 tbsp of the oil. Add the celery, chillies, spring onion and ginger to the wok and stir-fry for 1 minute. Add the chicken, remaining salt, sugar and rice wine or dry sherry. Cook for 1 minute, then add the sesame oil. Serve hot.

Chicken with Chinese Vegetables

This dish makes an excellent family main course served with rice or noodles, but also combines with a selection of other dishes to serve as part of a dinner party menu.

INGREDIENTS

Serves 4

225–275g/8–10oz boneless chicken, skinned
5ml/1 tsp salt
½ egg white, lightly beaten
10ml/2 tsp cornflour paste
60ml/4 tbsp vegetable oil
6–8 small dried shiitake mushrooms, soaked in hot water
115g/4oz canned sliced bamboo shoots, drained
115g/4oz mangetouts
1 spring onion, cut into short sections
few small pieces of fresh root ginger
5ml/1 tsp light brown sugar
15ml/1 tbsp light soy sauce
15ml/1 tbsp Chinese rice wine or dry sherry
few drops of sesame oil

1 Cut the chicken into thin slices, each about the size of an oblong postage stamp. Place it in a bowl and mix with a pinch of the salt, the egg white and the cornflour paste.

2 Heat the oil in a preheated wok, add the chicken and stir-fry over medium heat for about 30 seconds, then remove with a slotted spoon and keep warm.

3 Add the vegetables to the wok and stir-fry over high heat for about 1 minute. Add the remaining salt, the sugar and chicken. Blend, then add the soy sauce and rice wine or dry sherry. Stir for a further 1 minute. Sprinkle with the sesame oil and serve.

Fu-yung Chicken

Because the egg whites mixed with milk are deep fried in a wok, they have prompted some imaginative cooks to refer to this dish as "Deep Fried Milk"!

INGREDIENTS

Serves 4

175g/6oz chicken breast fillet, skinned
5ml/1 tsp salt
4 egg whites, lightly beaten
15ml/1 tbsp cornflour paste
30ml/2 tbsp milk
vegetable oil, for deep frying
1 lettuce heart, separated into leaves
about 120ml/4fl oz/½ cup stock
15ml/1 tbsp Chinese rice wine or dry sherry
15ml/1 tbsp green peas
few drops sesame oil
5ml/1 tsp minced ham, to garnish

1 Finely mince the chicken meat, then mix with a pinch of the salt, the egg whites, cornflour paste and milk. Blend well until smooth.

2 Heat the oil in a very hot wok, bu before the oil gets too hot, gently spoon the chicken and egg white mixture into the oil in batches. Do no stir, otherwise it will scatter. Stir the o from the bottom of the wok so that th egg whites will rise to the surface. Remove as soon as the colour turns bright white. Drain.

3 Pour off the excess oil, leaving about 15ml/1 tbsp in the wok. Stir-fry the lettuce leaves with the remaining salt for 1 minute, add the stock and bring to the boil.

4 Add the chicken to the wok with the rice wine and peas, and blend well. Sprinkle with sesame oil, garnish with ham and serve immediately.

Szechuan Chicken

wok is the ideal cooking pot or this stir-fried chicken dish. he flavours emerge wonderfully nd the chicken is fresh and crisp.

NGREDIENTS

rves 4

50g/12oz chicken thigh, boned and skinned
5ml/¼ tsp salt
egg white, lightly beaten
0ml/2 tsp cornflour paste
green pepper, cored and seeded
0ml/4 tbsp vegetable oil
-4 whole dried red chillies, soaked in water for 10 minutes
spring onion, cut into short sections
w small pieces of fresh root ginger, peeled
5ml/1 tbsp sweet bean paste or hoi-sin sauce
ml/1 tsp chilli bean paste
5ml/1 tbsp Chinese rice wine or dry sherry
15g/4oz roasted cashew nuts
w drops sesame oil

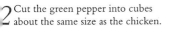

1 Cut the chicken meat into small cubes, each about the size of a ıgar lump. Mix together the chicken, ılt, egg white and cornflour paste a bowl.

2 Cut the green pepper into cubes about the same size as the chicken.

3 Heat the oil in a preheated wok. Stir-fry the chicken cubes for about 1 minute, or until the colour changes. Remove from the wok with a slotted spoon and keep warm.

4 Add the green pepper, chillies, spring onion and ginger and stir-fry for about 1 minute. Then add the chicken, sweet bean paste or hoi-sin sauce, chilli bean paste and rice wine or sherry. Blend well and cook for 1 minute more. Finally add the cashew nuts and sesame oil. Serve hot.

Indonesian-style Satay Chicken

Satay traditionally forms part of a *Rijsttafel* – literally rice table – a vast feast of as many as 40 different dishes served with a large bowl of plain rice. However, for the less ambitious, creamy coconut satay makes these chicken pieces a mouth-watering dish to present at the table at any time of the day.

Ingredients

Serves 4

50g/2oz raw peanuts
45ml/3 tbsp vegetable oil
1 small onion, finely chopped
2.5cm/1in fresh root ginger, peeled and finely chopped
1 clove garlic, crushed
675g/1½lb chicken thighs, skinned and cut into cubes
90g/3½oz creamed coconut, roughly chopped
15ml/1 tbsp chilli sauce
60ml/4 tbsp crunchy peanut butter
5ml/1 tsp soft dark brown sugar
150ml/¼ pint/⅔ cup milk
1.5ml/¼ tsp salt

1 Shell the peanuts and remove the skins by rubbing them between the palms of the hands. Put them in a small bowl, add just enough water to cover and soak for 1 minute. Drain the nuts and cut them into slivers.

2 Heat the wok and add 5ml/1 tsp oil. When the oil is hot, stir-fry the peanuts for 1 minute until crisp and golden. Remove with a slotted spoon and drain on kitchen paper.

3 Add the remaining oil to the hot wok. When the oil is hot, add the onion, ginger and garlic and stir-fry for 2–3 minutes until softened but not browned. Remove with a slotted spoon and drain on kitchen paper.

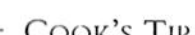

Cook's Tip

Soak bamboo skewers in cold water for at least 2 hours, or preferably overnight, so that they do not char when keeping the threaded chicken warm in the oven.

4 Add the chicken pieces to the wok and stir-fry for 3–4 minutes until crisp and golden on all sides. Thread on to pre-soaked bamboo skewers and keep warm.

5 Add the creamed coconut to the hot wok in small pieces and stir-fry until melted. Add the chilli sauce, peanut butter and ginger mixture and simmer for 2 minutes. Stir in the sugar, milk and salt, and simmer for a further 3 minutes. Serve the skewered chicken hot, with a dish of the hot dipping sauce sprinkled with the roasted peanuts.

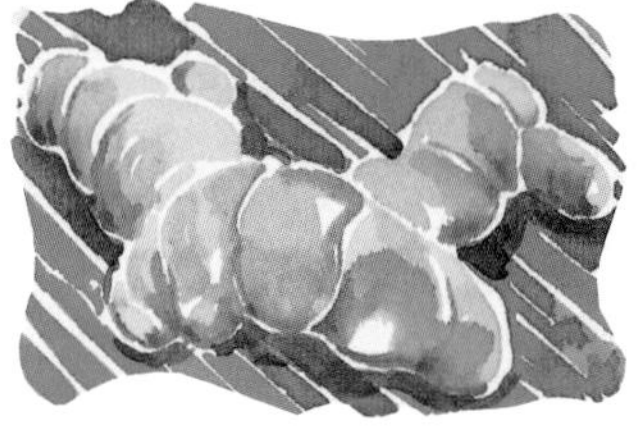

Hot Chilli Chicken

A tantalizing mixture of lemon grass and ginger provides the flavourings for this chicken feast. The ingredients are gently simmered in a wok to achieve a superb end effect.

Ingredients

Serves 4–6

3 chicken legs, thighs and drumsticks
15ml/1 tbsp vegetable oil
2cm/¾in fresh root ginger, peeled and finely chopped
1 clove garlic, crushed
1 small red chilli, seeded and finely chopped
5cm/2in lemon grass stalk, shredded
150ml/¼ pint/⅔ cup chicken stock
15ml/1 tbsp fish sauce (optional)
10ml/2 tsp sugar
2.5ml/½ tsp salt
juice of ½ lemon
50g/2oz raw peanuts
2 spring onions, shredded
rind of 1 mandarin orange or satsuma, shredded
30ml/2 tbsp chopped fresh mint, to garnish
rice or rice noodles, to serve

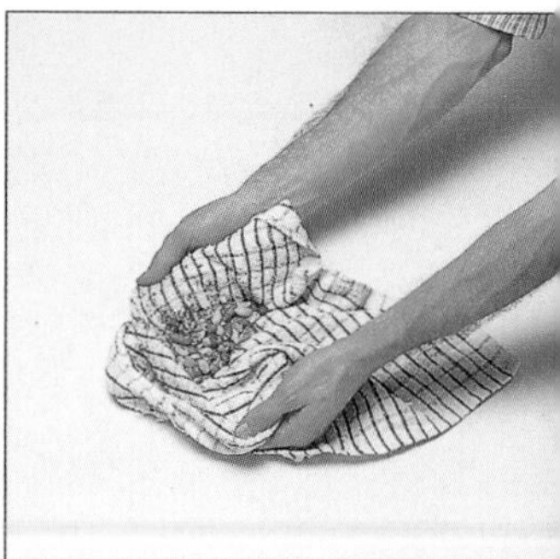

1 With the heel of the knife, chop through the narrow end of the drumsticks. Remove the jointed parts of the drumsticks and thigh bones, then remove the skin.

2 Heat the oil in a large preheated wok. Add the chicken, ginger, garlic, chilli and lemon grass and cook for 3–4 minutes. Add the chicken stock, fish sauce, if using, sugar, salt and lemon juice. Lower the heat, cover and simmer for 30–35 minutes.

3 To prepare the peanuts for the topping, grill or roast them under steady heat until evenly brown, for about 2–3 minutes. Turn the nuts out on to a dish towel and rub briskly to loosen the skins.

4 Serve the chicken scattered with roasted peanuts, shredded spring onions and the rind of the mandarin orange or satsuma. Garnish with mint and serve with rice or rice noodles.

Cook's Tip

This dish can also be prepared using duck legs. Be sure to remove the jointed parts of the drumsticks and thigh bones to make the meat easier to eat with chopsticks.

Stir-fried Chicken with Basil and Chillies

his quick and easy chicken dish an excellent introduction to hai cuisine. Deep frying the ısil adds another dimension to ıis dish. Thai basil, which is ›metimes known as Holy basil, ıs a unique, pungent flavour ıat is both spicy and sharp. The ıll leaves have serrated edges.

IGREDIENTS

rves 4–6

ml/3 tbsp vegetable oil
garlic cloves, sliced
-4 red chillies, seeded and chopped
0g/1lb chicken, cut into
bite-size pieces
)–45ml/2–3 tbsp fish sauce
)ml/2 tsp dark soy sauce
nl/1 tsp sugar
)–12 Thai basil leaves
red chillies, finely sliced, to garnish
) Thai basil leaves, deep fried
(optional)

1 Heat the oil in a wok or large frying pan and swirl it around.

COOK'S TIP

To deep fry Thai basil leaves, make sure that the leaves are completely dry. Deep fry in hot oil for about 30–40 seconds, lift out and drain on kitchen paper.

2 Add the garlic and chillies and stir-fry until golden.

3 Add the chicken and stir-fry until it changes colour.

4 Season with fish sauce, soy sauce and sugar. Continue to stir-fry for 3-4 minutes or until the chicken is cooked. Stir in the fresh Thai basil leaves. Garnish with sliced chillies and the deep fried basil, if using.

Chicken and Cashew Nut Stir-fry

Hoi-sin sauce lends a sweet yet slightly hot note to this chicken stir-fry, while cashew nuts add a pleasing contrast of texture.

INGREDIENTS

Serves 4

75g/3oz cashew nuts
1 red pepper
450g/1lb skinless chicken breast fillets
45ml/3 tbsp groundnut oil
4 garlic cloves, finely chopped
30ml/2 tbsp Chinese rice wine or dry sherry
45ml/3 tbsp hoi-sin sauce
10ml/2 tsp sesame oil
5–6 spring onions, green parts only, cut into 2.5cm/1in lengths

1 Heat a wok until hot, add the cashew nuts and dry fry over a low to medium heat for 1–2 minutes until golden brown. Remove and set aside.

COOK'S TIP

Use blanched almonds instead of cashew nuts, if you prefer. If you prefer a slightly less sweet taste, you could substitute light soy sauce for the hoi-sin sauce.

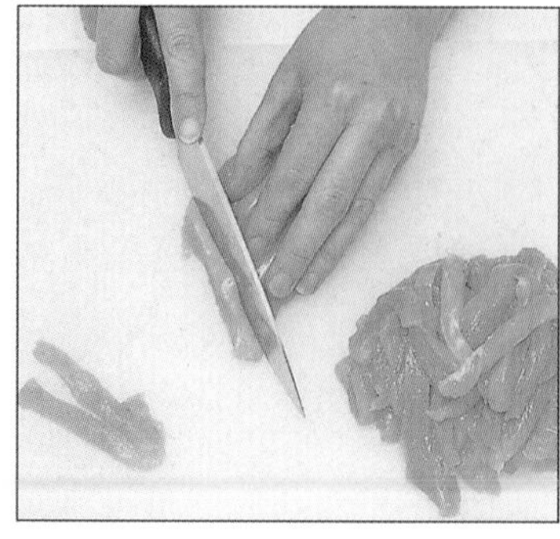

2 Cut the red pepper in half and remove the core and seeds. Slice into thin strips. Cut the chicken fillet into thin finger-length strips.

3 Heat the wok again until hot, add the oil and swirl it around. Add the garlic and let it sizzle in the oil for a few seconds. Add the pepper and chicken and stir-fry for 2 minutes.

4 Add the rice wine or sherry and hoi-sin sauce. Continue to stir-fry until the chicken is tender and all the ingredients are evenly glazed.

5 Stir in the sesame oil, toasted cashew nuts and spring onion tips. Serve immediately.

Chicken, Ham and Broccoli Stir-fry

The charmingly poetic Chinese name for this pretty and colourful dish – *jin hua yi shu ji* – means "golden flower and jade tree chicken". It is a marvellous, cold-buffet-style stir-fry to serve on any occasion.

INGREDIENTS

Serves 6–8

1 chicken, about 1–1.35kg/2¼–3lb
2 spring onions
2–3 pieces fresh root ginger
15ml/1 tbsp salt
275g/8oz honey-roast ham
285g/10oz broccoli
45ml/3 tbsp vegetable oil
5ml/1 tsp light brown sugar
10ml/2 tsp cornflour

1 Place the chicken in a large pan and cover it with cold water. Add the spring onions, ginger and about 10ml/2 tsp of the salt. Bring to the boil, then reduce the heat and simmer for 10–15 minutes under a tightly-fitting lid. Turn off the heat and let the chicken cook itself in the hot water for at least 4–5 hours; do not lift the lid as this will let out the residual heat.

2 Remove the chicken from the pan reserving the liquid, and carefully cut the meat away from the bones, keeping the skin on. Slice both the chicken and ham into pieces, each the size of a matchbox, and arrange the meats in alternating layers on a plate.

3 Cut the broccoli into small florets and stir-fry in the hot oil with the remaining salt and the sugar for about 2–3 minutes. Arrange the broccoli between the rows of chicken and ham and around the edge of the plate, making a border for the meat.

4 Heat 30ml/2tbsp of the chicken stock and thicken it with the cornflour. Stir until smooth, then pour it evenly all over the chicken and ham to form a thin coat of transparent jelly. Allow to cool before serving.

Stir-fried Sweet and Sour Chicken

his all-in-one stir-fry has a ›uth-east Asian influence, and it ideal for today's cook who is so ten short of time.

IGREDIENTS

rves 4

5g/10oz Chinese egg noodles
ml/2 tbsp vegetable oil
spring onions, chopped
garlic clove, crushed
5cm/1in fresh root ginger, peeled and grated
nl/1 tsp hot paprika
nl/1 tsp ground coriander
chicken breast fillets, sliced
5g/4oz sugar snap peas, topped and tailed
5g/4oz baby sweetcorn, halved
25g/8oz fresh beansprouts
5ml/1 tbsp cornflour
5ml/3 tbsp soy sauce
5ml/3 tbsp lemon juice
5ml/1 tbsp sugar
lt
5ml/3 tbsp chopped fresh coriander or spring onion tops, to garnish

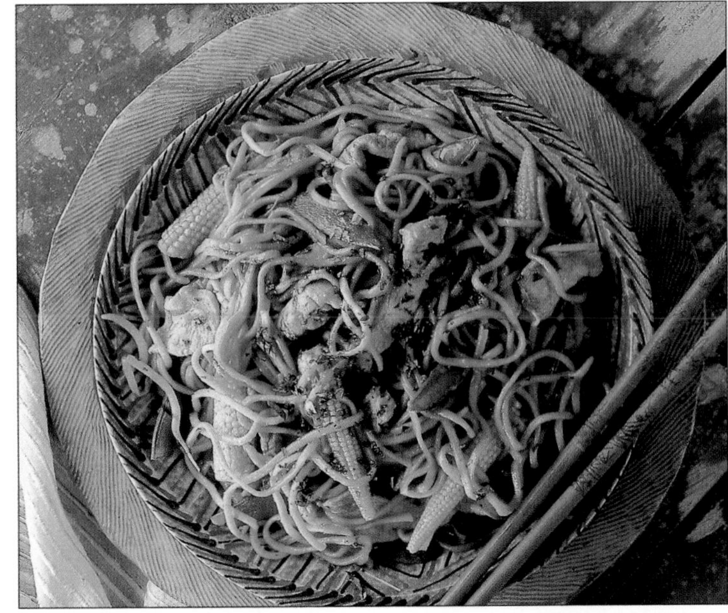

1 Bring a large saucepan of salted water to the boil. Add the noodles id cook according to the packet structions if using dried noodles. If sing fresh egg noodles, cook for a few inutes only, stirring occasionally to parate. Drain thoroughly, cover and eep warm.

2 Heat the oil in a pre-heated wok. Add the spring onions and cook over a gentle heat. Mix in the garlic, ginger, paprika, coriander and chicken, then stir-fry for 3–4 minutes.

3 Add the peas, baby sweetcorn and beansprouts, cover and cook briefly. Add the noodles.

4 Combine the cornflour, soy sauce, lemon juice and sugar in a small bowl. Add to the wok and simmer briefly to thicken. Serve immediately, garnished with chopped coriander or spring onion tops.

COOK'S TIP

Large wok lids are cumbersome and can be difficult to store in a small kitchen. Consider placing a circle of greaseproof paper against the food surface to keep the cooking juices in.

Balti Chicken with Lentils

This is rather an unusual combination of flavours, but it is certainly worth trying! The mango powder gives a delicious tangy flavour to this spicy dish.

INGREDIENTS

Serves 4–6
75g/3oz split yellow lentils
60ml/4 tbsp corn oil
2 medium leeks, chopped
6 large dried red chillies
4 curry leaves
5ml/1 tsp mustard seeds
10ml/2 tsp mango powder
2 medium tomatoes, chopped
2.5ml/½ tsp chilli powder
5ml/1 tsp ground coriander
450g/1lb boneless chicken, skinned and cubed
salt
15ml/1 tbsp chopped fresh coriander, to garnish
paratha, to serve

1 Put the lentils in a sieve and wash carefully under plenty of cold running water.

2 Put the lentils in a saucepan and add just enough water to cover. Bring to the boil and cook for 10 minutes or until they are soft but not mushy. Drain thoroughly, transfer to a bowl and set aside.

3 Heat the oil in a pre-heated wok until hot. Lower the heat and add the leeks, dried red chillies, curry leaves and mustard seeds and stir-fry gently for 2–3 minutes.

4 Add the mango powder, tomatoes, chilli powder, ground coriander and chicken. Season with salt and stir-fry for 7–10 minutes.

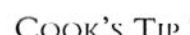

COOK'S TIP

Split yellow lentils, known as chana dhal, are available from Asian stores. However, if you cannot get them, split yellow peas are a good substitute.

5 Mix in the cooked lentils and fry for a further 2 minutes or until the chicken is cooked through.

6 Garnish with fresh coriander and serve immediately with paratha.

Aromatic Chicken from Madura

Magadip is best cooked ahead so that the flavours permeate the chicken flesh making it even more delicious. A cool cucumber salad is a good accompaniment.

Ingredients

Serves 4

1.5kg/3–3½lb chicken, cut in quarters, or 4 chicken quarters
5ml/1 tsp sugar
30ml/2 tbsp coriander seeds
10ml/2 tsp cumin seeds
6 whole cloves
2.5ml/½ tsp ground nutmeg
2.5ml/½ tsp ground turmeric
1 small onion
2.5cm/1in fresh root ginger, peeled and sliced
300ml/½ pint/1¼ cups chicken stock or water
salt and freshly ground black pepper
boiled rice and Deep-fried Onions, to serve

1 Cut each chicken quarter in half to obtain eight pieces. Place in a flameproof casserole, sprinkle with sugar and salt and toss together. This helps release the juices in the chicken. Use the backbone and any remaining carcass to make chicken stock for use later in the recipe, if you like.

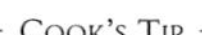

Cook's Tip

Add a large piece of bruised ginger and a small onion to the chicken stock to ensure a good flavour.

2 Dry-fry the coriander, cumin and whole cloves until the spices give off a good aroma. Add the nutmeg and turmeric and heat briefly. Grind in a food processor or a pestle and mortar.

3 If using a processor, process the onion and ginger until finely chopped. Otherwise, finely chop the onion and ginger and pound to a paste with a pestle and mortar. Add the spices and stock or water and mix well.

4 Pour over the chicken in the flameproof casserole. Cover with a lid and cook over a gentle heat until the chicken pieces are really tender, about 45–50 minutes.

5 Serve portions of the chicken, with the sauce, on boiled rice, scattered with crisp Deep-fried Onions.

Chicken with Turmeric

GREDIENTS

ves 4

kg/3–3½lb chicken, cut in 8 pieces,
or 4 chicken quarters, each halved
ml/1 tbsp sugar
nacadamia nuts or 6 almonds
arlic cloves, crushed
arge onion, quartered
cm/1in fresh *lengkuas*, peeled and
liced, or 5ml/1 tsp *lengkuas* powder
2 lemon grass stems, lower 5cm/2in
liced, top bruised
m/½ in cube *terasi*
n/1½ in fresh turmeric, peeled and
liced, or 15ml/1 tbsp
ground turmeric
ml/1 tbsp tamarind pulp, soaked in
150ml/¼ pint/⅔ cup warm water
–90ml/4–6 tbsp oil
0ml/14fl oz/1⅔ cups coconut milk
t and freshly ground black pepper
ep-fried Onions, to garnish

1 Rub the chicken joints with a little sugar and set them aside.

2 Grind the nuts and garlic in a food processor with the onion, *lengkuas*, sliced lemon grass, *terasi*, and turmeric. Alternatively, pound the ingredients to a paste with a pestle and mortar. Strain the tamarind pulp and reserve the juice.

3 Heat the oil in a wok and cook the paste, without browning, until it gives off a spicy aroma. Add the pieces of chicken and toss well in the spices. Add the strained tamarind juice. Spoon the coconut cream off the top of the milk and set it to one side.

4 Add the coconut milk to the pan. Cover and cook for 45 minutes, or until the chicken is tender.

5 Just before serving, stir in the coconut cream while coming to the boil. Season and serve at once, garnished with Deep-fried Onions.

Spiced Chicken Stir-fry

Ingredients

Serves 4

1.5kg/3–3½lb chicken, cut in 8 pieces
5ml/1 tsp each salt and freshly ground black pepper
2 garlic cloves, crushed
150ml/¼ pint/⅔ cup sunflower oil

For the sauce

25g/1oz butter
30ml/2 tbsp sunflower oil
1 onion, sliced
4 garlic cloves, crushed
2 large, ripe beefsteak tomatoes, sliced and chopped, or 400g/14oz can chopped tomatoes with chilli, drained
600ml/1 pint/2½ cups water
50ml/2fl oz/¼ cup dark soy sauce
salt and freshly ground black pepper
sliced fresh red chilli, to garnish
Deep-fried Onions, to garnish (optional)
boiled rice, to serve

1 Preheat the oven to 190°C/375°F/Gas 5. Make two slashes in the fleshy part of each chicken piece. Rub well with the salt, pepper and garlic. Drizzle with a little of the oil and bake for 30 minutes, or shallow-fry, in hot oil for 12–15 minutes, until brown.

2 To make the sauce, heat the butter and oil in a wok and fry the onion and garlic until soft. Add the tomatoes, water, soy sauce and seasoning. Boil briskly for 5 minutes, to reduce the sauce and concentrate the flavour.

3 Add the chicken to the sauce in the wok. Turn the chicken piece over in the sauce to coat them well. Continue cooking slowly for about 20 minutes until the chicken pieces a tender. Stir the mixture occasionally.

4 Arrange the chicken on a warm serving platter and garnish with t sliced chilli and Deep-fried Onions, i using. Serve with boiled rice.

Stir-fried Chicken with Pineapple

Ingredients

Serves 4–6

500g/1¼lb boneless, skinless chicken breasts, thinly sliced at an angle
30ml/2 tbsp cornflour
60ml/4 tbsp sunflower oil
1 garlic clove, crushed
5cm/2in fresh root ginger, peeled and cut in matchsticks
1 small onion, thinly sliced
1 fresh pineapple, peeled, cored and cubed, or 425g/15oz can pineapple chunks in natural juice
30ml/2 tbsp dark soy sauce or 15ml/1 tbsp *kecap manis*
1 bunch spring onions, white bulbs left whole, green tops sliced
salt and freshly ground black pepper

1 Toss the strips of chicken in the cornflour with a little seasoning. Fry in hot oil until tender.

2 Lift out of the wok or frying pan and keep warm. Reheat the oil and fry the garlic, ginger and onion until soft, but not browned. Add the fresh pineapple and 120ml/4fl oz/½ cup water, or the canned pineapple pieces together with their juice.

3 Stir in the soy sauce or *kecap man* and return the chicken to the pa to heat through.

4 Taste and adjust the seasoning. St in the whole spring onion bulbs and half of the sliced green tops. Toss well together and then turn the chicken stir-fry on to a serving platte Serve garnished with the remaining sliced green spring onions.

Soy-braised Chicken

As the chicken is braised in the wok, so the spicy ginger sauce releases its flavour into the meat to create a succulent dish. Enjoy it hot or cold.

INGREDIENTS

Serves 6–8
1 chicken, about 1.5kg/3–3½lb
15ml/1 tbsp ground Szechuan peppercorns
30ml/2 tbsp minced fresh root ginger
45ml/3 tbsp light soy sauce
30ml/2 tbsp dark soy sauce
45ml/3 tbsp Chinese rice wine or dry sherry
15ml/1 tbsp light brown sugar
vegetable oil, for deep frying
about 600ml/1 pint/2½ cups stock or water
10ml/2 tsp salt
25g/1oz crystal sugar
lettuce leaves, to serve

1 Rub the chicken both inside and out with the ground pepper and fresh ginger. Marinate the chicken with the soy sauces, rice wine or sherry and sugar for at least 3 hours, turning it several times.

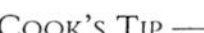

COOK'S TIP

Any sauce that is left over can be stored, covered, in the refrigerator to be re-used again and again.

2 Heat the oil in a preheated wok, remove the chicken from the marinade and deep-fry for 5–6 minutes, or until brown all over. Remove and drain.

3 Pour off the excess oil, add the marinade with the stock or water, salt and rock sugar and bring to the boil. Cover and braise the chicken in the sauce for 35–40 minutes, turning once or twice.

4 Remove the chicken from the wo and let it cool down a little before chopping it into approximately 30 bit sized pieces. Arrange on a bed of lettuce leaves, then pour some of the sauce over the chicken and serve.

Chicken with Spices and Soy Sauce

. very simple recipe, called *yam Kecap,* which will often ɔpear as one of the dishes on a adang restaurant menu. Any ftovers taste equally good when :heated the following day.

IGREDIENTS

erves 4

- 5kg/3–3½lb chicken, jointed and cut in 16 pieces
- onions, sliced
- ɔout 1 litre/1¾ pints/4 cups water
- garlic cloves, crushed
- -4 fresh red chillies, seeded and sliced, or 15ml/1 tbsp chilli powder
- 5–60ml/3–4 tbsp oil
- 5ml/½ tsp ground nutmeg
- whole cloves
- nl/1 tsp tamarind pulp, soaked in 45ml/3 tbsp warm water
-)–45ml/2–3 tbsp dark or light soy sauce
- lt
- esh red chilli shreds, to garnish
- ɔiled rice, to serve

1 Prepare the chicken and place the pieces in a large pan with one of ıe onions. Pour over enough water to ıst cover. Bring to the boil and then :duce the heat and simmer gently for) minutes.

2 Grind the remaining onions, with the garlic and chillies, to a fine ıste in a food processor or with a estle and mortar. Heat a little of the l in a wok or frying pan and cook the ıste to bring out the flavour, but do ɔt allow to brown.

3 When the chicken has cooked for 20 minutes, lift it out of the stock in the pan using a draining spoon and put it straight into the spicy mixture. Toss everything together over a fairly high heat so that the spices permeate the chicken pieces. Reserve 300ml/½ pint/1¼ cups of the chicken stock to add to the pan later.

4 Stir in the nutmeg and cloves. Strain the tamarind and add the tamarind juice and the soy sauce to the chicken. Cook for a further 2–3 minutes, then add the reserved stock.

5 Taste and adjust the seasoning and cook, uncovered, for a further 25–35 minutes, until the chicken pieces are tender.

6 Serve the chicken in a bowl, topped with shredded chilli, and eat with boiled rice.

COOK'S TIP

Dark soy sauce is thicker and more salty than light. Adding the dark variety will give a deeper colour to the chicken.

Thai Stir-fry Chicken Curry

Here chicken and potatoes are simmered in a wok filled with coconut milk, one of the essential ingredients of Thai cuisine. The end result is a superb flavoursome curry.

INGREDIENTS

Serves 4

1 onion
15ml/1 tbsp groundnut oil
400ml/14fl oz/$1^2/_3$ cups coconut milk
30ml/2 tbsp red curry paste
30ml/2 tbsp Thai fish sauce (*nam pla*)
15ml/1 tbsp soft light brown sugar
225g/8oz tiny new potatoes
450g/1lb skinless chicken breasts, cut into chunks
15ml/1 tbsp lime juice
30ml/2 tbsp chopped fresh mint
15ml/1 tbsp chopped fresh basil
salt and ground black pepper
2 kaffir lime leaves, shredded and 1–2 fresh red chillies, seeded and finely shredded, to garnish

1 Cut the onion into wedges, using a sharp knife.

COOK'S TIP

You can use boneless chicken thighs instead of breasts. Simply skin them, cut the flesh into chunks and cook in the coconut milk with the potatoes.

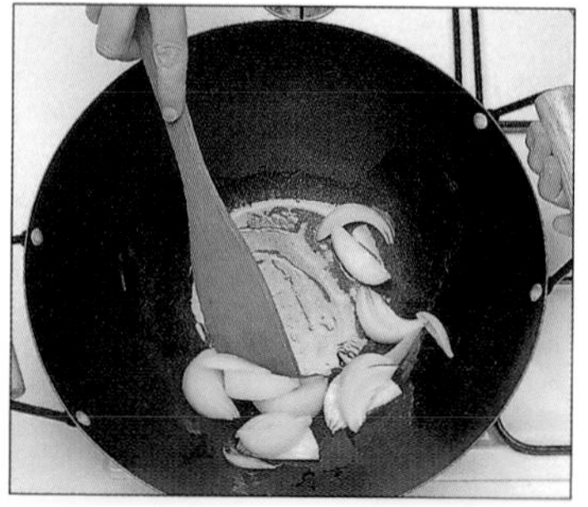

2 Heat a wok until hot, add the oil and swirl it around. Add the onion and stir-fry for 3–4 minutes.

3 Pour in the coconut milk, then bring to the boil, stirring. Stir in the curry paste, fish sauce and sugar.

4 Add the potatoes and seasoning, cover and simmer gently for about 20 minutes.

5 Add the chicken chunks, cover and cook over a low heat for a further 10–15 minutes, until the chicken and potatoes are tender.

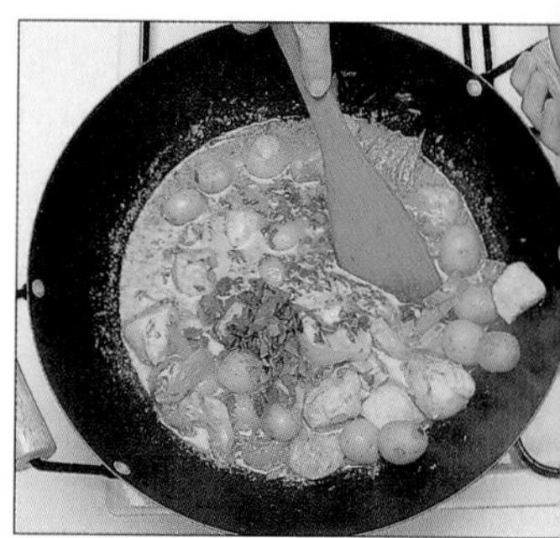

6 Stir in the lime juice, chopped mint and basil. Serve at once, sprinkled with the shredded kaffir lime leaves and red chillies.

Khara Masala Balti Chicken

Whole spices – *khara* – are used in this recipe, giving it a wonderfully rich flavour. This is a dry dish, so it is best served with raita and paratha.

INGREDIENTS

Serves 4
3 curry leaves
1.5ml/¼ tsp mustard seeds
1.5ml/¼ tsp fennel seeds
1.5ml/¼ tsp onion seeds
2.5ml/½ tsp crushed dried red chillies
2.5ml/½ tsp white cumin seeds
1.5ml/¼ tsp fenugreek seeds
2.5ml/½ tsp crushed pomegranate seeds
5ml/1tsp salt
5ml/1 tsp shredded ginger
3 garlic cloves, sliced
60ml/4 tbsp corn oil
4 fresh green chillies, slit
1 large onion, sliced
1 medium tomato, sliced
675g/1½lb chicken, skinned, boned and cubed
15 ml/1 tbsp chopped fresh coriander, to garnish
paratha, to serve

1 Mix together the curry leaves, mustard seeds, fennel seeds, onion seeds, crushed red chillies, cumin seeds, fenugreek seeds and crushed pomegranate seeds in a large bowl. Add the salt.

2 Add the shredded ginger and garlic cloves to the bowl.

3 Heat the oil in a preheated wok. When the oil is hot, add the spice mixture, then the green chillies.

4 Add the onion to the wok and stir-fry over a medium heat for 5–7 minutes.

5 Add the tomato and chicken pieces to the wok and cook over a medium heat for about 7 minutes or until the chicken is cooked through and the sauce has reduced slightly.

6 Stir the mixture over the heat for a further 3–5 minutes, then garnish with the chopped fresh coriander and serve with the paratha.

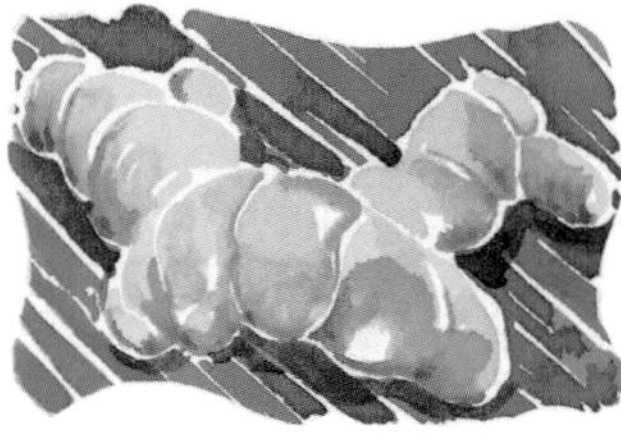

Chicken Pot

This nourishing main course combines meat with beans in a spicy sauce.

INGREDIENTS

Serves 4–6

175g/6oz dried haricot beans
3 chicken legs
15ml/1 tbsp vegetable oil
350g/12oz lean pork, diced
1 chorizo (optional)
1 small carrot, peeled and roughly chopped
1 onion, roughly chopped
1.75 litres/3 pints/7½ cups water
1 clove garlic, crushed
30ml/2 tbsp tomato purée
1 bay leaf
2 chicken stock cubes
350g/12oz sweet potatoes or new potatoes, peeled and cubed
10ml/2 tsp chilli sauce
30ml/2 tbsp white wine vinegar
3 firm tomatoes, skinned, seeded and chopped
225g/8oz Chinese leaves, shredded
salt and ground black pepper
3 spring onions, shredded, to garnish
boiled rice, to serve

1 Put the haricot beans in a bowl, cover with plenty of cold water and set aside to soak for 8 hours or overnight.

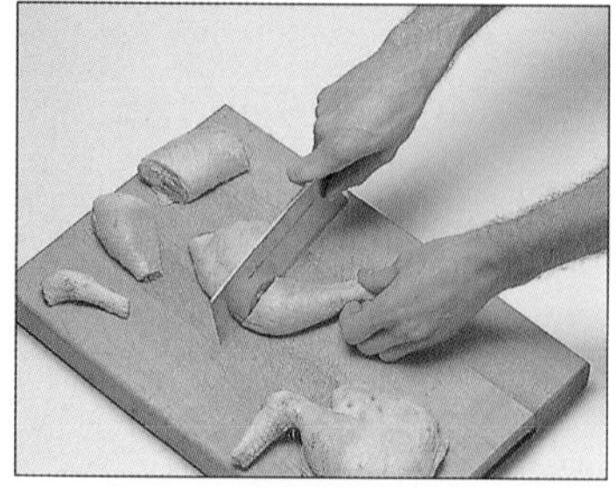

2 Separate the chicken drumsticks from the thighs. Chop off the narrow end of each drumstick and discard.

3 Heat the vegetable oil in a preheated wok, add the chicken, pork, sliced chorizo, if using, carrot and onion, then brown evenly.

4 Drain the haricot beans and add to the wok with fresh water, the garlic, tomato purée and bay leaf and stir to mix. Bring to the boil, lower the heat and simmer for 2 hours until the beans are almost tender.

5 Crumble the chicken stock cubes into the wok, add the sweet or new potatoes and the chilli sauce, then simmer for 15–20 minutes until the potatoes are cooked.

6 Add the vinegar, tomatoes and Chinese leaves to the wok, then simmer for 1–2 minutes. Season to taste with salt and pepper. Garnish with the spring onions and serve with the rice.

COOK'S TIP

This dish is intended to provide enough liquid to be served as a soup for the first course, rather like a French *pot au feu*. This is followed by a main course of the meat and vegetables, served with rice.

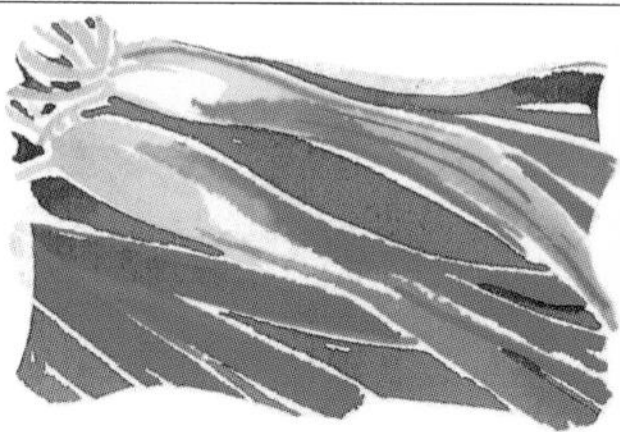

Balti Baby Chicken in Tamarind Sauce

The tamarind in this recipe gives the dish a sweet and sour flavour; this is also quite a hot Balti.

INGREDIENTS

Serves 4–6

60ml/4 tbsp tomato ketchup
15ml/1 tbsp tamarind paste
60ml/4 tbsp water
7.5ml/1½ tsp chilli powder
7.5ml/1½ tsp salt
15ml/1 tbsp sugar
7.5ml/1½ tsp ginger pulp
7.5ml/1½ tsp garlic pulp
30ml/2 tbsp desiccated coconut
30ml/2 tbsp sesame seeds
5ml/1 tsp poppy seeds
5ml/1 tsp ground cumin
7.5ml/1½ tsp ground coriander
2 x 450g/1lb baby chickens, skinned and cut into 6–8 pieces
75ml/5 tbsp corn oil
120ml/8 tbsp curry leaves
2.5ml/½ tsp onion seeds
3 large dried red chillies
2.5ml/½ tsp fenugreek seeds
10–12 cherry tomatoes
45ml/3 tbsp chopped fresh coriander
2 fresh green chillies, chopped

1 Put the tomato ketchup, tamarind paste and water into a large mixing bowl and blend together with a fork.

2 Add the chilli powder, salt, sugar, ginger, garlic, coconut, sesame seeds, poppy seeds, ground cumin and ground coriander to the mixture.

3 Add the chicken pieces to the bowl and stir until they are well coated with the spice mixture. Set aside.

4 Heat the oil in a preheated wok. When it is hot, add the curry leaves, onion seeds, dried red chillies and fenugreek seeds and fry for 1 minute.

5 Lower the heat to medium and ad the chicken pieces, together with their sauce, 2 or 3 pieces at a time. When all the chicken has been added to the wok, stir to mix well.

6 Simmer gently for 12–15 minutes or until the chicken is thoroughly cooked through.

7 Add the tomatoes, fresh coriander and green chillies to the wok and serve immediately.

Thai-style Chicken Livers

Chicken liver is a good source of iron and is a popular meat, especially in the north-east of Thailand. Serve this dish as a starter with salad, or as part of a main course with jasmine rice.

INGREDIENTS

Serves 4–6

45ml/3 tbsp vegetable oil
450g/1lb chicken livers, trimmed
4 shallots, chopped
2 garlic cloves, chopped
15ml/1 tbsp roasted ground rice
45ml/3 tbsp fish sauce
45ml/3 tbsp lime juice
5ml/1 tsp sugar
2 stalks lemon grass, bruised and finely chopped
30ml/2 tbsp chopped coriander
10–12 mint leaves, to garnish
2 red chillies, chopped, to garnish

1 Heat the oil in a wok or large frying pan. Add the livers and fry over a medium-high heat for about 4 minutes, until the liver is golden brown and cooked, but still pink inside.

2 Move the liver to one side of the pan and add the shallots and garlic. Fry for about 1–2 minutes.

3 Add the roasted ground rice, fish sauce, lime juice, sugar, lemon grass and coriander. Stir to combine. Remove from the heat and serve garnished with mint leaves and chillie

Barbecued Chicken

Barbecued chicken is served almost everywhere in Thailand, from portable roadside stalls to sports stadiums and beaches.

INGREDIENTS

Serves 4–6

1 chicken, about 1.5kg/3–3½ lb, cut into 8–10 pieces
2 limes, cut into wedges, to garnish
2 red chillies, finely sliced, to garnish

For the marinade

2 stalks lemon grass, chopped
2.5cm/1in piece fresh root ginger
6 garlic cloves
4 shallots
½ bunch coriander roots
15ml/1 tbsp palm sugar
120ml/4fl oz/½ cup coconut milk
30ml/2 tbsp fish sauce
30ml/2 tbsp soy sauce

1 To make the marinade, put all the ingredients into a food processor and process until smooth.

2 Put the chicken pieces in a dish and pour over the marinade. Leave in a cool place to marinate for at least 4 hours or overnight.

3 Barbecue the chicken over glowir coals, or place on a rack over a baking tray and bake at 200°C/400°F, Gas 6 for about 20–30 minutes or unt the chicken is cooked and golden brown. Turn the pieces occasionally and brush with the marinade.

4 Garnish with lime wedges and finely sliced red chillies.

Duck and Ginger Chop Suey

Chicken can also be used in this recipe, but duck gives a richer contrast of flavours.

INGREDIENTS

Serves 4

2 duck breasts, about 175g/6oz each
45ml/3 tbsp sunflower oil
1 small egg, lightly beaten
1 garlic clove
175g/6oz beansprouts
2 slices fresh root ginger, cut into matchsticks
10ml/2 tsp oyster sauce
2 spring onions, cut into matchsticks
salt and ground black pepper

For the marinade

15ml/1 tbsp clear honey
10ml/2 tsp Chinese rice wine or dry sherry
10ml/2 tsp light soy sauce
10ml/2 tsp dark soy sauce

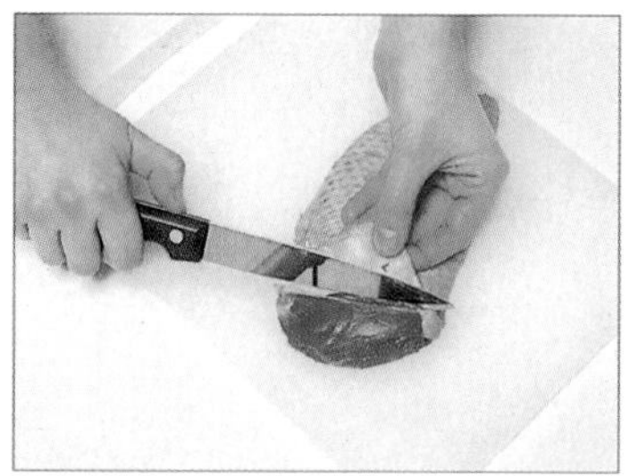

1 Remove the fat and skin from the duck, cut the breasts into thin strips and place in a bowl. Mix the marinade ingredients together, pour over the duck, cover, chill and marinate overnight.

2 Next day, make the egg omelette. Heat a small frying pan and add 15ml/1 tbsp of the oil. When the oil is hot, pour in the egg and swirl around to make an omelette. Once cooked, leave it to cool and then cut into strips. Drain the duck and discard the marinade.

3 Bruise the garlic with the flat blade of a knife. Heat 10ml/2 tsp of the oil in a preheated wok. When the oil is hot, add the garlic and fry for 30 seconds, pressing it to release the flavour. Discard. Add the beansprouts with seasoning and stir-fry for 30 seconds. Transfer to a heated dish, draining off any liquid.

4 Heat the remaining oil in a preheated wok. When the oil is hot, stir-fry the duck for 3 minutes until cooked. Add the ginger and oyster sauce and stir-fry for a further 2 minutes. Add the beansprouts, egg strips and spring onions, stir-fry briefly and serve.

Mandarin Sesame Duck

uck is a high-fat meat but it is ossible to get rid of a onsiderable proportion of the fat y cooking it in this way. (If you move the skin completely, the eat can be dry.) For a special ccasion, duck breasts are an xcellent choice, but they are ore expensive.

NGREDIENTS

erves 4

duck legs or boneless breasts
0ml/2 tbsp light soy sauce
5ml/3 tbsp clear honey
5ml/1 tbsp sesame seeds
mandarin oranges
ml/1 tsp cornflour
lt and ground black pepper
ixed vegetables, to serve

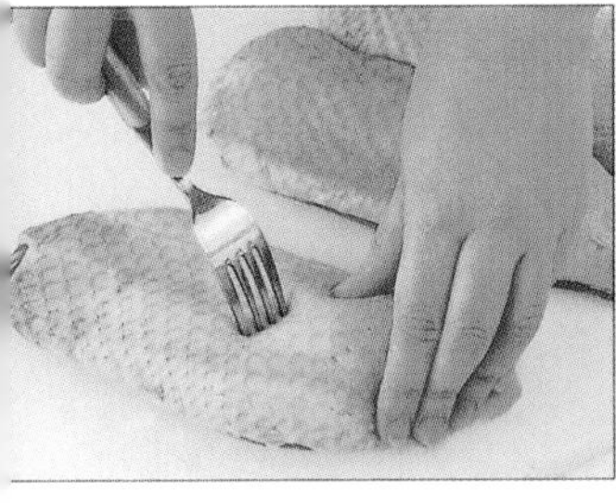

1 Prick the duck skin all over. If using breasts, slash the skin iagonally at intervals with a small, arp knife.

2 Place the duck on a rack in a roasting tin and roast for 1 hour in a preheated oven at 180°C/350°F/ Gas 4. Mix 15ml/1 tbsp of the soy sauce with 30ml/2 tbsp of the honey and brush over the duck. Sprinkle with sesame seeds. Roast for 15–20 minutes, until golden brown.

3 Meanwhile, grate the rind from 1 mandarin and squeeze the juice from 2. Mix together the rind, juice and cornflour, then stir in the remaining soy sauce and honey. Heat, stirring, until thickened and clear. Season to taste. Peel and slice the remaining mandarins. Serve the duck, with the mandarin slices and the sauce, accompanied by mixed vegetables.

Peking Duck

This has to be the *pièce de résistance* of any Chinese banquet. It is not too difficult to prepare and cook at home – the secret is to use duckling with a low-fat content. Also, make sure that the skin of the duck is absolutely dry before you start to cook – the drier the skin, the crispier the duck.

Ingredients

Serves 6–8

2.25kg/5–5¼lb oven-ready duckling
30ml/2 tbsp maltose or honey, dissolved in 150ml/¼ pint/⅔ cup warm water

For the duck sauce

30ml/2 tbsp sesame oil
90–120ml/6–8 tbsp yellow bean sauce, crushed
30–45ml/2–3 tbsp light brown sugar

To serve

20–24 thin pancakes
6–8 spring onions, thinly shredded
½ cucumber, thinly shredded

Cook's Tip

If preferred, serve Peking Duck with plum sauce in place of the duck sauce. Plum sauce is available from oriental stores and larger supermarkets. Duck sauce can also be bought ready-prepared.

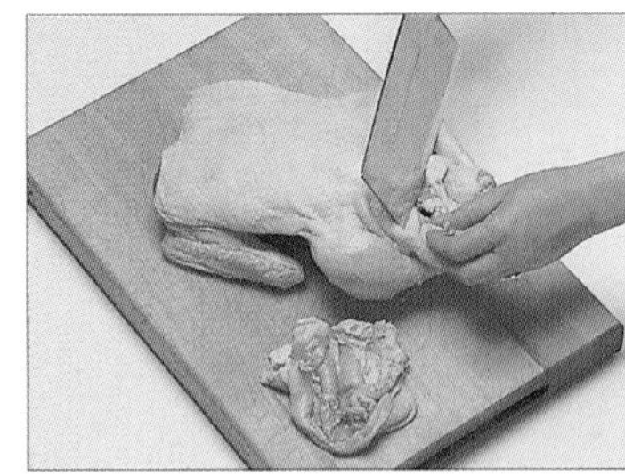

1 Remove any feather studs and any lumps of fat from inside the vent of the duck. Plunge the duck into a saucepan of boiling water for 2–3 minutes to seal the pores. This will make the skin airtight, thus preventing the fat from escaping during cooking. Remove and drain well, then dry thoroughly.

2 Brush the duck all over with the dissolved maltose or honey, then hang the bird up in a cool place for at least 4–5 hours.

3 Place the duck, breast side up, on a rack in a roasting tin and cook in a preheated oven at 200°C/400°F/Gas 6 for 1½–1¾ hours without either basting or turning.

4 Meanwhile, make the duck sauce. Heat the sesame oil in a small saucepan. Add the crushed yellow bean sauce and the light brown sugar. Stir until smooth and allow to cool.

5 To serve, peel off the crispy duck skin in small slices using a sharp carving knife or cleaver, then carve the juicy meat in thin strips. Arrange the skin and meat on separate serving plates

6 Open a pancake on each plate, spread about 5ml/1 tsp of the chosen sauce in the middle, with a few strips of shredded spring onions and cucumber. Top with 2–3 slices each of duck skin and meat. Roll up and eat.

Crispy and Aromatic Duck

Because this dish is often served with pancakes, spring onions, cucumber and duck sauce, many people mistakenly think this is Peking Duck. This recipe, however, uses quite a different cooking method. The result is just as crispy but the delightful aroma makes this dish particularly distinctive. Plum sauce may be substituted for the duck sauce.

INGREDIENTS

Serves 6–8

1.75–2.25kg/4–5¼lb oven-ready duckling
10ml/2 tsp salt
5–6 whole star anise
15ml/1 tbsp Szechuan peppercorns
5ml/1 tsp cloves
2–3 cinnamon sticks
3–4 spring onions
3–4 slices fresh root ginger, unpeeled
75–90ml/5–6 tbsp Chinese rice wine or dry sherry
vegetable oil, for deep-frying

To serve

lettuce leaves
20–24 thin pancakes
120ml/4fl oz/½ cup duck sauce
6–8 spring onions, thinly shredded
½ cucumber, thinly shredded

1 Remove the wings from the duck. Split the body in half down the backbone.

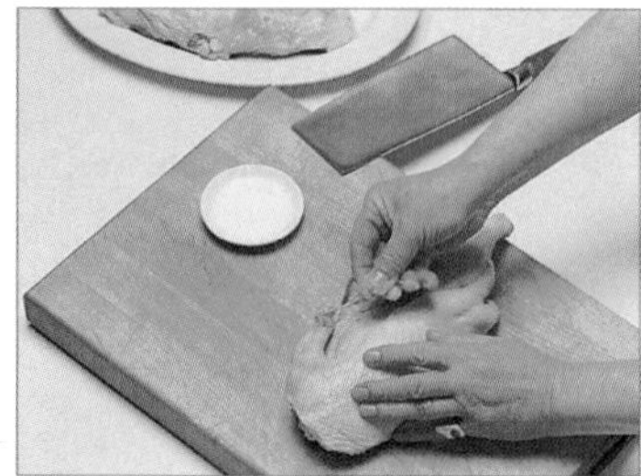

2 Rub salt all over the two duck halves, taking care to rub it well in.

3 Place the duck in a dish with the star anise, peppercorns, cloves, cinnamon, spring onions, ginger and rice wine or dry sherry and set aside to marinate for at least 4–6 hours.

4 Place the duck with the marinade in a steamer positioned in a wok partly filled with boiling water and steam vigorously for 3–4 hours (longer if possible). Remove the duck from the cooking liquid and leave to cool for at least 5–6 hours. The duck must be completely cold and dry or the skin will not become crispy.

5 Heat the oil in a preheated wok until smoking, place the duck pieces in the oil, skin side down, and deep-fry for 5–6 minutes or until crisp and brown, turning just once at the very last moment.

6 Remove, drain, take the meat off the bone and place on a bed of lettuce leaves. To serve, wrap a portion of duck in each pancake with a little sauce, shredded spring onion and cucumber. Eat with your fingers.

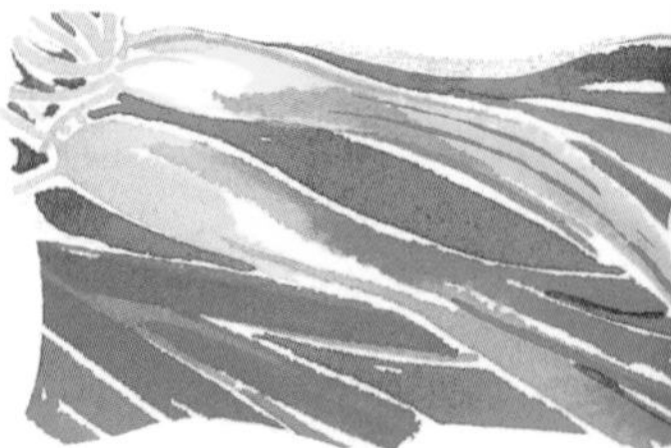

Chilli Duck with Crab and Cashew Sauce

This spicy dish would be delicious served with Thai rice, which is slightly aromatic.

INGREDIENTS

Serves 4–6

2.75kg/6lb duck
1.2 litres/2 pints/5 cups water
2 kaffir lime leaves
7.5ml/1½ tsp salt
2–3 small fresh red chillies, seeded and finely chopped
25ml/5 tsp sugar
30ml/2 tbsp coriander seeds
5ml/1 tsp caraway seeds
115g/4oz/1 cup raw cashew nuts, chopped
7.5cm/3in lemon grass
2.5cm/1in galangal or fresh root ginger, finely chopped
2 garlic cloves, crushed
4 shallots or 1 medium onion, finely chopped
2cm/¾in square shrimp paste
25g/1oz coriander white root or stem, finely chopped
175g/6oz frozen white crab meat, thawed
50g/2oz creamed coconut
1 small bunch fresh coriander, chopped, to garnish
boiled rice, to serve

1 Remove the legs from the duck, separate the thighs from the drumsticks and chop each thigh and drumstick into two pieces. Trim away the lower half of the duck with kitchen scissors. Cut the breast piece in half down the middle, then chop each half into four pieces.

2 Put the duck flesh and bones into a large saucepan and cover with the water. Add the lime leaves and 5ml/1 tsp of the salt, bring to the boil and simmer for 30–45 minutes, until the meat is tender. Discard the duck bones. Skim off the fat from the stock and set the stock aside.

3 Grind together the chillies, sugar and remaining salt in a mortar with a pestle or in a food processor. Dry-fry the coriander seeds, caraway seeds and cashew nuts in a preheated wok for 1–2 minutes to release their flavour. Add the seeds and nuts to the chilli mixture, together with the lemon grass, galangal or ginger, garlic and shallots or onion and reduce to a smooth paste. Add the shrimp paste and coriander root or stem and mix well.

4 Add 250ml/8fl oz/1 cup of the reserved stock and blend to make a thin paste.

5 Pour the spice mixture into the saucepan with the duck and mix thoroughly. Bring to the boil, lower the heat and simmer for 20–25 minutes.

6 Add the crab meat and creamed coconut and simmer briefly to heat through. Turn out on to a warmed serving dish, garnish with the chopped coriander and accompany with boiled rice.

Balinese Spiced Duck

There is a delightful hotel on the beach at Sanur which cooks this delicious duck dish perfectly.

INGREDIENTS

Serves 4

8 duck portions, fat trimmed and reserved
50g/2oz desiccated coconut
175ml/6fl oz/¾ cup coconut milk
salt and freshly ground black pepper
Deep-fried Onions and salad leaves or fresh herb sprigs, to garnish

For the spice paste

1 small onion or 4–6 shallots, sliced
2 garlic cloves, sliced
2.5cm/½ in fresh root ginger, peeled and sliced
1cm/½ in fresh *lengkuas*, peeled and sliced
2.5cm/1in fresh turmeric or 2.5ml/½ tsp ground turmeric
1–2 red chillies, seeded and sliced
4 macadamia nuts or 8 almonds
5ml/1 tsp coriander seeds, dry-fried

1 Place the duck fat trimmings in a heated frying pan, without oil, and allow the fat to render. Reserve the fat.

2 Dry-fry the desiccated coconut in a preheated pan until crisp and brown in colour.

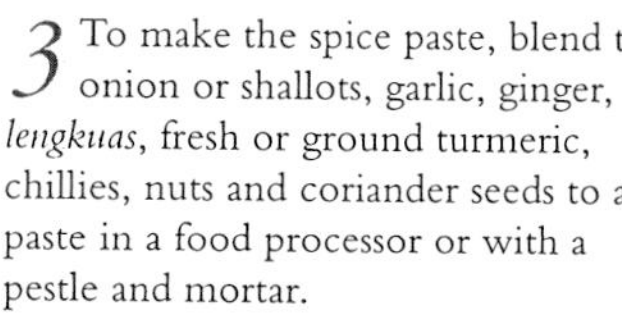

3 To make the spice paste, blend t onion or shallots, garlic, ginger, *lengkuas*, fresh or ground turmeric, chillies, nuts and coriander seeds to a paste in a food processor or with a pestle and mortar.

4 Spread the spice paste over the duck portions and leave to marinate in a cool place for 3–4 hou Preheat the oven to 160°C/325°F/ Gas 3. Shake off the spice paste and transfer the duck breasts to an oiled roasting tin. Cover with a double lay of foil and cook the duck in the oven for 2 hours.

5 Turn the oven temperature up to 190°C/375°F/Gas 5. Heat the reserved duck fat in a pan, add the spice paste and fry for 1–2 minutes. St in the coconut milk and simmer for 2 minutes. Discard the duck juices th cover the duck with the spice mixtur and sprinkle with the toasted coconut Cook in the oven for 20–30 minutes.

6 Arrange the duck on a warm serving platter and sprinkle with the Deep-fried Onions. Season to tast and serve with the salad leaves or fres herb sprigs of your choice.

Duck with Chinese Mushrooms and Ginger

ucks are often seen, comically rded in single file, along the ater channels between the rice ddies throughout the country. ne substantial Chinese pulation in Indonesia is rticularly fond of duck and the licious ingredients in this cipe give it an oriental flavour.

GREDIENTS

ves 4

5kg/5½lb duck
nl/1 tsp sugar
ml/2fl oz/¼ cup light soy sauce
garlic cloves, crushed
dried Chinese mushrooms, soaked in 350ml/12fl oz/1½ cups warm water for 15 minutes
onion, sliced
m/2in fresh root ginger, sliced and cut in matchsticks
0g/7oz baby sweetcorn
bunch spring onions, white bulbs left whole, green tops sliced
–30ml/1–2 tbsp cornflour, mixed to a paste with 60ml/4 tbsp water
t and freshly ground black pepper
iled rice, to serve

1 Cut the duck along the breast, open it up and cut along each side the backbone. Use the backbone, ings and giblets to make a stock, to e later in the recipe. Any trimmings fat can be rendered in a frying pan, use later in the recipe. Cut each leg d each breast in half. Place in a bowl, b with the sugar and then pour over e soy sauce and garlic.

2 Drain the mushrooms, reserving the soaking liquid. Trim and discard the stalks.

3 Fry the onion and ginger in the duck fat, in a frying pan, until they give off a good aroma. Push to one side. Lift the duck pieces out of the soy sauce and fry them until browned. Add the mushrooms and reserved liquid.

4 Add 600ml/1 pint/2½ cups of the duck stock or water to the browned duck pieces. Season, cover and cook over a gentle heat for about 1 hour, until the duck is tender.

5 Add the sweetcorn and the white part of the spring onions and cook for a further 10 minutes. Remove from the heat and add the cornflour paste. Return to the heat and bring to the boil, stirring. Cook for 1 minute until glossy. Serve, scattered with the spring onion tops, with boiled rice.

VARIATION

Replace the corn with chopped celery and slices of drained, canned water chestnuts.

Sweet-sour Duck with Mango

Mango adds natural sweetness to this colourful stir-fry. Crispy deep-fried noodles make the perfect accompaniment.

INGREDIENTS

Serves 4

225–350g/8–12oz duck breasts
45ml/3 tbsp dark soy sauce
15ml/1tbsp Chinese rice wine or dry sherry
5ml/1 tsp sesame oil
5ml/1 tsp Chinese five-spice powder
15ml/1 tbsp soft brown sugar
10ml/2 tsp cornflour
45ml/3 tbsp Chinese rice vinegar
15ml/1 tbsp tomato ketchup
1 mango, not too ripe
3 baby aubergines
1 red onion
1 carrot
60ml/4 tbsp groundnut oil
1 garlic clove, sliced
2.5cm/1in fresh root ginger, cut into shreds
75g/3oz sugar snap peas

1 Thinly slice the duck breasts and place in a bowl. Mix together 15ml/1 tbsp of the soy sauce with the rice wine or sherry, sesame oil and five-spice powder. Pour over the duck, cover and leave to marinate for 1–2 hours. In a separate bowl, blend together the sugar, cornflour, rice vinegar, ketchup and remaining soy sauce. Set aside.

2 Peel the mango, slice the flesh from the stone, then cut into thick strips. Slice the aubergines, onion and carrot into similar-sized pieces.

3 Heat a wok until hot, add 30ml/2 tbsp of the oil and swirl it around. Drain the duck, reserving the marinade. Stir-fry the duck slices over a high heat until the fat is crisp and golden. Remove and keep warm. Add 15ml/1 tbsp of the oil to the wok and stir-fry the aubergine for 3 minutes until golden.

4 Add the remaining oil and fry the onion, garlic, ginger and carrot fc 2–3 minutes, then add the sugar snap peas and stir fry for a further 2 minut

5 Add the mango and return the duck with the sauce and reserved marinade to the wok. Cook, stirring, until the sauce thickens slightly. Serve at once.

COOK'S TIP

If baby aubergines are not available, use the smallest you can find. Sprinkle with salt after slicing and set aside in a colander for the bitter juices to drain off. Rinse thoroughly before cooking.

Stir-fried Turkey with Broccoli and Mushrooms

This is a really easy, tasty supper dish which works well with chicken too.

INGREDIENTS

Serves 4

115g/4oz broccoli florets
4 spring onions
5ml/1 tsp cornflour
45ml/3 tbsp oyster sauce
15ml/1 tbsp dark soy sauce
120ml/4fl oz/½ cup chicken stock
10ml/2 tsp lemon juice
45ml/3 tbsp groundnut oil
450g/1lb turkey steaks cut into strips, about 5mm x 5cm/¼ x 2in
1 small onion, chopped
2 garlic cloves, crushed
10ml/2 tsp grated fresh root ginger
115g/4oz fresh shiitake mushrooms, sliced
75g/3oz baby sweetcorn, halved lengthways
15ml/1 tbsp sesame oil
salt and ground black pepper
egg noodles, to serve

1 Divide the broccoli florets into smaller sprigs and cut the stalks into thin diagonal slices.

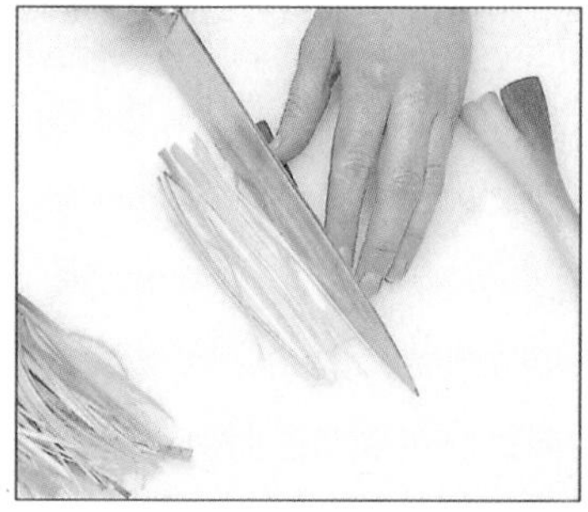

2 Finely chop the white parts of the spring onions and slice the green parts into thin shreds.

3 In a bowl, blend together the cornflour, oyster sauce, soy sauce, stock and lemon juice. Set aside.

4 Heat 30ml/2 tbsp of the groundnut oil in a preheated wok. Add the turkey and stir-fry for 2 minutes until golden and crisp at the edges. Remove from the wok and keep warm.

5 Add the remaining groundnut oil to the wok and stir-fry the chopped onion, garlic and ginger over a medium heat for about 1 minute. Increase the heat to high, add the broccoli, mushrooms and sweetcorn and stir-fry for 2 minutes.

6 Return the turkey to the wok, then add the sauce with the chopped spring onion and seasoning. Cook, stirring, for about 1 minute until the sauce has thickened. Stir in the sesame oil. Serve immediately on a bed of egg noodles with the finely shredded spring onion scattered on top.

COOK'S TIP

Cook fresh egg noodles in salted boiling water, stirring occasionally to prevent them from sticking. They are ready within a few minutes. Follow the packet instructions for cooking dried egg noodles.

Stir-fried Turkey with Mangetouts

Turkey is often a rather disappointing meat with a bland flavour. Here it is enlivened with a delicious marinade and combined with crunchy nuts to provide contrasting textures.

Ingredients

Serves 4

30ml/2 tbsp sesame oil
90ml/6 tbsp lemon juice
1 garlic clove, crushed
1cm/½in fresh root ginger, grated
5ml/1 tsp clear honey
450g/1lb turkey fillets, skinned and cut into strips
115g/4oz mangetouts
30ml/2 tbsp groundnut oil
50g/2oz cashew nuts
6 spring onions, cut into strips
225g/8oz can water chestnuts, drained and thinly sliced
salt
saffron rice, to serve

1 Mix together the sesame oil, lemon juice, garlic, ginger and honey in a shallow, non-metallic dish. Add the turkey and mix well. Cover and leave to marinate for 3–4 hours.

2 Blanch the mangetouts in boiling salted water for 1 minute. Drain, refresh under cold running water and set aside.

3 Drain the marinade from the turkey strips and reserve the marinade. Heat the groundnut oil in a preheated wok or large frying pan, add the cashew nuts and stir-fry for about 1–2 minutes, until golden brown. Remove the cashew nuts from the wok or frying pan, using a slotted spoon, and set aside.

4 Add the turkey to the wok or frying pan and stir-fry for 3–4 minutes, until golden brown. Add th spring onions, mangetouts, water chestnuts and reserved marinade. Co for a few minutes, until the turkey is tender and the sauce is bubbling and hot. Stir in the cashew nuts and serve with saffron rice.

Honey-glazed Quail with a Five-spice Marinade

lthough the quail is a relatively nall bird – 115–150g/4–5oz – it surprisingly meaty. One bird is sually quite sufficient for one rving.

IGREDIENTS

rves 4

oven-ready quails
pieces star anise
)ml/2 tsp ground cinnamon
)ml/2 tsp fennel seeds
)ml/2 tsp ground Szechuan or Chinese pepper
nch of ground cloves
small onion, finely chopped
garlic clove, crushed
ml/4 tbsp clear honey
)ml/2 tbsp dark soy sauce
spring onions, roughly chopped, finely shredded rind of 1 mandarin orange or satsuma and radish and carrot "flowers", to garnish
nana leaves, to serve

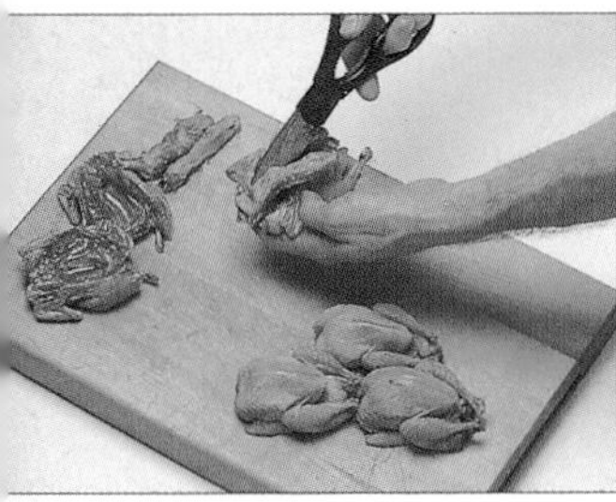

1 Remove the backbones from the quails by cutting down either side ith a pair of kitchen scissors.

2 Flatten the birds with the palm of your hand and secure each one ith two bamboo skewers.

3 Grind together the star anise, cinnamon, fennel seeds, pepper and cloves in a mortar with a pestle. Add the onion, garlic, honey and soy sauce and combine well.

4 Place the quails on a flat dish, cover with the spice mixture and set aside to marinate for at least 8 hours.

5 Cook the quails under a preheated grill or on a barbecue for 7–8 minutes on each side, basting from time to time with the marinade.

6 Arrange the quails on a bed of banana leaves and garnish with the spring onion, orange rind and radish and carrrot "flowers".

VEGETABLES

Unusual ways of preparing familiar vegetables, as well as dishes using more exotic ingredients, can spice up Western grills and roasts or form part of a Chinese meal. Stir-frying is an especially good way of cooking vegetables without losing flavour, texture, colour and valuable nutrients. There are recipes for all tastes: palate-tingling Pak Choi with Lime Dressing, Cooked Vegetable Gado-Gado with its colourful, crunchy mix of ingredients, Chinese Garlic Mushrooms, the perfect vegetarian snack, and even Chinese-style Brussels sprouts!

Stir-fried Chinese Leaves with Mushrooms

You can stir-fry fresh button mushrooms in this recipe, if you prefer them or if fresh or canned straw mushrooms are not available.

INGREDIENTS

Serves 4
225g/8oz fresh straw mushrooms or 350g/12oz can straw mushrooms, drained
60ml/4 tbsp vegetable oil
400g/14oz Chinese leaves, cut in strips
5ml/1 tsp salt
5ml/1 tsp light brown sugar
15ml/1tbsp cornflour paste
120ml/4fl oz/½ cup milk

1 Cut the mushrooms in half lengthways. Heat half the oil, stir-fry the Chinese leaves for 2 minutes, then add half the salt and half the sugar. Stir for 1 minute.

2 Transfer the Chinese leaves to a warm serving dish. Add the mushrooms to the wok and stir-fry for 1 minute. Add the remaining salt and sugar, cook for 1 minute, then thicken with the cornflour paste and milk. Serve with the Chinese leaves.

COOK'S TIP

The Chinese approach cooking with the same overall desire for harmony and balance that characterizes their ancient philosophy. Recipes for stir-fried vegetables are not simply an arbitrary combination of whatever is to hand – they should balance and complement each other in both colour and texture. The delicious slipperiness of straw mushrooms complements the crunchier texture of the Chinese leaves, so it is best to use them if at all possible. Canned straw mushrooms are available from oriental food stores. Do not overcook or the harmony and balance will be lost.

Stir-fried Beansprouts

'his is an easy way to cook up ome tasty beansprouts in a wok. t is not necessary to top and tail hem. Simply rinse in a bowl of old water and discard any husks hat float to the surface.

NGREDIENTS

erves 4

–3 spring onions
25g/8oz fresh beansprouts
5ml/3 tbsp vegetable oil
ml/1 tsp salt
.5ml/½ tsp light brown sugar
ew drops sesame oil (optional)

1 Cut the spring onions into short sections about the same length as he beansprouts.

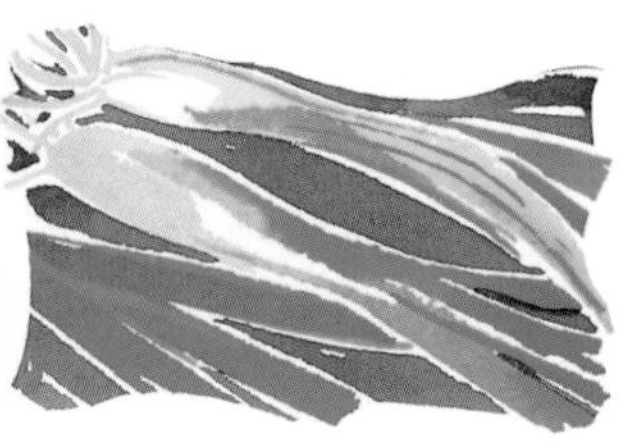

2 Heat the oil in a wok and stir-fry the beansprouts and spring onions for about 1 minute. Add the salt and sugar and continue stirring for 1 minute. Sprinkle with the sesame oil, if using, and serve. Do not overcook or the beansprouts will go soggy.

COOK'S TIP

Fresh and canned bean sprouts are readily available, but they can easily be grown at home for a constant and completely fresh supply. Scatter mung beans on several layers of damp kitchen paper on a small plate. Keep moist in a fairly warm place and the beans will sprout in a few days.

Braised Chinese Vegetables

The original recipe calls for no less than 18 different ingredients to represent the 18 Buddhas (*Lo Han*). Later, this was reduced to eight, but nowadays anything between four and six items is regarded as quite sufficient to put in a wok.

INGREDIENTS

Serves 4

10g/¼oz dried Chinese mushrooms
75g/3oz straw mushrooms
75g/3oz sliced bamboo shoots, drained
50g/2oz mangetouts
1 packet tofu
175g/6oz Chinese leaves
45–60ml/3–4 tbsp vegetable oil
5ml/1 tsp salt
2.5ml/½ tsp light brown sugar
15ml/1 tbsp light soy sauce
few drops sesame oil

1 Soak the Chinese mushrooms in cold water for 20–25 minutes, then rinse and discard the hard stalks, if any. Cut the straw mushrooms in half lengthways, if they are large, keep them whole, if they are small. Rinse and drain the bamboo shoot slices. Top and tail the mangetouts. Cut the tofu into about 12 small pieces. Cut the Chinese leaves into small pieces about the same size as the mangetouts.

2 Harden the tofu pieces by placing them in a wok of boiling water for about 2 minutes. Remove and drain.

3 Discard the water and heat the oil in the wok. a saucepan or a flameproof casserole. Lightly brown the tofu pieces on both sides. Remove with a slotted spoon and keep warm.

4 Stir-fry all the vegetables in the wok or pan for about 1½ minutes, then add the tofu, salt, sugar and soy sauce. Continue stirring for 1 minute, then cover and braise for 2–3 minutes. Sprinkle with sesame oil and serve.

Aubergine in Spicy Sauce

ubergines are given a royal eatment in this recipe, where ey are stir-fried with seasonings iore commonly associated with sh cooking.

NGREDIENTS

rves 4

50g/1lb aubergines
-4 whole dried red chillies, soaked in water for 10 minutes
egetable oil, for deep frying
clove garlic, finely chopped
ml/1 tsp finely chopped fresh ginger
ml/1 tsp finely chopped spring onion, white part only
15g/4oz lean pork, thinly shredded (optional)
5ml/1 tbsp light soy sauce
5ml/1 tbsp light brown sugar
5ml/1 tbsp chilli bean sauce
5ml/1 tbsp Chinese rice wine or dry sherry
5ml/1 tbsp rice vinegar
0ml/2 tsp cornflour paste
ml/1 tsp finely chopped spring onions, green part only, to garnish
ew drops sesame oil

1 Cut the aubergines into short strips the size of chips – the skin can either be peeled off or left on, whichever you prefer. Cut the soaked ed chillies into two or three small pieces and discard the seeds.

2 Heat the oil in a preheated wok and deep fry the aubergine chips for about 3–4 minutes or until limp. Remove and drain.

3 Pour off the excess oil, leaving about 15ml/1 tbsp in the wok. Add the garlic, ginger, white spring onions and chillies, stir a few times, then add the pork, if using. Stir-fry the meat for about 1 minute or until it becomes pale, almost white, in colour. Add all the seasonings, then increase the heat and bring the mixture to the boil.

4 Add the aubergines to the wok, blend well and braise for 30–40 seconds, then thicken the sauce with the cornflour paste, stirring until smooth. Garnish with the green spring onions and sprinkle with sesame oil.

COOK'S TIP

Soaking dried chillies in water will reduce their spicy flavour. If you prefer a milder chilli taste, soak for longer than the recommended 10 minutes.

Szechuan Spicy Tofu

The meat used in this popular wok recipe can be omitted to create a purely vegetarian dish, if you prefer.

INGREDIENTS

Serves 4
3 packets tofu
1 leek
45ml/3 tbsp vegetable oil
115g/4oz minced beef
15ml/1 tbsp black bean sauce
15ml/1 tbsp light soy sauce
5ml/1 tsp chilli bean sauce
15ml/1 tbsp Chinese rice wine or dry sherry
about 45–60ml/3–4 tbsp stock or water
10ml/2 tsp cornflour paste
ground Szechuan peppercorns, to taste
few drops of sesame oil

1 Cut the tofu into 1cm/½in square cubes. Fill a wok with boiling water, add the tofu cubes and bring back to the boil. Cook for 2–3 minutes to harden. Remove and drain. Cut the leek into short sections.

2 Empty the wok. Preheat and add the oil. When hot, stir-fry the minced beef until the colour changes, then add the leek and black bean sauce. Add the tofu with the soy sauce, chilli bean sauce and rice wine or sherry. Stir gently for 1 minute.

3 Add the stock or water, bring to the boil and braise for 2-3 minutes.

4 Stir in the cornflour paste and cook, stirring, until thickened. Season with ground Szechuan pepper, sprinkle with the sesame oil and serve immediately.

Karahi Shredded Cabbage with Cumin

ıis cabbage is only lightly ıced and makes a good companiment to most other lti dishes.

GREDIENTS

ves 4
ml/1 tbsp corn oil
g/2oz butter
ml/½ tsp crushed coriander seeds
ml/½ tsp white cumin seeds
lried red chillies
mall Savoy cabbage, shredded
mangetouts
resh red chillies, seeded and sliced
baby sweetcorn
t
g/1oz flaked almonds, toasted
ınd 15ml/1 tbsp chopped fresh
coriander, to garnish

Heat the oil and butter in a preheated wok and, when the tter has melted, add the crushed riander seeds, cumin seeds and dried l chillies.

Add the shredded cabbage and mangetouts to the wok and stir-fry r about 5 minutes.

3 Add the fresh red chillies, baby sweetcorn and salt and stir-fry for a further 3 minutes.

4 Garnish the cabbage with toasted almonds and fresh coriander and serve hot.

COOK'S TIP

Unlike many parts of the Indian sub-continent, Pakistan – whence Balti recipes come – is generally a meat-eating nation. Vegetable dishes are, therefore, usually cooked as side dishes, rather than as a main dish, much in the way they are in the West. Consequently, this delicious, slightly spicy treatment of cabbage would go as well with a traditional western roast as it would with a Balti curry or stir-fry.

Spicy Balti Potatoes

Potatoes often form an integral part of a Balti meal. Rice is not always served or may be served in addition to potatoes, which are frequently treated as just another vegetable, rather than as a staple.

Ingredients

Serves 4
45ml/3 tbsp corn oil
2.5ml/½ tsp white cumin seeds
3 curry leaves
5ml/1 tsp crushed dried red chillies
2.5ml/½ tsp mixed onion, mustard and fenugreek seeds
2.5ml/½ tsp fennel seeds
3 garlic cloves, thinly sliced
2.5ml/½ tsp shredded fresh root ginger
2 medium onions, sliced
6 new potatoes, cut into 5mm/¼in slices
15ml/1 tbsp chopped fresh coriander
1 fresh red chilli, seeded and sliced
1 fresh green chilli, seeded and sliced

1 Heat the oil in a preheated wok. When hot, lower the heat and add the cumin seeds, curry leaves, dried red chillies, onion, mustard and fenugreek seeds, fennel seeds, garlic and ginger. Stir-fry for about 1 minute, then add the onions and fry for 5 minutes or until the onions are golden brown.

2 Add the potatoes, coriander and fresh red and green chillies to the wok and mix well. Cover tightly with lid or foil, making sure the foil does n touch the food. Cook over a very low heat for about 7 minutes or until the potatoes are tender.

3 Remove the lid or foil and serve straight from the pot in the traditional manner.

Okra with Green Mango and Lentils

If you like okra, you will love this tangy and spicy dish.

Ingredients

Serves 4
115g/4oz yellow lentils
45ml/3 tbsp corn oil
2.5ml/½ tsp onion seeds
2 medium onions, sliced
2.5ml/½ tsp ground fenugreek
5ml/1 tsp ginger pulp
5ml/1 tsp garlic pulp
7.5ml/1½ tsp chilli powder
1.5ml/¼ tsp ground turmeric
5ml/1 tsp ground coriander
1 unripe mango, peeled and stoned
450g/1lb okra, chopped
2 fresh red chillies, seeded and sliced
30ml/2 tbsp chopped fresh coriander
1 tomato, sliced

1 Wash the lentils thoroughly and put into a saucepan with just enough water to cover. Bring to the boil and cook until soft but not mushy. Drain and set aside.

2 Heat the oil in a preheated wok. Add the onion seeds and fry until they begin to pop. Add the onions an fry until they are golden brown. Low the heat and add the ground fenugree ginger, garlic, chilli powder, ground turmeric and ground coriander.

3 Slice the mango, then add with th okra. Stir well and add the red chillies and fresh coriander. Stir-fry fo about 3 minutes or until the okra is well cooked. Stir in the cooked lentils and sliced tomato, then cook for a further 3 minutes. Serve immediately.

Crispy Cabbage

This makes a wonderful accompaniment to meat or vegetable dishes – just a couple of spoonfuls adds a crunchy texture to a meal. It goes especially well with prawn dishes.

INGREDIENTS

Serves 4
4 juniper berries
1 large Savoy cabbage
60ml/4 tbsp vegetable oil
1 clove garlic, crushed
5ml/1 tsp caster sugar
5ml/1 tsp salt

1 Finely crush the juniper berries, in a mortar with a pestle.

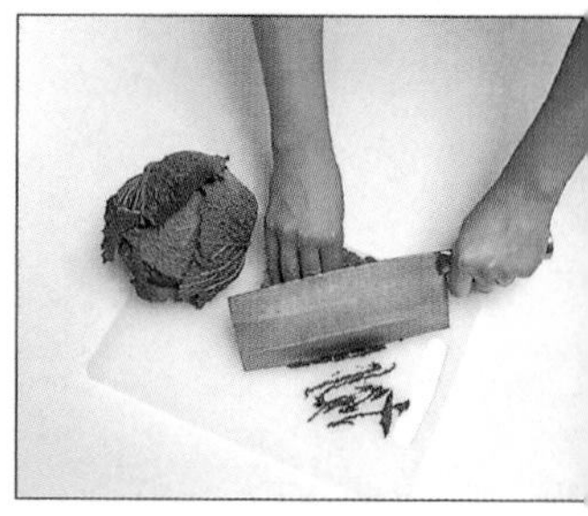

2 Finely shred the cabbage.

3 Heat a wok, then add the oil. When the oil is hot, stir-fry the garlic for 1 minute. Add the cabbage and stir-fry for 3–4 minutes until cris[p]. Remove from the wok and pat dry with kitchen paper.

4 Reheat the wok and return the cabbage to it. Add the sugar, salt and crushed juniper berries and toss t[he] cabbage so that it is well coated and thoroughly mixed with the flavouring[s]. Serve either hot or cold.

Stir-fried Greens

ıail's eggs look very attractive *Chah Kang Kung*, but you can bstitute some baby sweetcorn, lved at an angle.

GREDIENTS

ves 4

ɔunches spinach or chard or 1 head Chinese leaves or 450g/1lb curly kale
ɡarlic cloves, crushed
m/2in fresh root ginger, peeled and cut in matchsticks
–60ml/3–4 tbsp groundnut oil
5g/4oz boneless, skinless chicken breast, or pork fillet, or a mixture of both, very finely sliced
quail's eggs, hard-boiled and shelled
fresh red chilli, seeded and shredded
–45ml/2–3 tbsp oyster sauce
ml/1 tbsp brown sugar
ml/2 tsp cornflour, mixed with 50ml/2fl oz/¼ cup cold water
t

COOK'S TIP

As with all stir-fries, don't start cooking until you have prepared all the ingredients and arranged them to hand. Cut everything into small, even-size pieces so the food can be cooked very quickly and all the colours and flavours preserved.

1 Wash the chosen leaves well and shake them dry. Strip the tender aves from the stems and tear them ıto pieces. Discard the lower, tougher ırt of the stems and slice the emainder evenly.

2 Fry the garlic and ginger in the hot oil, without browning, for a minute. Add the chicken and/or pork and keep stirring it in the wok until the meat changes colour. When the meat looks cooked, add the sliced stems first and cook them quickly; then add the torn leaves, quail's eggs and chilli. Spoon in the oyster sauce and a little boiling water, if necessary. Cover and cook for 1–2 minutes only.

3 Remove the cover, stir and add sugar and salt to taste. Stir in the cornflour and water mixture and toss thoroughly. Cook until the mixture is well coated in a glossy sauce.

4 Serve immediately, while still very hot and the colours are bright and positively jewel-like.

Water Spinach with Brown Bean Sauce

Water spinach, often known as Siamese watercress, is a green vegetable with arrowhead-shaped leaves. If you can't find it, use spinach, watercress, pak choy or even broccoli, and adjust the cooking time accordingly. There are excellent variations to this recipe using black bean sauce, shrimp paste or fermented bean curd instead of brown bean sauce.

INGREDIENTS

Serves 4–6

1 bunch water spinach, about 1kg/2¼lb in weight
45ml/3 tbsp vegetable oil
15ml/1 tbsp chopped garlic
15ml/1 tbsp brown bean sauce
30ml/2 tbsp fish sauce
15ml/1 tbsp granulated sugar
freshly black ground pepper

1 Trim and discard the bottom coarse, woody end of the water spinach. Cut the remaining part into 5cm/2in lengths, keeping the leaves separate from the stems.

2 Heat the oil in a wok or large frying pan. When it starts to smoke, add the chopped garlic and toss for 10 seconds.

3 Add the stem part of the water spinach, let it sizzle and cook for 1 minute, then add the leafy parts.

4 Stir in the brown bean sauce, fish sauce, sugar and pepper. Toss and turn over the spinach until it begins to wilt, about 3–4 minutes. Transfer to a serving dish and serve immediately.

Mixed Vegetables in Coconut Milk

A most delicious way of cooking vegetables. If you don't like highly spiced food, use fewer red chilli peppers.

INGREDIENTS

Serves 4–6

450g/1lb mixed vegetables, such as aubergines, baby sweetcorn, carrots, snake beans and patty pan squash
8 red chillies, seeded
2 stalks lemon grass, chopped
4 kaffir lime leaves, torn
30ml/2 tbsp vegetable oil
250ml/8fl oz/1 cup coconut milk
30ml/2 tbsp fish sauce
salt
15–20 Thai basil leaves, to garnish

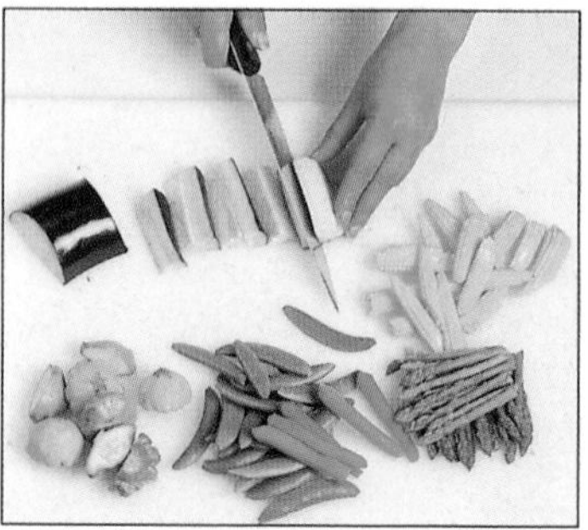

1 Cut the vegetables into similar size shapes using a sharp knife.

2 Put the red chillies, lemon grass and kaffir lime leaves in a mortar and grind together with a pestle.

3 Heat the oil in a wok or large deep frying pan. Add the chilli mixture and fry for 2–3 minutes.

4 Stir in the coconut milk and bring to the boil. Add the vegetables and cook for about 5 minutes or until they are tender. Season with the fish sauce and salt, and garnish with basil leaves.

Szechuan Aubergines

INGREDIENTS

Serves 4
2 small aubergines
5ml/1 tsp salt
3 dried red chillies
groundnut oil, for deep frying
3–4 garlic cloves, finely chopped
1cm/½in fresh root ginger, finely chopped
4 spring onions, chopped and white and green parts separated
15ml/1 tbsp Chinese rice wine or dry sherry
15ml/1 tbsp light soy sauce
5ml/1 tsp sugar
1.5ml/¼ tsp ground roasted Szechuan peppercorns
15ml/1 tbsp Chinese rice vinegar
5ml/1 tsp sesame oil

1 Trim the aubergines and cut into strips, about 4cm/1½in wide and 7.5cm/3in long. Place the aubergines in a colander and sprinkle with the salt. Leave for 30 minutes, then rinse them thoroughly under cold running water. Pat dry with kitchen paper.

2 Meanwhile soak the chillies in warm water for 15 minutes. Drain then cut each chilli into three or four pieces, discarding the seeds.

3 Half-fill a wok with oil and heat to 180°C/350°F. Deep fry the aubergine until golden brown. Drain on kitchen paper. Pour off most of the oil from the wok. Reheat the oil and add the garlic, ginger and white part of the spring onions.

4 Stir-fry for 30 seconds. Add the aubergine and toss, then add the wine or sherry, soy sauce, sugar, ground Szechuan peppercorns and rice vinegar. Stir-fry for 1–2 minutes. Sprinkle over the sesame oil and green spring onion.

Root Vegetables with Spiced Salt

ll kinds of root vegetables can e finely sliced and deep fried to ıake "crisps". Serve as an :companiment to an oriental-yle meal or simply by ıemselves as much tastier nibbles ıan commercial snacks with re-dinner drinks.

NGREDIENTS

rves 4–6

carrot
parsnips
raw beetroots
sweet potato
roundnut oil, for deep frying
5ml/¼ tsp chilli powder
ml/1 tsp sea salt flakes

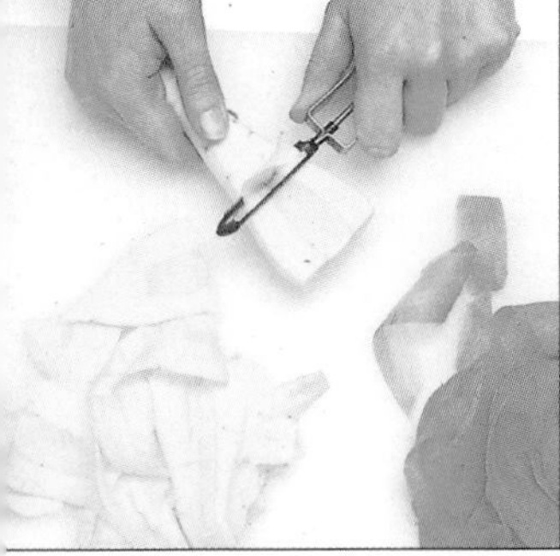

1 Peel the carrot, parsnips, beetroots and sweet potato. Slice the carrot ıd parsnips into long, thin ribbons. :ut the beetroots and sweet potato into ıin rounds. Pat dry on kitchen paper.

2 Half-fill a wok with oil and heat to 180°C/350°F. Add the vegetable slices in batches and deep-fry for 2–3 minutes until golden and crisp. Remove and drain on kitchen paper.

3 Place the chilli powder and sea salt flakes in a mortar and grind them together with a pestle to form a coarse powder.

4 Pile up the vegetable "crisps" on a serving plate and sprinkle over the spiced salt.

COOK'S TIP

To save time, you can slice the vegetables using a mandoline, blender or food processor with a thin slicing disc attached.

Spiced Cauliflower Braise

A delicious vegetable stew, known as *Sambal Kol Kembang,* which combines coconut milk with spices and is perfect as a vegetarian main course or as part of a buffet.

INGREDIENTS

Serves 4

1 cauliflower
2 medium or 1 large tomato(es)
1 onion, chopped
2 garlic cloves, crushed
1 fresh green chilli, seeded
2.5ml/½ tsp ground turmeric
1cm/½ in cube *terasi*
30ml/2 tbsp sunflower oil
400ml/14fl oz coconut milk
250ml/8fl oz/1 cup water
5ml/1 tsp sugar
5ml/1 tsp tamarind pulp, soaked in 45ml/3 tbsp warm water
salt

1 Trim the stalk from the cauliflower and divide into tiny florets. Skin the tomato(es) if liked. Chop the flesh into 1–2.5cm/½–1in pieces.

2 Grind the chopped onion, garlic, green chilli, ground turmeric and *terasi* together to a paste in a food processor or with a pestle and mortar. Heat the sunflower oil in a wok or large frying pan and fry the spice paste to bring out the aromatic flavours, without allowing it to brown.

3 Add the cauliflower florets and to well to coat in the spices. Stir in the coconut milk, water, sugar and sal to taste. Simmer for 5 minutes. Strain the tamarind and reserve the juice.

4 Add the tamarind juice and chopped tomatoes to the pan the cook for 2–3 minutes only. Taste and check the seasoning and serve.

Spicy Scrambled Eggs

This is a lovely way to liven up scrambled eggs. When making *Orak Arik,* prepare all the ingredients ahead so that the vegetables retain all their crunch and colour.

INGREDIENTS

Serves 4

30ml/2 tbsp sunflower oil
1 onion, finely sliced
225g/8oz Chinese leaves, finely sliced or cut in diamonds
200g/7oz can sweetcorn kernels
1 small fresh red chilli, seeded and finely sliced (optional)
30ml/2 tbsp water
2 eggs, beaten
salt and freshly ground black pepper
Deep-fried Onions, to garnish

1 Heat a wok, add the oil and fry the onion, until soft but not browned.

2 Add the Chinese leaves and toss well together. Add the sweetcorn, chilli and water. Cover with a lid and cook for 2 minutes.

3 Remove the lid and stir in the beaten eggs and seasoning. Stir constantly until the eggs are creamy and just set. Serve on warmed plates, scattered with crisp Deep-fried Onio

Spiced Coconut Mushrooms

Here is a simple and delicious way to cook mushrooms. They can be served with almost any oriental meal as well as with traditional western grilled or roasted meats and poultry.

Ingredients

Serves 4

30ml/2 tbsp groundnut oil
2 garlic cloves, finely chopped
2 fresh red chillies, seeded and sliced into rings
3 shallots, finely chopped
225g/8oz brown-cap mushrooms, thickly sliced
150ml/¼ pint/⅔ cup coconut milk
30ml/2 tbsp chopped fresh coriander
salt and ground black pepper

1 Heat a wok until hot, add the oil and swirl it round the wok. Add the garlic and chillies, then stir-fry for a few seconds.

2 Add the shallots and stir-fry for 2–3 minutes until softened. Add the mushrooms and stir-fry for 3 minutes.

Cook's Tip

Use snipped fresh chives instead of chopped fresh coriander, if you wish.

3 Pour in the coconut milk and brin to the boil. Boil rapidly over a hig heat until the liquid has reduced by about half and coats the mushrooms. Season to taste with salt and pepper.

4 Sprinkle over the chopped coriander and toss the mushrooms gently to mix. Serve at once.

Mixed Vegetable Pickle

f you can obtain fresh turmeric, : makes such a difference to the olour and appearance of *Acar Campur*. You can use almost any egetable, bearing in mind that ou need a balance of textures, avours and colours.

NGREDIENTS

lakes 2–3 x 300g/11oz jars

fresh red chilli, seeded and sliced
onion, quartered
garlic cloves, crushed
cm/½ in cube *terasi*
macadamia nuts or 8 almonds
.5cm/1in fresh turmeric, peeled and sliced, or 5ml/1 tsp ground turmeric
0ml/2fl oz/¼ cup sunflower oil
75ml/16fl oz/2 cups white vinegar
50ml/8fl oz/1 cup water
5–50g/1–2oz granulated sugar
carrots
25g/8oz green beans
small cauliflower
cucumber
25g/8oz white cabbage
15g/4oz dry-roasted peanuts, roughly crushed
alt

1 Place the chilli, onion, garlic, *terasi*, nuts and turmeric in a food rocessor and blend to a paste, or ound in a mortar with a pestle.

2 Heat the oil and stir-fry the paste to release the aroma. Add the vinegar, water, sugar and salt. Bring to he boil. Simmer for 10 minutes.

3 Cut the carrots into flower shapes. Cut the green beans into short, neat lengths. Separate the cauliflower into neat, bite-size florets. Peel and seed the cucumber and cut the flesh in neat, bite-size pieces. Cut the cabbage in neat, bite-size pieces.

4 Blanch each vegetable separately, in a large pan of boiling water, for 1 minute. Transfer to a colander and rinse with cold water, to halt the cooking. Drain well.

COOK'S TIP

This pickle is even better if you make it a few days ahead.

5 Add the vegetables to the sauce. Slowly bring to the boil and allow to cook for 5–10 minutes. Do not overcook – the vegetables should still be crunchy.

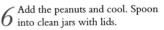

6 Add the peanuts and cool. Spoon into clean jars with lids.

Black Bean and Vegetable Stir-fry

The secret of a quick stir-fry is proper preparation of all the ingredients first. It is important that the ingredients are added to the wok in the right order so that the larger or thicker pieces have a longer cooking time than the smaller pieces – even if this is a difference of only a few millimetres and a few seconds!

INGREDIENTS

Serves 4
8 spring onions
225g/8oz button mushrooms
1 red pepper
1 green pepper
2 large carrots
60ml/4 tbsp sesame oil
2 garlic cloves, crushed
60ml/4 tbsp black bean sauce
90ml/6 tbsp warm water
225g/8oz beansprouts
salt and ground black pepper

1 Thinly slice the spring onions and button mushrooms.

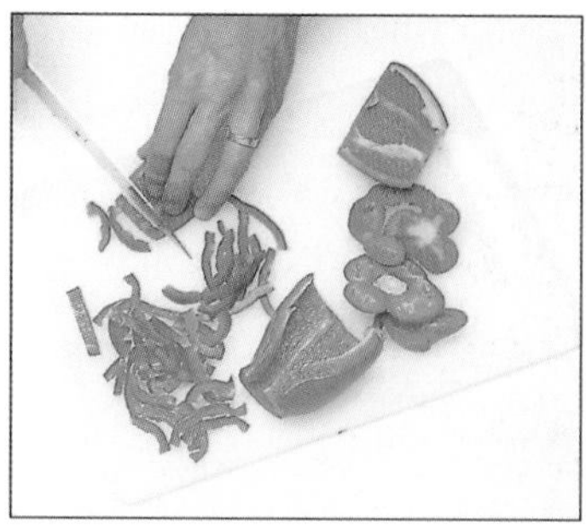

2 Cut both the peppers in half, remove the seeds and slice the flesh into thin strips.

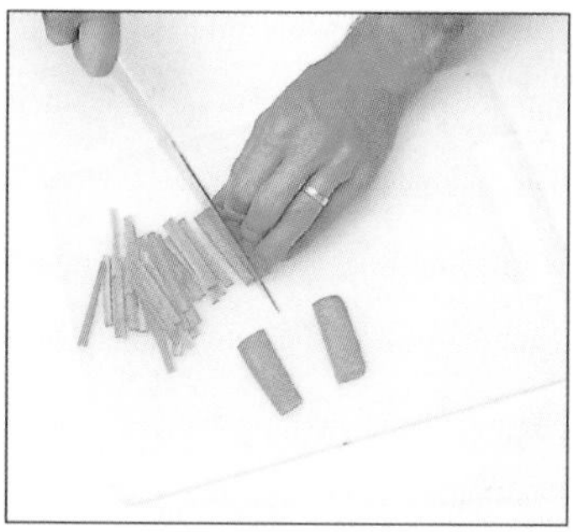

3 Cut the carrots in half. Cut each half into thin strips lengthways. Stack the slices and cut through them to make very fine strips.

4 Heat the oil in a large preheated wok until very hot. Add the spring onions and garlic and stir-fry for 30 seconds.

5 Add the mushrooms, peppers and carrots. Stir-fry for 5–6 minutes over a high heat until the vegetables a just beginning to soften.

6 Mix the black bean sauce with th water. Add to the wok and cook for 3–4 minutes. Stir in the beansprou and cook for 1 minute more, until all the vegetables are coated in the sauce. Season to taste, then serve at once.

COOK'S TIP

Black bean sauce is made from salted black beans – which have a very distinctive flavour – that have been crushed and mixed with a variety of spices, such as ginger and chilli. It is quite a thick paste and readily available in jars, bottles and cans from large supermarkets and oriental food stores. Store in the refrigerator after opening.

Stir-fried Spinach with Garlic and Sesame Seeds

The sesame seeds add a crunchy texture which contrasts well with the wilted spinach in this easy vegetable dish.

INGREDIENTS

Serves 2

225g/8oz fresh spinach, washed
25ml/1½ tbsp sesame seeds
30ml/2 tbsp groundnut oil
1.5ml/¼ tsp sea salt flakes
2–3 garlic cloves, sliced

COOK'S TIP

Take care when adding the spinach to the hot oil as it will spit furiously.

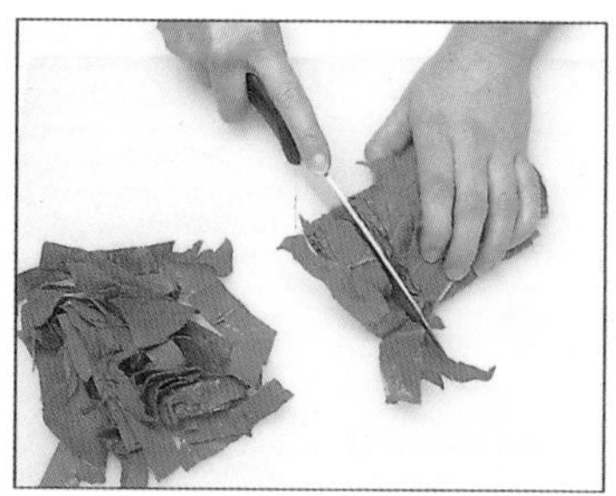

1 Shake the spinach to get rid of any excess water, then remove the stalks and discard any yellow or damaged leaves. Lay several spinach leaves one on top of another, roll up tightly and cut crossways into wide strips. Repeat with the remaining leaves.

2 Heat a wok to a medium heat, ad the sesame seeds and dry fry, stirring constantly, for 1–2 minutes until golden brown. Transfer to a smal bowl and set aside.

3 Add the oil to the wok and swirl i around. When hot, add the salt, spinach and garlic and stir-fry for 2 minutes until the spinach just wilts anc the leaves are coated in oil.

4 Sprinkle over the dry-fried sesame seeds and toss well. Serve at once.

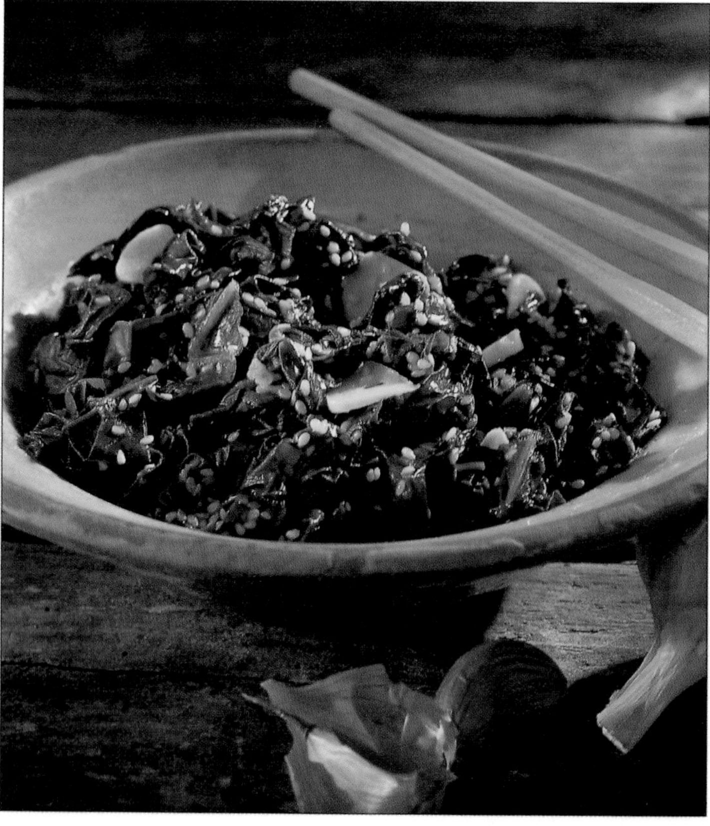

Chinese Leaves with Oyster Sauce

Iere, Chinese leaves are prepared
a a very simple way – stir-fried
nd served with oyster sauce.
'his Cantonese combination
nakes a simple, quickly prepared
nd tasty accompaniment to
riental or western seafood
lishes. Vegetarians may prefer to
ubstitute light soy or hoi-sin
auce for the oyster sauce used in
his recipe.

NGREDIENTS

erves 3–4
50g/1lb Chinese leaves
0ml/2 tbsp groundnut oil
5–30ml/1–2 tbsp oyster sauce

1 Trim the Chinese leaves, removing any discoloured leaves and damaged tems. Tear into manageable pieces.

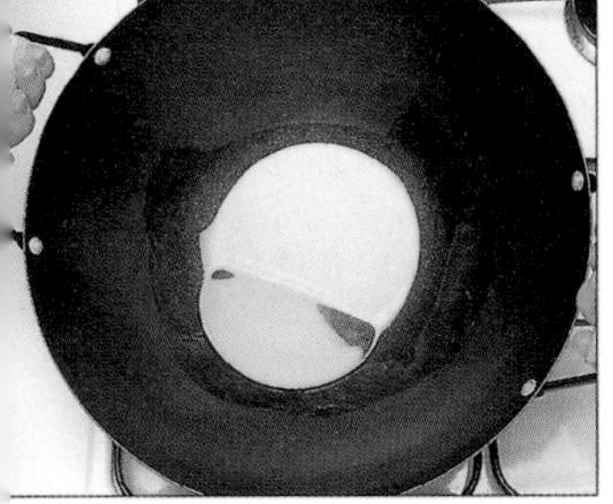

2 Heat a wok until hot, add the oil and swirl it around.

3 Add the Chinese leaves and stir-fry for 2–3 minutes until they have wilted a little.

4 Add the oyster sauce and continue to stir-fry for a few seconds more until the leaves are cooked but still slightly crisp. Serve immediately.

COOK'S TIP

You can replace the Chinese leaves with Chinese flowering cabbage, which is also known by its Cantonese name *choi sam*. It has bright green leaves and tiny yellow flowers, which are also eaten along with the leaves and stalks. It is available from oriental supermarkets.

Tofu Stir-fry

The tofu has a pleasant creamy texture, which contrasts delightfully with the crunchy stir-fried vegetables. Make sure you buy firm tofu which is easy to cut neatly.

INGREDIENTS

Serves 2–4

115g/4oz hard white cabbage
2 green chillies
225g/8oz firm tofu
45ml/3 tbsp vegetable oil
2 cloves garlic, crushed
3 spring onions, chopped
175g/6oz French beans, topped and tailed
175g/6oz baby sweetcorn, halved
115g/4oz beansprouts
45ml/3 tbsp smooth peanut butter
25ml/1½ tbsp dark soy sauce
300ml/½ pint/1¼ cups coconut milk

1 Shred the white cabbage. Carefully remove the seeds from the chillies and chop finely. Wear rubber gloves to protect your hands, if necessary.

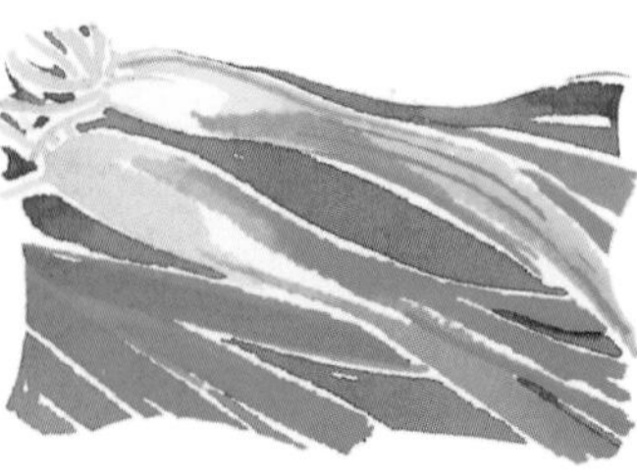

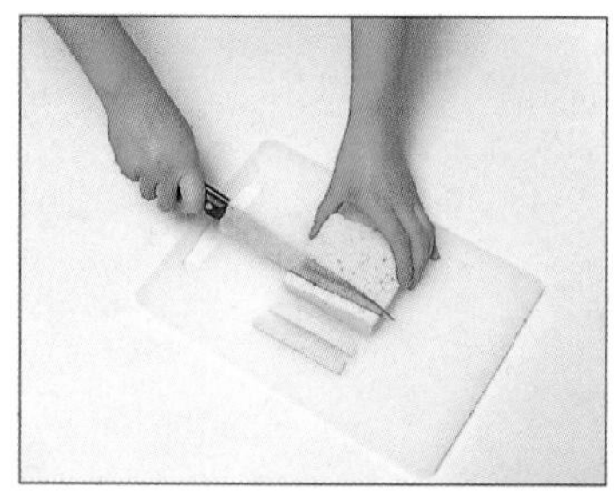

2 Cut the tofu into strips.

3 Heat the wok, then add 30ml/2 tbsp of the oil. When the oil is hot, add the tofu, stir-fry for 3 minutes and remove. Set aside. Wipe out the wok with kitchen paper.

4 Add the remaining oil. When it is hot, add the garlic, spring onions and chillies and stir-fry for 1 minute. Add the French beans, sweetcorn and beansprouts and stir-fry for a further 2 minutes.

5 Add the peanut butter and soy sauce to the wok. Stir well to coat the vegetables. Add the tofu to the vegetables in the wok.

6 Pour the coconut milk over the vegetables, simmer for 3 minutes and serve immediately.

COOK'S TIP

There are literally hundreds of varieties of chilli. Generally speaking, dark green chillies are hotter than paler green ones, which are, in turn, hotter and less sweet than red chillies – but this is not a hard-and-fast rule and it is possible to be caught out by an unfamiliar variety. The "heat factor" of chillies is measured in Scoville units, with sweet peppers at 0 at the bottom of the scale and Mexican habanero chillies at 300,000, the hottest at the top. Most oriental recipes call for medium to hot chillies. Some Indonesian and Thai dishes can be very fiery, but Chinese recipes tend to use fairly mild fresh green or red chillies.

Cooked Vegetable Gado-Gado

Instead of putting everything on a large platter, you can serve individual servings of this salad. It is a perfect recipe for lunchtime or informal gatherings.

INGREDIENTS

Serves 6

225g/8oz waxy potatoes, cooked
450g/1lb mixed cabbage, spinach and beansprouts, in equal proportions, rinsed and shredded
½ cucumber, cut in wedges, salted and set aside for 15 minutes
2–3 eggs, hard-boiled and shelled
115g/4oz fresh bean curd
oil for frying
6–8 large prawn crackers
lemon juice
Deep-fried Onions, to garnish
Peanut Sauce, see Vegetable Salad with Hot Peanut Sauce

1 Cube the potatoes and set aside. Bring a large pan of salted water to the boil. Plunge one type of raw vegetable at a time into the pan for just a few seconds to blanch. Lift out the vegetables with a large draining spoon or sieve and run under very cold water. Or plunge them into iced water and leave for 2 minutes. Drain thoroughly. Blanch all the vegetables, except the cucumber, in this way.

2 Rinse the cucumber pieces and drain them well. Cut the eggs in quarters. Cut the bean curd into cube

3 Fry the bean curd in hot oil in a wok until crisp on both sides. Lift out and drain on kitchen paper.

4 Add more oil to the pan and then deep-fry the Prawn Crackers one or two at a time. Reserve them on a tray lined with kitchen paper.

5 Arrange all the cooked vegetables attractively on a platter, with the cucumber, hard-boiled eggs and bean curd. Scatter with the lemon juice and Deep-fried Onions at the last minute.

6 Serve with the prepared Peanut Sauce and hand round the fried Prawn Crackers separately.

Spicy Courgette Fritters with Thai Salsa

'he Thai salsa goes just as well ·ith plain stir-fried salmon strips r stir-fried beef as it does with ıese courgette fritters.

NGREDIENTS

erves 2–4

0ml/2 tsp cumin seeds
0ml/2 tsp coriander seeds
50g/1lb courgettes
15g/4oz chick-pea (gram) flour
.5ml/½ tsp bicarbonate of soda
20ml/4fl oz/½ cup groundnut oil
ılt and ground black pepper
resh mint sprigs, to garnish

'or the Thai salsa

½ cucumber, diced
spring onions, chopped
radishes, cubed
0ml/2 tbsp fresh mint, chopped
.5cm/1in fresh root ginger, peeled and grated
5ml/3 tbsp lime juice
0ml/2 tbsp caster sugar
cloves garlic, crushed

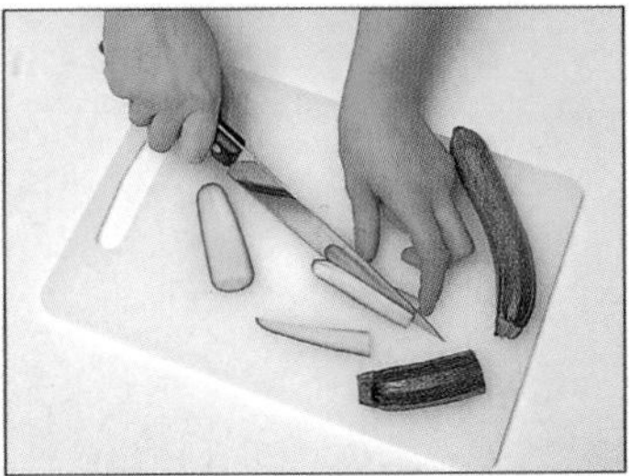

1 Heat the wok, then dry fry the cumin and coriander seeds. Cool :hem, then grind well, using a pestle ınd mortar.

COOK'S TIP

You can substitute mooli, also known as daikon and white radish, for the round radishes in the salsa.

2 Cut the courgettes into 7.5cm/3in sticks. Place in a bowl.

3 Process the flour, bicarbonate of soda, spices and salt and pepper in a food processor or blender. Add 120ml/4fl oz warm water with 15ml/1 tbsp groundnut oil and process again.

4 Coat the courgettes in the batter, then leave to stand for 10 minutes.

5 To make the salsa, mix together the cucumber, spring onions, radishes, mint, ginger and lime juice in a bowl. Stir in the sugar and the garlic.

6 Heat the wok, then add the remaining oil. When the oil is hot, stir-fry the courgettes in batches. Drain well on kitchen paper, then serve hot with the Thai salsa, garnished with fresh mint sprigs.

Spiced Vegetables with Coconut

This spicy and substantial stir-fry could be served as a starter, or as a vegetarian main course for two. Eat it with spoons and forks, and provide hunks of granary bread for mopping up the delicious coconut milk.

Ingredients

Serves 2–4

1 red chilli
1 bulb fennel
2 large carrots
6 celery sticks
30ml/2 tbsp grapeseed oil
2.5cm/1in fresh root ginger, peeled and grated
1 clove garlic, crushed
3 spring onions, sliced
1 x 400ml/14fl oz can thin coconut milk
15ml/1 tbsp chopped fresh coriander
salt and ground black pepper
fresh coriander sprigs, to garnish

Cook's Tip

When buying fennel, look for well-rounded bulbs; flatter ones are immature and will not have developed their full aniseed-like flavour. The bulbs should be white with overlapping ridged layers. Avoid any that look damaged or bruised. The fennel should be dry, but not desiccated.

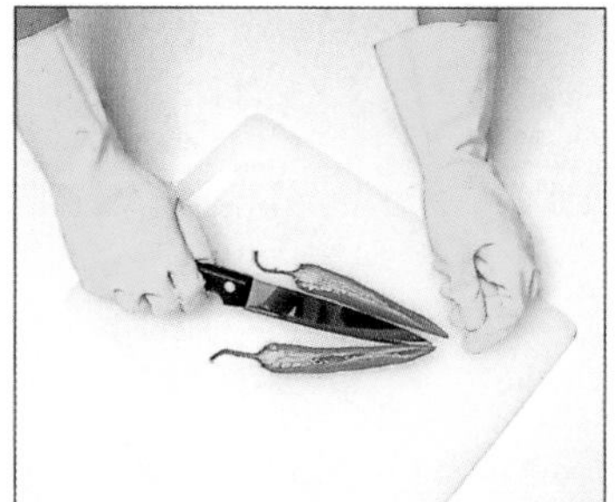

1 Halve, seed and finely chop the chilli. If necessary, wear rubber gloves to protect your hands.

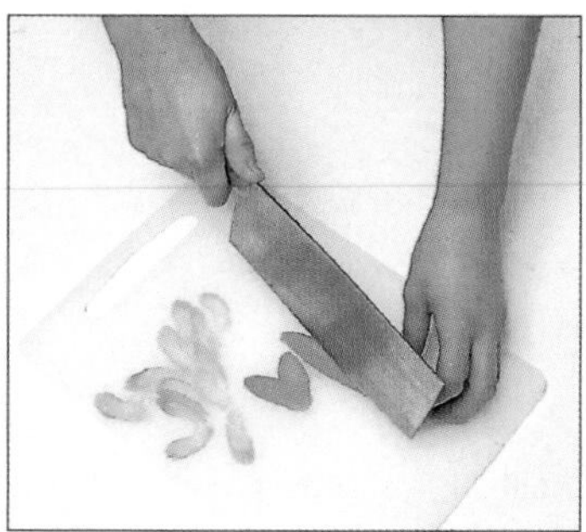

2 Thinly slice the carrots and the celery sticks on the diagonal.

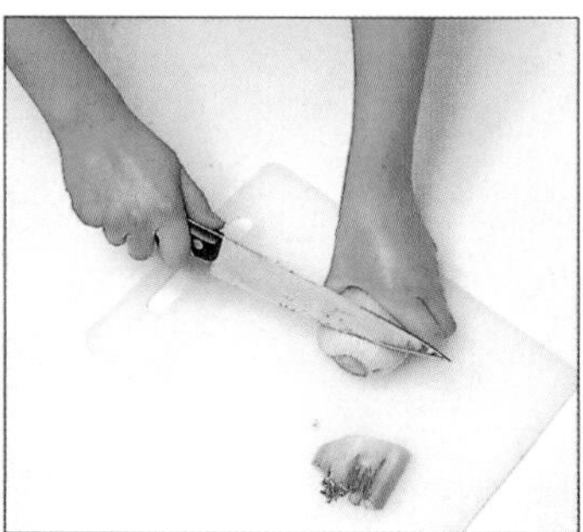

3 Trim the fennel bulb and slice roughly, using a sharp knife.

4 Heat the wok, then add the oil. When the oil is hot, add the chilli, fennel, carrots, celery, ginger, garlic and spring onions and stir-fry for 2 minutes.

5 Stir in the coconut milk with a large spoon and bring to the boil.

6 Stir in the coriander and salt and pepper, and serve garnished with coriander sprigs.

Pak Choi and Mushroom Stir-fry

Try to buy all the varieties of mushroom for this dish – wild oyster and shiitake mushrooms have particularly distinctive, delicate flavours that work well when stir-fried.

INGREDIENTS

Serves 4

4 dried black Chinese mushrooms
150ml/¼ pint/⅔ cup hot water
450g/1lb pak choi
50g/2oz oyster mushrooms, preferably wild
50g/2oz shiitake mushrooms
15ml/1 tbsp vegetable oil
1 clove garlic, crushed
30ml/2 tbsp oyster sauce

1 Soak the black Chinese mushrooms in the hot water for 15 minutes to soften.

COOK'S TIP

Pak choi, also called bok choi, pok choi and spoon cabbage, is an attractive member of the cabbage family, with long, smooth white stems and dark green leaves. It has a pleasant flavour which does not, in any way, resemble that of cabbage.

2 Tear the pak choi into bite-sized pieces with your fingers.

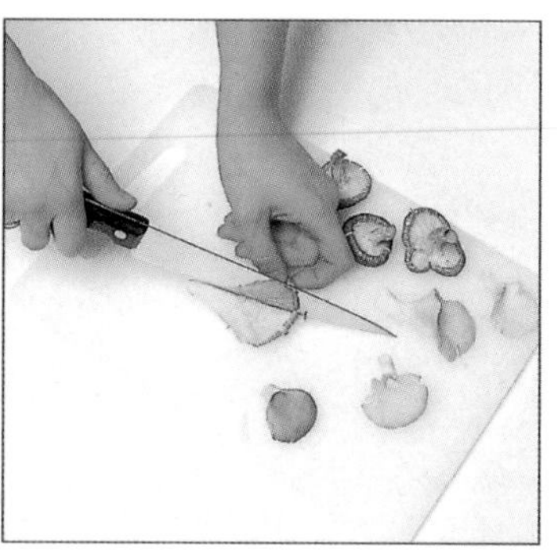

3 Halve any large oyster and shiitake mushrooms, using a sharp knife.

4 Strain the Chinese mushrooms. Heat the wok, then add the oil. When the oil is hot, stir-fry the garlic until softened but not coloured.

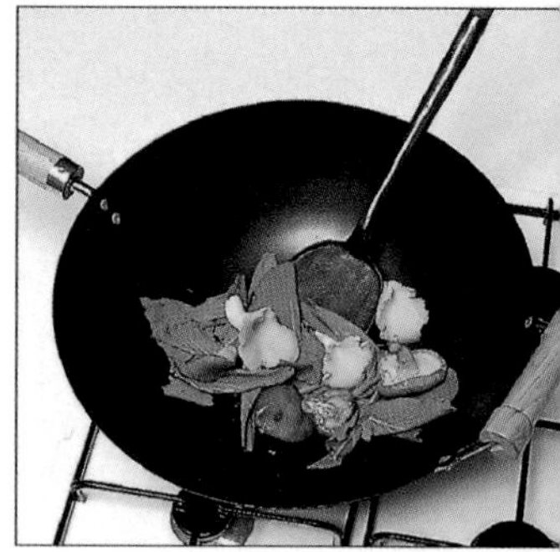

5 Add the pak choi to the wok and stir-fry for 1 minute. Mix in all the mushrooms and stir-fry for 1 minute.

6 Add the oyster sauce, toss well and serve immediately.

Red-cooked Tofu with Chinese Mushrooms

Red-cooked is a term applied to Chinese dishes cooked with a dark soy sauce. This tasty dish can be served as either a side dish or main meal.

INGREDIENTS

Serves 4

225g/8oz firm tofu
45ml/3 tbsp dark soy sauce
30ml/2 tbsp Chinese rice wine or dry sherry
10ml/2 tsp soft dark brown sugar
1 garlic clove, crushed
15ml/1 tbsp grated fresh root ginger
2.5ml/½ tsp Chinese five-spice powder
pinch of ground roasted Szechuan peppercorns
6 dried Chinese black mushrooms
5ml/1 tsp cornflour
30ml/2 tbsp groundnut oil
5–6 spring onions, sliced into 2.5cm/1in lengths, white and green parts separated
small fresh basil leaves, to garnish
rice noodles, to serve

1 Drain the tofu, pat dry with kitchen paper and cut into 2.5cm/1in cubes. Place in a shallow dish. In a small bowl, mix together the soy sauce, rice wine or sherry, sugar, garlic, ginger, five-spice powder and Szechuan peppercorns. Pour the marinade over the tofu, toss well and leave to marinate for about 30 minutes. Drain, reserving the marinade.

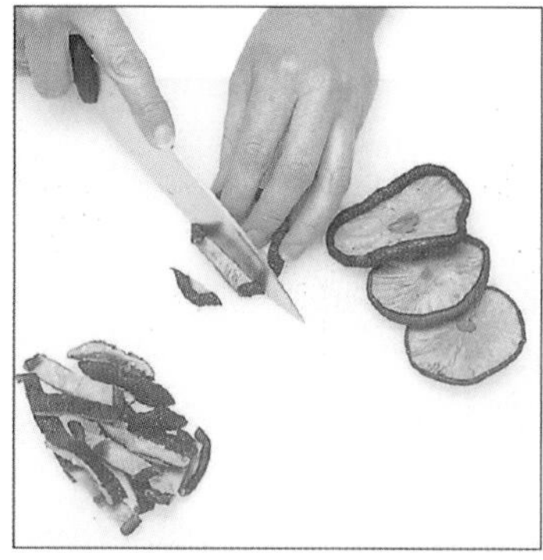

2 Meanwhile soak the dried black mushrooms in warm water for 20–30 minutes until soft. Drain, reserving 90ml/6 tbsp of the soaking liquid. Squeeze out any excess liquid from the mushrooms, remove the tough stalks and slice the caps. In a small bowl, blend the cornflour with the reserved marinade and mushroom soaking liquid.

3 Heat a wok until hot, add the oil and swirl it around. Add the tofu and stir-fry for 2–3 minutes until evenly golden. Remove from the wok and set aside.

4 Add the mushrooms and white parts of the spring onions to the wok and stir-fry for 2 minutes. Pour the marinade mixture and stir for 1 minute until thickened.

5 Return the tofu to the wok with the green parts of the spring onions. Simmer gently for 1–2 minut Scatter over the basil leaves and serve once with rice noodles.

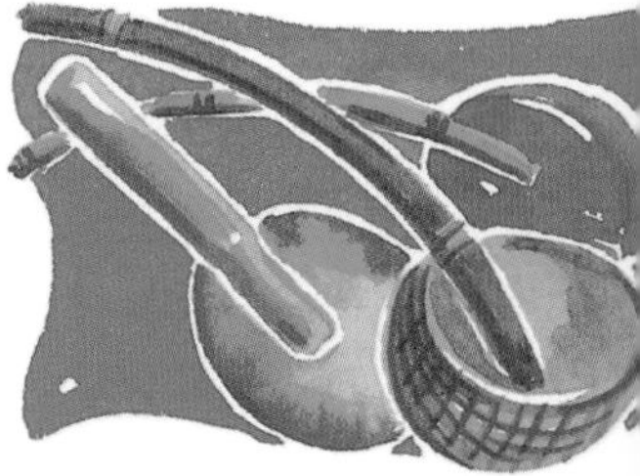

Pancakes with Stir-fried Vegetables

To serve, each person spreads a little hoi-sin sauce over a pancake, adds a helping of the filling from the wok and rolls up the pancake.

INGREDIENTS

Serves 4

3 eggs
30ml/2 tbsp water
60ml/4 tbsp groundnut oil
25g/1oz dried Chinese black mushrooms
25g/1oz dried wood ears
10ml/2 tsp cornflour
30ml/2 tbsp light soy sauce
30ml/2 tbsp Chinese rice wine or dry sherry
10ml/2 tsp sesame oil
2 garlic cloves, finely chopped
1cm/½in fresh root ginger, cut into thin shreds
75g/3oz canned sliced bamboo shoots, drained and rinsed
175g/6oz beansprouts
4 spring onions, finely shredded
salt and ground black pepper
Chinese pancakes and hoi-sin sauce, to serve

1 Whisk the eggs, water and seasoning in a small bowl. Heat 15ml/1 tbsp of the groundnut oil in a wok and swirl it around. Pour in the eggs, then tilt the wok so that they spread to an even layer. Continue to cook over a high heat for about 2 minutes until set. Turn on to a board and, when cool, roll up and cut into thin strips. Wipe the wok clean.

COOK'S TIP

Chinese pancakes are available from oriental supermarkets. Reheat them in a bamboo steamer for 2–3 minutes just before serving.

2 Meanwhile put the black mushrooms and wood ears into separate bowls. Pour over enough warm water to cover, then leave to soak for 20–30 minutes until soft. Drain the dried mushrooms, reserving their soaking liquid. Squeeze the excess liquid from each of them.

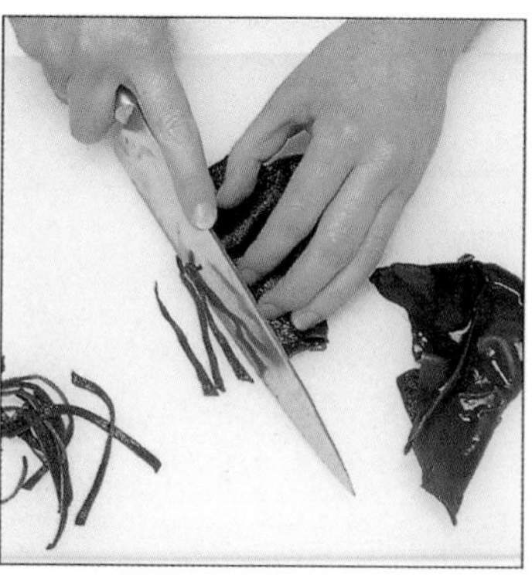

3 Remove the tough stalks and thinly slice the black mushrooms. Finely shred the wood ears. Set aside. Strain the reserved soaking liquid through muslin into a jug; reserve 120ml/4fl oz/½cup of the liquid. In a bowl, blend the cornflour with the reserved liquid, soy sauce, rice wine or sherry and sesame oil.

4 Heat the wok over a medium hea add the remaining groundnut oil and swirl it around. Add the wood ea and black mushrooms and stir-fry for about 2 minutes. Add the garlic, ging bamboo shoots and beansprouts and stir-fry for 1–2 minutes.

5 Pour in the cornflour mixture and cook, stirring, for 1 minute until thickened. Add the spring onions and omelette strips and toss gently. Adjust the seasoning, adding more soy sauce, needed. Serve at once with the Chinese pancakes and hoi-sin sauce.

Stir-fried Vegetables with Coriander Omelette

A wok is the ideal utensil for cooking an omelette as the heat is evenly distributed over the wide surface. This is a great supper dish for vegetarians. The glaze is intended to give the vegetables an appealing shine and does not constitute a sauce.

INGREDIENTS

Serves 3–4

For the omelette

2 eggs
30ml/2 tbsp water
45ml/3 tbsp chopped fresh coriander
salt and ground black pepper
15ml/1 tbsp groundnut oil

For the glazed vegetables

15ml/1 tbsp cornflour
30ml/2 tbsp dry sherry
15ml/1 tbsp sweet chilli sauce
120ml/4 fl oz/½ cup vegetable stock
30ml/2 tbsp groundnut oil
5ml/1 tsp grated fresh root ginger
6–8 spring onions, sliced
115g/4oz mangetouts
1 yellow pepper, seeded and sliced
115g/4oz fresh shiitake or button mushrooms
115g/4oz canned water chestnuts, drained and rinsed
115g/4oz beansprouts
½ small Chinese cabbage, roughly shredded

COOK'S TIP

Vary the combination of vegetables used according to availability and taste, but make sure that you slice or chop them to approximately the same size and thickness.

1 To make the omelette, whisk the eggs, water, coriander and seasoning in a small bowl. Heat the oil in a wok. Pour in the eggs, then tilt the wok so that the mixture spreads in an even layer. Cook over a high heat until the edges are slightly crisp.

2 Flip the omelette over with a spatula and cook the other side for about 30 seconds until lightly browned. Turn the omelette on to a board and leave to cool. When cold, roll up loosely and cut into thin slices. Wipe the wok clean.

3 In a bowl, blend together the cornflour, sherry, chilli sauce and stock to make the glaze. Set aside.

4 Heat the wok until hot, add the o and swirl it around. Add the ging and spring onions and stir-fry for a fe seconds to flavour the oil. Add the mangetouts, sliced pepper, mushroom and water chestnuts and stir-fry for 3 minutes.

5 Add the beansprouts and Chinese cabbage and stir-fry for 2 minutes.

6 Pour in the glaze ingredients and cook, stirring for about 1 minute until the glaze thickens and coats the vegetables. Turn the vegetables on to a warmed serving plate and top with the omelette shreds. Serve at once.

Broccoli in Oyster Sauce

The broccoli florets retain their vivid shade of green and crunchy texture, as well as much of their vitamin and mineral content, when given the wok treatment here. Vegetarians may prefer to substitute light soy sauce for the oyster sauce.

Ingredients

Serves 4

450g/1lb broccoli
45–60ml/3–4 tbsp vegetable oil
2.5ml/½ tsp salt
2.5ml/½ tsp light brown sugar
30–45ml/2–3 tbsp stock or water
30ml/2 tbsp oyster sauce

1 Cut the broccoli heads into florets, remove the rough skin from the stalks and slice the florets diagonally into diamond-shaped chunks.

2 Heat the oil in a preheated wok and add the salt, then stir-fry the broccoli for about 2 minutes. Add the sugar and stock or water, and continue stirring for 1 minute. Finally add the oyster sauce, blend well and serve.

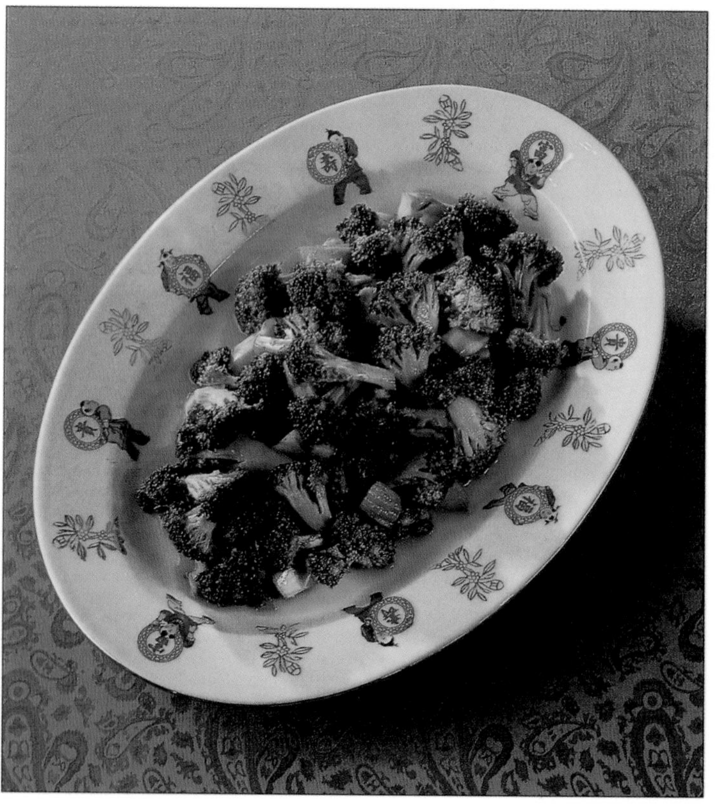

Cook's Tip

Always choose healthy-looking broccoli with firm stems that are neither woody nor wrinkled. Look for tightly packed, well-coloured flower heads with no signs of yellowing. Broccoli is best eaten on the day it was purchased or, better still, picked. It deteriorates rapidly in storage and loses many of the vitamins for which it is especially valued, as well as its crispness.

Deep Fried Onions

:nown as *bawang goreng*, these are traditional accompaniment and arnish to many Indonesian lishes. Oriental stores sell them eady-prepared, but it is simple to nake them at home, using fresh nions. The small red onions that nay be bought in Asian food tores are excellent when deep ried as they contain less water nan most European varieties.

NGREDIENTS

Iakes 450g/1lb
50g/1lb onions
il for deep frying

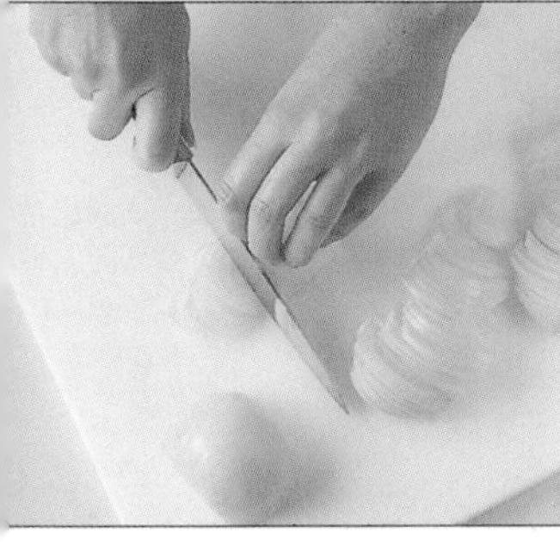

1 Peel and slice the onions as evenly and finely as possible.

2 Spread out thinly on kitchen paper in an airy place and leave to dry for 0 minutes–2 hours.

3 Heat the oil in a wok to 190°C/375°F. Fry the onions in batches, turning all the time, until they are crisp and golden. Drain well on kitchen paper and cool. Deep fried onions can be stored in an airtight container.

COOK'S TIP

Garlic can also be prepared and cooked in the same way or some can be fried with the last batch of onions. Deep fried garlic gives an added dimension in flavour as a garnish for many dishes.

An even faster way to prepare home-made deep fried onions is to use a 75g/3oz packet of quick-dried onions, which you can fry in about 250ml/8fl oz/1 cup sunflower oil. This gives you 115g/4oz of fried onion flakes.

Bamboo Shoots and Chinese Mushrooms

Another name for this dish is "twin winter vegetables" because both bamboo shoots and mushrooms are at their best then. For that reason, try using canned winter bamboo shoots and extra "fat" mushrooms.

INGREDIENTS

Serves 4

50g/2oz dried Chinese mushrooms
275g/10oz can winter bamboo shoots
45ml/3 tbsp vegetable oil
1 spring onion, cut into short sections
30ml/2 tbsp light soy sauce or oyster sauce
15ml/1 tbsp Chinese rice wine or dry sherry
2.5ml/½ tsp light brown sugar
10ml/2 tsp cornflour paste
few drops sesame oil

1 Soak the mushrooms in cold water for at least 3 hours. Squeeze dry and discard any hard stalks, reserving the water. Cut the mushrooms in half or in quarters if they are large – keep them whole if small.

2 Rinse and drain the bamboo shoots, then cut them into small, wedge-shaped pieces.

3 Heat the oil in a preheated wok and stir-fry the mushrooms and bamboo shoots for about 1 minute. Add the spring onion, soy or oyster sauce, rice wine or sherry and the sugar, with about 2–3 tbsp of the reserved mushroom soaking liquid. Bring to the boil and braise for a further 1–2 minutes. Stir in the cornflour paste to thicken, sprinkle with the sesame oil and serve at once.

Stir-fried Tomatoes, Cucumber and Eggs

The cucumber can be replaced by a green pepper or courgettes if you prefer.

INGREDIENTS

Serves 4

175g/6oz firm tomatoes, skinned
½ cucumber, unpeeled
4 eggs
5ml/1 tsp salt
1 spring onion, finely chopped
60ml/4 tbsp vegetable oil
10ml/2 tsp Chinese rice wine or dry sherry (optional)

1 Cut the tomatoes and cucumber in half, then cut across into small wedges. In a bowl, beat the eggs with a pinch of salt and a few pieces of the chopped spring onion.

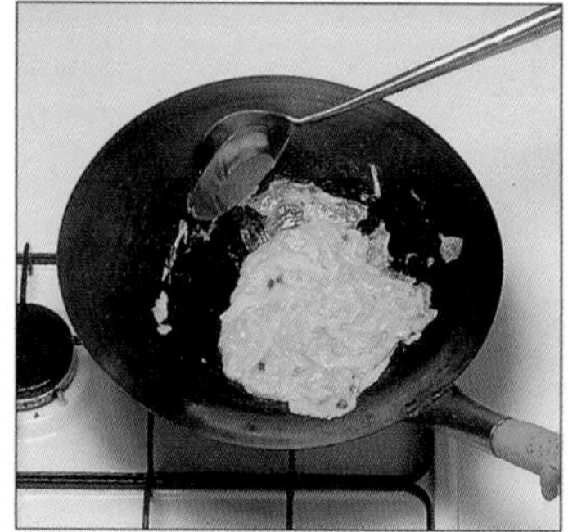

2 Heat about half the oil in a preheated wok, then pour in the eggs and scramble lightly over a moderate heat until set, but not too dry. Remove the scrambled egg from the wok and keep warm.

3 Add the remaining oil to the wok and heat over a high heat. Add the vegetables and stir-fry for 1 minute. Add the remaining salt, then the scrambled eggs and wine or sherry if using. Serve at once.

Mooli, Beetroot and Carrot Stir-fry

This is a dazzlingly colourful dish with a crunchy texture and fragrant taste.

INGREDIENTS

Serves 4

25g/1oz/¼ cup pine nuts
115g/4oz mooli, peeled
115g/4oz raw beetroot, peeled
115g/4oz carrots, peeled
25ml/1½ tbsp vegetable oil
juice of 1 orange
30ml/2 tbsp chopped fresh coriander
salt and ground black pepper

1 Place the pine nuts in a preheated wok and toss until golden brown. Remove and set aside.

2 Cut the mooli, beetroot and carrots into long, thin strips.

3 Heat the oil in a preheated wok. When the oil is hot, stir-fry the mooli, raw beetroot and carrots for 2–3 minutes. Remove the vegetables from the wok and set aside.

4 Pour the orange juice into the wok and simmer for 2 minutes. Remove and keep warm.

5 Arrange the vegetables attractively on a warmed platter, sprinkle over the coriander and season to taste with salt and pepper.

6 Drizzle over the orange juice, sprinkle with the pine nuts, and serve immediately.

Pak Choi with Lime Dressing

or this Thai recipe, the coconut ressing is traditionally made sing fish sauce, but vegetarians ould use mushroom sauce nstead. Beware, the red chillies nake this a fiery dish!

NGREDIENTS

erves 4
spring onions
pak choi
0ml/2 tbsp oil
fresh red chillies, cut into thin strips
garlic cloves, thinly sliced
5ml/1 tbsp crushed peanuts

or the dressing
5–30ml/1–2 tbsp fish sauce
0ml/2 tbsp lime juice
50ml/8fl oz/1 cup coconut milk

1 To make the dressing, blend together the fish sauce and lime uice, then stir in the coconut milk.

2 Trim the spring onions, then cut diagonally into slices, including all ut the very tips of the green parts, but eeping the green and white parts eparate.

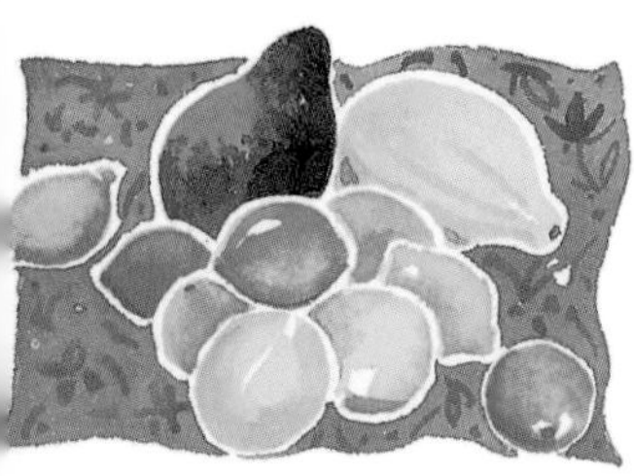

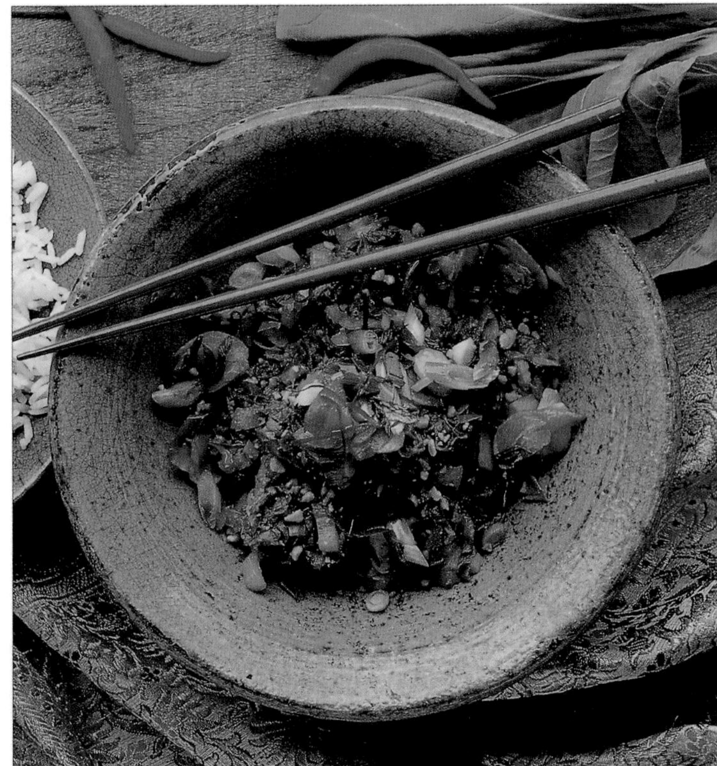

3 Using a large sharp knife, cut the pak choi into very fine shreds.

4 Heat the oil in a preheated wok and stir-fry the chillies for 2–3 minutes until crisp. Transfer to a plate using a slotted spoon. Stir-fry the garlic for 30–60 seconds until golden brown and transfer to the plate with the chillies. Stir-fry the white parts of the spring onions for about 2–3 minutes and then add the green parts and stir-fry for a further 1 minute. Add to the plate with the chillies and garlic.

5 Bring a large pan of salted water to the boil and add the pak choi. Stir twice and then drain immediately. Place the warmed pak choi in a large bowl, add the coconut dressing and stir well. Spoon into a large serving bowl and sprinkle with the crushed peanuts and the stir-fried chilli mixture. Serve immediately.

Stir-Fried Vegetables with Pasta

This colourful Chinese-style dish is easily prepared and, for a change, uses pasta instead of Chinese noodles.

INGREDIENTS

Serves 4

1 medium carrot
175g/6oz small courgettes
175g/6oz runner or other green beans
175g/6oz baby sweetcorn
450g/1lb ribbon pasta, such as tagliatelle
30ml/2 tbsp corn oil, plus extra for tossing the pasta
1cm/½in fresh root ginger, finely chopped
2 garlic cloves, finely chopped
90ml/6 tbsp yellow bean sauce
6 spring onions, sliced into 2.5cm/1in lengths
30ml/2 tbsp dry sherry
5ml/1 tsp toasted sesame seeds
salt

1 Slice the carrot and courgettes diagonally into chunks. Slice the beans diagonally. Cut the baby corn diagonally in half.

2 Cook the pasta in plenty of boiling salted water according to the manufacturer's instructions, drain, then rinse under hot water. Toss in a little oil to prevent sticking.

3 Heat 30ml/2 tbsp oil in a preheated wok or frying pan and add the ginger and garlic. Stir-fry for 30 seconds, then add the carrots, beans, baby sweetcorn and courgettes.

4 Stir-fry for 3–4 minutes, then stir in the yellow bean sauce. Stir-fry for 2 minutes, add the spring onions, dry sherry and pasta and stir-fry for a further 1 minute until piping hot. Sprinkle with sesame seeds and serve immediately.

Chinese Vegetable Stir-fry

This is a typical stir-fried vegetable dish popular all over China. Chinese leaves are like a cross between a cabbage and a crunchy lettuce, with a delicious peppery flavour.

INGREDIENTS

Serves 4

45ml/3 tbsp sunflower oil
15ml/1 tbsp sesame oil
1 garlic clove, chopped
225g/8oz broccoli florets, cut into small pieces
115g/4oz sugar snap peas
1 head Chinese leaves, about 450g/1lb, or Savoy cabbage, sliced
4 spring onions, finely chopped
30ml/2 tbsp soy sauce
30ml/2 tbsp Chinese rice wine or dry sherry
30–45ml/2–3 tbsp water
15ml/1 tbsp sesame seeds, lightly toasted

1 Heat the sunflower and sesame oils in a preheated wok or large frying pan, add the garlic and stir-fry for 30 seconds.

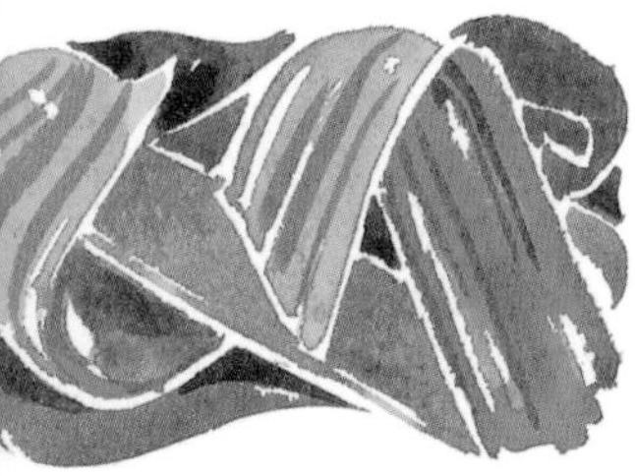

2 Add the broccoli florets and stir-fry for 3 minutes. Add the sugar snap peas and cook for 2 minutes, then toss in the Chinese leaves or cabbage and the spring onions and stir-fry for a further 2 minutes.

3 Pour on the soy sauce, rice wine or dry sherry and water and stir-fry for a further 4 minutes, or until the vegetables are just tender. Sprinkle with the toasted sesame seeds and serve hot.

Indonesian Potatoes with Onions and Chilli Sauce

This adds another dimension to potato chips, with the addition of crisply fried onions and a hot soy sauce and chilli dressing. Eat *Kentang Gula* hot, warm or cold, as a tasty snack.

INGREDIENTS

Serves 6

3 large potatoes, about 225g/8oz each, peeled and cut into chips
sunflower or groundnut oil for deep-frying
2 onions, finely sliced
salt

For the dressing

1–2 fresh red chillies, seeded and ground
45ml/3 tbsp dark soy sauce

1 Rinse the potato chips and then pat dry very well with kitchen paper. Heat the oil and deep-fry the chips, until they are golden brown in colour and crisp.

2 Put the chips in a dish, sprinkle with salt and keep warm. Fry the onion slices in the hot oil until they are similarly crisp and golden brown. Drain well on kitchen paper and then add to the potato chips.

3 Mix the chillies with the soy sauce and heat gently.

4 Pour over the potato and onion mixture and serve as suggested.

VARIATION

Alternatively, boil the potatoes in their skins. Drain, cool and slice them and then shallow-fry until golden. Cook the onions and pour over the dressing, as above.

Courgettes with Noodles

Any courgette or member of the squash family can be used in this *Oseng Oseng,* which is very similar to a dish enjoyed in Malaysia, whose cuisine has strong links with Indonesia.

INGREDIENTS

Serves 4–6

450g/1lb courgettes, sliced
1 onion, finely sliced
1 garlic clove, finely chopped
30ml/2 tbsp sunflower oil
2.5ml/½ tsp ground turmeric
2 tomatoes, chopped
45ml/3 tbsp water
115g/4oz cooked, peeled prawns (optional)
25g/1oz cellophane noodles
salt

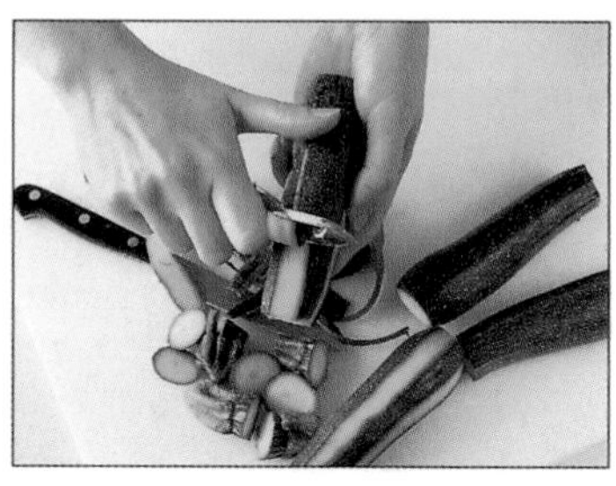

1 Use a potato peeler to cut thin strips from the outside of each courgette. Cut them in neat slices. Set the courgettes on one side. Fry the onion and garlic in hot oil; do not allow to brown.

2 Add the turmeric, courgette slices, chopped tomatoes, water and prawns, if using.

3 Put the noodles in a pan and pour over boiling water to cover, leave for a minute and then drain. Cut the noodles in 5cm/2in lengths and add to the vegetables.

4 Cover with a lid and cook in their own steam for 2–3 minutes. Toss everything well together. Season with salt to taste and serve while still hot.

Aubergine with Sesame Chicken

Young vegetables are prized in Japan for their sweet, delicate flavour. Here, small aubergines are stuffed with seasoned chicken.

INGREDIENTS

Serves 4

175g/6oz chicken breast or thighs, skinned
1 spring onion, green part only, finely chopped
15ml/1 tbsp dark soy sauce
15ml/1 tbsp mirin or sweet sherry
2.5ml/½ tsp sesame oil
2.5ml/½ tsp salt
4 small aubergines, about 10cm/4in long
15ml/1 tbsp sesame seeds
flour, for dusting
vegetable oil, for deep-frying

For the dipping sauce

60ml/4 tbsp dark soy sauce
60ml/4 tbsp *dashi* or vegetable stock
45ml/3 tbsp mirin or sweet sherry

1 Remove the chicken meat from the bone and mince it finely in a food processor for 1–2 minutes. Add the spring onion, soy sauce, mirin or sherry, sesame oil and salt.

2 Make four slits in each aubergine, so they remain joined at the stem. Spoon the minced chicken mixture into the aubergines, opening them slightly to accommodate it. Dip the fat end of each stuffed aubergine in the sesame seeds, then dust with flour. Set aside.

3 To make the dipping sauce, combine the soy sauce, *dashi* or stock and mirin or sherry. Pour into a shallow bowl and set aside.

4 Heat the vegetable oil in a wok o[r] deep-fryer to 196°C/385°F. Fry the aubergines, two at a time, for 3–4 minutes. Lift out with a slotted spoon and drain on kitchen paper. Serve wit[h] the dipping sauce.

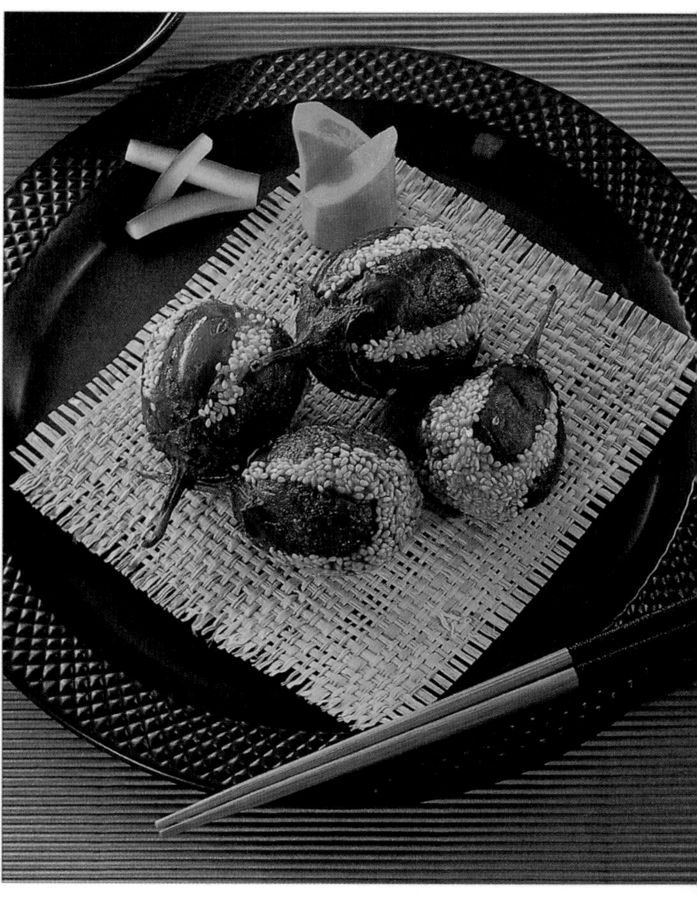

Chinese Potatoes with Chilli Beans

ast meets West. An American-tyle dish with a Chinese flavour - the sauce is particularly tasty. ry it as a quick supper dish vhen you fancy a meal with a ttle zing!

NGREDIENTS

erves 4

- medium potatoes, cut in thick chunks
- 0ml/2 tbsp sunflower or groundnut oil
- spring onions, sliced
- large fresh red chilli, seeded and sliced
- garlic cloves, crushed
- 00g/14oz can red kidney beans, drained
- 0ml/2 tbsp soy sauce
- 5ml/1 tbsp sesame oil
- alt and ground black pepper
- 5ml/1 tbsp sesame seeds and chopped fresh coriander or parsley, to garnish

1 Boil the potatoes until they are just tender. Take care not to overcook hem. Drain and reserve.

2 Heat the sunflower or groundnut oils in a preheated wok or large frying pan, stir-fry the spring onions and chilli for about 1 minute, then add the garlic and fry for a few seconds longer.

3 Add the potatoes, stirring well, then the beans and finally the soy sauce and sesame oil.

4 Season to taste and cook the vegetables until they are well heated through. Sprinkle with sesame seeds and coriander or parsley and serve.

Chinese Garlic Mushrooms

Tofu is high in protein and very low in fat, so it is an extremely useful and healthy food to keep handy for quick meals and snacks like this one.

Ingredients

Serves 4
8 large open mushrooms
3 spring onions, sliced
1 garlic clove, crushed
30ml/2 tbsp oyster sauce
275g/10oz marinated tofu, cut into small dice
200g/7oz can sweetcorn kernels, drained
10ml/2 tsp sesame oil
salt and ground black pepper

1 Finely chop the mushroom stalks and mix with the spring onions, garlic and oyster sauce.

2 Stir in the diced, marinated tofu and sweetcorn, season well with salt and pepper, then spoon the filling into the mushrooms.

3 Brush the edges of the mushroom with the sesame oil. Arrange the stuffed mushrooms in a baking dish an bake in a preheated oven at 200°C/400°F/Gas 6 for 12–15 minutes, until the mushrooms are just tender, then serve at once.

Cook's Tip

If you prefer, omit the oyster sauce and use light soy sauce instead.

Stir-fried Mixed Vegetables

Vhen selecting different items ›r a stir-fried dish, never mix the ıgredients indiscriminately. The lea is to achieve a harmonious alance of colour and texture.

NGREDIENTS

erves 4
25g/8oz Chinese leaves
15g/4oz baby corn cobs
15g/4oz broccoli
medium or 2 small carrots
0ml/4 tbsp vegetable oil
ml/1 tsp salt
ml/1 tsp light brown sugar
asic Stock or water, if necessary
5ml/1 tbsp light soy sauce
w drops of sesame oil (optional)

1 Cut the vegetables into roughly similar shapes and sizes.

2 Heat the oil in a preheated wok and stir-fry the vegetables for about 2 minutes.

3 Add the salt and sugar and a little stock or water, if necessary, and continue stirring for another minute. Add the soy sauce and sesame oil, if using. Blend well and serve.

Tofu and Green Bean Red Curry

This is another curry that is simple and quick to make. This recipe uses green beans, but you can use almost any kind of vegetable such as aubergines, bamboo shoots or broccoli.

INGREDIENTS

Serves 4–6

600ml/1 pint/2½ cups coconut milk
15ml/1 tbsp red curry paste
45ml/3 tbsp fish sauce
10ml/2 tsp palm sugar
225g/8oz button mushrooms
115g/4oz green beans, trimmed
175g/6oz tofu, rinsed and cut into 2cm/¾in cubes
4 kaffir lime leaves, torn
2 red chillies, sliced
coriander leaves, to garnish

1 Put about one third of the coconut milk in a wok or saucepan. Cook until it starts to separate and an oily sheen appears.

2 Add the red curry paste, fish sauce and sugar to the coconut milk. Mix together thoroughly.

3 Add the mushrooms. Stir and cook for 1 minute.

4 Stir in the rest of the coconut milk and bring back to the boil.

5 Add the green beans and cubes of tofu and simmer gently for another 4–5 minutes.

6 Stir in kaffir lime leaves and chillies. Serve garnished with the coriander leaves.

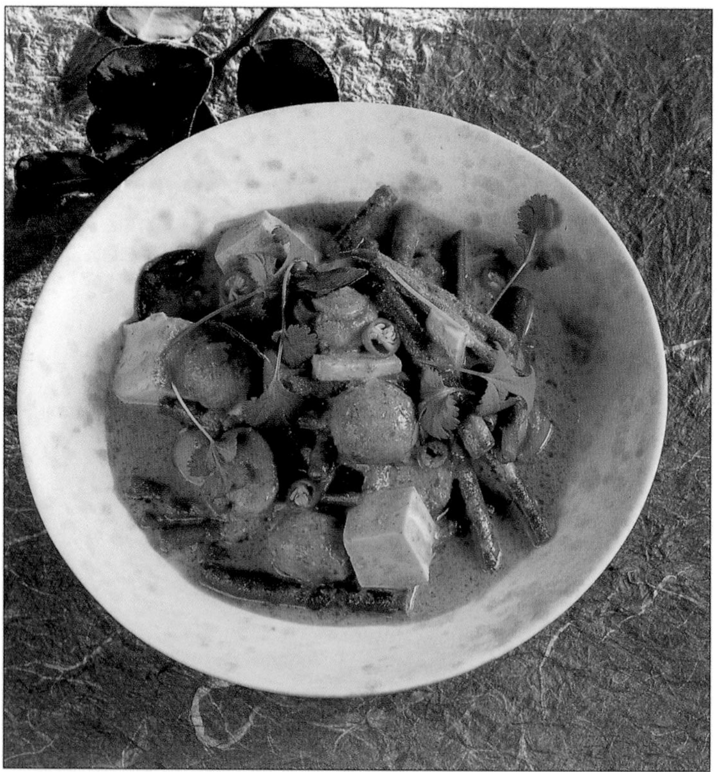

Chinese Leaves and Mooli with Scallops

. speedy stir-fry made using :hinese cabbage, mooli and :allops. Both the Chinese abbage and mooli have a leasant crunchy "bite". You eed to work quickly, so have verything prepared before you :art cooking.

NGREDIENTS

erves 4

0 prepared scallops
5ml/5 tbsp vegetable oil
garlic cloves, finely chopped
cm/½ in fresh root ginger, finely sliced
–5 spring onions, cut lengthways into 2.5cm/1in pieces
0ml/2 tbsp Chinese rice wine or dry sherry
½ mooli, cut into 1cm/½in slices
Chinese cabbage, chopped lengthways into thin strips
0ml/4 tbsp water

'or the marinade
ml/1 tsp cornflour
egg white, lightly beaten
inch of white pepper

'or the sauce
ml/1 tsp cornflour
0ml/4 tbsp water
5ml/3 tbsp oyster sauce

1 Rinse the scallops and separate the corals from the white meat. Cut each scallop into two pieces and slice he corals. Place them on two separate lishes. For the marinade, blend ogether the cornflour, egg white and vhite pepper. Pour half over the callops and the rest over the corals. Set side for 10 minutes.

2 To make the sauce, blend the cornflour with the water and the yster sauce and set aside.

3 Heat about 30ml/2 tbsp of the oil in a preheated wok, add half the garlic and let it sizzle, then add half the ginger and half the spring onions. Stir-fry for about 30 seconds, then stir in the scallops (not the corals). Stir-fry for ½–1 minute until the scallops start to become opaque. Reduce the heat and add 15ml/1 tbsp of the rice wine or dry sherry. Cook briefly and then spoon the scallops and the cooking liquid into a bowl and set aside.

4 Heat another 30ml/2 tbsp of the oil in the wok, add the remaining garlic, ginger and spring onions and stir-fry for 1 minute. Add the corals and the remaining rice wine or dry sherry, stir-fry briefly and transfer to a dish.

5 Heat the remaining oil and add the mooli. Stir-fry for about 30 seconds, then stir in the cabbage. Stir-fry for about 30 seconds and add the oyster sauce mixture and the water. Allow the cabbage to simmer briefly. Stir in the scallops and corals, together with all their liquid, and cook briefly to heat through.

Spiced Tofu Stir-fry

You could add any quickly cooked vegetable to this stir-fry – try mangetouts, sugar snap peas, leeks or thin slices of carrot.

INGREDIENTS

Serves 4

10ml/2 tsp ground cumin
15ml/1 tbsp paprika
5ml/1 tsp ground ginger
good pinch of cayenne pepper
15ml/1 tbsp caster sugar
275g/10oz firm tofu
oil, for frying
2 garlic cloves, crushed
1 bunch spring onions, sliced
1 red pepper, seeded and sliced
1 yellow pepper, seeded and sliced
225g/8oz brown-cap mushrooms, halved or quartered if very large
1 large courgette, sliced
115g/4oz fine green beans, halved
50g/2oz/½ cup pine nuts
15ml/1 tbsp lime juice
15ml/1 tbsp clear honey
salt and ground black pepper

1 Mix together the cumin, paprika, ginger, cayenne and sugar with plenty of seasoning. Cut the tofu into cubes and coat them thoroughly in the spice mixture.

2 Heat some oil in a preheated wok or large frying pan. Cook the tofu over a high heat for 3–4 minutes, turning occasionally. Take care not to break up the tofu too much. Remove with a slotted spoon. Wipe out the wok or pan with kitchen paper.

3 Add a little more oil to the wok or frying pan and stir-fry the garlic and spring onions for 3 minutes. Add the remaining vegetables and stir-fry over a medium heat for 6 minutes, or until beginning to soften and turn golden. Season well.

4 Return the tofu to the pan with the pine nuts, lime juice and honey. Heat through and serve.

Chinese Sprouts

f you are bored with plain oiled Brussels sprouts, try epping them up with this nusual stir-fried method, which ses the minimum of oil.

NGREDIENTS

erves 4
50g/1lb Brussels sprouts
ml/1 tsp sesame or sunflower oil
spring onions, sliced
.5ml/½ tsp Chinese five-spice powder
5ml/1 tbsp light soy sauce

1 Trim the Brussels sprouts, then shred them finely using a large harp knife or shred in a food rocessor.

2 Heat the oil in a preheated wok or frying pan and add the sprouts and nions, then stir-fry for 2 minutes, without browning.

3 Stir in the five-spice powder and soy sauce, then cook, stirring, for a further 2–3 minutes, until just tender.

4 Serve hot, with grilled meat or fish or with Chinese dishes.

COOK'S TIP

Brussels sprouts are rich in vitamin C, and this is a good way to cook them to preserve the nutrients. Larger sprouts cook particularly well by this method, and cabbage can be cooked in the same way.

SALADS

There is much more to Asian salads than a few Chinese leaves and a bunch of beansprouts. The superb collection of recipes here includes flamboyant combinations of raw fruit and vegetables, surprisingly refreshing warm salads, startling pairings of sweet and spicy ingredients, dramatic mixtures of crunchy and melt-in-the mouth textures and daring matching of flavours. Try Thai Fruit and Vegetable Salad, Warm Stir-fried Salad, Hot Coconut Prawn and Pawpaw Salad, Sesame Noodle Salad with Hot Peanuts or Hot-and-sour Chicken Salad.

Bean Curd and Cucumber Salad

Tahu Goreng Ketjap is a nutritious and refreshing salad with a hot, sweet and sour dressing. It is ideal for buffets.

Ingredients

Serves 4–6
1 small cucumber
oil for frying
1 square fresh or 115g/4oz long-life bean curd
115g/4oz beansprouts, trimmed and rinsed
salt

For the dressing
1 small onion, grated
2 garlic cloves, crushed
2.5ml/½ tsp chilli powder
30–45ml/2–3 tbsp dark soy sauce
15–30ml/1–2 tbsp rice-wine vinegar
10ml/2 tsp dark brown sugar
salt
celery leaves, to garnish

1 Trim the ends from the cucumber and then cut it in neat cubes. Sprinkle with salt and set aside, while preparing the remaining ingredients.

2 Heat a little oil in a pan and fry th bean curd on both sides until golden brown. Drain on absorbent kitchen paper and cut in cubes.

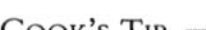

Cook's Tip

Beansprouts come from the mung bean and are easily grown at home on damp cotton or in a plastic bean sprouter. They must be eaten when absolutely fresh, so when buying from a shop check that they are crisp and are not beginning to go brown or soft. Eat within a day or two.

3 Prepare the dressing by blending together the onion, garlic and chi powder. Stir in the soy sauce, vinegar, sugar and salt to taste. You can do this in a screw-topped glass jar.

4 Just before serving, rinse the cucumber under cold running water. Drain and dry thoroughly. Toss the cucumber, bean curd and beansprouts together in a serving bow and pour over the dressing. Garnish with the celery leaves and serve the salad at once.

Vegetable Salad with Hot Peanut Sauce

wok is ideal for dry frying as ell as stir-frying, and here it is ›ed to great effect in making ›is wonderful peanut sauce.

IGREDIENTS

rves 4–6
potatoes, peeled
'5g/6oz French beans, topped and tailed

or the peanut sauce
50g/5oz peanuts
5ml/1 tbsp vegetable oil
shallots or 1 small onion, finely chopped
clove garlic, crushed
-2 small chillies, seeded and finely chopped
:m/½ in square shrimp paste, or 15ml/1 tbsp fish sauce (optional)
)ml/2 tbsp tamarind sauce
)0ml/4fl oz/½ cup canned coconut milk
5ml/1 tbsp clear honey

or the salad
75g/6oz Chinese leaves, shredded
iceberg or bib lettuce, separated into leaves
75g/6oz beansprouts, washed
› cucumber, cut into fingers
50g/5oz giant white radish, shredded
spring onions, trimmed
25g/8oz tofu, cut into large dice
hard-boiled eggs, quartered

1 Bring the potatoes to the boil in salted water and simmer for 20 ninutes. Cook the beans for 3–4 ninutes. Drain the potatoes and beans nd refresh under cold running water.

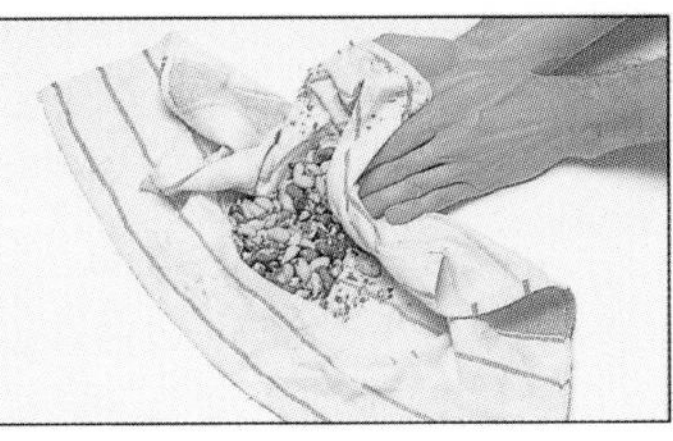

2 For the peanut sauce, dry fry the peanuts in a wok, or place under a moderate grill, tossing them all the time to prevent burning. Turn the peanuts on to a clean dish cloth and rub vigorously to remove the papery skins. Place the peanuts in a food processor or blender and process for 2 minutes.

3 Heat the vegetable oil in a wok and soften the shallots or onion, garlic and chillies without letting them colour. Add the shrimp paste or fish sauce if using, together with the tamarind sauce, coconut milk and honey. Simmer briefly, add to the peanuts and process in a food processor to form a thick sauce.

4 Arrange the salad ingredients, potatoes and beans on a large platter and serve with a bowl of the peanut sauce.

Thai Seafood Salad

This seafood salad with chilli, lemon grass and fish sauce is light and refreshing.

INGREDIENTS

Serves 4

225g/8oz ready-prepared squid
225g/8oz raw tiger prawns
8 scallops, shelled
225g/8oz firm white fish
30–45ml/2–3 tbsp olive oil
small mixed lettuce leaves and coriander sprigs, to serve

For the dressing

2 small fresh red chillies, seeded and finely chopped
5cm/2in lemon grass stalk, finely chopped
2 fresh kaffir lime leaves, shredded
30ml/2 tbsp Thai fish sauce (*nam pla*)
2 shallots, thinly sliced
30ml/2 tbsp lime juice
30ml/2 tbsp rice vinegar
10ml/2 tsp caster sugar

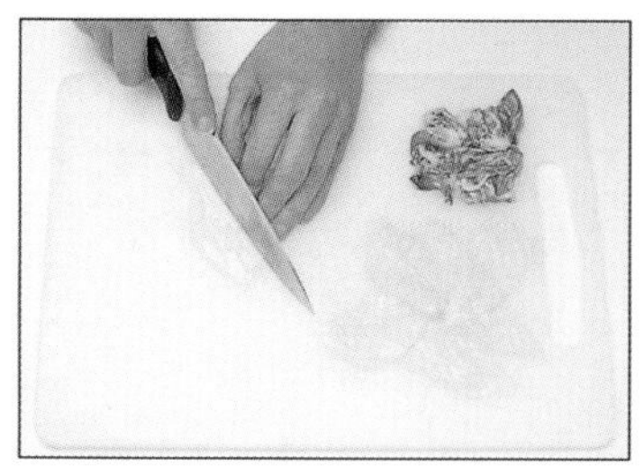

1 Prepare the seafood: slit open the squid bodies. Score the flesh with a sharp knife, then cut into square pieces. Halve the tentacles, if necessary. Peel and devein the prawns. Remove the dark beard-like fringe and tough muscle from the scallops. Cube the white fish.

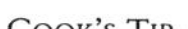

COOK'S TIP

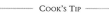

It is important to ensure that the prawns are cooked properly as undercooked prawns can carry infection.

2 Heat a wok until hot. Add the oi and swirl it around, then add the prawns and stir-fry for 2–3 minutes until pink. Transfer to a large bowl. Stir-fry the squid and scallops for 1–2 minutes until opaque. Remove and a to the prawns. Stir-fry the white fish for 2–3 minutes. Remove and add to the cooked seafood. Reserve any juic

3 Put all the dressing ingredients in small bowl with the reserved juic from the wok; mix well.

4 Pour the dressing over the seafoo and toss gently. Arrange the salad leaves and coriander sprigs on four individual plates, then spoon the seafood on top. Serve at once.

Cabbage Salad

A simple and delicious way of using cabbage. Other vegetables such as broccoli, cauliflower, beansprouts and Chinese cabbage can also be prepared this way.

INGREDIENTS

Serves 4–6

30ml/2 tbsp fish sauce
grated rind of 1 lime
30ml/2 tbsp lime juice
120ml/4fl oz/½ cup coconut milk
30ml/2 tbsp vegetable oil
2 large red chillies, seeded and finely cut into strips
garlic cloves, finely sliced
shallots, finely sliced
small cabbage, shredded
30ml/2 tbsp coarsely chopped roasted peanuts, to serve

1 Make the dressing by combining the fish sauce, lime rind and juice nd coconut milk. Set aside.

2 Heat the oil in a wok or frying pan. Stir-fry the chillies, garlic and shallots, until the shallots are brown nd crisp. Remove and set aside.

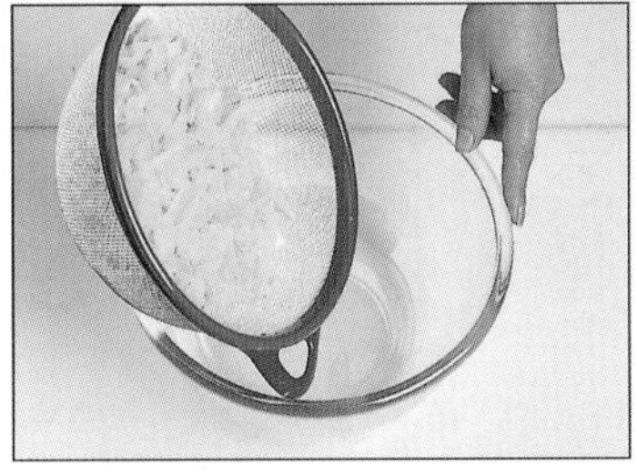

3 Blanch the cabbage in boiling salted water for about 2–3 minutes, drain and put into a bowl.

4 Stir the dressing into the cabbage, toss and mix well. Transfer the salad into a serving dish. Sprinkle with the fried shallot mixture and the chopped roasted peanuts.

Hot-and-sour Chicken Salad

INGREDIENTS

Serves 4–6
2 chicken breast fillets, skinned
1 small red chilli, seeded and finely chopped
1cm/½in piece fresh root ginger, peeled and finely chopped
1 garlic clove, chopped
15ml/1tbsp crunchy peanut butter
30ml/2 tbsp chopped fresh coriander leaves
5ml/1 tsp sugar
2.5ml/½ tsp salt
15ml/1 tbsp rice or white wine vinegar
60ml/4 tbsp vegetable oil
10ml/2 tsp fish sauce (optional)
115g/4oz beansprouts
1 head Chinese leaves, roughly shredded
2 medium carrots, cut into thin sticks
1 red onion, cut into fine rings
2 large gherkins, sliced

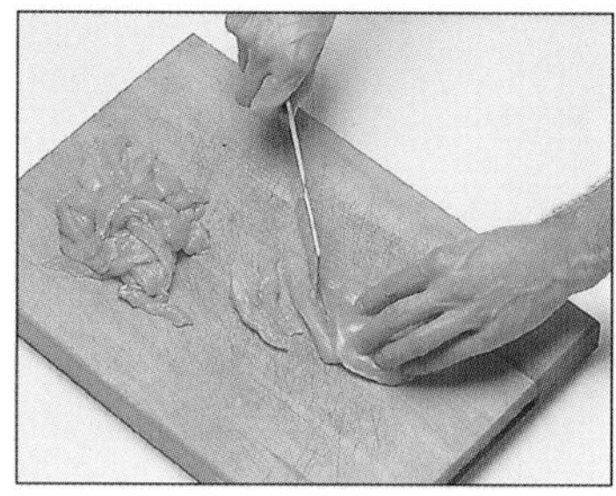

1 Slice the chicken thinly, place in a shallow bowl and set aside. Grind the chilli, ginger and garlic in a mortar with a pestle. Add the peanut butter, coriander, sugar and salt.

2 Add the vinegar, 30ml/2 tbsp of the oil and the fish sauce if using. Combine well. Cover the chicken with the spice mixture and leave to marinate for at least 2–3 hours.

3 Heat the remaining 2 tbsp of oil i a preheated wok. Add the chicke and fish sauce, if using, and cook for 10–12 minutes, turning the meat occasionally. Meanwhile, arrange the beansprouts, Chinese leaves, carrots, onion rings and gherkins decoratively on a serving platter. Serve the chicke arranged on the salad.

Alfalfa Crab Salad with Crispy Fried Noodles

INGREDIENTS

Serves 4–6
vegetable oil, for deep frying
50g/2oz Chinese rice noodles
2 dressed crabs, or 150g/5oz frozen white crab meat, thawed
115g/4oz alfalfa sprouts
1 small iceberg lettuce
4 sprigs fresh coriander, chopped
1 tomato, skinned, seeded and diced
4 sprigs fresh mint, roughly chopped

For the sesame lime dressing
45ml/3 tbsp vegetable oil
15ml/1 tbsp sesame oil
½ red chilli, seeded and finely chopped
1 piece stem ginger in syrup, cut in strips
10ml/2 tsp stem ginger syrup
10ml/2 tsp soy sauce
juice of ½ lime

1 To make the dressing, combine the vegetable and sesame oils in a bowl. Add the chilli, stem ginger, stem ginger syrup and soy sauce with the lime juice.

2 Heat the oil in a preheated wok to 190°C/375°F. Fry the noodles, one handful at a time, until crisp. Lift out and drain on kitchen paper.

3 Flake the white crab meat into a bowl and mix well with the alfalfa sprouts. Put the lettuce, coriander, tomato and mint in a serving bowl, pour over the dressing and toss lightly. Place a nest of noodles on top and finally add the crab and alfalfa sprouts.

Egg Noodle Salad with Sesame Chicken

INGREDIENTS

Serves 4–6
400g/14oz fresh thin egg noodles
1 carrot, cut into long fine strips
50g/2oz mange-touts, topped, tailed, cut into fine strips and blanched
115g/4oz beansprouts, blanched
30ml/2 tbsp olive oil
225g/8oz skinless, boneless chicken breasts, finely sliced
30ml/2 tbsp sesame seeds, toasted
2 spring onions, finely sliced diagonally and coriander leaves, to garnish

For the dressing
45ml/3 tbsp sherry vinegar
75ml/5 tbsp soy sauce
60ml/4 tbsp sesame oil
90ml/6 tbsp light olive oil
1 garlic clove, finely chopped
5ml/1 tsp grated fresh root ginger
salt and freshly ground black pepper

1 To make the dressing. Combine all the ingredients in a small bowl with a pinch of salt and mix together well using a whisk or a fork.

2 Cook the noodles in a large saucepan of boiling water. Stir them occasionally to separate. They will only take a few minutes to cook: be careful not to overcook them. Drain, rinse under cold running water and drain well. Tip into a bowl.

3 Add the vegetables to the noodles. Pour in about half the dressing, then toss the mixture well and adjust the seasoning according to taste.

4 Heat the oil in a large frying pan. Add the chicken and stir-fry for 3 minutes, or until cooked and golden. Remove from the heat. Add the sesame seeds and drizzle in some of the remaining dressing.

5 Arrange the noodles on individual serving plates, making a nest on each plate. Spoon the chicken on top. Sprinkle with the sliced spring onions and the coriander leaves and serve any remaining dressing separately.

Potato and Cellophane Noodle Salad

NGREDIENTS

erves 4

medium potatoes, peeled and cut into eighths
75g/6oz cellophane noodles, soaked in hot water until soft
0ml/4 tbsp vegetable oil
onion, finely sliced
ml/1 tsp ground turmeric
0ml/4 tbsp gram flour
ml/1 tsp grated lemon rind
0–75ml/4–5 tbsp lemon juice
5ml/3 tbsp fish sauce
spring onions, finely sliced
lt and freshly ground black pepper

1 Place the potatoes in a saucepan. Add water to cover, bring to the oil and cook for about 15 minutes ntil tender but firm. Drain the otatoes and set them aside to cool.

2 Meanwhile, cook the drained noodles in a saucepan of boiling vater for 3 minutes. Drain and rinse nder cold running water. Drain well.

3 Heat the oil in a frying pan. Add the onion and turmeric and fry for about 5 minutes until golden brown. Drain the onion, reserving the oil.

4 Heat a small frying pan. Add the gram flour and stir constantly for about 4 minutes until it turns light golden brown in colour.

5 Mix the potatoes, noodles and fried onion in a large bowl. Add the reserved oil and the toasted gram flour with the lemon rind and juice, fish sauce and spring onions. Mix together well and adjust the seasoning to taste if necessary. Serve at once.

Curry Fried Pork and Rice Vermicelli Salad

Pork crackles add a delicious crunch to this popular salad.

INGREDIENTS

Serves 4
225g/8oz lean pork
2 garlic cloves, finely chopped
2 slices fresh root ginger, finely chopped
30–45ml/2–3 tbsp rice wine
45ml/3 tbsp vegetable oil
2 lemon grass stalks, finely chopped
10ml/2 tsp curry powder
175g/6oz beansprouts
225g/8oz rice vermicelli, soaked in warm water until soft
½ lettuce, finely shredded
30ml/2 tbsp mint leaves
lemon juice and fish sauce, to taste
salt and freshly ground black pepper
2 spring onions, chopped, 25g/1oz roasted peanuts, chopped, and pork crackles (optional), to garnish

1 Cut the pork into thin strips. Place in a shallow dish with half the garlic and ginger. Season with salt and pepper, pour over 30ml/2 tbsp rice wine and marinate for at least 1 hour.

2 Heat the oil in a frying pan. Add the remaining garlic and ginger and fry for a few seconds until fragrant. Stir in the pork, with the marinade, and add the lemon grass and curry powder. Fry until the pork is golden and cooked through, adding more rice wine if the mixture seems too dry.

3 Place the beansprouts in a sieve. Blanch them by lowering the siev into a saucepan of boiling water for 1 minute, then drain and refresh unde cold running water. Drain again. Usir the same water, cook the drained rice vermicelli for 3–5 minutes until tende drain and rinse under cold running water. Drain well and tip into a bowl.

4 Add the beansprouts, shredded lettuce and mint leaves to the rice vermicelli. Season with the lemon juic and fish sauce. Toss lightly.

5 Divide the noodle mixture among individual serving plates, making a nest on each plate. Arrange the pork mixture on top. Garnish with spring onions, roasted peanuts and pork crackles, if using.

Larp of Chiang Mai

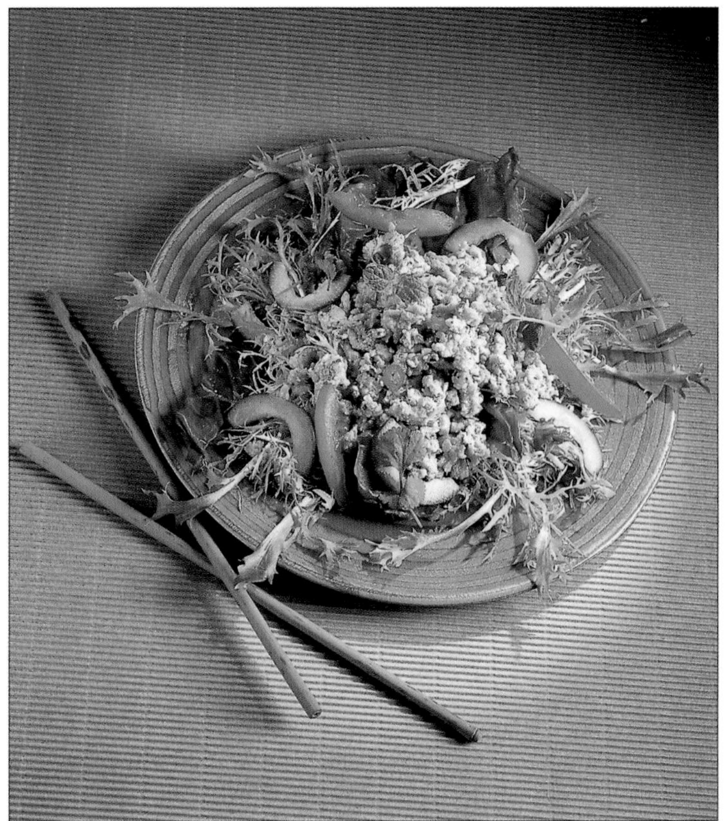

:hiang Mai is a city in the ›orth-east of Thailand. The city ; culturally very close to Laos nd famous for its chicken salad, vhich was originally called Laap" or "Larp". Duck, beef or ›ork can be used instead.

NGREDIENTS

erves 4–6

50g/1lb minced chicken
stalk lemon grass, finely chopped
kaffir lime leaves, finely chopped
red chillies, seeded and chopped
0ml/4 tbsp lime juice
0ml/2 tbsp fish sauce
5ml/1 tbsp roasted ground rice
spring onions, chopped
0ml/2 tbsp coriander leaves
ıixed salad leaves, cucumber and
tomato slices, to serve
few sprigs of mint, to garnish

1 Heat a large non-stick frying pan. Add the minced chicken and cook ı a little water.

COOK'S TIP

Use sticky, or glutinous, rice to make roasted ground rice. Put the rice in a frying pan and dry-roast until golden brown. Remove and grind to a powder in a pestle and mortar or in a food processor. Keep in a glass jar in a cool and dry place and use as required.

2 Stir constantly until cooked; this will take about 7–10 minutes.

3 Transfer the cooked chicken to a large bowl and add the rest of the ingredients. Mix thoroughly.

4 Serve on a bed of mixed salad leaves, cucumber and tomato slices and garnish with sprigs of mint.

Chinese-style Chicken Salad

This delicious salad is a masterpiece of subtle flavours and contrasts in texture.

INGREDIENTS

Serves 4

4 boneless chicken breasts, about 175g/6oz each
60ml/4 tbsp dark soy sauce
pinch of Chinese five-spice powder
good squeeze of lemon juice
½ cucumber, peeled and cut into matchsticks
5ml/1 tsp salt
45ml/3 tbsp sunflower oil
30ml/2 tbsp sesame oil
15ml/1 tbsp sesame seeds
30ml/2 tbsp Chinese rice wine or dry sherry
2 carrots, cut into matchsticks
8 spring onions, shredded
75g/3oz beansprouts

For the sauce

60ml/4 tbsp crunchy peanut butter
10ml/2 tsp lemon juice
10ml/2 tsp sesame oil
1.5ml/¼ tsp hot chilli powder
1 spring onion, finely chopped

1 Put the chicken portions into a large pan and just cover with water. Add 15ml/1 tbsp of the soy sauce, the Chinese five-spice powder and lemon juice, cover and bring to the boil, then simmer for about 20 minutes.

2 Meanwhile, place the cucumber matchsticks in a colander, sprinkle with the salt and cover with a plate with a weight on top. Leave to drain for 30 minutes – set the colander in a bowl to catch the drips.

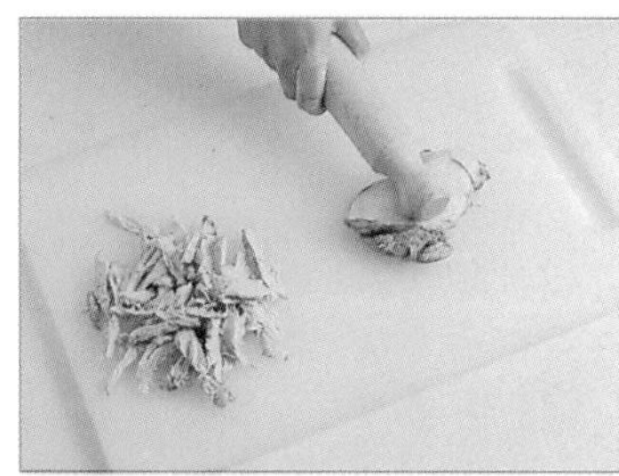

3 Lift out the poached chicken with a draining spoon and leave until cool enough to handle. Remove and discard the skin. Bang the chicken lightly with a rolling pin to loosen the fibres. Slice into thin strips and reserve.

4 Heat the sunflower and sesame oils in a preheated wok. Add the sesame seeds, fry for 30 seconds and then stir in the remaining soy sauce and the rice wine or dry sherry.

5 Add the carrots and stir-fry for 2–minutes, until just tender. Remove from the heat and reserve.

6 Rinse the cucumber well, pat dry with kitchen paper and place in a bowl. Add the spring onions, beansprouts, cooked carrots, pan juices and shredded chicken and mix together. Transfer to a shallow dish. Cover and chill for about 1 hour, turning the mixture in the juices once or twice.

7 To make the sauce, cream the peanut butter with the lemon juice, sesame oil and chilli powder, adding a little hot water to form a paste, then stir in the spring onion. Arrange the chicken mixture on a serving dish and serve with the peanut sauce.

Prawn Noodle Salad with Fragrant Herbs

\ light, refreshing salad with all
he tangy flavour of the sea.
nstead of prawns, try squid,
callops, mussels or crab.

NGREDIENTS

erves 4
15g/4oz cellophane noodles, soaked in hot water until soft
6 cooked prawns, peeled
small green pepper, seeded and cut into strips
½ cucumber, cut into strips
tomato, cut into strips
shallots, finely sliced
alt and freshly ground black pepper
oriander leaves, to garnish

or the dressing
5ml/1 tbsp rice vinegar
0ml/2 tbsp fish sauce
0ml/2 tbsp fresh lime juice
inch of salt
.5ml/½ tsp grated fresh root ginger
lemon grass stalk, finely chopped
red chilli, seeded and finely sliced
0ml/2 tbsp roughly chopped mint
ew sprigs tarragon, roughly chopped
5ml/1 tbsp snipped chives

1 Make the dressing by combining all the ingredients in a small bowl or jug; whisk well.

2 Drain the noodles, then plunge them in a saucepan of boiling water for 1 minute. Drain, rinse under cold running water and drain again well.

3 In a large bowl, combine the noodles with the prawns, pepper, cucumber, tomato and shallots. Lightly season with salt and pepper, then toss with the dressing.

4 Spoon the noodles on to individual plates, arranging the prawns on top. Garnish with a few coriander leaves and serve at once.

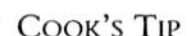

COOK'S TIP

Prawns are available ready-cooked and often shelled. To cook prawns, boil them for 5 minutes. Leave them to cool in the cooking liquid, then gently pull off the tail shell and twist off the head.

Warm Stir-fried Salad

Warm salads are becoming increasingly popular because they are delicious and nutritious. Arrange the salad leaves on four individual plates, so the hot stir-fry can be served quickly on to them, ensuring the lettuce remains crisp and the chicken warm.

INGREDIENTS

Serves 4

few large sprigs of fresh tarragon
2 boneless chicken breasts, about 225g/8oz each, skinned
5cm/2in root ginger, peeled and finely chopped
45ml/3 tbsp light soy sauce
15ml/1 tbsp sugar
15ml/1 tbsp sunflower oil
1 Chinese lettuce
½ frisée lettuce, torn into bite-sized pieces
115g/4oz/1 cup unsalted cashew nuts
2 large carrots, cut into fine strips
salt and ground black pepper

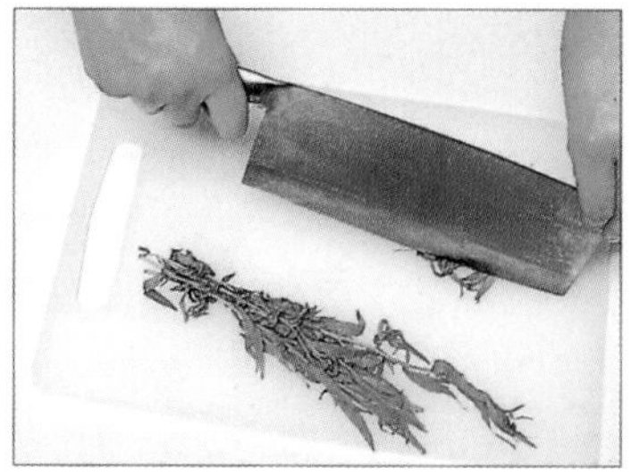

1 Strip the tarragon leaves from the stems and chop the leaves.

2 Cut the chicken into fine strips and place in a bowl.

3 To make the marinade, mix together in a bowl the tarragon, ginger, soy sauce, sugar and seasoning.

4 Pour the marinade over the chicken strips and leave for 2–4 hours in a cool place.

5 Strain the chicken and reserve the marinade. Heat the oil in a preheated wok. When the oil is hot, stir-fry the chicken for 3 minutes, add the marinade and allow to bubble for 2–3 minutes.

6 Slice the Chinese lettuce and arrange on a plate with the frisée. Toss the cashews and carrots together with the chicken, pile on top of the bed of lettuce and serve immediately.

Thai Beef Salad

A hearty salad of beef, laced with a chilli and lime dressing.

INGREDIENTS

Serves 4

2 x 225g/8oz sirloin steaks
1 red onion, finely sliced
½ cucumber, finely sliced into matchsticks
1 stalk lemon grass, finely chopped
juice of 2 limes
15–30ml/1–2 tbsp fish sauce
30ml/2 tbsp chopped spring onions
2–4 red chillies, finely sliced, to garnish
fresh coriander, Chinese mustard cress and mint leaves, to garnish

1 Pan-fry or grill the beef steaks to medium-rare. Allow to rest for 10–15 minutes.

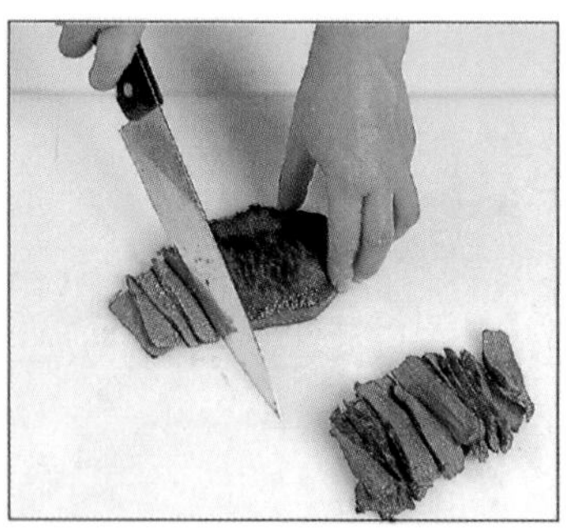

2 When cool, thinly slice the beef and put the slices in a large bowl.

3 Add the sliced onion, cucumber matchsticks and lemon grass.

4 Add the spring onions. Toss and season with lime juice and fish sauce. Serve at room temperature or chilled, garnished with the chillies, coriander, mustard cress and mint.

Tangy Chicken Salad

his fresh and lively dish typifies
ıe character of Thai cuisine. It is
leal for a starter or light lunch.

NGREDIENTS

rves 4–6

skinned, boneless chicken breasts
garlic cloves, crushed and roughly chopped
0ml/2 tbsp soy sauce
0ml/2 tbsp vegetable oil
20ml/4fl oz/½ cup coconut cream
0ml/2 tbsp fish sauce
ice of 1 lime
0ml/2 tbsp palm sugar
15g/4oz water chestnuts, sliced
0g/2oz cashew nuts, roasted
shallots, finely sliced
kaffir lime leaves, finely sliced
stalk lemon grass, finely sliced
ml/1 tsp chopped galangal
large red chilli, seeded and finely sliced
spring onions, finely sliced
0–12 mint leaves, torn
head of lettuce, to serve
prigs of coriander, to garnish
red chillies, seeded and sliced, to garnish

1 Trim the chicken breasts of any excess fat and put them in a large lish. Rub with the garlic, soy sauce ınd 15ml/1 tbsp of the oil. Leave to narinate for 1–2 hours.

2 Grill or pan-fry the chicken for 3–4 minutes on both sides or until cooked. Remove and set aside to cool.

3 In a small saucepan, heat the coconut cream, fish sauce, lime juice and palm sugar. Stir until all of the sugar has dissolved and then remove from the heat.

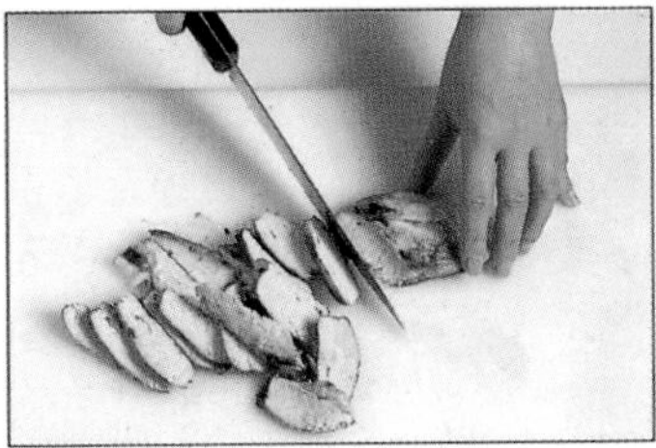

4 Cut the cooked chicken into strips and combine with the water chestnuts, cashew nuts, shallots, kaffir lime leaves, lemon grass, galangal, red chilli, spring onions and mint leaves.

5 Pour the coconut dressing over the chicken, toss and mix well. Serve the chicken on a bed of lettuce leaves and garnish with sprigs of coriander and sliced red chillies.

Noodles with Pineapple, Ginger and Chillies

INGREDIENTS

Serves 4

275g/10oz dried udon noodles
½ pineapple, peeled, cored and sliced into 4cm/1½in rings
45ml/3 tbsp soft light brown sugar
60ml/4 tbsp fresh lime juice
60ml/4 tbsp coconut milk
30ml/2 tbsp fish sauce
30ml/2 tbsp grated fresh root ginger
2 garlic cloves, finely chopped
1 ripe mango or 2 peaches, finely diced
freshly ground black pepper
2 spring onions, finely sliced, 2 red chillies, seeded and finely shredded, plus mint leaves, to garnish

1 Cook the noodles in a large saucepan of boiling water until tender, following the directions on the packet. Drain, refresh under cold water and drain again.

2 Place the pineapple rings on a flameproof dish, sprinkle with 30ml/2 tbsp of the sugar and grill for about 5 minutes or until golden. Cool slightly and cut into small dice.

3 Mix the lime juice, coconut milk and fish sauce in a salad bowl. Add the remaining brown sugar, with the ginger and garlic, and whisk well. Add the noodles and pineapple.

4 Add the mango or peaches and toss. Scatter over the spring onions, chillies and mint leaves before serving.

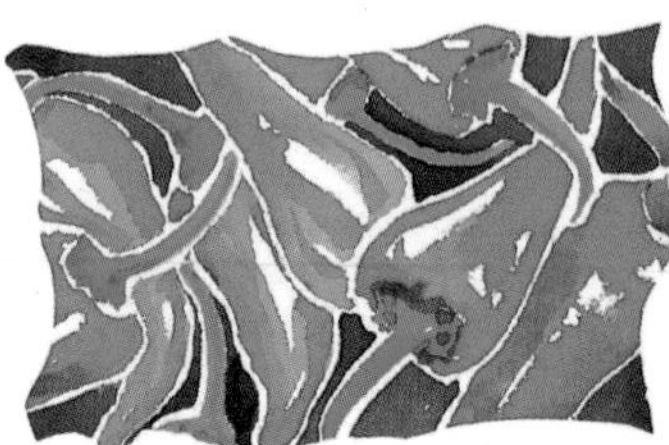

Buckwheat Noodles with Smoked Salmon

Young pea sprouts are only available for a short time. You can substitute watercress, mustard cress, young leeks or your favourite green vegetable or herb in this dish.

INGREDIENTS

Serves 4

225g/8oz buckwheat or soba noodles
15ml/1 tbsp oyster sauce
juice of ½ lemon
30–45ml/2–3 tbsp light olive oil
115g/4oz smoked salmon, cut into fine strips
115g/4oz young pea sprouts
2 ripe tomatoes, peeled, seeded and cut into strips
15ml/1 tbsp snipped chives
salt and freshly ground black pepper

1 Cook the buckwheat or soba noodles in a large saucepan of boiling water, following the directions on the packet. Drain, then rinse under cold running water and drain well.

2 Tip the noodles into a large bowl. Add the oyster sauce and lemon juice and season with pepper to taste. Moisten with the olive oil.

3 Add the smoked salmon, pea sprouts, tomatoes and chives. Mix well and serve at once.

Sesame Duck and Noodle Salad

This salad is complete in itself and makes a lovely summer lunch. The marinade is a marvellous blend of spices.

INGREDIENTS

Serves 4

2 duck breasts
15ml/1 tbsp vegetable oil
150g/5oz sugar snap peas
2 carrots, cut into 7.5cm/3in sticks
225g/8oz medium egg noodles
6 spring onions, sliced
salt
fresh coriander leaves, to garnish

For the marinade

15ml/1 tbsp sesame oil
5ml/1 tsp ground coriander
5ml/1 tsp Chinese five-spice powder

For the dressing

15ml/1 tbsp garlic vinegar
5ml/1 tsp soft light brown sugar
5ml/1 tsp soy sauce
15ml/1 tbsp toasted sesame seeds
45ml/3 tbsp sunflower oil
30ml/2 tbsp sesame oil
ground black pepper

1 Slice the duck breasts thinly across and place them in a shallow dish. Mix all the ingredients for the marinade, pour over the duck and mix well to coat thoroughly. Cover and leave in a cool place for 30 minutes.

2 Heat the oil in a preheated wok or frying pan, add the slices of duck breast and stir-fry for 3–4 minutes until cooked. Set aside.

3 Bring a saucepan of lightly salted water to the boil. Place the sugar snap peas and carrots in a steamer that will fit on top of the pan. When the water boils, add the noodles, place the steamer on top and steam the vegetables while cooking the noodles for the time suggested on the packet. Set the steamed vegetables aside. Drai the noodles, refresh them under cold running water and drain again. Place them in a large serving bowl.

4 Make the dressing. Mix the vinegar, sugar, soy sauce and sesar seeds in a bowl. Season well with blac pepper, then whisk in the sunflower and sesame oils.

5 Pour the dressing over the noodle and mix well. Add the sugar snap peas, carrots, spring onions and duck slices and toss to mix. Scatter over the coriander leaves and serve.

Duck, Avocado and Raspberry Salad

.ich duck breasts are roasted ntil crisp with a honey and oy glaze to serve warm with esh raspberries and avocado. delicious raspberry and edcurrant dressing adds a onderful sweet-and-sour avour.

NGREDIENTS

erves 4

small or 2 large duck breasts, halved if large
5ml/1 tbsp clear honey
5ml/1 tbsp dark soy sauce
0ml/4 tbsp olive oil
5ml/1 tbsp raspberry vinegar
5ml/1 tbsp redcurrant jelly
election of salad leaves, such as lamb's lettuce, red chicory and frisée
avocados, stoned, peeled and cut into chunks
15g/4oz raspberries
alt and ground black pepper

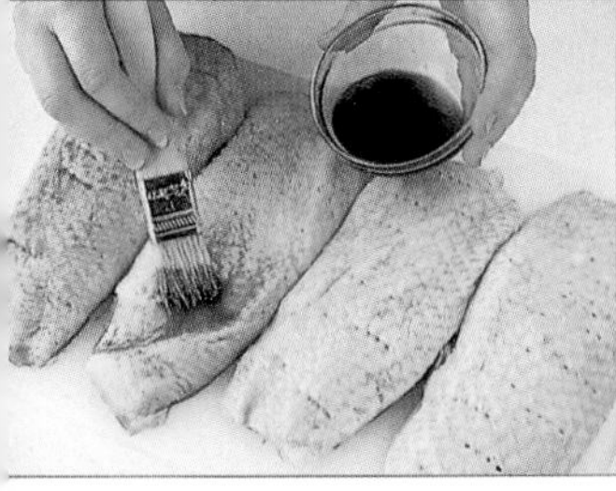

1 Prick the skin of each duck breast with a fork. Blend the honey and oy sauce together in a small bowl, then rush all over the skin.

2 Place the duck breasts on a rack set over a roasting tin and season with alt and pepper. Roast in a preheated ven at 220°C/425°F/Gas 7 for 15–20 minutes, until the skin is crisp and the neat is cooked.

3 Meanwhile, to make the dressing, put the oil, vinegar, redcurrant jelly and seasoning in a small bowl and whisk well until evenly blended.

4 Slice the duck breasts diagonally and arrange on individual plates with the salad leaves, avocados and raspberries. Spoon over the dressing and serve immediately.

Spicy Szechuan Noodles

INGREDIENTS

Serves 4

350g/12oz thick noodles
175g/6oz cooked chicken, shredded
50g/2oz roasted cashew nuts

For the dressing

4 spring onions, chopped
30ml/2 tbsp chopped coriander
2 garlic cloves, chopped
30ml/2 tbsp smooth peanut butter
30ml/2 tbsp sweet chilli sauce
15ml/1 tbsp soy sauce
15ml/1 tbsp sherry vinegar
15ml/1 tbsp sesame oil
30ml/2 tbsp olive oil
30ml/2 tbsp chicken stock or water
10 toasted Szechuan peppercorns, ground

1 Cook the noodles in a saucepan of boiling water until just tender, following the directions on the packet. Drain, rinse under cold running water and drain well.

2 While the noodles are cooking combine all the ingredients for the dressing in a large bowl and whisk together well.

3 Add the noodles, shredded chicken and cashew nuts to the dressing, tos gently to coat and adjust the seasoning to taste. Serve at once.

COOK'S TIP

You could substitute cooked turkey or pork for the chicken for a change.

Sesame Noodles with Spring Onions

This simple but very tasty warm salad can be prepared and cooked in just a few minutes.

INGREDIENTS

Serves 4

2 garlic cloves, roughly chopped
30ml/2 tbsp Chinese sesame paste
15ml/1 tbsp dark sesame oil
30ml/2 tbsp soy sauce
30ml/2 tbsp rice wine
15ml/1 tbsp honey
pinch of five-spice powder
350g/12oz soba or buckwheat noodles
4 spring onions, finely sliced diagonally
50g/2oz beansprouts
7.5cm/3in piece of cucumber, cut into matchsticks
toasted sesame seeds
salt and freshly ground black pepper

1 Process the garlic, sesame paste, oil, soy sauce, rice wine, honey and five-spice powder with a pinch each of salt and pepper in a blender or food processor until smooth.

2 Cook the noodles in a saucepan of boiling water until just tender, following the directions on the packet. Drain the noodles immediately and tip them into a bowl.

3 Toss the hot noodles with the dressing and the spring onions. To with the beansprouts, cucumber and sesame seeds and serve.

COOK'S TIP

If you can't find Chinese sesame paste, then use either tahini paste or smooth peanut butter instead.

Sweet-and-sour Fruit and Vegetable Salad

Acar bening makes a perfect accompaniment to many spicy dishes, with its clean taste and bright, jewel-like colours. Any leftover salad can be covered and stored in the refrigerator for up to two days. This is an ideal dish for buffets.

INGREDIENTS

Serves 8

1 small cucumber
1 onion
1 small ripe pineapple or 425g/15oz can pineapple rings
1 green pepper, seeded and thinly sliced
3 firm tomatoes, cut into wedges
25g/1oz golden granulated sugar
45–60ml/3–4 tbsp cider vinegar or white wine vinegar
120ml/4fl oz/½ cup water
salt

1 Peel the cucumber and cut in half lengthways. Remove the seeds with a small spoon. Cut the cucumber into even-sized pieces. Sprinkle with a little salt. Thinly slice the onion and sprinkle that also with a little salt. Leave both vegetables for a few minutes, then rinse and pat dry, and mix them together in a bowl.

2 Peel the fresh pineapple, if using, removing all the "eyes". Slice the pineapple thinly, then core the slices and cut in neat pieces. If using canned pineapple, cut the rings into similarly sized pieces. Add them to the bowl, together with the green pepper and tomato wedges.

3 Heat the sugar, vinegar and water until the sugar dissolves. Remove from the heat and leave to cool. When cool, add salt to taste and then pour over the fruit and vegetables. Cover and chill until required.

Rice Vermicelli and Salad Rolls

;oi Cuor is a hearty noodle salad 'rapped in rice sheets: it makes a ealthy change from a sandwich ıd is great for a picnic.

NGREDIENTS

lakes 8
)g/2oz rice vermicelli, soaked in warm water until soft
large carrot, shredded
iml/1 tbsp sugar
5–30ml/1–2 tbsp fish sauce
x 20cm/8in round rice sheets
large lettuce leaves, thick stalks removed
i0g/12oz roast pork, sliced
.5g/4oz beansprouts
ındful of mint leaves
cooked king prawns, peeled, deveined and halved
cucumber, cut into fine strips
riander leaves, to garnish

or the peanut sauce
iml/1 tbsp vegetable oil
garlic cloves, finely chopped
-2 red chillies, finely chopped
nl/1 tsp tomato purée
:0ml/4fl oz/½ cup water
ml/1 tbsp smooth peanut butter
ml/2 tbsp hoisin sauce
5ml/½ tsp sugar
ice of 1 lime
'g/2oz roasted peanuts, ground

1 Drain the noodles. Cook in a saucepan of boiling water for about -3 minutes until tender. Drain, rinse ıder cold running water, drain well. p into a bowl. Add the carrot and ıson with the sugar and fish sauce.

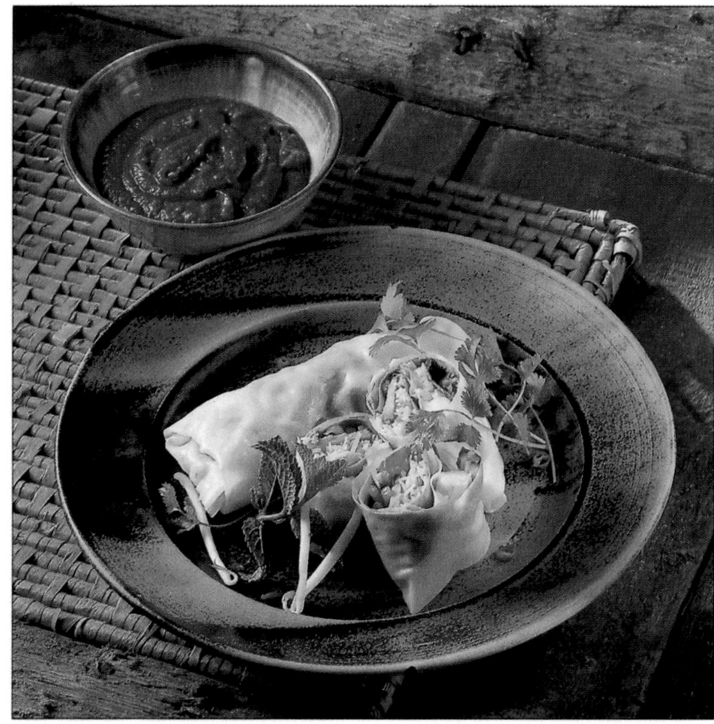

2 Assemble the rolls, one at a time. Dip a rice sheet in a bowl of warm water, then lay it flat on a surface. Place 1 lettuce leaf, 1–2 scoops of the noodle mixture, a few slices of pork, some of the beansprouts and several mint leaves on the rice sheet.

3 Start rolling up the rice sheet into a cylinder. When half the sheet has been rolled up, fold both sides of the sheet towards the centre and lay 2 pieces of prawn along the crease.

4 Add a few of strips of cucumber and some of the coriander leaves. Continue to roll up the sheet to make a tight packet. Place the roll on a plate and cover with a damp dish towel, so that it will stay moist while you make the remaining rolls.

5 Make the peanut sauce. Heat the oil in a small saucepan and fry the garlic, chillies and tomato purée for about 1 minute. Add the water and bring to the boil, then stir in the peanut butter, hoisin sauce, sugar and lime juice. Mix well. Reduce the heat and simmer for 3–4 minutes. Spoon the sauce into a bowl, add the ground peanuts and cool to room temperature.

6 To serve, cut each roll in half. Add a spoonful of the peanut sauce.

Fruit and Raw Vegetable Gado-gado

A banana leaf, which can be bought from oriental stores, can be used to line the platter for a special occasion.

INGREDIENTS

Serves 6

2 unripe pears, peeled at the last moment, or 175g/6oz wedge *bangkuang* (yambean), peeled and cut in matchsticks
1–2 eating apples
juice of ½ lemon
1 small, crisp lettuce, shredded
½ cucumber, seeded, sliced and salted, set aside for 15 minutes, then rinsed and drained
6 small tomatoes, cut in wedges
3 slices fresh pineapple, cored and cut in wedges
3 eggs or 12 quail's eggs, hard-boiled and shelled
175g/6oz egg noodles, cooked, cooled and chopped
deep-fried onions, to garnish

For the peanut sauce
2–4 fresh red chillies, seeded and ground
300ml/½ pint/1¼ cups coconut milk
350g/12oz crunchy peanut butter
15ml/1 tbsp dark soy sauce or dark brown sugar
5ml/1 tsp tamarind pulp, soaked in 45ml/3 tbsp warm water, strained and juice reserved
coarsely crushed peanuts
salt

1 To make the Peanut Sauce, put the chillies and coconut milk in a pan. Add the peanut butter and heat gently, stirring, until no lumps of peanut butter remain.

2 Allow to simmer gently until the sauce thickens, then add the soy sauce or sugar and tamarind juice. Season with salt to taste. Pour into a bowl and sprinkle with a few coarsely crushed peanuts.

3 To make the salad, peel and core the pears or *bangkuang* and apples. Slice the apples and sprinkle with lemon juice. Arrange the salad and fruit attractively on a flat platter. The lettuce can be used, instead of a banana leaf, to form a bed for the salad.

4 Add the sliced or quartered hard boiled eggs (leave quail's eggs whole), the chopped noodles and the deep-fried onions.

5 Serve at once, accompanied with bowl of the Peanut Sauce.

Sesame Noodle Salad with Hot Peanuts

.n Eastern-inspired salad with runchy vegetables and a light oy dressing. The hot peanuts nake a surprisingly successful nion with the cold noodles.

NGREDIENTS

erves 4

50g/12oz egg noodles
carrots, cut into fine julienne strips
½ cucumber, peeled, seeded and cut into 1cm/½in cubes
15g/4oz celeriac, peeled and cut into fine julienne strips
spring onions, finely sliced
canned water chestnuts, drained and finely sliced
75g/6oz beansprouts
small fresh green chilli, seeded and finely chopped
0ml/2 tbsp sesame seeds and 115g/4oz/1 cup peanuts, to serve

or the dressing

5ml/1 tbsp dark soy sauce
5ml/1 tbsp light soy sauce
5ml/1 tbsp clear honey
5ml/1 tbsp Chinese rice wine or dry sherry
5ml/1 tbsp sesame oil

1 Cook the egg noodles in boiling water, following the instructions on ne packet.

2 Drain the noodles, refresh in cold water, then drain again. Mix the oodles together with all of the repared vegetables.

3 Combine the dressing ingredients in a small bowl, then toss into the noodle and vegetable mixture. Divide the salad between 4 plates.

4 Place the sesame seeds and peanuts on separate baking trays and place in a preheated oven at 200°C/400°F/ Gas 6. Take the sesame seeds out after 5 minutes and continue to cook the peanuts for a further 5 minutes until evenly browned.

5 Sprinkle the sesame seeds and peanuts evenly over each portion and serve at once.

Thai Fruit and Vegetable Salad

This fruit salad is typically presented with the main course and serves as a cooler to counteract the heat of Thai curry.

INGREDIENTS

Serves 4–6

1 small pineapple
1 small mango, peeled, stoned and sliced
1 green apple, cored and sliced
6 ramboutans or lychees, peeled and stoned
115g/4oz French beans, halved
1 medium red onion, sliced
1 small cucumber, cut into short sticks
115g/4oz beansprouts
2 spring onions, sliced
1 ripe tomato, quartered
225g/8oz cos, Bibb or iceberg lettuce leaves, torn into pieces
salt

For the coconut dipping sauce

90ml/6 tbsp coconut cream
30ml/2 tbsp sugar
75ml/5 tbsp boiling water
1.5ml/¼ tsp chilli sauce
15ml/1 tbsp fish sauce
juice of 1 lime

1 To make the dipping sauce, place the coconut cream, sugar and boiling water in a screw-top jar. Add the chilli sauce, fish sauce and lime juice and shake to mix. Set aside.

2 Trim both ends of the pineapple with a serrated knife, then cut away the skin. Remove the central core with an apple corer, or cut the pineapple into four down the middle and remove the core with a knife. Roughly chop the pineapple and set aside with the other fruits.

3 Bring a small saucepan of lightly salted water to the boil and cook the beans for 3–4 minutes. Refresh under cold running water and set aside. To serve, arrange the fruits, vegetables and lettuce leaves in individual heaps in a serving bowl. Serve the dipping sauce separately.

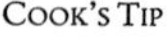

COOK'S TIP

The ramboutan or rambutan, cousin to the lychee, originated in Malaysia, but is now cultivated in much of South-east Asia and the USA. It has a dark reddish-brown, hairy skin with sweet, translucent flesh and an inedible stone. It is about 5cm/2in in diameter.

Bamboo Shoot Salad

'his salad, which has a hot and ıarp flavour, originated in orth-east Thailand. Use fresh oung bamboo shoots when ou can find them, otherwise ıbstitute canned bamboo shoots.

NGREDIENTS

erves 4

00g/14oz can whole bamboo shoots
5g/1oz glutinous rice
0ml/2 tbsp chopped shallots
5ml/1 tbsp chopped garlic
5ml/3 tbsp chopped spring onions
0ml/2 tbsp fish sauce
0ml/2 tbsp lime juice
ml/1 tsp granulated sugar
.5ml/½ tsp dried flaked chillies
0–25 small mint leaves
5ml/1 tbsp toasted sesame seeds

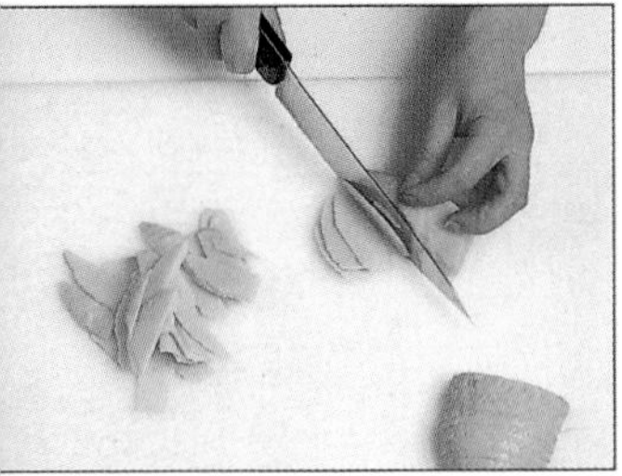

1 Rinse and drain the bamboo shoots, finely slice and set aside.

2 Dry roast the rice in a frying pan until it is golden brown. Remove ınd grind to fine crumbs with a pestle ınd mortar.

3 Tip the rice into a bowl, add the shallots, garlic, spring onions, fish sauce, lime juice, granulated sugar, chillies and half the mint leaves.

4 Mix thoroughly, then pour over the bamboo shoots and toss together. Serve sprinkled with sesame seeds and the remaining mint leaves.

Egg Pancake Salad Wrappers

One of Indonesia's favourite snack foods, pancakes are assembled according to taste and dipped in various sauces.

INGREDIENTS

Makes 12

2 eggs
2.5ml/½ tsp salt
5ml/1 tsp vegetable oil, plus extra for frying
115g/4oz/1 cup flour
300ml/½ pint/1¼ cups water
lettuce leaves, shredded, beansprouts, cucumber wedges, spring onions, shredded, cooked peeled prawns and coriander sprigs, to serve

For the filling

45ml/3 tbsp vegetable oil
1cm/½in fresh root ginger, chopped
1 garlic clove, crushed
1 small red fresh chilli, seeded and finely chopped
15ml/1 tbsp rice vinegar or white wine vinegar
10ml/2 tsp sugar
115g/4oz mooli, grated
1 medium carrot, grated
115g/4oz Chinese leaves, shredded
2 shallots or 1 small red onion, thinly sliced

1 Break the eggs into a bowl and stir in the salt, vegetable oil and flour until smooth; do not over-mix. Add the water, a little at a time, and strain into a jug. Allow the batter to stand for 15–20 minutes before use.

2 Moisten a small, non-stick frying pan with vegetable oil and heat. Pour in enough batter just to cover the base of the pan and cook for 30 seconds. Turn over and cook the other side briefly. Stack the pancakes on a plate, cover and keep warm.

3 Make the filling. Heat the oil in a preheated wok and add the ginger, garlic and chilli and stir-fry for 1–2 minutes. Add the vinegar, sugar, mooli, carrot, Chinese leaves or cabbage and shallots or onion. Cook for 3–4 minutes. Serve with the pancakes, prawns and salad ingredients.

Green Vegetable Salad with Coconut Mint Dip

'his dish is usually served as an ccompaniment to Singapore and Malaysian meat dishes.

NGREDIENTS

erves 4–6

15g/4oz mangetouts, halved
15g/4oz French beans, halved
cucumber, peeled, halved and sliced
15g/4oz Chinese leaves, roughly shredded
15g/4oz beansprouts
alt
ettuce leaves, to serve

'or the dressing

garlic clove, crushed
small fresh green chilli, seeded and finely chopped
0ml/2 tsp sugar
5ml/3 tbsp creamed coconut
5ml/5 tbsp boiling water
0ml/2 tsp fish sauce
5ml/3 tbsp vegetable oil
uice of 1 lime
0ml/2 tbsp chopped fresh mint

1 Bring a saucepan of lightly salted water to the boil. Blanch the nangetouts, French beans and cucumber for 4 minutes. Drain and efresh under cold running water. Drain and set aside.

2 To make the dressing, pound the garlic, chilli and sugar together in a mortar with a pestle. Add the creamed coconut, water, fish sauce, vegetable oil, lime juice and mint. Stir well.

3 Arrange the blanched vegetables, Chinese leaves and beansprouts on a bed of lettuce in a basket, pour the dressing into a shallow bowl and serve.

Aubergine Salad with Dried Shrimps and Egg

An appetizing and unusual salad that you will find yourself making over and over again.

INGREDIENTS

Serves 4–6

2 aubergines
15ml/1 tbsp oil
30ml/2 tbsp dried shrimps, soaked and drained
15ml/1 tbsp coarsely chopped garlic
30ml/2 tbsp freshly squeezed lime juice
5ml/1 tsp palm sugar
30ml/2 tbsp fish sauce
1 hard-boiled egg, shelled and chopped
4 shallots, finely sliced into rings
coriander leaves, to garnish
2 red chillies, seeded and sliced, to garnish

COOK'S TIP

For an interesting variation, try using salted duck's or quail's eggs, cut in half, instead of chopped chicken's eggs.

1 Grill or roast the aubergines until charred and tender.

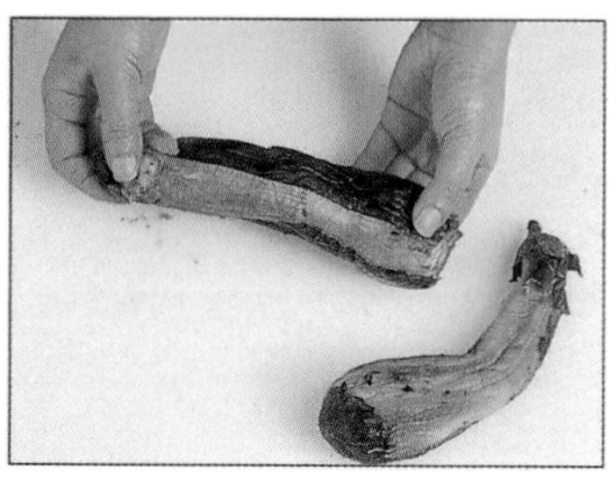

2 When cool enough to handle, peel away the skin and slice the flesh.

3 Heat the oil in a small frying pan add the drained shrimps and garli and fry until golden. Remove from tl pan and set aside.

4 To make the dressing, put the lin juice, palm sugar and fish sauce i small bowl and whisk together.

5 To serve, arrange the aubergine c a serving dish. Top with the egg, shallots and dried shrimp mixture. Drizzle over the dressing and garnish with coriander and red chillies.

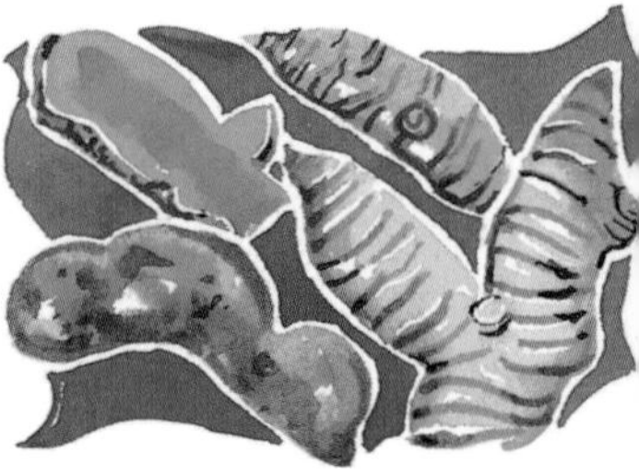

Hot Coconut Prawn and Pawpaw Salad

This Thai dish may be served as ın accompaniment to beef and :hicken dishes or on its own as a ight lunch in the summer.

NGREDIENTS

erves 4–6

225g/8oz raw or cooked prawn tails, peeled and deveined
2 ripe pawpaws
225g/8oz mixed salad leaves, such as Cos, Iceberg or Bib lettuce, Chinese leaves or young spinach
1 firm tomato, seeded and roughly chopped
3 spring onions, shredded

For the dressing

15ml/1 tbsp creamed coconut
30ml/2 tbsp boiling water
90ml/6 tbsp vegetable oil
uice of 1 lime
2.5ml/½ tsp hot chilli sauce
10ml/2 tsp fish sauce (optional)
5ml/1 tsp sugar
1 small bunch fresh coriander, shredded, and 1 large, fresh chilli, sliced, to garnish

1 First make the dressing: place the creamed coconut in a screw-top jar ınd add the boiling water. Add the vegetable oil, lime juice, chilli sauce, fish sauce, if using, and sugar. Shake well and set aside, but do not refrigerate.

2 If using raw prawns, place them in a saucepan and cover with water. Bring to the boil and simmer for 2 minutes. Drain and set aside.

3 To prepare the pawpaws, cut each in half from top to bottom and remove the black seeds with a teaspoon. Peel away the outer skin and cut the flesh into even-sized pieces. Wash the salad leaves and toss in a bowl. Add the other ingredients, pour over the dressing and serve.

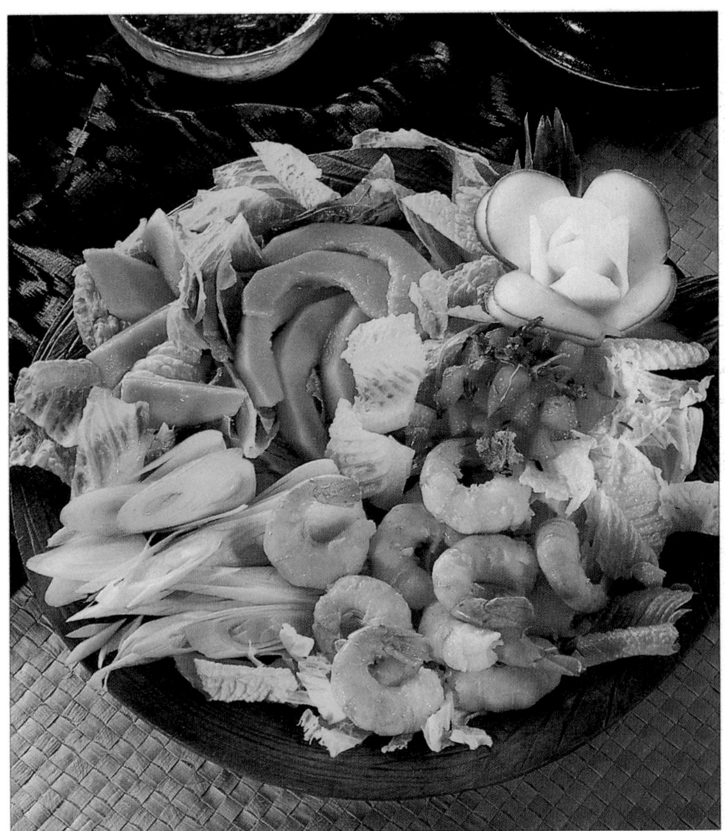

Seafood Salad with Fragrant Herbs

INGREDIENTS
Serves 4–6
250ml/8fl oz/1 cup fish stock or water
350g/12oz squid, cleaned and cut into rings
12 uncooked king prawns, shelled
12 scallops
50g/2oz bean thread noodles, soaked in warm water for 30 minutes
½ cucumber, cut into thin sticks
1 stalk lemon grass, finely chopped
2 kaffir lime leaves, finely shredded
2 shallots, finely sliced
juice of 1–2 limes
30ml/2 tbsp fish sauce
30ml/2 tbsp chopped spring onion
30ml/2 tbsp coriander leaves
12–15 mint leaves, roughly torn
4 red chillies, sliced
sprigs of coriander, to garnish

1 Pour the stock or water into a medium-size saucepan, set over a high heat and bring to the boil.

2 Cook each type of seafood separately in the stock for a few minutes. Remove and set aside.

3 Drain the bean thread noodles and cut them into short lengths, about 5cm/2in long. Combine the noodles with the cooked seafood.

4 Add all the remaining ingredients, mix together well and serve garnished with the coriander sprigs.

Pomelo Salad

Pomelo is a large fruit that resembles a grapefruit. It has a much sturdier and drier flesh.

INGREDIENTS
Serves 4–6
For the dressing
30ml/2 tbsp fish sauce
15ml/1 tbsp palm sugar
30ml/2 tbsp lime juice

For the salad
30ml/2 tbsp vegetable oil
4 shallots, finely sliced
2 garlic cloves, finely sliced
1 large pomelo
115g/4oz cooked shelled prawns
115g/4oz cooked crab meat
15ml/1 tbsp roasted peanuts
10–12 small mint leaves
2 spring onions, finely sliced
2 red chillies, seeded and finely sliced
coriander leaves, to garnish
shredded fresh coconut (optional)

1 Whisk together the fish sauce, palm sugar and lime juice and set aside.

2 Heat the oil in a small frying pan, add the shallots and garlic and fry until they are golden. Remove from the pan and set aside.

3 Peel the pomelo and break the flesh into small pieces, taking care to remove any membranes.

4 Coarsely grind the peanuts, then combine with the pomelo flesh, prawns, crab meat, mint leaves and the fried shallot mixture. Toss in the dressing and serve sprinkled with the spring onions, red chillies, coriander leaves and shredded coconut, if using.

NOODLES

Noodles are the original "fast food" in Asia and are eaten on almost every possible occasion, from weddings to funerals. There are numerous varieties and they are served both hot and cold, cooked in combination with vegetables, meat, poultry and seafood. They can be braised, deep-fried and stir-fried, as well as made into nests and cakes. Noodles may be served as a complete meal or simply as a side dish. Recipes here include Singapore Noodles, Special Chow Mein, Vegetarian Fried Noodles and Crisp Pork Meatballs Laced with Noodles.

Oriental Vegetable Noodles

Thin Italian egg pasta is a good alternative to oriental egg noodles; use it fresh or dried.

INGREDIENTS

Serves 6

500g/1¼lb thin tagliarini
1 red onion
115g/4oz shiitake mushrooms
45ml/3 tbsp sesame oil
45ml/3 tbsp dark soy sauce
15ml/1 tbsp balsamic vinegar
10ml/2 tsp caster sugar
salt
celery leaves, to garnish

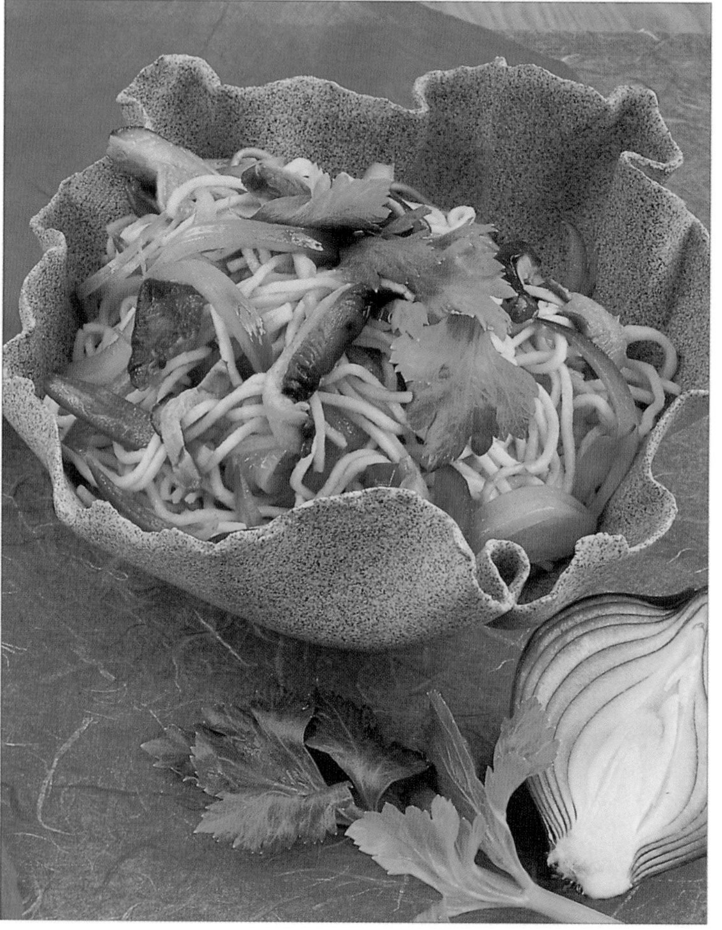

1 Cook the tagliarini in a large pan of salted boiling water, following the instructions on the pack.

2 Thinly slice the red onion and the mushrooms, using a sharp knife.

3 Heat 15ml/1 tbsp of the sesame oil in a preheated wok. When the oil is hot, stir-fry the onion and mushrooms for 2 minutes.

4 Drain the tagliarini, then add to the wok with the soy sauce, balsamic vinegar, sugar and salt to taste. Stir-fry for 1 minute, then add the remaining sesame oil, and serve garnished with celery leaves.

Peanut Noodles

\dd any of your favourite 'egetables to this recipe to make great, quick mid-week supper – nd increase the chilli, if you can ake the heat!

NGREDIENTS

erves 4
:00g/7oz medium egg noodles
›0ml/2 tbsp olive oil
garlic cloves, crushed
large onion, roughly chopped
red pepper, seeded and roughly chopped
yellow pepper, seeded and roughly chopped
›50g/12oz courgettes, roughly chopped
50g/5oz/1¼ cups roasted unsalted peanuts, roughly chopped

'or the dressing
›0ml/2 fl oz/¼ cup olive oil
rated rind and juice of 1 lemon
fresh red chilli, seeded and finely chopped
›0ml/4 tbsp chopped fresh chives
5–30ml/1–2 tbsp balsamic vinegar
ılt and ground black pepper

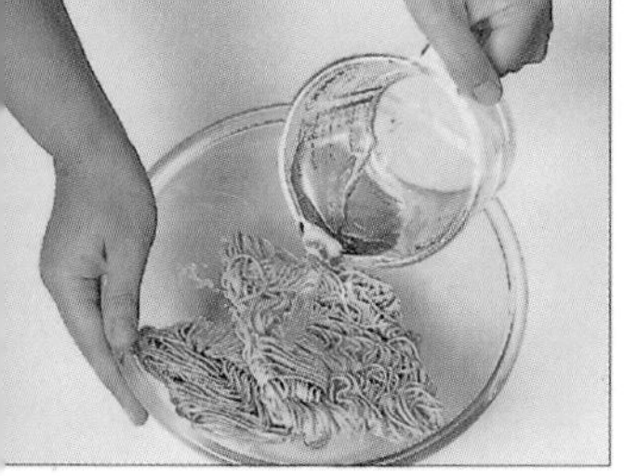

1 Soak the noodles according to the packet instructions and drain well.

2 Meanwhile, heat the oil in a preheated wok or very large frying pan and cook the garlic and onion for 3 minutes, or until beginning to soften. Add the peppers and courgettes and cook for a further 15 minutes over a medium heat until beginning to soften and brown. Add the peanuts and cook for a further 1 minute.

3 For the dressing, whisk together the olive oil, grated lemon rind and 45ml/3 tbsp lemon juice, the chilli, 45ml/3 tbsp of the chives, plenty of seasoning and balsamic vinegar to taste.

4 Toss the noodles into the vegetables and stir-fry to heat through. Add the dressing, stir to coat and serve immediately, garnished with the remaining chopped fresh chives.

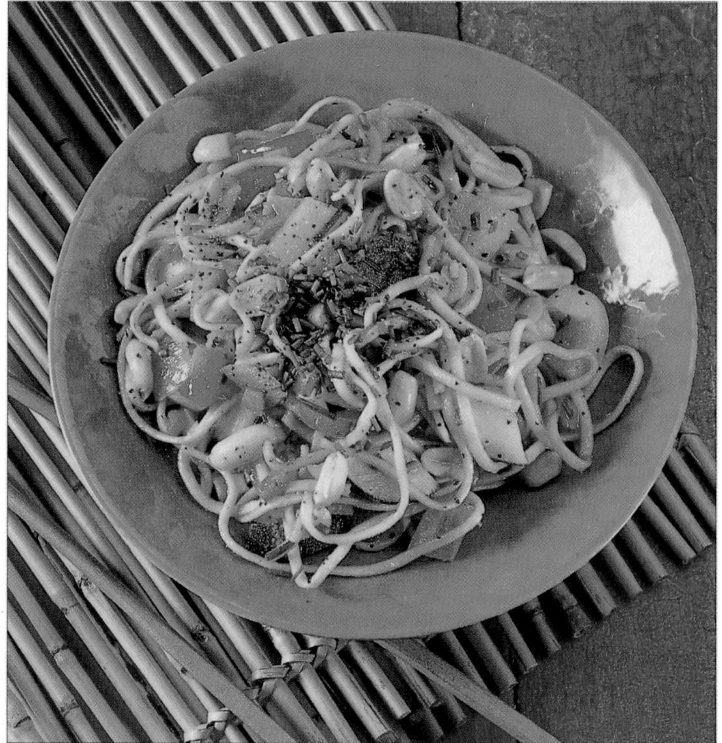

Soft Fried Noodles

This is a very basic dish for serving as an accompaniment or for those occasions when you are feeling a little peckish and fancy something simple. Break an egg into the noodles if you want to add protein. They are also good tossed with oyster sauce and a dollop of chilli black bean sauce.

INGREDIENTS

Serves 4–6
350g/12oz dried egg noodles
30ml/2 tbsp vegetable oil
30ml/2 tbsp finely chopped spring onions
soy sauce, to taste
salt and freshly ground black pepper

1 Cook the noodles in a large saucepan of boiling water until just tender, following the directions on the packet. Drain, rinse under cold running water and drain again thoroughly.

2 Heat the oil in a wok and swirl it around. Add the spring onions and fry for 30 seconds. Add the noodles, stirring gently to separate the strands.

3 Reduce the heat and fry the noodles until they are heated through, lightly browned and crisp on the outside, but still soft inside.

4 Season with soy sauce, salt and pepper. Serve at once.

Egg Fried Noodles

Yellow bean sauce gives these noodles a savoury flavour.

INGREDIENTS

Serves 4–6
350g/12oz medium-thick egg noodles
60ml/4 tbsp vegetable oil
4 spring onions, cut into 1 cm/½in rounds
juice of 1 lime
15ml/1 tbsp soy sauce
2 garlic cloves, finely chopped
175g/6oz skinless, boneless chicken breast, sliced
175g/6oz raw prawns, peeled and deveined
175g/6oz squid, cleaned and cut into rings
15ml/1 tbsp yellow bean sauce
15ml/1 tbsp fish sauce
15ml/1 tbsp soft light brown sugar
2 eggs
coriander leaves, to garnish

1 Cook the noodles in a saucepan of boiling water until just tender, then drain well and set aside.

2 Heat half the oil in a wok or large frying pan. Add the spring onions, stir-fry for 2 minutes, then add the noodles, lime juice and soy sauce and stir-fry for 2–3 minutes. Transfer the mixture to a bowl and keep warm.

3 Heat the remaining oil in the wok or pan. Add the garlic, chicken, prawns and squid. Stir-fry over a high heat until cooked.

4 Stir in the yellow bean paste, fish sauce and sugar, then break the eggs into the mixture, stirring gently until they set.

5 Add the noodles, toss lightly to mix, and heat through. Serve garnished with coriander leaves.

Lettuce Wraps with Sesame Noodles

Ingredients

Serves 4

15ml/1 tbsp vegetable oil
2 duck breasts, about 225g/8oz each, trimmed
60ml/4 tbsp saké
60ml/4 tbsp soy sauce
30ml/2 tbsp mirin
15ml/1 tbsp sugar
½ cucumber, halved, seeded and finely diced
30ml/2 tbsp chopped red onion
2 red chillies, seeded and finely chopped
30ml/2 tbsp rice vinegar
115g/4oz rice vermicelli, soaked in warm water until soft
15ml/1 tbsp dark sesame oil
15ml/1 tbsp black sesame seeds, toasted
handful of coriander leaves
12–16 large green or red lettuce leaves
handful of mint leaves
salt and freshly ground black pepper

1 Heat the oil in a large frying pan, add the duck breasts, skin side down and fry until golden. Turn each breast and fry the other side briefly. Remove the duck, rinse under hot water to remove excess oil, then drain.

2 Combine the saké, soy sauce, mirin and sugar in saucepan large enough to hold both duck breasts in a single layer. Bring to the boil, add the duck, skin side down, lower the heat and simmer for 3–5 minutes, depending on the thickness of the duck. Remove the pan from the heat and allow the duck to cool in the liquid.

3 Using a slotted spoon, transfer the duck to a board then slice thinly using a large sharp knife. Return the pan to a low heat and cook the sauce until it reduces and thickens slightly.

4 In a serving bowl, mix the diced cucumber with the red onion, chillies and rice vinegar. Set aside.

5 Cook the noodles in a saucepan of boiling water for about 3 minutes or until tender. Drain and rinse under cold running water. Drain again, then tip into a serving bowl and toss lightly with the sesame oil and seeds. Season with salt and pepper.

6 Place the thickened sauce and coriander leaves in separate serving bowls, alongside the bowls of noodles and the cucumber mixture. Arrange the lettuce leaves and sliced duck on individual serving plates.

7 To serve, place a few slices of duck, some noodles, cucumber, herbs and sauce inside a lettuce leaf, wrap and eat.

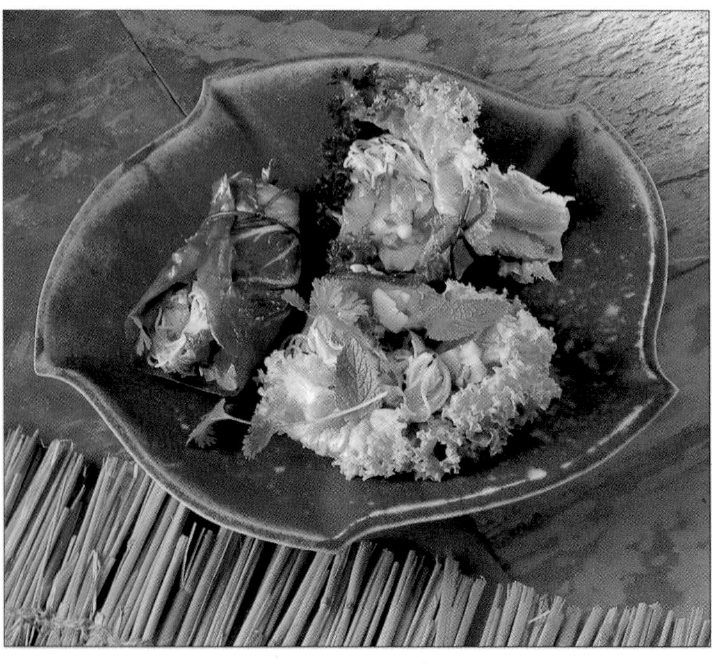

Singapore Noodles

)ried Chinese mushrooms add n intense flavour to this lightly :urried dish.

NGREDIENTS

'erves 4
0g/¾oz dried Chinese mushrooms
25g/8oz fine egg noodles
0ml/2 tsp sesame oil
5ml/3 tbsp groundnut oil
garlic cloves, crushed
small onion, chopped
fresh green chilli, seeded and thinly sliced
0ml/2 tsp curry powder
15g/4oz green beans, halved
15g/4oz Chinese leaves, thinly shredded
spring onions, sliced
0ml/2 tbsp soy sauce
15g/4oz cooked prawns, peeled and deveined
alt

1 Place the mushrooms in a bowl. cover with warm water and soak or 30 minutes. Drain, reserving 0ml/2 tbsp of the soaking water, hen slice.

2 Bring a saucepan of lightly salted water to the boil and cook the oodles according to the directions on he packet. Drain, tip into a bowl and oss with the sesame oil.

3 Heat the groundnut oil in a preheated wok. When it is hot, stir-fry the garlic, onion and chilli for 3 minutes. Stir in the curry powder and cook for 1 minute. Add the mushrooms, green beans, Chinese leaves and spring onions. Stir-fry for 3–4 minutes until the vegetables are tender, but still crisp.

4 Add the noodles, soy sauce, reserved mushroom soaking water and prawns. Toss over the heat for 2–3 minutes until the noodles and prawns are heated through.

COOK'S TIP

Ring the changes with the vegetables used in this dish. Try mangetouts, broccoli, peppers or baby corn cobs. The prawns can be omitted or replaced with ham or chicken, if wished.

Chinese Mushrooms with Cellophane Noodles

Red fermented bean curd adds extra flavour to this hearty vegetarian dish. It is brick red in colour, with a very strong, cheesy flavour, and is made by fermenting bean curd (tofu) with salt, red rice and rice wine. Look out for it in cans or earthenware pots at Chinese food markets.

INGREDIENTS

Serves 4

115g/4oz dried Chinese mushrooms
25g/1oz dried wood ears
115g/4oz dried bean curd
30ml/2 tbsp vegetable oil
2 garlic cloves, finely chopped
2 slices fresh root ginger, finely chopped
10 Szechuan peppercorns, crushed
15ml/1 tbsp red fermented bean curd
½ star anise
pinch of sugar
15–30ml/1–2 tbsp soy sauce
50g/2oz cellophane noodles, soaked in hot water until soft
salt

1 Soak the Chinese mushrooms and wood ears separately in bowls of hot water for 30 minutes. Break the dried bean curd into small pieces and soak in water according to the instructions on the packet.

COOK'S TIP

If you can't find Szechuan peppercorns, then use ordinary black ones instead.

2 Strain the mushrooms, reserving the liquid. Squeeze as much liquid from the mushrooms as possible, then discard the mushroom stems. Cut the cups in half if they are large.

3 The wood ears should swell to five times their original size. Drain them, rinse thoroughly and drain again. Cut off any gritty parts, then cut each wood ear into two or three pieces.

4 Heat the oil in a heavy-based pan. Add the garlic, ginger and Szechuan peppercorns. Fry for a few seconds, then add the mushrooms and red fermented bean curd. Mix lightly and fry for 5 minutes.

5 Add the reserved mushroom liqu to the pan, with sufficient water completely cover the mushrooms. Ac the star anise, sugar and soy sauce, th cover and simmer for 30 minutes.

6 Add the chopped wood ears and reconstituted bean curd pieces to the pan. Cover and cook for about 10 minutes.

7 Drain the cellophane noodles, ad them to the mixture and cook for a further 10 minutes until tender, adding more liquid if necessary. Add salt to taste and serve.

Thai Noodles with Chinese Chives

'his recipe requires a little time or preparation but the cooking ime is very fast. Everything is ooked speedily in a hot wok nd should be eaten at once.

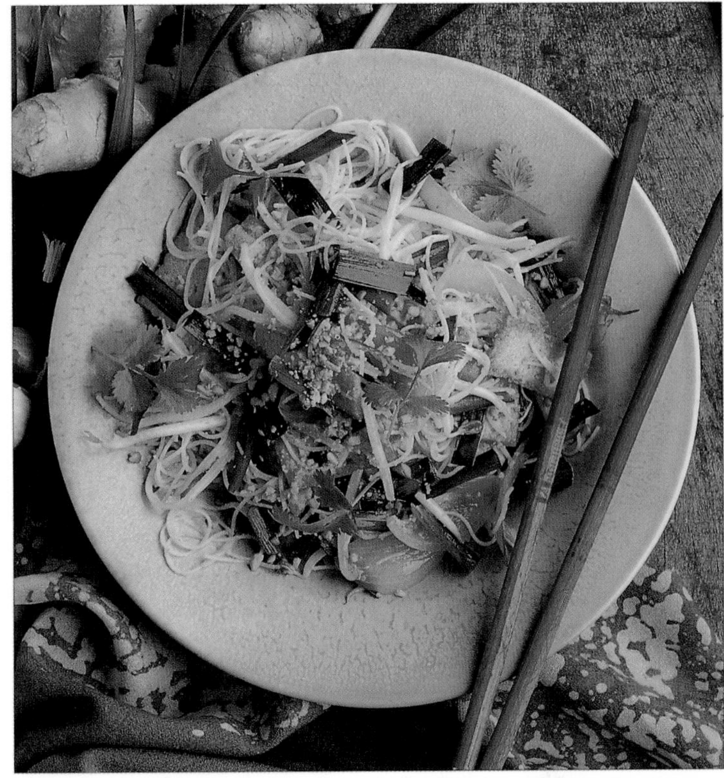

NGREDIENTS

erves 4

50g/12oz dried rice noodles
cm/½ in fresh root ginger, grated
0ml/2 tbsp light soy sauce
5ml/3 tbsp vegetable oil
25g/8oz Quorn, cut into small cubes
garlic cloves, crushed
large onion, cut into thin wedges
15g/4oz fried tofu, thinly sliced
fresh green chilli, seeded and finely sliced
75g/6oz beansprouts
15g/4oz Chinese chives, cut into 5cm/2in lengths
0g/2oz roasted peanuts, ground
0ml/2 tbsp dark soy sauce
esh coriander leaves, to garnish

1 Place the noodles in a large bowl, cover with warm water and soak or 20–30 minutes, then drain. Blend ogether the ginger, light soy sauce and 5ml/1 tbsp of the oil in a bowl. Stir n the Quorn and set aside for 10 ninutes. Drain, reserving the marinade.

2 Heat 15ml/1 tbsp of the oil in a preheated wok or frying pan and ry the garlic for a few seconds. Add the Quorn and stir-fry for 3–4 minutes. Transfer to a plate and set aside.

3 Heat the remaining oil in the wok or frying pan and stir-fry the onion for 3–4 minutes until softened and just beginning to colour. Add the tofu and chilli, stir-fry briefly and then add the noodles. Stir-fry for 4–5 minutes.

4 Stir in the beansprouts, Chinese chives and most of the ground peanuts, reserving a little for the garnish. Add the Quorn, the dark soy sauce and the reserved marinade.

5 When hot, spoon on to serving plates and garnish with the remaining ground peanuts and coriander leaves.

COOK'S TIP

Quorn makes this a vegetarian meal. However, thinly sliced pork or chicken could be used instead. Stir-fry them initially for 4–5 minutes.

Udon Pot

INGREDIENTS

Serves 4

350g/12oz dried udon noodles
1 large carrot, cut into bite-size chunks
225g/8oz chicken breasts or thighs, skinned and cut into bite-size pieces
8 raw king prawns, peeled and deveined
4–6 Chinese cabbage leaves, cut into short strips
8 shiitake mushrooms, stems removed
50g/2oz mange-touts, topped and tailed
1.5 litres/2½ pints/6¼ cups chicken stock or instant bonito stock
30ml/2 tbsp mirin
soy sauce, to taste
1 bunch spring onions, finely chopped, 30ml/2 tbsp grated fresh root ginger, lemon wedges, and extra soy sauce, to serve

1 Cook the noodles until just tender, following the directions on the packet. Drain, rinse under cold water and drain again. Blanch the carrot in boiling water for 1 minute, then drain.

2 Spoon the noodles and carrot chunks into a large saucepan or flameproof casserole, and arrange the chicken breasts or thighs, prawns, Chinese cabbage leaves, mushrooms and mange-touts on top.

3 Bring the stock to the boil in a saucepan. Add the mirin and enough soy sauce to taste. Pour the stock over the noodles. Cover the pan or casserole, bring to the boil over a moderate heat, then simmer gently for 5–6 minutes until all the ingredients are cooked.

4 Serve with chopped spring onions, grated ginger, lemon wedges and a little soy sauce.

Combination Chow Mein

INGREDIENTS

Serves 4–6

450g/1lb thick egg noodles
45ml/3 tbsp vegetable oil
2 garlic cloves, chopped
2 spring onions, cut into short lengths
50g/2oz pork fillet, sliced, or Chinese roast pork cut into short lengths
50g/2oz pig's liver, sliced
75g/3oz raw prawns, peeled and deveined
50g/2oz prepared squid, sliced
50g/2oz cockles or mussels
115g/4oz watercress, leaves stripped from the stems
2 red chillies, seeded and finely sliced
30–45ml/2–3 tbsp soy sauce
15ml/1 tbsp sesame oil
salt and freshly ground black pepper

1 Cook the egg noodles in a large saucepan of boiling water until just tender. Drain thoroughly.

2 Heat the oil in a wok and fry the garlic and spring onions for about 30 seconds. Add the pork fillet, if using, with the liver, prawns, squid and cockles or mussels. Stir-fry for 2 minutes over a high heat.

3 Add the watercress and chillies to the wok and stir-fry for a further 3–4 minutes, until the meat is cooked.

4 Add the drained noodles, stirring constantly but gently. Toss in the Chinese roast pork, if using, and add the soy sauce with salt and pepper to taste. Cook until the noodles are thoroughly heated through. Stir in the sesame oil, mix well and serve.

Cellophane Noodles with Pork

Unlike other types of noodles, cellophane noodles can be reheated successfully.

INGREDIENTS

Serves 3–4

115g/4oz cellophane noodles
4 dried Chinese black mushrooms
225g/8oz boneless lean pork
30ml/2 tbsp dark soy sauce
30ml/2 tbsp Chinese rice wine or dry sherry
2 garlic cloves, crushed
15ml/1 tbsp grated fresh root ginger
5ml/1 tsp chilli oil
45ml/3 tbsp groundnut oil
4–6 spring onions, chopped
5ml/1 tsp cornflour blended with 175ml/6fl oz/¾ cup chicken stock or water
30ml/2 tbsp chopped fresh coriander
salt and ground black pepper
fresh coriander sprigs, to garnish

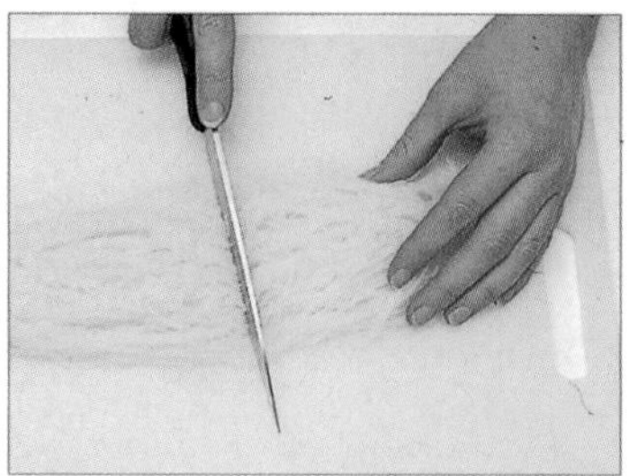

1 Put the noodles and mushrooms in separate bowls and pour over sufficient warm water to cover. Set aside to soak for 15–20 minutes, until soft. Drain well. Cut the noodles into 12.5cm/5in lengths using scissors or a knife. Squeeze out any excess water from the mushrooms, discard the stems and finely chop the caps.

2 Cut the pork into very small cube and place them in a bowl. Add the soy sauce, rice wine or dry sherry, garlic, ginger and chilli oil and mix well. Set aside to marinate for 15 minutes. Drain, reserving the marinade

3 Heat the groundnut oil in a preheated wok. Add the pork and mushrooms and stir-fry for 3 minutes. Add the spring onions and stir-fry for minute. Stir in the cornflour mixture and reserved marinade and season to taste. Cook for 1 minute.

4 Add the noodles and stir-fry for about 2 minutes, until the noodles have absorbed most of the liquid and the pork is cooked through. Stir in the chopped coriander. Serve immediately garnished with the coriander sprigs.

Noodles with Chicken, Prawns and Ham

gg noodles can be cooked up to 4 hours in advance and kept in bowl of cold water.

NGREDIENTS

erves 4–6

75g/10oz dried egg noodles
5ml/1 tbsp vegetable oil
medium onion, chopped
garlic clove, crushed
5cm/1in fresh root ginger, chopped
0g/2oz canned water chestnuts, drained and sliced
5ml/1 tbsp light soy sauce
0ml/2 tbsp fish sauce or strong chicken stock
75g/6oz cooked chicken breast, sliced
50g/5oz cooked ham, thickly sliced and cut into short fingers
25g/8oz cooked prawn tails, peeled
75g/6oz beansprouts
00g/7oz canned baby corn cobs, drained
limes, cut into wedges, and 1 small bunch coriander, shredded, to garnish

1 Cook the noodles according to the packet instructions. Drain well and et aside.

2 Heat the oil in a preheated wok or frying pan. Fry the onion, garlic and ginger for 3 minutes, or until soft but not coloured. Add the chestnuts, soy sauce, fish sauce or chicken stock, chicken breast, ham and prawns.

3 Add the noodles, beansprouts and baby corn cobs and stir-fry for 6–8 minutes, until heated through. Transfer to a warmed serving dish, garnish with the lime wedges and shredded coriander and serve immediately.

Seafood Chow Mein

This basic recipe can be adapted using different items for the "dressing".

INGREDIENTS

Serves 4
75g/3oz squid, cleaned
75g/3oz raw prawns
3–4 fresh scallops
½ egg white
15ml/1 tbsp cornflour paste
250g/9oz egg noodles
75–90ml/5–6 tbsp vegetable oil
50g/2oz mangetouts
2.5ml/½ tsp salt
2.5ml/½ tsp light brown sugar
15ml/1 tbsp Chinese rice wine or dry sherry
30ml/2 tbsp light soy sauce
2 spring onions, finely shredded
Basic Stock, if necessary
few drops of sesame oil

1 Open up the squid and score the inside in a criss-cross pattern with a sharp knife. Cut the squid into pieces, each about the size of a postage stamp. Soak the squid in a bowl of boiling water until all the pieces curl up. Rinse in cold water and drain.

2 Peel and devein the prawns, then cut each in half lengthways.

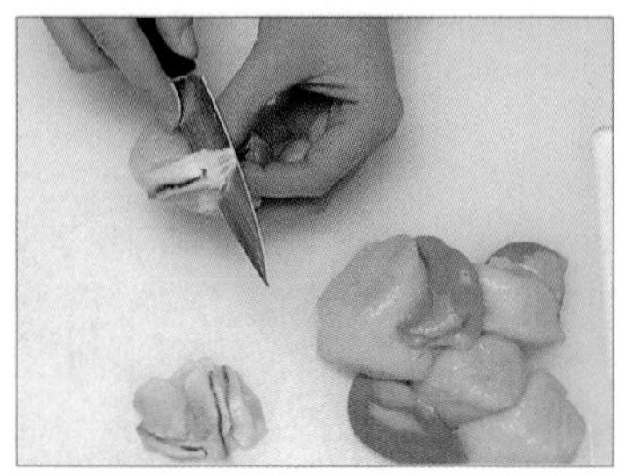

3 Cut each scallop into 3–4 slices. Mix together the scallops, prawns, egg white and cornflour paste.

4 Cook the noodles in boiling water according to the packet instructions. Drain and refresh under cold water. Mix with about 15ml/1 tbsp of the oil.

5 Heat 30–45ml/2–3 tbsp of the remaining oil in a preheated wok Stir-fry the mangetouts, squid and prawn mixture for about 2 minutes, then add the salt, sugar, rice wine or dry sherry, half the soy sauce and the spring onions. Blend well and add a little stock, if necessary. Remove from the wok and keep warm.

6 Heat the remaining oil in the wo and stir-fry the noodles for 2–3 minutes with the remaining soy sauce Place in a large serving dish, pour the "dressing" on top and sprinkle with a little sesame oil. Serve hot or cold.

富
貴
福

Special Chow Mein

Lap cheong is a special air-dried Chinese sausage. It is available from most Chinese supermarkets. If you cannot buy it, substitute with either diced ham, chorizo or salami.

INGREDIENTS

Serves 4–6

45ml/3 tbsp vegetable oil
2 garlic cloves, sliced
5ml/1 tsp chopped fresh root ginger
2 red chillies, chopped
2 lap cheong, about 75g/3oz, rinsed and sliced (optional)
1 boneless chicken breast, thinly sliced
16 uncooked tiger prawns, peeled, tails left intact, and deveined
115g/4oz green beans
225g/8oz beansprouts
50g/2oz garlic chives
450g/1lb egg noodles, cooked in boiling water until tender
30ml/2 tbsp soy sauce
15ml/1 tbsp oyster sauce
salt and freshly ground black pepper
15ml/1 tbsp sesame oil
2 spring onions, shredded, to garnish
15ml/1 tbsp coriander leaves, to garnish

1 Heat 15ml/1 tbsp of the oil in a wok or large frying pan and fry the garlic, ginger and chillies. Add the lap cheong, chicken, prawns and beans. Stir-fry for about 2 minutes over a high heat or until the chicken and prawns are cooked. Transfer the mixture to a bowl and set aside.

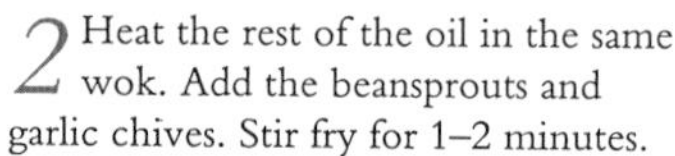

2 Heat the rest of the oil in the same wok. Add the beansprouts and garlic chives. Stir fry for 1–2 minutes.

3 Add the noodles and toss and stir to mix. Season with soy sauce, oyster sauce, salt and pepper.

4 Return the prawn mixture to the wok. Reheat and mix well with the noodles. Stir in the sesame oil. Serve garnished with spring onions and coriander leaves.

Chicken Chow Mein

:how Mein is arguably the best :nown Chinese noodle dish in :e West. Noodles are stir-fried :ith meat, seafood or vegetables.

:NGREDIENTS

:rves 4
:50g/12oz noodles
:25g/8oz skinless, boneless chicken breasts
:5ml/3 tbsp soy sauce
:5ml/1 tbsp rice wine or dry sherry
:5ml/1 tbsp dark sesame oil
:0ml/4 tbsp vegetable oil
: garlic cloves, finely chopped
:0g/2oz mange-touts, topped and tailed
:15g/4oz beansprouts
:0g/2oz ham, finely shredded
: spring onions, finely chopped
:lt and freshly ground black pepper

1 Cook the noodles in a saucepan of boiling water until tender. Drain, :inse under cold water and drain well.

2 Slice the chicken into fine shreds about 5cm/2in in length. Place in a :owl and add 10ml/2 tsp of the soy :auce, the rice wine or sherry and :esame oil.

3 Heat half the vegetable oil in a wok or large frying pan over a high heat. When it starts smoking, add the chicken mixture. Stir-fry for 2 minutes, then transfer the chicken to a plate and keep it hot.

4 Wipe the wok clean and heat the remaining oil. Stir in the garlic, mange-touts, beansprouts and ham, stir-fry for another minute or so and add the noodles.

5 Continue to stir-fry until the noodles are heated through. Add the remaining soy sauce to taste and season with salt and pepper. Return the chicken and any juices to the noodle mixture, add the chopped spring onions and give the mixture a final stir. Serve at once.

Rice Noodles with Beef and Black Bean Sauce

This is an excellent combination – beef with a chilli sauce tossed with silky smooth rice noodles.

INGREDIENTS

Serves 4

450g/1lb fresh rice noodles
60ml/4 tbsp vegetable oil
1 onion, finely sliced
2 garlic cloves, finely chopped
2 slices fresh root ginger, finely chopped
225g/8oz mixed peppers, seeded and cut into strips
350g/12oz rump steak, finely sliced against the grain
45ml/3 tbsp fermented black beans, rinsed in warm water, drained and chopped
30ml/2 tbsp soy sauce
30ml/2 tbsp oyster sauce
15ml/1 tbsp chilli black bean sauce
15ml/1 tbsp cornflour
120ml/4fl oz/½ cup stock or water
2 spring onions, finely chopped, and 2 red chillies, seeded and finely sliced, to garnish

1 Rinse the noodles under hot water; drain well. Heat half the oil in a wok or large frying pan, swirling it around. Add the onion, garlic, ginger and mixed pepper strips. Stir-fry for 3–5 minutes, then remove with a slotted spoon and keep hot.

2 Add the remaining oil to the wok. When hot, add the sliced beef and fermented black beans and stir-fry over a high heat for 5 minutes or until they are cooked.

3 In a small bowl, blend the soy sauce, oyster sauce and chilli black bean sauce with the cornflour and stock or water until smooth. Add the mixture to the wok, then return the onion mixture to the wok and cook, stirring, for 1 minute.

4 Add the noodles and mix lightly. Stir over a medium heat until the noodles are heated through. Adjust the seasoning if necessary. Serve at once, garnished with the chopped spring onions and chillies.

Straw Noodle Prawns in a Sweet Ginger Dip

'rawns are a popular feature in ıpanese cooking. Rarely are they ıore delicious than when vrapped in crispy noodles.

NGREDIENTS

erves 4–6

5g/3oz somen noodles or vermicelli
sheets nori
2 large raw prawn tails, peeled and deveined
egetable oil, for deep-frying

or the dipping sauce

0ml/6 tbsp soy sauce
0ml/2 tbsp sugar
cm/¾in fresh root ginger, grated

1 Cover the somen noodles, if using, with boiling water and leave to oak for 1–2 minutes. Drain and dry ıoroughly with kitchen paper. Cut the oodles into 7.5cm/3in lengths. If sing vermicelli, cover with boiling vater and leave to soak for 1–2 minutes ɔ soften. Drain and set aside. Cut the ori into 1 x 5cm/½ x 2in strips and et aside.

2 To make the dipping sauce, bring the soy sauce to the boil in a small ıucepan with the sugar and ginger. immer for 2–3 minutes, strain and set side to cool.

3 Line up the noodles or vermicelli on a wooden board. Straighten ach prawn by pushing a bamboo kewer through its length. Roll the rawn in the noodles or vermicelli so ıat they adhere in neat strands.

4 Moisten one end of the nori strips and secure the noodles at the fat end of each prawn. Set aside.

5 Heat the vegetable oil in a preheated wok with a wire draining rack or in a deep-fryer to 180°C/350°F. Fry the prawns in the oil, two at a time, until the noodles or vermicelli are crisp and golden.

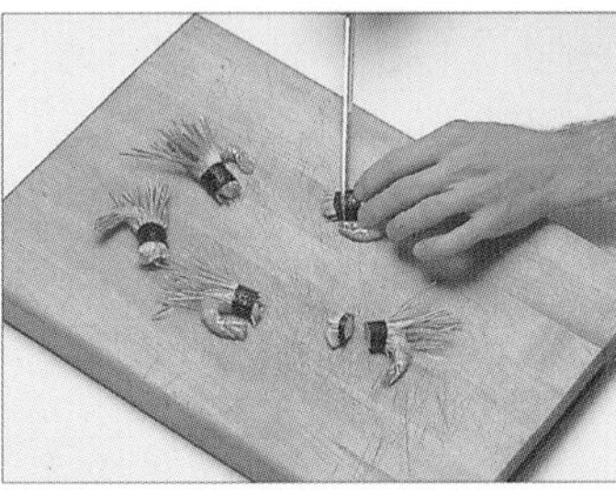

6 To finish, cut through the band of nori with a sharp knife, exposing a clean section of prawn. Drain on kitchen paper and serve with the dipping sauce in a small dish.

Main Course Spicy Prawn and Noodle Soup

This dish is served as a hot coconut broth with a separate platter of prawns, fish and noodles. Diners are invited to add their own choice of accompaniment to the broth.

Ingredients

Serves 4–6

25g/1oz/¼ cup raw cashew nuts
3 shallots or 1 medium onion, sliced
5cm/2in lemon grass, shredded
2 garlic cloves, crushed
150g/5oz laksa noodles (spaghetti-sized rice noodles), soaked for 10 minutes before cooking
30ml/2 tbsp vegetable oil
1cm/½in square shrimp paste or 15ml/1 tbsp fish sauce
15ml/1 tbsp mild curry paste
400g/14oz can coconut milk
½ chicken stock cube
3 curry leaves (optional)
450g/1lb white fish fillet, such as cod, haddock or whiting
225g/8oz raw or cooked prawn tails, peeled
1 small Cos lettuce, shredded
115g/4oz beansprouts
3 spring onions, shredded
½ cucumber, sliced and shredded
prawn crackers, to serve

1 Grind the cashew nuts with the shallots or onion, lemon grass and garlic in a mortar with a pestle or in a food processor. Cook the noodles according to the instructions on the packet.

2 Heat the oil in a large preheated wok or saucepan, add the cashew nut mixture and stir-fry for 1–2 minutes, or until the nuts are just beginning to brown.

3 Add the shrimp paste or fish sauce and curry paste, followed by the coconut milk, stock cube and curry leaves, if using. Simmer for 10 minutes.

4 Cut the white fish into bite-size pieces. Add the fish and prawns t the simmering coconut stock and co for 3–4 minutes.

5 To serve, line a large serving plat with the shredded lettuce leaves. Arrange the beansprouts, spring onio and cucumber in neat piles, together with the cooked fish and noodles. Serve the salad with a bowl of prawn crackers and the broth in a stoneware closed-rim pot.

Cook's Tip

When cooking the fish and prawns, yo may find it easier to put them in a larg frying-basket before immersing them i the coconut stock.

Special Fried Noodles

Mee goreng is, perhaps, the best-known dish of Singapore. It is prepared from a wide range of ingredients.

INGREDIENTS

Serves 4–6

275g/10oz egg noodles
1 boneless chicken breast, skinned
115g/4oz lean pork
30ml/2 tbsp vegetable oil
175g/6oz raw or cooked prawn tails, peeled
4 shallots or 1 medium onion, chopped
2cm/¾in fresh root ginger, thinly sliced
2 garlic cloves, crushed
45ml/3 tbsp light soy sauce
5–10ml/1-2 tsp chilli sauce
15ml/1 tbsp rice vinegar or white wine vinegar
5ml/1 tsp sugar
2.5ml/½ tsp salt
115g/4oz Chinese leaves, shredded
115g/4oz spinach, shredded
3 spring onions, shredded

1 Bring a large saucepan of lightly salted water to the boil and cook the noodles according to the instructions on the packet. Drain and set aside. Place the chicken breast and pork in the freezer for 30 minutes to firm, but not freeze.

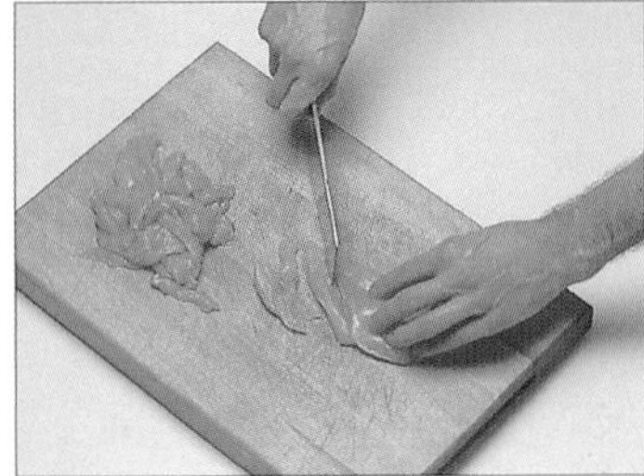

2 Slice the meat thinly against the grain. Heat the oil in a preheated wok and stir-fry the chicken, pork and prawns for 2–3 minutes. Add the shallots or onion, ginger and garlic and stir-fry for 2–3 minutes, until softened but not coloured.

3 Add the soy sauce, chilli sauce, vinegar, sugar and salt. Bring to a simmer. Add the Chinese leaves, spinach and spring onions, cover and cook for 3–4 minutes. Add the noodles, heat through and serve.

Crisp Pork Meatballs Laced with Noodles

These little meatballs, decoratively coated with a lacing of noodles, look very impressive, but are actually extremely easy to make.

INGREDIENTS

Serves 4

400g/14oz minced pork
2 garlic cloves, finely chopped
30ml/2 tbsp chopped fresh coriander
15ml/1 tbsp oyster sauce
30ml/2 tbsp fresh breadcrumbs
1 egg, beaten
175g/6oz fresh thin egg noodles
oil, for deep-frying
salt and ground black pepper
fresh coriander leaves, to garnish
spinach leaves and chilli sauce or tomato sauce, to serve

1 Mix together the pork, garlic, chopped coriander, oyster sauce, breadcrumbs and egg. Season with salt and pepper.

2 Knead the pork mixture until it is sticky, then form into balls about the size of a walnut.

3 Blanch the noodles in a saucepan of boiling water for 2–3 minutes. Drain, rinse under cold running water and drain well.

4 Wrap 3–5 strands of noodles securely around each meatball in a criss-cross pattern.

5 Heat the oil in a deep-fryer or preheated wok. Deep-fry the meatballs in batches until golden brown and cooked through to the centre. As each batch browns, remove with a slotted spoon and drain well on kitchen paper. Serve hot on a bed of spinach leaves, garnished with fresh coriander leaves and with chilli sauce or tomato sauce in a small dish.

Noodles, Chicken and Prawns in Coconut Broth

his typical Indonesian dish has everal different components rom which the diners may help hemselves, making a complete neal in itself.

NGREDIENTS

erves 8

onions, quartered
.5cm/1in fresh root ginger, sliced
garlic cloves
macadamia nuts or 8 almonds
–2 fresh chillies, seeded and sliced
lemon grass stems, lower 5cm/2in sliced
cm/2in fresh turmeric, peeled and sliced, or 5ml/1 tsp ground turmeric
5ml/1 tbsp coriander seeds, dry-fried
0ml/4 tbsp sunflower oil
00ml/14fl oz can coconut milk
.5 litres/2½ pints/6¼ cups chicken stock
50g/12oz rice noodles, soaked in cold water
50g/12oz cooked tiger prawns, peeled and deveined
alt and ground black pepper

or the garnish

hard-boiled eggs, shelled and quartered
25g/8oz cooked chicken, chopped
25g/8oz beansprouts
bunch spring onions, shredded
onion, finely sliced and deep-fried

1 Place the quartered onions, ginger, garlic and nuts in a food processor with the chillies, lemon grass and turmeric. Process to a paste. Alternatively, pound all the ingredients in a mortar with a pestle. Grind the coriander seeds coarsely and add to the paste.

2 Heat the oil in a preheated wok or frying pan and fry the spice paste, without allowing it to colour, to bring out the flavours. Add the coconut milk, stock and seasoning. Simmer for 5–10 minutes.

3 Meanwhile, drain the noodles and plunge them into a large pan of salted boiling water for 2 minutes. Remove from the heat and drain thoroughly. Rinse well with plenty of cold water. Add the tiger prawns to the soup just before serving and heat through for a minute or two.

4 Arrange the garnishes in separate bowls. Each person takes a helping of noodles, tops them with soup, eggs, chicken or beansprouts, then scatters shredded spring onions and fried onions on top.

Noodles in Soup

In China, noodles in soup are far more popular than fried noodles. This is a basic recipe which you can adapt by using different ingredients.

INGREDIENTS

Serves 4

225g/8oz chicken or pork fillet
3–4 dried Chinese mushrooms, soaked
115g/4oz can sliced bamboo shoots, drained
115g/4oz spinach leaves, lettuce hearts or Chinese leaves
2 spring onions
375g/12oz dried egg noodles
600ml/1 pint/2½ cups Basic Stock
30ml/2 tbsp vegetable oil
5ml/1 tsp salt
2.5ml/½ tsp light brown sugar
15ml/1 tbsp light soy sauce
10ml/2 tsp Chinese rice wine or dry sherry
few drops of sesame oil

1 Thinly shred the meat. Squeeze dry the mushrooms and discard any hard stalks. Thinly shred the mushroom caps, bamboo shoots, spinach, lettuce hearts or Chinese leaves and the spring onions. Keep the meat, the spring onions and the other ingredients in three heaps.

2 Cook the noodles in boiling water according to the instructions on the packet, then drain and rinse in cold water. Place in a serving bowl.

3 Bring the stock to the boil and pour over the noodles. Keep warm.

4 Heat the oil in a preheated wok, add the spring onions and the mea and stir-fry for about 1 minute.

5 Add the mushrooms, bamboo shoots and spinach, lettuce or Chinese leaves and stir-fry for 1 minute or until the meat is cooked through. Add the salt, sugar, soy sauce, rice wine or dry sherry and sesame oil and blend well

6 Pour the "dressing" over the noodles and serve.

Vegetable and Egg Noodle Ribbons

Serve this elegant, colourful dish with a tossed green salad as a light lunch or as a starter for six to eight people.

INGREDIENTS

Serves 4

1 large carrot, peeled
2 courgettes
50g/2oz butter
15ml/1 tbsp olive oil
6 fresh shiitake mushrooms, finely sliced
50g/2oz frozen peas, thawed
350g/12oz broad egg ribbon noodles
10ml/2 tsp chopped mixed herbs (such as marjoram, chives and basil)
salt and freshly ground black pepper
25g/1oz Parmesan cheese, to serve (optional)

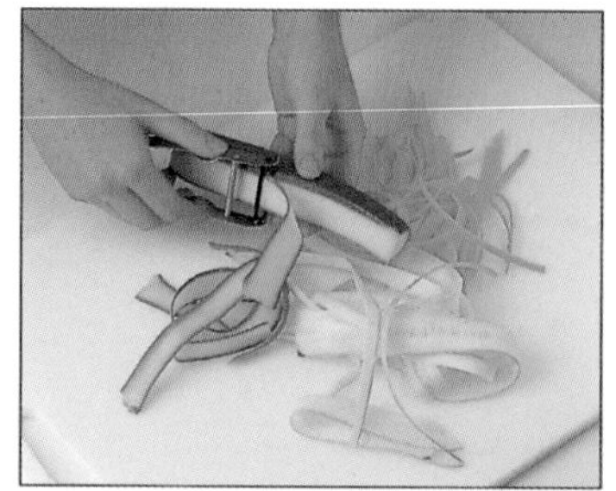

1 Using a vegetable peeler, carefully slice thin strips from the carrot and from the courgettes.

2 Heat the butter with the olive oil in a large frying pan. Stir in the carrots and shiitake mushrooms; fry for 2 minutes. Add the courgettes and peas and stir-fry until the courgettes are cooked, but still crisp. Season with salt and pepper.

3 Meanwhile, cook the noodles in a large saucepan of boiling water until just tender. Drain the noodles well and tip them into a bowl. Add th vegetables and toss to mix.

4 Sprinkle over the fresh herbs and season to taste. If using the Parmesan cheese, grate or shave it ove the top. Toss lightly and serve.

Buckwheat Noodles with Goat's Cheese

When you don't feel like doing a lot of cooking, try this good fast supper dish. The earthy flavour of buckwheat goes well with the nutty, peppery taste of rocket leaves, offset by the deliciously creamy goat's cheese.

INGREDIENTS

Serves 4

350g/12oz buckwheat noodles
50g/2oz butter
2 garlic cloves, finely chopped
4 shallots, sliced
75g/3oz hazelnuts, lightly roasted and roughly chopped
large handful rocket leaves
175g/6oz goat's cheese
salt and freshly ground black pepper

1 Cook the noodles in a large saucepan of boiling water until just tender. Drain well.

2 Heat the butter in a large frying pan. Add the garlic and shallots and cook for 2–3 minutes, stirring all the time, until the shallots are soft.

3 Add the hazelnuts and fry for about 1 minute. Add the rocket leaves and, when they start to wilt, tos in the noodles and heat through.

4 Season with salt and pepper. Crumble in the goat's cheese and serve immediately.

Shanghai Noodles with Lap Cheong

Lap cheong are firm, cured waxy pork sausages, available from Chinese food markets. Sweet and savoury, they can be steamed with rice, chicken or pork, added to an omelette or stir-fried with vegetables.

INGREDIENTS

Serves 4

30ml/2 tbsp vegetable oil
115g/4oz rindless back bacon, cut into bite-size pieces
2 lap cheong, rinsed in warm water, drained and finely sliced
2 garlic cloves, finely chopped
2 spring onions, roughly chopped
225g/8oz Chinese greens or fresh spinach leaves, cut into 5cm/2in pieces
450g/1lb fresh Shanghai noodles
30ml/2 tbsp oyster sauce
30ml/2 tbsp soy sauce
freshly ground black pepper

1 Heat half the oil in a wok or large frying pan. Add the bacon and lap cheong with the garlic and spring onions. Stir fry for a few minutes until golden. Using a slotted spoon, remove the mixture from the wok or pan and keep warm.

2 Add the remaining oil to the wok or pan. When hot, stir-fry the Chinese greens or spinach over a high heat for about 3 minutes until it just starts to wilt.

3 Add the noodles and return the lap cheong mixture to the wok or pan. Season with oyster sauce, soy sauce and pepper. Stir-fry until the noodles are heated through.

COOK'S TIP

You can buy rindless bacon already cut into bite-size pieces. To remove the rind from bacon rashers cut it off with sharp kitchen scissors.

Noodles with Tomatoes, Sardines and Mustard

Serve this simple dish hot or at room temperature.

INGREDIENTS

Serves 4

350g/12oz broad egg noodles
60ml/4 tbsp olive oil
30ml/2 tbsp lemon juice
15ml/1 tbsp wholegrain mustard
1 garlic clove, finely chopped
225g/8oz ripe tomatoes, roughly chopped
1 small red onion, finely chopped
1 green pepper, seeded and finely diced
60ml/4 tbsp chopped parsley
225g/8oz canned sardines, drained
salt and freshly ground black pepper
croûtons, made from 2 slices of bread, to serve (optional)

1 Cook the noodles in a large saucepan of boiling water for about 5–8 minutes until just tender.

2 Meanwhile, to make the dressing, whisk the oil, lemon juice, mustard and garlic in a small bowl with salt and pepper to taste.

3 Drain the noodles, tip into a large bowl and toss with the dressing. Add the tomatoes, onion, pepper, parsley and sardines and toss lightly again. Season to taste and serve with crisp croûtons, if using.

Vegetarian Fried Noodles

When making this dish for non-vegetarians, or for vegetarians who eat fish, add a piece of *blacan* (compressed shrimp paste). A small chunk about the size of a stock cube, mashed with the chilli paste, will add a deliciously rich, aromatic flavour.

INGREDIENTS

Serves 4

2 eggs
5ml/1 tsp chilli powder
5ml/1 tsp turmeric
60ml/4 tbsp vegetable oil
1 large onion, finely sliced
2 red chillies, seeded and finely sliced
15ml/1 tbsp soy sauce
2 large cooked potatoes, cut into small cubes
6 pieces fried bean curd, sliced
225g/8oz beansprouts
115g/4oz green beans, blanched
350g/12oz fresh thick egg noodles
salt and freshly ground black pepper
sliced spring onions, to garnish

1 Beat the eggs lightly, then strain them into a bowl. Heat a lightly greased omelette pan. Pour in half of the egg to cover the bottom of the pan thinly. When the egg is just set, turn the omelette over and fry the other side briefly. Slide on to a plate, blot with kitchen paper, roll up and cut into narrow strips. Make a second omelette in the same way and slice. Set the omelette strips aside for the garnish.

COOK'S TIP

Always be very careful when handling chillies. Keep your hands away from your eyes as chillies will sting them. Wash your hands thoroughly after touching chillies.

2 In a cup, mix together the chilli powder and turmeric. Form a paste by stirring in a little water.

3 Heat the oil in a wok or large frying pan. Fry the onion until soft. Reduce the heat and add the chilli paste, sliced chillies and soy sauce. Fry for 2–3 minutes.

4 Add the potatoes and fry for about 2 minutes, mixing well with the chillies. Add the bean curd, then the beansprouts, green beans and noodles.

5 Gently stir-fry until the noodles are evenly coated and heated through. Take care not to break up the potatoes or the bean curd. Season with salt and pepper. Serve hot, garnished with the reserved omelette strips and spring onion slices.

Fried Cellophane Noodles

IGREDIENTS

rves 4

75g/6oz cellophane noodles
5ml/3 tbsp vegetable oil
garlic cloves, finely chopped
15g/4oz cooked prawns, peeled
lap cheong, rinsed, drained and finely diced
eggs
celery sticks, including leaves, diced
15g/4oz beansprouts
15g/4oz spinach, cut into large pieces
spring onions, chopped
5–30ml/1–2 tbsp fish sauce
ml/1 tsp sesame oil
5ml/1 tbsp sesame seeds, toasted, to garnish

1 Soak the cellophane noodles in hot water for about 10 minutes or until soft. Drain and cut the noodles into 10cm/4in lengths.

2 Heat the oil in a wok, add the garlic and fry until golden brown. Add the prawns and lap cheong; stir-fry for 2–3 minutes. Stir in the noodles and fry for 2 minutes more.

3 Make a well in the centre of the prawn mixture, break in the eggs and slowly stir them until they are creamy and just set.

4 Stir in the celery, beansprouts, spinach and spring onions. Season with fish sauce and stir in the sesame oil. Continue to stir-fry until all the ingredients are cooked, mixing well.

5 Transfer to a serving dish. Sprinkle with sesame seeds to garnish.

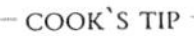

COOK'S TIP

This is a very versatile dish. Vary the vegetables if you wish and substitute ham, chorizo or salami for the lap cheong.

Crispy Noodles with Mixed Vegetables

In this dish, rice vermicelli noodles are deep fried until crisp, then tossed into a colourful selection of stir-fried vegetables.

Ingredients

Serves 4

2 large carrots
2 courgettes
4 spring onions
115g/4oz yard-long beans or green beans
115g/4oz dried vermicelli rice noodles or cellophane noodles
groundnut oil, for deep frying
2.5cm/1in fresh root ginger, shredded
1 fresh red chilli, sliced
115g/4oz fresh shiitake or button mushrooms, thickly sliced
few Chinese cabbage leaves, roughly shredded
75g/3oz beansprouts
30ml/2 tbsp light soy sauce
30ml/2 tbsp Chinese rice wine or dry sherry
5ml/1 tsp sugar
30ml/2 tbsp roughly torn fresh coriander leaves

Cook's Tip

Vermicelli rice noodles, which are thin and brittle, look like a bundle of white hair. They cook almost instantly in hot liquid, provided they have first been soaked in warm water. Rice noodles can also be deep fried. Cellophane noodles, which are made from ground mung beans, look a little like bundles of candy floss. They are opaque white when dried and expand and become translucent after soaking. Cellophane noodles are also known as bean thread, transparent and glass noodles. Dried noodles must be soaked for 5 minutes in hot water before cooking.

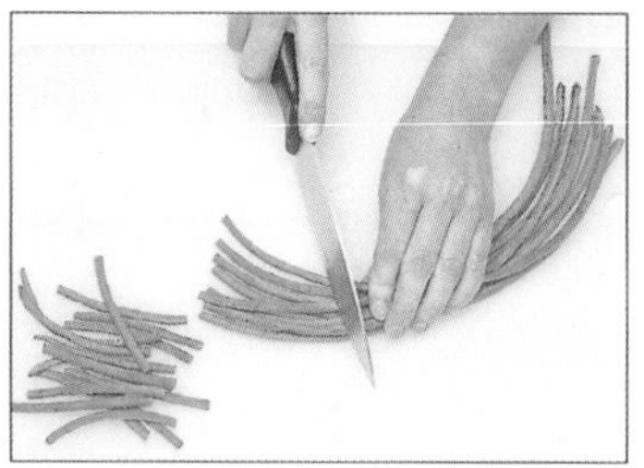

1 Cut the carrots and courgettes into fine sticks. Shred the spring onions into similar-sized pieces. Trim the beans and cut them into short lengths.

2 Break the noodles into lengths of about 7.5cm/3in. Half-fill a wok with oil and heat it to 180°C/350°F. Deep fry the raw noodles, a handful at a time, for 1–2 minutes until puffed and crispy. Drain on kitchen paper. Pour off all but 30ml/2 tbsp of the oil.

3 Reheat the oil in the wok. When hot, add the beans and stir-fry for 2–3 minutes.

4 Add the ginger, red chilli, mushrooms, carrots and courgettes and stir-fry for 1–2 minutes. Add the Chinese cabbage, beansprouts and spring onions. Stir-fry for 1 minute, then add the soy sauce, rice wine or sherry and sugar. Cook, stirring, for about 30 seconds.

5 Add the noodles and coriander and toss to mix, taking care not to crush the noodles too much. Serve at once, piled up on a plate.

Noodles with Meatballs

Mie Rebus is a one-pot meal, for which the East is renowned. It's fast food, served from street stalls.

INGREDIENTS

Serves 6

450g/1lb Spicy Meatball mixture
350g/12oz dried egg noodles
45ml/3 tbsp sunflower oil
1 large onion, finely sliced
2 garlic cloves, crushed
2.5cm/1in fresh root ginger, peeled and cut in thin matchsticks
1.2 litres/2 pints/5 cups stock
30ml/2 tbsp dark soy sauce
2 celery sticks, finely sliced, leaves reserved
6 Chinese leaves, cut in bite-size pieces
1 handful mange-touts, cut in strips
salt and freshly ground black pepper

1 Prepare the meatballs, making them quite small. Set aside.

2 Add the noodles to a large pan of salted, boiling water and stir so that the noodles do not settle at the bottom. Simmer for 3–4 minutes, or until *al dente.* Drain in a colander and rinse with plenty of cold water. Set aside.

3 Heat the oil in a wide pan and fry the onion, garlic and ginger until soft but not browned. Add the stock and soy sauce and bring to the boil.

4 Add the meatballs, half-cover and allow to simmer until they are cooked, about 5–8 minutes depending on size. Just before serving, add the sliced celery and, after 2 minutes, add the Chinese leaves and mange-touts. Taste and adjust the seasoning.

5 Divide the noodles among soup bowls, add the meatballs and vegetables and pour the soup on top. Garnish with the reserved celery leaves

Stir-fried Rice Noodles with Chicken and Prawns

hellfish have a natural affinity vith both meat and poultry. This 'hai-style recipe combines hicken with prawns and has the haracteristic sweet, sour and alty flavour.

NGREDIENTS

erves 4

25g/8oz dried flat rice noodles
20ml/4fl oz/½ cup water
0ml/4 tbsp fish sauce
5ml/1 tbsp sugar
5ml/1 tbsp fresh lime juice
ml/1 tsp paprika
inch of cayenne pepper
5ml/3 tbsp oil
garlic cloves, finely chopped
skinless, boneless chicken breast, finely sliced
raw prawns, peeled, deveined and cut in half
egg
0g/2oz roasted peanuts, coarsely crushed
spring onions, cut into short lengths
75g/6oz beansprouts
oriander leaves and 1 lime, cut into wedges, to garnish

1 Place the rice noodles in a large bowl, cover with warm water and oak for 30 minutes until soft. Drain.

2 Combine the water, fish sauce, sugar, lime juice, paprika and ayenne in a small bowl. Set aside intil required.

3 Heat the oil in a wok. Add the garlic and fry for 30 seconds until it starts to brown. Add the chicken and prawns and stir-fry for 3–4 minutes until cooked.

4 Push the chicken and prawn mixture in the wok out to the sides. Break the egg into the centre, then quickly stir to break up the yolk and cook over a medium heat until the egg is just lightly scrambled.

5 Add the drained noodles and the fish sauce mixture to the wok. Mix together well. Add half the crushed peanuts and cook, stirring frequently, until the noodles are soft and most of the liquid has been absorbed.

6 Add the spring onions and half of the beansprouts. Cook, stirring for 1 minute more. Spoon on to a platter. Sprinkle with the remaining peanuts and beansprouts. Garnish with the coriander and lime wedges and serve.

Thai Fried Noodles

Phat Thai has a fascinating flavour and texture. It is made with rice noodles and is considered one of the national dishes of Thailand.

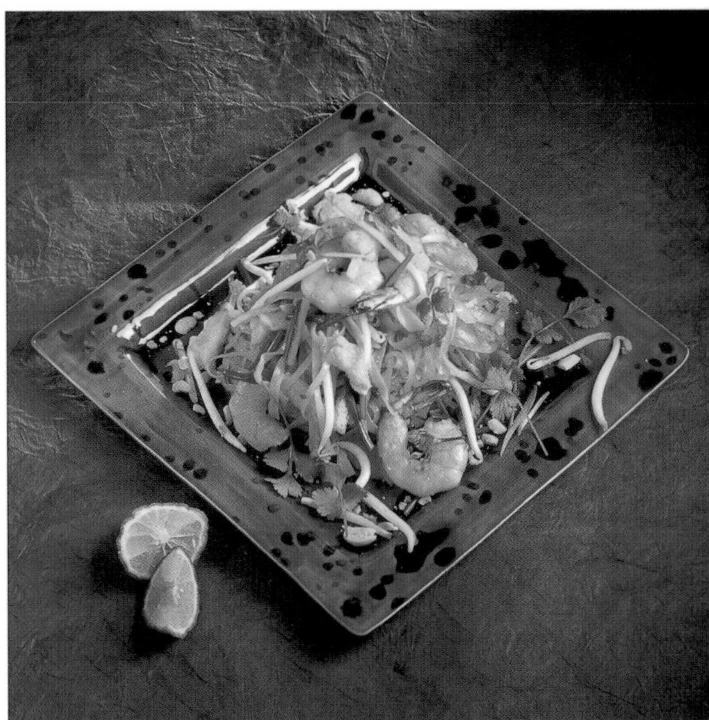

Ingredients

Serves 4–6

350g/12oz rice noodles
45ml/3 tbsp vegetable oil
15ml/1 tbsp chopped garlic
16 uncooked king prawns, shelled, tails left intact and deveined
2 eggs, lightly beaten
15ml/1 tbsp dried shrimps, rinsed
30ml/2 tbsp pickled white radish
50g/2oz fried bean curd, cut into small slivers
2.5ml/½ tsp dried chilli flakes
115g/4oz garlic chives, cut into 5cm/2in lengths
225g/8oz beansprouts
50g/2oz roasted peanuts, coarsely ground
5ml/1 tsp granulated sugar
15ml/1 tbsp dark soy sauce
30ml/2 tbsp fish sauce
30ml/2 tbsp tamarind juice
30ml/2 tbsp coriander leaves, to garnish
1 kaffir lime, to garnish

1 Soak the noodles in warm water for 20–30 minutes, then drain.

2 Heat 15ml/1 tbsp of the oil in a wok or large frying pan. Add the garlic and fry until golden. Stir in the prawns and cook for about 1–2 minutes until pink, tossing from time to time. Remove and set aside.

3 Heat another 15ml/1 tbsp of oil in the wok. Add the eggs and tilt the wok to spread them into a thin sheet. Stir to scramble and break the egg into small pieces. Remove from the wok and set aside with the prawns.

4 Heat the remaining oil in the same wok. Add the dried shrimps, pickled radish, bean curd and dried chillies. Stir briefly. Add the soaked noodles and stir-fry for 5 minutes.

5 Add the garlic chives, half the beansprouts and half the peanuts. Season with the granulated sugar, soy sauce, fish sauce and tamarind juice. Mix well and cook until the noodles a heated through.

6 Return the prawn and egg mixtur to the wok and mix with the noodles. Serve garnished with the rest of the beansprouts, peanuts, coriander leaves and lime wedges.

Bamie Goreng

his fried noodle dish is 'onderfully accommodating. o the basic recipe you can add ther vegetables, such as ıushrooms, tiny pieces of ıayote, broccoli, leeks or eansprouts, if you prefer. As 'ith fried rice, you can use hatever you have to hand, earing in mind the need to :hieve a balance of colours, avours and textures.

ıGREDIENTS

rves 6–8

i0g/1lb dried egg noodles
boneless, skinless chicken breast
.5g/4oz pork fillet
.5g/4oz calves' liver (optional)
eggs, beaten
)ml/6 tbsp oil
;g/1oz butter or margarine
garlic cloves, crushed
15g/4oz cooked, peeled prawns
15g/4oz spinach or Chinese leaves
celery sticks, finely sliced
spring onions, shredded
ɔout 60ml/4 tbsp chicken stock
ırk soy sauce and light soy sauce
lt and freshly ground black pepper
'eep-fried Onions and celery leaves, to garnish
weet and Sour Fruit and Vegetable ılad, to serve (optional)

1 Cook the noodles in salted, boiling water for 3–4 minutes. Drain, rinse ith cold water and drain again. Set ide until required.

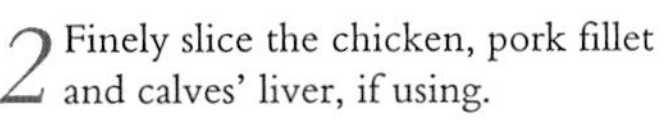

2 Finely slice the chicken, pork fillet and calves' liver, if using.

3 Season the eggs. Heat 5ml/1 tsp oil with the butter or margarine in a small pan until melted and then stir in the eggs and keep stirring until scrambled. Set aside.

4 Heat the remaining oil in a wok and fry the garlic with the chicken, pork and liver for 2–3 minutes, until they have changed colour. Add the prawns, spinach or Chinese leaves, celery and spring onions, tossing well.

5 Add the cooked and drained noodles and toss well again so that all the ingredients are well mixed. Add enough stock just to moisten and dark and light soy sauce to taste. Finally, stir in the scrambled eggs.

6 Garnish the dish with Deep-fried Onions and celery leaves. Serve with Sweet and Sour Fruit and Vegetable Salad, if using.

Somen Noodles with Courgettes

A colourful dish with lots of flavour. Pumpkin or patty pan squashes can be used as an alternative to courgettes.

INGREDIENTS

Serves 4
2 yellow courgettes
2 green courgettes
60ml/4 tbsp pine nuts
60ml/4 tbsp extra virgin olive oil
2 shallots, finely chopped
2 garlic cloves, finely chopped
30ml/2 tbsp capers, rinsed
4 sun-dried tomatoes in oil, drained and cut into strips
300g/11oz somen noodles
60ml/4 tbsp chopped mixed herbs (such as chives, thyme and tarragon)
grated rind of 1 lemon
50g/2oz Parmesan cheese, finely grated
salt and freshly ground black pepper

1 Slice the courgettes diagonally into rounds the same thickness as the noodles. Cut the courgette slices into matchsticks. Toast the pine nuts in an ungreased frying pan over a medium heat until golden in colour.

2 Heat half the oil in a large frying pan. Add the shallots and garlic and fry until fragrant. Push the shallot mixture to one side of the pan, add the remaining oil and, when hot, stir-fry the courgettes until soft.

3 Stir thoroughly to incorporate the shallot mixture and add the capers, sun-dried tomatoes and pine nuts. Remove the pan from the heat.

4 Cook the noodles in a large saucepan of boiling, salted water until just tender, following the directions on the packet. Drain well and toss into the courgette mixture, adding the herbs, lemon rind and Parmesan, with salt and pepper to taste. Serve at once.

Noodles Primavera

INGREDIENTS

Serves 4
225g/8oz dried rice noodles
115g/4oz broccoli florets
1 carrot, finely sliced
225g/8oz asparagus, cut into 5cm/2in lengths
1 red or yellow pepper, seeded and cut into strips
50g/2oz baby corn cobs
50g/2oz sugar snap peas, topped and tailed
45ml/3 tbsp olive oil
15ml/1 tbsp chopped fresh ginger
2 garlic cloves, chopped
2 spring onions, finely chopped
450g/1lb tomatoes, chopped
1 bunch rocket leaves
soy sauce, to taste
salt and freshly ground black pepper

1 Soak the noodles in hot water for about 30 minutes until soft. Drain.

2 Blanch the broccoli florets, sliced carrot, asparagus, pepper strips, baby corn cobs and sugar snap peas separately in boiling, salted water. Drain them, rinse under cold water, then drain again and set aside.

3 Heat the olive oil in a frying pan. Add the ginger, garlic and onions. Stir-fry for 30 seconds, then add the tomatoes and stir-fry for 2–3 minutes.

4 Add the noodles and stir-fry for 3 minutes. Toss in the blanched vegetables and rocket leaves. Season with soy sauce, salt and pepper and cook until the vegetables are tender.

Egg Noodles with Tuna and Tomato Sauce

Raid the store cupboard, add a few fresh ingredients and you can produce a scrumptious main meal in moments.

INGREDIENTS

Serves 4

45ml/3 tbsp olive oil
2 garlic cloves, finely chopped
2 dried red chillies, seeded and chopped
1 large red onion, finely sliced
175g/6oz canned tuna, drained
115g/4oz pitted black olives
400g/14oz can plum tomatoes, mashed, or 400g/14oz can chopped tomatoes
30ml/2 tbsp chopped parsley
350g/12oz medium-thick noodles
salt and freshly ground black pepper

1 Heat the oil in a large frying pan. Add the garlic and dried chillies; fry for a few seconds before adding the sliced onion. Fry, stirring, for about 5 minutes until the onion softens.

2 Add the tuna and black olives to the pan and stir until well mixed. Stir in the tomatoes and any juices. Bring to the boil, season with salt and pepper, add the parsley, then lower the heat and simmer gently.

3 Meanwhile, cook the noodles in boiling water until just tender, following the directions on the packe Drain well, toss the noodles with the sauce and serve at once.

Stir-fried Noodles with Wild Mushrooms

The greater the variety of wild mushrooms you have available, the more interesting this dish will be. Of course, if you can't find wild mushrooms, then a mixture of cultivated mushrooms can be used instead.

INGREDIENTS

Serves 4

350g/12oz broad flat egg noodles
45ml/3 tbsp vegetable oil
115g/4oz rindless back or streaky bacon, cut into small pieces
225g/8oz wild mushrooms, trimmed and cut in half
115g/4oz garlic chives, snipped
225g/8oz beansprouts
15ml/1 tbsp oyster sauce
15ml/1 tbsp soy sauce
salt and freshly ground black pepper

1 Cook the noodles in a large saucepan of boiling water for about 3–4 minutes or until just tender. Drain, rinse under cold water and drain well.

2 Heat 15ml/1tbsp of the oil in a wok or large frying pan. Add the bacon and fry until golden.

3 Using a slotted spoon, transfer the cooked bacon to a small bowl and set aside until needed.

4 Add the rest of the oil to the wok or pan. When hot, add the mushrooms and fry for 3 minutes. Ad the garlic chives and beansprouts to tl wok and fry for 3 minutes, then add the drained noodles.

5 Season with salt, pepper, oyster sauce and soy sauce. Continue to stir-fry until the noodles are thorougl heated through. Sprinkle the crispy bi of bacon on top and serve.

Noodles with Sun-dried Tomatoes and Prawns

INGREDIENTS

Serves 4
350g/12oz somen noodles
45ml/3 tbsp olive oil
20 uncooked king prawns, peeled and deveined
2 garlic cloves, finely chopped
45–60ml/3–4 tbsp sun-dried tomato paste
salt and freshly ground black pepper

For the garnish
handful of basil leaves
30ml/2 tbsp sun-dried tomatoes in oil, drained and cut into strips

COOK'S TIP

Ready-made sun-dried tomato paste is readily available, however you can make your own simply by processing bottled sun-dried tomatoes with their oil. You could also add a couple of anchovy fillets and some capers if you like.

1 Cook the noodles in a large saucepan of boiling water until tender, following the directions on the packet. Drain.

2 Heat half the oil in a large frying pan. Add the prawns and garlic and fry them over a medium heat for 3–5 minutes, until the prawns turn pink and are firm to the touch.

3 Stir in 15ml/1 tbsp of the sun-dried tomato paste and mix well. Using a slotted spoon, transfer the prawns to a bowl and keep hot.

4 Reheat the oil remaining in the pan. Stir in the rest of the oil with the remaining sun-dried tomato paste. You may need to add a spoonful of water if the mixture is very thick.

5 When the mixture starts to sizzle, toss in the noodles. Add salt and pepper to taste and mix well.

6 Return the prawns to the pan and toss to combine. Serve at once garnished with the basil and strips of sun-dried tomatoes.

Mixed Rice Noodles

. delicious noodle dish made xtra special by adding avocado ıd garnishing with prawns.

ıGREDIENTS

:rves 4

5ml/1 tbsp sunflower oil
.5cm/1in fresh root ginger, peeled and grated
cloves garlic, crushed
5ml/3 tbsp dark soy sauce
25g/8oz peas, thawed if frozen
50g/1lb rice noodles
50g/1lb spinach, stalks removed
0ml/2 tbsp smooth peanut butter
0ml/2 tbsp tahini
50ml/¼ pint/⅔ cup milk
ripe avocado, peeled and stoned
ɔasted peanuts and peeled, cooked prawns, to garnish

1 Heat the wok, then add the oil. When the oil is hot, stir-fry the inger and garlic for 30 seconds. Add 5ml/1 tbsp of the soy sauce and 50ml/¼ pint/⅔ cup boiling water.

COOK'S TIP

Do not peel, stone or slice the avocado much in advance of using as the flesh quickly discolours. Sprinkling with a little lemon or lime juice helps prevent this.

2 Add the peas and noodles, then cook for 3 minutes. Stir in the spinach. Remove the vegetables and noodles, drain and keep warm.

3 Stir the peanut butter, remaining soy sauce, tahini and milk together in the wok, and simmer for 1 minute.

4 Add the vegetables and noodles, slice in the avocado and toss together. Serve piled on individual plates. Spoon some sauce over each portion and garnish with roasted peanuts and prawns.

Noodles with Asparagus and Saffron Sauce

A rather elegant summery dish with fragrant saffron cream.

Ingredients

Serves 4

450g/1lb young asparagus
pinch of saffron threads
25g/1oz butter
2 shallots, finely chopped
30ml/2 tbsp white wine
250ml/8fl oz/1 cup double cream
grated rind and juice of ½ lemon
115g/4oz peas
350g/12oz somen noodles
½ bunch chervil, roughly chopped
salt and freshly ground black pepper
grated Parmesan cheese (optional)

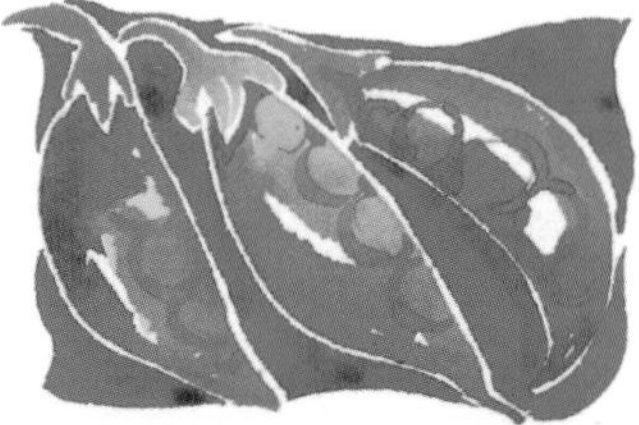

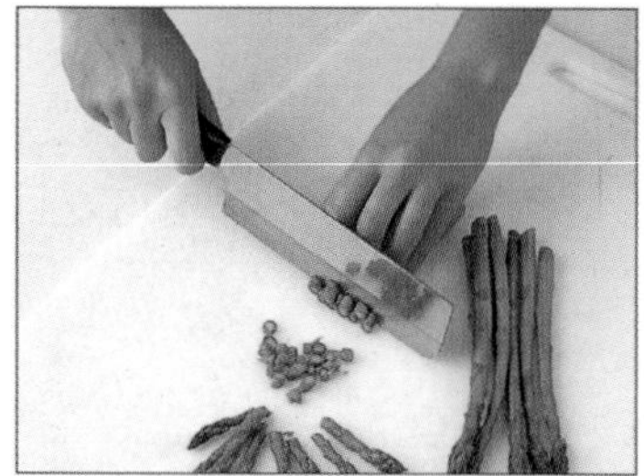

1 Cut off the asparagus tips (about 5cm/2in in length), then slice the remaining spears into short rounds. Steep the saffron in 30ml/2 tbsp boiling water in a cup.

2 Melt the butter in a saucepan, add the shallots and cook over a low heat for 3 minutes until soft. Add the white wine, cream and saffron infusion. Bring to the boil, reduce the heat and simmer gently for 5 minutes or until the sauce thickens to a coating consistency. Add the grated lemon rind and juice, with salt and pepper to taste.

3 Bring a large saucepan of lightly salted water to the boil. Blanch t asparagus tips, scoop them out and ad them to the sauce, then cook the pea and short asparagus rounds in the boiling water until just tender. Scoop them out and add to the sauce.

4 Cook the somen noodles in the same water until just tender, following the directions on the packet Drain, place in a wide pan and pour the sauce over the top.

5 Toss the noodles with the sauce and vegetables, adding the chervil and more salt and pepper if needed. Finally, sprinkle with the grated Parmesan, if using, and serve hot.

Fried Noodles with Beansprouts and Asparagus

Soft fried noodles contrast beautifully with crisp beansprouts and asparagus.

INGREDIENTS

Serves 4

115g/4oz dried egg noodles
60ml/4 tbsp vegetable oil
1 small onion, chopped
2.5cm/1in fresh root ginger, peeled and grated
2 garlic cloves, crushed
175g/6oz young asparagus spears, trimmed
115g/4oz beansprouts
4 spring onions, sliced
45ml/3 tbsp soy sauce
salt and ground black pepper

1 Bring a pan of salted water to the boil. Add the noodles and cook for 2–3 minutes, until tender. Drain and toss them in 30ml/2 tbsp of the oil.

2 Heat the remaining oil in a preheated wok until very hot. Add the onion, ginger and garlic and stir-fry for 2–3 minutes. Add the asparagus and stir-fry for a further 2–3 minutes.

3 Add the noodles and beansprouts and stir-fry for 2 minutes.

4 Stir in the spring onions and soy sauce. Season to taste, adding salt sparingly as the soy sauce will add quite a salty flavour. Stir-fry for 1 minute, then serve at once.

Noodles with Ginger and Coriander

Here is a simple noodle dish that goes well with most oriental dishes. It can also be served as a snack for two or three people.

Ingredients

Serves 4–6
handful fresh coriander sprigs
225g/8oz dried egg noodles
45ml/3 tbsp groundnut oil
5cm/2in fresh root ginger, finely shredded
6–8 spring onions, shredded
30ml/2 tbsp light soy sauce
salt and ground black pepper

Cook's Tip

Many of the dried egg noodles available are sold packed in layers. As a guide, allow 1 layer of noodles per person as an average portion for a main dish.

1 Strip the leaves from the coriander sprigs. Pile them on a chopping board and chop them roughly, using a cleaver or large sharp knife.

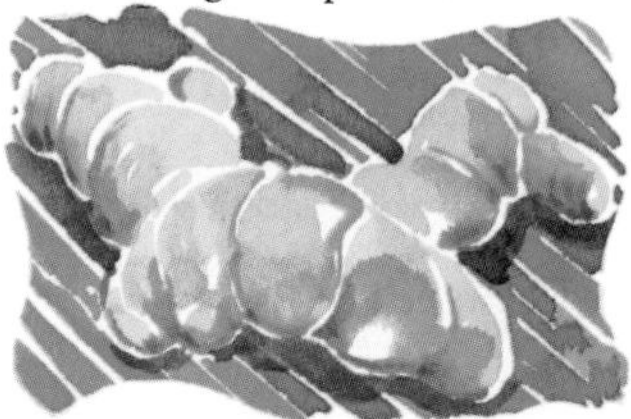

2 Cook the noodles according to the packet instructions. Rinse under cold water and drain well. Toss them in 15ml/1 tbsp of the oil.

3 Heat a wok until hot, add the remaining oil and swirl it around. Add the ginger and stir-fry for a few seconds, then add the noodles and spring onions. Stir-fry for 3–4 minutes until hot.

4 Sprinkle over the soy sauce, coriander and seasoning. Toss well, then serve at once.

Stir-fried Tofu and Beansprouts with Noodles

'his is a satisfying dish, which is oth tasty and easy to make.

NGREDIENTS

erves 4
25g/8oz firm tofu
roundnut oil, for deep frying
75g/6oz medium egg noodles
5ml/1 tbsp sesame oil
ml/1 tsp cornflour
0ml/2 tsp dark soy sauce
0ml/2 tbsp Chinese rice wine or dry sherry
ml/1 tsp sugar
–8 spring onions, cut diagonally into 2.5cm/1in lengths
garlic cloves, sliced
fresh green chilli, seeded and sliced
15g/4oz Chinese cabbage leaves, roughly shredded
0g/2oz beansprouts
0g/2oz toasted cashew nuts, to garnish

1 Drain the tofu and pat dry with kitchen paper. Cut the tofu into .5cm/1in cubes. Half-fill a wok with roundnut oil and heat to 180°C/ 50°F. Deep fry the tofu in batches for –2 minutes until golden and crisp.)rain on kitchen paper. Carefully pour ll but 30ml/2 tbsp of the oil from he wok.

2 Cook the noodles. Rinse them thoroughly under cold water and drain well. Toss them in 10ml/2 tsp of the sesame oil and set aside. In a bowl, blend together the cornflour, soy sauce, rice wine or sherry, sugar and remaining sesame oil.

3 Reheat the 30ml/2 tbsp of groundnut oil and, when hot, add the spring onions, garlic, chilli, Chinese cabbage and beansprouts. Stir-fry for 1–2 minutes.

4 Add the tofu with the noodles and sauce. Cook, stirring, for about 1 minute until well mixed. Sprinkle over the cashew nuts. Serve at once.

Tossed Noodles with Seafood

INGREDIENTS

Serves 4–6

350g/12oz thick egg noodles
60ml/4 tbsp vegetable oil
3 slices fresh root ginger, grated
2 garlic cloves, finely chopped
225g/8oz mussels or clams
225g/8oz raw prawns, peeled
225g/8oz squid, cut into rings
115g/4oz oriental fried fish cake, sliced
1 red pepper, seeded and cut into rings
50g/2oz sugar snap peas, topped and tailed
30ml/2 tbsp soy sauce
2.5ml/½ tsp sugar
120ml/4fl oz/½ cup stock or water
15ml/1 tbsp cornflour
5–10ml/1–2 tsp sesame oil
salt and freshly ground black pepper
2 spring onions, chopped, and 2 red chillies, seeded and chopped, to garnish

1 Cook the noodles in a large saucepan of boiling water until just tender. Drain, rinse under cold water and drain well.

2 Heat the oil in a wok or large frying pan. Fry the ginger and garlic for 30 seconds. Add the mussels or clams, prawns and squid and stir-fry for about 4–5 minutes until the seafood changes colour. Add the fish cake slices, red pepper rings and sugar snap peas and stir well.

3 In a bowl, mix the soy sauce, sugar, stock or water and cornflo Stir into the seafood and bring to the boil. Add the noodles and cook until they are heated through.

4 Add the sesame oil to the wok or pan and season with salt and pepp to taste. Serve at once, garnished wit the spring onions and red chillies.

Noodles with Spicy Meat Sauce

INGREDIENTS

Serves 4–6

30ml/2 tbsp vegetable oil
2 dried red chillies, chopped
5ml/1 tsp grated fresh root ginger
2 garlic cloves, finely chopped
15ml/1 tbsp chilli bean paste
450g/1lb minced pork or beef
450g/1lb broad flat egg noodles
15ml/1 tbsp sesame oil
2 spring onions, chopped, to garnish

For the sauce
1.25ml/¼ tsp salt
5ml/1 tsp sugar
15ml/1 tbsp soy sauce
5ml/1 tsp mushroom ketchup
15ml/1 tbsp cornflour
250ml/8fl oz/1 cup chicken stock
5ml/1 tsp shaohsing wine or dry sherry

1 Heat the vegetable oil in a large saucepan. Add the dried chillies, ginger and garlic. Fry until the garlic starts to colour, then gradually stir in the chilli bean paste.

2 Add the minced pork or beef, breaking it up with a spatula or wooden spoon. Cook over a high heat until the minced meat changes colour and any liquid has evaporated.

3 Mix all the sauce ingredients in a jug. Make a well in the centre of the pork mixture. Pour in the sauce mixture and stir together. Simmer fo 10–15 minutes until tender.

4 Meanwhile, cook the noodles in large saucepan of boiling water f 5–7 minutes until just tender. Drain well and toss with the sesame oil. Serve, topped with the meat sauce a garnished with the spring onions.

Tomato Noodles with Fried Egg

Ingredients

Serves 4

350g/12oz medium-thick dried noodles
60ml/4 tbsp vegetable oil
2 garlic cloves, very finely chopped
4 shallots, chopped
2.5ml/½ tsp chilli powder
5ml/1 tsp paprika
2 carrots, finely diced
115g/4oz button mushrooms, quartered
50g/2oz peas
15ml/1 tbsp tomato ketchup
10ml/2 tsp tomato purée
salt and freshly ground black pepper
butter for frying
4 eggs

1 Cook the noodles in a saucepan of boiling water until just tender. Drain, rinse under cold running water and drain well.

2 Heat the oil in a wok or large frying pan. Add the garlic, shallots, chilli powder and paprika. Stir-fry for about 1 minute, then add the carrots, mushrooms and peas. Continue to stir-fry until the vegetables are cooked.

3 Stir the tomato ketchup and puré into the vegetable mixture. Add the noodles and cook over a medium heat until the noodles are heated through and have taken on the reddis tinge of the paprika and tomato.

4 Meanwhile melt the butter in a frying pan and fry the eggs. Seasc the noodle mixture, divide it among four serving plates and top each portion with a fried egg.

Curry Fried Noodles

On its own bean curd (tofu) has a fairly bland flavour, but it takes on the flavour of the curry spices wonderfully.

Ingredients

Serves 4

60ml/4 tbsp vegetable oil
30–45ml/2–3 tbsp curry paste
225g/8oz smoked bean curd, cut into 2.5cm/1in cubes
225g/8oz green beans, cut into 2.5cm/1in lengths
1 red pepper, seeded and cut into fine strips
350g/12oz rice vermicelli, soaked in warm water until soft
15ml/1 tbsp soy sauce
salt and freshly ground black pepper
2 spring onions, finely sliced, 2 red chillies, seeded and chopped, and 1 lime, cut into wedges, to garnish

1 Heat half the oil in a wok or large frying pan. Add the curry paste and stir-fry for a few minutes, then add the bean curd and continue to fry until golden brown. Using a slotted spoon remove the cubes from the pan and set aside until required.

2 Add the remaining oil to the wok or pan. When hot, add the green beans and red pepper. Stir-fry until the vegetables are cooked. You may need to moisten them with a little water.

3 Drain the noodles and add them to the wok or frying pan. Contin to stir-fry until the noodles are heate through, then return the curried bear curd to the wok. Season with soy sauce, salt and pepper.

4 Transfer the mixture to a serving dish. Sprinkle with the spring onions and chillies and serve the lime wedges on the side.

Rice

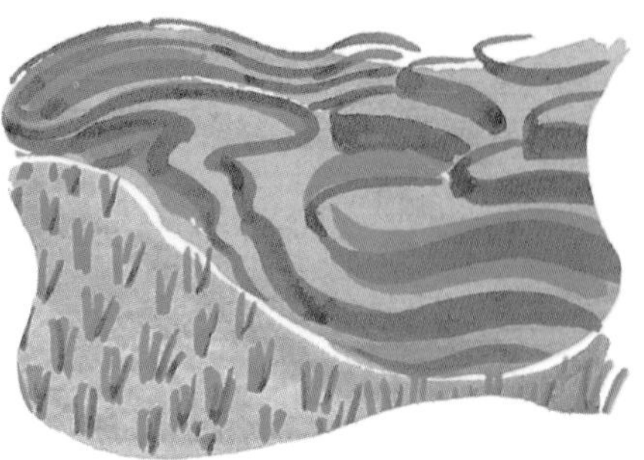

Rice is a staple food throughout much of China and Asia. While plain boiled rice is a useful accompaniment that goes well with a wide variety of dishes, it is easy to combine rice with vegetables, eggs and a range of flavourings and spices to create a rather more special meal. Rice dishes from each country and region have their own unique flavours. Try Chinese Special Fried Rice, Sushi from Japan, Thai Coconut Rice or Rice Porridge with Chicken from Indonesia. Don't overlook Coconut Rice Fritters, a sweet snack from the Philippines.

Plain Rice

Use long-grain or patna rice or fragrant rice from Thailand. Allow 50g/2oz raw rice per person. If you use fragrant Thai rice, omit the salt.

INGREDIENTS

Serves 4
225g/8oz/generous 1 cup rice
about 250ml/8fl oz/1 cup water
pinch of salt
2.5ml/½ tsp vegetable oil

1 Wash and rinse the rice. Place the rice in a saucepan and add the water. There should be no more than 2cm/¾in of water above the surface of the rice.

2 Bring to the boil, add the salt and oil, then stir to prevent the rice sticking to the bottom of the pan. Reduce the heat to very, very low, cover and cook for 15–20 minutes.

3 Remove from the heat and leave to stand, still covered, for 10 minutes. Fluff up the rice with a fork or spoon just before serving.

Egg-fried Rice

Use rice with a fairly firm texture. Ideally, the raw rice should be soaked in water for a short time before cooking.

INGREDIENTS

Serves 4
3 eggs
5ml/1 tsp salt
30–45ml/2–3 tbsp vegetable oil
450g/1lb cooked rice
2 spring onions, finely chopped
115g/4oz frozen peas

1 In a bowl, lightly beat the eggs with a pinch of the salt and a few pieces of the spring onions.

2 Heat the oil in a preheated wok, and lightly scramble the eggs.

3 Add the cooked rice and stir to make sure that each grain of rice is separated. Add the remaining salt, spring onions and the peas. Blend well, allow to heat through and serve.

Chinese Special Fried Rice

This recipe combines a tasty mixture of chicken, prawns and vegetables with fried rice.

INGREDIENTS

Serves 4

175g/6oz/scant 1 cup long-grain white rice
45ml/3 tbsp groundnut oil
350ml/12fl oz/1½ cups water
1 garlic clove, crushed
4 spring onions, finely chopped
115g/4oz cooked chicken, diced
115g/4oz cooked prawns, peeled
50g/2oz frozen peas
1 egg, lightly beaten
50g/2oz lettuce, shredded
30ml/2 tbsp light soy sauce
pinch of caster sugar
salt and ground black pepper
15ml/1 tbsp chopped roasted cashew nuts, to garnish

1 Rinse the rice in two to three changes of warm water to wash away some of the starch. Drain well.

2 Put the rice in a saucepan and add 15ml/1 tbsp of the oil and the water. Cover and bring to the boil, stir once, then cover and simmer for 12–15 minutes, until nearly all the water has been absorbed. Turn off the heat and leave, covered, to stand for 10 minutes. Fluff up with a fork and leave to cool.

3 Heat the remaining oil in a preheated wok or frying pan, add the garlic and spring onions and stir-fry for 30 seconds.

4 Add the chicken, prawns and peas and stir-fry for 1–2 minutes, then add the cooked rice and stir-fry for a further 2 minutes. Pour in the egg and stir-fry until just set. Stir in the lettuce, soy sauce, sugar and seasoning.

5 Transfer to a warmed serving bow[l], sprinkle with the chopped cashew nuts and serve immediately.

Egg Foo Yung

A great way of turning a bowl of leftover cooked rice into a meal for four, this dish is tasty and full of texture.

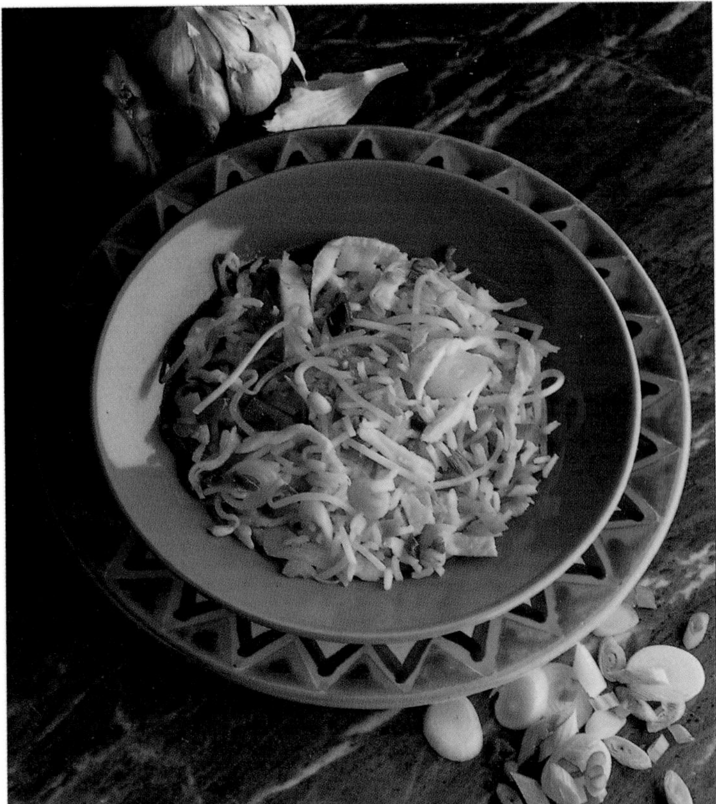

Ingredients

Serves 4

3 eggs, beaten
pinch of Chinese five-spice powder (optional)
45ml/3 tbsp groundnut or sunflower oil
4 spring onions, sliced
1 garlic clove, crushed
1 small green pepper, seeded and chopped
115g/4oz beansprouts
225g/8oz/generous 1 cup white rice, cooked
45ml/3 tbsp light soy sauce
15ml/1 tbsp sesame oil
salt and ground black pepper

1 Season the eggs with salt and pepper to taste and beat in the five-spice powder, if using.

2 Heat 15ml/1 tbsp of the oil in a preheated wok or large frying pan and, when quite hot, pour in the egg. Cook rather like an omelette, pulling the mixture away from the sides and allowing the rest to slip underneath.

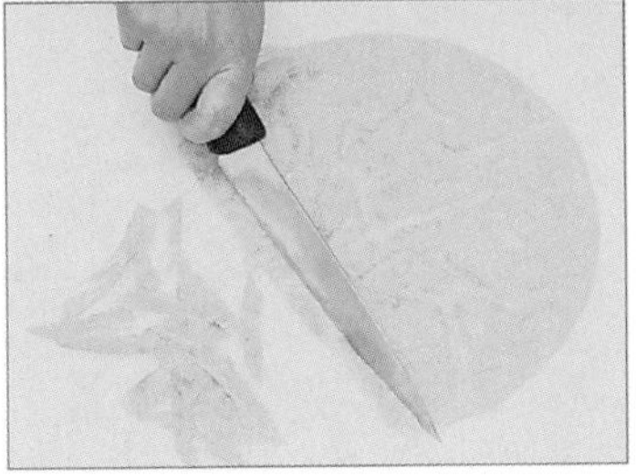

3 Cook the egg until firm, then tip out. Chop the omelette into small strips and set aside.

4 Heat the remaining oil and stir-fry the onions, garlic, green pepper and beansprouts for about 2 minutes, stirring and tossing continuously.

5 Mix in the cooked rice and heat thoroughly, stirring well. Add the soy sauce and sesame oil, then return the egg strips and mix in well. Serve immediately, piping hot.

Malacca Fried Rice

There are many versions of this dish throughout the East, all of which make use of leftover rice. Ingredients vary according to what is available, but prawns are a popular addition.

INGREDIENTS

Serves 4–6
2 eggs
45ml/3 tbsp vegetable oil
4 shallots or 1 medium onion, finely chopped
5ml/1 tsp finely chopped fresh root ginger
1 garlic clove, crushed
225g/8oz raw or cooked prawn tails, peeled and deveined
5–10ml/1–2 tsp chilli sauce (optional)
3 spring onions, green part only, roughly chopped
225g/8oz frozen peas
225g/8oz thickly sliced roast pork, diced
45ml/3 tbsp light soy sauce
350g/12oz/1⅔ cups long-grain rice, cooked
salt and ground black pepper

1 In a bowl, beat the eggs well and season to taste with salt and pepper. Heat 15ml/1 tbsp of the oil in a large, non-stick frying pan, pour in the eggs and cook for about 30 seconds, without stirring, until set. Roll up the omelette, cut into thin strips and set aside.

2 Heat the remaining oil in a large preheated wok, add the shallots or onion, ginger, garlic and prawn tails and cook for 1–2 minutes, ensuring that the garlic does not burn.

3 Add the chilli sauce, spring onions, peas, pork and soy sauce. Stir to heat through, then add the cooked rice. Fry the rice over a moderate heat for 6–8 minutes. Turn into a dish and decorate with the egg strips.

Oriental Fried Rice

This is a great way to use leftover cooked rice. Make sure the rice is very cold before attempting to fry it, as warm rice will become soggy. Some supermarkets sell frozen cooked rice.

INGREDIENTS

Serves 4–6

75ml/5 tbsp oil
115g/4oz shallots, halved and thinly sliced
3 garlic cloves, crushed
1 red chilli, seeded and finely chopped
5 spring onions, finely chopped
1 red pepper, seeded and finely chopped
225g/8oz white cabbage, finely shredded
175g/6oz cucumber, finely chopped
50g/2oz frozen peas, thawed
3 eggs, beaten
5ml/1 tsp tomato purée
30ml/2 tbsp lime juice
1.5ml/¼ tsp Tabasco sauce
675g/1½lb cooked white rice, cooled
115g/4oz/1 cup cashew nuts, roughly chopped
30ml/2 tbsp chopped fresh coriander, plus extra to garnish
salt and ground black pepper

1 Heat the oil in a large preheated wok or non-stick frying pan and cook the shallots until very crisp and golden. Remove with a slotted spoon and drain on kitchen paper.

2 Add the garlic and chilli and cook for 1 minute. Add the spring onions and red pepper and cook for 3–4 minutes, or until the onions are beginning to soften.

3 Add the cabbage, cucumber and peas and cook for a further 2 minutes.

4 Make a gap in the ingredients in the wok or frying pan and add the beaten eggs. Scramble the eggs, stirring occasionally, and then stir them into the vegetables.

5 Add the tomato purée, lime juice and Tabasco sauce and stir well to combine.

6 Increase the heat and add the cooked rice, cashew nuts, coriander and plenty of seasoning. Stir-fry for 3–4 minutes, until piping hot. Serve garnished with the crisp shallots and extra fresh coriander, if liked.

COOK'S TIP

675g/1½lb cooked rice is equivalent to 225g/8oz raw weight.

Sushi

INGREDIENTS

Makes 8–10

For the tuna sushi

3 sheets nori (paper-thin seaweed)
150g/5oz fresh tuna fillet, cut into fingers
5ml/1 tsp wasabi (Japanese horseradish)
6 young carrots, blanched
450g/1lb/6 cups cooked Japanese rice

For the salmon sushi

2 eggs
2.5ml/½ tsp salt
10ml/2 tsp sugar
5 sheets nori
450g/1lb/6 cups cooked Japanese rice
150g/5oz fresh salmon fillet, cut into fingers
5ml/1 tsp wasabi paste
½ small cucumber, cut into strips

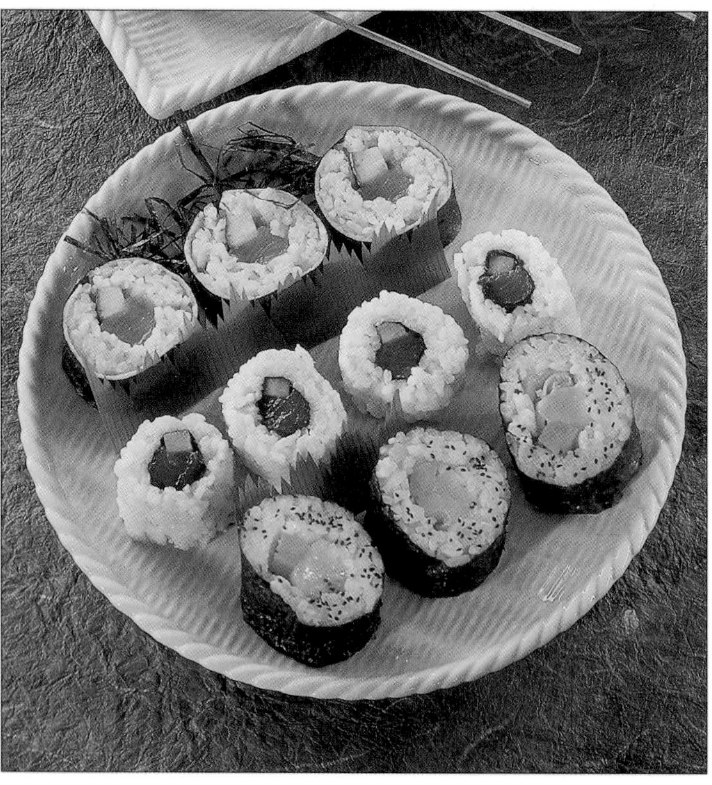

1 To make the tuna sushi, spread half a sheet of nori on to a bamboo mat, lay strips of tuna across the full length and season with the thinned wasabi. Place a line of blanched carrot next to the tuna and roll tightly. Moisten the edge with water and seal.

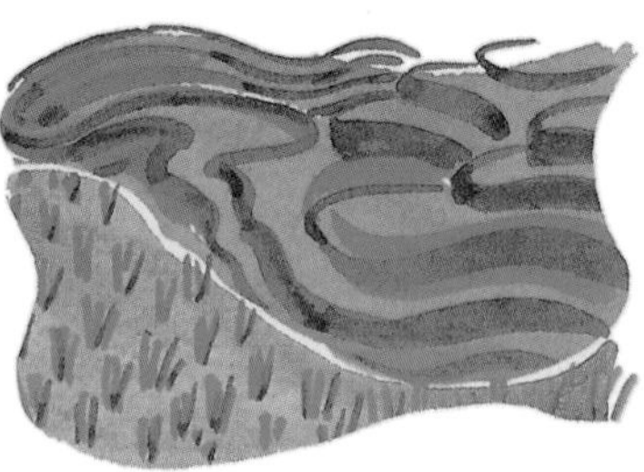

2 Place a square of damp wax paper on to the bamboo mat, then spread evenly with sushi rice. Place the nori-wrapped tuna along the centre and wrap tightly, enclosing the nori completely. Remove the paper and cut into neat rounds with a wet knife.

3 To make the salmon sushi, make a simple flat omelette by beating together the eggs, salt and sugar. Heat a large non-stick pan, pour in the egg mixture, stir briefly and allow to set. Transfer to a clean dish towel and cool.

4 Place the nori on to a bamboo mat, cover with the omelette, and trim to size. Spread a layer of rice over the omelette, then lay strips of salmon across the width. Season the salmon with the thinned wasabi, then place a strip of cucumber next to the salmon. Fold the bamboo mat in half. Cut into neat rounds with a wet knife.

Shiitake Fried Rice

hiitake mushrooms have a trong, meaty, mushroomy aroma nd flavour. This is a very easy ecipe to make, and although it is side dish, it can almost be a neal in itself.

NGREDIENTS

erves 4

eggs
5ml/1 tbsp water
5ml/3 tbsp vegetable oil
50g/12oz shiitake mushrooms
spring onions, sliced diagonally
garlic clove, crushed
½ green pepper, seeded and chopped
5g/1oz/2 tbsp butter
75–225g/6–8oz/about 1 cup long-grain rice, cooked
5ml/1 tbsp medium-dry sherry
0ml/2 tbsp dark soy sauce
5ml/1 tbsp chopped fresh coriander
alt

1 Beat the eggs with the water and season with a little salt.

2 Heat 15ml/1 tbsp of the oil in a preheated wok or large frying pan, pour in the eggs and cook to make a arge omelette. Lift the sides of the omelette and tilt the wok so that the uncooked egg can run underneath and be cooked. Roll up the omelette and slice thinly.

3 Remove and discard the mushroom stalks, if they are tough. Slice the caps thinly, halving them if they are large.

4 Heat 15ml/1 tbsp of the remaining oil in the wok and stir-fry the spring onions and garlic for 3–4 minutes until softened but not brown. Transfer them to a plate using a slotted spoon and set aside.

5 Add the green pepper and stir-fry for about 2–3 minutes, then add the butter and the remaining oil. As the butter begins to sizzle, add the mushrooms and stir-fry over a moderate heat for 3–4 minutes until both vegetables are soft.

6 Loosen the rice grains as much as possible. Pour the sherry over the mushrooms and then stir in the rice.

7 Heat the rice over a moderate heat, stirring all the time to prevent it sticking. If the rice seems very dry, add a little more oil. Stir in the cooked spring onions, garlic and omelette slices, the soy sauce and chopped coriander. Cook for a few minutes until heated through and serve.

Coconut Rice Fritters

These delicious fritters from the Philippines can be served at any time and go especially well with coffee or hot chocolate.

INGREDIENTS

Makes 28

150g/5oz/⅔ cup long-grain rice, cooked
30ml/2 tbsp coconut milk powder
45ml/3 tbsp sugar
2 egg yolks
juice of ½ lemon
75g/3oz desiccated coconut
oil, for deep-frying
icing sugar, for dusting

1 Place 75g/3oz of the cooked rice in a mortar and pound with a pestle until smooth and sticky. Alternatively, process in a food processor. Turn out into a bowl and mix in the remaining rice, the coconut milk powder, sugar, egg yolks and lemon juice.

2 Spread out the desiccated coconut on a tray or plate. With wet hands, divide the rice mixture into thumb-sized pieces and roll them in the coconut to make neat balls.

3 Heat the oil in a wok or deep-fryer to 180°C/350°F. Fry the coconut rice balls, three or four at a time, for 1–2 minutes, until the coconut is evenly browned. Transfer to a plate and dust with icing sugar. Place a wooden skewer in each fritter and serve in the traditional way, as an afternoon snack.

COOK'S TIP

In the Philippines, hot chocolate is made by preparing a syrup with 30ml/2 tbsp sugar and 120ml/4fl oz/½ cup water and then melting 115g/4oz pieces of best-quality plain chocolate in it. Finally, 200ml/7fl oz/scant 1 cup evaporated milk is whisked in over a low heat. This luxurious drink serves 2.

Rice Porridge with Chicken

his dish is often served as ıstaining breakfast fare. It can be ·rved simply, with just the hicken stirred into it. Hearty ıters tuck into helpings of orridge drizzled with a little soy ıuce, with strips of chicken, rawns, garlic and strips of fresh hilli, topped with a lightly fried gg and garnished with celery ·aves and fried onion.

NGREDIENTS

erves 6

kg/2¼lb chicken, cut into 4 pieces, or 4 chicken quarters
.75 litres/3 pints/7½ cups water
large onion, quartered
.5cm/1in fresh root ginger, halved and bruised
50g/12oz Thai fragrant rice, rinsed
ılt and ground black pepper
ooked peeled prawns, strips of fresh chilli, deep-fried onion and celery leaves, to garnish (optional)

1 Place the chicken pieces in a large saucepan with the water, onion quarters and ginger. Season with salt nd pepper, bring to the boil and immer for 45–50 minutes, until the hicken is tender. Remove the chicken rom the pan and reserve the stock. Remove the skin from the chicken ieces. Cut the meat from the bones nd then into bite-sized pieces.

2 Strain and measure the reserved chicken stock. Make the quantity up to 1.75 litres/3 pints/7½ cups with water and transfer to a clean saucepan.

3 Add the rice to the stock and bring to the boil, stirring constantly. Lower the heat and simmer gently for 20 minutes. Stir, cover and cook for a further 20 minutes, stirring from time to time, until the rice is soft.

4 Stir the chicken pieces into the porridge and heat through for 5 minutes. Serve as it is or with any of the garnishes suggested.

Coconut Rice

This rich dish is usually served with a tangy papaya salad.

Ingredients

Serves 4–6

450g/1lb/2 cups jasmine rice
250ml/8fl oz/1 cup water
475ml/16fl oz/2 cups coconut milk
2.5ml/½ tsp salt
30ml/2 tbsp granulated sugar
fresh shredded coconut, to garnish (optional)

1 Wash the rice in several changes of cold water until it runs clear. Place the water, coconut milk, salt and sugar in a heavy-bottomed saucepan.

2 Add the rice, cover and bring to the boil. Reduce the heat to low and simmer for about 15–20 minutes or until the rice is tender to the bite and cooked through.

3 Turn off the heat and allow the rice to rest in the saucepan for a further 5–10 minutes.

4 Fluff up the rice with chopsticks before serving.

Pineapple Fried Rice

When buying a pineapple, look for a sweet-smelling fruit with an even brownish/yellow skin. To test for ripeness, tap the base – a dull sound indicates that the fruit is ripe. The flesh should also give slightly when pressed.

Ingredients

Serves 4–6

1 pineapple
30ml/2 tbsp vegetable oil
1 small onion, finely chopped
2 green chillies, seeded and chopped
225g/8oz lean pork, cut into small dice
115g/4oz cooked shelled prawns
675–900g/1½–2 lb/3–4 cups cooked cold rice
50g/2oz roasted cashew nuts
2 spring onions, chopped
30ml/2 tbsp fish sauce
15ml/1 tbsp soy sauce
10–12 mint leaves, to garnish
2 red chillies, sliced, to garnish
1 green chilli, sliced, to garnish

1 Cut the pineapple in half lengthways and remove the flesh from both halves by cutting round inside the skin. Reserve the skin shells. You need 115g/4oz of fruit, chopped finely (keep the rest for a dessert).

Cook's Tip

This dish is ideal to prepare for a special occasion meal. Served in the pineapple skin shells, it is sure to be the talking point of the dinner.

2 Heat the oil in a wok or large frying pan. Add the onion and chillies and fry for about 3–5 minutes until softened. Add the pork and cook until it is brown on all sides.

3 Stir in the prawns and rice and tos well together. Continue to stir-fry until the rice is thoroughly heated.

4 Add the chopped pineapple, cashew nuts and spring onions. Season with fish sauce and soy sauce.

5 Spoon into the pineapple skin shells. Garnish with shredded mint leaves and red and green chillies.

Thai Rice with Beansprouts

Thai rice has a delicate fragrance that is delicious hot or cold.

INGREDIENTS

Serves 6

225g/8oz/1 cup Thai fragrant rice
30ml/2 tbsp sesame oil
30ml/2 tbsp fresh lime juice
1 small red chilli, seeded and chopped
1 garlic clove, crushed
10ml/2 tsp grated fresh root ginger
30ml/2 tbsp light soy sauce
5ml/1 tsp clear honey
45ml/3 tbsp pineapple juice
15ml/1 tbsp wine vinegar
2 spring onions, sliced
2 canned pineapple rings, chopped
150g/5oz/1¼ cups sprouted lentils or beansprouts
1 small red pepper, sliced
1 stick celery, sliced
50g/2oz/½ cup cashew nuts, chopped
30ml/2 tbsp toasted sesame seeds
salt and ground black pepper

1 Soak the Thai fragrant rice for 20 minutes, then rinse in several changes of water. Drain, then boil in salted water for 10–12 minutes until tender. Drain and set aside.

2 Whisk together the sesame oil, lime juice, chilli, garlic, ginger, soy sauce, honey, pineapple juice and wine vinegar in a large bowl. Stir in the rice.

3 Add the spring onions, pineapple rings, sprouted lentils or beansprouts, red pepper, celery, cashew nuts and the toasted sesame seeds and mix well. If the rice grains stick together on cooling, simply stir them with a metal spoon. This dish can be served warm or lightly chilled and is a good accompaniment to grilled or barbecued meats and fish.

COOK'S TIP

Sesame oil has a strong, nutty flavour and is used for seasoning, marinating or flavouring rather than for cooking. Because the taste is so distinctive, sesame oil can be mixed with grapeseed or other light-flavoured oils.

Spicy Peanut Rice Cakes

Serve these spicy, Indonesian rice cakes with a crisp green salad and a dipping sauce, such as Hot Tomato Sambal.

INGREDIENTS

Makes 16

- 1 garlic clove, crushed
- 1cm/½in fresh root ginger, finely chopped
- 1.5ml/¼ tsp ground turmeric
- 5ml/1 tsp sugar
- 2.5ml/½ tsp salt
- 5ml/1 tsp chilli sauce
- 10ml/2 tsp fish sauce or soy sauce
- 30ml/2 tbsp chopped fresh coriander
- juice of ½ lime
- 115g/4oz/generous ½ cup long-grain rice, cooked
- 75g/3oz/¾ cup raw peanuts, chopped
- vegetable oil, for deep-frying

1 Pound together the garlic, ginger and turmeric in a mortar with a pestle or in a food processor. Add the sugar, salt, chilli sauce, fish or soy sauce, coriander and lime juice.

2 Add 75g/3oz of the cooked rice and pound until smooth and sticky. Stir the mixture into the remaining rice and mix well. With wet hands, shape 16 thumb-sized balls.

3 Spread the chopped peanuts out on a plate and roll the balls in them to coat evenly. Set aside.

4 Heat the oil in a preheated wok or deep frying pan. Deep-fry the rice cakes, three at a time, until crisp and golden. Remove and drain on kitchen paper. Serve immediately.

Rice with Seeds and Spices

This dish provides a change from plain boiled rice, and is a colourful accompaniment to serve with curries or grilled meats.

INGREDIENTS

Serves 4

5ml/1 tsp sunflower oil
2.5ml/½ tsp ground turmeric
6 green cardamom pods, lightly crushed
5ml/1 tsp coriander seeds, lightly crushed
1 garlic clove, crushed
200g/7oz/1 cup basmati rice
400ml/14fl oz/1⅔ cups stock
115g/4oz/½ cup natural yogurt
15ml/1 tbsp toasted sunflower seeds
15ml/1 tbsp toasted sesame seeds
salt and ground black pepper
coriander leaves, to garnish

1 Heat the oil in a non-stick frying pan and fry the spices and garlic for 1 minute, stirring all the time.

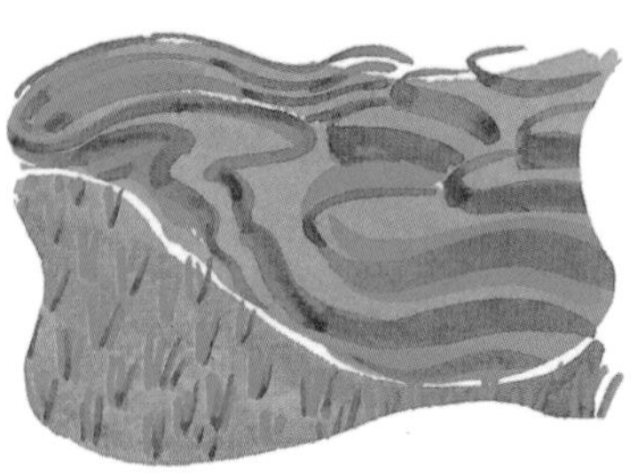

2 Add the rice and stock, bring to the boil, then cover and simmer for 15 minutes or until just tender.

3 Stir in the yogurt and the toasted sunflower and sesame seeds. Adjust the seasoning and serve the rice hot, garnished with coriander leaves.

Nasi Goreng

ne of the most familiar and vell-known Indonesian dishes. This is a marvellous way to use ip leftover rice, chicken and neats such as pork. It is mportant that the rice is quite old and the grains separate efore adding the other ngredients, so it's best to cook he rice the day before.

NGREDIENTS

erves 4–6

50g/12oz dry weight long-grain rice, such as basmati, cooked and allowed to become completely cold
eggs
0ml/2 tbsp water
05ml/7 tbsp oil
25g/8oz pork fillet or fillet of beef
15g/4oz cooked, peeled prawns
75g–225g/6–8oz cooked chicken, chopped
–3 fresh red chillies, seeded and sliced
cm/½in cube *terasi*
garlic cloves, crushed
onion, sliced
0ml/2 tbsp dark soy sauce or 45–60ml/3–4 tbsp tomato ketchup
alt and freshly ground black pepper
elery leaves, Deep-fried Onions and coriander sprigs, to garnish

1 Once the rice is cooked and cooled, fork it through to separate he grains and keep it in a covered pan r dish until required.

2 Beat the eggs with seasoning and the water and make two or three omelettes in a frying pan, with a minimum of oil. Roll up each omelette and cut in strips when cold. Set aside.

3 Cut the pork or beef into neat strips and put the meat, prawns and chicken pieces in separate bowls. Shred one of the chillies and reserve it.

4 Put the *terasi*, with the remaining chilli, garlic and onion, in a food processor and grind to a fine paste. Alternatively, pound together using a pestle and mortar.

5 Fry the paste in the remaining hot oil, without browning, until it gives off a rich, spicy aroma. Add the pork or beef, tossing the meat all the time, to seal in the juices. Cook for 2 minutes, stirring constantly. Add the prawns, cook for 2 minutes and then stir in the chicken, cold rice, dark soy sauce or ketchup and seasoning to taste. Stir all the time to keep the rice light and fluffy and prevent it from sticking.

6 Turn on to a hot platter and garnish with the omelette strips, celery leaves, onions, reserved shredded chilli and the coriander sprigs.

Thai Fried Rice

This hot and spicy dish is easy to prepare and makes a complete meal in itself.

Ingredients

Serves 4

225g/8oz Thai fragrant rice
45ml/3 tbsp vegetable oil
1 onion, chopped
1 small red pepper, seeded and cubed into 2cm/¾in cubes
350g/12oz skinless, boneless chicken breasts, cut into 2cm/¾in cubes.
1 garlic clove, crushed
15ml/1 tbsp mild curry paste
2.5ml/½ tsp paprika
2.5ml/½ tsp ground turmeric
30ml/2 tbsp Thai fish sauce (*nam pla*)
2 eggs, beaten
salt and ground black pepper
fried basil leaves, to garnish

1 Put the rice in a sieve and wash well under cold running water. Put the rice in a heavy-based pan with 1.5 litres/2½ pints/6¼ cups boiling water. Return to the boil, then simmer uncovered, for 8–10 minutes; drain well. Spread out the grains on a tray and leave to cool.

2 Heat a wok until hot, add 30ml/2 tbsp of the oil and swirl it around. Add the onion and red pepper and stir-fry for 1 minute.

3 Add the chicken cubes, garlic, curry paste and spices and stir-fry for 2–3 minutes.

4 Reduce the heat to medium, add the cooled rice, fish sauce and seasoning. Stir-fry for 2–3 minutes until the rice is very hot.

5 Make a well in the centre of the rice and add the remaining oil. When hot, add the beaten eggs, leave to cook for about 2 minutes until lightly set, then stir into the rice.

6 Scatter over the fried basil leaves and serve at once.

Cook's Tip

Among the various types of rice available, Thai fragrant rice is one of the more popular, especially in Thai, Vietnamese and some other South-east Asian recipes. It does, in fact, have a particularly special fragrance and is generally served on feast days and other important occasions.

Chinese Jewelled Rice

This rice dish, with its many different, interesting ingredients, can make a meal in itself.

INGREDIENTS

Serves 4

350g/12oz long grain rice
45ml/3 tbsp vegetable oil
1 onion, roughly chopped
115g/4oz cooked ham, diced
175g/6oz canned white crab meat
75g/3oz canned water chestnuts, drained and cut into cubes
4 dried black Chinese mushrooms, soaked, drained and diced
115g/4oz peas, thawed if frozen
30ml/2 tbsp oyster sauce
5ml/1 tsp sugar
salt

1 Rinse the rice, then cook for 10–12 minutes in 700–900ml/ 1¼ –1½pints/3–3¾ cups salted water in a saucepan with a tight-fitting lid. When cooked, refresh under cold water. Heat half the oil in a preheated wok, then stir-fry the rice for 3 minutes. Remove and set aside.

2 Add the remaining oil to the wok. When the oil is hot, cook the onion until softened but not coloured.

3 Add all the remaining ingredients and stir-fry for 2 minutes.

4 Return the rice to the wok and stir-fry for 3 minutes, then serve.

Indonesian Fried Rice

This fried rice dish makes an deal supper on its own or as an ccompaniment to another dish.

NGREDIENTS

erves 4–6
- shallots, roughly chopped
- fresh red chilli, seeded and chopped
- garlic clove, chopped
- hin sliver of dried shrimp paste
- 5ml/3 tbsp vegetable oil
- 25g/8oz boneless lean pork, cut into fine strips
- 75g/6oz long grain white rice, boiled and cooled
- –4 spring onions, thinly sliced
- 15g/4oz cooked peeled prawns
- 0ml/2 tbsp sweet soy sauce (*kecap manis*)
- hopped fresh coriander and fine cucumber shreds, to garnish

1 In a mortar pound the shallots, chilli, garlic and shrimp paste with a pestle until they form a paste.

COOK'S TIP

Shrimp paste, sometimes called dried shrimp paste, is a strong-smelling and flavoursome paste made from fermented shrimps that is used extensively in many oriental cuisines. Always use sparingly. It is available from most oriental food stores and Chinese supermarkets.

2 Heat a wok until hot, add 30ml/2 tbsp of the oil and swirl it around. Add the pork and stir-fry for 2–3 minutes. Remove the pork from the wok, set aside and keep warm.

3 Add the remaining oil to the wok. When hot, add the spiced shallot paste and stir-fry for about 30 seconds.

4 Reduce the heat. Add the rice, sliced spring onions and prawns. Stir-fry for 2–3 minutes. Add the pork and sprinkle over the soy sauce. Stir-fry for 1 minute. Serve at once, garnished with chopped fresh coriander and cucumber shreds.

Festive Rice

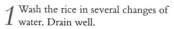

Nasi Kuning is served at special events – weddings, birthdays or farewell parties.

Ingredients

Serves 8

450g/1lb Thai fragrant rice
60ml/4 tbsp oil
2 garlic cloves, crushed
2 onions, finely sliced
5cm/2in fresh turmeric, peeled and crushed
750ml/1¼ pints/3 cups water
400ml/14fl oz can coconut milk
1–2 lemon grass stems, bruised
1–2 *pandan* leaves (optional)
salt

For the accompaniments
omelette strips
2 fresh red chillies, shredded
cucumber chunks
tomato wedges
Deep-fried Onions
prawn crackers

1 Wash the rice in several changes of water. Drain well.

2 Heat the oil in a wok and gently fry the crushed garlic, the finely sliced onions and the crushed fresh turmeric for a few minutes until soft but not browned.

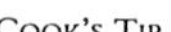

Cook's Tip

It is the custom to shape the rice into a cone (to represent a volcano) and then surround with the accompaniments. Shape with oiled hands or use a conical sieve.

3 Add the rice and and stir well so that each grain is thoroughly coated. Pour in the water and coconut milk and add the lemon grass, *pandan* leaves, if using, and salt.

4 Bring to the boil, stirring well. Cover and cook gently for about 15–20 minutes, until all of the liquid has been absorbed.

5 Remove from the heat. Cover with a dish towel, put on the lid and leave to stand in a warm place, for 15 minutes. Remove the lemon grass and *pandan* leaves.

6 Turn on to a serving platter and garnish with the accompaniments.

Special Fried Rice

Special fried rice is so substantial and tasty that it is another rice dish that is almost a meal in itself.

INGREDIENTS

Serves 4

50g/2oz peeled, cooked prawns
50g/2oz cooked ham
115g/4oz green peas
3 eggs
5ml/1 tsp salt
2 spring onions, finely chopped
60ml/4 tbsp vegetable oil
15ml/1 tbsp light soy sauce
15ml/1 tbsp Chinese rice wine or dry sherry
450g/1lb cooked rice

1 Pat dry the prawns with kitchen paper. Cut the ham into small dice about the same size as the peas.

2 In a bowl, lightly beat the eggs with a pinch of the salt and a few pieces of the spring onions.

3 Heat about half of the oil in a preheated wok, stir-fry the peas, prawns and ham for 1 minute, then add the soy sauce and rice wine or sherry. Remove and keep warm.

4 Heat the remaining oil in the wok and lightly scramble the eggs. Add the rice and stir to make sure that each grain of rice is separated. Add the remaining salt, spring onions and the prawns, ham and peas. Blend well and serve either hot or cold.

Jasmine Rice

A naturally aromatic, long grain white rice, jasmine rice is the staple of most Thai meals. If you eat rice regularly, you might want to invest in an electric rice cooker.

INGREDIENTS

Serves 4–6

450g/1lb/2 cups jasmine rice
750ml/1¼ pint/3 cups cold water

COOK'S TIP

An electric rice cooker cooks the rice and keeps it warm. Different sizes and models of rice cookers are available. The top of the range is a non-stick version, which is expensive, but well worth the money

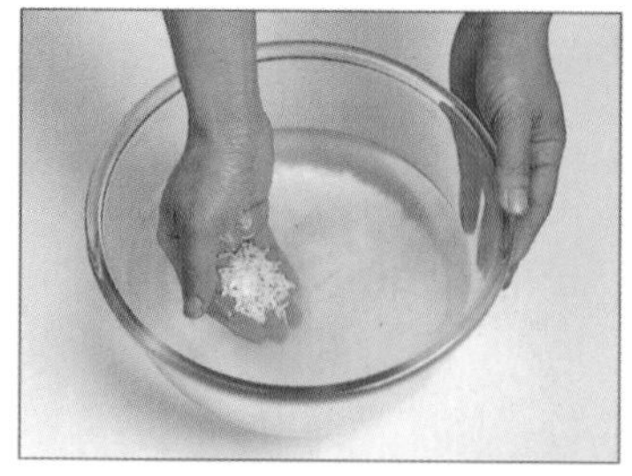

1 Rinse the rice thoroughly at least three times in cold water until the water runs clear.

2 Put the rice in a heavy-based saucepan and add the water. Bring the rice to a vigorous boil, uncovered, over a high heat.

3 Stir and reduce the heat to low. Cover and simmer for up to 20 minutes, or until all the water has been absorbed. Remove from the heat and leave to stand for 10 minutes.

4 Remove the lid and stir the rice gently with a rice paddle or a pair of wooden chopsticks, to fluff up and separate the grains.

Fried Jasmine Rice with Prawns and Thai Basil

Thai basil (*bai grapao*), also known as Holy basil, has a unique, pungent flavour that is both spicy and sharp. It can be found in most Oriental food markets.

INGREDIENTS

Serves 4–6

45ml/3 tbsp vegetable oil
1 egg, beaten
1 onion, chopped
15ml/1 tbsp chopped garlic
15ml/1 tbsp shrimp paste
1kg/2¼lb/4 cups cooked jasmine rice
350g/12oz cooked shelled prawns
50g/2oz thawed frozen peas
oyster sauce, to taste
2 spring onions, chopped
15–20 Thai basil leaves, roughly snipped, plus an extra sprig, to garnish

1 Heat 15ml/1 tbsp of the oil in a wok or frying pan. Add the beaten egg and swirl it around the pan to set like a thin pancake.

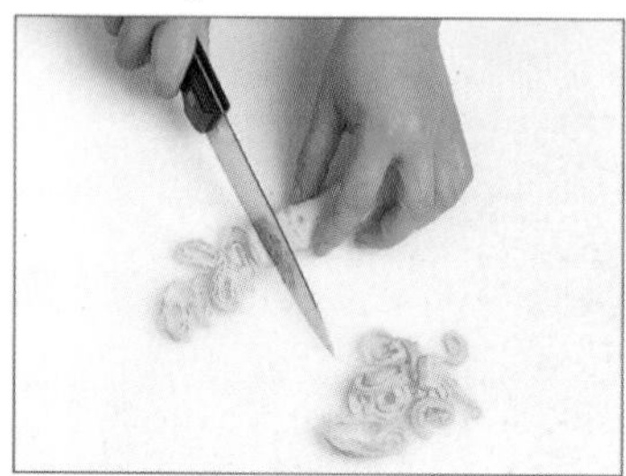

2 Cook until golden, slide out on to a board, roll up and cut into thin strips. Set aside.

3 Heat the remaining oil in the wok, add the onion and garlic and fry for 2–3 minutes. Stir in the shrimp paste and mix well.

4 Add the rice prawns and peas and toss and stir together, until everything is heated through.

5 Season with oyster sauce to taste, taking great care as the shrimp paste is salty. Add the spring onions anc basil leaves. Transfer to a serving dish and serve topped with the strips of egg pancake. Garnish with a sprig of basil.

Fried Rice with Pork

If liked, garnish with strips of egg omelette, as in the Jasmine Rice with Prawns and Holy Basil.

INGREDIENTS

Serves 4–6

45ml/3 tbsp vegetable oil
1 onion, chopped
15ml/1 tbsp chopped garlic
115g/4oz pork, cut into small cubes
2 eggs, beaten
1kg/2¼lb/4 cups cooked rice
30ml/2 tbsp fish sauce
15ml/1 tbsp dark soy sauce
2.5 ml/½ tsp caster sugar
4 spring onions, finely sliced, to garnish
2 red chillies, sliced, to garnish
1 lime, cut into wedges, to garnish
egg omelette, to garnish (optional)

1 Heat the oil in a wok or large frying pan. Add the onion and garlic and cook for about 2 minutes until softened.

2 Add the pork to the softened onion and garlic. Stir-fry until the pork changes colour and is cooked.

3 Add the eggs and cook until scrambled into small lumps.

4 Add the rice and continue to stir and toss, to coat it with the oil and prevent it from sticking.

5 Add the fish sauce, soy sauce and sugar and mix well. Continue to fry until the rice is thoroughly heated. Garnish with sliced spring onion, red chillies and lime wedges. Top with a few strips of egg omelette, if you like.

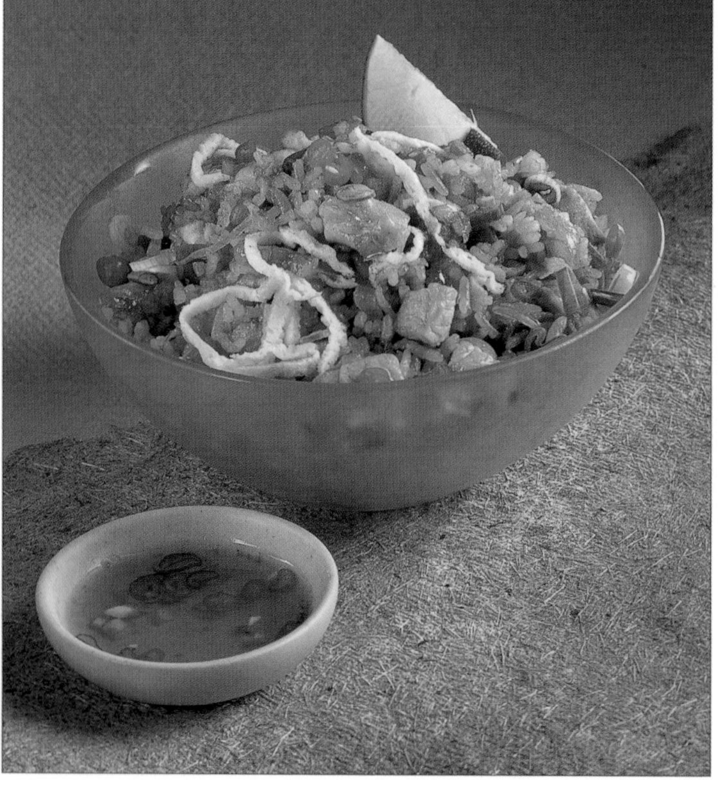

Red Fried Rice

'his vibrant rice dish owes its ppeal as much to the bright olours of red onion, red pepper nd cherry tomatoes as it does to heir distinctive flavours.

NGREDIENTS

erves 2
15g/4oz basmati rice
0ml/2 tbsp groundnut oil
small red onion, chopped
red pepper, seeded and chopped
25g/8oz cherry tomatoes, halved
eggs, beaten
alt and ground black pepper

1 Wash the rice several times under cold running water. Drain well. Bring a large pan of salted water to the boil, add the rice and cook for 10–12 minutes until tender.

2 Meanwhile, heat the oil in a wok until very hot. Add the onion and red pepper and stir-fry for 2–3 minutes. Add the cherry tomatoes and stir-fry for a further 2 minutes.

3 Pour in the beaten eggs all at once. Cook for 30 seconds without stirring, then stir to break up the egg as it sets.

4 Drain the cooked rice thoroughly, add to the wok and toss it over the heat with the vegetable and egg mixture for 3 minutes. Season the fried rice with salt and pepper to taste.

Spicy Fried Rice Sticks with Prawns

This well-known recipe is based on the classic Thai noodle dish called *pad Thai*. Popular all over Thailand, it is enjoyed morning, noon and night.

INGREDIENTS

Serves 4

15g/½oz dried shrimps
15ml/1 tbsp tamarind pulp
45ml/3 tbsp Thai fish sauce *(nam pla)*
15ml/1 tbsp sugar
2 garlic cloves, chopped
2 fresh red chillies, seeded and chopped
45ml/3 tbsp groundnut oil
2 eggs, beaten
225g/8oz dried rice sticks, soaked in warm water for 30 minutes, refreshed under cold running water and drained
225g/8oz cooked, peeled king prawns
3 spring onions cut into 2.5cm/1in lengths
75g/3oz beansprouts
30ml/2 tbsp roughly chopped roasted unsalted peanuts
30ml/2 tbsp chopped fresh coriander
lime slices, to garnish

1 Put the dried shrimps in a small bowl and pour over enough warm water to cover. Leave to soak for 30 minutes until soft, then drain.

2 Put the tamarind pulp in a bowl with 60ml/4 tbsp hot water. Blend together, then press through a sieve to extract 30ml/2 tbsp thick tamarind water. Mix the tamarind water with the fish sauce and sugar.

3 Using a mortar and pestle, pound the garlic and chillies to form a paste. Heat a wok over a medium heat, add 15ml/1 tbsp of the oil, then add the beaten eggs and stir for 1–2 minutes until the eggs are scrambled. Remove and set aside. Wipe the wok clean.

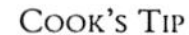

COOK'S TIP

For a vegetarian dish, omit the dried shrimps and replace the king prawns with cubes of deep-fried tofu.

4 Reheat the wok until hot, add the remaining oil, then the chilli paste and dried shrimps and stir-fry for 1 minute. Add the rice sticks and tamarind mixture and stir-fry for 3–4 minutes.

5 Add the scrambled eggs, prawns, spring onions, beansprouts, peanuts and coriander, then stir-fry for 2 minutes until well mixed. Serve at once, garnishing each portion with lime slices.

Fried Rice with Spices

This dish is mildly spiced, suitable as an accompaniment to any curried dish. The whole spices – cloves, cardamom, bay leaf, cinnamon, peppercorns and cumin – are not intended to be eaten.

INGREDIENTS

Serves 3–4

175g/6oz basmati rice
2.5ml/½ tsp salt
15ml/1 tbsp ghee or butter
8 whole cloves
4 green cardamom pods, bruised
1 bay leaf
7.5cm/3in cinnamon stick
5ml/1 tsp black peppercorns
5ml/1 tsp cumin seeds

1 Put the rice in a colander and wash under cold running water until the water clears. Put in a bowl and pour 600ml/1 pint/2½ cups fresh water over the rice. Leave the rice to soak for 30 minutes; then drain thoroughly.

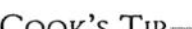

COOK'S TIP

You could add 2.5ml/½ tsp ground turmeric to the rice in step 2 of the recipe to colour it yellow.

2 Put the rice, salt and 600ml/1 pint/2½ cups water in a heavy-based pan. Bring to the boil, then cov and simmer for about 10 minutes. Th rice should be just cooked with a littl bite to it. Drain off any excess water, fluff up the grains with a fork, then spread it out on a tray and leave aside to cool.

3 Heat the ghee or butter in a wok until foaming, add the spices and stir-fry for 1 minute.

4 Add the cooled rice and stir-fry fc 3–4 minutes until warmed throug Serve at once.

Nutty Rice and Mushroom Stir-fry

This delicious and substantial upper dish can be eaten hot or old with salads.

NGREDIENTS

erves 4–6
50g/12oz long grain rice, preferably basmati
5ml/3 tbsp sunflower oil
small onion or shallot, roughly chopped
25g/8oz field mushrooms, sliced
0g/2oz hazelnuts, roughly chopped
0g/2oz pecan nuts, roughly chopped
0g/2oz almonds, roughly chopped
0ml/4 tbsp fresh parsley, chopped
alt and ground black pepper

1 Rinse the rice, then cook for 10–12 minutes in 700–900ml/ 1¼–1½ pints/3–3¾ cups salted water in a saucepan with a tight-fitting lid. When cooked, refresh under cold water. Heat the wok, then add half the oil. Stir-fry the rice for 2–3 minutes. Remove and set aside.

2 Add the remaining oil and stir-fry the onion or shallot for 2 minutes until softened but not coloured. Mix in the field mushrooms and stir-fry for 2 minutes.

3 Add all the nuts and stir-fry for 1 minute. Return the rice to the wok and stir-fry for 3 minutes. Season with salt and pepper. Stir in the parsley and serve at once.

COOK'S TIP

Of all the types of long grain rice, basmati is undoubtedly the king. This long, thin, aromatic grain grows in India, where its name means fragrant. Basmati rice benefits from rinsing in a bowl with plenty of cold water and a light soaking for 10 minutes.

Desserts

Surprise the family with something completely different with these melt-in-the-mouth dessert recipes collected from all over China and Asia. Exotic Fruit Salad from Vietnam tastes just as wonderful – and tropical – as it looks. Old or young, few can resist the delicious little Japanese Sweet Potato and Chestnut Candies. Thailand offers an intriguing variation on an international favourite with Steamed Coconut Custard and the combination of crisp batter and soft, warm fruit in Indonesian Deep-fried Bananas is quite simply magical.

Chinese Fruit Salad

For an unusual fruit salad with an oriental flavour, try this mixture of fruits in a tangy lime and lychee syrup, topped with a light sprinkling of toasted sesame seeds.

INGREDIENTS

Serves 4

115g/4oz/½ cup caster sugar
300ml/½ pint/1¼ cups water
thinly pared rind and juice of 1 lime
400g/14oz can lychees in syrup
1 ripe mango, peeled, stoned and sliced
1 eating apple, cored and sliced
2 bananas, chopped
1 star fruit, sliced (optional)
5ml/1 tsp sesame seeds, toasted

1 Place the sugar in a saucepan with the water and the lime rind. Heat gently until the sugar dissolves, then increase the heat and boil gently for about 7–8 minutes. Remove from the heat and set aside to cool.

2 Drain the lychees and reserve the juice. Pour the juice into the cooled lime syrup with the lime juice Place all the prepared fruit in a bowl and pour over the lime and lychee syrup. Chill for about 1 hour. Just before serving, sprinkle with toasted sesame seeds.

COOK'S TIP

To prepare a mango, cut through the fruit lengthways, about 1cm/½in either side of the centre. Then, using a sharp knife, cut the flesh from the central piece from the stone. Make even criss-cross cuts in the flesh of both side pieces. Hold one side piece in both hands, bend it almost inside out and remove the cubes of flesh with a spoon. Repeat with the other side piece.

Date and Walnut Crisps

Try this sweet version of fried wontons; they make a truly scrumptious snack or dessert.

INGREDIENTS

Makes 15

25–30 dried dates, stoned
50g/2oz/½ cup walnuts
30ml/2 tbsp light brown sugar
pinch of ground cinnamon
30 wonton wrappers
1 egg, beaten
oil, for deep-frying
fresh mint sprigs, to decorate
icing sugar, for dusting

1 Chop the dates and walnuts roughly. Place them in a bowl and add the sugar and cinnamon. Mix well.

2 Lay a wonton wrapper on a flat surface. Centre a spoonful of the filling on the wrapper, brush the edges with beaten egg and cover with a second wrapper. Lightly press the edges together to seal. Make more filled wontons in the same way.

3 Heat the oil to 180°C/350°F in a wok or deep-fryer. Deep-fry the wontons, a few at a time, until golden. Do not crowd the pan. Remove them with a slotted spoon and drain on kitchen paper. Serve warm, decorated with mint and dusted with icing sugar.

Thin Pancakes

Thin pancakes are not too difficult to make, but quite a lot of practice and patience are needed to achieve the perfect result. Nowadays, even restaurants buy frozen, ready-made ones from Chinese supermarkets.
If you decide to use ready-made pancakes, or are reheating home-made ones, steam them for about 5 minutes, or microwave on high (650 watts) for 1–2 minutes.

INGREDIENTS

Makes 24–30

450g/1lb/4 cups plain flour, plus extra for dusting
about 300ml/½ pint/1¼ cups boiling water
5ml/1 tsp vegetable oil

1 Sift the flour into a mixing bowl, then pour in the boiling water very gently, stirring as you pour. Mix with the oil and knead the mixture into a firm dough. Cover with a damp cloth and let stand for about 30 minutes.

2 Lightly dust a work surface with flour. Knead the dough for about 5–8 minutes, or until smooth, then divide it into 3 equal portions. Roll out each portion into a long "sausage", cut each into 8–10 pieces and roll each into a ball. Using the palm of your hand, press each piece into a flat pancake. With a rolling pin, gently roll each into a 15cm/6in circle.

3 Heat an ungreased frying pan unti hot, then reduce the heat to low and place the pancakes, one at a time, in the pan. Remove the pancakes whe small brown spots appear on the underside. Keep under a damp cloth until all the pancakes are cooked.

Red Bean Paste Pancakes

If you are unable to find red bean paste, sweetened chestnut purée or mashed dates are possible substitutes.

INGREDIENTS

Serves 4

about 120ml/8 tbsp sweetened red bean paste
8 Thin Pancakes
30–45ml/2–3 tbsp vegetable oil
granulated or caster sugar, to serve

1 Spread about 15ml/1 tbsp of the red bean paste over about three-quarters of each pancake, then roll the pancake over three or four times.

2 Heat the oil in a preheated wok or frying pan and fry the pancake rolls until golden brown, turning once.

3 Cut each pancake roll into three o four pieces and sprinkle with sugar to serve.

Almond Curd Junket

Also known as almond float, this is usually made from agar-agar or isinglass, although gelatine can also be used.

INGREDIENTS

Serves 4–6

10g/¼oz agar-agar or isinglass or 25g/1oz gelatine powder
about 600ml/1 pint/2½ cups water
60ml/4 tbsp granulated or caster sugar
300ml/½ pint/1¼ cups milk
5ml/1 tsp almond essence
fresh or canned mixed fruit salad with syrup, to serve

1 In a saucepan, dissolve the agar-agar or isinglass in about half the water over a gentle heat. This will take at least 10 minutes. If using gelatine, follow the packet instructions.

2 In a separate saucepan, dissolve the sugar in the remaining water over medium heat. Add the milk and the almond essence, blending well. Do not allow the mixture to boil.

3 Mix the milk and sugar with the agar-agar, isinglass or gelatine mixture in a serving bowl. When cool, place in the refrigerator for 2–3 hours to set.

4 To serve, cut the junket into small cubes and spoon into a serving dish or into individual bowls. Pour the fruit salad, with the syrup, over the junket and serve.

Stewed Pumpkin in Coconut Cream

Stewed fruit is a popular dessert in Thailand. Use the firm-textured Japanese kabocha pumpkin for this dish, if you can. Bananas and melons can also be prepared in this way and you can even stew sweetcorn kernels or pulses such as mung beans and black beans in coconut milk.

INGREDIENTS

Serves 4–6

1kg/2¼lb kabocha pumpkin
750ml/1¼ pint/3 cups coconut milk
175g/6oz granulated sugar
pinch of salt
pumpkin seed kernels, toasted, and mint sprigs, to decorate

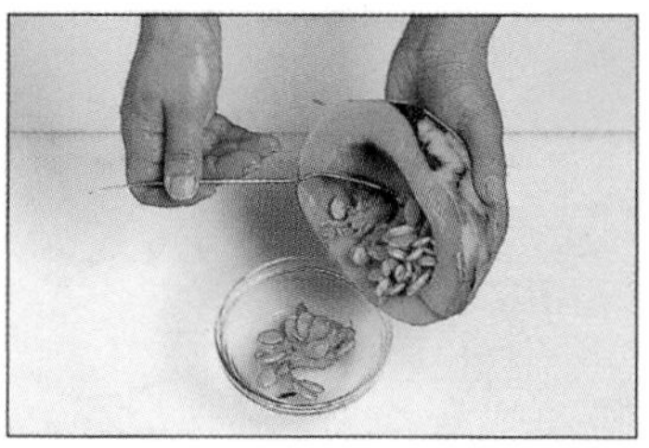

1 Wash the pumpkin skin and cut off most of it. Scoop out the seeds.

COOK'S TIP

Any pumpkin can be used for this dish, as long as it has a firm texture. Jamaican or New Zealand varieties both make good alternatives to kabocha pumpkin.

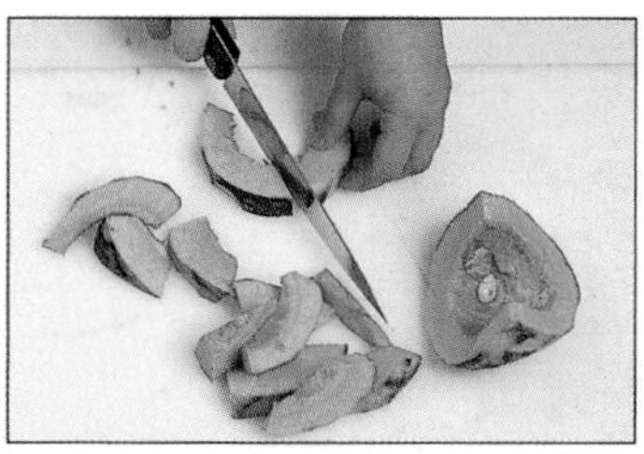

2 Using a sharp knife, cut the flesh into pieces about 5cm/2in long and 2cm/¾in thick.

3 In a saucepan, bring the coconut milk, sugar and salt to the boil.

4 Add the pumpkin and simmer for about 10–15 minutes until the pumpkin is tender. Serve warm. Decorate each serving with a mint sprig and a few toasted pumpkin seed kernels.

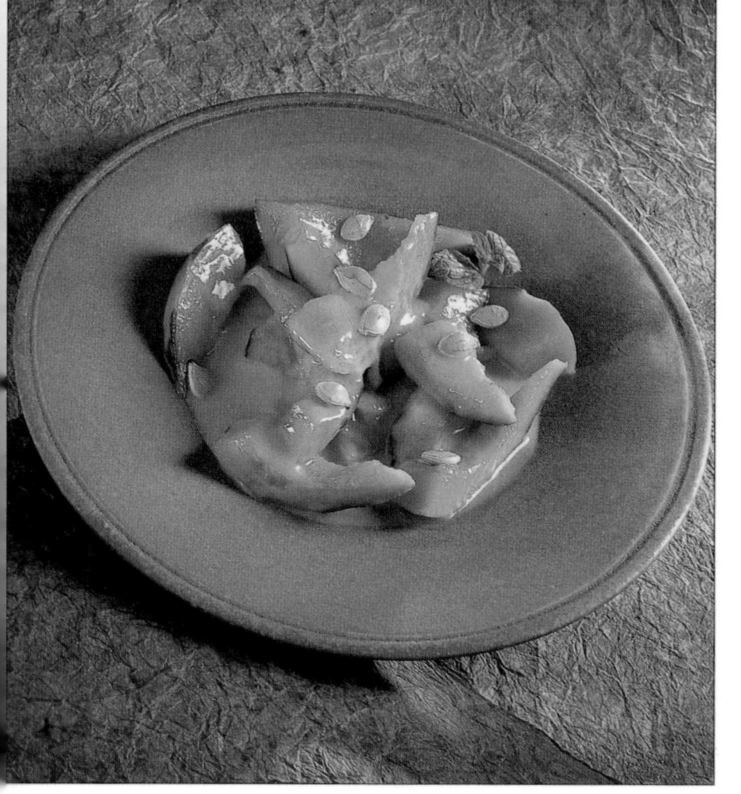

Celebration Cake

A mouth-watering gâteau made from fragrant Thai rice covered with a tangy cream icing. Top with fresh berry fruits or pipe on a greeting in melted chocolate.

INGREDIENTS

Serves 8–10

225g/8oz/generous 1 cup Thai fragrant or Jasmine rice
1 litre/1¾ pints/4 cups milk
115g/4oz/¾ cup caster sugar
6 cardamom pods, crushed open
2 bay leaves
300ml/½ pint/1¼ cups whipping cream
6 eggs, separated

For the topping

300ml/½ pint/1¼ cups double cream
200g/7oz/scant 1 cup quark
5ml/1 tsp vanilla essence
grated rind of 1 lemon
30g/1½oz/3 tbsp caster sugar
soft berry fruits and sliced star or kiwi fruits, to decorate

1 Grease and line a deep 25cm/10in round cake tin. Boil the rice in unsalted water for 3 minutes, then drain well.

COOK'S TIP

If you prefer something simpler, turn the cake out and top with sliced fruits or a lovely tumble of berries and stoned cherries. Serve the topping separately, thinning it down slightly with a little milk.

2 Return the rice to the pan with the milk, 115g/4oz/generous ½ cup of the sugar, the cardamom and bay leaves. Bring to the boil, then lower the heat and simmer the mixture for 20 minutes, stirring occasionally.

3 Allow the mixture to cool, then remove the bay leaves and any cardamom husks. Turn into a large bowl. Beat in the whipping cream and then the egg yolks.

4 Whisk the egg whites until they form soft peaks and fold into the rice mixture. Spoon into the prepared tin and bake in a preheated oven at 180°C/350°F/Gas 4 for 45–50 minutes, until risen and golden brown. The centre should be slightly wobbly – it will firm up as it cools.

5 Chill overnight in the tin. Turn out on to a large serving plate. For the topping, whip the double cream until stiff, then mix in the quark, vanilla essence, lemon rind and sugar.

6 Cover the top and sides of the cake with the cream, swirling it attractively. Decorate with soft berry fruits and sliced star or kiwi fruits.

Steamed Coconut Custard

Srikaya is a very popular dessert that pops up all over South-east Asia, rather as crème caramel is found all over Europe or, indeed, wherever Europeans have settled.

INGREDIENTS

Serves 8

400ml/14fl oz can coconut milk
75ml/5 tbsp water
25g/1oz sugar
3 eggs, beaten
25g/1oz cellophane noodles, soaked in warm water for 5 minutes
4 ripe bananas or plantains, peeled and cut in small pieces
salt
vanilla ice cream, to serve (optional)

1 Stir the coconut milk, water and sugar into the beaten eggs and whisk well together.

2 Strain into a 1.75 litre/3 pint/ 7½ cup heatproof soufflé dish.

3 Drain the noodles well and cut them into small pieces with scissors. Stir the noodles into the coconut milk mixture, together with the chopped bananas or plantains. Stir in a pinch of salt.

4 Cover the dish with foil and place in a steamer for about 1 hour, or until set. Test by inserting a thin, small knife or skewer into the centre. Serve hot or cold, on its own or topped with vanilla ice cream.

Sweet Potato and Chestnut Candies

It is customary in Japan to offer special bean paste candies with tea. The candies tend to be very sweet by themselves, but contrast well with Japanese green tea. They also make an unusual dessert at the end of a special evening meal.

INGREDIENTS

Makes 18

450g/1lb sweet potatoes, peeled and chopped
1.5ml/¼ tsp salt
2 egg yolks
200g/7oz/1 cup sugar
60ml/4 tbsp water
75ml/5 tbsp rice flour or plain flour
5ml/1 tsp orange flower or rose water (optional)
200g/7oz can chestnuts in heavy syrup, drained
caster sugar, for dusting
2 strips candied angelica
10ml/2 tsp plum or apricot preserve
3–4 drops red food colouring

1 Place the sweet potatoes in a heavy saucepan, cover with cold water and add the salt. Bring to the boil and simmer for 20–25 minutes, until the sweet potatoes are tender. Drain and return to the pan. Mash until smooth or rub through a wire strainer. Place the egg yolks, sugar and water in a bowl, then mix in the flour and orange flower or rose water, if using. Add the potato purée and stir over a gentle heat for about 3–4 minutes. Turn the paste out on to a tray and allow to cool.

2 To shape the paste, place 10ml/ 2 tsp of the mixture in the centre of a wet, cotton napkin. Enclose the paste in the napkin and twist into a nut shape. Make sure the napkin is properly wet or the mixture will stick to it.

3 To prepare the chestnuts, rinse off the syrup and dry well. Roll the chestnuts in caster sugar and decorate with strips of angelica. To finish the sweet potato candies, colour the plum or apricot preserve with red food colouring and decorate each candy with a spot of colour.

COOK'S TIP

Sugar-coated chestnuts will keep for up to 5 days in a sealed container at room temperature. Store sweet potato candies in a sealed container in the refrigerator.

Baked Rice Pudding, Thai-style

Black glutinous rice, also known as black sticky rice, has long black grains and a nutty taste similar to wild rice. This baked pudding has a distinct character and flavour all of its own.

Ingredients

Serves 4–6

175g/6oz white or black glutinous (sticky) rice
30ml/2 tbsp soft light brown sugar
475ml/16fl oz/2 cups coconut milk
250ml/8fl oz/1 cup water
3 eggs
30ml/2 tbsp granulated sugar

1 Combine the glutinous rice, brown sugar, half the coconut milk and all the water in a saucepan.

2 Bring to the boil and simmer for about 15–20 minutes or until the rice has absorbed most of the liquid, stirring from time to time. Preheat the oven to 150°C/300°F/Gas 3.

3 Transfer the rice into one large ovenproof dish or divide it between individual ramekins. Mix together the eggs, remaining coconut milk and sugar in a bowl.

4 Strain and pour the mixture evenly over the par-cooked rice.

5 Place the dish in a baking tin. Pour in enough boiling water to come halfway up the sides of the dish.

6 Cover the dish with a piece of foil and bake in the oven for about 35 minutes to 1 hour or until the custard is set. Serve warm or cold.

Mango with Sticky Rice

Everyone's favourite dessert. Mangoes, with their delicate fragrance, sweet and sour flavour and velvety flesh, blend especially well with coconut sticky rice. You need to start preparing this dish the day before.

Ingredients

Serves 4

115g/4oz sticky (glutinous) white rice
175ml/6fl oz/¾ cup thick coconut milk
45ml/3 tbsp granulated sugar
pinch of salt
2 ripe mangoes
strips of lime rind, to decorate

1 Rinse the glutinous rice thoroughly in several changes of cold water, then leave to soak overnight in a bowl of fresh, cold water.

2 Drain and spread the rice in an even layer in a steamer lined with cheesecloth. Cover and steam for about 20 minutes or until the grains of rice are tender.

3 Meanwhile, reserve 45ml/3 tbsp of the top of the coconut milk and combine the rest with the sugar and salt in a saucepan. Bring to the boil, stirring until the sugar dissolves, then pour into a bowl and leave to cool a little.

4 Turn the rice into a bowl and pour over the coconut mixture. Stir, then leave for about 10–15 minutes.

5 Peel the mangoes and cut the flesh into slices. Place on top of the rice and drizzle over the reserved coconut milk. Decorate with strips of lime rind.

Sugar Bread Rolls

These delicious sweet rolls reveal the influence of Spain on the cooking of the Philippines. They make an unusual end to a meal or a tea-time treat.

INGREDIENTS

Makes 10

350g/12oz/3 cups strong white bread flour
5ml/1 tsp salt
15ml/1 tbsp caster sugar
5ml/1 tsp dried yeast
150ml/¼ pint/⅔ cup hand-hot water
3 egg yolks
50g/2oz/4 tbsp unsalted butter, softened
75g/3oz/¾ cup Cheddar cheese, grated
30ml/2 tbsp melted unsalted butter
50g/2oz/generous ¼ cup sugar

1 Sift the flour, salt and caster sugar into a food processor fitted with a dough blade or the bowl of an electric mixer fitted with a dough hook. Make a well in the centre. Dissolve the yeast in the hand-hot water and pour into the well. Add the egg yolks and leave for a few minutes until bubbles appear on the surface of the liquid.

2 Mix the ingredients for 30–45 seconds to form a firm dough. Add the softened butter and knead for 2–3 minutes in a food processor, or for 4–5 minutes with an electric mixer, until smooth. Turn the dough out into a floured bowl, cover and leave in a warm place to rise until doubled in volume.

3 Turn the dough out on to a lightly floured surface and divide it into 10 pieces. Spread the grated cheese over the surface. Roll each of the dough pieces into 12.5cm/5in lengths, incorporating the cheese as you do so. Coil into snail shapes and place on a lightly greased high-sided tray measuring 30 x 20cm/12 x 8in.

4 Cover the tray with a loose-fitting plastic bag and leave in a warm place for 45 minutes or until the dough has doubled in volume. Bake in a preheated oven at 190°C/375°F/Gas 5 for 20–25 minutes. Brush with the melted butter, sprinkle with the sugar and allow to cool. Separate the rolls before serving.

Exotic Fruit Salad

\ variety of fruits can be used for hisVietnamese dessert, depending)n what is available. Look out ŏr mandarin oranges, star fruit,)awpaw and passion fruit.

NGREDIENTS

erves 4–6

'5g/3oz/scant ½ cup sugar
00ml/½ pint/1¼ cups water
0ml/2 tbsp stem ginger syrup
pieces star anise
.5cm/1in cinnamon stick
clove
uice of ½ lemon
fresh mint sprigs
mango
bananas, sliced
fresh or canned lychees
25g/8oz strawberries, hulled and halved
pieces stem ginger, cut into sticks
medium pineapple

1 Put the sugar, water, ginger syrup, star anise, cinnamon, clove, lemon ıice and mint into a saucepan. Bring o the boil and simmer for 3 minutes. train into a bowl and set aside to cool.

2 Remove the top and bottom from the mango and remove the outer kin. Stand the mango on one end and emove the flesh in two pieces either de of the flat stone. Slice evenly and dd to the syrup. Add the bananas, ychees, strawberries and ginger.

3 Cut the pineapple in half down the centre. Loosen the flesh with a small serrated knife and remove to form two boat shapes. Cut the flesh into chunks and place in the syrup.

4 Spoon some of the fruit salad into the pineapple halves and serve on a large dish. There will be sufficient fruit salad to refill the pineapple halves.

Black Glutinous Rice Pudding

This very unusual rice pudding, *Bubor Pulot Hitam,* which uses bruised fresh root ginger, is quite delicious. When cooked, black rice still retains its husk and has a nutty texture. Serve in small bowls, with a little coconut cream poured over each helping.

INGREDIENTS

Serves 6
115g/4oz black glutinous rice
475ml/16fl oz/2 cups water
1cm/½in fresh root ginger, peeled and bruised
50g/2oz dark brown sugar
50g/2oz caster sugar
300ml/½ pint/1¼ cups coconut milk or cream, to serve

1 Put the rice in a sieve and rinse well under cold running water. Drain and put in a large pan, with the water. Bring to the boil and stir to prevent the rice from settling on the base of the pan. Cover and cook for about 30 minutes.

2 Add the ginger and both the brown and caster sugar. Cook for further 15 minutes, adding a little mor water if necessary, until the rice is cooked and porridge-like. Remove th ginger and serve warm, in bowls, topped with coconut milk or cream.

Deep-fried Bananas

Known as *Pisang Goreng*, these delicious deep-fried bananas should be cooked at the last minute, so that the outer crust of batter is crisp in texture and the banana is soft and warm inside.

INGREDIENTS

Serves 8
115g/4oz self-raising flour
40g/1½oz rice flour
2.5ml/½ tsp salt
200ml/7fl oz /scant 1 cup water
finely grated lime rind (optional)
8 small bananas
oil for deep-frying
sugar and 1 lime, cut in wedges, to serve

1 Sift both the flours and the salt together into a bowl. Add just enough water to make a smooth, coating batter. Mix well, then add the lime rind, if using.

2 Peel the bananas and dip them into the batter two or three times.

3 Heat the oil to 190°C/375°F or when a cube of day-old bread browns in 30 seconds. Deep-fry the battered bananas until crisp and golde Drain and serve hot, dredged with sugar and with the lime wedges to squeeze over the bananas.

Thai Coconut Cream

This traditional dish can be baked or steamed and is often served with sweet sticky rice and a selection of fruit such as mango and tamarillo.

INGREDIENTS

Serves 4–6

4 eggs
75g/3oz soft light brown sugar
250ml/8fl oz/1 cup coconut milk
5ml/1 tsp vanilla, rose or jasmine extract
mint leaves, to decorate
icing sugar, to decorate

1 Preheat the oven to 150°C/300°F/Gas 2. Whisk the eggs and sugar in a bowl until smooth. Add the coconut milk and vanilla or other extract and blend well together.

2 Strain the mixture and pour into individual ramekins or a cake tin.

3 Stand the ramekins or tin in a roasting pan. Carefully fill the pan with hot water to reach halfway up the outsides of the ramekins or tin.

4 Bake for about 35–40 minutes or until the custards are set. Test with a fine skewer or cocktail stick.

5 Remove from the oven and leave to cool. Turn out onto a plate, and serve with sliced fruit. Decorate with mint leaves and icing sugar.

Apples and Raspberries in Rose Pouchong Syrup

This delightfully fragrant and quick-to-prepare Asian dessert couples the subtle flavours of apples and raspberries, both of which belong to the rose family, within an infusion of rose-scented tea.

INGREDIENTS

Serves 4

5ml/1 tsp rose pouchong tea
5ml/1 tsp rose water (optional)
50g/2oz/¼ cup sugar
5ml/1 tsp lemon juice
5 dessert apples
175g/6oz/1½ cups fresh raspberries

1 Warm a large tea pot. Add the rose pouchong tea and 900ml/1½ pints/3¾ cups of boiling water together with the rose water, if using. Allow to stand and infuse for 4 minutes.

2 Measure the sugar and lemon juice into a stainless steel saucepan. Strain in the tea and stir to dissolve the sugar.

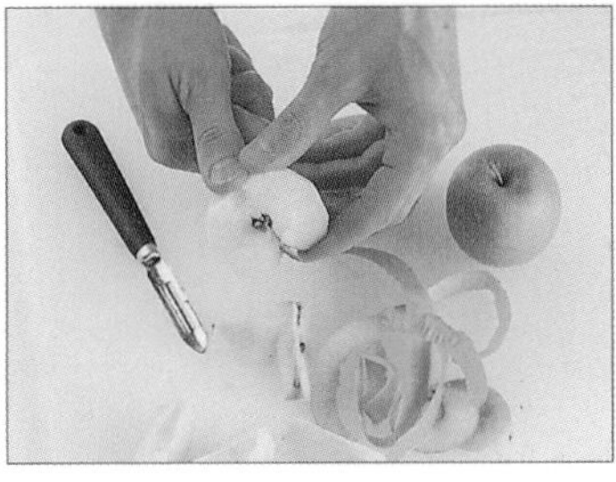

3 Peel and core the apples, then cut into quarters.

4 Poach the apples in the syrup for about 5 minutes.

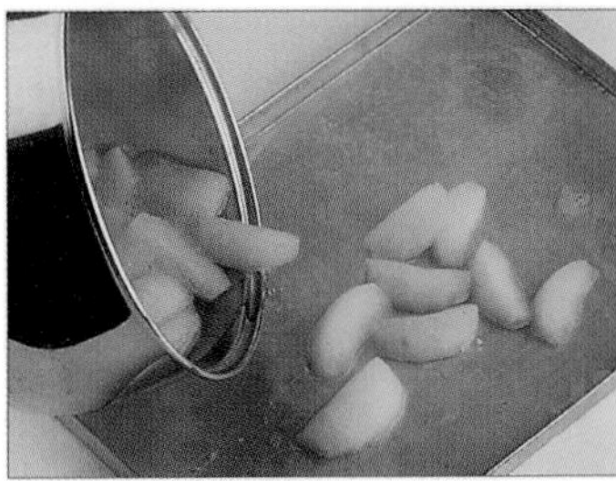

5 Transfer the apples and syrup to a large metal tray and leave to cool to room temperature.

6 Pour the cooled apples and syrup into a bowl, add the raspberries and mix to combine. Spoon into individual dishes or bowls and serve immediately.

Pancakes Filled with Sweet Coconut

Traditionally, the pale green colour in the batter for *Dadar Gulung* was obtained from the juice squeezed from *pandan* leaves – a real labour of love. Green food colouring can be used as the modern alternative to this lengthy process.

INGREDIENTS

Makes 12–15 pancakes

175g/6oz dark brown sugar
450ml/15fl oz/scant 2 cups water
1 *pandan* leaf, stripped through with a fork and tied into a knot
175g/6oz desiccated coconut
oil for frying
salt

For the pancake batter

225g/8oz plain flour, sifted
2 eggs, beaten
2 drops of edible green food colouring
few drops of vanilla essence
450ml/15fl oz/scant 2 cups water
45ml/3 tbsp groundnut oil

1 Dissolve the sugar in the water with the *pandan* leaf, in a pan over gentle heat, stirring all the time. Increase the heat and allow to boil gently for 3–4 minutes, until the mixture just becomes syrupy. Do not let it caramelize.

2 Put the coconut into a wok with a pinch of salt. Pour over the prepared sugar syrup and cook over a very gentle heat, stirring from time to time, until the mixture becomes almc dry; this will take 5–10 minutes. Set aside until required.

3 To make the batter, blend togeth the flour, eggs, food colouring, vanilla essence, water and oil either b hand or in a food processor.

4 Brush an 18cm/7in frying pan w oil and cook 12–15 pancakes. Ke the pancakes warm. Fill each pancakc with a generous spoonful of the coconut mixture, roll up and serve them immediately.

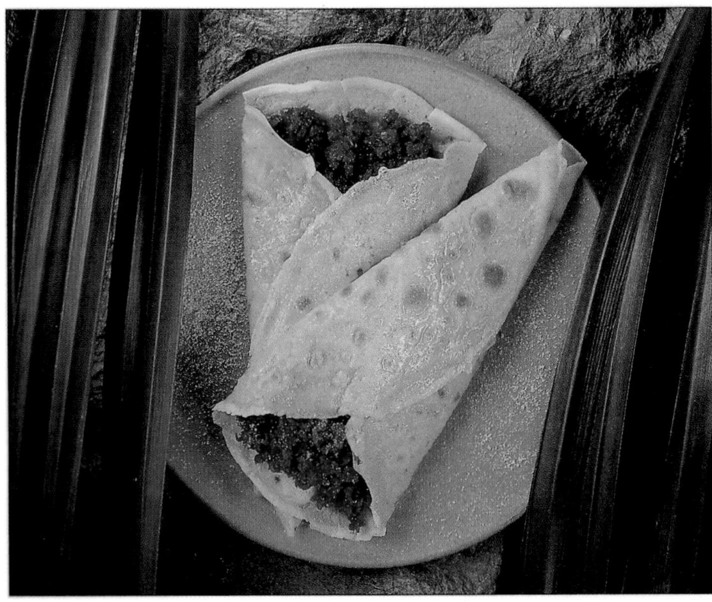

Toffee Apples

A variety of fruits, such as bananas and pineapple, can be prepared and cooked in this way.

INGREDIENTS

Serves 4

4 firm eating apples
115g/4oz plain flour
about 120ml/4fl oz/½ cup water
1 egg, beaten
vegetable oil, for deep frying, plus 30ml/2 tbsp for the toffee
115g/4oz sugar

1 Peel and core each apple and cut into eight pieces. Dust each piece of apple with a little of the flour.

2 Sift the remaining flour into a mixing bowl, then slowly add the cold water and stir well to make a smooth batter. Add the beaten egg and blend well.

3 Heat the oil for deep frying in a wok. Dip the apple pieces in the batter and deep fry for about 3 minutes or until golden. Remove and drain. Drain off the oil.

4 Heat the remaining oil in the wok, add the sugar and stir continuously until the sugar has caramelized. Quickly add the apple pieces and blend well so that each piece of apple is thoroughly coated with the toffee. Dip the apple pieces in cold water to harden before serving.

Mango and Coconut Stir-fry

Choose a ripe mango for this recipe. If you buy one that is a little under-ripe, leave it in a warm place for a day or two before using.

Ingredients

Serves 4

¼ coconut
1 large, ripe mango
juice of 2 limes
rind of 2 limes, finely grated
15ml/1 tbsp sunflower oil
15g/½ oz butter
30ml/2 tbsp clear honey
crème fraîche, to serve

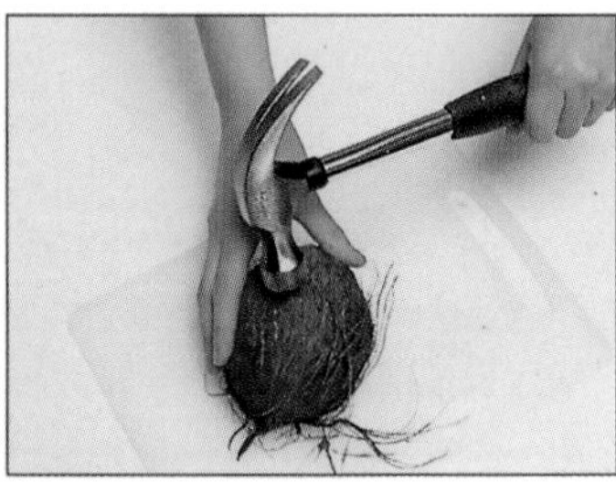

1 Prepare the coconut flakes by draining the milk from the coconut and peeling the flesh with a vegetable peeler.

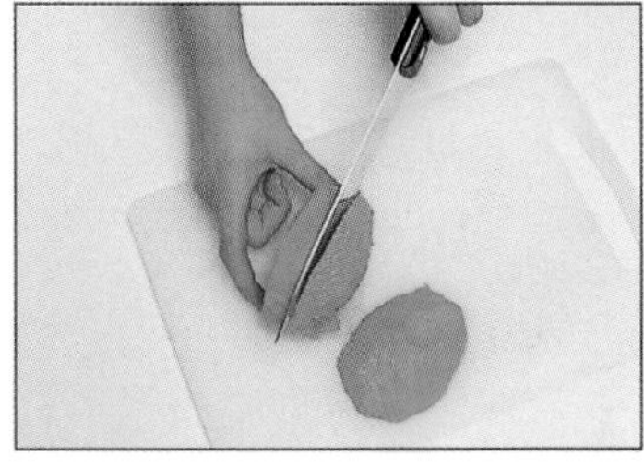

2 Peel the mango. Cut the stone out of the middle of the fruit. Cut each half of the mango into slices.

3 Place the mango slices in a bowl and pour over the lime juice and rind, to marinate them.

4 Meanwhile heat a wok, then add 10ml/2 tsp of the oil. When the oil is hot, add the butter. When the butter has melted, stir in the coconut flakes and stir-fry for 1–2 minutes until the coconut is golden brown. Remove and drain on kitchen paper. Wipe out the wok. Strain the mango slices, reserving the juice.

5 Heat the wok and add the remaining oil. When the oil is hot, add the mango and stir-fry for 1–2 minutes, then add the juice and allow to bubble and reduce for 1 minute. Stir in the honey, sprinkle on the coconut flakes and serve with crème fraîche.

Cook's Tip

You can sometimes buy "fresh" coconut that has already been cracked open and is sold in pieces ready for use from supermarkets, but buying the whole nut ensures greater freshness. Choose one that is heavy for its size and shake it so that you can hear the milk sloshing about. A "dry" coconut will almost certainly have rancid flesh. You can simply crack the shell with a hammer, preferably with the nut inside a plastic bag, but it may be better to pierce the two ends with a sharp nail or skewer first in order to collect and save the coconut milk. An alternative method is to drain the milk first and then heat the nut briefly in the oven until it cracks. Whichever method you choose, it is then fairly easy to extract the flesh and chop or shave it.

Wonton Twists

These little twists are perfect when you want a quick snack.

INGREDIENTS

Makes 24
12 wonton wrappers
1 egg, beaten
15ml/1 tbsp black sesame seeds
oil for deep frying
icing sugar for dusting (optional)

1 Cut the wonton wrappers in half and make a lengthways slit in the centre of each piece with a sharp knife.

COOK'S TIP

Use ordinary sesame seeds in place of the black ones if you prefer.

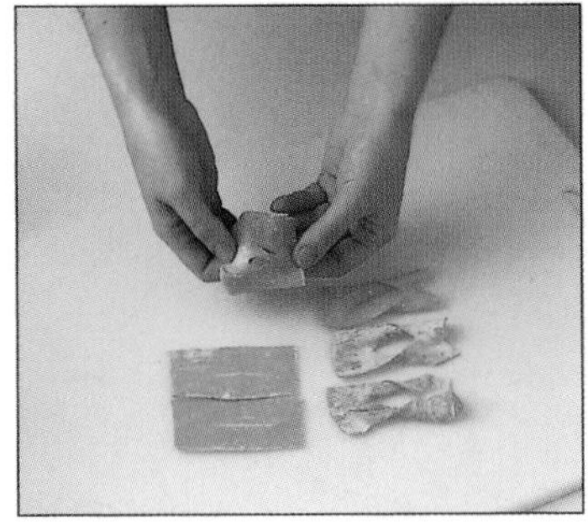

2 Take one wonton at a time and pull one end through the slit, stretching it a little as you go.

3 Brush each twist with a little beaten egg. Dip the wonton twists briefly in black sesame seeds to coat them lightly.

4 Heat the oil in a deep fryer or large saucepan to 190°C/375°F. Add a few wonton twists at a time so they do not overcrowd the pan. Fry for about 1–2 minutes on each side until crisp and light golden brown. Remove each twist and drain on kitchen paper. Dust the wonton twists with icing sugar, if you like, and serve at once.

Fried Wontons and Ice Cream

Americans have their cookies and ice cream – here is the Chinese equivalent. Serve it with fresh or poached fruits or fruit sauces for an impressive treat.

INGREDIENTS

Serves 4
oil for deep frying
12 wonton wrappers
8 scoops of your favourite ice cream

COOK'S TIP

Try using two flavours of ice cream – chocolate and strawberry perhaps, or vanilla and coffee. For a sophisticated adults-only treat, drizzle over a spoonful of your favourite liqueur.

1 Heat the oil in a deep fryer or large saucepan to 190°C/375°F.

2 Add a few wonton wrappers at a time so that they do not crowd the pan too much. Fry for 1–2 minutes on each side until the wrappers are crisp and light golden brown.

3 Leave the cooked wontons to drain on kitchen paper.

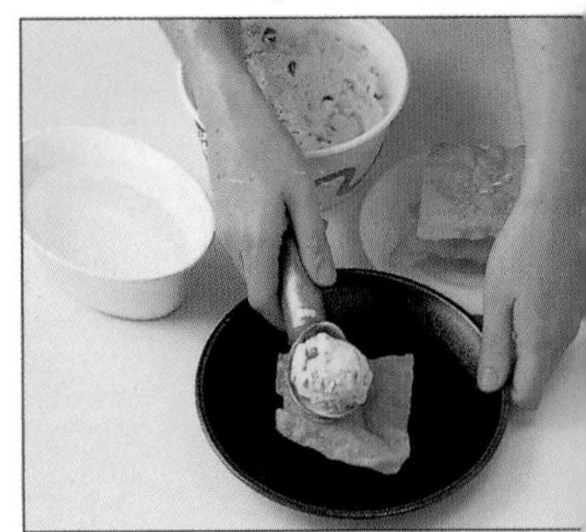

4 To serve, place one wonton on each plate. Place a scoop of ice cream on top of each wonton. Top with a second wonton, then add another ball of ice cream and finish with a final wonton. Serve at once.

Tapioca Pudding

This pudding, made from large pearl tapioca and coconut milk and served warm, is much lighter than the western-style version. You can adjust the sweetness to your taste. Serve with lychees or the smaller, similar-tasting logans – also known as 'dragon's eyes'.

INGREDIENTS

Serves 4
115g/4oz tapioca
475ml/16fl oz/2 cups water
175g/6oz granulated sugar
pinch of salt
250ml/8fl oz/1 cup coconut milk
250g/9oz prepared tropical fruits
finely shredded rind of 1 lime, to decorate

1 Soak the tapioca in warm water for 1 hour so the grains swell. Drain.

2 Put the water in a saucepan and bring to the boil. Stir in the sugar and salt.

3 Add the tapioca and coconut milk and simmer for 10 minutes or until the tapioca turns transparent.

4 Serve warm with some tropical fruits and decorate with lime zest strips and coconut shavings, if using.

Fried Bananas

These delicious treats are a favourite among children and adults alike. They are sold as snacks throughout the day and night at portable roadside stalls and market places. Other fruits such as pineapple and apple work just as well.

INGREDIENTS

Serves 4
115g/4oz plain flour
2.5ml/½ tsp bicarbonate of soda
pinch of salt
30ml/2 tbsp granulated sugar
1 egg
90ml/6 tbsp water
30ml/2 tbsp shredded coconut or 15ml/1 tbsp sesame seeds
4 firm bananas
oil for frying
30ml/2 tbsp honey, to serve (optional)
sprigs of mint, to decorate

1 Sift the flour, bicarbonate of soda and salt into a bowl. Stir in the granulated sugar. Whisk in the egg and add enough water to make quite a thin batter.

2 Whisk in the shredded coconut or sesame seeds.

3 Peel the bananas. Carefully cut each one in half lengthways, then in half crossways.

4 Heat the oil in a wok or deep frying pan. Dip the bananas in the batter, then gently drop a few into the oil. Fry until golden brown.

5 Remove from the oil and drain on kitchen paper. Serve immediately with honey, if using, and decorate with sprigs of mint.

Sauces, Sambals and Accompaniments

Dipping sauces are often served with spring rolls, meat, fish, salads and vegetables. Sometimes, they provide a cooling or creamy contrast to hot spiced dishes. More often, they add piquancy and may be very fiery. Sambals, pungent relishes that originated in southern India, are now served throughout South-east Asia and are often quite substantial, containing vegetables, poultry or seafood. Whether raw or cooked, they are invariably very hot. Finally, no Balti dish would be complete without freshly cooked bread and a spicy chutney.

Sambal Goreng

Traditional flavourings for this dish are fine strips of calves' liver, chicken livers, green beans or hard-boiled eggs. A westernized version is shown here.

INGREDIENTS

Makes 900ml/1½ pints/3¾ cups

2.5cm/1in cube *terasi*
2 onions, quartered
2 garlic cloves, crushed
2.5cm/1in fresh *lengkuas*, peeled and sliced
2 fresh red chillies, seeded and sliced
1.5ml/¼ tsp salt
30ml/2 tbsp oil
45ml/3 tbsp tomato purée
600ml/1 pint/2½ cups stock or water
60ml/4 tbsp tamarind juice
pinch sugar
45ml/3 tbsp coconut milk or cream

1 Grind the *terasi*, with the onions and garlic, to a paste in a food processor or with a pestle and mortar. Add the sliced *lengkuas*, sliced red chillies and salt. Process or pound to a fine paste.

2 Fry the paste in hot oil for 1–2 minutes, without browning, until the mixture gives off a rich aroma.

3 Add the tomato purée and the stock or water and cook for about 10 minutes. Add 350g/12oz cooked chicken pieces and 50g/2oz cooked and sliced French beans, or one of the flavouring variations below, to half the quantity of the sauce. Cook in the sauce for 3–4 minutes, then stir in the tamarind juice, sugar and coconut milk or cream at the last minute, before tasting and serving.

VARIATIONS

Tomato *Sambal Goreng* – Add 450g/1lb of skinned, seeded and coarsely chopped tomatoes, before the stock.

Prawn *Sambal Goreng* – Add 350g/12oz cooked, peeled prawns and 1 green pepper, seeded and chopped.

Egg *Sambal Goreng* – Add 3 or 4 hard-boiled eggs, shelled and chopped, and 2 tomatoes, skinned, seeded and chopped.

Sweet-and-sour Ginger Sambal

This sambal is especially delicious with fish, chicken or pork – but beware, it is extremely hot.

INGREDIENTS

Makes 90ml/6 tbsp

4–5 small fresh red chillies, seeded and chopped
2 shallots or 1 small onion, chopped
2 garlic cloves
2cm/¾in fresh root ginger
30ml/2 tbsp sugar
1.5ml/¼ tsp salt
45ml/3 tbsp rice vinegar or white wine vinegar

1 Pound together the chillies and shallots or onion in a mortar with a pestle. Alternatively, grind them in a food processor.

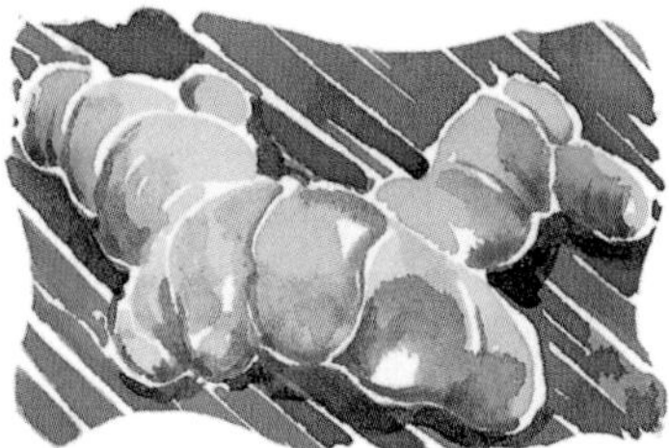

2 Add the garlic, ginger, sugar and salt and continue to pound or grind until smooth. Stir in the vinegar and mix well.

COOK'S TIP

This sambal can be stored in a screw-topped jar in the refrigerator.

Satay Sauce

There are many versions of this tasty peanut sauce. This one is very speedy and it tastes delicious drizzled over grilled or barbecued skewers of chicken. For parties, spear chunks of chicken with cocktail sticks and arrange around a bowl of warm satay sauce.

INGREDIENTS

Serves 4

200ml/7fl oz/scant 1 cup coconut cream
60ml/4 tbsp crunchy peanut butter
5ml/1 tsp Worcestershire sauce
few drops of Tabasco sauce
fresh coconut, to garnish (optional)

1 Pour the coconut cream into a small saucepan and heat it gently over a low heat for about 2 minutes.

2 Add the peanut butter and stir vigorously until the mixture is thoroughly blended. Continue to heat, but do not allow to boil.

3 Add the Worcestershire sauce and Tabasco sauce to taste. Pour into a serving bowl.

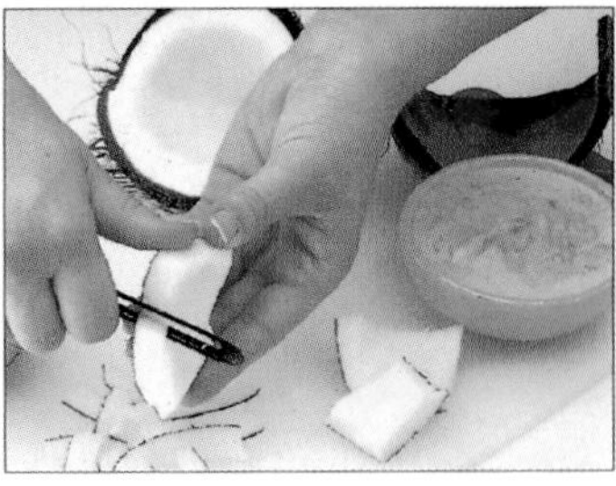

4 Use a potato peeler to shave thin strips from a piece of fresh coconut, if using. Scatter the coconut over the sauce and serve immediately.

Vietnamese Dipping Sauce

Serve this dip in a small bowl as an accompaniment to spring rolls or meat dishes.

INGREDIENTS

Makes 150ml/¼ pint/⅔ cup

1–2 small fresh red chillies, seeded and finely chopped
1 garlic clove, crushed
15ml/1 tbsp roasted peanuts
60ml/4 tbsp coconut milk
30ml/2 tbsp fish sauce
juice of 1 lime
10ml/2 tsp sugar
5ml/1 tsp chopped fresh coriander

1 Pound the chilli or chillies with the garlic in a mortar with a pestle.

2 Add the peanuts and pound until crushed. Add the coconut milk, fish sauce, lime juice, sugar and coriander. Mix well.

Thai Dipping Sauce

Nam prik is the most common dipping sauce in Thailand. It has a fiery strength, so use it with caution.

INGREDIENTS

Makes 120ml/4fl oz/½ cup

15ml/1 tbsp vegetable oil
1cm/½in square shrimp paste or 15ml/1 tbsp fish sauce
2 garlic cloves, finely sliced
2cm/¾in fresh root ginger, finely chopped
3 small fresh red chillies, seeded and chopped
15ml/1 tbsp finely chopped coriander root or stem
20ml/4 tsp sugar
45ml/3 tbsp dark soy sauce
juice of ½ lime

1 Heat the vegetable oil in a preheated wok. Add the shrimp paste or fish sauce, garlic, ginger and chillies and stir-fry for 1–2 minutes, until softened, but not coloured.

2 Remove from the heat and add the chopped coriander, sugar, soy sauce and lime juice.

COOK'S TIP

Thai Dipping Sauce will keep for up to 10 days in a screw-topped jar in the refrigerator.

Hoisin Dip

This speedy dip needs no cooking and can be made in just a few minutes – it tastes great with Mini Spring Rolls or prawn crackers.

INGREDIENTS

Serves 4
4 spring onions
4cm/1½in fresh root ginger
2 fresh red chillies
2 garlic cloves
60ml/4 tbsp hoisin sauce
120ml/4fl oz/½ cup passata
5ml/1 tsp sesame oil (optional)

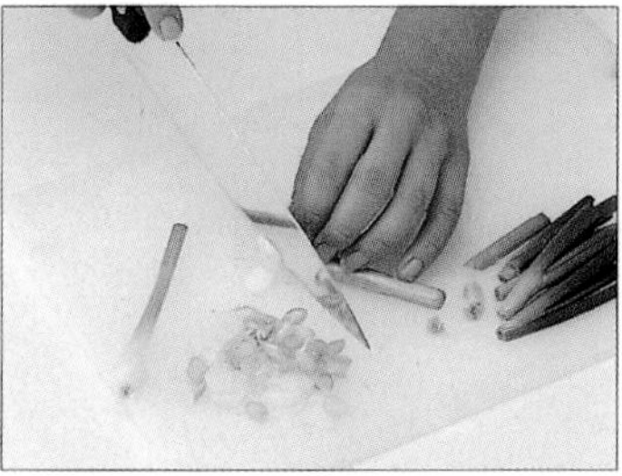

1 Trim off and discard the green ends of the spring onions. Slice the white parts very thinly.

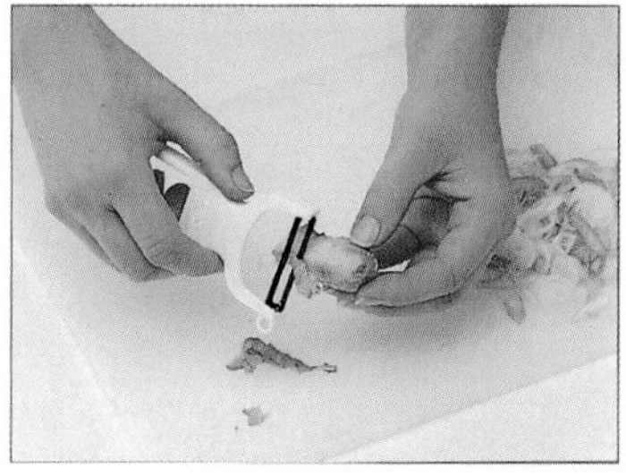

2 Peel and finely chop the ginger.

3 Halve and seed the chillies. Slice finely. Finely chop the garlic.

4 Stir together the hoisin sauce, passata, spring onions, ginger, chillies, garlic and sesame oil, if using. Serve within 1 hour.

Cucumber Sambal

This sauce has a piquant flavour and does not have the heat of chillies found in other sambals.

INGREDIENTS

Makes 150ml/¼ pint/⅔ cup
1 garlic clove, crushed
5ml/1 tsp fennel seeds
10ml/2 tsp sugar
2.5ml/½ tsp salt
2 shallots or 1 small onion, finely sliced
120ml/4fl oz/½ cup rice vinegar or white wine vinegar
¼ cucumber, finely diced

1 Pound together the garlic, fennel seeds, sugar and salt in a mortar with a pestle. Alternatively, grind them together in a food processor.

2 Stir in the shallots or onion, vinegar and cucumber and set aside for at least 6 hours to allow the flavours to combine.

Tomato Sambal

Sambal Tomaat, from Surabaya, can be used as a dip to eat with fritters and snack foods.

INGREDIENTS

Makes about 300ml/½ pint/1¼ cups

2 large beefsteak tomatoes, about 400g/14oz, peeled if liked
1 fresh red chilli, seeded, or 2.5ml/½ tsp chilli powder
2–3 garlic cloves
60ml/4 tbsp dark brown sugar
45ml/3 tbsp sunflower oil
15ml/1 tbsp lime or lemon juice
salt

1 Cut the tomatoes in quarters and remove the cores. Place in a food processor, with the chilli or chilli powder, garlic, sugar and salt to taste. Process to a purée.

2 Fry the tomato pureé in hot oil, stirring all the time, until the mixture thickens and has lost its raw taste. Add the lime or lemon juice. Cool, then season. Serve warm or co

Carrot and Apple Salad

Known as *Selada Bortel*, this simple, crunchy salad is always a perfect accompaniment to spicy Indonesian food. It's best to grate the apple at the last minute and sprinkle it liberally with lemon juice to prevent discoloration. Cover the salad with clear film and store in the fridge until needed.

INGREDIENTS

Serves 6

3 large carrots
1 green apple
juice of 1 lemon
45ml/3 tbsp sunflower oil
5ml/1 tsp sugar
salt and freshly ground black pepper

VARIATION

For a tangy flavour, add lime juice and a little grated lime rind to the apple.

1 Coarsely grate the carrot and set aside. Grate the apple, including the skin and drizzle it with the lemon juice to prevent discoloration. Mix gently with your hand to evenly coat the apple with the lemon juice.

2 Add the sunflower oil and sugar t the apple mixture. Season to taste with salt and black pepper, then stir i the grated carrot.

3 Cover the salad with clear film ar chill in the fridge for a short time until required.

Apricot Chutney

Chutneys can add zest to most meals and cooks in Pakistan often serve a choice of different kinds in tiny bowls.

INGREDIENTS

Makes about 450g/1lb
450g/1lb dried apricots, finely diced
5ml/1 tsp garam masala
275g/10oz soft light brown sugar
450ml/¾ pint/scant 2 cups malt vinegar
1 tsp ginger pulp
1 tsp salt
75g/3oz/½ cup sultanas
450ml/¾ pint/scant 2 cups water

1 Put all the ingredients into a medium-sized saucepan and mix together thoroughly.

2 Bring to the boil, then lower the heat and simmer gently for 30–35 minutes, stirring occasionally.

3 When the chutney has thickened to a fairly stiff consistency, transfer into 2–3 warm, clean jars and set aside to cool completely. Cover and store in the refrigerator.

Tasty Toasts

These crunchy toasts are excellent served as part of a weekend brunch. They are especially delicious served with grilled tomatoes.

INGREDIENTS

Makes 8
4 eggs
300ml/½ pint/1¼ cups milk
2 fresh green chillies, finely chopped
30ml/2 tbsp chopped fresh coriander
75g/3oz Cheddar or mozzarella cheese, grated
4 slices bread
salt and freshly ground black pepper
corn oil, for frying

1 Break the eggs into a medium bowl and whisk together. Slowly add the milk and whisk again. Add the chillies, chopped coriander and cheese and season with salt and pepper.

2 Cut the bread slices in half diagonally and soak them, one at a time, in the egg mixture.

3 Heat the oil in a frying pan and fry the bread triangles over a medium heat, turning them once or twice, until they are golden brown.

4 Drain off any excess oil as you remove the toasts from the pan and serve immediately.

Paratha

Paratha is an unleavened bred with rich, flaky layers. The preparation time is quite lengthy and, as the parathas are best served fresh from the pan, you will need to plan your menu well ahead. They can be served as an accompaniment to almost any Balti dish.

Ingredients

Makes about 8

225g/8oz chapati flour or wholemeal flour, plus extra for dusting
2.5ml/½ tsp salt
200ml/7fl oz/scant 1 cup water
115g/4oz vegetable ghee, melted

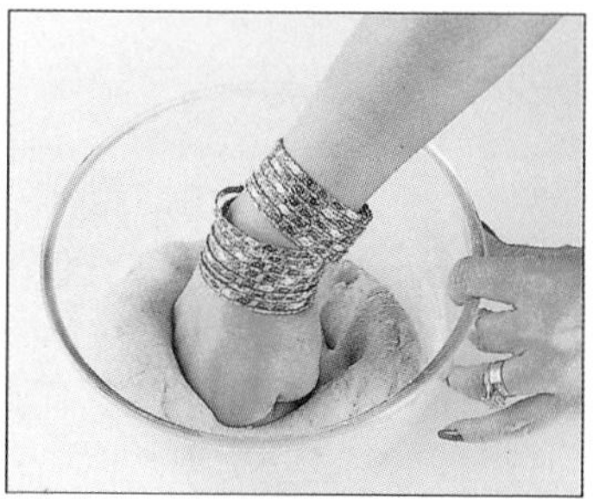

1 Put the flour and salt into a large mixing bowl. Make a well in the centre and add the water, a little at a time, to make a soft, but pliable, dough. Knead well for a few minutes, then cover and leave to rest for about 1 hour.

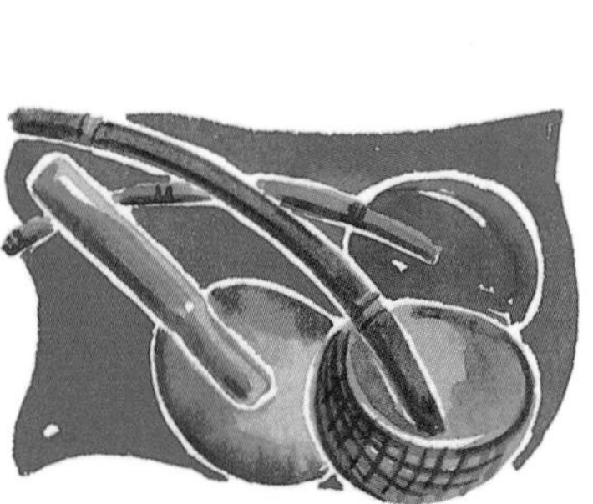

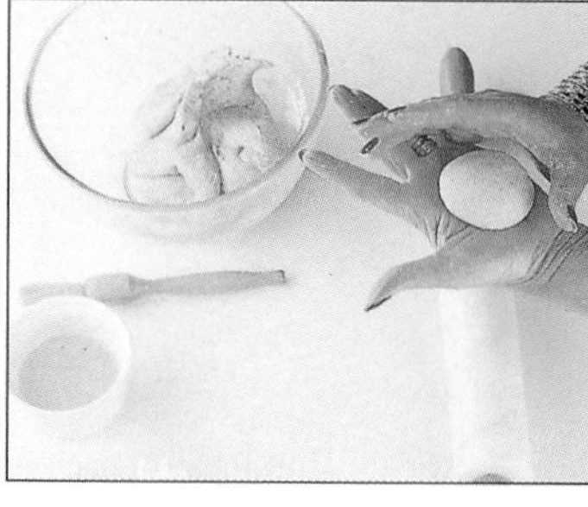

2 Divide the dough into 8 even portions. Roll each one out on a lightly floured surface into a round about 10cm/4in in diameter. Brush the middle of each with about 2.5ml/½ tsp vegetable ghee.

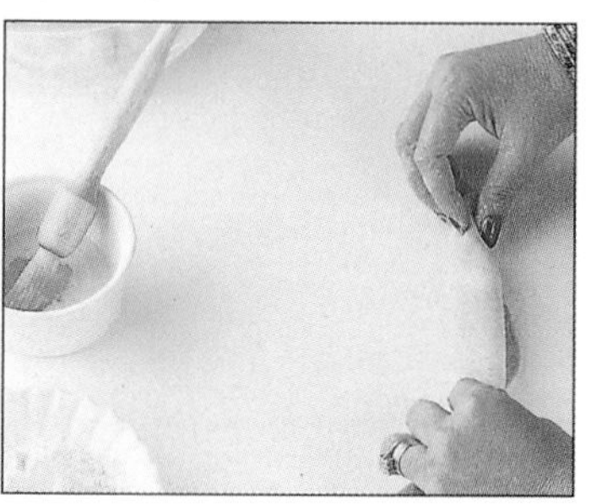

3 Fold each round in half and roll up into a tube.

4 Flatten slightly between your palms, then roll around your finger to form a coil. Roll out again into a round about 18cm/7in in diameter, dusting with extra flour as necessary.

5 Heat a heavy-based frying pan and slap a paratha on to it. Move it gently around the pan to ensure that it is evenly exposed to the heat. Turn it over and brush with about 5ml/1 tsp of the ghee.

6 Cook for about 1 minute, then turn it over again and cook for about 30 seconds, moving it constantly.

7 Remove from the pan and wrap in foil to keep warm. Fry the remaining parathas in the same way. Serve warm.

Index

A

alfalfa crab salad with crispy fried noodles, 352
almond curd junket, 472
apples: apples and raspberries in rose pouchong syrup, 485
  carrot and apple salad, 500
  toffee apples, 487
apricot chutney, 502
aromatic chicken from Madura, 258
asparagus: chicken and asparagus soup, 31
  fried noodles with beansprouts and, 427
  noodles with asparagus and saffron sauce, 426
  stir-fried scallops with asparagus, 156
aubergines: aubergine in spicy sauce, 295
  aubergine salad with dried shrimps and egg, 378
  aubergine with sesame chicken, 338
  beef and aubergine curry, 222
  green beef curry with Thai aubergine, 214
  Szechuan aubergines, 304
avocado: duck, avocado and raspberry salad, 367
  mixed rice noodles, 425

B

Balinese spiced duck, 282
Balinese vegetable soup, 43
Balti baby chicken in tamarind sauce, 270
Balti chicken with lentils, 256
Balti fish fillets in spicy coconut sauce, 118
Balti fried fish, 114
Balti lamb tikka, 226
bamboo shoots: bamboo shoot salad, 375
  bamboo shoots and Chinese mushrooms, 330
bamie goreng, 419
banana leaves, baked fish in, 156
bananas: deep-fried bananas, 482

  fried bananas, 492
barbecue-glazed chicken skewers, 97
barbecued chicken, 272
barbecued pork spareribs, 196
basil: chilli beef with basil, 216
  fried jasmine rice with prawns and Thai basil, 458
  stir-fried chicken with basil and chillies, 251
battered fish, prawns and vegetables, 133
bean curd see tofu
beansprouts: duck and ginger chop suey, 274
  egg foo yung, 439
  fried noodles with beansprouts and asparagus, 427
  stir-fried beansprouts, 293
  stir-fried tofu and beansprouts with noodles, 429
  Thai rice with beansprouts, 448
beef: beef and aubergine curry, 222
  beef and vegetables in a table-top broth, 210
  beef noodle soup, 26
  beef saté with hot mango dip, 213
  beef stir-fry with crisp parsnips, 200
  beef strips with orange and ginger, 203
  beef with Cantonese oyster sauce, 202
  braised beef in a rich peanut sauce, 209
  chilli beef with basil, 216
  clear soup with meatballs, 42
  dry fried shredded beef, 221
  fragrant Thai meatballs, 194
  green beef curry with Thai aubergine, 214
  Hanoi beef and noodle soup, 28
  noodles with meatballs, 416
  noodles with spicy meat sauce, 430
  Oriental beef, 215
  Peking beef and pepper stir-fry, 198
  rice noodles with beef and black bean sauce, 400
  sesame steak, 206
  sizzling beef with celeriac straw, 218
  sizzling steak, 205
  spicy meat-filled parcels, 91
  spicy meat fritters, 196
  spicy meat patties with coconut, 92
  spicy meatballs, 217
  stir-fried beef and broccoli, 199
  stir-fried beef in oyster sauce, 220
  stir-fried beef with mangetouts, 208
  stuffed Thai omelette, 194
  sukiyaki beef, 212
  Szechuan spicy tofu, 296
  Thai beef salad, 362
  thick beef curry in sweet peanut sauce, 204
black bean and vegetable stir-fry, 310
black bean sauce: baked lobster with black beans, 165
  rice noodles with beef and black bean sauce, 400
  squid with green pepper and black bean sauce, 171
black glutinous rice pudding, 482
boemboe Bali of fish, 117
bon-bon chicken with sesame sauce, 96
braised Chinese vegetables, 294
bread rolls, sugar, 480
broccoli: broccoli in oyster sauce, 328
  chicken, ham and broccoli stir-fry, 254
  stir-fried beef and broccoli, 199
  stir-fried prawns with broccoli, 144
  stir-fried turkey with broccoli and mushrooms, 286
brown bean sauce, water spinach with, 302
Brussels sprouts: Chinese sprouts, 345
buckwheat noodles with goat's cheese, 408
buckwheat noodles with smoked salmon, 364
butterfly prawns, 68

C

cabbage: cabbage salad, 351
  crispy cabbage, 300
  hot-and-sour cabbage, 86
  karahi shredded cabbage with cumin, 297
cake, celebration, 474
carrots: carrot and apple salad,

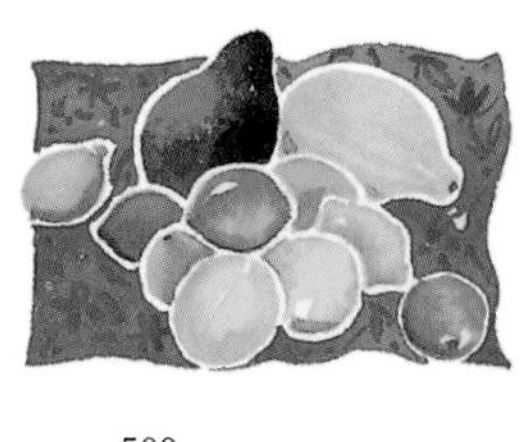

500
  mooli, beetroot and carrot stir-fry, 332
cashew nuts: chicken and cashew nut stir-fry, 252
cauliflower braise, spiced, 306
celebration cake, 474
celeriac straw, sizzling beef with, 218
celery, shredded chicken with, 244
cellophane noodles with pork, 394
chayote: prawns with chayote in turmeric sauce, 136
cheese: buckwheat noodles with goat's cheese, 408
  paneer Balti with prawns, 142
  sugar bread rolls, 480
chestnuts: sweet potato and chestnut candies, 477
Chiang Mai noodle soup, 45
chicken: aromatic chicken from Madura, 258
  aubergine with sesame chicken, 338
  Balti baby chicken in tamarind sauce, 270
  Balti chicken with lentils, 256
  barbecue-glazed chicken skewers, 97
  barbecued chicken, 272
  basic stock, 16
  bon-bon chicken with sesame sauce, 96
  Chiang Mai noodle soup, 45
  chicken and asparagus soup, 31
  chicken and buckwheat noodle soup, 40
  chicken and cashew nut stir-fry, 252
  chicken and sticky rice balls, 99
  chicken chow mein, 399
  chicken cooked in coconut milk, 242
  chicken curry with rice vermicelli, 236
  chicken, ham and broccoli stir-fry, 254

chicken livers, Thai-style, 272
chicken pot, 268
chicken teriyaki, 243
chicken with Chinese vegetables, 244
chicken with spices and soy sauce, 263
chicken with turmeric, 259
chicken wonton soup with prawns, 17
Chinese-style chicken salad, 358
egg noodle salad with sesame chicken, 354
fu-yung chicken, 246
ginger, chicken and coconut soup, 46
gingered chicken noodles, 236
green curry coconut chicken, 241
hot-and-sour chicken salad, 352
hot-and-sour soup, 33
hot chilli chicken, 250
Indonesian-style satay chicken, 248
khara masala Balti chicken, 266
larp of Chiang Mai, 357
noodles, chicken and prawns in coconut broth, 405
noodles with chicken, prawns and ham, 395
rice porridge with chicken, 445
rice noodles with beef and black bean sauce, 400
shredded chicken with celery, 244
soy-braised chicken, 262
spiced chicken stir-fry, 260
spiced honey chicken wings, 94
spicy chicken stir-fry, 238
spicy clay-pot chicken, 240
spicy Szechuan noodles, 368
stir-fried chicken with basil and chillies, 251
stir-fried chicken with pineapple, 260
stir-fried rice noodles with chicken and prawns, 417
stir-fried sweet-and-sour chicken, 255
sweetcorn and chicken soup, 30
Szechuan chicken, 247
tangy chicken salad, 363
Thai chicken soup, 18
Thai fried rice, 452
Thai stir-fry chicken curry, 264
three delicacy soup, 36
warm stir-fried salad, 360
chillies: aubergine in spicy sauce, 295
braised whole fish in chilli and garlic sauce, 119
chilli beef with basil, 216
chilli crabs, 164
chilli duck with crab and cashew sauce, 280
chilli prawns, 152
Chinese potatoes with chilli beans, 339
clay pot of chilli squid and noodles, 170
hot chilli chicken, 250
hot chilli prawns, 50
spring rolls with sweet chilli dipping sauce, 51
stir-fried chicken with basil and chillies, 251
Thai dipping sauce, 498
Vietnamese dipping sauce, 498
Chinese crispy spring rolls, 56
Chinese fruit salad, 468
Chinese garlic mushrooms, 340
Chinese jewelled rice, 454
Chinese leaves: Chinese leaves with oyster sauce, 313
Chinese leaves and mooli with scallops, 343
stir-fried Chinese leaves with mushrooms, 292
Chinese mushrooms with cellophane noodles, 390
Chinese potatoes with chilli beans, 339
Chinese special fried rice, 438
Chinese-spiced fish fillets, 103
Chinese sprouts, 345
Chinese-style chicken salad, 358
Chinese sweet-and-sour pork, 186
Chinese tofu and lettuce soup, 19
Chinese vegetable stir-fry, 335
Chinese vegetables, braised, 294
chow mein: chicken, 399
combination, 392
pork, 181
seafood, 396
special, 398
clams: fried clams with chilli and yellow bean sauce, 84
clear soup with meatballs, 42
coconut: Balti fish in spicy coconut sauce, 118
coconut rice fritters, 444
Indonesian-style satay chicken, 248
Malaysian fish curry, 128
mango and coconut stir-fry, 488
pancakes filled with sweet coconut, 486
spiced prawns with coconut, 141
spicy meat patties with, 92
coconut, creamed: green vegetable salad with coconut mint dip, 377
hot coconut prawn and paw-paw salad, 379
satay sauce, 497
coconut milk: chicken cooked in coconut milk, 242
coconut rice, 446
green curry coconut chicken, 241
mixed vegetables in coconut milk, 302
spiced coconut mushrooms, 308
spiced vegetables with coconut, 318
steamed coconut custard, 476
stewed pumpkin in coconut cream, 473
tapioca pudding, 492
Thai coconut cream, 484
Thai stir-fry chicken curry, 264
coriander: noodles with ginger and coriander, 428
sliced fish and coriander soup, 34
stir-fried vegetables with coriander omelette, 326
corn and crab meat soup, 32
courgettes: courgettes with noodles, 336
somen noodles with courgettes, 420
spicy courgette fritters with Thai salsa, 317
stir-fried pork with tomatoes and courgettes, 190
crab: alfalfa crab salad with crispy fried noodles, 352
baked crab with spring onions and ginger, 162
chilli crabs, 164
Chinese jewelled rice, 454
corn and crab meat soup, 32
crab and egg noodle broth, 20
crab and tofu dumplings, 59
crab, pork and mushroom spring rolls, 71
crab spring rolls and dipping sauce, 52
crisp-fried crab claws, 74
hot spicy crab claws, 72
crispy cabbage, 300
crispy noodles with mixed vegetables, 414
crispy "seaweed", 88
cucumber: bean curd and cucumber salad, 348
cucumber sambal, 499
fish cakes with cucumber relish, 77
lamb and cucumber soup, 36
pickled sweet-and-sour cucumber, 86
stir-fried tomatoes, cucumber and eggs, 330
cumin, karahi shredded cabbage with, 297
curries: beef and aubergine curry, 222
chicken curry with rice vermicelli, 236
curried prawns in coconut milk, 160
curry fried noodles, 432
curry fried pork and rice vermicelli salad, 356
green beef curry with Thai aubergine, 214
green curry coconut chicken, 241
green curry of prawns, 134
Malaysian fish curry, 128
pineapple curry with prawns and mussels, 160
prawn curry with quail's eggs, 147
Thai stir-fry chicken curry, 264
thick beef curry in sweet peanut sauce, 204
tofu and green bean red curry, 343
custard: steamed coconut custard, 476
Thai coconut cream, 484

D

date and walnut crisps, 469
deep fried onions, 329
deep-frying, 13
desserts, 466–93

dim sum, 60
dip, hoisin, 499
doedoeh of fish, 136
dry fried shredded beef, 221
duck: Balinese spiced duck, 282
chilli duck with crab and cashew sauce, 280
crispy and aromatic duck, 278
duck and ginger chop suey, 274
duck, avocado and raspberry salad, 367
duck with Chinese mushrooms and ginger, 283
lettuce wraps with sesame noodles, 388
mandarin sesame duck, 275
Peking duck, 276
sesame duck and noodle salad, 366
sweet-sour duck with mango, 284
dumplings: crab and tofu, 59
dim sum, 60
pork, 62

E
eggs: aubergine salad with dried shrimps and egg, 378
egg foo yung, 439
egg-fried rice, 436
egg pancake salad wrappers, 376
fu-yung chicken, 246
lacy duck egg nets, 83
pork with eggs and mushrooms, 182
prawn fu-yung, 122
son-in-law eggs, 84
special fried rice, 457
spicy scrambled eggs, 306
stir-fried tomatoes, cucumber and eggs, 330
stir-fried vegetables with coriander omelette, 326
stuffed Thai omelette, 194
equipment, 12
exotic fruit salad, 481

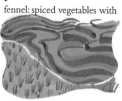

F
fennel: spiced vegetables with coconut, 318
fenugreek, karahi prawns and, 140
festive rice, 456
fish, 100-73
baked fish in banana leaves, 156
Balti fish fillets in spicy coconut sauce, 119
battered fish, prawns and vegetables, 133
boemboe Bali of fish, 117
braised fish fillet with mushrooms, 122
braised whole fish in chilli and garlic sauce, 119
Chinese-spiced fish fillets, 103
fish balls with Chinese greens, 112
fish cakes with cucumber relish, 77
fish with a cashew ginger marinade, 111
Malaysian fish curry, 128
sesame baked fish with a hot ginger marinade, 105
sizzling Chinese steamed fish, 107
sliced fish and coriander soup, 34
spicy fish, 172
steamed fish with ginger and spring onions, 102
sweet-and-sour fish, 125
Thai fish cakes, 124
Thai fish stir-fry, 116
vinegar fish, 129
whole fish with sweet-and-sour sauce, 104
see also sea bass, tuna etc
five-spice lamb, 231
fragrant Thai meatballs, 194
fritters: coconut rice, 444
spicy courgette fritters with Thai salsa, 317
spicy meat, 196
sweetcorn, 92
vegetable tempura, 78
fruit: celebration cake, 474
Chinese fruit salad, 468
exotic fruit salad, 481
fruit and raw vegetable gado-gado, 372
Thai fruit and vegetable salad, 374
see also individual types of fruit
fu-yung chicken, 247

G
gado-gado: cooked vegetable, 316
fruit and raw vegetable, 372
garlic: braised whole fish in chilli and garlic sauce, 118
stir-fried spinach with garlic and sesame seeds, 312
ginger: beef strips with orange and ginger, 203
duck and ginger chop suey, 274
duck with Chinese mushrooms and ginger, 283
ginger, chicken and coconut soup, 46
gingered chicken noodles, 236
gingered seafood stir-fry, 151
noodles with ginger and coriander, 428
Oriental scallops with ginger relish, 154
scallops with ginger, 152
sweet-and-sour ginger sambal, 497
glazed lamb, 225
goat's cheese, buckwheat noodles with, 408
golden pouches, 74
green beef curry with Thai aubergine, 214
green curry of prawns, 135
greens, stir-fried, 301

H
ham: chicken, ham and broccoli stir-fry, 254
Chinese jewelled rice, 454
special fried rice, 457
three delicacy soup, 36
Hanoi beef and noodle soup, 28
hoisin dip, 499
honey-glazed quail with a five-spice marinade, 289
hot-and-sour chicken salad, 352
hot-and-sour prawn soup with lemon grass, 46
hot-and-sour soup, 33

I
ice cream, fried wontons and, 490
Indonesian fried rice, 455
Indonesian potatoes with onions and chilli sauce, 336
Indonesian-satay chicken, 248
ingredients, 8-11

J
junket, almond curd, 472

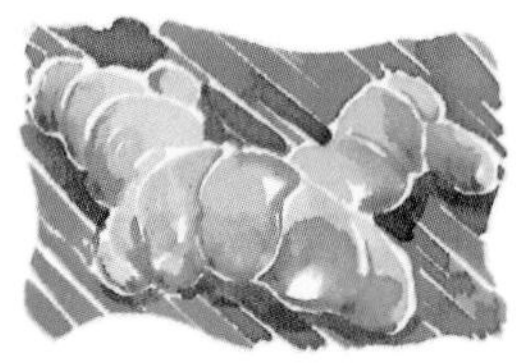

K
karahi prawns and fenugreek, 140
karahi shredded cabbage with cumin, 297
khara masala Balti chicken, 266

L
laksa, seafood, 39
lamb: Balti lamb tikka, 226
Balti minced lamb koftas with vegetables, 232
braised birthday noodles with hoisin lamb, 223
five-spice lamb, 231
glazed lamb, 225
lamb and cucumber soup, 36
lamb satés, 98
minted lamb stir-fry, 229
paper-thin lamb with spring onions, 228
spiced lamb with spinach, 224
stir-fried lamb with spring onions, 230
lap cheong, Shanghai noodles with, 410
larp of Chiang Mai, 357
lemon grass: lemon-grass-and-basil-scented mussels, 159
lemon grass pork, 176
lemon grass prawns on crisp noodle cake, 151
lentils, Balti chicken with, 256
lettuce wraps with sesame noodles, 388
lion's head casserole, 190
lobster: baked lobster with black beans, 165
lychees, stir-fried pork with, 177

M
mackerel: doedoeh of fish, 136
salt-grilled mackerel, 109
Malacca fried rice, 440
Malaysian fish curry, 128
mandarin sesame duck, 275
mangetouts: stir-fried beef with mangetouts, 208
stir-fried turkey with mangetouts, 288
mangoes: beef saté with hot

mango dip, 213
mango and coconut stir-fry, 488
mango with sticky rice, 478
sweet-sour duck with mango, 284
meat, 174-233
see also beef; lamb; pork
meatballs: clear soup with meatballs, 42
crisp pork meatballs laced with noodles, 404
fragrant Thai meatballs, 194
lion's head casserole, 190
noodles with meatballs, 416
spicy meatballs, 217
minted lamb stir-fry, 229
miso breakfast soup, 23
monkfish: fried monkfish coated with rice noodles, 110
mooli: Chinese leaves and mooli with scallops, 342
mooli, beetroot and carrot stir-fry, 332
mushrooms: braised Chinese vegetables, 294
braised fish fillet with mushrooms, 122
Chinese garlic mushrooms, 340
Chinese mushrooms with cellophane noodles, 390
duck with Chinese mushrooms and ginger, 283
hot-and-sour soup, 33
nutty rice and mushroom stir-fry, 465
pak choi and mushroom stir-fry, 320
pancakes with stir-fried vegetables, 324
pork with eggs and mushrooms, 182
red-cooked tofu with Chinese mushrooms, 322
shiitake fried rice, 443
spiced coconut mushrooms, 308
stir-fried noodles with wild mushrooms, 422
stir-fried turkey with broccoli and mushrooms, 286

mussels: lemon-grass-and-basil-scented mussels, 159
pan-steamed mussels with Thai herbs, 163
mustard, noodles with tomatoes, sardines and, 410
mustard greens: pork and pickled mustard greens soup, 41

N

nasi goreng, 451
noodles, 382-433
alfalfa crab salad with crispy fried noodles, 352
beef noodle soup, 26
braised birthday noodles with hoisin lamb, 223
buckwheat noodles with goat's cheese, 408
buckwheat noodles with smoked salmon, 364
cellophane noodles with pork, 394
cheat's shark's fin soup, 22
Chiang Mai noodle soup, 45
chicken and buckwheat noodle soup, 40
chicken chow mein, 399
chicken curry with rice vermicelli, 236
Chinese mushrooms with cellophane noodles, 390
clay pot of chilli squid and noodles, 170
combination chow mein, 392
courgettes with noodles, 336
crab and egg noodle broth, 20
crisp pork meatballs laced with noodles, 404
crispy noodles with mixed vegetables, 414
curry fried noodles, 432
curry fried pork and rice vermicelli salad, 356
egg fried noodles, 386
egg noodle salad with sesame chicken, 354
egg noodles with tuna and tomato sauce, 422
fried cellophane noodles, 413
fried monkfish coated with rice noodles, 110
fried noodles with beansprouts and asparagus, 427
gingered chicken noodles, 237
Hanoi beef and noodle soup, 28
lemon grass prawns on crisp noodle cake, 150
lettuce wraps with sesame noodles, 388
main course spicy prawn and noodle soup, 402
mixed rice noodles, 425
noodle soup with pork and Szechuan pickle, 24
noodles, chicken and prawns in coconut broth, 405
noodles in soup, 406
noodles primavera, 420
noodles with asparagus and saffron sauce, 426
noodles with chicken, prawns and ham, 395
noodles with ginger and coriander, 428
noodles with meatballs, 416
noodles with pineapple, ginger and chillies, 364
noodles with spicy meat sauce, 430
noodles with sun-dried tomatoes and prawns, 424
noodles with tomatoes, sardines and mustard, 410
Oriental vegetable noodles, 384
peanut noodles, 385
pork and noodle broth with prawns, 27
pork chow mein, 181
potato and cellophane noodle salad, 355
prawn noodle salad with fragrant herbs, 359
pumpkin and coconut soup, 44
rice noodles with beef and black bean sauce, 400
rice vermicelli and salad rolls, 371
seafood chow mein, 396
seafood laksa, 39
sesame duck and noodle salad, 366
sesame noodle salad with hot peanuts, 373
sesame noodles with spring onions, 368
Shanghai noodles with lap cheong, 410
Singapore noodles, 389
soft fried noodles, 386
somen noodles with courgettes, 420
special chow mein, 398
special fried noodles, 403
spicy Szechuan noodles, 368
stir-fried noodles with chicken and prawns, 417
stir-fried noodles with wild mushrooms, 422
stir-fried sweet-and-sour

chicken, 255
stir-fried tofu and beansprouts with noodles, 429
stir-fried vegetables with pasta, 334
straw noodle prawns in a sweet ginger dip, 401
sukiyaki beef, 212
Thai fried noodles, 418
Thai noodles with Chinese chives, 391
tomato noodles with fried egg, 432
tossed noodles with seafood, 430
udon pot, 392
vegetable and egg noodle ribbons, 408
vegetarian fried noodles, 412
nori: sushi, 443
nutty rice and mushroom stir-fry, 465

O

okra: okra with green mango and lentils, 298
omelette, stuffed Thai, 194
onions: deep fried onions, 329
red fried rice, 461
Oriental beef, 215
Oriental fried rice, 441
Oriental scallops with ginger relish, 154
Oriental vegetable noodles, 384
oyster sauce: beef with Cantonese oyster sauce, 202
broccoli in oyster sauce, 328
Chinese leaves with oyster sauce, 313

P

pak choi: pak choi and mushroom stir-fry, 320
pak choi with lime dressing, 333
pancakes: crispy and aromatic duck, 278
egg pancake salad wrappers, 376
pancakes filled with sweet coconut, 486

pancakes with stir-fried vegetables, 324
Peking duck, 276
red bean paste pancakes, 470
thin pancakes, 470
paneer Balti with prawns, 142
paratha, 504
parsnips, beef stir-fry with crisp, 200
pawpaws: hot coconut prawn and pawpaw salad, 378
peanuts: braised beef in a rich peanut sauce, 209
fruit and raw vegetable gado-gado, 372
peanut noodles, 385
satay sauce, 497
sesame noodle salad with hot peanuts, 373
spicy peanut rice cakes, 449
tamarind soup with peanuts and vegetables, 29
thick beef curry in sweet peanut sauce, 204
Peking beef and pepper stir-fry, 198
Peking duck, 276
peppers: peanut noodles, 388
Peking beef stir-fry, 198
red fried rice, 461
squid with green pepper and black bean sauce, 171
stuffed green peppers, 192
pickles: mixed vegetable pickle, 309
pickled sweet-and-sour cucumber, 86
pies, savoury pork, 188
pineapple: noodles with pineapple, ginger and chillies, 364
pineapple curry with prawns and mussels, 160
pineapple fried rice, 446
stir-fried chicken with pineapple, 260
sweet-and-sour fruit and vegetable salad, 370
pomelo salad, 380
pork: barbecued pork spareribs, 196
cellophane noodles with pork, 394

Chinese sweet-and-sour pork, 186
crab, pork and mushroom spring rolls, 71
crisp pork meatballs laced with noodles, 404
curry fried pork and rice vermicelli salad, 356
deep-fried ribs with spicy salt and pepper, 82
fragrant Thai meatballs, 194
fried rice with pork, 460
golden pouches, 74
hot-and-sour pork, 184
hot-and-sour soup, 33
Indonesian fried rice, 455
lemon grass pork, 176
lion's head casserole, 190
noodle soup with pork and Szechuan pickle, 24
noodles with spicy meat sauce, 430
pork and noodle broth with prawns, 27
pork and pickled mustard greens soup, 41
pork and vegetable stir-fry, 187
pork chow mein, 181
pork dumplings, 62
pork satay, 95
pork with eggs and mushrooms, 182
savoury pork pies, 188
savoury pork ribs with snake beans, 178
spicy spareribs, 80
steamed pork and water chestnut wontons, 65
stir-fried pork with lychees, 177
stir-fried pork with tomatoes and courgettes, 190
stir-fried pork with vegetables, 193
stir-fried Thai omelette, 194
stuffed green peppers, 192
sweet-and-sour pork and prawn soup, 188
Thai sweet-and-sour pork, 180
wonton soup, 38
potatoes: Chinese potatoes with chilli beans, 339
Indonesian potatoes with onions and chilli sauce, 336
potato and cellophane noodle salad, 355
spicy Balti potatoes, 298
spicy meat fritters, 196
poultry, 234–89
see also chicken; duck; turkey
prawns: Balti prawns and vegetables in thick sauce, 148
Balti prawns in hot sauce, 132
battered fish, prawns and vegetables, 133
butterfly prawns, 68
chicken wonton soup with prawns, 17
chilli prawns, 152
curried prawns in coconut milk, 160
fried jasmine rice with prawns and Thai basil, 458
green curry of prawns, 134
hot-and-sour prawn soup with lemon grass, 46
hot chilli prawns, 50
hot coconut prawn and pawpaw salad, 379
Indonesian fried rice, 455
karahi prawns and fenugreek, 140
lemon grass prawns on crisp noodle cake, 150
main course spicy prawn and noodle soup, 402
mixed rice noodles, 425
noodles, chicken and prawns in coconut broth, 405
noodles with sun-dried tomatoes and prawns, 424
paneer Balti with prawns, 142
prawn crackers, 50
prawn curry with quail's eggs, 147
prawn fu-yung, 122
prawn noodle salad with fragrant herbs, 359
prawn satés, 135
prawns with chayote in turmeric sauce, 136
quick-fried prawns with hot spices, 70
red and white prawns with green vegetables, 138
satay prawns, 146
sesame seed prawn toasts, 88
Singapore noodles, 389
special fried noodles, 403
special fried rice, 457
spiced prawns with coconut, 141
spicy fried rice sticks with prawns, 462
stir-fried prawns with broccoli, 144
stir-fried prawns with tamarind, 145
stir-fried rice noodles with chicken and, 417
straw noodle prawns in a sweet ginger dip, 401

sweet-and-sour pork and prawn soup, 188
sweet potato and pumpkin prawn cakes, 90
Thai seafood salad, 350
three delicacy soup, 36
wonton soup, 38
pumpkin: pumpkin and coconut soup, 44
stewed pumpkin in coconut cream, 473
sweet potato and pumpkin prawn cakes, 90

Q

quail: honey-glazed quail with a five-spice marinade, 289
quail's eggs, prawn curry with, 147

R

ragout of shellfish with sweet-scented basil, 166
raspberries: apples and raspberries in rose pouchong syrup, 485
duck, avocado and raspberry salad, 367
red bean paste pancakes, 470
red-cooked tofu with Chinese mushrooms, 322
red fried rice, 461
red kidney beans: Chinese potatoes with chilli beans, 339
red snapper: sesame baked fish with a hot ginger marinade, 105
snapper, tomato and tamarind noodle soup, 24
rice, 434–65
black glutinous rice pudding, 482
celebration cake, 474
chicken and sticky rice balls, 99
Chinese jewelled rice, 454
Chinese special fried rice, 438
coconut rice, 446
coconut rice fritters, 444
egg foo yung, 439
egg-fried rice, 436

festive rice, 456
fried jasmine rice with prawns and Thai basil, 458
fried rice with pork, 460
fried rice with spices, 464
Indonesian fried rice, 455
jasmine rice, 458
Malacca fried rice, 440
mango with sticky rice, 478
nasi goreng, 451
nutty rice and mushroom stir-fry, 465
Oriental fried rice, 441
pineapple fried rice, 446
plain rice, 436
red fried rice, 461
rice cakes with spicy dipping sauce, 76
rice porridge with chicken, 445
rice with seeds and spices, 450
shiitake fried rice, 443
special fried rice, 457
spicy fried rice sticks with prawns, 462
spicy peanut rice cakes, 449
sushi, 442
baked rice pudding Thai-style, 478
Thai fried rice, 452
Thai rice with beansprouts, 448
root vegetables with spiced salt, 305

S
saffron: noodles with asparagus and saffron sauce, 426
salads, 346-381
alfalfa crab salad with crispy fried noodles, 352
aubergine salad with dried shrimps and egg, 37
bamboo shoot salad, 375
bean curd and cucumber salad, 348
cabbage salad, 351
carrot and apple salad, 500
Chinese-style chicken salad, 358
curry fried pork and rice vermicelli salad, 356
duck, avocado and raspberry salad, 367
egg noodle salad with sesame chicken, 354
egg pancake salad wrappers, 376
fruit and raw vegetable gado-gado, 372
green vegetable salad with coconut mint dip, 377
hot-and-sour chicken salad, 352
hot coconut prawn and paw-paw salad, 379
larp of Chiang Mai, 357
pomelo salad, 380
potato and cellophane noodle salad, 355
prawn noodle salad with fragrant herbs, 359
rice vermicelli and salad rolls, 371
seafood salad with fragrant herbs, 380
sesame duck and noodle salad, 366
sesame noodle salad with hot peanuts, 373
sesame noodles with spring onions, 368
spicy Szechuan noodles, 368
sweet-and-sour fruit and vegetable salad, 370
tangy chicken salad, 363
Thai beef salad, 362
Thai fruit and vegetable salad, 374
Thai seafood salad, 350
warm stir-fried salad, 360
salmon: salmon sushi, 442
salmon teriyaki, 108
spiced salmon stir-fry, 126
sambals: cucumber, 499
sambal goreng, 496
sweet-and-sour ginger, 497
tomato, 500
sardines, noodles with tomatoes, mustard and, 410
satay: Indonesian-style satay chicken, 248
lamb satés, 98
pork satay, 95
prawn satés, 135
satay prawns, 146
satay sauce, 497
sauces, 494-505
satay sauce, 497
Thai dipping sauce, 498
Vietnamese dipping sauce, 498
scallops: Chinese leaves and mooli with scallops, 343
Oriental scallops with ginger relish, 154
scallops with ginger, 152
seared scallops with wonton crisps, 66
spiced scallops in their shells, 158
stir-fried scallops with asparagus, 156
sea bass: fish with a cashew ginger marinade, 111
sea bass with Chinese chives, 106
steamed fish with ginger and spring onions, 102
seafood, 100-73
gingered seafood stir-fry, 151
ragout of shellfish with sweet-scented basil, 166
seafood Balti with vegetables, 120
seafood chow mein, 396
seafood laksa, 39
seafood salad with fragrant herbs, 380
seafood wontons with coriander dressing, 64
steamed seafood packets, 73
Thai seafood salad, 350
tossed noodles with seafood, 430
see also crab; prawns etc
"seaweed", crispy, 88
sesame: egg noodle salad with sesame chicken, 354
lettuce wraps with sesame noodles, 388
mandarin sesame duck, 275
sesame baked fish with a hot ginger marinade, 105
sesame duck and noodle salad, 366
sesame noodle salad with hot peanuts, 373
sesame noodles with spring onions, 368
sesame seed prawn toasts, 88
sesame steak, 206
Shanghai noodles with lap cheong, 410
shark's fin soup, cheat's, 22
shellfish ragout with sweet-scented basil, 166
shiitake fried rice, 443
shrimps *see* prawns
Singapore noodles, 389
sizzling beef with celeriac straw, 218
sizzling steak, 205
smoked salmon, buckwheat noodles with, 364
snake beans, savoury pork ribs with, 178
somen noodles with courgettes, 420

son-in-law eggs, 84
soups, 14-47
Balinese vegetable soup, 43
beef noodle soup, 26
cheat's shark's fin soup, 22
Chiang Mai noodle soup, 45
chicken and asparagus soup, 31
chicken and buckwheat noodle soup, 40
chicken wonton soup with prawns, 17
Chinese tofu and lettuce soup, 19
clear soup with meatballs, 42
corn and crab meat soup, 32
crab and egg noodle broth, 20
ginger, chicken and coconut soup, 46
Hanoi beef and noodle soup, 28
hot-and-sour prawn soup with lemon grass, 46
hot-and-sour soup, 33
lamb and cucumber soup, 36
main course spicy prawn and noodle soup, 402
miso breakfast soup, 23
noodle soup with pork and Szechuan pickle, 24
noodles in soup, 406
pork and noodle broth with prawns, 27
pork and pickled mustard greens soup, 41
seafood laksa, 39
sliced fish and coriander soup, 34
snapper, tomato and tamarind noodle soup, 24
spinach and tofu soup, 34
sweet-and-sour pork and prawn soup, 188
sweetcorn and chicken soup, 30
tamarind soup with peanuts and vegetables, 29
Thai chicken soup, 18
three delicacy soup, 36
wonton soup, 38
soy sauce: chicken with spices and soy sauce, 263
soy-braised chicken, 262
special chow mein, 398
special fried rice, 457

spinach: spiced lamb with spinach, 224
spinach and tofu soup, 34
stir-fried spinach with garlic and sesame seeds, 312
water spinach with brown bean sauce, 302
spring greens: crispy "seaweed", 88
spring onions: baked crab with spring onions and ginger, 162
paper-thin lamb with spring onions, 228
sesame noodles with spring onions, 368
stir-fried lamb with spring onions, 230
spring rolls: Chinese crispy spring rolls, 56
crab, pork and mushroom spring rolls, 71
crab spring rolls and dipping sauce, 52
mini spring rolls, 54
spring rolls with sweet chilli dipping sauce, 51
Thai spring rolls, 55
Vietnamese spring rolls with nuoc cham sauce, 58
squid: clay pot of chilli squid and noodles, 170
deep fried squid with spicy salt and pepper, 69
squid from Madura, 172
squid with green pepper and black bean sauce, 171
stir-fried five-spice squid, 169
Vietnamese stuffed squid, 168
starters, 48-99
steaming, 13
stir-frying, 13
stock, 16
straw noodle prawns in a sweet ginger dip, 401
sugar bread rolls, 480
sukiyaki beef, 212
sushi, 442
sweet-and-sour fish, 125
sweet-and-sour fruit and vegetable salad, 370
sweet-and-sour ginger sambal, 497

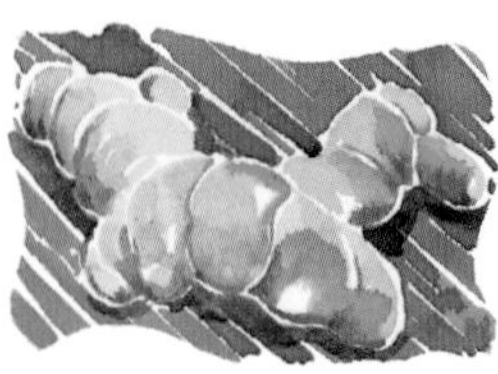

sweet-and-sour pork and prawn soup, 188
sweet potatoes: sweet potato and chestnut candies, 477
sweet potato and pumpkin prawn cakes, 90
sweet-sour duck with mango, 284
sweetcorn: corn and crab meat soup, 32
sweetcorn and chicken soup, 30
sweetcorn fritters, 92
swordfish: fragrant with ginger and lemon grass, 130
Szechuan aubergines, 304
Szechuan spicy tofu, 296

T

tamarind: Balti baby chicken in tamarind sauce, 270
stir-fried prawns with tamarind, 145
tamarind soup with peanuts and vegetables, 29
tapioca pudding, 492
tasty toasts, 502
tea: apples and raspberries in rose pouchong syrup, 485
tempura: battered fish, prawns and vegetables, 133
vegetable tempura, 78
Thai-style baked rice pudding, 478
Thai beef salad, 362
Thai chicken soup, 18
Thai dipping sauce, 498
Thai fish cakes, 124
Thai fish stir-fry, 116
Thai fried noodles, 418
Thai fried rice, 452
Thai fruit and vegetable salad, 374
Thai noodles with Chinese chives, 391
Thai rice with beansprouts, 448
Thai seafood salad, 350
Thai spring rolls, 55
Thai stir-fry chicken curry, 264
Thai sweet-and-sour pork, 180
three delicacy soup, 36
toffee apples, 487
tofu: bean curd and cucumber salad, 348
braised Chinese vegetables, 294
Chinese garlic mushrooms, 340
Chinese tofu and lettuce soup, 19
crab and tofu dumplings, 59
red-cooked tofu with Chinese mushrooms, 322
spiced tofu stir-fry, 344
spinach and tofu soup, 34
stir-fried tofu and beansprouts with noodles, 429
Szechuan spicy tofu, 296
tofu and green bean red curry, 342
tofu stir-fry, 314
tomatoes: noodles with sun-dried tomatoes and prawns, 424
noodles with tomatoes, sardines and mustard, 410
red fried rice, 461
stir-fried pork with tomatoes and courgettes, 190
tomato noodles with fried egg, 432
tomato sambal, 500
tossed noodles with seafood, 430
trout: sizzling Chinese steamed fish, 107
tuna: egg noodles with tuna and tomato sauce, 422
tuna sushi, 443
turkey: stir-fried turkey with broccoli and mushrooms, 286
stir-fried turkey with mangetouts, 288
turmeric, chicken with, 259

U

udon pot, 392

V

vegetables, 290-345
Balinese vegetable soup, 43
beef and vegetables in a table-top broth, 210
beef with Cantonese oyster sauce, 202
black bean and vegetable stir-fry, 310
chicken with Chinese vegetables, 244
Chinese vegetable stir-fry, 335
cooked vegetable gado-gado, 316
crispy noodles with mixed vegetables, 414
fish balls with Chinese greens, 112
mixed vegetable pickle, 309
mixed vegetables in coconut milk, 302
Oriental fried rice, 441
pancakes with stir-fried vegetables, 324
pork and vegetable stir-fry, 187
root vegetables with spiced salt, 305
seafood Balti with vegetables, 120
spiced tofu stir-fry, 344
spiced vegetables with coconut, 318
spicy courgette fritters with Thai salsa, 317
stir-fried mixed vegetables, 341
stir-fried pork with vegetables, 193
stir-fried vegetables with pasta, 334
tamarind soup with peanuts and vegetables, 29
vegetable and egg noodle ribbons, 408
vegetable salad with hot peanut sauce, 349
vegetable tempura, 78
vegetarian fried noodles, 412
vermicelli: rice vermicelli and salad rolls, 371
Vietnamese dipping sauce, 498
Vietnamese spring rolls with nuoc cham sauce, 58
Vietnamese stuffed squid, 168
vinegar fish, 129

W

walnuts: date and walnut crisps, 469
water chestnuts, bamboo shoots and, 330
water spinach with brown bean sauce, 302
whiting: battered fish, prawns and vegetables, 133
woks, 12
wontons: fried wontons and ice cream, 490
seafood wontons with coriander dressing, 64
seared scallops with wonton crisps, 66
steamed pork and water chestnut wontons, 65
wonton flowers with sweet-and-sour sauce, 67
wonton soup, 38
wonton twists, 490